# MUSEUM
# REVOLUTIONS

UNIVERSITY COLL'

A leading group of museum professionals and academics from around the world explore the ways in which museums are shaped and configured and how they themselves attempt to shape and change the world around them. Together, the authors reveal the diverse and subtle means by which museums engage in society and in so doing change and are changed; in *Museum Revolutions*, museums are constantly in flux. Spanning more than 200 years, the authors discuss national museums, ecomuseums, society museums, provincial galleries, colonial museums, the showman's museum, and science centres, and range across such topics as disciplinary practices, ethnic representation, postcolonial politics, economic aspiration, social reform, indigenous models, conceptions of history, urban regeneration, sustainability, sacred objects, a sense of place, globalisation, identities, social responsibility, controversy, repatriation, human remains, drama, learning and education.

While change has been on the museum professional's agenda for twenty years, this book is the first to reveal its complexity and frame it in the context of contemporary museum studies. In doing so, it captures the richness of the field of museum studies at a time when it has achieved a new level of maturity and international cohesiveness. *Museum Revolutions* is the ideal text for Museum Studies courses, providing a wide range of interlinked themes and the latest thought and research from experts in the field. It is invaluable for those students, researchers and museum professionals who want to understand the past, present and future of the museum and the intellectual richness and diversity of the field of museum studies.

**Simon Knell** is Professor of Museum Studies and Director of the Department of Museum Studies at the University of Leicester. He previously worked in museums. His books include: *Museums and the Future of Collecting, Museums in the Material World* and *The Culture of English Geology 1815–1851: A Science Revealed Through Its Collecting.*

**Suzanne MacLeod** is a lecturer in the Department of Museum Studies at the University of Leicester where she is Programme Director of Art Museum and Gallery Studies. She is editor of *Reshaping Museum Space: Architecture, Design, Exhibitions* (Routledge, 2005).

**Sheila Watson** is a lecturer in the Department of Museum Studies at the University of Leicester. Until 2003 she worked in museums. She is the editor of *Museums and Their Communities* (Routledge, 2007).

# MUSEUM REVOLUTIONS

How museums change and are changed

*Edited by*
*Simon J. Knell, Suzanne MacLeod*
*and Sheila Watson*

Routledge
Taylor & Francis Group

LONDON AND NEW YORK

First published 2007
by Routledge
2 Park Square, Milton Park, Abingdon, Oxon OX14 4RN

Simultaneously published in the USA and Canada
by Routledge
270 Madison Ave, New York, NY 10016

*Routledge is an imprint of the Taylor & Francis Group, an informa business*

Reprinted 2009

Typeset in Goudy by
Book Now Ltd, London
Printed and bound in Great Britain by
CPI Antony Rowe Chippenham, Wiltshire

*British Library Cataloguing in Publication Data*
A catalogue record for this book is available from the British Library

*Library of Congress Cataloging in Publication Data*
Knell, Simon J.
Museum revolutions: How museums change and are changed / Simon
J. Knell, Suzanne MacLeod and Sheila E.R. Watson.
p. cm.
Includes bibliographical references and index.
1. Museums–Social aspects. 2. Museum exhibits–Social aspects.
3. Museums–Philosophy. 4. Museum visitors. I. Macleod, Suzanne.
II. Watson, Sheila E. R. III. Title.
AM7.K56 2007
069–dc22                                   2007010340

ISBN 10: 0–415–44466–7 (hbk)
ISBN 10: 0–415–44467–5 (pbk)
ISBN 10: 0–203–93264–3 (ebk)

ISBN 13: 978–0–415–44466–8 (hbk)
ISBN 13: 978–0–415–44467–5 (pbk)
ISBN 13: 978–0–203–93264–1 (ebk)

# CONTENTS

CONTENTS

CONTENTS

# ILLUSTRATIONS

## Figures

## Tables

# CONTRIBUTORS

**Marta Anico** is a lecturer in anthropology at the Instituto Superior de Ciências Sociais e Políticas/Universidade Técnica de Lisboa. She co-organised the 1st International Conference on Heritage and Identities, held in Lisbon in 2004. She is co-editor of the book *Patrimónios e Identidades: Ficções Contemporâneas* (Celta, 2006) and author of several chapters and articles in her research areas. Her main topics of interest include heritage, museums and cultural representations, namely representations of power and identity.

**Mary M. Brooks** is a reader at the University of Southampton and Programme Leader of the MA Museums and Galleries. She has published widely on textile conservation and her recent publications include another paper with co-author Rumsey: Brooks, M. M. and Rumsey C. 'The body in the museum', in V. Cassman, N. Odegaard and J. Powell (eds) *Human Remains: A Guide for Conservators, Museums, Universities, and Law Enforcement Agencies* (AltaMira Press, 2006). Mary has a special interest in the contribution that object-based research and conservation approaches can make to the wider interpretation and presentation of cultural artefacts.

**David Butts** is the Programme Coordinator of the Museum Studies Programme in the School of People, Environment and Planning at Massey University, Palmerston North, New Zealand. His research interests include the regional heritage strategies, contemporary issues in collection management, the role of government in the heritage sector, museum governance, museums and indigenous peoples. He is currently investigating heritage retention and access strategies in marginalised regions with widely distributed small population centres.

**Fiona Cameron** is Research Fellow, Museum and Cultural Heritage Studies, at the Centre for Cultural Research, University of Western Sydney. Fiona's research interests embrace the idea of the museum and interrelationships between institutions and contemporary societies in an increasingly complex, diverse and globalising world. These interests fall into two research fields. The first examines the social, civic and political roles and agency of museums in the representation of topics of societal significance and importance. The second investigates digital technologies and museum collections. Major publications include a co-edited collection, *Theorizing Digital Cultural Heritage: A Critical Discourse* (MIT Press, April 2007) and numerous book chapters and articles in leading journals. Fiona was a lecturer in Museum Studies at the University of Sydney and has worked as a museum director, social history curator and curatorial consultant on projects in Australia, New Zealand, Singapore and Vanuatu.

**Chia-Li Chen** is currently an assistant professor at the Graduate School of Museum Studies, Taipei National University of the Arts, Taiwan. She is the author of *Wound on Exhibition: Notes on Memory and Trauma of Museums* and co-editor of *Collecting: Nostalgia and Popular* (Artco Publisher, Taiwan). Her research interests include contemporary popular collecting, community museum history and visitors' museum experiences in relation to the shaping of cultural identities and memories.

**Peter Davis** is Professor of Museology at Newcastle University and Guest Professor of Museology at Museion, University of Gothenburg, Sweden. His books include *Museums and the Natural Environment* (1996), *Ecomuseums: A Sense of Place* (1999) and (with Christine Jackson) *Sir William Jardine: A Life in Natural History* (2001). His recent work on ecomuseums has led him to a close involvement with developments in East Asia, particularly Japan and China, including Taiwan. His research interests focus on three main areas: the history of museums; natural history museums and environmentalism; and ecomuseums.

**Jem Fraser** is currently Project Director of the £46.4m capital project to refurbish the Royal Museum in the National Museums Scotland, Edinburgh. Her new model of the museum visitor experience forms the basis for the £7m new displays. She has managed a variety of large-scale exhibition projects, is experienced in securing grants through funding bids, and was formerly Head of Education in the National Museums of Scotland and previously at Glasgow Museums and Art Galleries, Glasgow. Her main research interests are in the field of visitor studies and she is interested in applying theory to practice. She is a Fellow of the Museums Association and a founder member of the Capital Projects Network Group, which promotes the sharing of good practice in capital projects in museums.

**Viv Golding** is a lecturer in Museum Education and Communication in the Department of Museum Studies at the University of Leicester. Her recent publications include 'Carnival connections: challenging racism as the unsaid at the museum/school frontiers with feminist-hermeneutics' in M. Inglilleri (ed.) *Swinging Her Breasts at History* (Mango Publishing, 2006) and 'The museum clearing: a metaphor for new museum practice' in D. Atkinson and P. Dash (eds) *Social and Critical Practice in Art Education* (Trentham Books, 2006). Previously she developed formal educational provision at the Horniman Museum, London, and worked on arts education programmes in London.

**Kate Gregory** is a post-doctoral research associate for an Australian Research Council project 'Place, Taste and Tradition: a history of ideas about heritage in Western Australia as a foundation for change', based in Fremantle, Western Australia. Her research charts a history of heritage interpretation through the practices of the National Trust of Australia (W.A.). Kate's research interests include the effect of contemporary art on new exhibitionary forms across a range of museum sites and the representation of the museum within art practices since the 1960s. She has worked for heritage sites and museums, including Fremantle Prison, a convict-built heritage site, and continues to combine curatorial practice with her research pursuits.

**Eilean Hooper-Greenhill** is Professor of Museum Studies at the University of Leicester and was formerly Head of Department and Director of the Research Centre for Museums and Galleries. She has written *Museum and Gallery Education* (Leicester University Press,

1991), *Museums and the Shaping of Knowledge* (Routledge, 1992), *Museums and their Visitors* (Routledge, 1994) and *Museums and the Interpretation of Visual Culture* (Routledge, 2000). In addition she has edited *Museum: Media: Message* (Routledge, 1995), *Cultural Diversity: Developing Museum Audiences in Britain* (Leicester University Press, 1997) and *The Educational Role of the Museum* (Routledge, 1994, 1999). She is editor (with Flora Kaplan) for the Routledge *Museum Meanings* series.

**Robert R. Janes** is the Editor-in-Chief of *Museum Management and Curatorship*, an adjunct professor at the University of Calgary and a museum consultant. His recent books include *Museums and the Paradox of Change* (1995, 1997), *Looking Reality in the Eye: Museums and Social Responsibility* (2005, with Gerald Conaty) and *Museum Management and Marketing* (2007, with Richard Sandell). He was the President and Chief Executive Officer of the Glenbow Museum in Calgary, Canada (1989–2000). In addition to his museum work, Robert is the Chair of the Board of Directors of the Biosphere Institute of the Bow Valley in Canmore, Alberta, an organisation committed to the ecological integrity of the Bow Valley watershed.

**Lynda Kelly** is the Head of Audience Research at the Australian Museum. She has published widely in the field of audience research, including four books about museum audiences: *Energised, engaged, everywhere: Older Australians and Museums* (2002), *Indigenous Youth and Museums: A Report on the Indigenous Youth Access Project* (2002), *Knowledge Quest: Australian families visit museums* (2004) and *Many Voices Making Choices: Museum Audiences with Disabilities* (2005). Lynda is particularly interested in indigenous evaluation, visitor experiences and learning and how these can be measured, use of digital media in research and evaluation, as well as the strategic uses of audience research in organisational change.

**Simon J. Knell** is Professor and Head of the Department of Museum Studies at the University of Leicester. His books on museums and material culture include *The Culture of English Geology, 1815–1851: A Science Revealed Through its Collecting* (Ashgate, 2000), *Museums and the Future of Collecting* (Ashgate, 1999, 2004), and *Care of Collections* (Routledge, 1994). His *Museums in the Material World* (Routledge, 2007) is in press, and he is preparing *Pander's Tooth* (Chicago, 2007/8), a book examining how scientists use material culture to negotiate progress. He is involved, in various capacities, in the journals, M, *Museos de México del Mundo, Museum and Society* and the *Museum History Journal*. He is series editor for Leicester Readers in Museum Studies (Routledge).

**Bronwyn Labrum** is a senior lecturer in the School of Visual and Material Culture, Massey University, Wellington, New Zealand. She is the co-editor of *Fragments: New Zealand Social and Cultural History* (2000) and *Looking Flash: Clothing in Aotearoa/New Zealand* (2007) and a contributor to *The New Oxford History of New Zealand* (2008), and has written widely on the history of women, welfare and mental health. She is currently working on a history of the material culture of post-war New Zealand, which includes consideration of the representation of history in museums.

**Margaret A. Lindauer** is Associate Professor and Museum Studies Coordinator in the Department of Art History at Virginia Commonwealth University. She holds an interdisciplinary PhD in Curriculum Studies from Arizona State University, where she was the Curator of Exhibitions at the Museum of Anthropology. Her current research, for which she was awarded a 2004 Fellowship from the Smithsonian Center for Education and Museum Studies, focuses on social, cultural and curatorial implications of the ways in which museums historically have been characterised as educational institutions.

**Beth Lord** is lecturer in Philosophy at the University of Dundee, Scotland. Her work on Foucault and the museum as a space of representation has been published in the journals *Museum and Society* and *Museum Management and Curatorship* and in the collection *Reshaping Museum Space* (S. MacLeod (ed.), 2005). Her research on philosophy and museums complements research interests in seventeenth- and eighteenth-century metaphysics and aesthetics and contemporary continental philosophy. She is currently developing a new way to think about time and history in the museum, based on the thoughts of Foucault and philosopher Gilles Deleuze.

**Conal McCarthy** is Director of the Museum and Heritage Studies programme in the School of Art History, Classics and Religious Studies at Victoria University of Wellington, New Zealand. His first book, a study of colonial architecture in North Otago, was published in 2002, and his second book *Exhibiting Māori* appeared in 2007. He has written articles for a number of journals, including *Art New Zealand, Sites, The Journal of Australian Art Education, New Zealand Sociology, The Journal of New Zealand Literature* and *Museum Management and Curatorship*. His research interests include New Zealand art and architecture, museum history and theory, visitor research and heritage issues.

**Suzanne MacLeod** is a lecturer and Programme Director for Art Museum and Gallery Studies in the Department of Museum Studies at the University of Leicester. She recently edited the volume *Reshaping Museum Space* (Routledge 2005). Current projects include two co-authored volumes for the Leicester Readers in Museum Studies series on *Museums and Exhibitions* and *Art in Museums* as well as research into the histories of English provincial art galleries. She teaches on art curation, museum design and museum histories.

**Ali Mozaffari** is an Iranian architect, currently based in Australia, and has been affiliated with universities in Iran and Australia in different teaching capacities. He is conducting his PhD research at the University of Western Australia. His publications include 'Tradition and the formation of the intangible morphology of cities in Iran', in A. Leach and G. Matthewson (eds) *Celebration*, The Society of Architectural Historians of Australia and New Zealand (SAHANZ) 22nd Annual Conference proceedings (Napier, New Zealand, 2005). Ali's broader research interests include the application of critical theory to architectural criticism, theory of heritage and museums in non-Western countries and traditional cultures, and theories of Islamic cities.

**Savithri Preetha Nair** is an AHRC post-doctoral research assistant on the 'Guide to Sources in the India Office Records for the History of Science and Environment in India (1780–1920)' in the Department of History, School of Oriental and African Studies, University of London. Among her publications she has co-authored (with Richard Axelby), *Science and the Changing Environment in India 1780–1920: A Guide to Sources in the India Office Records* (British Library, 2007: forthcoming). Preetha is interested in all aspects of science, technology and medicine in colonial India and has been specifically focusing on colonialism and its impact on the collecting sciences: geology, botany and zoology.

**Susan Pearce** is now Emeritus Professor of Museum Studies at Leicester, and has been elected a Senior Research Fellow of Somerville College, Oxford. She is the author of a number of books and papers on museum studies and the formation of collections in the late eighteenth and early nineteenth centuries. She is now working on C. Cockerell and his collecting activities in Greece. She has served as a Vice-President of the Society of Antiquaries of London, as a Pro-Vice-Chancellor at the University of Leicester, and as President of the Museums Association.

**Elsa Peralta** is a lecturer in anthropology at the Instituto Superior de Ciências Sociais e Políticas/Universidade Técnica de Lisboa. She is co-editor of the book *Patrimónios e Identidades: Ficções Contemporâneas* (Celta, 2006) and author of several chapters and articles in her research areas: culture and identity; heritage, museums, power and memory. She co-organised the 1st International Conference on Heritage and Identities, held in Lisbon in 2004. She is currently researching the construction of Portuguese national identity and is also interested in comparative national memories in Europe.

**Michael Pickering** is the Program Director of the Aboriginal and Torres Strait Islander Program and the Repatriation Program of the National Museum of Australia. He has worked extensively in Australia as an anthropologist and archaeologist. His research interests and publications include studies on material culture, cannibalism, hunter-gatherer anthropology and archaeology, heritage management, and repatriation.

**Claire Rumsey** is Learning and Access Officer for the National Motor Museum, Beaulieu. She has had other museum roles and worked as an Arts Development Officer since completing her MA Museum Studies degree in 2001. Originally a freelance prop and model maker, Claire created replica artefacts for museum displays nationally and internationally, such as Roman items for the 'High Street Londinium' exhibition at the Museum of London in 2000. Her recent publications include Brooks, M. M. and Rumsey C. 'The body in the museum', in V. Cassman, N. Odegaard and J. Powell (eds) *Human Remains: A Guide for Conservators, Museums, Universities, and Law Enforcement Agencies* (AltaMira Press, 2006). She has a particular interest in the ethics of exhibiting human remains in museums.

**Moira G. Simpson** is lecturer in Arts Education, School of Education, University of South Australia. Her publications include *Making Representations: Museums in the Post-Colonial Era* (Routledge, 1996, revised 2001), *Museums and Repatriation* (Museums Association, 1997), 'Revealing and concealing: museums, objects and the transmission of knowledge in Aboriginal Australia' in J. Marstine (ed.) *New Museum Theory and Practice: An Introduction* (Blackwell Publishing, 2006), and 'Bunjilaka' in C. Healy and A. Witcomb (eds) *South Pacific Museums: Experiments in Culture* (Monash University Press, 2007). Her current research focuses on spiritual heritage and culturally appropriate museology, Indigenous museum models in Aboriginal communities in Canada and Australia, and the use of non-Western artefacts and art works in inter-cultural arts education.

**Philippe Taquet** is Professor of Palaeontology at the Muséum national d'histoire naturelle, Paris. He is a member of the French Académie des Sciences and of the Royal Academy Hassan II of Science and Technology of Morocco, and a foreign member of the Academy of Lisboa (Portugal); he is also President of the International Commission for the History of Geology. A dinosaur specialist, he is internationally known for his work on the

Iguanodontid *Ouranosaurus nigeriensis* and of the giant crocodile *Sarcosuchus imperator*. His most recent publications include *Dinosaur Impressions: Postcards from a Paleontologist* (Cambridge University Press, 1998) and *Georges Cuvier: Naissance d'un Génie* (Odile Jacob, 2006).

**Evelyne Ngwaelung Tegomoh** is based at the University of Buea, Cameroon. Before that she worked with the Norwegian Peace Corps, Fredskorpset, attached to the Tromsoe University Museum, during which she made the film *Let's Share the Beauty*. She is working on a new film whilst working with marginal coastal communities in Norway, as part of a research project under the direction of Professor Reidar Bertelsen. Her research interests include material culture, cultural heritage, social change, gender and the use of still and moving images.

**Richard Toon** is a Senior Research Analyst at Morrison Institute for Public Policy, School of Public Affairs, Arizona State University. He has authored a variety of research reports on issues of public policy in Arizona (see www.asu.edu/copp/morrison/). Before joining the Morrison Institute, Richard was the Education and Research Director at the Arizona Science Center, in Phoenix. His publications include 'The search for learning outcomes: beyond the deficit model', *ASTC Dimensions* (November/December 2005), and 'Black box science in black box science centers' in S. MacLeod (ed.) *Reshaping Museum Space: Architecture, Design, Exhibitions* (Routledge, 2005).

**Sheila Watson** is a lecturer in the Department of Museum Studies at the University of Leicester. She joined the Department in 2003 after working for Norfolk Museums and Archaeology Service. She managed several museums in Great Yarmouth, where she championed the use of focus groups as part of the consultation with local communities that guided the development of the museums. She is the editor of *Museums and Their Communities* (Routledge 2007). Her research interests are focused around the role of museums as sites of national and local identity formation.

**Christopher Whitehead** is senior lecturer in Museum, Gallery and Heritage Studies at the University of Newcastle. He has worked previously as a curator and as a lecturer in Art History. He publishes on the history, architecture and theory of museums and galleries, with particular emphasis on questions of display and knowledge construction. He is the author of *The Public Art Museum in 19th Century Britain: the development of the National Gallery* (Ashgate, 2005) as well as various papers on the V&A in the nineteenth century. He also publishes in the fields of contemporary gallery education and learning and art interpretation in museums and galleries.

**Andrea Witcomb** is an associate professor in the Research Institute for Citizenship and Globalisation at Deakin University in Melbourne, Australia. She is the author of *Re-Imagining the Museum: Beyond the Mausoleum* (Routledge, 2003) and co-editor with Chris Healy of *South-Pacific Museums: Experiments in Culture* (Monash University ePress, 2006). Her research interests cover the areas of museum history and theory, relations between museums and media and practices of interpretation. She is currently working with Kate Gregory on an Australian Research Council funded project entitled 'Place, taste and tradition: A history of ideas about heritage in Western Australia as a foundation for change'.

# PREFACE

The origins of this book lie in an international conference organised to celebrate 40 years of the Department of Museum Studies, at University of Leicester, held in April 2006. That conference acted as a springboard for the papers contained in this volume. This is not, however, a conference volume: all of the papers have been significantly developed since that meeting and represent the fully developed views of contributors at the time this book went to press. It is also a distillation of the huge number of presentations at the conference and a considerable number of submissions for inclusion in the book – nearly twice the number the book contains. We are especially grateful to all those authors who prepared this material for inclusion but who, for reasons of the book's shape and direction, could not be included.

This book is, in a variety of ways, about change, as is explained in the introductory chapter. This was not, however, the subject of the conference but rather a uniting theme that emerged in the preparation of the book. As editors we have been keen to keep the diversity of perspectives contained in these submissions and we have not directed authors to theme their work around change or revolution. By this means, we hope we have preserved the richness of perspectives concerning how museums change and are changed.

Simon Knell, Suzanne MacLeod and Sheila Watson
20 February 2007

# ACKNOWLEDGEMENTS

Simon Knell would like to thank his co-organiser, Barbara Lloyd, for her outstanding contribution to making the conference, *The Museum: A World Forum*, such a success. Simon would also like to thank those who gave their organisational support and expertise, in particular: Jim Roberts, Bob Ahluwalia, Elizabeth Rudge, Ross Parry, Andy Sawyer, Gus Dinn, Katy Garfitt, Ceri Jones and Amy Barnes.

We would also like to thank our conference sponsors and supporters for their essential contributions: The British Academy, The Arts Council, East Midlands Museums, Libraries and Archives Council, MWR, Haley Sharpe Design and Hanwell Instruments.

In various ways the content of this book has been influenced by all the contributions at the conference, and many individuals listed here made significant contributions afterwards to the shaping of this book: Geoffrey Lewis, Awhina Tamarapa, Julien Bastoen, Geoffrey Hancock, Dr Masaaki Morishita, Georgios Alexopoulos, Dr Rinella Cere, Konstantinos Arvanitis, Kostas Kotsakis, Paraskevi Nitsiou, Matoula Scaltsa, Maria Triantafyllidou, Panos Tzonos, Lia Yoka, Kalliopi Fouseki, Zenobia R. Kozak, Carlofilippo Frateschi, Elisabetta Lazzaro, Angela Jannelli, Laila Skjøthaug, Yuka Shimamura-Willcocks, Clara Masriera, Joan Santacana, Montserrat Sebastia, Eva Delgado, Marion Endt, Padmini Sebastian, Laura McAtackney, Sophia Bakogianni, Michelle Foggett, Scarpati Dario, Leopardi Andrea, Benedettucci Francesco, Alessandra Carnovale, Barbara Wenk, Elizabeth Rankin, Heather Hollins, Richard Sandell, Jocelyn Dodd, Ceri Jones, Annie Delin, Pippa Little, Dr Craig Douglas, Arnon Golan, Žarka Vujic, Darko Babiæ, Georgos Karadedos, Paraskevi Nitsiou, Malamatenia Scaltsa, Valasia Amiridou, Evaggeli Mamouri, Ifigenia Anagnostou, Efthalia Ioannidou, Kalliopi Hante, António Ribeiro da Costa, Professor Panos Tzonos, Ela Beaumont, Xatziri Peña Licea, Kate Pontin, Matthew Tyler-Jones, Anna Chrusciel, Katerina Gioftsali, Vasiliki Tzibazi, Alice Semedo, Alexandra Lekka, Theodore Alexiou, Maria Sotirakou, Giannis Gailas, Nadia Arbach, Keiko Kuroiwa, Emma Sullivan, Martin Philips, Sérgio Lira, Alexandra Bounia, Eleni Myrivili, Jeffrey Abt, Linda Young, Alexandra Badzak, Alexandra Stara, Nancy Dallet, Kolokesa Māahina-Tuai, Stephen Brown, Jared Bryson, Juliet Edwards, Myriam Proulx, Outi Turpeinen, Alisdair Hinshelwood, Bill Haley, Emmeline Leary, Lisanne Gibson, Núria Serrat Antoli, Dagny Stuedahl, Palmyre Pierroux, Eva van Moer, Nick Poole, Robin Boast, Jennifer Crowe, Scott Paterson, Martin Bazley, John Benfield and John Pratty. We would like to thank them all.

Finally, we would like to thank the contributors to this book for their efficient timekeeping and patience with the editors, and also to thank our editor at Routledge, Matt Gibbons.

# INTRODUCTION

It would be foolish to consider museums as unchanging but their very existence implies a commitment to stasis. Museums were established to capture and concretise progress – to gather up things as they became known and valued and keep them unchanged. By keeping real things they gave knowledge an underpinning framework and as such they became a pervasive networked technology which interlinked this knowledge and assured the visitor of its veracity. We may now ask 'Who's truth?' and question the practice in a multitude of ways, but nevertheless this empirical attitude remains fundamental to what museums are.

But museums are not solely about collections, indeed, they are rather less about collections than we tend to believe. Museums are about people, and collections are merely manifestations of human desires. As human products of different times, places, values, media, cultures and so on, museums themselves are more variable in time and space than we sometimes credit. And inevitably they must change more than we realise, and it is this which this book wishes to demonstrate. There is no central thesis to this book beyond exploring the ways in which museums are shaped and configured and how they themselves attempt to shape and change the world around them. The attempts of people to shape museums and the effects of a constantly changing museum context ensure that the museum remains in flux.

This book also challenges and questions a notion of change which sees the modern museum as the product of a linear development, from cabinets of curiosity, through the disciplinary museum, to modern conceptions of the living, eco-, digital or post-museum. It is easy to locate in their similarities a path of evolution, but two populations situated either side of a revolutionary moment always have much in common. Many museums – perhaps most new museums – are the product of rejecting the perceived norms of museum practice as much as they are about adopting them. The present array of museums does not bear witness to a survival of the fittest, but rather to repeated attempts to reinvent and redefine. This can be called mutation, in the sense that museums are always reacting to a perceived future – they are all opportunists – but yet they must also reflect upon their past and on the inertia that surrounds them. As such, no biological metaphor really offers a sensible way to visualise this change. Museums are in revolt. Revolution here then is a process which objectifies a set of values and an imagined past, and then follows a future that in some ways is oppositional and new. Or to put it another way, the museum sees two possible futures, one that reflects the present trajectory and one that can be obtained by reinvention. One needs to understand that this is in many respects a managing of myths, as neither past nor future are neutral or factual; both are political.

Museum revolutions – or museum changes more generally – have rarely addressed the fundamental question 'Why?' Museums are accepted and valued and therefore are more likely to ask 'How?' and 'For whom?' As revolutionary questions, these seem to belong to a genteel and professionalised middle class; they lack the anarchy that calls for the erection of barricades and the raising of flags and banners. In *Museum Revolutions*, museums are constantly in flux, and change is often fine scale rather than pervasive. Nevertheless, each change incrementally, and sometimes fundamentally, changes the institution. Spanning more than 200 years, *Museum Revolutions* discusses national museums, ecomuseums, society museums, provincial galleries, colonial museums, the showman's museum and science centres, and ranges across such topics as disciplinary practices, ethnic representation, post-colonial politics, economic aspiration, social reform, indigenous models, conceptions of history, urban regeneration, sustainability, sacred objects, a sense of place, globalisation, identities, social responsibility, controversy, repatriation, human remains, drama, learning and education. The product of this exploration is the revisualisation of the museum not as a static cultural monument but as fluid and responsive, dynamic, shaping, political, particular and complex.

The book begins with contributions that are essentially about change as invention. In the language of revolutions, these are about manifestos and their implementation. Philippe Taquet describes how Georges Cuvier reinvented a museum in the Jardin du Roi in Paris as a manifestation of his own ideals and intellectual ambition. The Muséum d'Histoire Naturelle became the paradigm for the museum across Europe and her colonies, and Cuvier the very model for the heroic savant. Sue Pearce discusses a rather different inventor who, although often portrayed as a sensationalist, began to probe the visual language of exhibition. Out of sheer necessity, William Bullock needed to understand the nature of audience appeal and soon understood that science alone was insufficient to create attention-grabbing interpretation. At a time when the museum in Britain was still an emerging phenomenon, Bullock's methods seem to have been given serious consideration among the literati. It was only a matter of time, however, before the museum as serious scientific and educational enterprise distinguished itself from the amateur collector's mania or the London shows' attempt to reach beyond the fact. More than a century later, however, museums began to study and understand their audiences much as Bullock had. What followed were carefully designed and immersive galleries that pushed academic pedantry and collections into the background. Conversations much like those that surrounded Bullock's activity again emerged and attempted to reassert the roles of scholarship and the object. The museums that Simon Knell explores grew up in the shadow of Cuvier, who was widely considered – by those who did not feel in competition with the French – the greatest savant of the day. Knell considers a longer period of change and merges manifesto with context to explore change that is partly modelled and partly beyond control. Locating institutions and practices in relation to the contemporary desires and expectations of society, the individual and the emergent discipline of geology, Knell detects change, and even revolution. The first part of the nineteenth century is, as a result, exposed as a period when the museum was being repeatedly reformulated. The lens of a single discipline is also useful to Chris Whitehead, who attempts to understand the making of a national museum. His interest is reflexive and revealing: both discipline and museum are formed as bounded, divided and ordered intellectual and physical spaces. It reveals that, while museums are inevitably victims of change, at moments in their history individuals take control and establish a manifesto, which like an architectural plan gives a structure with long-term impact. Knell's geologists also sense a map but can never be fully cognisant of the widely felt cultural consequences of their actions. Cuvier seems certain, however, that the rigour of his efforts will ensure their long-term impact.

Preetha Nair's Indian museums also emerge from individual visions, but she sees them more broadly in terms of the geography of social transformation ('spaces of modernity') which has largely been overlooked by historians seeking to understand the formation of the modern country. There is here a drive for mass access and education, which was also affecting the largely private museum culture in Britain at the same time. Underpinning these developments was an economic drive which, although present to some degree in the formation of Britain's Museum of Practical Geology, was more pervasive in developments in India, reflecting the desires of the industrialised British to extend their possession of natural resources through colonial expansion. Here in India we also see Cuvier's museum acting as a paradigm.

The Walker Art Gallery in Liverpool, discussed here by Suzanne MacLeod, is perhaps the only institution in this book that sees the masses in revolt and taking possession of a museum. Although brutally put down, this was hardly a call to arms; it was rather a clash of class values. As MacLeod reveals, the Walker is a curiously elite product of an industry which fed the development of a drinking culture that contemporary society then deemed unacceptable. For MacLeod, however, this is but one moment in a study which examines the changing Gallery through the modelling of space and the politics of control. As MacLeod explains, this is not a standard architectural history, but rather one that shows how the material nature of the institution naturally resists change, producing an inertia which repeatedly has to been addressed through acts of appropriation and renewal. This was recognised by Ali Mozaffari in his study of the National Museum of Iran, the only chapter in this book to discuss a museum that experienced national revolution – in this case during the Islamic Revolution of 1979. As Mozaffari explains, Iran long found itself in difficult encounters with the West, and as a result it developed its own notions of national identity built around tangible heritage. Before the revolution this heritage was used as part of a process of modernisation and secularisation; after the revolution it held potential for rejecting Western influences and for the reinterpretation of a traditional and religiously observant past. At the National Museum of Iran today, two buildings materialise and represent this ideological revolution: one reflecting the old Iran, the other representing the new.

Just as Iran's museums reflect a cultural ideology, so Richard Toon's American science centres might be understood to materialise that nation's faith in science, economy and private patronage. Toon investigates the shaping of these institutions, and in doing so locates rather different influences from those often repeated in the long established heroic history of the science centre movement. Toon locates some contextual necessities, such as the Cold War, and internal ideologies, such as decontextualised ahistoricism, which the movement had to locate as defining principles. The American science centre movement also constructed and manipulated its heroes as it spread its influence around the world. Often formulaic in their construction – each centre in some ways a clone of those that have gone before – science centres give a rather different perspective on change. Set against Nair's Indian museums and juxtaposed with an Iranian view, the science centre might be seen as a kind of cultural imperialism – though, of course, adopters are welcoming the phenomenon with open arms and their own money. It is a globalising influence. It has also tested the resolve of professionals to see the museum as essentially collection based.

In terms of revolutionary impact of museum exhibitions, few have acquired the status of the 'Te Maori' exhibition at the Met in New York in 1984. Here, Conal McCarthy reveals that the revered status of that exhibition relies on the production of a self-perpetuating mythology. 'Te Maori' signalled the birth of a postcolonial present and an objectified ahistorical colonial past. History was to be politically manipulated into black and white: self-determination and equality replacing White supremacy and exploitation. Returning to documents written in the Māori language, McCarthy re-examines the period before 'Te Maori' and demonstrates that the politics of representation were never so clear cut, that the revolution was a product of presentism.

This section ends with a modern day manifesto produced by Bob Janes which reflects modern-day concerns. No longer Cold War or colonial, for Janes there is a need to re-evaluate purpose rather than slip into the endless business-driven model of a heritage industry. This model is most developed in North America, but it has been adopted by many other countries and heritage organisations in a world in which service and cost can no longer be kept apart. Janes shows how this business-driven model of heritage forces the museum to lose sight of its original purpose and its relationship to the needs of the community. In order to convince us of the importance of ideals and responsibilities, Janes takes the reader on a journey that leaves the museum and enters wider political debate regarding society's activities and values. For example, you might feel you have good reason to doubt that gas-guzzling SUVs have anything to do with a museum debate, but Janes is keen to demonstrate relationships, and that these issues have the same root. Janes unashamedly admits to that anathema of the economist, idealism, but he does so as the basis for a uniting philosophy that can turn an institution into a socially relevant and effective organisation rather than merely a place to attract and entertain. An experienced and influential manager, Janes is here giving an alternative business vision which attempts to displace the necessity of merely becoming a business with a return to purpose.

The step into the second section of the book is not a huge one. Many of the chapters here might also be considered to be about agendas and contextual shaping. The emphasis in this section is the role of museums in shaping identities – in changing places and people. A universally applicable notion, one could also locate it in Whitehead's art gallery visionaries, Knell's fossil-obsessed philosophers, Nair's new India, Toon's science centres and Mozaffari's various Iranian museum incarnations. Here, Bronwyn Labrum takes the reader back into the rich New Zealand context already explored by McCarthy. Labrum looks at one of the hothouses of postcolonial museological debate: the Pakeha – the settler communities – and the role of museums in the production of histories, where she shows that histories were renegotiated according to changing context. Here, museums are to be understood as key public intellectual frontiers which challenged past conceptions among communities which imagined a pioneer age. Sheila Watson's exploration of a socially deprived English coastal resort is also about a renegotiation of history, but here the museum is active and the history overtly democratic. If Labrum's actors are participating in a reconfiguring of a country then undergoing overt self assessment, Watson's public do not live in such a society and an act of proactive and open public engagement is necessary in order to locate agenda for change. What Watson's museum ends up valuing is the inevitably poetic past as much as the hard data. The history produced is no more fictional than any other history, but if history is a process of foregrounding aspects of the past in order to construct a narrative, then here that narrative is one which centres on identity, local pride and the use of history for social and urban regeneration. Some might suggest this is a manipulation of heritage, perhaps forgetting that the very notion 'heritage' conceals that very act.

It is the manipulative aspect of heritage that so often makes historians run from it. The historian worries that heritage production is a modernising activity, which constructs fake façades from surviving material and in the process eradicates any material truth or poetic value. It does this in the interests of public consumption or a heritage industry of the kind that so concerns Janes. Yet others believe the past is there to be used, and not all uses need to corrupt and distort. Many chapters here discuss this production of heritage. Marta Anico and Elsa Peralta explore the manipulation of heritage in the formation of identities in modern Portugal. Like Mozaffari's Iran, Portugal also experienced a political revolution, and also like Iran, an engagement with Western conceptions of modernity and modernisation was central. However, the two countries have moved in opposite directions: the Portuguese sought a liberal Western democracy and all that came with it. As with Watson in Great Yarmouth, Anico and Peralta are dealing with changed communities and changed places, and they consider how heritage is exploited to manufacture identities that resonate with an imagined past. Modern Taiwan has similarly, and perhaps more extensively, undergone a period of rapid social change. As Chia-Li Chen explains, its museums have been fundamental to establishing a Taiwanese identity, with the necessary unpacking of ethnic difference, waves of immigration, a renegotiated past and relationships to the People's Republic of China. Unlike Watson's museums, where an attempt has been made to make the museum a reflection of the people, Chen's museums have been established from a more traditional understanding of heritage and the necessity of memorialisation. Yet, the impact of the museums on an individual's sense of place and identity is no less profound. Peter Davis's communities have also engaged with heritage with open eyes, becoming part of what Davis calls a 'movement' – a term which suggests a shared philosophy, ideology or set of values. Despite playing a key role in this movement, Davis remains a dispassionate observer who wishes to understand rather than take on the role of advocate. He can define its very being in terms of characteristics, such as sustainability, which lie at the heart of the vision. It is these characteristics which he then tests by studying the implementation of the ecomuseum model in diverse national and regional contexts. In terms of revolution, the ecomuseum model can fundamentally alter communities, yet Davis is also interested in how the model itself is changed. Rather than believing in an orthodoxy, one suspects that his past as a biologist makes him amenable to evolutionary adaptation.

For Anico and Peralta, the context of globalisation is important, and indeed it has given a sense of urgency to the ecomuseum movement and its desire to capture and preserve the essence of traditional (unmodernised) communities. But to what extent do we fail to question Western notions of the museum and heritage? We have already pointed to the globalising aspect of the science centre; more than a century earlier the museum found itself in that role and one cannot deny that it continues to function in this way. In Australia and New Zealand, the museum has been at the heart of a debate about the nature of heritage which has affected museum process, re-evaluated the nature of engagement and implementation, and reversed past acts of appropriation. This is driven by a respect and privileging of first peoples and indigenous knowledge. In a material way this can be seen in staffing, boards of management, narrative voice and so on. The aim has been to replace imposition with community autonomy over place. David Butts, however, raises concerns about the museum implications of a political backlash which attempts to counter a highly developed biculturalism with a sense of one nation equality. More fundamentally, this shifts expertise from an appreciation of lived indigenous expertise to abstract knowledge of indigenous communities. The philosophical difference is profound and one cannot separate this from a longer political struggle between coloniser and indigenous resistance. The exchanges may be more tempered than in the past, but these are still battles over territory, self-determination or, as we discuss them in this section, place and identity. In contrast to Australia and New Zealand, countries in Africa have been far more doubting of the role of the Western museum. Indeed, Evelyne Tegomoh might well share many a Western historian's concerns about the corrupting effect of turning the past into heritage. Tegomoh's chapter shows that there is much in indigenous culture that values and preserves without ever needing to 'museumise' in any Western sense. The conflict she describes is not immediately to be seen as one of imperialism, colonialism or Western appropriation, but this is implicitly what it is. It is the construction of the museum as a universally valid concept in and using it as a signifier of civilisation, which turns the museum into an instrument of globalisation and homogenisation. But as communities around the world cannot evade the pervasive and insidious economic impact of the developed world, so inevitably such threats to indigenous values must be resisted. Clearly, the selling of souls in order to satiate the Western desire for accessible heritage must be challenged. The West's object fetishism and obsession with knowing other people's business needs to be questioned, and the museum perhaps challenged.

Moira Simpson would certainly empathise with Tegomoh, but she sees the museum as adaptive and even essential as a place of safekeeping in the context of a globalised art market and the worldwide pillaging of sites. Such models of the museum challenge traditional definitions, and where they prevent public access they also challenge government endorsed funding models which relate funding to public service. Mike Pickering's chapter also has a relationship to Tegomoh's because Pickering is attempting to reverse actions which Tegomoh's actors are attempting to resist. Pickering, a practitioner who has unparalleled experience of the issues surrounding the museum possession of indigenous human remains, notes that professionals, for a range of reasons, tend to distance themselves from these issues. Repatriation becomes a process: a matter of professional obligation and logistical necessity. Repatriation has been seen by museum workers as being at the edge of practice for at least 20 years. This is not because it is new or as contentious as it once was, but professionals still fear its ethical, legal and political complexities and implications. Pickering sees these matters otherwise, and does so from within the process. For him, these matters are the everyday and real rather than imagined. He has certainly witnessed and been a part of a revolutionary change in practice, which has now left the whispered conversations of coffee rooms and entered wider public discussion – discussion that is no longer merely political. Ever the pragmatist, Pickering can nevertheless show the positives of the repatriation process in terms of building of long-term relationships between museums and indigenous communities and media impact. In some ways, it echoes Janes's marrying of responsibility with a re-evaluation of goals.

The third section of this book is concerned with the ways in which museums attempt to instigate change in their publics. Clearly, this is a theme shared with many of the preceding chapters, and many authors here relate their work to questions of identity. Kate Gregory and Andrea Witcomb's study returns us to the nature of heritage, and here to its affective qualities. It is a quality underutilised and barely understood in museums but which forms a central communicative thread in the creative arts and, most relevantly for museums, in theatre and film. This affective engagement is clearly present in Watson's and Chen's museums and must be an implicit principle guiding the ecomuseum movement. Its semiotics are also understood by shopping mall architects and other 'Disneyfiers'. In museums, however, the preference has been for aesthetics, and the journey by Gregory and Witcomb into the other manifestations is fraught with difficulties in terms of understanding outcomes or considering their utility. It is here that there seems to remain a huge gulf between the affective possibilities of the real (in the museum or heritage environment) and film, theatre, literature and other immersive narrative media. Uncovering and realising the possibilities returns us to Bullock's concerns with engagement and communication, as discussed by Pearce. In many respects this work exists at the edge of practice, but here it might be usefully informed by practices in rather different communication media.

Lynda Kelly's study of museum visitors as learners also addresses the active role of visitors' identities. Her research revealed that a visitor's learning image was fluid – that context shaped how they performed as learners. Kelly attempts to understand this by establishing a five-component model of museum learning. Jem Fraser offers her own model of the visitor engagement, again locating identity as a key component of performance. Fraser is here implicitly locating affective change. While Pierre Bourdieu's class-based analyses of the museum also saw power and identity as fundamental to the rejection and acceptance of museums, Fraser considers how such things can be turned into meaningful rituals. Fraser begins her discussion with 'critical pedagogy', and this also forms the central idea critically discussed by Peggy Lindauer. Critical pedagogy, Lindauer explains, uses teaching techniques for socially activist purposes, to deal with such things as social inequalities and exclusion. It is worth noting at this point that outsiders, when they see such notions, accuse museum studies of indulging in advocacy rather than research. But as Lindauer's chapter admirably demonstrates, museums can be seen as manifestations of social policy, and their research agendas can thus be socially moulded, much as educationalists research the approaches to literacy or sociologists consider the mechanics of socially inclusive societies. If these projects in some sense have a notion of progress towards a goal, they are no different from scientific studies aimed at renewable energy or better insulation for the space shuttle. It does, however, position the museum as an active participant in fields that possess essentially caring and socially responsible ideologies. Lindauer considers how this socially active perspective affects modern perceptions of such things as the post-museum, recognising – as historians have long done and as this book purposefully illustrates – that museums are constantly in flux, complex and messy. Museums have never conformed to single paradigms and they never will. In a closely argued chapter, Lindaur searches for a sense of how critical pedagogy might be manifested in the museum exhibition, locating many blind alleys along the way.

Viv Golding certainly sees museums playing a key role in the production of a more equal society. Her work is particularly concerned with educational programming, and it draws upon her own Black and feminist-inspired studies of the museum as a neutral space – a clearing, away from formal education and home life – within which new relationships, new ways of seeing, new opportunities, can be explored and can counter other negative media portrayals. Here it is as easy for the museum to address difference positively and to do so by exploiting the values of multiculturalism, which, as Butts shows, are now challenged in New Zealand, just as they are in the United Kingdom. In the museum, Golding shows, this enabled museum workers to turn self-perception on its head and fundamentally address issues of low self-esteem and exclusion.

Fiona Cameron takes the reader on another tack by examining the supposed apolitical stance of the museum. Social responsibility, however, might suggest a political positioning – at least as much as Golding's stance on education does. Cameron asks how well museums are positioned to deal with controversial subjects, and she begins by taking issue with Janes's view that museums can work outside government policy. Noting examples from Canada, Australia and Britain, it is easy to demonstrate that governments can control museum discourses – either through financial incentive or penalty. In many countries, of course, the museum director is often a political appointment and so individuals come and go with the regularity of city mayors. In this situation, it would be extremely dangerous for a museum director to raise subjects that might leave a political patron exposed. It is far safer to be a machine for generally recognised public benefit and goodwill. Politicians cannot use the museum for their own political ends – though clearly political appointments are aimed at a supportive cultural infrastructure – but nor can they feel compromised by the politics of unelected professionals.

Yet as Cameron discusses, there can be a morally illegitimate position in some topical areas which make a centre-ground objective view appear leftfield. Thus, if museums are instrumental in changing society, their messages do not always conform to the middle ground; museums court acceptability, they wish for patronage. Cameron concludes that museums do have a role in the projects Janes so desires, not as advocates but as providers of information. One should not, however, underestimate the political difficulties of attempting this.

Mary Brooks and Claire Rumsey's contribution acts as an example of the controversial in museum practice and reveals how fundamentally acceptable practices in museums have changed over the past decade or so. Their focus is the body, an object that remains very much at the museum edge in terms of affect and instrumental use. Its place is utterly perplexing: moral obligations unaffected by the secularisation of society; the bones of the long dead rehumanised; the flesh of the recently living objectified as art; bodies controlled by codes; and bodies used for sensation. If the body is the most contentious of museum objects, it is also an object which needs relatively little explanation.

Beth Lord's contribution continues the theme of museum communication, and in philosophical mood she turns to Michel Foucault's work to consider the perceived dichotomy in the production of museum histories between 'objective' didacticism and 'subjective' aestheticism. She considers, contrasts, and unites Platonism and hermeneutics, which seem to define past and present values for communicators – which might be simplified as a move from fact to meaning. Here, it is Foucault's effective history which most interests Lord, with the opportunities for visitors to work with objects to construct history rather than to visit the monuments of written history. Lord's assertion is for object first and active meaning-making second, with the removal of traditional tools of narrative, empathy or memory. This looks like another manifesto.

From the chapters in this section, it is no surprise that Eilean Hooper-Greenhill sees museum education as a field 'trying to establish new paradigms in relation to long-established frameworks'. One might not separate museum education from wider ambitions to communicate more effectively (or affectively). Hooper-Greenhill takes an overview of change in the field, while admitting that a history of museum education, from which to understand this change, has not been written. One cannot deny, even if the comparative data are not fully available, that there have been fundamental changes to ideas about learning – that the field has a disconcerting theoretical fluidity. One cannot escape the politics of learning and knowledge, or social control of the process. Hooper-Greenhill fears that the ghosts of the past might be inescapable, and certainly the politics of provision – if we reflect on the contributions by Janes, Cameron or Butts – suggest that past values can return into vogue. What is inescapable, however, is that museums will change, never simply heading to become the post-museum or to reinvent themselves as cabinets for the curious; never gaining finality but remaining in flux, ready to be appropriated and remodelled, and perhaps to experience revolution.

# Part 1

# SHAPING MUSEUMS
# AND MANIFESTOS

# 1

# ESTABLISHING THE PARADIGMATIC MUSEUM

## Georges Cuvier's Cabinet d'anatomie comparée in Paris

*Philippe Taquet*

Georges Cuvier was born on the 23 August 1769 to a modest middle class family in the city of Montbéliard in the east of France. The status of this Lutheran city, at that time attached to the duchy of Wurtemberg, gave Cuvier the opportunity to acquire an excellent education at the Caroline University. In 1788, newly appointed as a tutor in Normandy, Cuvier devoted his free time to his passion for natural history. While the rest of France was in revolution, Cuvier collected plants and insects and dissected fishes, birds and marine organisms (Taquet 2006).

An avid reader of the works of Aristotle, Cuvier soon began to elaborate a new plan for a general natural history: 'searching for the relationships between all living animals with Nature'. His inspirations were many: he became an admirer of the Swedish taxonomist Carolus Linnaeus and his methods of classification; he discovered German Gottlieb Conrad Storr's essay on mammal classification; he was impressed by the German naturalist Karl Friedrich Kielmeyer; he gained an understanding of the scope of comparative anatomy from the works of the French savant Louis Jean Marie Daubenton; he consumed enthusiastically the works of Antoine Laurent Lavoisier, who proposed a new approach to chemistry, and Antoine Laurent de Jussieu, whose new natural method for classifying plants suggested correlations between the different parts of the organism. Cuvier felt, for example, that by applying Jussieu's botanical approaches he could transform zoology from a science of memory and nomenclature into something new, within which could be located combinations and affinities like those seen in chemistry and the problem solving utilised in geometry.

Cuvier understood that the realisation of this grand project required the acknowledgement of the scientific community, particularly those Parisian naturalists working at the Cabinet d'histoire naturelle in the Jardin du Roi, an institution which became known, in 1793, as the Muséum d'Histoire Naturelle. Understanding that the museum's treasure house of zoological specimens was key to his plans, Cuvier sent manuscripts of his work to the entomologist Guillaume Antoine Olivier and the zoologists Bernard Germain Etienne de Lacepède and Etienne Geoffroy Saint-Hilaire. These demonstrated his capabilities in natural history and his talents as observer and artist. The museum was then recovering from the disorder of The Terror and saw in Cuvier a young naturalist free from any links with the old regime; a follower of Linné rather than Buffon. As a consequence of these fortuitous circumstances and being an already prodigious talent, Cuvier – then only 26 years old – became engaged at the museum in July 1795 as assistant to Jean Claude Mertrud, who held the chair of animal anatomy. Almost immediately, he began work on his 'Tableau élémentaire de l'Histoire naturelle des animaux', which was to take on material form in a new Cabinet d'anatomie, supported by a team of efficient preparators and assistants.

## Cuvier's Cabinet d'anatomie

Noting the relationship to Lavoisier's science, Cuvier defined his programme as follows:

> Chemistry exposes the laws according to which elementary molecules of substances act one upon the other at short distances . . . The natural history of any organisms, to be perfect, must include,
>
> a) The description of all sensible properties of this organism, and of all its parts
> b) The relationships of all these parts between themselves, the movements which are in action, and the modifications they are submitted to during their union
> c) The active and passive relationships of this organism with all other organisms of the Universe
> d) And finally the explanation of all these phenomena
>
> Natural history considers from only one point of view all natural living beings and the common result of all their actions in the great overall picture of Nature. Natural History determines the laws of coexistence of their properties . . . It establishes the degrees of similarity which exist between the different organisms, and the groups according to degrees. Natural History can only reach its perfection when completed by the specific history of all natural living beings.
>
> (Cuvier 1797)

On arriving at the museum, Cuvier made an inventory of the comparative anatomy collection, which had been assembled as a direct result of the works of Buffon.

> The Great man had conceived a plan for the history of animals, more ambitious than his predecessors; he wanted the whole organization to be known, and it is possible to say that, with the help of Daubenton, he started to realize this project, in a correct way, for the viviparous quadrupedal animals.
>
> Daubenton, who was in charge of the dissections, worked to preserve as much as possible of parts of the animals, in alcohol or dried. Of these the skeletons, which were described and figured in the main edition of the *Histoire Naturelle*, had been kept.
>
> However, Buffon abandoned this part of his plan in his *Histoire Naturelle des Oiseaux* and in the supplements of the *Histoire des Animaux Quadrupèdes*. There was no part devoted to anatomy and the collection did not increase. Instead, the quadruped skeletons were put into storage in order to make space for more spectacular artefacts which were then being added to all parts of the Cabinet. As a consequence the skeletons suffered considerable damage. The situation stayed like this for many years.
>
> (Cuvier 1803)

Cuvier's rise in Paris was meteoric, with Cuvier eventually taking over Mertrud's chair of animal anatomy in 1802, and in so doing gaining control of the anatomy collections: 'So it is from that time that I really began the collection in the Jardin du Roi' (Cuvier 1822). He noted at the time that: 'It was lacking a room for the exhibition. The soft preparations were arranged in the Cabinet with the complete skeletons. The skeletons were partly in the basement, partly in the attic, and nobody knew where to put the new preparations' (Cuvier 1803). Later, Cuvier remembered:

> The Garden had just acquired large buildings occupied by storehouses which had formerly been used for the management of cabs and which were just against the house were I was living. I managed to make a hole in the wall. I ordered three or four skeletons that Mertrud had prepared to be moved from the attic into the new space. I also collected ... what was left from the old skeletons prepared by Daubenton for Buffon, which were piled up like faggots. And it was while completing this enterprise, sometimes helped by professors of the Museum, annoyed sometimes by others, that I succeeded in increasing my collection so much that nobody was opposed to its enlargement.
>
> (Cuvier 1822)

To manage his enterprise successfully, Cuvier surrounded himself with efficient and devoted collaborators:

> there was no assistant anatomist for the manual tasks as there was for the other collections, but the zeal of the citizen Rousseau supplied the lack of help [Pierre Rousseau, 1756–1829, followed by his son Emmanuel Rousseau, 1788–1868]. In spite of the modest salary it was possible to give to him, pushed by the love of anatomy, he worked very hard to increase the treasure, modest at the beginning, which was trusted to him.
>
> (Cuvier 1803)

Cuvier called for his relations from Montbéliard to help him in Paris: his brother Frédéric (1773–1838), who became professor and first keeper of the chair of comparative physiology of the museum; his cousin Georges Duvernoy (1777–1855), who worked by Cuvier's side from 1802 to 1805; Charles Léopold Laurillard (1783–1853), who was placed in charge of the anatomical drawings from 1804; and Constant Duméril (1774–1860), who helped with the writing the of first two volumes of the Leçons d'Anatomie Comparée, a role later taken on by Georges Duvernoy for the final three volumes.

Cuvier later called upon his daughter-in-law Sophie Duvaucel and his daughter Clémentine, who were both put in charge of drawing fishes. His wife was also called upon; she made the catalogue of the preparations given to the Royal College of Surgeons in London. Cuvier would also later surround himself with foreign collaborators: Miss Sarah Lee, the widow of the explorer Thomas Bowdich, and Joseph Barclay Pentland, an Irish naturalist who worked with Cuvier for many years before becoming a diplomat of the British Foreign Office in Bolivia.

Despite all the help he would receive there was little hint initially of the grandeur of the project. As one of his helpers later recalled: 'often at the beginning, he and his brother were obliged to saw and fix the almost unpolished boards themselves, onto which the skeletons were then placed in order' (Laurillard 1836). His collecting had begun with the dead animals of the menagerie, as well as those given or sent by private individuals, those bought specially from the market or elsewhere, and those in the zoological collections that were unused (Cuvier 1803). He had the building, which was composed of two huge rooms, divided into several smaller rooms. Embryonic British geologist Charles Lyell reflected on the spatial arrangement when he spent two months in Paris in 1823. Clearly, the ordering and control of people, space, books and objects was fundamental to Cuvier's way of working:

> I got into Cuvier's *sanctum sanctorum* yesterday, and it is truly characteristic of the man. In every part it displays that extraordinary power of methodising which is the grand secret of the prodigious feats which he performs annually without appearing to give himself the least trouble. But before I introduce you to this study, I should tell you that there is first the museum of natural history opposite his house, and admirably arranged by himself, then the anatomy museum connected with his dwelling. In the latter is a library disposed in a suite of rooms, each containing works on one subject. There is one where there are all the works on ornithology, in another room all on ichthyology, in another osteology, in another law books, etc. etc. When he is engaged in such works as require continual reference to a variety of authors, he has a stove shifted into one of these rooms, in which everything on that subject is systematically arranged, so that in the same work he often makes the round of many apartments. But the ordinary studio contains no bookshelves. It is a longish room, comfortably furnished, lighted from above, and furnished with eleven desks to stand to, and two low tables, like a public office for so many clerks. But all is for one man, who multiplies himself as author, and admitting no one into this room, moves as he finds necessary, or as fancy inclines him, from one occupation to another. Each desk is furnished with a complete establishment of inkstand, pens, etc., pins to pin Manuscripts together, the works immediately in reading and the Manuscript in hand, and on shelves behind all the Manuscripts of the same work. There is a separate bell to several desks. The low tables are to sit at when he is tired. The collaborators are not numerous, but always chosen well. They save him every mechanical labour, find references, etc., are rarely admitted to the study, receive orders, and speak not.
>
> (Lyell 1888)

## Anatomy of the Cabinet

In 1802, Cuvier gave an inventory of the skeletons and preparations that could be seen in the new Cabinet d'anatomie comparée (Figure 1.1). Of the 2,898 preparations, 526 were complete skeletons, of which 102 were old preparations. These formed nearly half of the 1,239 osteological specimens. In addition, there were 1,136 soft preparations preserved in alcohol and a further 523 preparations of invertebrates.

An inventory made by Joseph Barclay Pentland and Achille Valenciennes on Cuvier's death, in 1832, reveals that the collection continued to grow prodigiously. By then it contained 16,665 preparations (Valenciennes, Laurillard and Pentland 1833). This included, among other things: 2,625 complete skeletons, 2,150 skulls and 1,389 disarticulated heads (Figure 1.2). It also held 56 human skeletons from all parts of the world: Papous from New Guinea, Aborigines from Australia, Indians from Canada, Patagons and Araucans

*Figure 1.1* The Cabinet d'anatomie comparée in the Jardin des Plantes in Paris. Behind Georges Cuvier's house is the building that was transformed for the presentation of the comparative anatomy collection. On the first floor are the rooms where Cuvier worked.

Photo: the author.

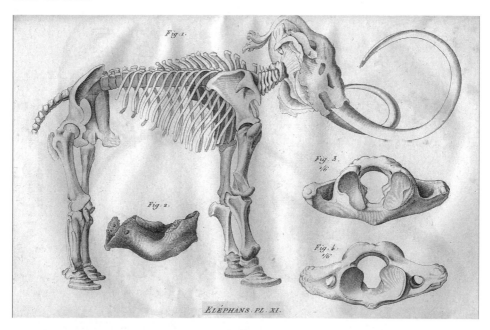

*Figure 1.2* Eléphans. One of the plates of the *Recherches sur les Ossemens Fossiles* volumes. Plate XI, T.I, 1821.

Photo: D. Geffard.

from South America, two Bushmen, two Guanches from Tenerife, one Dutchman, one Flemish, 25 French, one Italian and one English. There was also the skeleton of Soleyman el Haleby, who assassinated the famed General Kléber in Cairo in 1800. It had been brought back by Napoleon's surgeon, Baron Larrey. Among the collection of apes were two orangutans (though, of course, no gorilla, which was not described until 1847). The collection also contained eight complete skeletons of cetaceans, including a cape whale and a right whale. In total, the collection held 7,626 mammal specimens, 2,310 specimens of birds, 800 skeletons of fishes and 906 arthropods. There were also fossil animals: the remains of *Palaeotherium* and *Anoplotherium* from the gypsum of Montmartre and bones of *Anthracotherium*, *Lophiodon*, mammoths, mastodons, hippopotamus and rhinoceros (Figure 1.3).

As Cuvier's status grew he relied rather less on the animals of the local menagerie. He became connected into a network through which flowed specimens from around the world. For example, he received material from Nicolas Baudin's expedition to Australia, and from the naturalist François Péron and illustrator Charles Alexandre Lesueur after their exhibition at La Malmaison Castle, where they were presented to Napoleon's first wife, Josephine de Beauharnais. Pierre Antoine Delalande brought Cuvier a tapir from Brazil and, from the Cape of Good Hope, a rhinoceros, hippopotamus and two large and beautiful species of whale. His son-in-law, Alfred Duvaucel, with his friend Pierre Médard Diard, sent him an Indian rhinoceros, gibbons, a dugong and numerous species of mammals from Asia. He was

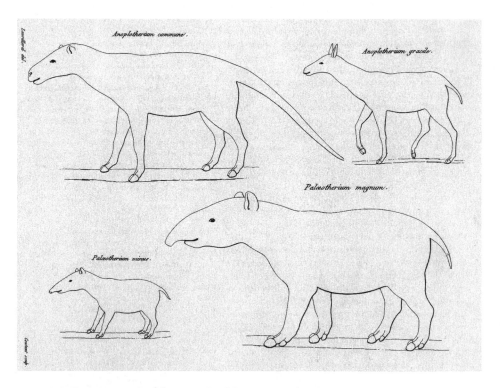

*Figure 1.3* Reconstitution of the animals of the gypsum of Montmartre. Plate LXVI, T.III, 1822, *Ossemens Fossiles.*

Photo: D. Geffard.

offered the skeleton of the walrus collected during Captain William Edward Parry's expedition to the Arctic. The list of naturalist travellers willing to donate to Cuvier's project grew: Leschenault, Quoy, Gaimard, Lesson, Garnot, Reynaud, Rang, Milbert, Dussumier and so on.

Cuvier took in these objects and placed them in a systematic arrangement of his own design: 'The preparations have been made and placed in physiological arrangement. This means that they are distributed not according to the animals from which they are originated, but according to the organs from which their structure can be understood' (Cuvier 1803). As noted by Philippe Sloan (1997), the purpose of the arrangement was not to compare organs across different subkingdoms (such as the eye of a cephalopod with that of a mammal) but rather to show that inside each class, or subkingdom, organs share relationships and functions. Cuvier's aim was to illustrate and prove the assertions of his groundbreaking *Règne Animal*, which drew upon this mode of analysis to promote a natural distribution of species, genera and families inside the different classes.

It was in this book that Cuvier explained his method, its application to natural history and its utility as an introduction to comparative anatomy.

> Here, I go partly climbing from the lower divisions to the upper divisions, by the way of comparison and rapprochement; in part also going down from the upper to the lower by the way of the subordination of the characters; comparing precisely the results of the two methods, verifying the one by the other, and establishing always the connection between the external and the internal forms, which all together are an integral part of the essential being of each animal.
>
> (Cuvier 1817)

Cuvier was here probably also taking into account recent observations of Etienne Geoffroy Saint-Hilaire, who was making links between oviparous vertebrates, through an analysis of the composition of the different skulls. However, Cuvier fundamentally disagreed with Geoffroy's assertion that there existed a single body plan. Geoffroy was then making bold connections between the structure of the vertebrates and that of molluscs, such as the octopus. For Cuvier, the 'embranchements' (subkingdoms) were very distinctive entities, which could not be united together in this way.

The result of Cuvier's huge effort to prepare, study and arrange the collection was his proud proposal, in 1812, of the different classes, to be articulated in *Le Règne Animal Distribué d'Après Son Organisation, Pour Servir de Base à l'Histoire Naturelle des Animaux et d'Introduction à l'Anatomie Compare*. It divided nature into four subkingdoms: vertebrata, molluscs, articulata (arthropods) and zoophytes or radiata.

As William Coleman wrote:

> The *Règne Animal* was to be a logical and complete exposition of all known animals. It was not what is today called a taxonomic key. On the contrary, the experienced naturalist used Cuvier's work in order to gain more profound knowledge of a specimen, or a species, or any zoological unit whose identity he already knew. Using the index or his knowledge of the plan of the work he could turn, for example, to a detailed description of the elephant or to a discussion of the structure and habits of the various mollusks.
>
> (Coleman 1964)

The *Règne Animal* was an attempt to formulate a natural classification guaranteed by the principle of correlation of parts and by the subordination of characters. In it Cuvier introduced brevity and clarity into natural history, with the aim of reproducing accurately the actual order of animals in the creation.

> The basic presupposition of this practice was that each kind of animal in nature enjoyed an individual identity. Each was a unique complex of morphological resemblances separated by unmistakable gaps from all other forms. Cuvier believed that the zoological species were real, in a literal sense of the world. The *natural* system was merely an intelligent ordering of the zoological *types* so as best to preserve the *real* order of nature.
>
> (Coleman 1964)

It was this approach that would permit Cuvier to extend zoological understanding into the realm of extinct animals. The four embranchements, expressed in terms of types, were regarded in 1812 as an enormous advance in the classification of animals, which also began a recognition of the diversity and singularity of non-vertebrate life. The *Règne Animal* was translated into English and German, and parts of it into Italian, Hungarian and Welsh. The Cabinet d'anatomie comparée, which had opened in 1806, revealed to the public the results Cuvier's inventory of nature.

## Cuvier and the Hunterian Museum

When Cuvier was only 21 years old he had already discovered the works of the distinguished British surgeon John Hunter and knew of his significant personal museum. In a letter sent from Normandy to his German friend Christoph Heinrich Pfaff, in August 1790, Cuvier explained that he had read John Hunter's work, published in 1786, in which Hunter explained the definition of 'species', and separated the wolf, dog and jackal into distinct species (Taquet 2006). Later, writing on the history of natural sciences, Cuvier (1841) remarks on William Hunter and then on his brother John:

> the most important thing we credit to him is the founding in London of a school of anatomy and a museum which became very rich and very famous . . . his younger and better known brother, John Hunter . . . devoted himself with passion to comparative anatomy. He started with the collection of his brother which formed the base of a beautiful and tremendous collection of the Museum of Surgeons established in London, in a very nice building where the anatomical preparations are arranged in a very useful manner for study.
>
> (Cuvier 1841)

The museum included numerous physiological and pathological preparations, and rare animals from different parts of the world, including the aardvark or Cape anteater, the armadillo and a young kangaroo. It also held the extraordinary skeleton of Charles Byrne, the Irish giant. A few years after Hunter's death in 1793, the collection was moved from Leicester Square to Lincoln's Inn Field, and into the custodianship of the newly reconstituted Royal College of Surgeons. Its first curator, or Conservator, was William Clift, who had previously been Hunter's assistant and had continued to look after the collection imme-diately following Hunter's sudden death. However, Clift's task was simply to maintain an historical monument. In contrast to Cuvier's new Cabinet in Paris, Hunter's collection in London presented physiological series of isolated organs and structures from very different animals, including both vertebrates and invertebrates. A guide to the museum printed in 1818 shows an arrangement where each group of organs made a distinct series, linked in a chain of progressive gradation from the most simple to the most complex (Sloan 1997). This arrangement was different from that suggested and implemented by Cuvier, who wanted to show the impossibility of the Chain of Being and of progressive series.

Taking advantage of the possibilities of travel to Britain, which became possible with the end of the Napoleonic wars in 1815, Cuvier crossed the Channel to visit London and Oxford. On the 12th June 1818, Cuvier wrote to George Greenough in London in order to finalise his stay in the capital, and also expressing his wish to meet the University of Oxford geologist William Buckland in London. Six days later, Cuvier was in London and writing to Buckland, with a view to arranging a rendezvous at the Royal College of Surgeons for the following morning at 11.00.

While at the museum, Cuvier made drawings of some fossil bones that interested him greatly; it was in London that he discovered the presence of a group of unknown marine fossil reptiles, different from the *Mosasaurus* which he had sensationally described some years before. The new bones belonged to what would be known as the *Plesiosaurus* (Knell, this volume), which would become a fossil sensation in the next decade. It was a project Cuvier would happily have taken up, commenting to a German colleague, Samuel Thomas Soemmerring, on the 13th September 1818:

> During a small trip I just made in Great Britain, I saw countless remains of an extremely remarkable genus, of which Sir Everard Home has already described several pieces. Unfortunately the English people have not enough elements for comparison, and I have not enough time for a detailed study. If I had only 3 months in their country, I would have started this work. I think I saw among these numerous fragments the remains of two or three species.
>
> (Taquet 2003)

Cuvier later gave orders to have some material purchased at the auction of the fossil collec-tion of the Bullock Museum.

Cuvier was in London with his wife, his daughter and his faithful assistant and preparator Charles Léopold Laurillard, who gave what seems – until we understand that the British as a nation were inclined to agree – a chauvinistic opinion of the country he was visiting:

> We travelled, as you know, in Great Britain which was very interesting for Mr Cuvier and his family. We saw very nice things in Natural History, especially amongst the fossils. Their collections are, however, not to be compared with ours. The Surgeons College exhibits very nice presentations made by Hunter and also some skeletons, but the English anatomists, and also the naturalists are not so good in zoology and in comparative anatomy, such that they don't even know the value of their treasures. In general, the scientific institutions are nearly zero in Great Britain; the government is just interested in the art of earning money, which is in

this country elevated to the perfection. All is a question of money: painting collections, natural history cabinets, view of the monuments; all must be paid for in Great Britain, all bring back money, and all is connected with money.

(Taquet 1983)

Cuvier had been permitted make drawings of the preparations in the museum, but he noted in his diary that even this had required special permission and that a demand to the board had normally to be asked. This was, however, only the beginning of Cuvier's engagement with Hunter's collections, and soon a regular exchange of information was being transmitted across the Channel. In 1820, for example, Clift, who wrote frequently to Cuvier, sent him specially made drawings of orang-utan skulls; in January 1822, Cuvier sent the Hunterian Museum 17 casts of fossil specimens (bones and teeth), together with a list prepared by Joseph Pentland. Six months later, a second set of casts was sent. The result of these exchanges became apparent on the 30th September 1829, when Clift reported to Cuvier that he had adopted Cuvier's classification in the osteological catalogue of the Hunterian. Cuvier only returned to the museum once more in his life, during a visit to London in the summer of 1830. He did, however, return posthumously, when in 1833 a marble sculpture was placed beside the anatomical exhibits.

However, before Cuvier's death, Clift's young assistant, Richard Owen, travelled to Paris for the first anniversary of the reign of Louis Philippe. Owen was working with Clift on a descriptive and illustrated catalogue of the Hunterian Museum and had noted that the collection seemed at that time to:

refer only to the functions of digestion or assimilation, and reproduction, without which no species of organized being could exist. But the preparations imply a different signification, viz., all those organs that an individual organism makes use of for its own convenience and preservation; and exemplify parts concerned in functions not essential to existence as an organized body, viz., the instruments of locomotion and of the Senses.

(Sloan 1997)

In Paris, Owen spent four days visiting Cuvier's Cabinet d'anatomie comparée, returning to London convinced that the Hunterian collections needed to be rearranged and re-presented. The resulting transformation contributed significantly to the enlargement of the museum and to raising its significance as a scientific institution. The museum had shifted from historical monument to an important mirror of Cuvier's work in Paris, but now its anatomy was changing again, this time to reflect Owen's own burgeoning intellect:

The task of arranging and cataloguing the osteological part of the Hunterian Museum enforced a reconsideration of Cuvier's conclusions to which I had previously yielded assent. To demonstrate the evidence of the community of organisation, I found that the artifice of an archetype vertebrate animal was as essential as those of the archetype plan had been to Goethe in expressing analogous ideas.

(Sloan 1997)

Owen was now using the reorganised Hunterian to shape his own vision of the natural world, one that would distance him and the museum from Cuvier and Geoffroy. Yet in many respects he could not. Cuvier's museum became the paradigm for museums around the world. They too wished to adopt a view of the museum as active experiment rather than passive representation. The British in particular looked across the channel in admiration; Cuvier himself was as much a paradigm for science as was his museum. Following Cuvier's death some would refer to Owen – who would transform the natural history departments of the British Museum – as the 'English Cuvier'. It was a measure not simply of Owen's growing status as an encyclopaedic naturalist but also of the significance of Cuvier's influence as a paradigm for how science should be conducted, represented and lived.

After Cuvier's death, the museum continued its development, but not as quickly as formerly (Crémière 2005). In 1889, the galleries of zoology, which housed the inheritance of the Cabinet of Buffon, were considered too old and too decayed, and were replaced by a large building which attempted to show the political power of the French Republic. This building, designed by architect Jules André, displayed its collections of animals in accordance with the classification of Cuvier; Darwin's evolutionary ideas did not pass through its doors. These galleries were closed to the public in 1960 due to a lack of funding, and they remained closed for 25 years. It was only in 1988 that a program of renovation started, with the building reopening in 1992 as the highly acclaimed Grande Galerie de l'Evolution and attracting some 600,000 visitors a year.

Cuvier's comparative anatomy survived on the other side of the Jardin des Plantes in new galleries of comparative anatomy and palaeontology, designed by architect Frederic Dutert and opened in 1898 (Figure 1.4). These inherited Cuvier's collections and display 10,000

*Figure 1.4* The new Galerie d'Anatomie Comparée today.
Photo: the author.

skeletons, arranged as a huge herd, with a statue of Cuvier, by David d'Angers, standing in the middle as a tribute to the reformer of the *Règne Animal*.

## Bibliography

Allen, E. (1993) *A Guide to the Hunterian Museum*, Bicentenary edition, London: The Royal College of Surgeons of England.

Coleman, W. (1964) *Georges Cuvier Zoologist, A Study in the History of Evolution Theory*. Cambridge, MA: Harvard University Press.

Crémière, C. (2005) 'La galerie d'Anatomie comparée du Muséum de Paris: 1745–1898, jalons d'un projet', in C. Colin-Fromont and J.-L. Lacroix (eds) *Muséums en Rénovation: Les Sciences de la Terre et l'Anatomie Comparée Face aux Publics*, Paris: Editions du Muséum et Ocim., 155–67.

Cuvier, G. (1797) *Tableau élémentaire de l'Histoire Naturelle des Animaux*, Paris: Beaudouin.

—— (1803) 'Notice sur l'établissement de la collection d'anatomie comparée du Muséum', *Annales du Muséum*, 2: 409–14.

—— (1810) *Rapport Historique sur les Progrès des Sciences Naturelles depuis 1789, et sur leur Etat Actuel, Présenté à Sa Majesté l'Empereur et Roi, en son Conseil d'Etat, le 6 Février 1808, par la Classe des Sciences Physiques et Mathématiques de l'Institut*, Paris: Imprimerie Impériale.

—— (1817) *Le Règne Animal Distribué d'Après son Organisation, Pour Servir de Base à l'Histoire Naturelle des Animaux et d'Introduction à l'Anatomie Comparée*, Paris: Deterville.

—— (1822) Autobiographie, unpublished manuscript, Paris: Bibliothèque de l'Institut.

—— (1841) *Histoire des Sciences Naturelles Depuis leur Origine Jusqu'à Nos Jours Chez Tous les Peuples Connus*, Paris: Fortin, Masson.

Laurillard, C.-L. (1836) 'Cuvier' *Biographie Universelle Michaud*, 9: 590–600.

Lyell, Mrs. (1888) *Life, Letters and Journals of Sir Charles Lyell*, London, I, 249–50.

Sloan, P. (1997) 'Le Muséum de Paris vient à Londres', in C. Blanckaert *et al.* (eds) Le Muséum au premier siècle de son histoire, *Archives*, Paris: Muséum National d'Histoire Naturelle, 607–34.

Taquet, P. (1983) 'Cuvier, Buckland, Mantell et les dinosaures', in E. Buffetaut, J.M. Mazin and E. Salmon (eds) *Actes du Symposium Paléontologique G. Cuvier*, Montbéliard, 525–38.

—— (2003) 'Quand les Reptiles marins anglais traversaient la Manche. Mary Anning et Georges Cuvier, deux acteurs de la découverte et de l'étude des Ichthyosaures et des Plésiosaures', *Annales de Paléontologie*, 89: 37–64.

—— (2006) *Georges Cuvier: Naissance d'un Génie*, Paris: Odile Jacob.

Valenciennes, A., Laurillard, C.-L. and Pentland, J.B. (1833) 'Catalogue des préparations anatomiques laissées dans le Cabinet d'anatomie comparée du Muséum d'Histoire naturelle, faisant suite à la notice insérée dans le tome II des Annales du Muséum', *Nouvelles Annales du Muséum*, 2: 417–508.

# 2

# WILLIAM BULLOCK

## Inventing a visual language of objects

*Susan Pearce*

On Thursday, 29 April 1819, at the Egyptian Hall, Piccadilly, London, William Bullock began to auction off his museum collection. At a conservative estimate, by then the museum had been visited by several hundred thousand people, a figure which includes a very large proportion of 'the upper ten thousand', the educated opinion formers and consumers living at the time in London and the country. The eventual destinations of Bullock's material have attracted considerable attention (Kaeppler 1978) but the significance of his collection and his museum has been relatively neglected. This is, in large part, because Bullock was a showman as well as a natural philosopher and a collector, and as such his intellectual respectability as a player in the history of ideas was only marginal. Yet the style of the displays that he mounted can fairly be claimed to have invented a new visual language of objects, one which museums across the globe have, one way or another, been working through ever since. This chapter endeavours to trace the changes Bullock initiated in his collecting and exhibition practices between 1795 and 1819, and to draw out their wider implications.

### Bullock's collecting practices

The Bullock family had probably originated in Birmingham, England. William's parents, Elizabeth and George, ran a travelling waxworks, and William seems to have been born in the early 1780s (Baigent 2004–6). He started collecting in about 1795, by which time the family was resident in Sheffield, and by 1799 he took it seriously enough to produce a *Companion* to his exhibition, which was published in 1801 (Bullock 1801). Its full title established his intentions: *Companion to Bullock's Museum, containing a description of upwards of Three Hundred Curiosities. Intended principally for the Information of those who visit his Cabinet, and to enable them to describe it afterwards to their friends*. The Cabinet was on show, presumably at the Bullock home, and probably he charged an entrance fee. Bullock intended that the collection would be the subject of discussion, presumably in some detail, among the local population. The *Companion* was intended to be a catalogue, listing the objects and giving information about them, so that the visitor could walk round with it in hand and keep it afterwards as a useful work of reference. Part of the material seems to have derived from Captain Cook's voyages of twenty years earlier (Kaeppler 1978). Other pieces, particularly the arms and armour, had come from the collection of Dr Richard Greene of Lichfield, when part of it was sold following his death in 1793 (Altick 1978: 235). In buying up an existing collection, Bullock was typical of his period, when a number of important holdings were collections comprising several earlier collections. By the mid-eighteenth century, the owners of collections formed at the end of the seventeenth and through the earlier eighteenth century, who themselves had been inspired by men such as the Tradescants, were dying out, and their collections were often sold to younger collectors in their entirety, or at least in large blocks. In this way, to take only two obvious examples, Sir Hans Sloane's collection included the herbaria of Leonard Plukenet and Adam Buddle, the natural history of James Petiver and the scientific material of Christopher Merret; Sir Joseph Bank's herbaria included those of Clifford, Hermann, Clayton and Miller, among others (Edwards 1870: 290, 509). Bullock was to buy at auction from another collection in 1806, when he purchased material from the Leverian Museum, some from the original collection of Sir Ashton Lever and some from among those objects from Captain Cook's voyages which had been given to its then owner, Mr James Parkinson, by Sir Joseph Banks. Important material from the Pacific survives in the British Museum (Kaeppler 1978) and other museums (Pearce 1973: 2) in Britain because it has come down through these chains of collections.

By 1801 William and his brother George, a cabinet maker, had moved to Liverpool, and William set up his museum in his house at 24 Lord Street, and in about 1804 it was moved to specially fitted premises on the corner of Church Street and Whitechapel. He stayed in Liverpool from 1801 to 1809, describing himself primarily as a silversmith and jeweller, and by 1808 claiming the patronage of 'his royal Highness, the Duke of Gloucester' (Bullock 1808). During this time, the collection grew steadily to over four thousand items. In the sixth edition of the *Companion*, of 1808, Bullock lists sixty-three men and women of Liverpool (Bullock 1808) and one hundred from outside the city (Bullock 1808: iv) who had presented material to him, it would seem in single objects or small groups. Probably he supplemented these gifts by letting it be known on the Liverpool Pierhead that he would buy curiosities brought back by sea. Many of the additions seem to have arrived by these means.

The market supply of whole collections containing 'natural and artificial curiosities', rather than fine and applied art, had dwindled through natural causes, and this was one of the reasons why Bullock embarked on the first of his expeditions into the field to gather new material. In May 1807 he travelled to Bass Island in the Firth of Forth and there took two tufted shags, and he returned that August to collect 'gannets in different stages of plumage' (Bullock 1808: 41; Hunt 1815: 2, 9). The new specimens meant that there were new displays for visitors to see, always crucial for a large museum, especially one which depends upon payment at the door, and the range of gannets meant that the species could be fully represented, and displays which showed family groups of male, female and young were possible. These acquisitions extended both the scientific scope of the museum and its popular appeal.

In 1812, he made two journeys to Orkney. On the second, in August, he made his famous hunt for the sole surviving specimen of the great auk in Orkney, at Papa Westray, but he failed to shoot it. However, he received the same bird in 1813, 'finely preserved and sent to me by Miss Trail of that island, a lady to whom I am under considerable obligation for procuring me many valuable and rare subjects from the Northern Isles, and much interesting information regarding their habits'. It is interesting that Bullock had such a 'local correspondent' from whom material came to London. Miss Trail was not alone: in his paper to the Linnaean Society, on 17 November 1812, Bullock tells us that his snowy owl came to him from a young Shetland ornithologist called Mr L. Edmondson, although he procured this when he was in the islands (Bullock 1814: 75). By 1813, Bullock described his Egyptian goose and white-headed eagle as living 'for some time in the Queen's menagerie at Frogmore and were graciously presented to the Museum by Her Majesty'. A rhinoceros and an elephant also came from the Pollito managerie, open to the public at Exeter 'Change near the Strand' (Bullock 1813).

## Approaches to exhibition

The sixth edition of Bullock's *Companion* shows that a separate 'apartment' was devoted to works of art and models (Bullock 1808: 11–15) but access to the rest of the material seems to have been continuous. The *Companion* was organised in the same order as the exhibition, so the first items the visitor saw were glass cases with material culture from the Pacific, including, in the largest case, the famous green feather cloak from Hawaii. A bell glass of shells and another of another of humming birds followed, and then came a case of Chinese 'curiosities', including the celebrated Tartar whistling arrows (Bullock 1808: 15–21). It is obvious that Bullock deliberately placed some of the most tempting material at the entrance; it may even have been partially visible from the street. The bulk of the collection, the natural history, came next, with a series of cases containing preserved animals displayed in broad groups: birds, amphibians, serpents, lizards, fish, insects, crabs and worms (Bullock 1808: 22–80). Towards the end came a collection described as 'uncommon animals', with an Egyptian mummy and minerals (Bullock 1808). Finally, there were ninety-five pieces of arms and armour, described as the 'armoury', most of which had come from Greene. The cloak was perhaps displayed on one of the parental waxworks, and perhaps some wax models were used to provide naturalistic perches and wallows for some of the cased animal specimens, but this is only speculation.

What we do know is that by 1808 'a general objection having been made against the Linnaean classification . . . the Evil complained of . . . has been in some degree removed, by arranging the whole of the objects in a numerical manner' (Bullock 1808: ii). Clearly, Bullock had tried to identify the material on display by organising it in a Linnaean sequence, and by selling the *Companion* which carried numbers. Experience suggests that from the viewer's perspective, this would have been confusing not only because of the need to understand the system itself, but also because Bullock's presentation of it must have been inevitably bitty and disjointed, given the large gaps in his collection. He needed to please his public, and matching numbers on the objects and in the catalogue *Companion* proved much more intelligible. He retained this approach right up to 1819, but by 1813 he had created a good compromise by also showing the specimens 'in the order in which they stand in the *Systema Naturae*' (Bullock 1813: 15 and preface). It is not clear whether the material carried Linnaean labels as well as numbers, but the handbooks and the sales catalogue of 1819 certainly had both. By this time the collection was much bigger, and Bullock had studied natural philosophers such as Buffon, Sloane and Clusius (Bullock 1813: 156–78) and was himself a Fellow of the Linnaean Society, elected in 1810, and had lectured to the Society, giving 'An account of four rare species of British birds' two years later. By this time too, as we shall see, he had solved the problem of combining appeal with sound scientific information.

The second issue of the seventh edition of the *Companion* (1809) tells us that what came to be called the London Museum had been transferred to London and was 'now open at 22 Piccadilly', which was on the north side of Piccadilly, near its junction with Regent Street. The site had housed Philip Astley's Chinese Shadows show, together with an auctioneers and a Baptist congregation, and probably Bullock had had to time his relocation so that he could go into suitable premises in a suitable location. The move was a major commercial risk for Bullock, but the transfer to London gave him access to the hub of the collecting world and to a new and much larger paying public. It also offered the enlarged scope that would enable him to develop ambitious plans. The speculation paid off brilliantly. The museum became one of the sights of London, and a compulsory experience for those visiting the Metropolis who wished to be in the social swim. In early 1810, *Bell's Weekly Messenger* reported that the museum had become 'the most fashionable place of amusement in London; more than 22,000 have already visited it during the month it has been opened' (Abrahams 1906: 61–4). Jane Austen visited it in April 1811 and wrote to her sister, Cassandra, that she had found 'some amusement' there (Chapman 1952: 267). By the tenth *Companion* of 1811, the collection had 'upwards of 10,000' items.

Most interestingly, an aquatint published by Ackerman in 1810 – *Repository of Arts* (1810) – almost certainly of the principal gallery, shows us what the exhibition looked like (Figure 2.1). The room, judging by the representations of human figures, was roughly 9 m by 7 m, and it was lit by a large, oval, domed ceiling light. The centre of the room is dominated by a large uncased display area surrounded by a substantial rail, equipped with at least two built-in seating areas. Within this is a naturalistic ground cover, on which five ceiling-height artificial trees, one a coconut palm, are dotted about; two of the trees have very large snakes twined up them and two have birds in their branches. Between the trees stand large animals and birds, including an elephant, a zebra, a bear, a kangaroo and a least four birds, including what seems to be a black swan. Around the sides of the room are wall cases, clearly

BULLOCK'S MUSEUM,
22, Piccadilly.

*Figure 2.1* Part of Bullock's natural history display (and also some other visible material) in his museum at 22 Piccadilly, London. Aquatint in *Ackermann's Repository of Arts*, 1810.

Author's collection.

over 2 m high, with more individual specimen cases put on top of them. The wall cases have three shelves, giving four display areas, and probably twelve panes of glass held by bars, but the quality of the glass was good enough to see through adequately without opening the doors. On the visible long side, these cases, and the smaller ones above, hold simple displays of single, standing birds, and on the wall above is hung ethnographic material. The narrow end has more bird cases, and a display of arms and armour, including a full size armoured horse and rider and a standing suit of armour. The central display cunningly gives the appearance of creating a natural setting by putting the animals together with the floor cover and the artificial trees, and this was enormously impressive for the visiting public; nothing like it had been seen in London before. But, as Bullock must have known, the naturalism was illusory. Animals unrelated by either geography or genus stood side by side, amidst equally alien mock vegetation. Better was to come.

## The collection at the Egyptian Hall

Bullock may well have intended to develop his own premises when he decided to move to London. In any event, by late 1810 he was making plans for the erection of a permanent building on the south side of Piccadilly, opposite the end of Bond Street, a prime site. The result was the building known variously as the London Museum, the Egyptian Temple or Hall, or Bullock's Museum. The famous, exotic façade, by Peter Robinson (Sheppard 1960: 29: 266–70), was in the Egyptian style, with three tall, narrow pylons rising in front of a broad pylon, cut by a curved cornice. The upper part of the central pylon created a deep recess that framed Coade stone statues of Isis and Osiris, and above them was another cornice surmounted by two carved sphinxes and a large scarab; the face also had a range of Egyptianising detail. As the re-creation of an Egyptian building, the museum would not have struck a later viewer as very convincing, but Bullock was evidently pleased with it, and it did its job as a sensational advertisement for what lay within. The museum occupied an L-shaped plot (National Archives CRES 6/115), with a narrow, semicircular entrance leading through to the first exhibition gallery approximately 6 m by 18 m. On the right, a narrow corridor led to a second single-story exhibition room, approximately 8 m by 17 m (Figure 2.2).

It is difficult to follow the detailed history of exactly what was displayed where and when, because evidently the rooms were revamped from time to time with various dividing arrangements, and the material was redisplayed and moved around also. However, the general dispositions can be reconstructed. The room above the entrance area, the only part of the museum which had an upper story, was set up in the style of a medieval hall, and in it were displayed the arms and armour. It seems likely that the first room contained the bulk of the birds, with probably the amphibians, fish, insects and fossils, and perhaps at least some of the ethnography and assorted curios. An account not published until 1866 remembered this room as containing:

> 3,000 birds set up with similar accuracy, and attended by well-selected accessories, so as to afford sufficient ideas of their motions, food, and mode of feeding, and peculiarities of every description – from eagles to humming birds (of the latter of which there were ninety different species); . . . the whole were so perfect in plumage and disposition, that the aviary, if it might be so called, presented a scene of wonderful beauty to the eye.
>
> (Jerdan 1866: 70)

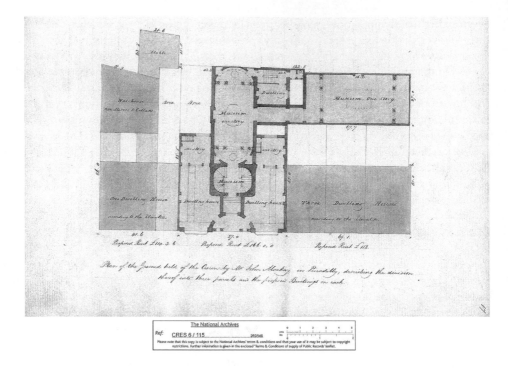

*Figure 2.2* Architect's drawing for the building of the Egyptian Hall, showing the ground plan. The actual building may not have followed the plan in every detail, but the principal areas seem to have been as planned.

Public Record Office CRES 6/115.

By now Bullock had returned to the Linnaean system, so presumably the birds were in systematic order, and, as the humming birds showed, displayed in as complete a record as the collection permitted. Evidently, also, as the gannet collecting in 1807 on Bass Rock demonstrates, care was taken to create adult and juvenile groups, and the mounting allowed some to be shown with their wings extended, and others in typical feeding positions, with appropriate props, to show the roles of the different beak and claw types. It was both a wonderful spectacle and a highly significant educational tool, which must have introduced a great many people, quite painlessly, to the notion that the natural world was inherently organised in a range of ways, the cross-cutting of which had produced species designed to fit their own habitat niches, and that knowledge could be created by setting out specimens in classificatory patterns. It is difficult to believe that this exhibition was not part of the context that shaped the intellectual giants of the later nineteenth century.

In the gallery on the right, a new exhibition 'completed with much labour and great expense' (Bullock 1812: iv) named The Pantherion was opened in 1812. It was devoted to the larger animals: 'The Pantherion is an exhibition of Natural History on a plan entirely novel, intended to display the whole of the known quadrupeds, in a manner that will convey a more perfect idea of their haunts and mode of life than has hitherto been done' (Bullock 1812: 1–2). The animals were 'exhibited as ranging in their native wilds; whilst exact models, both in figure and colour of the rarest and most luxuriant plants from every clime, give all the appearance of reality' (Bullock 1812: 1). The narrow access corridor was turned to advantage: 'The visitor is introduced through a basaltic cavern (of the same kind as the Giant's Causeway or Fingall's Cave, in the Isle of Staffa) into an Indian hut situated in a tropical forest' (Bullock 1812: 2). Before him lay 'most of the quadrupeds described by naturalists . . . the whole assisted by an appropriate panoramic effect of distance, which makes the illusion produced so strong, that the surprised visitor finds himself suddenly transported from a crowded metropolis to the depths of an Indian forest, every part of which is occupied by its various savage inhabitants' (Bullock 1812: 2). Bullock tells us that 'the Linnaean arrangement of quadrupeds commences at the first opening on the left-hand side of the entrance' (Bullock 1812: 2) making it clear that the exhibition, like the birds but on a more ambitious scale, combined the ideas of classification and habitat, in a display that was both fun and educational.

This first exhibit (assuming, as seems very likely, that the order of material in the *Companion* followed that in the display) was sixty specimens of the genus Simia, the monkeys, 'dispersed on rocks and the branches of a large orange tree' (Bullock 1812: 3–8). As throughout the text, the species details are given for each specimen. Next to the monkeys were anteaters, near a model of an African termites' nest. Facing the entrance 'in dens and on large rocks . . . are the whole of the feline tribe' (Bullock 1812: 21). In a cavern were a lion and her cub, with bats in front of it, a panther was emerging from its den, and walking on the rocks above the lions' den were a leopard, a puma, a tiger cat and serval, and two lynx. A bottle gourd was arranged to trail over the rocks of the den (Bullock 1812: 51). At the end of these rocks followed the weasels and the otter. Near this whole rocky group (backing onto it and facing the end wall?) was another similar group, showing a wolf from Hudson's Bay in a 'low den', a hyena, three jackals, a black fox, and two arctic foxes, one in summer fur and the other with a white winter coat. At one point, there was a painted 'sea view' backdrop, depicting waves breaking on a rocky coast, and in front of this were a common seal, rough seal cubs and three Patagonian penguins, all arranged in a naturalistic group (Figure 2.3). This display was illustrated in the twelfth *Companion* (Bullock 1812: opp. 55) and is clearly very well done. Near this exhibit, 'on the right hand side, is seen, as descending from a rock, the white or Greenland bear' (Bullock 1812: 46).

The 'Botanical Subjects' in the Pantherion are listed separately, although they were all integrated into the rest of the exhibition. They included trees, of which there seem to have been some twenty examples, and smaller plants, such as the green tea and the papyrus (Bullock 1812: 55–6). They seem generally to have been selected because they provided useful fruit or other products. The list of trees includes the Seville orange, breadfruit, five-fingered lemon, banana and cork (Bullock 1812: 49–53). The description of one of the orange trees gives us some interesting detail:

> Fronting the last window on this side, is a beautiful, though diminutive, species of orange, modelled from a drawing in the possession of Sir Joseph Banks . . . as, from Sir Joseph's personal directions, the use of his library and valuable collection of fruit, the principal part of these vegetables were modelled.
>
> (Bullock 1812: 54)

Evidently, all the trees were modelled, with the fruit and leaves, at least, presumably made of wax; here Bullock was able to draw on his earliest skills and on his knowledge of the waxworks trade to employ sufficiently skilful modellers, working both from illustrations and from life. Bullock tells us that, 'embracing the stem of the cocoa[nut] is a beautiful

*Figure 2.3* Engraving of the exhibition of seals and penguins in the Egyptian Hall, probably in the Pantherium. The caption reads ' 1. Common Seal. 2. Young of the Rough Seal. 3. Patagonian Penguins.' Facing p. 45, in Bullock's *Companion …to the Museum*, 12th edition, 1812.

British Library.

variegated species of gourd, cast from a specimen raised in this country' (Bullock 1812: 54). It is interesting that Banks, the dominant figure of the day in intellectual politics, was willing to give Bullock the run of his books, collections and expertise, as well as making him a number of donations. Banks could be arrogant and difficult, especially where commercial enterprises were concerned, but he was probably the only man in England who could have provided the level of help Bullock needed to create the large range of accurate models. It suggests that Banks saw Bullock's venture as at least approaching serious science.

Interestingly, 'the cocoa-nut tree 60' high crowned with a bunch of ten or twelve beautiful leaves' (Bullock: 1812: 54) seems to have been one of the trees made earlier to form part of the central display at 22 Piccadilly. Probably quite a number of these earlier exhibits were transferred – perhaps with a makeover, since the cocoa-nut seems to have had extra leaves added – to the Egyptian Hall.

## Specimens and displays

None of the models and only a handful of the animal specimens are now known to exist. Sweet (1970: 31–2), for example, was able to identify about forty Bullock specimens in the register of the old Natural History Museum, Edinburgh, of which only the baby African elephant survives (Figure 2.4). Another specimen survives in Rossendale Museum, Rawtenstall, Lancashire, and is of very great interest (Hancock 1980). This comprises an animal group in a fine mahogany and glass case, the wood now painted over. The exhibit shows:

The Royal Tiger (*F. tigrina*). This is represented expiring in one of those dreadful combats which sometimes take place betwixt this powerful and sanguinary destroyer of the human species, and the immense serpent of India, called the Boa Constrictor, in whose enormous folds its unavailing strength is nearly exhausted, its bones crushed and broken by the strength and weight of its tremendous adversary.

(Bullock 1813: 123)

*Figure 2.4* Young African elephant, on display in Edinburgh, one of the few surviving prepared animals, which have been identified as from Bullock's collection.

Royal Scottish Museum, 1818/19.8.

The fifteenth *Companion* tells us that the tiger and snake were one of the group of felines in and around the lions' den, where it was listed as No. 2; this suggests that it was uncased, since these large quadrupeds seem to have been free-standing. By the sale of 1819, it was described as:

A most superb and finely prepared specimen of the Royal or Bengal Tiger seized by a Boa Constrictor. The beautiful manner in which this group is preserved, renders it worthy of a place in the first museum in the world. A fine picture of it by the Chevalier de Barde, is now in the Louvre. It is enclosed in a large mahogany glass case.

(*Catalogue of the London Museum of Natural History . . . which will be sold by Auction*, Part Second, 1819, 69)

Alexandre de Barde held an exhibition of his works, of which this picture probably formed a part, entitled *Large Water Colour Drawings*, shown at the Egyptian Hall in 1814 (Hancock 1980: 173–5) and possibly the group was cased up as part of this project.

A carnivorous, twining snake was one of Bullock's favourite motifs, combining as it does the picturesque and the horrific. Three appeared around trees at 22 Piccadilly, two confronting each other and the third eying a bird. The twelfth *Companion* lists two more with animals, interestingly both exhibits listed not under the Pantherion but under the museum. There was a great boa 'preserved in the act of destroying a deer, which is crushed and expiring in the enormous folds of its merciless enemy' and a plate (Bullock 1812: 103) shows a large snake crushing a panther, with the caption 'Gigantic coluber seizing a panther'. Bullock had an unerring eye for what made a telling illustration, and these were obviously chosen for their dramatic content. Perhaps the recurrent 'snake scene' in nine-teenth-century adventure fiction and early twentieth-century cinema descends in part from Bullock's taste in display.

The Rossendale exhibit raises a further question (Figure 2.5). The snake appears to be *Python reticulates* (Schneider 1801: 351), a genuine species from the Indian sub-continent, but it was a made-up specimen; or to put the matter less kindly, a fake. It was constructed from two specimens, joined together to give the right kind of length for its species at 5.7 m (Hancock 1980: 171), and was given a carved wooden head. In a letter of 24 January 1819, Bullock wrote to Professor Robert Jameson of Edinburgh University saying, among other matters, that this 'Boa Constrictor' is the only fake in the collection (Sweet 1970: 22–3). This was not completely true. Dr Walter Adams, who bid for Jameson at the sale in April of that year, wrote to him on 21 May that one of the petrels sold that day had a pair of duck's feet. When the animals arrived in Edinburgh, it was found that the rhinoceros' ear had come off in transit, and it had the wrong horn, and that a bird of paradise was found to be a compound. Adams evidently had to defend the baby African elephant, of which he wrote, 'the little elephant is real observe the ears' and he says, quite specifically, that there were many 'pieces of manufacture in the sale' (Sweet 1970: 30).

Part of the problem arose from the difficulties of preparing and preserving skins and other parts and mounting the animals satisfactorily, forcing Bullock to fall back on composites and 'manufacture' in order to maintain a show that was as complete as possible. As was (and is) usual, Bullock received most of his specimens as skins, and there was a market in such material: in his letter of 14 May 1819, for example, Adams recounts that Dr Leach, a curator at the British Museum, was offering thirty antelope skins brought by Mr Burchell from

*Figure 2.5* Display group showing a tiger and a large snake in mortal combat, identified as from Bullock's collection. Rossendale Museum, Rawtenstall.

Lancashire Museums.

Africa for £80 (Sweet 1970: 27). The condition in which skins arrived in Britain must often have been relatively poor, especially those sold by ordinary sailors, from whom Bullock had bought in Liverpool. Bullock developed his own recipe for a preservative with which skins could be painted (Bullock 1817), and Dr Leach had his own for killing insects and for the composition of barites paint for coating cases and bird stands (Sweet 1970: 27). There are also references to Bullock's specimens being 'baked' (Sweet 1970: 30). Each collector seems to have had his own pet recipes, and as these mostly involved arsenic they did succeed in keeping insect infestation down (whatever else they may have done), but the various applications, and the baking, will have had their own adverse effects on the specimens. The Rossendale snake, for example, is so dark with varnish that it is impossible to see that it has any markings. A good number of Bullock's exhibits were prepared from skins in house. The larger animals were supported on metal armatures and then stuffed (with what is not clear), and the various preparations and procedures were probably undertaken at various stages, and probably repeated as necessary. The result is likely to have been objects which were hard, stiff and brittle. All taxidermy specimens damage easily, and the impression given by the Egyptian Hall is that all the large areas were used as galleries, with no provision for storage.

These difficulties had their impact on the possible displays. In his description of the display of felids, Bullock refers to 'a panther issuing from a den' (Bullock 1812: 21), and this will almost certainly have been an arrangement designed to get the best out of a very imperfect specimen. We may suspect that similar ruses were employed throughout the museum, with foliage overlapping or judiciously placed. By 1819, when some of the animals had been on continuous open display in industrial Liverpool and London for over twenty years, and those exhibits that came from older collections probably considerably longer, it is clear that many were in a bad state. In his letter to Jameson of 18 May 1819, Adams says he did not buy some things because they were bad specimens, and this letter makes it clear that Jameson was disappointed with the earlier purchases, which by then had arrived in Edinburgh. Adams writes in his own defence that some of the items were in such poor condition that he would not have felt justified in biding for them: the baboon he did buy was 'vile', and 'the pigmy antelope is miserable to be sure. I was quite ashamed of it when it came home'. He hopes that the Bullock pieces will fill gaps in the Edinburgh collection until better specimens can be obtained, and advises that the poor, presumably infested, animals should be kept separate from the rest until they are 'washed with sublimate' (Sweet 1970: 29–30).

These problems are undoubtedly one of the reasons why so few of the animals can now be identified in contemporary collections, although hard specimens such as fossils and corals may yet be. The Edinburgh giraffe had to be destroyed on 2 February 1949, and many others had certainly gone before it (Sweet 1970: 32). Bullock probably had several reasons for selling up in 1819: he wanted to move on, as obsessive collectors sometimes find they must, and the museum had lost its early impact, which will have had commercial repercussions however much he tried to ring small changes and bring in new attractions. But it seems, also, that the quality of the most eye-catching specimens was deteriorating, suggesting that by early 1819 it was clear that if a considerable sum was to be achieved, the sale had to happen soon. In 1818, Bullock had been discussing the sale of the collection as a whole with both Edinburgh University and the British Museum, but neither wished to buy, and although funds were a problem, the state of the material may also have been important.

## Some conclusions

Bullock did not abandon the Egyptian Hall in 1819; he continued to put on important shows there, both those he organised himself and those put on by others as business arrangements, until he sold his interest in the building in 1825. But he never again mounted a serious exhibition of natural history. The critical feature of Bullock's natural history and Pantherion exhibitions was the solution he found to the problem of creating a display that united essential popular attraction with genuine scientific endeavour. He was not the first museum man to devise naturalistic settings for his specimens; Charles Willson Peale had done this in Philadelphia more than a decade earlier. But he was the first to marry a natural-style setting with a Linnean-based arrangement of the animals, which drew attention to their interrelationships. In his rocks and grass, he brought together members of the same genus, he was able to show the variations of family groups, and he explained the reasons why different species had different forms of claw and beak and different colour coats. The animals emerge not merely as scientific or hunting trophies, or as pieces on a classificatory games board designed to set out the process (and the prowess) of knowledge. They stand as creatures in their own right, essential inhabitants of a real world to which they are adapted. Ironically, it was the limitations of Bullock's background and education, and his need to make spectacle bring in a respectable living, that stimulated this leap of imagination, and helped to bring a fresh vision of the world into being.

# Bibliography

Abrahams, A. (1906) 'The Egyptian Hall, Piccadilly, 1813–73', *Antiquary*, 42: 61–230.

Altick, R. (1978) *The Shows of London*, Harvard, MA: Belnap Press.

Baigent, E. (2004–6) 'William Bullock' *Oxford Dictionary of National Biography*, Oxford: Oxford University Press.

Bullock, W. (1801–1819) *Companions to Bullock's Museum*, Liverpool and London, seventeen editions.

—— (1801) *Companion to Bullock's Museum*, first edition, Liverpool.

—— (1808) *Companion to Bullock's Museum*, sixth edition, Liverpool.

—— (1812) *Companion to Bullock's Museum*, twelfth edition, London.

—— (1813) *Companion to Bullock's Museum*, fifteenth edition, London.

—— (1817) *A Concise and Easy Method of Preserving Objects of Natural History*, London.

—— (1819) *Catalogue of the Roman Gallery, of Antiquities and Works of Art, and the London Museum of Natural History at the Egyptian Hall in Piccadilly, Which will be sold by Auction.* London.

—— (1824) *Catalogue of the Exhibition, called modern Mexico: containing a panoramic view of the city, with specimens of the natural history of New Spain . . . at the Egyptian Hall, Piccadilly.* London.

Chapman, R. (ed.) (1952) *Jane Austen's Letters to her Sister Cassandra and Others.* Oxford: Oxford University Press.

Edwards, E. (1870) *Lives of the Founders of the British Museum*, London: Trubner.

Hancock, E. (1980) 'One of those dreadful combats – a surviving display from William Bullock's London Museum, 1807–18', *Museums Journal*, 74(4): 172–5.

Hunt, J. (1815) *British Ornithology*, London.

Jerdan, W. (1866) *Men I have Known*, London.

Kaeppler, A. (1978) 'Artificial Curiosities': *Being an Exposition of Native Manufactures Collected on the three Pacific Voyages of Captain James Cook*, Honolulu, HI: Bishop Museum Press.

Mullens, W. (1917–18) 'Some museums of old London. II. William Bullock's London Museum', *Museums Journal*, 17: 51–6, 132–87.

Pearce, S. (1973) *Arts of Polynesia*, Exeter City Museum.

Schneider, J. (1801) *Historiae Amphibiorum Naturalis et Literaiae*, Parts 1 and 2, Jena.

Sheppard, F. H. W. (1960) *Survey of London, 29: St. James, Westminster*, London: Athlone Press.

Sweet, J. 1970. 'William Bullock's collection and the University of Edinburgh, 1819', *Annals of Science*, 26: 23–32.

# 3

# MUSEUMS, FOSSILS AND THE CULTURAL REVOLUTION OF SCIENCE

## Mapping change in the politics of knowledge in early nineteenth-century Britain

*Simon J. Knell*

This chapter is about the reflexive relationships between objects, institutions and practices, and what these tell us about change in the production and control of knowledge. In the first half of the nineteenth century a pattern of scientific engagement based on private cabinets was replaced by one centred on private learned society museums, and this in turn was replaced by the system of publicly funded institutions we still see today. In Britain, the birth of the modern science of geology was strongly associated with these changes. It was, moreover, a science that reached the heights of fashion in the 1820s and 1830s and which privileged the fossil as its central resource. But, as shall be suggested in this chapter, this fashionability – of which museums were an important part – necessitated a political revolution in the new discipline. This revolution paralleled that then taking place in wider society, as the country underwent social and political reform. Geology experienced a similar struggle in the late 1830s, which shifted power out of the hands of a social hegemony and into the control of the employed middle-class bureaucrat. To effect this change the infrastructure of the science had to be changed: museums and fossils – the forums and fuel of the old economy – were fundamentally altered. They thus become indicative of the political progress of a 'cultural revolution'. This chapter charts that revolution through those museums and their fossils. It is stressed that the kind of revolution described here is not that concerned with the replacement of essential intellectual paradigms. These have had the full attention of the scholars of the history and philosophy of science (Cohen 1985). A cultural revolution is something different, which results in a reshaping of a science's constitution and institutions and relationships between actors. Certainly this can happen as a result of intellectual change, but it can also result from tensions in the politics of participation.

## Locating the scientific subconscious

In modern society, fossils are understood as scientifically significant objects – a position they have occupied for more than two centuries (see, for example, Rudwick 1972; 1985; 2005; Secord 1986). It is, however, also possible to see the fossil as a social resource, and to read its role and place culturally (Knell 2000; 2002; Knell and Taylor 2006). Rather than charting a 'progress' of ideas, histories which adopt this viewpoint investigate, for instance: the roles and functions of actors (book and paper writers, amateur scientists, collectors, dilettantes, artisans, dealers and elder statesmen); the primary material objects of study (rocks, minerals and fossils); locations for activity (journals, societies, museums and landscapes); and the nature of interpretation (language, performance, aesthetics). These things are the products of disciplinary formation within wider society. They also reflect the possibilities and constraints of social and individual aspiration. Thus we have three factors useful to this present investigation: the *individual*, with his or her particular motives, positions, opportunities, abilities and relationships; the *social* aspects of society, with its roles as critical judge of legitimate and value actions, as nurturer of fashions and producer of social structures; and the *discipline* of geology itself, with its particular objectives, values, processes, methods and language. All three are constantly in flux and each is partially shaped by the others (Figure 3.1).

As has been explained elsewhere, if we can view the formation of a scientific discipline, such as geology, in this cultural sense, then this discipline becomes open to a form of spatial analysis, as its growth and development can be seen as a process of colonisation followed by 'civilization' (Knell 2000: 308–9). It is within the cultural space of the discipline (shaded in Figure 3.1) that the attributes of science are shaped, and since this space is clearly political, its study is essentially one of political geography.

To locate and trace change within this cultural space one must isolate the relevant indicative structures: institutions and material things which marry the intellectual ideal with the practical possibilities of contemporary society. For geology, museums and the specimens in their collections are obvious examples. But if one is to use museums (and their objects) in this way then it is critically important to focus on the moment of the birth of these institutions as only then do they holistically embody the ideals and potentials of making knowledge. It often took only a few years for a museum to develop into an uneasy balance between the ideals of its founding, the more conservative notions of tradition and inheritance, and the latest – and sometimes radically different – ideals and aspirations of its current operators.

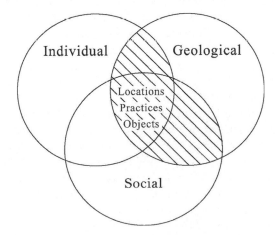

*Figure 3.1* Reflexive relationships. Disciplinary locations, practices and objects formed where the intellectual goals of science meet with wider socialised and individual interpretive perspectives.

The whole was then further constrained by the inertia imposed by the physical and financial burdens of the building and its collection. One only need look at the Whitby Literary and Philosophical Society and its museum to see this. Born in 1822, today it is essentially a beautiful relic. It undoubtedly reflects the values of a portion of the modern town and of a wider population, but these are very different from the values which shaped the institution in the early nineteenth century, though doubtless a residue of these earlier values remains.

How then can we recover something of the moment when this learned society and its museum were born? Studying directly what is left of the buildings, objects and collections can be informative, but these things alone can retain little sense of their former meanings. Indeed, in many respects museum collections were built on principles which ensured they were rather immune to meanings; they were established to weather change, to remain true and relevant. To look, for example, for evidence of the Darwinian revolution in fossil collections is largely futile. The exhibitions that accompanied the growing acceptance of this new orthodoxy have long gone, while the collections themselves were largely unchanged by the event – their ordering relied rather more on their revealed characters than on grander theory. Science constituted collections to be understood as curated bits of reality, although we, as historians and museologists, might question the implicit idealism that permits science to see such things as uncontaminated, 'disinterested' and objective (Knell 2007). Collections are, like the real world in totality, the ultimate test of theory; they are meant to be objective and empirical truths beyond mere understanding. Darwin simply gave an alternative explanation to an order easily located in Nature. That explanation may have had rather less need for the notion of a designer God that had been so useful to museum makers thirty years earlier – and no one did look at the stuffed monkeys in the same way again – but in museums the same objects sat in the same serried rows, physical representations of life gathered at a time and place, there to be drawn as evidence into any world view.

So rather than reading the order, which has survived in museums to the present day and which says relatively little that is historically useful to us, we need to uncover the 'looking' (the interpretive frame) of the founders (Knell 2007). Order alone gives a sense that museums were locked into an abstract 'Enlightenment project', but order was only ever required to give science a common language and, as shall be explained here, science was never, at this point of major museum expansion, the closed and arcane world sometimes discussed in the museum studies literature. The Enlightenment museum is an imagined museum, the product of the moral idealism of museum founders combined with historical interpretation of the ordered relic we can see today. The presence of the idealist in the past – the Yorkshire Philosophical Society, for example, was to 'acquire' and 'diffuse a more perfect knowledge of the works of creation' (Yorkshire Philosophical Society 1828; Knell 2000) – gives plausibility to the notion of the Enlightenment or 'modernist' museum. It permits the construction of an ahistorical black box that serves to encapsulate an imagined extreme and blinkered scientific rationalism. This black box was constructed as an oppositional Other by which postmodernism could perform its own revolution in museum studies. Although this revolution was essential to the intellectual maturity of the discipline, it concealed a number of ironies. It depended, for example, upon a particular brand of scientism that claimed evidence from past acts of representation (with its empowered and subjugated parties) but which simultaneously denied the presence of diversity and democracy in the past. Rather, it was to claim these as inventions of the postmodern era. The aim here is not to deny or undermine the importance of postmodernism to museum studies, but rather to reveal that it – like all revolutions – required the construction of a political myth, an Other that could be painted in black and white. Disciplinary revolution then becomes a political act of constructing black boxes in order to control, and, indeed, it recognises that control is central to disciplinarity. This, perhaps, gives political extension to Bruno Latour's groundbreaking investigation of black-box making in science of a few years ago (Latour 1987). In its revolutionary form, the black box relies upon an act of decontextualisation and the construction of an oppositional form. By this means the new, favoured, alternative must position itself as a morally and politically elevated (according the subconscious of the time) paradigm. By this means a discipline can undergo revolution. It happened to museum studies in the late 1980s and early 1990s, and, as shall be argued below, it happened in geology 150 years earlier, when it had a considerable impact on museums and their objects.

To understand the nineteenth-century science culture within which that revolution took place we need to interrogate a considerable range of materials (newspaper reviews, annual reports, scientific publications, accession registers, correspondence, field notebooks, museum labels, collecting instructions) in order to sense the contemporary interpretive outlook, as each kind of document encapsulates different values and perspectives. By these means we can locate the cultural *subconscious* of science. To value this notion is to suggest that decisions that shaped early nineteenth-century science culture in the English city of York, for example, were influenced by regional actions (such as the mob burning hayricks on distant Yorkshire farms), local civic disputes (such as that concerning the refurbishment of York Minster) and national perceptions (such as the universally low reputation of some of the nation's greatest cultural institutions). These things contribute to the doing of science; affecting the things it values, the form and appropriateness of its practices and the shape of its institutions. Only through a study of language can we hope to reveal this subconscious (here highlighted with italics):

> As *England* is not only the most affluent of *modern* nations, but the grand centre of commercial activity and *communication* between *distant* portions of the globe . . . we may *naturally* ask why her *museums* do not display a proportional extent and magnificence, and set all foreign *rivalry* at *defiance*?
>
> (Lyell 1826a: 155)

Here the words of geological theorist and populariser Charles Lyell remain accessible today, but that accessibility creates an illusion. In fact, his words conceal that complex individual subconscious that merges those three perceptions discussed above. Similarly, William Vernon Harcourt, President of the Yorkshire Philosophical Society and a founder of the British Association for the Advancement of Science (BAAS), noted the opinion of Alexander von Humboldt at the first meeting of the BAAS in York in 1831. He remarked: 'There is not a country in the *world* which had such opportunities for making *collections* as England. Yet how *wretched* were the collections of the *British Museum*' (*York Courant*, 27 September 1831). This statement relies upon tacit comparisons, shared knowledge and values, paradigms and so on. What is being referred to here is not merely context, but an absorbed and digested sense of one's world. It also depends on an individually specific reading, not simply a generalised zeitgeist. This individual and social subconscious is critical to unravelling science and its museums and objects in this earlier period. To illustrate this point a little further, the next section explores and expands the meaning of fossils – a subject dealt with at length a few years ago (Knell 2000). This might be tackled by asking 'What would it mean to find a stone nodule on a British beach in 1830?'

## Fossils of the subconscious

Brown, smooth and rounded, a nodule of stone, although aesthetically pleasing – even curious – is ordinary and everyday, and indistinguishable from the many other pebbles that accompany it on the beach. But what if, with one hammer blow, that nodule is split in two to reveal a fossil? How would our conception of the unopened nodule change? When distinguished television naturalist David Attenborough re-enacted this moment in a Leicestershire quarry as a scene from his childhood, he turned to camera and remarked how breathtaking it was to look at a trace of life which in perhaps the 200 million years of its existence no human eyes had seen. For Attenborough, as for those who performed the same act nearly two centuries before, it was to peer into a primeval world. Attenborough's life became a succession of such revelatory moments as he sought to be the first to bring extraordinary animals and animal behaviour to our screens (Attenborough 2002). But when Attenborough saw his first fossil, sometime before the Second World War, he would have had little difficulty relating it to the wider natural world, so adequately represented by his growing menagerie of captive animals. In contrast, the finder of a nodule in 1830 lived in a world that was only then discovering the true nature of the fossil past, a past that often revealed the totally unexpected. In 1821, for example, the discovery of hyena remains in Kirkdale Cave in Yorkshire produced a national sensation. It assured Oxford University's William Buckland – the man who turned this discovery into an animated scene from the distant past – of great public celebrity. Similarly, in 1824 the skeleton of a monstrously proportioned beast, without any modern analogue, arrived in London having been shipped directly from the site of its exhumation at Lyme Regis in Dorset. This was the plesiosaur, an animal that Buckland's friend William Conybeare had been piecing together for some time. Having presented the discovery to an excited audience, Conybeare told his friend and helper Henry De la Beche of the find, signalling the triumph also in terms of his own performance: 'I made my beast roar almost as loud as Buckland's Hyenas' (Knell 2000: 197). In the early nineteenth century, the boundaries that limited the expectations of what might be found within a nodule were far less clearly drawn than today. The nodule was clearly understood for its revelatory potential, and for the celebrity a mere hit of the hammer might bring. It was this possibility that fuelled a succession of short-term collecting fads and fashions in natural history, and which taken more broadly kept the discipline alive (Allen 1994).

While there was much about the past world that geology could reveal as extraordinary, the science also made the commonplace significant. In the late eighteenth century, land and mineral surveyor William Smith had discovered that rocks have a natural order, or sequence, and that each contains its own peculiar fossils. Thus given similar looking rocks, fossils provided the key to identifying the rock and its position in the sequence. In other words, fossils permitted rocks to be seen as a time sequence – a historical record. One could now imagine a world stretching back through time, from the modern age, through a history of kings and queens and into a past recorded in those documents that permitted the writing of the Bible, and then back still further to Buckland's hyenas, and beyond to the world of Conybeare's plesiosaur. Fossils were both the page numbers in a great history book and the most remarkable actors in that newly discovered history. As Buckland noted:

> the documents of geology record the warfare of ages antecedent to the creation of the human race, of which in their later days the geologist becomes the first and only historiographer. And the documents of his history are not sculptured imita-

tions of marble, but they are the actual substance and bodies of the bones themselves, mineralized and converted to imperishable stone.

(Rupke 1983: 60)

Buckland's counterpart in Cambridge, Adam Sedgwick, was similarly taken with the historical implications:

Phenomena like these have a tenfold interest, when regarded as the extreme link
of a great chain, binding the present order of things to that of older periods in
which the existing forms of animated nature seem one after another to disappear.

(Sedgwick 1830)

This was a fundamentally new intellectual world and individuals rushed in to stake a claim
(Knell 2000). Those who could succeed in this world required a number of qualities as
regards social group and income, but they were also required to be great communicators.
Buckland, Sedgwick and Lyell certainly possessed these attributes. Participants were keen to
reap the social rewards of participation, to grow an audience, and thus naturally acquire an
influential place in an enlarged science. Even in 1830, the language was infectious and
could effortlessly construct images to appeal to the contemporary mind; mere nondescript
fragments emerged from the page as 'winged dragons from fabulous legends' (Lyell 1876b:
524). The world of human antiquities, by comparison, paled: 'with how much intenser feelings of wonder and humility must the Geologist view these interesting discoveries, which
place before him not the relics of a departed age, but the petrified mementos of a former
world!' (*York Courant*, 27 September 1831).

In this period, then, the value of the fossil was extended, but what has been described
thus far is a rather unremarkable interpretation. We have long known something of the
science's fashionability, its fossil discoveries, and the impact of Smith's big idea. This interpretation does not take us far from established discourses of the history of science. But what
if we step out of the science, its ideas and its popularity, and consider the fossil as an object
and place it in a world of institutions? Let us imagine that our object was found on the
Yorkshire coast and that, perhaps in order to reap its novelty or scientific value, the finder
decides to give it to a local museum. There were plenty from which to choose: Leeds, York,
Scarborough, Whitby, Hull, Wakefield and Sheffield could each offer such a repository,
though they were not all equal in this regard. There is also one other complication we would
need to consider: these were not public museums in the modern sense. Rather, these
museums belonged to private philosophical societies, which had sprung up across Britain in
the 1820s. What could our fossil mean now?

To answer that question, we need to select a specific museum as, while all shared some
common characteristics, each was the product of its own geography. Previous histories of
these societies have tended to underplay or simply not detect the role of the emergent
science of geology in their birth and development. The Yorkshire Philosophical Society in
York, for example, openly admitted to being principally a geological society. The societies
in Scarborough and Whitby, and those in many other parts of the country, also placed
geology well ahead of their other interests. The Kirkdale discoveries notably stimulated the
birth of many Yorkshire societies and several appeared at the same moment, each competing
with its neighbours for the status and resources (collections) available to those who are first.

The formation of a York society was already being discussed, unknown to the local newspaper's editor, when he commented on the formation of a rival society in Sheffield:

> Do not these useful institutions, which are daily forming around us, convey a severe reproof to the tardiness of our own city? York . . . presents none of the characteristics of an enlightened and scientific people. Her mental energies are either suffered to lay dormant, or only exerted in solitary and unassisted instances . . . .
>
> (*York Courant*, 24 December 1822)

At the heart of the larger societies – such as that in York – was a core membership, usually composed of honorary officers and curators and supported by a paid curator who attempted to turn their leisure interests into real science. However, viewed holistically these societies were rather more interested in the 'notion of science' – as cultural signifier and cultivating influence – than in real scientific output, such as the production of scientific papers. As a reporter for the *York Courant* observed in his best – twice published – prose:

> The museum standing between the mouldering remains of Roman strength and grandeur, and the venerable ruins of a now desolated Christian temple, and rearing its front above the crumbling walls of dilapidated palaces, whose dark outlines were dimly shadowed forth by the solitary lanterns scattered through the grounds, whilst a halo of light emanating from the gas within rendered its proportions distinctly visible, forced upon the mind the imperishable nature of 'science' . . . .
>
> (*York Courant*, 27 September 1831)

It was not, however, necessarily an indication of superficiality to value science for its image. Image construction was important both to civic society and to the individual, not merely for puff and pose but because it could affect one's material and social prospects. In the setting of the Yorkshire Philosophical Society, it provided a motive for social relations on both sides: those who wished to rise and those who wished to be seen as patron. The society was built from the top down, first locating its aristocratic patrons and then its president and vice presidents from the gentry and country elite. A representative portion of the nation's scientific literati were then made honorary members, together with collectors who would help fill the society's museum. The society in Sheffield used the same methods: 'From the respectable names already entered as subscribers, there can be no doubt that the projected institution will meet with that patronage which will ensure its success' (*York Courant*, 24 December 1822). By these means the societies constructed honeypots to attract an established elite and social climbers in a country experiencing the rapid emergence of a self-made middle class who wished to join the establishment (Bentley 1985: 21; Dinwiddy 1986: 2).

In York, the society's core membership was composed of those who patronised other cultural and charitable projects in the city and county, such as the theatre and schools. In that sense these were already men of power, though they were not of the same religious or political persuasion and there was no single institution in which to house them. This power distribution was not, for example, adequately represented in the governing Corporation of York; before the reform acts of the 1830s, this latter relic of a bygone age operated on long-established nepotism and self interest. York, however, had long been considered a Whig stronghold. In contrast, Scarborough's corrupt corporation had long been in Tory hands, its incestuous practices stretching back over centuries (Binns 2003:159). Until the passing of the Municipal Corporations Act 1835, the new philosophical societies therefore provided a forum for the civic elite. Effectively, they were local parliaments. They were inclusive organisations and, unlike contemporary legislation, they made no distinctions on the basis of religion or, indeed, politics. To foster this inclusive forum, politics and religion were banned as topics of discussion. Instead, these subjects were replaced by the natural sciences, geology in particular: it was topical and fashionable, it provided opportunities for significant discovery and a vehicle for oratory and debate, it was inexpensive and, critically, it was politically and religiously neutral.

However, banning politics did not make these organisations apolitical. Externally, the societies fostered an image of civic cultivation. Whitby could proudly claim, for example: 'This important discovery has excited intense interest in the literary world our fossil croco-dile being superior to any kind now existing in Britain or perhaps any other country' (Anon. 1825). However, internally these societies were strongly individualistic. While this resulted in inevitable disputes over the interpretation of scientific evidence, it also meant that a society and its museum were very much about social positioning, identity creation, network building and various kinds of liaison. And if the attractions of science, the necessities of city and county politics, and the honeypot of social elevation were not sufficient to pull together a coherent group, then there were also the external pressures of a country ill-served on a long list of issues by the Westminster parliament (Dinwiddy 1986: 11–12).

Nor could the groundswell for reform be ignored. The growth of Manchester outstripped that of all other towns and cities, and similarly in Yorkshire, Leeds grew at a prodigious pace compared with the county town of York. This brought with it poor working conditions, low wages and exploitative employers – the conditions for political dissatisfaction. Membership of the philosophical societies was politically mixed but included a large number who were pro-reform: reform of both national and local electoral representation. Scarborough's society was led by Sir John Johnstone and Sir George Cayley, both reformists. Similarly, Lord Milton, a political liberal and one of the most powerful and popular politicians in the country, was soon installed as President of the York society. In contrast, the York society's patron, the Archbishop of York (who was also the father of the society's first president, William Vernon Harcourt), found his palace under assault by an angry mob of several thou-sand, who broke his windows, vandalised his gardens and burnt his effigy, when the Reform Bill failed to be passed in May 1832.

Regardless of party politics, these societies were peopled by individuals wedded to notions of change and progress at a time when both national and local governance seemed incapable of moving into the modern age and when civic and rural society seemed increasingly unstable. And, if still further encouragement were needed, there was also a sense that Britain was in competition with its neighbours, and that actions locally to address such deficiencies as science would ultimately improve the nation's competitiveness and greatness.

It is in this vastly expanded world that our fossil would arrive in York. But still we have not expanded our view sufficiently. Placing a material object in this world adds still further to the complexity. In the 1820s, fossils were arriving in York almost daily and by various routes, utilising a network of contacts and drawing upon a range of social and commercial relationships (Figure 3.2). Each linkage in the network, whether between the included (i.e. a member of the society) or between the included and the excluded (primarily on grounds of class), saw a social transaction (with its indebtedness engineering and the manipulation of value and perception). The society needed to play a complex social game in order to achieve

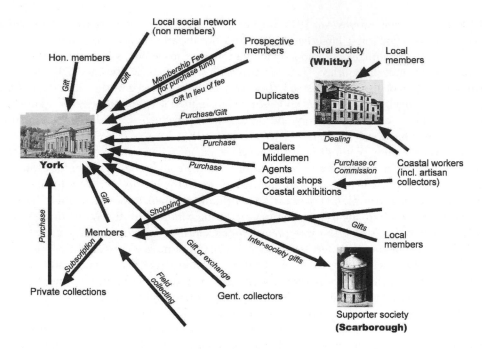

*Figure 3.2* The flow of fossils into York in the 1820s and 1830s.

its multiple and interrelated objectives. The ultimate repayment – excepting those who received a direct payment for fossils – was recognition.

What, then, would it mean to find a nodule in this world? We know the answer to this question precisely and have seen it many times over. Perhaps one of the best examples comes not from Yorkshire but from the tiny northern Scottish town of Cromarty. Here, and later in Edinburgh, a former stonemason and erstwhile banker, Hugh Miller, became one of Scotland's most celebrated authors of popular non-fiction, a great campaigner on numerous subjects, a newspaper editor and much more besides, and we might argue that his break came, in large part, from breaking open nodules. In these he found extraordinary tortoise-like fish, which he described in his first book on Scottish legends and myths (Miller 1835) and recounted again in one of his most famous books, *The Old Red Sandstone* (Miller 1841: 130):

> The first nodule laid open contained a bituminous-looking mass, in which I could trace a few pointed bones and few minute scales. The next abounded in rhomboidal and finely-enamelled scales, of much larger size and more distinct character. I wrought on with the eagerness of a discoverer entering for the first time in a *terra incognita* of wonders.

Miller dreamed of being a great Scottish poet – the equivalent perhaps of William Cowper, one of his English favourites – but he lacked the necessary economy of words and found instead an extraordinary ability with prose which placed the reader in the landscape and in imagined fossil pasts (Knell and Taylor 2006). Through the finding of fossils a man could rise up in society in a variety of ways, each finding his own route. Miller was not alone in using fossils to locate a literary path, though no other writer integrated the geological past so seamlessly into the mind of Victorian Britain (Taylor 2007).

Now, if we consider our nodule again, in this expanded scientific world, perhaps we can see that the nodule, unopened with its contents concealed, is a supremely powerful thing. It is at least as powerful, in terms of its contribution to scientific progress, as the nodule that has already been split, its fossil contents studied and published. In that moment, before the nodule is broken open, we see its true potential. It is that same moment that occurs before the consumption of any thing: a moment of anticipation, before reality provides a slap in the face (Campbell 1987). In this moment, the thing within isn't any one thing but everything: it doesn't need to belong to the real, it can be fantastic, mythological, its possibilities only limited by imagination – particularly at this time when the fossil world was only partially known and understood. This fantastic thing conjured up in the mind is not fantastic because of the former life it might reveal but because its finding may result in the intellectual, social and material transformation of the finder.

## The museum succession

So the fossil, in the early nineteenth century subconscious, was rather more than it might now seem. Indeed, a study of the consumption of fossils can permit us to understand the cultural depth of geology. The same might be acquired through studying the museum, and it is to this institution that we now turn in order to locate change in the culture of geology during the first fifty years of the nineteenth century. In order to do so, we must examine the succession of institutions produced to support the developing science, in the belief that the institution society (i.e. the wider community) chooses to build is itself indicative of its disciplinary, social and individual values and perceptions (its subconscious). First, it is necessary to point out that each incarnation of the museum was not an *evolution* of the concept but the result of reflection on all that had gone before; the product of that reflection was sometimes a revolutionary break and at other times a reinterpretation. By locating the values embedded in the founding moment, one might detect change in the science itself – change brought about not by any intellectual paradigm shift but by the changing politics of participation.

In order to give some consistency to the survey that follows, it is helpful to follow the development of these institutions through the experiences of a single individual. John Phillips, who was born on Christmas Day, 1800, is particularly useful for this purpose because he became closely associated with the professionalisation of the science and with its museum aspects (Morrell 2005). Out of financial necessity his career was very much geared to the changing opportunities the science threw up. His natural talents, peculiar apprenticeship, eloquence, modesty and diplomacy enamoured him to his contemporaries; he became the perfect employee even before the science had established a consistent means of employment. Phillips was adaptable, and from the outset very much the model of the educated middle-class professional who would people the country's public institutions later in the century; Phillips was not the product of an old conservatism.

The first museums Phillips encountered were those of private gentlemen. These were essentially the products of an eighteenth-century approach to natural history, and fossils sat within these collections as biological, rather than geological, entities. In 1808, Phillips was orphaned and came under the guardianship of his uncle, William Smith, who was then a successful mineral surveyor reaping the practical rewards of his discovery (of geological sequence, as discussed above). Although Smith began disseminating his idea almost immediately and largely by word of mouth, and particularly utilising his own collection, his discovery had not been accompanied by a clap of thunder. There had been no geological revolution. Rather, the idea seeped out, from 1799 onwards, into the emergent community of dilettante geologists. Nevertheless, Smith was relatively prosperous and he ensured that his nephew gained a good education. However, by Phillips's thirteenth year, both Smith and the school were in financial decline, and Phillips was sent to study under Smith's friend, the gentleman naturalist Benjamin Richardson, near Bath (Morrell 2005: 13).

Here, Phillips learned the gentlemanly science of collections: its language and authors, methods and resources. He later reflected on this period:

> to his talk on plants, shells, and fossils, to his curiously rich old library, and sympathy with all good knowledge, I may justly attribute whatever may be thought to have been my own success in following pursuits which he opened to my mind.
>
> (Anon. 1874: 597)

This phase of his education was, however, short, and a year later he joined his now impoverished uncle in London. Here, one of Phillips's first jobs was to identify and label Smith's collection of fossils prior to its sale to the British Museum (Eyles 1967). This was the lowest period in Smith's career, although it was prefaced by the publication of a remarkable geological map, A *Delineation of the Strata of England and Wales with part of Scotland* (1815) – the first modern national geological map of any country – and illustrated explanations of his geological methods (Eyles 1969). These ventures did nothing to mitigate his financial insecurity, and he was soon forced to quit London for the North before his published work could bring him notice, but not before enduring a spell in debtors' prison.

Another kind of geology had begun when Phillips was only seven years old. This was a new socialised – but yet strongly individualistic – gentlemanly geology constructed by the Geological Society of London, the first national geological society in the world. It began well enough, adopting a strongly empirical methodology. This new science of 'geology' was the society's to develop – it was the membership's amusement, it was *their* geology, and the members begged, borrowed and stole information and ideas with impunity. To their eyes this was just a social pursuit, though they had hopes for its potential. Initially, when the science and the society lacked recognition, geological intelligence was a relatively weak currency. Indeed, in 1807, who could say what the new science would become? It had little language of its own, and no single theoretical outlook. Many thought its future might be found in the study of mineral collections. Others thought the future lay in artistic illustration (Knell 2000). In time, however, with the addition of wealthy, empowered, young and enthusiastic members, the society's geology became geology in general, and the society – or rather its individual members – became legitimisers of practice by default. Built around individualism and empiricism, this society established an internal culture built around discovery and open competition. In time this broke out into open warfare, especially as the competition became funnelled into solving a reducing list of great geological questions. This competitive individualism, in the vast new intellectual territory that opened up, where so little was settled, became the engine that drove British geology forward, but at a considerable price. Phillips did not know this world until his late twenties or early thirties, when it had begun to take on absurd characteristics. He noted on one trip to London: 'The jealousy among the men of Science here is wonderful and you feel to walk on a cavity, and to be grasped by a hand of friendship no firmer than a ghost's shadow' (Edmonds 1975: 273). Another of the new geologists, George Cumberland, noted that 'The fault of the age is jealousy of discovery, men are every day tripping one another up, there is too little honour among us, and too much setting up of Gods' (Knell 2000: 32). Buckland warned others of this competitive world in 1839: 'there are living as well as fossil sharks with prodigiously voracious teeth' (Morrell and Thackray 1981: 424).

This, however, takes us a little ahead of ourselves: in the first twenty years of the century geology made steady but unremarkable progress. It was in the early 1820s that the field began to make a more striking social impact: the philosophical societies that formed in most major towns and cities across the country have already been mentioned. The timing had much to do with towns protecting local treasures and, particularly in Yorkshire, with the sensationalism of the Kirkdale discoveries. Something of the politics of these institutions has already been discussed, but it has not been mentioned that by this time Smith and Phillips became almost permanently resident in Yorkshire, there transformed into peripatetic lecturers and curators. Hawking his ideas around the philosophical societies, the anecdotal Smith, ably supported by his eloquent disciple, had a revolutionary impact. Communities were converted overnight to the new utilitarian potential of fossils as time markers. It gave local 'philosophers' an ideal science: purposeful and within reach of the everyman. It was here that Smith was finally raised shoulder high, the iconic father of an English science (Morrell 2005. 73).

By the 1830s, the more straightforward strata were largely understood and mapped, although often only coarsely. Refinement of the understanding of these rocks became a secondary consideration, and was perceived as second-class science (Bulwer-Lytton 1830). The cutting edge of geology continued to shift. It could now be drawn as a 'Western Front', separating the known world of lowland England from a geological wilderness of complex folded, faulted and metamorphosed rocks in Devon and Cornwall, Wales and Cumberland. It was to these that certain members of the Geological Society now turned their attentions. In Devon, as elsewhere in these territories, there were no society collections to help; only the collections of private individuals. When the metropolitan geologists failed to crack Devon's complex geology and developed into bickering factions, local collectors began to foster their own ambitions. They had hoped to ride to fame on the coat-tails of whichever London geologist might resolve the controversy – this, they understood, was the way the science was prosecuted, with every 'organism' in the science's ecology having its own particular role. But now there grew a sense that their own musings on the subject were equally valid. Such thinking, of course, might have seemed quite natural in a Britain where liberal interests were overriding entrenched conservatism in a succession of reforming acts of parliament. The warning signs that the science was becoming overtaken by a new democratic popularism are apparent in Cambridge academic William Whewell's and astronomer John Herschel's opinions that science should be interpreted by learned and perhaps institutional experts (Yeo 1986: 268). Phillips, too, saw the landscape changing, and a gulf emerging between the local fact collector and those who made true science (Knell 2000: 167). Elsewhere, local geologists were also rethinking the limited rewards of their subservient role (Thackray 1979; Torrens 1990). Men such as Roderick Murchison demonstrated that through the collection, curation and publication of fossils an individual could produce founding concepts with all the merits of universal laws. These laws could then be used to claim and name major portions of time and space. This ability to invent such universal laws, although seen as desirable and perhaps inevitable in the early years of the Geological

Society ([Fitton] 1817: 72), had only become a reality in the 1830s. This began with the eventual reconstitution, by this society, of Smith as the founder of an English science of geology. Indeed, Smith's fossil utilitarianism was to be regarded as the most significant and fundamental contribution to the science for the first century of its modern existence. Utilising Smith's methods, Murchison had given a large sequence of rocks the name Silurian. In doing so he moved beyond the arcane detail of lithology and fossils, to more conceptual views of Nature, to something for wide public digestion. In many respects Murchison's (1835) generalisable world of the Silurian was no less capable of sensation than Buckland's cave of more familiar hyenas. Lyell's reclamation of James Hutton's 'uniformitarian' ideas and reworking of countless examples of geological processes similarly permitted the construction of a monumental work, but one that was, however, entirely accessible to the general reader (Lyell 1830–3). Murchison's success relied not only on the ideas of Smith but also on the networking model so effectively exploited by the Geological Society and its philosophical society imitators, and on his ability to master the general over the particular.

However, the assurances that geology could achieve progress through a reward system based on individualism and recognition had pushed the science to a point of high tension, which came to a head in Devon. Unfortunately for this heroic and individualistic world of science, the Government's first experiment in funding the new science, represented by the one man geological survey of Henry De la Beche, with Phillips as an external helper, took place in Devon, where De la Beche became one of the chief protagonists. As the controversy played out on the public stage of the BAAS, so De la Beche became increasingly worried for his new enterprise and saw the fault in the science's competitive culture: 'To advance science we must allow men to work from all sorts of motives, but "every gentleman for his peculiar fame" is sad work' (Knell 2000: 232). However, the survey survived, and it did so in expanded form, institutionalised as the Geological Survey of Great Britain. So when the survey entered Wales in the early 1840s, it did so as a company of men within which the whole culture of geology – from fossil collecting and mapping, to direction, debate and publication – was internalised. Almost immediately, this new way began to be perceived as a better way, and the ambitions of both gentleman geologist and local philosopher began to dissolve.

The institutional impact of this change was profound. De la Beche soon found himself in charge of a growing empire of publicly funded geological institutions, which culminated in the establishment of a new national museum – the Museum of Practical Geology – in 1851. What underpinned these developments was a new belief that government could fund public institutions without risk of corruption. Before reform it was an open secret that 'jobbery' – self-interest, nepotism and corruption – was rife. Reform put in place mechanisms to contain the opportunities for corruption, though never perfectly so. Nevertheless, the landscape had changed: geology was institutionalised and inevitably professionalised in a way it had not previously been; it no longer required a free economy based on fame from discovery.

In what sense, then, can museums and fossils – situated in their broader social context – tell us of this disciplinary revolution, a revolution that was political rather than a shift of intellectual paradigm? Geology had undergone a political change, and one that not only reflected the national trend towards public institutionalisation and professional employment, but which also utilised this trend in order to wrest control of geology from the anarchic democracy of the masses. The following section reviews this period of change again, but this time tries to see it in terms of the relationships between the science, the individual and the socialised aspects of society (including the production of its institutions).

## Mapping the politics of knowledge

Whether we consider the practical man's (Smith's) collection or the gentleman naturalist's (Richardson's) collection, we essentially see a personal 'museum' that represents the values and personal knowledge of the individual. This is not to dismiss external influences, but collection building is here the activity of an individual, though clearly it reflects wider social norms. The collection permitted the man to make and represent himself, whether to potential clients, students, visitors or neighbours. Figure 3.3 suggests a relationship between these things, with 'geology' essentially shaped by a personal perception and the museum a personal representation of that understanding.

These personal 'museums' did not die out with the emergence of more socialised and structured institutions. However, the rise of these communal ventures undoubtedly altered public perceptions of the individual collector, and in many cases altered the collectors themselves. If an individual was interested in the representative qualities of collections and collecting, then involvement in a socialised and networked venture would surely open up new opportunities for participation. The formation of the Geological Society saw these individualistic gentlemanly interests and values brought together into an institution that valued evidence and individualism but which placed a greater emphasis on performance. Its membership had quite varying views on what would constitute the new geological science, but they shared a belief that a properly formulated museum was key to locating an empirical truth. As Figure 3.4 shows, the science was here internalised – legitimised within a private club which both made it and kept possession of it.

By the 1820s, the science was rapidly gaining popularity, helped by spectacular and accessible discoveries and the still new 'everyman' geology of Smith. Inevitably, the new philosophical societies began to shape their own science according to the social and political needs of their locations. Thus the historian sometimes finds the persistence of rather outdated views depending upon each society's links into and respect for the nascent science of the Geological Society or practical men like Smith and others. In Leeds and Hull, for example, presidents opened proceedings with the kind of 'Theory of the Earth' fashionable in an earlier era. In Whitby, there was a pocket of biblical literalism which saw the Flood of Genesis as an explanation for its local rocks, while one of its most proficient artisan collectors remained convinced that the Earth was flat. However, most local natural philosophers rapidly adopted a shared conception of the science built on Smith's ideas ideas which even

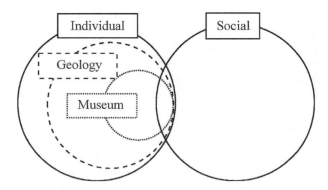

*Figure 3.3* The private cabinet circa 1805. Here 'geology' is personally understood, and the museum is a representation of that understanding.

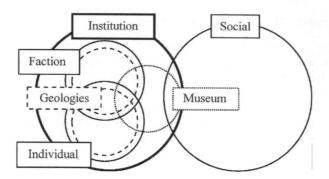

*Figure 3.4* The Geological Society of London, circa 1810. In the early days of the Society there was no single notion of geology; the discipline was embryonic and indefinite. Individuals and factions managed their own perceptions but shared the museum as a repository and as a representation of the empirical truth of material things. The operation of this geological world was within a private club – wider society was excluded.

then were not wholly adopted by the Geological Society of London. Figure 3.5 shows this shared conception of the science in an institution shaped by the needs of wider society. Here, geological engagement could not be separated from civic and individual ambition, both of which saw social elevation as being central to existence. To achieve these social ends, societies were willing to recognise and legitimise a diversity of roles and practices, from shopping to field excavation, from dilettante gift-giving to the solution of local geological puzzles, from publisher of original findings to orator of derivative views. The museum, composed of what were indisputably real things, was a key stabilising influence within the organisation, just as the philosophical society itself acted to bring political stability at a time of social tension.

When the science came to investigate Devon in the 1830s, there were no stabilising museums. The geology was difficult and geographically localised. Progress had ensured that the cutting edge of geology would end up in a geographical and temporal bottleneck in the older rocks of the West of England (Rudwick 1985; Knell 2000). William Buckland was well aware that the science was increasingly competitive: 'being anticipated in these days of philosophical scrambling for subjects to write about' (Morrell and Thackray 1981: 424 n.215). By this time, the rewards of participation in the science were considerable, and beyond the wildest dreams of those who founded the London society a quarter century before. The difficulty of Devonian geology, the science's high public profile and the proven social rewards of success produced a volatile mixture. The dispute that developed centred on the interpretation of fossils, and before long the considerable social weight of the science became centred on their possession; the fossils themselves became incredibly powerful.

The Devonian free-for-all, however, saw this hierarchy of participation challenged. The Geological Society's nurturing of a competitive model, and an appreciative audience, ensured that the social rewards of participation overshadowed the intellectual gains. In a scientific hierarchy, the social aspects of participation can be controlled; progress involved the curation not just of fossils but also of people. The failure of 'the wise master builders' to resolve the geological problem meant that their power to curate the participants was also diminished. Matters were not helped by a pervasive reformist social subconscious that was

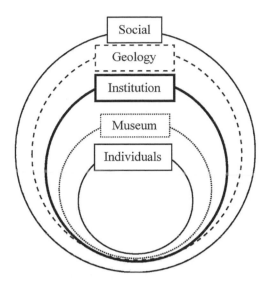

*Figure 3.5* The northern philosophical societies circa 1824. Under the influence of William
Smith, the societies were plugged into a shared conception of geology which could be
understood as universal and existing within wider society. Each institution was a
component in this larger geological world and its own museum was its central
resource. This resource spoke the same empirical truth known to the London geologists but it also spoke of an individual's knowledge and commitment, and of a town's
cultural status.

doubting cliques and inherited power. Now the very thing that had permitted British
science to progress so effectively was inhibiting its progress. Figure 3.6 conceptualises what
was an unhappy state of affairs for those who had invested time in the development of a
largely self-funded geological career.

On the rebound, scarred by his Devonian experiences, De la Beche acquired additional
funding for a reconfigured Geological Survey in 1841. Now the entire culture of geology was
internalised; all that lay outside was an audience (Figure 3.7). In some respects this internal-
isation was a mirror of that achieved by the Geological Society, though internally the two
organisations could not be more different. Individualism remained important to motivation,
but now it was contained and constrained by officer hierarchy and a career ladder (such as
there was). Geology was back in the hands of the scientific hegemony and free from debili-
tating pressures of democratic influence. However, that hegemony was composed of the now
fully emerged middle-class bureaucrat, and although these men were often gentleman, this
was no longer the gentlemanly science of earlier decades which had then fed off the social
politics of participation. Now all De la Beche needed to do was play the political game
known to directors of all public utilities, a political game of ensuring government patronage.
In this De la Beche was unsurpassed. With the rise of publicly funded science and a way of
doing which was soon understood to surpass anything that could be achieved by individuals
working alone, the local philosopher and gentleman geologist faded into the background.
The rage for geology had by then almost burnt itself out as a popular sport, but it had burned
most ferociously in its final stages.

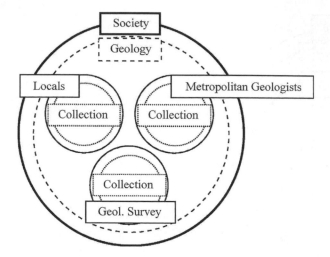

*Figure 3.6* Geology in Devon in 1835. Here participants worked with a common conception of geology but now each faction was clustered around separate resources. In past conceptions of the science the museum's universalism was central to stability and progress, and a political world surrounded and interacted with that resource. In Devon, the museum was drawn into the politics and thus could not function in this way.

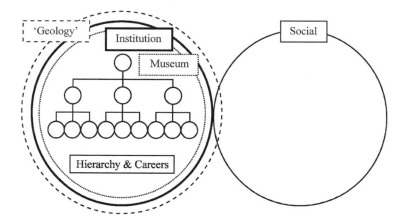

*Figure 3.7* The Geological Survey of Great Britain in 1842. Here the science is removed from the social world. It is internalised within a career, reporting and decision making infrastructure.

## A geological revolution

What the science saw in the 1830s was a system under stress and which could only be stabilised by transformation into something else. It was a catastrophic failure of a particularly British way of conducting the new science, which had located progress in individual enterprise. The necessary conditions for its success involved the internal and then external socialisation of geology. A landscape rich in the intellectual building blocks of reputation emerged as a result, while the spark of sensation lifted the science out of the mundane of the everyday. To these were added the simple everyman concepts of Smith and a coterie of able popularisers and romantics who made the science approachable. The emergence of provincial learned societies reflected this new subconscious and catalysed the science's development. It placed geology on the path towards popularism – a popularism that would test the very basis of participation. Science demanded its hegemony and its lines of respect. Only by this means could it build on what had gone before and bring together a growing body of ordered knowledge; the free market tended to subvert these goals.

The reformulated Geological Survey can by these means be understood as revolutionary, as a means to assert control when deference to the wise master was no longer sufficient. But the new Geological Survey was not an untried model. In an earlier period the topographical mapmaking Ordnance Survey, which parented De la Beche's early survey work, had long been organised around delegated team working. Geology also had its own model, located within the learned societies, where paid curators provided science and expertise. It was this particular expertise – in fossil identification – that De la Beche first acquired for his nascent Geological Survey in the form of John Phillips. A pre-eminently political animal, De la Beche was then able to operate within the corridors of Whitehall to grow a public empire and a recognisably modern practice of geology. His greatest achievement, however, was one of cultural revolution, which determined who controlled the new science. The science had flown the nest.

This was not a revolution in method or interpretation as both had been established long before. Indeed, the Geological Survey in 1842 used the same working methods as were applied by Smith and Phillips a quarter of a century earlier. De la Beche's revolution placed geology in the hands of the 'public', as understood in an ordered democratic state – that is funded by public taxation – rather than a public who claimed participation out of equality of opportunity. In this regard it reflected the wider revolution resulting from political reform, which created an ordered democracy and prevented the rule of the mob. The two seem to

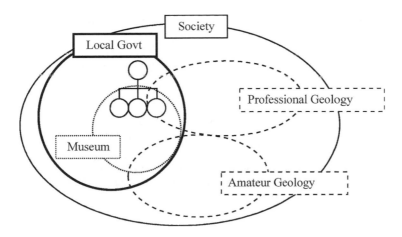

Figure 3.8 The museum in local government, 1850. Here, too, control of the science is internalised in a particular strain of professional geology linked into the web of local government bureaucracy and public service. Many of those who were once engaged in a gentlemanly science now found themselves firmly isolated as relatively powerless amateurs in a discipline shaped by careered professionals.

reflect and resolve a similar struggle; they perhaps reflect the same subconscious and the wider zeitgeist.

The museums which had been at the heart of this age may have looked very similar, but their true identities were defined by people and not, as we sometimes assume, by collections. Each was formed in response to all that had gone before; as such they 'progressed' by revolution rather than evolution, often overtly rejecting the values of an earlier era (Knell 1996). Political reform had, by the late 1830s, ensured that most philosophical societies no longer had the same social currency. Their museums looked to a future under local government completely divorced from the world that had produced them, and with much of their earlier meaning stripped from them. While some survived, their parent societies often merged with more fashionable archaeological societies or newer natural history societies and field clubs, under the now identifiable banner of the amateur (see Figure 3.8 on previous page). The fossil, which had been so fundamental to the science as a politically powerful object, had also changed. Now it was simply a fossil. As such it remained what it had always been (and rather more than it is commonly believed to be): a material signifier of the condition of science.

## Bibliography

Allen, D.E. (1994) *The Naturalist in Britain: A Social History*, Princeton, NJ: Princeton University Press.

Anon. (1825) 'Report of meeting of Whitby Literary and Philosophical Society', *Whitby Repository*, 1(3): 19.

—— (1874) 'Prof. John Phillips', *The Athenaeum*, 2427, 2 May: 597–8.

Attenborough, D. (2002) *Life on Air: Memoirs of a Broadcaster*, London: BBC.

Bentley, M. (1985) *Politics Without Democracy*, Oxford: Blackwell/Fontana.

Binns, J. (2003) *The History of Scarborough*, Pickering: Blackthorn Press.

Bulwer-Lytton, E. (1830) *England and the English*, 2 volumes, facsimile reprint 1970, Shannon: Irish University Press.

Campbell, C. (1987) *The Romantic Ethic and the Spirit of Modern Consumerism*, Oxford: Blackwell.

Cohen, I. B. (1985) *Revolution in Science*, Cambridge, MA: Belknap.

Dinwiddy, J. R. (1986) *From Luddism to the First Reform Bill*, Oxford: Blackwell.

Edmonds, J. M. (1975) 'The first geological lecture course at the University of London, 1831', *Annals of Science*, 32: 257–75.

Eyles, J. M. (1967) 'William Smith: the sale of his collection to the British Museum', *Annals of Science*, 23: 177–212.

—— (1969) 'William Smith (1769–1839): A bibliography of his published writings, maps and geological sections, printed and lithographed', *Journal of the Society for the Bibliography of Natural History*, 5: 87–109.

[Fitton, W. H.]. (1817) 'Transactions of the Geological Society, vol. III', *Edinburgh Review*, 29: 71–94.

Knell, S. J. (1996) 'The roller-coaster of museum geology', in S. M. Pearce (ed.) *Exploring Science in Museums*, New Research in Museum Studies, London: Athlone, 29–56.

—— (2000) *The Culture of English Geology, 1815–1851: A Science Revealed Through Its Collecting*, Aldershot: Ashgate.

—— (2002) 'Collecting, conservation and conservatism: late twentieth century developments in the culture of British geology', in D. R. Oldroyd (ed.) *The Earth Inside and Out: Some Major Contributions to Geology in the Twentieth Century*, London: Geological Society, 329–51.

—— (2007) 'Museums, reality and the material world', in S. J. Knell (ed.) *Museums in the Material World*, London: Routledge.

—— and Taylor, M. A. (2006) 'Hugh Miller: fossils, landscape and literary geology', *Proceedings of the Geologists Association*, 117: 85–98.

Latour, B. (1987) *Science in Action: How to Follow Scientists and Engineers through Society*, Milton Keynes: Open University Press.

Lyell, C. (1826a) 'Scientific institutions', *Quarterly Review*, 34: 153–79.

—— (1826b) 'Transactions of the Geological Society of London', *Quarterly Review*, 34: 507–40.

—— (1830–3) *Principles of Geology*, 3 volumes, London: Murray.

Miller, H. (1835) *Scenes and Legends of the North of Scotland; or, The Traditional History of Cromarty*, Edinburgh: Black.

—— (1841) *The Old Red Sandstone, or, New Walks in an Old Field*, Edinburgh: John Johnstone.

Morrell, J. B. (2005) *John Phillips and the Business of Victorian Science*, Aldershot: Ashgate.

—— and Thackray, A. (1981) *Gentlemen of Science: Early Years of the British Association for the Advancement of Science*, Oxford: Clarendon.

Murchison, R. I. (1835) 'On the Silurian System of rocks', *Philosophical Magazine* (3rd series), 7: 46–53.

Rudwick, M. J. S. (1972) *The Meaning of Fossils*, Chicago, IL: University of Chicago Press.

—— (1985) *The Great Devonian Controversy: The Shaping of Scientific Knowledge among Gentlemanly Specialists*, Chicago, IL: University of Chicago Press.

—— (2005) *Bursting the Limits of Time: The Reconstruction of Geohistory in the Age of Revolution*, Chicago, IL: University of Chicago Press.

Rupke, N. A. (1983) *The Great Chain of History: William Buckland and the English School of Geology*, Oxford: Clarendon.

Secord, J. A. (1986) *Controversy in Victorian Geology: The Cambrian-Silurian Debate*, Princeton, NJ: Princeton University Press.

Sedgwick, A. (1830) 'Presidential Address, 19 February 1830', *Proceedings of the Geological Society*, London, 15: 197.

Taylor, M. A. (2007) *Hugh Miller*, Edinburgh: National Museums of Scotland.

Thackray, John C. (1979) 'T.T. Lewis and Murchison's Silurian System', *Transactions of the Woolhope Naturalists Field Club*, 42: 186–93.

Torrens, H. S. (1990) 'The scientific ancestry and historiography of the Silurian System', *Journal of the Geological Society*, London, 147: 657–62.

Yeo, R. (1986) 'Scientific method and the rhetoric of science in Britain, 1830–1917', in J. Schuster and R. Yeo (eds) *The Politics and Rhetoric of Scientific Method: Historical Studies*, Dordrecht: Kluwer.

Yorkshire Philosophical Society (1828) *Annual Report for 1827*, York: YPS.

# 4

# ESTABLISHING THE MANIFESTO

## Art histories in the nineteenth-century museum

*Christopher Whitehead*

This chapter examines three proposals for the reconfiguration of the national museums in London dating from the 1850s and considers some of the issues they raise in relation to the study of the history and theory of museums and disciplinarity. The purpose of this is to focus on the importance of the museum as a forum for the development of the disciplinary practices of art history in mid-nineteenth-century Britain. This chapter argues that the curatorial act of representing art history in museum display – situating collected objects three dimensionally, in relation to the transit and forms of engagement of imagined visitors – was actually constitutive of certain intellectual approaches and practices of art history as a discipline. This chapter also argues that the project of art museum display brought with it certain unique ways of thinking about, and configuring, art history, and these have been important for the intellectual and professional legacies of disciplinarity of which art historians are possessed, which guide and delimit practices and which govern where we site, and how we view, objects and history in or through objects. In this sense, this chapter is one attempt to analyse some of the complexities of the interrelationships between the art museum and the discipline of art history as recently hinted at by Preziosi (2005: 50–1):

> Never entirely distinct institutionally, professionally, or personally, their similarities and differences are not easily articulated: art history is not satisfactorily reduced to being the 'theory' to the museum's 'practice,' nor the ghost in the museum's machinery. Nor is the museum simply – if at all – the exemplification or application of art history, or merely the staging or stagecraft of the dramaturgies of art historical analysis and synthesis. If anything, their relations are anamorphic – each transforming the other – rather than direct or transitive.

## The project of display and the organisation of knowledge

Imagine this scenario. The date is 1853. What if the institutional identities of the British Museum and the National Gallery, together with their accreted conventions of collecting and display, were somehow suddenly dissolved, leaving us with their collections alone? Given the opportunity of such a *tabula rasa*, would we choose to situate the British Museum's

Egyptian, classical or prehistoric 'antiquities' and the post-medieval paintings of the National Gallery together, or at least in relation to one another? If, after the hypothetical orphaning of the collections, we were tasked with their rehoming, what would we do? Would we seek to reorganise them, and, in so doing, potentially reorganise the knowledges they represent? What boundaries would we impose, what categories of material culture would we seek to identify and what stories of the past would we tell?

This chapter will now focus on a crucial historical moment in 1850s England, when such questions were being asked; when, for example, the disciplines of art history and archaeology were not yet clearly defined or differentiated from one another in terms of their respective purviews of material culture, and when such a *tabula rasa* was a possibility. Prominent within parliamentary and literary debate about cultural provision in the 1850s was the so-called 'site question'. This centred around the location of the National Gallery collection in a building which was seen to be insufficiently spacious or architecturally meretricious; this building itself was and is sited in Trafalgar Square – then one of the busiest and most polluted areas of London. Its position led to concerns both about the safety of the paintings from an environmental perspective and about the uses made of the gallery by those visitors less interested in engaging with the paintings than with other leisure pursuits, such as picnicking in the gallery and 'lounging' (Prior 2002: 88–94; Whitehead 2005a: 79–61)

The British Museum's collection also appeared to suffer from problems caused by pollution, which led to the idea that it might be expedient to relocate both institutions, potentially allowing for them and their collections to come into closer relationship, or even to be integrated (Whitehead 2005a: 69–87). In effect this would have dissolved the historical identities of the two museums, eradicating, for example, any sense of their foundational collections and the private individuals responsible for them – Sir Hans Sloane and John Julius Angerstein respectively. Ultimately, the debate led to few obvious outcomes, for the two museums were not relocated or combined, as a result of circumstances which are as adventitious as they are intellectual or ideological (for example, the withdrawal of an offer to the Government of land for the construction of a new museum or cluster of museums, changes in government administration, etc.). For reasons of space these circumstances will not be discussed in detail here – this has been done elsewhere (Whitehead 2005a); it suffices to state that for some time in the 1850s, the project of entirely recasting the national museums, of rethinking their boundaries and those of the knowledges they invoked, was very seriously and lengthily contemplated. In practical terms this meant, for example, that in the various government inquiries about the future of the national museums, witnesses were repeatedly quizzed about the benefits of being able to refer between paintings and other categories of objects, such as antique and modern sculpture, ceramics and so on (Select Committee 1853).

In order to characterise something of this discussion, this chapter will now examine three of the many museological proposals from the 1850s that responded and contributed to the debate about the site question by proposing specific divisions of material culture in pursuit of different knowledges and disciplinary territories and practices. As stated, this chapter will look particularly at the conceptual and physical segregation of *painting* as a special category of material culture. The questions which this chapter addresses thus become: why is *painting* given the status of a discrete body of material culture? Why is it dislocated, in a discrete type of museum, from other things? What histories are pursued through its dislocation? How might this influence our historical understandings and disciplinary practices?

Each of the statements to be discussed was made in the context of parliamentary investigations into what should be done with the national collections. Their authors were some of the leading figures in the world (or worlds) of museums, art and archaeology in the 1850s. They are: Charles Lock Eastlake and Ralph Nicholson Wornum, who in 1855 would become respectively the first director of the National Gallery and its Keeper and Secretary; the archaeologist and British Museum curator Charles Newton; and the critic and author John Ruskin. In their respective statements these figures discussed topics such as the relationships between what we would now call art history and archaeology, the internal structures of the histories of material culture with which they were concerned, and the role of the museum in configuring these things. The plans envisaged the selective accumulation of objects and their sequential display, where the sequence of objects and the visitor's temporal movement from one object to another, or from one room to another – akin to what Bennett has termed 'organized walking as evolutionary practice' – could be used to suggest relationships, histories and geographies (Bennett 1995: 177–208). As stated, the choreography involved in this was an enabling means in the constitution of knowledge; something, in other words, capable not just of representing discourse (for example in the form of one historical narrative or another) but of potentialising and delimiting it.

In 1853, Eastlake and Wornum produced a *Plan for a Collection of Paintings, Illustrative of the History of the Art*. This provided a roadmap for the development of the collection, and was published as an appendix to a Select Committee report on the future of the national collections (Select Committee 1853). Notwithstanding its title, the authors noted in their introduction that it would also be desirable to acquire drawings, intarsia, painted glass and tapestry. However, this was not reflected in the *Plan* itself, and of course bore no relation to future collecting at the National Gallery (Select Committee 1853: 793). The *Plan for a Collection of Paintings* constituted, peopled and characterised a particular story of art. The story was diachronic and focused on stylistic developments in painting, which were articulated through biographical accounts of artists and genealogical accounts of artists' influence upon one another (see Whitehead 2005b for discussion of Gustav Friedrich Waagen's seminal 1853 essay, 'Thoughts on the new building to be erected for the National Gallery', which proposed a similar system, also limited to painting). In terms of display, this meant the physical ordering of works to represent both the periodised oeuvres of key artists, such as Raphael, and the relationships of tuition and influence between different artists, between 'schools', and so on (for a discussion of the use of the term 'school' at the National Gallery, see Whitehead 2005a: 24). After a preamble explaining its purpose, the plan is made up of two columns, the principal of which simply lists the 'Schools' of painting (Florentine, Venetian, Umbrian, etc.) within which are listed the artists who belonged to them, in roughly chronological order, incorporating notes on master–student relations. Alongside these lists, a second column gives occasional explanatory remarks pointing out the characteristics of certain schools or groups of artists and their stylistic similarities with, and differences from, others. For example:

> The Sienese School, in its earlier character [i.e. from the early thirteenth century], was remarkable for a religious tendency, not merely as regards the choice of subjects (which were everywhere of the same kind), but in a certain devotional fervour of expression; resembling, in this respect, Angelico da Fiesole, and also the painters of the Umbrian School. The works of all these painters, though conveying the

impression of deep feeling, do not exhibit that variety of form and study of nature which are conspicuous in the Florentines generally, to whom Angelico da Fiesole is thus to be regarded as an exception. With the Sienese, the prevailing tendency of feeling referred to involved a certain limitation in the forms and the character of heads.

(Select Committee 1853: 795)

It is apparent that the scheme was concerned with form and not with content in painting, with authorship and not with social context, and with a history of the production rather than of the use or social roles of works of art (and obviously all of these might now be seen as false dichotomies). In the above quotation the issue of subject matter is entirely subsidiary to the rather minute deliberations on stylistic differentiation and accounts of exceptions to the rules, and there is no attempt to consider the relationships between the production and consumption of paintings and social, political, religious or economic contexts of thirteenth-century Siena. Notably, the *Plan* is also a list of artists and not of works of art. This functions to bestow importance on the identity of the artist himself (for the list is almost entirely male) as subject and catalyst of intellectual evolution, while also making it possible for paintings within the gallery to act as signifiers of their authors. In so doing, the *Plan* corresponds to a long historiographical tradition based on the comprehension of the past through the study of great men (comprehending protagonists as varied as Plutarch, Paolo Giovio, Giorgio Vasari and Thomas Carlyle), although the biographies of the artists involved in the *Plan* are limited to their place within trajectories of tuition and influence. The emphasis on artists rather than works of art also responded to a practical imperative, in that it meant that different galleries could represent the same history of art by each collecting different 'specimens' of the same artist's work, thus ensuring the feasibility of executing the *Plan* within the context of the competitive European market for 'Old Masters'.

Eastlake's approach to the question of quality was somewhat innovative; the scheme included early works, conventionally perceived to be of a lower artistic quality (see Steegman 1950: 61–74; Hoeniger 1999), where they were seen to illustrate the historical narratives discussed above. This is not to say that quality was an unimportant criterion, but that it was ultimately subordinate as a structuring principle to a certain kind of comprehensiveness in historical ordering. Indeed, the rhetoric of comprehensiveness in a genealogical history of art was important in justifying the acquisition for the National Gallery of medieval paintings such as Margarito d'Arezzo's *Virgin and Child Enthroned* of 1255 (purchased during Eastlake's directorship in 1857), conventionally seen as 'primitive' and generally undesirable. (Margarito d'Arezzo is one of only six artists listed in the *Plan* under the heading 'early Italian specimens influenced by Byzantine art'). The particular stories of art which Eastlake and Wornum proposed to tell also isolated paintings into a discrete narrative, distinguished from other forms of material culture and from architectural and socio-historical contexts. The notion of the *purpose* of historical organisation is particularly important. The authors made it clear that the hypothetical collection of painting they were sketching *could* be studied in different contexts, for example the 'connection' of the paintings with 'Religion, History, Poetry, Natural History . . . Physiognomy, Costume and other facts'. However, for Eastlake and Wornum these were 'general uses', subsidiary to the 'special purposes' of the collection, which were to represent the development of 'well adapted and durable technical processes' and style, understood as 'artistic merit, considered in relation to periods and schools [and] the illustration of the connexion between various modes of representation' (Select Committee 1853: 792).

The archaeologist and British Museum curator Charles Newton's letter to the same Select Committee is rather different. Whereas Eastlake opted to segregate painting, Newton was concerned with uniting what he saw as three classes of material culture: 'Monuments of Fine Art, or productions of what are called the Fine Arts'; 'Inscribed Monuments' of any material; and 'Monuments of Handicraft, or production of the useful and decorative arts'. In fact Newton's letter was an appeal to conserve the heterogeneity of the British Museum collections in any future large-scale redevelopment of the national museums, for only through the 'felicitous combination of the monuments of many races' could 'a vast scheme of historical relations [be] suddenly disclosed and demonstrated' (Select Committee 1853: 781).

In discussing material culture Newton uses relatively conventional classifications, such as 'fine art', but they are placed within a system of reciprocal illustration. For example, Assyrian relief sculptures and cylinder seals belonged respectively to the categories of fine art and handicraft, and indeed both belonged to the class of inscribed monuments, but, as Newton pointed out:

> The same peculiar style of art, the same figures and groups, the same cuneiform characters which we find in the larger friezes, reappear on a reduced scale in the cylinders and seals; one system of mythography and of historical record pervades the whole of the art.
>
> (Select Committee 1853: 773)

There is, then, a clear appeal to attend to the relatedness of apparently different things. For Newton the rationale behind this approach was the greater understanding of what he called the 'motive and meaning' of objects, for which different sorts of objects needed to be available for cross referencing. Newton gave an example of his interrogative approach in his interpretation of the Parthenon marbles. Rather than seeing their style as an autonomous characteristic, Newton pointed out that they could not be appreciated without an understanding of their original physical placement, which influenced their formal qualities and the nature of spectatorship. Proceeding from this, Newton emphasised the importance above all of a contextual reading of the frieze as 'a celebration of the glory of Athena as the tutelary goddess of the Athenian people'. And indeed, much of Newton's letter was an appeal to the primacy of *meaning* as an interpretative key:

> How much, for instance, has the interest of the figure in the Gallery of Florence, commonly called 'The Listening Slave,' been enhanced since this figure has been recognised as part of a group representing the flaying of Marsyas by Apollo[?].
>
> (Select Committee 1853: 775)

When Newton discussed medieval painting he noted, along with Eastlake and Wornum, that 'unattractive' specimens should be acquired and displayed because of their place within historical narratives of development, but for Newton the narrative of most interest concerned iconography and meaning, and not style. In contrast with Eastlake and Wornum, Newton privileged a more inclusive approach to material culture – one which still relied on categorisation, but which involved greater referentiality among categories. Importantly though, the ultimate purpose of study, and of display, was still the comprehension of the object.

The last proposal to be examined here is John Ruskin's evidence before the Royal Commission of 1857 on the Site for the National Gallery (Royal Commission 1857). This post-dates the statements discussed above by four years, but it is situated within precisely the same debate and is unquestionably in dialogue with them.

Ruskin's proposal was more explicitly inclusive than Newton's, in aiming to reconstitute the national collections into two museums of art *and* archaeology – one 'Pagan' and the other 'Christian' (a proposal also advanced by Antonio Panizzi, principal librarian at the British Museum (Royal Commission 1857: qu. 1526)). Notably, the boundary between the two was the birth of Christ, meaning that the Christian museum would also contain Islamic art – because, as Ruskin noted, 'it seems to me that the history of Christianity is complicated perpetually by that which it was affecting' (Royal Commission 1857: qu. 2488). This is clearly a religiocentric and indeed Christocentric orientation for the organisation of material culture, but it permitted multiple foci, including, for Ruskin, sculpture, painting, architectural drawings and models, iron work, ceramics and woodwork; indeed, when pressed, Ruskin noted that a new national gallery should contain: 'Everything, pots and pans, and salt cellars and knives' (Royal Commission 1857: qu. 2481).

Although Ruskin also emphasised the importance of classification and the inclusion of inferior specimens of art, his interrogative focus was quite different from Eastlake's or Newton's. As he put it:

> One of the main uses of Art . . . is not so much as Art, but as teaching us the feelings of nations. History only tells us what they did. Art tells us their feelings, and why they did it: whether they were energetic and fiery, or whether they were, as in the case of the Dutch, imitating minor things, quiet and cold.
>
> (Royal Commission 1857: qu. 2437)

He went on:

> [A country] may be urged by an ambitious king to become a warrior nation . . . and its character at that time may materially depend upon that one man, but in its art all the mind of the nation is more or less expressed: it can be said, that was what the peasant sought to, when he went into the city to the cathedral in the morning . . . that was the sort of picture he prayed to. All of which involves infinitely more considerations than common history.
>
> (Royal Commission 1857: qu. 2475)

It is clear from this that Ruskin saw art objects as inherently documentary and thus useful for the study of topics beyond themselves. While to some extent this is romantically oriented, particularly in the notion that different peoples have inherent characteristics which are revealed by art, it also recognises the wider social network in which the production and consumption of art was situated, for example in the idea that the interpretational value of a religious painting resided in its location in a cathedral, in its relation to a viewer, and in its use within social and religious practices. This is a very different history of objects from those we saw earlier, which focused on stylistic development and the development of 'meaning'.

## Perspectives on art museum work as disciplinary practice

What this chapter has examined so far are three different statements about two interrelated problems: how to manage material culture and what information it should be used to produce. While the statements differ about the point of studying objects and which histories should be pursued, they involve certain commonalities. First, they all insist on classificatory organisation. Second, they attempt to rethink the notion of value, so that objects seen to be of inferior artistic quality and taste were admissible within classificatory structures, which made them legible. Third, and related to these last points, the statements involved the taxonomic labour of positioning and locating objects in relation to one another, involving:

> The fabrication of a central data mass, a universally extensible archive within which every possible object of study might *find its place* and locus relative to others, within which, in other words, every item might be *seen* as bearing the *traces* of others: as referencing or indexing another or others.
>
> (Preziosi 1993: 220)

Of interest here is the point that the three museological proposals invoke different criteria for relations, or, as Preziosi puts it elsewhere, 'dimensions of meaningful reference' (Preziosi 1993: 218) (style, meaning and use), which lead their authors to set different boundaries as to the kinds of objects their systems include and exclude and to engage in different critical practices predicated on different 'anamorphic positions':

> from which the history of art may be seen as unfolding, almost magically, before [one's] eyes. The archival mass, in other words, is made accessible from particular prefabricated stances designed to elicit (confer) additional sense from (on) the diachronic and differential system. Common anamorphic perspectives include artistic biography, periodization, stylistic evolution, and the evolution of particular thematic or semantic contents.
>
> (Preziosi 1993: 223)

One of the frameworks which can be employed to think about this comes from studies concerning the formation of disciplinarity in academia. A primary contention of such studies is that disciplines are constructs, built of politics and circumstance as well as intellectual endeavour; thus they are not natural recipients for certain apparently hermetic, self-forming bodies of knowledge and forms and methods of enquiry. In this context Messer-Davidow *et al.* note:

> If disciplines are such by virtue of a historically contingent, adventitious coherence of dispersed elements, then to study that coherence is necessarily to begin questioning portrayals of disciplines as seamless, progressive, or naturally 'about' certain topics. In studying disciplinarity, one defamiliarizes disciplines; one distances oneself from them and problematizes their very existence.
>
> (Messer-Davidow *et al.* 1993: 3)

Indeed, this kind of critical position is beginning to find analogue expression in museum historiography. Hill, for example, notes:

> We use different categories, such as 'natural history' or 'fine art', to analyse the shape and development of museums, but those categories could be largely created by the museums themselves . . . any category . . . is not an absolute division corresponding to a 'real' group in the material world, but rather an imposition on that world created by structures of knowledge.
>
> (Hill 2005: 73; see also, Jordanova 1989: 23–4; Sherman and Rogoff 1994: xi)

Another key concept in studies of disciplinarity is 'boundary work', which can be defined as the development of arguments and strategies to justify particular divisions of knowledge and the strategies used to construct, maintain and push boundaries. While current use of this concept is limited to studies of academia, it may be worthwhile to use the notion of boundary work differently, to understand what museums collect and display and why and how they do so as a form of boundary work.

Ruskin's proposal for 'Pagan' and 'Christian' museums is especially interesting in the context of boundary work. On the one hand its boundaries are immense, as Ruskin proposes the use of a uniform approach to objects normally seen to be of vastly different type (e.g. paintings and 'pots and pans'). On the other hand, within this broad territory he argues for certain divisions of knowledge (which, in disciplinary terms, might be called 'fields') based on a specific 'demarcation criterion' (Fuller 1993: 126–7). It can be argued that demarcation criteria are invariably complex and inherently political, and the use of the Pagan versus Christian criterion is a clear example of this, as, for that matter, is the more conventional criterion of 'art' versus 'non-art'. In this alone the acts of differencing within disciplinarity are problematic.

However, the museological proposals that this chapter has explored were also competitive. One theory of discipline is that it is a principle of limitation. In the words of Amariglio *et al.* (1993: 150–1), who have discussed the formation of economics as a discipline, 'A discipline arises in the course of struggles to limit the discourses involved in the production of formal knowledge'. They go on to discuss that while limitation may arise from agreement, it more often results from the silencing of discourses. In this context it could be argued that Eastlake's emphasis on a dislocated and discrete history of painting, itself organised around an overriding notion of style in exclusion of other interrogative foci, is a clear attempt to limit discourses; this might be termed *reductive* boundary work as opposed to the *expansive* boundary work attempted by Newton and, above all, by Ruskin. (It should be noted, however, that Eastlake did not oppose plans to amalgamate national collections (Select Committee 1853: qu. 6520–42).) It might also be argued that circumstances (political and other), enabled the silencing of the sorts of discourse in which Newton and Ruskin participated, concerning the integration of bodies of material culture within the museum. As stated earlier, to a certain extent their silencing was adventitious, contingent upon opportunities (such as the availability of funds and land for the kind of new museum complex imagined by Ruskin) which, for reasons that were sometimes banal rather than intellectual, were not taken up. Arguably, though, these contingencies co-existed with political and intellectual reasons for the silencing of discourse. However, it is difficult to find any open acknowledgment of such reasons in contemporary writing, so they must be understood to be speculative.

For example, the integration of paintings into wider museum collections would have weakened the crucial nineteenth-century discourse about their transcendental and moral agency, which was of great concern to policy makers in relation to the perceived need to 'improve' new electorates. If placed alongside 'pots and pans, and salt cellars and knives' – or even in the same building – paintings might have become just another category of material culture, and this could have been difficult to countenance, given the importance of their use within broader socio-political projects. Indeed, the intensity of government attention to the management and development of the National Gallery in the mid-nineteenth century was unprecedented and has never been matched since: between 1848 and 1861 the National Gallery alone was the subject of no less than five major government enquiries, involving the convocation of hundreds of witnesses and the production of thousands of pages of material in report form. This is an indication of the political investment in the collecting and display of paintings in various contexts, such as the ongoing project of electoral reform and cultural competition with other industrialised nation states, whose galleries and collections were a constant reference point in the development of policy in Britain (Whitehead 2005a: 12–16).

So far this chapter has accounted for segregation. But why style rather than meaning or context? There are a number of possible reasons, all of which seem to interrelate on close analysis. For example, the identification of style was a key determinant in contemporary practices of attribution, meaning that there was a strong economic imperative involved in perfecting this ostensibly intellectual practice; considerable sums of government money (relatively speaking) were spent on paintings, which, if proven to be misattributed to one artist or another, could turn out to be the source of embarrassment both nationally and internationally (see Robertson 1978: 84–7). Also, as has been argued elsewhere, the identification of stylistic characteristics has much in common with contemporary scientific practices and ocular culture (Whitehead 2005a: 8–10). Further, the focus on style hinged on the question of (largely) beneficial tuition and positive influence, which bears relation both with the importance of work- and studio-based teaching and learning in nineteenth-century Britain (both in terms of the apprenticeship system and the formal education of 'artisans', for example at the Schools of Design) and with the broader teleological discourse surrounding the identity of Britain in relation to colonised Others (Whitehead 2005b: 193). This is to suggest that wider contemporary values and concerns were present within art historical practices.

Another of the benefits of the emphasis on style is that it de-emphasised content, helping to neutralise the encounters between working-class visitors, who were seen as excitable and easily led, and paintings with potentially dangerous subject matter. An example is the *Adoration of the Shepherds* (NG 232), bought as a Velasquez during the 1853 Select Committee proceedings (attributed today to the Neapolitan School c.1630). Perhaps because of the unidealised representation of figures and the sheer griminess of the scene, this painting was seen by some to represent a sacred subject inappropriately, in such a way as to debase visitors' morals and excite inappropriate feelings (and here one should consider all of the dark hints at mass action and popular uprising that such a view must have conveyed in 1850s Britain), the proposition being, as one Select Committee member put it:

> That the taste of the mass of the people, who frequent the National Gallery, and who are not used, or but little used to see objects of that kind [i.e. the subject matter] treated in the way in which they ought to be treated, is likely to be deteriorated by having placed before them a very large picture treating a very sublime and very sacred object in a very low and undignified manner.
>
> (Select Committee 1853: qu. 5400)

When quizzed about this controversial acquisition during the proceedings, the insistent appeal of some witnesses to the primacy of style as interpretive key effectively defused this controversy (Whitehead 2005a: 138–9). In a sense, the culturally problematic aspects of the painting in mid-nineteenth-century Britain were thus cleaned away by its siting within a museum context and within a museological system. (McClellan (1999: 16) discusses a similar act of purification in revolutionary France.) This is indicative of a certain problem. On the one hand paintings were held up as quasi magical objects with agency all of their own, capable of exerting beneficial moral influence upon individuals (and particularly upon those who were seen to be most in need of it) (see also, McClellan 2003: 8; Robertson 2004: 4). On the other hand, the subject matter of historical paintings was potentially dangerous (for example, consider the question of morality in Greek mythology, or of religious doctrine in catholic imagery), and hinted at past and/or foreign societal mores and practices which would have been largely unacceptable in mid-nineteenth-century Britain and which policy makers would have had no wish to promote, either inadvertently or otherwise. Given this tension, the adherence to style seems almost to represent a national strategy for understanding paintings – the imposition of a dominant 'anamorphic perspective' – in which subject matter and the social histories of paintings were effectively suppressed as 'dimensions of meaningful reference'.

Lastly, in contrast with the rationales for style discussed above, which are reminiscent in many ways of the debate in contemporary museum historiography regarding knowledge–power relations (see, for example, Hooper-Greenhill 1992; Bennett 1995; Sherman and Rogoff 1994; Conn 1998; Trodd 2003; Hill 2005; Starn 2005), it is worth entertaining the possibility that the visitor's engagement with disciplinary practice (be it coerced or not), for example in relation to the understanding and appreciation of style in paintings, was a sensual, and in some way pleasurable, participation in the intellectual systems of art history as experienced in the museum. It should be noted, however, that museum historiography has so far provided us with few methodological tools to think in such ways – in other words to think about affect in the museum rather than about museum representations as hegemonic expressions of power. It might indeed be easier to find frameworks for such novel forms of historical study in other fields (for example, Csikszentmihalyi and Robinson's (1991) psychological accounts of the 'aesthetic encounter').

## Conclusions

While defining the term 'disciplinarity', Messer-Davidow *et al.* (1993: 3) state: 'To borrow from Foucault, we could say that disciplinarity is the means by which ensembles of diverse parts are brought into particular types of knowledge relations with each other'. This chapter has explored just some of the ways in which the physical, institutional and public spaces of the museum allowed individuals to marshal such ensembles of diverse parts (which here can be understood to stand for aims, practices and material objects) in specific ways, and to establish specific knowledge relations unavailable through other means. In this sense it is possible to view museum display, notional or real, as a form of theorising, through the relations between 'diverse parts' one seeks to establish and the boundaries one sets. Crucially, however, this intellectual endeavour is politically and circumstantially contingent. It is also potentially divisive, for in bringing together some objects (physically, intellectually and territorially) it separates others; in enabling some kinds of knowledge relations, it disables others. To point out what may seem a banal example – the nineteenth-century project of museum display, because of its inherently spatial nature, privileged an art history articulated through art *objects*. What alternative art histories did this obscure?

The outcomes of the site question – the silencing of discourses surrounding the integration of different types of objects, and the segregation of painting and its interrogation in terms of style – have been profoundly influential, providing the intellectual foundations for the National Gallery in London and for others which were modelled upon it. The art history thus proposed was one of products (works of art) rather than the processes (of production, siting and consumption) in which material culture can be situated. At the same time, the 'products' signified their makers in various ways (as being 'by' a certain artist, as 'belonging' to a certain geographical school, and so on), engendering an art history interested in human individuals and networks. Style, accounted for in terms of geography, chronology, tuition and influence, enabled the construction of a relational matrix whose workings predicate later practices of comparison in other historiographical media – the textbook, the slide lecture and the photographic library. Lastly, we must consider boundaries – what is the relationship between the isolation of painting from other forms of material culture in the museum and the boundaries of disciplinary study?

In this way the museum figures within emerging questions about the narrow foci of some forms of art history until relatively recent decades (in particular that which deals with, and thus works to define, post-classical 'art'), and the invisible but tangible divides between what has been studied under the banner of disciplines such as art history, archaeology and others, such as anthropology. More recent endeavours in art history can to some extent be read as attempts to overcome the disciplinary boundaries implicated in historical museological discourse; for example, the New Art History has worked hard to recapture a sense of paintings as objects of social use rather than as transcendental objects, detached from everyday life, while the parameters of what is studied in art history curricula have broadened over the past decades to supersede the biographical and genealogical emphases typical of much nineteenth- and twentieth-century practice (indeed, some have perceived a growing chasm between the 'two art histories' in the contemporary museum and in academia respectively (Haxthausen 2002)). Tracing links between historical museum practice and contemporary disciplinary practice is inevitably suppositional – especially if one considers the lack of unity with art history as a discipline which some have identified (Preziosi 1993: 216–17) – but this is not to devalue it in enabling new reflective understandings of both.

To conclude, it may be worth briefly considering the role of museological projects as disciplinary boundary work in more recent chronological contexts, thereby offering some orientations for attending to boundaries as they continue to shift. For example, the Victoria and Albert Museum's 'Day of Record', which have taken place from 2000, have celebrated and documented forms of human adornment – such as nail decoration, hair weaves, tattoos, carnival outfits and goth style, dress and accoutrements – by inviting, photographing and interviewing visitors from the communities associated with them. This is not something that would have been considered or taken seriously in the discipline of art history until recently, when broader disciplinary premises have gradually become more acceptable, through the consolidation and sharing of attitudes implicit in developments such as the New Art History and Visual Culture Studies, both of which have involved critiques (implicit and explicit) of canonicity. In this way the workings of some communities of art historical practice have (at least for themselves) shifted disciplinary boundaries to include and engage with different forms of cultural activity and production.

In another instance, the recent exhibition dedicated to the work of the mid-twentieth-century flower arranger Constance Spry at the Design Museum in London can be seen to push the boundary of what can be studied and exhibited under the banner of 'design history'. The controversy surrounding this exhibition, however, is an indication of the potentially difficult and contested nature of such boundary work, not to mention its interrelationship with cultural and commercial politics (see, for example, Sudjic 2004).

Moving into the future (at the time of writing), the V&A will shortly hold an exhibition, developed by the Arts Centre, Melbourne, dedicated to the material culture associated with the pop singer Kylie Minogue; 'featuring costumes, accessories, photographs, sound and video' (V&A website). The ratio of daring boundary work to commercially oriented programming is difficult to assess here, but the exhibition nevertheless indicates a challenge to entrenched understandings of what art is or can be, at least on the part of its producers. In part this could be attributed to the peculiar eclecticism of the V&A, which, according to Robertson 'will always look like many museums, and never one museum', and in which 'the experience of walking through the costume exhibition halls on the way to Raphael cartoons should stretch anyone's notion of the category [of art] to the snapping point' (Robertson 2004: 6). To this one might counter that stretching the category of art towards a 'snapping point' (which in itself is not a historical constant) is something which art museums can usefully do.

## Bibliography

Amariglio, J., Resnick, S. and Wolff, R. D. (1993) 'Division and difference in the "discipline" of economics', in E. Messer-Davidow, D. R. Shumway and D. J. Sylvan (eds) *Knowledges: Historical and Critical Studies in Disciplinarity*, Charlottesville, VA: University of Virginia Press, 150–184.

Bennett, T. (1995) *The Birth of the Museum: History, Theory, Politics*, London: Routledge.

Conn, S. (1998) *Museums and American Intellectual Life, 1876–1925*, Chicago, IL: University of Chicago Press.

Csikszentmihalyi, M. and Robinson, R. E. (1991) *The Art of Seeing: An Interpretation of the Aesthetic Encounter*, Malibu, CA: Getty Trust Publications.

Fuller, S. (1993) 'Disciplinary Boundaries and the Rhetoric of the Social Sciences', in E. Messer-Davidow, D. R. Shumway and D. J. Sylvan (eds) *Knowledges: Historical and Critical Studies in Disciplinarity*, Charlottesville, VA: University of Virginia Press, 125–149.

Haxthausen, C. W. (2002) 'Introduction', in C. W. Haxthausen (ed.) *The Two Art Histories: The Museum and the University*, New Haven, CT: Yale University Press, ix–xxv.

Hill, K. (2005) *Culture and Class in English Public Museums, 1850–1914*, Aldershot: Ashgate,

Hoeniger, C. (1999) 'The restoration of early Italian "Primitives" during the twentieth century: valuing art and its consequences', *Journal of the American Institute for Conservation*, 38: 144–161.

Hooper-Greenhill, E. (1992) *Museums and the Shaping of Knowledge*, London: Routledge.

Jordanova, L. (1989) 'Objects of knowledge: a historical perspective on museums', in P. Vergo (ed.) *The New Museology*, London: Reaktion Books, 22–40.

McClellan, A. (1999) *Inventing the Louvre: Art, Politics and the Origins of the Modern Museum in Eighteenth-Century Paris*, Berkeley, CA: University of California Press.

—— (2003) 'A brief history of the art museum public', in A. McClellan (ed.) *Art and its Publics: Museum Studies at the Millennium*, London: Blackwell Publishing, 1–50.

Messer-Davidow, E., Shumway, D. R. and Sylvan, D. J. (1993) 'Introduction: disciplinary ways of knowing', in E. Messer-Davidow, D. R. Shumway and D. J. Sylvan (eds) *Knowledges: Historical and Critical Studies in Disciplinarity*, Charlottesville, VA: University of Virginia Press, 1–21.

Preziosi, D. (1993) 'Seeing through art history', in E. Messer-Davidow, D. R. Shumway and D. J. Sylvan (eds) *Knowledges: Historical and Critical Studies in Disciplinarity*, Charlottesville, VA: University of Virginia Press, 215–31.

—— (2005) 'Art history and museology: rendering the visible legible', in S. Macdonald (ed.) *A Companion to Museum Studies*, London: Blackwell Publishing, 50–63.

Prior, N. (2002) *Museums and Modernity: Art Galleries and the Making of Modern Culture*, Oxford: Berg, 88–94.

Robertson, B. (2004) 'The South Kensington Museum in context: an alternative history', *Museum & Society*, 2(1): 1–14.

Robertson, D. (1978) *Sir Charles Eastlake and the Victorian Art World*, Princeton, NJ: Princeton University Press.

Royal Commission (1857) *Report, Proceedings and Minutes of Evidence of the Royal Commission of 1857 on the Site for the National Gallery*, London.

Select Committee (1853) *Report, Proceedings and Minutes of Evidence of the Select Committee Appointed to Inquire into the Management of the National Gallery; also to Consider in what Mode the Collective Monuments of Antiquity and Fine Art Possessed by the Nation may be most Securely Preserved, Judiciously Augmented, and Advantageously Exhibited to the Public*, London.

Sherman D. J. and Rogoff, I. (1994) 'Introduction: frameworks for critical analysis', in D. J. Sherman and I. Rogoff (eds) *Museum Culture: Histories, Discourses, Spectacles*, London: Routledge, ix–xx.

Starn, R. (2005) 'A historian's brief guide to new museum studies', *The American Historical Review*, 110(1): 68–98.

Steegman, J. ([1950] 1987) *Consort of Taste/Victorian Taste: A Study of the Arts and Architecture from 1830 to 1870*, London: Century.

Sudjic, D. (2004) 'How a flower arrangement caused fear and loathing' *The Observer*, 3 October. Online. Available at: http://observer.guardian.co.uk/review/story/0,6903,1318273,00.html (accessed 7 August 2006).

Trodd, C. (2003) 'The discipline of pleasure; or, how art history looks at the art museum', *Museum & Society*, 1(1): 17–29.

Whitehead, C. (2005a) *The Public Art Museum in Nineteenth-Century Britain: The Development of the National Gallery*, Aldershot: Ashgate.

—— (2005b) 'Architectures of display at the National Gallery: the Barry Rooms as art historiography', *Journal of the History of Collections*, 17, 189–211.

# 5

# ECONOMIC LOGIC VERSUS ENLIGHTENMENT RATIONALITY

## Evolution of the museum–zoo–garden complex and the modern Indian city, 1843–1900

*Savithri Preetha Nair*

The colonial museum has hardly attracted the attention of historians, even as museum history as a field of research continues to attract a growing number of students and scholars. Sheets-Pyenson's (1988a) cross-colonial comparison of natural history museums was a pioneering attempt to understand museums in the colonies, and remains till today the only substantial work on the subject (see also, Kohlstedt 1991; Lopes and Podgorny 2001). However, Sheets-Pyenson's study focused in particular on Australian, Canadian and Latin American natural history museums. Museums in colonial India received only passing reference, being regarded as institutions of little significance for science or society. This chapter acts as a corrective by attempting to locate the public museum in India as a key site of modernity in the non-western context.

Public museums exclusively devoted to natural history of the kind that appeared in Europe, America and even the colonies examined in Sheets-Pyenson's work did not exist in India. Some of the earliest museums in India were founded in connection with scientific societies such as the Asiatic Society of Bengal and assumed a heterogeneous nature, with contents ranging from natural history specimens to economic products and antiquities. Importantly, access to these museums was exclusive, restricted to members, most of whom were British East India Company officials and itinerant naturalists. This changed in 1843, however, when, for the first time in India, a public museum allowing access to all, irrespective of class, race, caste or gender, was proposed. This at a time when the larger society remained deeply stratified and divided. Ironically, the tremendous significance of this development for understanding the experience of modernity in India has gone completely unnoticed by scholars. Studies of modernity in India have largely been concerned with producing grand theories of the modern experience, its temporal characteristics and its ontology (studies of literature, film, social practices, art, science and the making of the 'nation') (see, for example, Niranjana *et al.* 1993 and Mitchell 2000). Geographies as products of social transformations in India, or, to use Pollock's term, 'spaces of modernity', remain wholly unexplored (for other contexts see Lefebvre 1991; Pollock 1988; Ogborn 1998). By contextualising one such space of modernity, the public museum in India, this chapter is intended to contribute to a new perspective on the colonial modern.

It is argued here that the public museum in India was born and shaped by the dialectical tension between an economic logic and 'enlightenment rationality', which gave rise to a dominant spatial modernity as yet unrecognised by scholars. The public museum, public garden and zoo – three western and modern institutions with past lives of their own – intersected at the heart of the colonial Indian city in the late nineteenth century to produce a modern public 'network space'. This democratic space of modernity has passed so much into public habit today that visitors and scholars alike simply take it for granted, as if it were a natural rather than a social construct and a product of history.

Modernity eludes an easy or consensual definition but it is not possible nor necessary here to outline the various theoretical attempts to understand it. It suffices to state that modernity is associated with 'newness, artificiality and emancipation' in contrast to tradition, nature and establishment (Secretan 1984: 126). It is an 'experience of space and time', providing an 'environment that promises us adventure, power, joy, growth, transformation of ourselves and the world' (Berman 1983). This chapter adopts the notion that there are multiple modernities – rather than a singular monolithic phenomenon – and that 'differentiated geographies are made in the relationships *between* places and *across* places' (Ogborn 1998: 19). Revealing the operation of what Latour (1993) calls 'networks' – of people, the state, ideas, and institutions – this chapter explores one such space of modernity in India, the museum–zoo–garden complex.

## Birth of the public museum in India

Unlike in Europe, where the museum became a key agent of social identity and emancipation, the public museum in India was predominantly conceived as an agent of economic progress; it made the systematic exploitation of resources possible. It was not founded as a result of accumulated capital in the colony, as argued by Sheets-Pyenson (1988b). The earliest public museums to emerge in India in the 1850s were all essentially 'economic museums', holding mainly geological collections, with the social argument remaining no more than rhetorical. This section will consider not only the socio-historical context of the founding of public museums in the Presidencies of British India, that is, Madras, Bombay and Bengal, but also of native states such as Travancore, which were not under the direct control of the British, and yet were in the forefront of this modernising development.

### The Presidencies

As early as 1818, the scientific society of Madras, the Madras Literary Society, had suggested the establishment of a museum in the Presidency. Sanctioned only in 1827, the society's museum was located in a rent-free room at the College of Fort St George. After about twenty-five years, in late 1843, the society addressed the government on the subject of the formation of what it now called a Museum of Economic Geology. It was hoped that the institution under the superintendence of a curator – 'a person of scientific attainments possessing knowledge of geology, mineralogy and chemistry' – would facilitate and encourage scientific enquiry and commerce, both of which it was claimed were at their lowest ebb. The museum was to be equipped with a laboratory where chemical analysis of minerals could be conducted. From 1840, a 'Museum of Economic Geology for India' had already begun functioning in Calcutta under the curatorship of Henry Piddington. However, the Madras Society argued that the inhabitants of its Presidency found it uneconomical and impractical to forward the results of their researches to as distant a Presidency as Bengal.[1]

About the same time, Major General William Cullen, the Resident of Travancore, submitted a memorandum to the Madras government suggesting the establishment of a network of museums in the Madras Presidency to aid the systematic collection of economic products and resources.[2] Cullen, trained at the Royal Military Academy, Woolwich, had arrived in Madras in 1804, where he became Superintendent of the Gun Carriage Manufactory, Military Auditor-General and Commissary General, before becoming Resident in 1840. His memorandum, although specific to the Madras Presidency, was a response to a circular from the Asiatic Society of Bengal, which requested help in the collection of systematic information on mineral, vegetable and other products and resources of the Indian Empire. Cullen drew the attention of the government to the lack of a 'system of concert or cooperation' in collecting information, to which he attributed the slow progress of science and commerce in the Madras Presidency. He wrote of the opportunities for exploration for the purposes of science, pleasure or profit, but saw the concentration of resources on Madras as problematic. His solution was the establishment of subsidiary or district museums, attached to a central museum in Madras. He added that there were great advantages to be enjoyed if local museums were to be situated in public buildings under the charge of the Collector because it would provide free access to every person interested, including itinerant naturalists and influential natives, who would be convinced of its benefits in the promotion of agriculture and trade. The new system of appointing civil engineers to the several districts was also expected to contribute greatly to the systematic collection of general statistical, scientific and commercial information, and not just minerals. To 'complete the chain of communication', Cullen suggested that the central museum be placed under the Board of Revenue and the Civil Engineering Department of the Presidency. In a minute, dated 28 February 1844, Henry Chamier, Member of Council of the Madras government discussed the suggestions put forward by the Madras Literary Society and Resident Cullen, recommending their suggestions to the Court of Directors of the East India Company. The government expressed hope that native surveyors and engineers taking up their first appointments in the Mofussils and native youths at the Madras University would also gain from local public museums.[3]

Convinced of the benefits that would accrue from such a scheme, the Court of Directors finally granted their consent in 1846 for the establishment of the Madras Government Central Museum, the first public museum to be established in India. The Literary Society appealed to the government that the Central Museum be conceived as a wide-ranging collection, covering many useful subjects rather than just economic geology. It was to contain objects of 'almost every description usually found in large public museums in Europe' and was to combine the objects of a museum of practical or economic geology and a museum of natural history. Though this gained immediate approval, the society's wishes that the Central Museum be attached to the Polytechnic Institution, with which it was thought the society would eventually amalgamate, were ignored. The Madras government on the other hand believed that for 'creating by degrees a general taste and appreciation of science', it would be most beneficial if the museum were attached to the Madras University.[4] This plan was also abandoned as the location of the university was thought disadvantageous as far as public access was concerned. In the end, the Madras government resolved that the society's collections, which were mainly geological, be used to lay the 'foundation or nucleus' for the new public museum[5] and that the museum, at least till the time the university was fully established, be treated as a separate institution.[6]

In early 1851, the Central Museum, under the honorary superintendence of Assistant

Surgeon Edward Green Balfour and functioning from rooms at the Fort St George College, was eventually thrown open to the public 'as a new idea or at best another of a series of experiments'. Even though the mobilisation of economic products from the Madras Presidency forwarded to London for display at the Great Exhibition in 1851 helped to add a substantial number of articles to the museum, it was hardly the source of the idea itself. Even Britain had to wait until 1851, Balfour remarked, to realise the importance of an economic museum to the commerce of a country.[7] It was through a public announcement that contributions to the museum were invited.[8] Balfour also appealed to friends in England and, importantly, to Madras mercantilists, engineers and medical officers to contribute generously to the museum and make it a source of pride to Madras, as the Felix Meritis was to Amsterdam (Madras Government Museum 1951: 6–9). If the 'Museum of Economic Geology' was intended to extend among the community information on the raw and manufactured products of India and the world in general, the other branch, the 'Museum of Natural History', was intended for public instruction.[9] If at all articles were to be purchased, they were to be 'specimens possessing a value either for their rarity or beauty in the estimation of a naturalist'.

Balfour's suggestion for the institution of a chair of natural history in connection with the museum,[10] – with a view to instruct 'the youth who are receiving education at the High School . . . who are studying at the Medical College . . . [and] those who are being educated for employment in the revenue and engineering departments' – though given due attention to by the government, was thought difficult to accomplish.[11] Balfour's request for a separate museum building in a more central locality, close to places of public instruction and the community, was also rejected on the grounds that funds were not available. As a result, by the end of 1853, the museum's collections were at the point of overflow. An appeal for the use of the central hall of the college was also rejected. As the Madras Museum continued to evolve rapidly, so public museums began to be founded in the surrounding districts and provinces.[12] These local museums were to act not only as repositories of local products and resources but also as feeders for the Central Museum at Madras (Madras Government Museum 1951: 10).

In 1855, the museum was moved, for reasons of space, to the Pantheon in the central part of the city (Srinvasachari 1999). When even this space began to fill up, the government called upon the Military Board to submit a plan for building upper rooms over the wings of the Pantheon and for improvements to the institution's external appearance.[13] An interesting turn in the course of events took place at this time. As an experiment, Balfour displayed a live 'Ourang-Outang' at the museum which had been sent to him by a friend. He noticed that the number of visitors to the museum almost doubled from the very next day. Convinced that a live zoological collection would not only greatly increase the source of amusement to visitors but also interest them in the study of animal behaviour, Balfour wrote to the government that 'the wishes of the people are entitled to consideration, . . . because . . . all Governments at all ages, have recognised the duty of providing liberally amusements for the people'. He argued that it was not only European Residents in the Madras Presidency who had generously contributed to the museum but also the natives, making it all the more necessary to fulfil their wishes. Advocating an establishment for a collection of live animals in the gardens of the museum did not mean, he explained, a compromise of the primary aims of the public museum, namely science and education. To ensure this, he suggested that the accounts of the two institutions be kept separate, even while the museum and the zoological garden remained under one management.

The government approved the plan and, just as in the case of the museum, it invited the public to contribute animals. The acceptance of public gifts of animals meant that admission had to be offered free 'for all classes of people'. The idea of a public zoological garden was entirely new to India, and Balfour's vision was based on what he had seen, or knew of, in Europe. The *Jardin des Plantes* in Paris, established at the turn of the eighteenth century, with its dispersion of animals through landscaped gardens and its accessibility to the public was deeply influential. It had spawned an imitator in 1828 in the menagerie at Regent's Park in London, which led to the subsequent invention of the term 'zoological garden' (Baratay and Hardouin-Fugier 2002: 82–83).

Balfour's plan was to display the animals in 'as Natural a state as possible', scattering them over the museum grounds 'tastefully, in groups, with pretty paths well gravelled and neatly kept, winding amongst them and, where possible, with trellised creepers over-head for shade . . . the carnivorous animals [in] grottoes and caves . . . protected by iron railings'. One or two large aviaries were to be constructed around trees in the garden, to display every bird species to be found in India. A 'highly interesting collection of the Monkey tribe' and a collection of snakes were also thought fit additions to the gardens. Through an arrangement of living animals in characteristic groups in the dwellings or 'gardens', it was claimed that not only could animals live in a free and natural state but 'the student and the sight seer [could] equally find profit and amusement'.[14] Balfour in fact expressed disdain for the term 'menagerie' used in the official communications on the subject, preferring 'the Greek derived word [rather] than the French'. His argument was that however small or big a collection, it 'must still relate to "zoon" and all its various derived words, namely zoological, zoology, zoography etc.' and not a menagerie.[15] The zoological collection in the museum's grounds proved such a success that Balfour could claim far more visitors to the Madras Museum and Gardens than to the British Museum, the Regent's Park and the Kew Gardens combined.[16] Indeed, visitor records were kept on a regular basis, and divided into two groups: those who could sign their names and those who could not. These numbers were used to demonstrate the relevance of the institution to the general public, irrespective of class and race.

Despite pressures to remove the museum to the college and to restrict its interests to local products (based on the belief that a museum of a wider scope was difficult to realise at a remote outstation like Madras), Balfour stuck to his view that a government Central Museum, 'which is open to all classes, and contains articles calculated to amuse and instruct all classes' could not be reduced to a departmental institution of a college open to a select few. By 1858–9, at the beginning of Crown rule, Madras could boast of a 'Museum of Natural History' with zoological gardens attached, a 'Museum of Geographical Geology', a 'Museum of Economic Geology' and a library. That this site of modernity had 'gained the entire confidence of the native community' was evident, according to Balfour, in the great number of native women visitors.[17]

The earliest reference to a public museum in the Bombay Presidency may be traced to 1848, when surgeon George Buist, as chairman of the Polytechnic Institute, proposed the establishment of an economic museum in Bombay for the 'exhibition of the productions of the East and maintained by public contribution, to be managed by Trustees, and placed under the charge of the Polytechnic Institute'. It was intended to contain specimens of every kind of resource, raw or manufactured, vegetable or mineral. The articles were to be arranged under a double system of classification, the first referring to the locality from which they were obtained and the second to their characteristics. It was hoped that in this way a stranger in Bombay would 'discover at a glance the whole contents of . . . bazaars'. Reports on the museum were to be published periodically in the newspapers or as reports of the Chamber of Commerce, and eventually formed a dictionary of 'Oriental Arts and Manufactures'. In his introduction to the plan of the Economic Museum at Bombay, Buist observed that there was scarcely one European capital city which did not possess a public museum for the instruction and amusement of the people.[18]

Buist's plan remained on paper until 1854, the year of the Paris Exposition. It was on the basis of duplicates of the materials sent to the Exposition from the Bombay Presidency, and a belief that it was 'not worthy of Bombay to be behind the sister Presidencies in the pursuit of social progress and enlightenment',[19] that a new 'Central Museum of Natural History and Economic Museum of Geology, Industry and the Arts' was established. It was hoped that the museum would ultimately become 'a perfect and useful Institution and a lasting memorial of the foresight as well as of the liberal spirit of the Government'. It was to contribute to 'the great national scheme of Education' and 'popular recreation and amusement, enlisting seekers of pleasure as well as the studious'.[20]

Tony Bennett's (1995: 87) belief that the nineteenth-century state took a 'soft approach' by educating by example rather than through coercion is well reflected in the Council Secretary's view that the museum in Bombay was paving the way for a gradual diffusion of popular science into people of all classes, simply through an exercise of their free will, and with the least exertion.[21] Following the example of the Museum of Practical Geology in London, Lumsden insisted that to be successful the Bombay Museum 'should originate with the Government and be for sometime under its control'. Approving the establishment of a public museum, the Bombay Governor stressed the importance of practical native education. He felt the natives should be directed away from 'abstract and metaphysical subjects' and introduced to the empirical sciences of botany, mineralogy and geology, keeping in mind the improvement of agriculture and commerce. Interestingly, he was of the opinion that it was premature to discuss the establishment of zoological and botanical gardens as they did not 'necessarily form part of the project'.[22]

In 1858, after two failed attempts to formally establish a pubic museum, a meeting was held at the Bombay Town Hall which aimed to establish an economic museum, with natural history and pleasure gardens, largely funded through public subscription. It was hoped that the museum would aid the development of the raw products:

> of this colossal and as yet unknown empire, in stimulating and improving its slow and crude manufactures, in supplying resorts of healthy recreation to the densely crowded inhabitants of Bombay, in ornamenting the town, inciting amongst the masses habits of observation and taste for rational pleasures . . . and above all, in affording the means of bringing Europeans and Natives more frequently and familiarly together.
>
> (Birdwood 1864: 14)

In 1859, George Birdwood, the museum's first paid curator, hoped that the museum when completed and handed over to the government could begin 'its higher career' as a 'College of Inquiry'. It was to 'become a standard repository of all that relate[d] to the economic productions of the East' and an agency for the organisation of periodic exhibitions of the industries of India and of countries trading with Bombay. Disinterested research into natural history was to be eschewed. Instead, curators were expected to be 'men of tried science . . . capable of prosecuting original researches' that would further economic progress, and in support of such a mission a Bombay merchant offered to endow a professorship of economic science connected to the museum.

Bengal Presidency's first public museum came to be established in Calcutta only as late as 1857, when geological collections from the Asiatic Society were transferred to a Museum of Economic Geology, under the charge of the Geological Survey of India (GSI) (Piddington 1842). Its purpose was to illustrate the geology, the mineral wealth and the manufacturing resources of the Empire. The museum was to function as a centre, connecting and directing colonial naturalists, merchants, miners, farmers, manufacturers and other 'practical men', such as the officers of the engineering and revenue survey departments, to aid the systematic exploration of economic resources of India. To enable the analysis of minerals and soils, a laboratory was to be attached to the museum and, for study and reference, a library. This museum was thrown open to the public, free of charge, everyday but Sundays.[23]

### The Native States

Of the native states in India, Travancore was the first to successfully establish a public museum. Although, Kolhapur, within the jurisdiction of the Bombay Presidency, founded a 'Native Library, Museum and Reading Room' as early as 1851, there is no evidence that the institution became fully established.[24] In 1852, John Allan Broun, Astronomer to the Maharaja of Travancore, proposed the establishment of a public museum to Cullen. The Maharaja, Uttram Thirunal, immediately approved the proposal and a collection of mineralogical specimens in the possession of Cullen was used as the nucleus for a museum. The museum acquired official status in 1855, when a public meeting held with the encouragement from the Madras Museum resolved to form a Museum Committee to study publications on scientific subjects that would aid the development of resources of the country and the mental and physical status of the natives.[25]

In 1857, the museum and library were opened to the public free of charge. Unlike in Madras or Bombay, and contrary to what was expected of local museums, the scope of the Travancore collections took on a general nature after its initial 'economic' intent. It was now to aid 'the Natives in their efforts to gain a practical knowledge of the Arts and Sciences of Europe, and of preserving the rapidly decaying illustrations of the ancient manners and customs of the country'.[26] The observatory, which was situated on a small hill very close to the museum, was also thrown open to the public, for fixed hours each day except Sundays. From the statistics collected by Broun, we learn that more farmers visited the observatory than merchants or soldiers, and more foreigners than Travancoreans (Broun 1865: 107–9).

As early as 1852, Broun had additionally recommended the use of the large compound occupied by the museum building for a public park, 'containing useful trees of the country'. He had proposed the planting of 'young forest trees of kinds remarkable for their utility as timber trees, or for their products' and the formation of a 'popular Botanic Garden'. During a visit to Madras in 1855, Broun had also learnt from Balfour that a display of live animals had the potential to increase the number of museum visitors, particularly the natives. The 'enlightened' *Dewan* of Travancore,[27] Tanjore Madhav Rao, when consulted was only too ready to support a public zoological collection in the state. Losing no time, the surrounding grounds of the museum were adapted for the purpose, and efforts were made to acquire a selection of animals 'whose form and habits' were least known to the native population.[28] The museum–zoo–garden complex in Travancore did not, however, attain a state of completion until the late 1860s.

## Calcutta: the imperial capital mirrors London

In 1858, the Asiatic Society of Bengal proposed the establishment of a museum in Calcutta for the 'advancement of science', to which it could transfer its general (including zoological and archaeological) collections in order to form a museum of a 'national character'.[29] By 'national', Calcutta, the imperial capital, was to be recognised as the 'centre of science' for the colony and in this respect analogous to London. After prolonged negotiations, on 8 January 1865 a provisional committee of trustees was formed, composed of twelve individuals, with eight nominated by the government and the rest by the Asiatic Society. Dr John Anderson, professor of comparative anatomy at the Medical College in Calcutta, was given the additional duties of curator of the new 'Imperial Museum'.[30] The transfer of the society's zoological, archaeological and geological collections was realised through the 1866 ACT XVII and the new national museum – to be known as the 'Indian Museum' – was born, controlled by a Board of Trustees. Building work began on a plot adjacent to the Asiatic Society in the city centre, but it took a decade for the new museum to be fully realised.

Meanwhile, in 1867, the society's Dr Schwendler proposed the establishment of a zoological gardens worthy of the imperial capital, both for the instruction, recreation and amusement of all classes, and to facilitate scientific observation of animals and acclimatisation and breeding experiments. After many years of discussions and negotiations, the zoological gardens was established at Alipore in 1875, a short distance from the city centre (Mitra 1975). A botanic garden on the city outskirts at Sibpur, established by the British East India Company for mercantile reasons in 1786, soon began to function as a public garden. However, these three allied national institutions were managed separately – unlike those in Madras, Bombay or Travancore they were not conceived as a unified space or project. In this respect, the imperial capital Calcutta strikingly mirrored its metropolitan counterpart, London, which had its British Museum in the city centre, the Kew Gardens on the outskirts and the zoological garden in the Regent's Park. However, rather than interpret this as a case of transference of a model of modernity from a London centre to a Calcutta periphery, it does demonstrate 'the crucial ways in which . . . geographies of connection are moments in the making of modernities'; that modernity's geographies are not place-specific in any unique way (Ogborn 1998: 18–19).

## Constructed nature and the modern Indian city (1880s): A Parisian 'network space' emerges as the colonial modern

'The modern' according to Latour is not a sudden transformation in the zeitgeist but the product of an enrichment of 'networks' as they extend themselves to involve more actors and more sites, and thus produce concrete and representational elements. The more extensive the networks, the more 'rational' the emergent model of modernity, which then readily yields to replication and expansion. In other words, the geography of modernity is not a self-consciously planned space but evolves itself in response to, and as an agent of, material transformations. The late nineteenth century witnessed a sharp increase in the number of public museums being founded in India (and the world over) as the social argument for the establishment of these institutions gained in strength. Heterogeneous in the nature of their content, and located within public gardens that could also boast of a live animal collection, public museums articulated a post-Enlightenment rationality that combined entertainment with instruction.

After years of social experimentation, initiated in the 1850s, a preferred spatial 'model', based on the Parisian city centre museum–zoo–garden complex, arrived in India to become the modern Indian city's defining feature. Each of the 'spaces of modernity' discussed here – in Madras, Bombay, Travancore and Calcutta – functioned as 'a crucible in which the new crystallised out of the ongoing' to give rise to a new spatial model (Pred 1995: 19; Ogborn 1998: 28). 'The domination of post-Enlightenment rationalism was such that by the end of the nineteenth century nature was only permitted to exist at the cost of its cooption by the social' (Oliver 2000: 228).

Even older museums, such as the Trivandrum museum in the Travancore State, began to transform themselves in the 1880s in keeping with the modernising development. Interestingly, the princely states were at the forefront of this, even competing with each other in the establishment of these new urban complexes. 'Enlightened' native Dewans such as Madhav Rao played crucial roles in the successful duplication of this model. By the end of the century, Hyderabad, Gwalior, Jaipur, Udaipur, Baroda, Indore, Alwar, Kapurthala and Patiala, to name some of the more important examples, could boast of modern public gardens, where 'nature' was recreated within a democratic social space. This artificially constructed nature in the city centre was seen as a 'great boon to [the city's] dense and crowded population'.[31] Such recreational public spaces were increasingly understood as important for the promotion of public health and for the intellectual and moral improvement of the public.

An urbanisation of nature, the public garden with its museum and zoo reconfigured the Indian city (see also Swyngedouw and Kaïka 2000). European horticulturists were hired and leading gardening encyclopaedias consulted; the newly established museums were designed by some of the leading colonial architects of the day who took inspiration from the local environment (such as in Baroda, Jaipur and Travancore), and paid curators were employed to oversee the institutions.

A concomitant development was the increase in the number of animal dealers, commercial horticultural establishments, model makers and taxidermists setting up shop in India in the late nineteenth century. It had become easier to 'grow' institutions of this kind with the trade and exchange in natural history objects. Exotic seeds could be easily imported from seedsmen abroad. Public gardens, most of which also incorporated a botanic and economic garden, received seeds, plants and advice at hardly any cost from the larger botanic gardens and agri-horticultural societies. By 1900, these complexes – public 'network spaces' on a Parisian pattern – were full established in the big cities of colonial India.

## Conclusion

To conclude, then, the public museum in India was born and shaped by the dialectical tension between an economic logic and an 'enlightenment rationality', which gave rise to a specific model of spatial modernity by the late nineteenth century. The public museum, public garden and zoo, three western and modern institutions with their own histories, intersected at the heart of the colonial Indian city to produce a modern public 'network space'. In this 'network space' civilised forms of behaviour could be learnt and diffused; nature had been artificially recreated and urbanised for entertainment and instruction.

Modernity is a project, but the geography of modernity is not self-consciously planned or entirely contrived, rather evolves in response to and as an agent of material processes. Ever changing and evolving, in the early twentieth century, new allied institutions, such as aquaria, art galleries and planetaria, began to be added to this 'network space'. However, the opposite also happened: in Madras and Bangalore the zoological collections were moved to the outskirts.

The period saw city planning gather momentum and again the princely states were in the forefront of this trend. As a consequence of these modernising and urbanising develop‑ ments, 'civics' as a university discipline, with its association with urban planning, came to gain official recognition in India. The University of Bombay established a chair for 'Civics and Sociology' in 1919, along the same lines as it had for Economic Science in the mid‑ nineteenth century. The first occupant of this chair was none other than Patrick Geddes, the great Scottish sociologist and town planner, and a worthy successor to fellow Scots, Balfour, Buist, Birdwood and Broun.

In his book the *Birth of the Museum*, Bennett remarks that 'the opening of the National Museum of Victoria in the 1850s coincided with Melbourne's acquisition of its first perma‑ nent menagerie, an establishment housed in a commercial amusement park' (Bennett 1995: 3). Now with the strength of evidence from India, it is worth reflecting on whether such a formation (namely, a museum and zoo housed within a public garden) was a mere historical coincidence or perhaps something more significant, from which we might gain a better understanding of the experience of modernity.

## Notes

1  From L. Minchin, Secretary, Madras Literary Society to Government of Madras, dated 10 Nov. 1843, British Library, India Office Records (hereafter BL, IOR): F/4/2133 no101367.
2  From Major General W. Cullen to the Government of Madras, dated 5 Dec. 1843 in BL, IOR: F/4/2133 no101367.
3  Minute by the Hon. H. Chamier of the Government of Madras, dated 28 Feb.1844, BL, IOR: F/4/2133 no101367.
4  Public letter to Fort St George, dated 20 May 1846, BL, IOR: F/4/2214 no109562.
5  Public letter from Fort St George, dated 11 March 1847, BL, IOR: F/4/2214 no109562.
6  BL, IOR: F/4/2358 no124805, dated 16 July 1849.
7  Government Museum (Madras, India) (1854) *Appendix to the Report of the Government Central Museum*, Madras: Pharoah.
8  BL, IOR: F/4/2511 no143289, dated 7 Aug. 1851.
9  Ibid.
10  Ibid., dated 24 July 1852.
11  Ibid., dated 22 Oct. 1853.
12  BL, IOR: F/4/2675 no180375.
13  BL, IOR: F/4/2648 no172302, dated 27 March 1855. The building of the upper storeys was completed only in 1864.
14  BL, IOR: F/4/2681 no183456, dated 4 Sep. 1855.
15  Ibid. dated 9 Nov. 1855.
16  BL, IOR: F/4/2681 no183457, dated 1 July 1856.
17  Government of Madras (1859) 'Report of the Government Central Museum', *Madras Administration Report*, 1858–59, Madras: Government Press.
18  Maharashtra State Archives (MSA), General Dept., Vol. 43, 1848.
19  BL, IOR: F/4/2678 no182124, dated 1 Aug. 1855.
20  Ibid.
21  Ibid.
22  Ibid. dated 31 Aug. 1855.
23  The Indian Museum (1914) *The Indian Museum, 1814–1914*, Calcutta: The Indian Museum, pp. 54–57.
24  See BL, IOR: F/4/2467 no137843.

25 Anon (1856) *Proceedings of the Trevandrum Museum Society*, Trevandum.
26 Ibid.
27 The *Dewan* of a Native State was the equivalent of a Prime Minister.
28 Kerala State Archives (KSA), Cover File, Bundle No. 30, File No. 239 of 1859.
29 National Archives of India (NAI): Atkinson to C. Beadon, Secretary to Government of India, Home Dept/Pub. Cons: 1 Sep. 1863, nos. 1–3 (A).
30 NAI: Atkinson to Beadon, Home Dept/Pub. Cons: 17 April 1865, nos. 61–62 (A).
31 Dewan Madhav Rao on the Baroda Public Gardens, Gujarat State Record Office, Baroda, Public Works Dept., File no. 173/10, Daftar no. 530, dated 8 April 1876.

# Bibliography

Baratay, E. and Hardouin-Fugier, E. (2002) *A History of Zoological Gardens in the West*, London: Reaktion.

Bennett, T. (1995) *The Birth of the Museum: History, Theory, Politics*, London: Routledge.

Berman, M. (1983) *All that is Solid Melts into Air: The Experience of Modernity*, London: Verso.

Birdwood, G. (1864) *Report on the Government Central Museum and on the Agricultural and Horticultural Society of Western India for 1863*, Bombay.

Broun, J. A. (1865) *Reports on the Observatories, Public Museum, Public Park and Gardens of the H. H. Maharajah of Travancore*, London.

Kohlstedt, S. G. (1991) 'International exchange in the natural history enterprise: museums in Australia and the United States', in R. W. Home and S. G. Kohlstedt (eds) *International Science and National Scientific Identity: Australia Between Britain and America*, Dordrecht: Kluwer, 121–49.

Latour, B. (1993) *We Have Never Been Modern*, Hemel Hempstead: Harvester Wheatsheaf.

Lefebvre, H. (1991) *The Production of Space*, Oxford: Basil Blackwell.

Lopes, M. M. and Podgorny, I. (2001) 'The shaping of Latin American museums of natural history, 1850–1900', in R. MacLeod (ed.) *Nature and Empire: Science and the Colonial Enterprise*, Chicago, IL: University of Chicago Press, 108–18.

Madras Government Museum (1951 [1999]) *Centenary Souvenir (1851–1951)*, Chennai.

Mitchell, T. (ed.) (2000) *Questions of Modernity*, Minneapolis, MN: University of Minnesota.

Mitra, D. K. (1975) *100 Years of the Calcutta Zoo (1875–1975)*, Calcutta.

Niranjana, T., Sudhir, P. and Dhareshwar, V. (eds) (1993) *Interrogating Modernity: Culture and Colonialism in India*, Calcutta: Seagull.

Ogborn, M. (1998) *Spaces of Modernity: London's Geographies 1680–1780*, London: Guilford Press.

Oliver, S. (2000) 'The Thames Embankment and the disciplining of nature in modernity', *Geographical Journal*, 166(3): 227–38.

Piddington, H. (1842) 'Museum of Economic Geology of India', *Journal of the Asiatic Society of Bengal*, 11: 322–25.

Pollock, G. (1988) *Vision and Difference: Femininity, Feminism and the Histories of Art*, London: Routledge.

Pred, A. (1995) *Recognizing European Modernities: A Montage of the Present*, London: Routledge.

Secretan, P. (1984) 'Elements for a theory of modernity', *Diogenes*, 126: 71–90.

Sheets-Pyenson, S. (1988a) 'How to "grow" a natural history museum: the building of colonial collections, 1850–1900', *Archives of Natural History*, 15(2): 121–47

—— (1988b) *Cathedrals of Science: The Development of Colonial Natural History Museums during the Late Nineteenth Century*, Kingston, Ont.: McGill Queen's University Press.

Srinvasachari, C. S. (1999) 'The Pantheon Hodie Museum' in Madras Government Museum (1951 [1999]), *Centenary Souvenir (1851–1951)*, Chennai, 18–20.

Swyngedouw, E. and Kaïka, M. (2000) 'The environment of the city . . . or the urbanization of nature' in G. Bridge and S. Watson (eds) *A Companion to the City*, Oxford: Blackwell Publishers, 566–80.

# 6

# OCCUPYING THE ARCHITECTURE OF THE GALLERY

## Spatial, social and professional change at the Walker Art Gallery, Liverpool, 1877–1933

*Suzanne MacLeod*

The twenty-first century museum sits within a museum landscape that has been transformed in recent decades through rebuilding and renovation on an international scale, and the architecture of the museum has been challenged and rewritten through numerous high-profile projects. Buildings such as the Guggenheim in Bilbao illustrate the ways in which architects have sought to create a new vocabulary of museum design. In the UK, Heritage Lottery Fund (HLF) monies have brought architectural changes to the majority of large regional museums as they have sought to respond to new demands and expectations placed against them. The complexity of these projects has not gone unremarked; museums and galleries today are shaped by architects, designers, engineers, funding bodies, regional development agencies and other interested parties. This expansion of participants and stakeholders raises interesting questions about the social relations and plays of power shaping the contemporary museum (see, for example, Stevenson 2005).

It is, of course, no coincidence that the changed contexts within which the modern museum must operate have resulted in architectural change. Architecture is now recognised, in some quarters at least, as a social and cultural product continually re-made through use. Architecture can be conceived as the outcome of a perceived social need, located in the specifics of time, space and site (see, for example, King 1980). Architectures – the physical structures of buildings and the uses to which they are put – will be shaped as needs and priorities shift. As Anthony King (1980: 1) noted, buildings are informed by a society's ideas, its forms of social organisation, the beliefs and values that dominate at a particular moment and its distribution of resources. It is through space that society's groups shape social relations, inscribing space with social practices and relationships that are then reproduced though use (Hill 1998, 2003; Borden and Rendell 2000).

As this approach to architecture might suggest, recent architectural changes in museums mark only the latest phase in their development; the space of the museum has been reshaped continuously through rearrangement, refurbishment and, periodically, expansion. Each major reshaping, real or imagined, the remnants of which are often visible in the architectures of museums and galleries today, offers a clue to the changing social, political and professional contexts within which museums exist. A history of museum architecture then could potentially reveal the social contexts, processes and dominant practices within and through which the architecture of the museum has been continually reproduced.

Few architectural histories of the museum, however, focus on the social nature of museum space. A good number of texts have been written on the history of museum architecture, but none of these consider the ongoing history or process of change that has been, and continues to be, the reality for most museums. Existing histories of museum architecture tend to approach buildings as objects and architecture as describing the practice and activities of the architect. Architects, and architects alone, make architecture. It exists, in its idealised architectural state, as a pure object, not yet tainted by the impure communities of use (Till 1998).

Histories based upon this more traditional understanding of architecture invariably take us on a journey, from Durand's 1803 design for an art museum, to Leo von Klenze's Glypothek in Munich (1816–30), Schinkel's Altes Museum in Berlin (1823–30) and John Soane's Dulwich Picture Gallery, London (1811–14), each architect adding something new to the museum as a building type. For the majority of architectural historians, these architects established a typology of museum design and formal solutions in lighting and circulation which prevailed until the mid-twentieth century, and to which modern architects continue to refer (see, for example, Searing 1986). This stress on the progressive development of the museum as a building type consigns the museum buildings of Mies van der Rohe to the category of misguided interruption, properly redirected by Louis Kahn at Kimbell and Yale (Lampugnani 1999). Such readings of the museum welcome the return to historicism in the museum architecture of the late 1970s and 1980s, as it continues the historical narrative so rudely interrupted by the modernist architecture of the 1950s and 1960s. Here the stress is, in the main, placed on the shell of the 'finished' museum and on the skills of the canon of eminent architects.

As the museum has come, in the later decades of the twentieth century, to be consciously recognised as a driver for urban regeneration, so new demands have been placed on architects to create one-off high profile landmark buildings. Architecturally innovative solutions as diverse as the Pompidou Centre in Paris (Richard Rogers and Renzo Piano 1972–7) and Guggenheim Bilbao (Frank Gehry 1994–7) have challenged the established canon and led a number of architectural historians to attempt the development of alternate typologies (Lampugnani 1999; Newhouse 1998). Many of these new typologies appear forced and restrictive, illustrating the complexity of museum types and the difficulties of classification.

Architectural histories, as described above, tend to take us from one major museum development – one architectural precedent or exemplar – to another, reinforcing the dominant notion of architecture as artistic practice and closing down interpretations which see architectural history as subtle and complex, and embedded in site-specific change. Similarly, this dominant view of architecture as a privileged activity shields from view the range of people, groups and organisations involved in the making of museum architecture through their competing, and sometimes oppositional, values, beliefs and agendas. A focus on the great names in architecture has also led to a distinction between 'great' museum buildings and the rest, with the rest then falling outside of architectural histories of the museum. Provincial museums and galleries in Britain are rarely considered at all, reduced as they are to 'municipal' interpretations of real architecture, mean and parochial versions – often designed by the town architect – of the real thing. Existing architectural histories, by focusing on architecture as a physical object, fail to recognise its social and cultural nature.

Such histories legitimise the notion that architecture is something that other people do and obscure from view our active involvement in its production.

Taking its lead from a body of theory which explores the social nature of architecture and advocates a critical engagement with architectural history, this chapter adopts an approach which focuses on the stories of architectural change in specific museums and galleries; on the architectural changes undertaken or imagined during the life of the museum or gallery which often, if not always, accompany museum reform. Its focus is thus on the changing social, political and professional contexts which lead to reform and the people and organisations directly involved in the museum's spatial reshaping. It is an approach which asks the following questions: What are the forces driving architectural change? Who is making the decisions and according to what criteria? Where does the power lie? And what does this tell us about the social relations and identities programmed into the space? This is then the soft rather than the hard of architecture, the intangible rather than the concrete.

In this chapter, these ideas are explored through the early architectural history of the Walker Art Gallery in Liverpool, a gallery which has changed its shape many times as its social and professional contexts have shifted (Figure 6.1). Since it was founded in 1877 and a purpose-designed building was erected on Upper William Brown Street, the Walker has undergone a series of architectural and spatial transformations. The gallery was extended in the 1880s to accommodate the annual contemporary art exhibition – at that time the main activity of the gallery – as well as the growing permanent collection. In the early 1930s a significant extension was added to the gallery and the existing building was renovated: the small entrance hall and staircase were demolished and replaced with a large, open entrance hall with a sweeping staircase either side (Figure 6.2). Following the decade-long occupation of the gallery by the Ministry of Food during and after the Second World War, the Walker was again renovated, reopening in 1951. During the decades that followed, as new

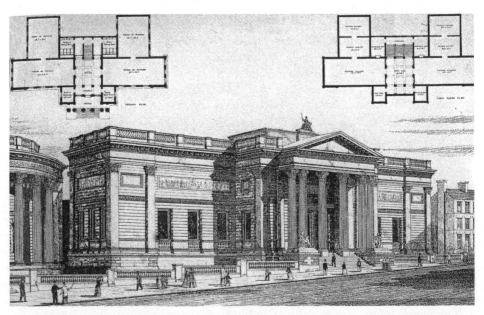

*Figure 6.1* The Walker Art Gallery, Liverpool.
*Building News*, September 1877.

*Figure* 6.2 The original entrance vestibule at the Walker Art Gallery and its transformation in 1933.

Reproduced with kind permission of the Walker Art Gallery, Liverpool.

museum functions such as conservation demanded physical space in the gallery, the amount of space given over to public programmes diminished. More recently, with the aid of HLF monies, spaces taken over for other purposes have been returned to public use, and the space between the 1884 structure and the 1930s extension has been enclosed to create a gateway to a series of newly refurbished temporary exhibitions galleries. Although small-scale in comparison to some HLF projects, this recent development has enabled the Walker to display its now national museum status – a status gained by Liverpool's Museums in 1986 following a funding crisis – permanent collection and deliver a changing programme of temporary exhibitions.

This chapter focuses on the early history of the gallery, from its initial building as a site for temporary exhibitions, genteel recreation and social improvement, to its later expansion and renovation in the 1930s as the gallery's audience and social role changed. In this latter section, the focus is particularly on the professionalisation of museum workers and the challenges this posed to sections of Liverpool's social elite who had, since the birth of the Walker in 1877 and in terms of earlier art patronage in Liverpool, ruled the local art world. It is argued here that, although subtle and complex, a significant shift in power occurred in the early decades of the twentieth century as the influence of the museums profession began to, quite literally, shape the space of the gallery.

## 'Art and Grog': establishing a gallery of art

Walker who has set apart
This grand Gallery of Art;
Walker, who the town doth fill
With his public houses still.
Feasting, fire-works, close the day –
Cheer for Art and Grog – hooray!
(Anon. 1877)

Existing research into the social conditions that led to the establishment of museums and galleries in the industrial towns and cities of the north and the Midlands begins to provide a context for the perceived need for a gallery of art in Liverpool (see, for example, Wolff and Seed 1988). By the early nineteenth century, the social problems brought about by industrialisation and urbanisation were signalling the need for civic reform. By the mid to late decades of the nineteenth century, governance in the provinces was shifting from local councils with relatively few powers, following the 1835 municipal reforms, to increasingly powerful and interventionist town and city councils actively involved in municipal development (Fraser 1979: 4). In the second half of the century, these organisations cleared slum housing, established higher sanitary standards and regulations, installed sewers and fresh water supplies, improved education provision and opened public parks. The development of public museums and galleries, made possible through legislation, was one part of this municipal development. Culture had come to be recognised by government as one possible solution to the country's increasingly difficult social problems (Minihan 1977).

The social problems brought about by industrialisation and urbanisation were evident in the extreme in Liverpool. A large proportion of the country's cotton and other trades passed through the town and, for an entrepreneurial few, fortunes were made. The majority of Liverpool's population, however, was composed of the mainly unskilled labouring classes, who were in industries chiefly devoted to distribution rather than manufacturing and which brought about, as Waller phrased it, 'irregular wages and irregular ways' (Waller 1981: xvi). Crime was high and alcohol abuse a cause for concern; in 1874 Liverpool could boast 1,929 public houses, 383 beer-houses . . . and 272 off-licenses and refreshment houses, outnumbering the combined total of all the other types of shop in the town (Waller 1981: 23).

Fuelled by headline-grabbing incidents of violence in the city, perceptions developed of Liverpool as an uncivilised, lawless place inhabited by a dangerous and fast-moving population. In 1839, a Royal Commission considering the need for police forces identified part of the Wirral as one of the most dangerous places in the country (Marriner 1982: 1). And in 1874, the town achieved notoriety following an incident in which a citizen was murdered in Tithebarn Street. The attack took place in front of an approving crowd, leading the *Daily Telegraph* to report that 'in all the pages of Dr Livingstone's experience among the negroes of Africa, there is no single instance approaching this Liverpool story, in savagery of mind and body, in bestiality of heart and act' (quoted in Waller 1981: 22).[1] In *The Times*, Liverpool's leading men were criticised for neglecting their responsibilities, as was so apparent in the town's frightening statistics of crime, disease and alcohol abuse (Waller 1981: 22). As the problems of Liverpool were publicised, and as the Conservative council followed a programme of public health improvements, actively taking an interest, albeit at a distance, in the public health of its citizens (Fraser 1979: 27), Liverpool Liberals focused on the temperance campaign, emphasising education and 'counter-attractions' such as free libraries and friendly societies. A gallery of art would offer yet another form of alternative recreation.

By the 1860s, in light of the negative image of Liverpool and amidst the continual threat of social unrest, the prospect of a gallery took on particular significance and gained public support. Even so, it would take a further fifteen years for the necessary social, economic and political conditions to come together. Early annual reports of the Free Public Library, Museum, and Gallery of Arts of the Borough of Liverpool illustrate the Art Committee's attempts throughout the 1860s to establish a gallery of art and begin the accumulation of a collection. In these reports, vacant land to the east of the library was noted as always having been intended for this purpose. The reports also record the actions taken to have blocks of housing there scheduled under the Improvement Act. A further step towards the establishment of the gallery came with the building of the William Brown Library and Museum in this period. It was the managers of this institution, together with the Town Council's Museum and Arts Committee that shaped plans to host an exhibition of contemporary art at the museum in 1871. The exhibition, which demanded the dismantling of two rooms in the museum, was a great success and became an annual fixture. Plans to develop a separate art gallery, and thus obviate the need for this annual disruption to the museum, finally became a real possibility in 1874 when Andrew Barclay Walker promised funds for a purpose-built gallery on the occasion of his becoming Mayor of Liverpool (Morris 1996: 2–4).

In order to understand the local structures that enabled the building of museums and galleries, one needs to understand the heady mix of public and private, of the civic and the individual, that shaped the Victorian city. Following the municipal reforms of the first half of the nineteenth century, power passed to the new economic urban elite; the merchants and industrialists previously denied the position of councillor, alderman, mayor or magistrate (Fraser 1979: 4). Through a series of urban networks and a culture of participation in public life, these men of wealth, for a whole complex of reasons and with large private incomes at their disposal, were able to establish a range of public institutions under corporate sanction. This play of power had effect within the committees of the town council. In terms of the direct shaping of the architecture of the Walker Art Gallery, in use as well as in form, power lay with the Arts Sub-Committee rather than with the first curator, Charles Dyall, who had few decision-making powers. Indeed, there are two particularly key individuals active in the early shaping of the gallery: the gallery's benefactor and Mayor of Liverpool, Andrew Barclay Walker, and the Treasurer and later Chair of the Arts Sub-Committee, Alderman Philip Henry Rathbone. These men characterise the range of interests and agendas, both individual and the civic, that came to shape the gallery.

For Walker, the giving of funds for the gallery added cultural provision to his public service record. In other respects, and although twice Mayor of Liverpool, Walker was not perceived as a particularly active politician. He was, however, reported to be the richest man in Liverpool. A driven and successful businessman, he had made his fortune through brewing and the selling of liquor through a large number of public houses in the city. As editorials in *The Argus* throughout September 1877 attest, there was an irony here that was not lost on the Liverpool press. Walker's business interests and social profile were undoubtedly aided by the investment in the gallery. Along with other members of the small social elite in Liverpool he attended royal openings and other social events at the gallery, including the annual autumn exhibition. Indeed, he became Sir Andrew shortly after its opening.

Walker undoubtedly held ambitions for Liverpool which were shared by his fellow councillors. Indeed, the architectural and spatial form of the gallery was linked directly to the desire on the part of a number of prominent Liverpool men, across the political spectrum, to raise the cultural profile of Liverpool. With this in mind, the gallery was based upon already existing precedents for what made good museum architecture, both in London and on the continent. On top of the building was placed a colossal female statue of commerce, symbolising the spirit of Liverpool, and to the sides of the entrance large sculptures of Raphael and Michelangelo made a claim to a prestigious artistic heritage. Bas-reliefs were placed along the front and sides of the gallery, representing a series of events in Liverpool's history – all with royal associations. There is no record of any committee discussion of the form the gallery should take, indeed the records suggest that it was simply accepted that it would be a gift from Walker, who promptly selected the architect of his private mansion to undertake the work.

Alderman Rathbone provided a dramatic contrast to Walker; concerns over the social conditions of the working classes informed his belief in the need for civic architecture that would act as a constant incentive to Liverpool's inhabitants to emulate the deeds of past times and become better citizens (Rathbone 1895: 40). Rathbone came from a family of Unitarians who regarded social service as part of their religion and who were actively involved in the temperance movement (Waller 1981: 160). His belief in the political value of art also informed the acquisitions policy whereby paintings recognised as holding popular appeal were selected over more esoteric works (Morris 1996: 6).

The architectural solution provided for the committee's basic requirements of access, circulation and display. Here, where almost the entire space was given over to display, people from all walks of Liverpool life would be exposed to the improving influence of art. However, the working classes were allocated a very specific description and location within this development. Far from entering the space on an equal footing with the great and the good, Rathbone imagined a space that would 'enable the individual to realize that he is a requisite element in a living organic whole [where] every man should feel that he had his defined place and use in the world' (Rathbone 1895: 38). This said, when the gallery opened its doors in 1877 the opportunity to view the pictures attracted a broad audience and visitor figures reached 2,349 a day in 1880, a figure not exceeded since (Morris 1994: 11).

In 1884 an extension was added to the gallery in order to make more space for the growing permanent collection. Even so, a large proportion of this was dismantled each year during the autumn exhibition and space would continue to be an issue in the annual reports from the later years of the nineteenth century onwards. Funds would finally become available, courtesy of gifts from two other long-standing committee members, to extend the gallery in the late 1920s, but by then Liverpool and the gallery would be very different places. This would warrant a complete reshaping.

## Depression, revolt and a new professionalism

By the 1920s, the fortunes and popularity of the Walker seem to have diminished as the gallery lost its traditional core audiences and became the subject of a good amount of criticism in the press. The successes of the early autumn exhibitions were then a distant memory and Liverpool was suffering from a downturn in the economy and declining trade, which resulted, by the 1920s, in high unemployment, strikes and civil unrest. The political ground had shifted dramatically since the Walker's foundation; the liberal values of free trade, individualism and philanthropy had given way, following the First World War, to increased state control and higher rates of taxation. The introduction of national assurance schemes in the early years of the century had, in part, alleviated some of the extreme poverty and 'the drink question' had diminished in importance (Waller 1981: 271).

It was against this background of economic uncertainty that the Walker became the site for one of the most significant political moments in the city's history. In September 1921, the gallery was 'rushed' and occupied by the National Unemployed Workers' Committee Movement (NUWCM) (Waller 1981: 290). The NUWCM was formed in the years following the First World War when thousands of men had returned from the trenches to be faced with mass unemployment. Resentment set in and, led by the Communist Party of Great Britain, the NUWCM was organised under the slogan of 'Work or Maintenance' and based upon principles of non-violent protest, tolerance and passive demonstration (Braddock and Braddock 1963: 32; Pridmore 2002). A series of demonstrations were organised in Liverpool: the first two involved taking over the Exchange Flags (the paved area behind the Town Hall where the merchants conducted their business) and marching, military style, through the streets of the city; the third was planned for Monday 12 September on St Georges Plateau.

In their memoirs, published in 1963, Jack and Bessie Braddock described the day's events. These began with speeches, after which the organisers of the protest, who included Bessie's mother, Ma Bamber, decided to take the assembled crowd to view the pictures in the Walker Art Gallery and stay there until the Lord Mayor gave permission for them to hold meetings in comfort in St George's Hall – a vast building and the town's most capacious and symbolic civic meeting place. Initially about two hundred protestors entered the Gallery, with a number (about fifty) immediately changing their minds and leaving (Braddock and Braddock 1963: 34) (Figure 6.3).

The events that followed were well documented in the Liverpool press. The men who remained in the gallery were shut in the vestibule by the police, who arrived quickly and in number. Doors and windows were closed and the unemployed protestors, according to all reports, were given a severe beating. The *Liverpool Daily Post and Mercury* reported:

When an attempt to force an exit was made by those shut in the vestibule, the police drew their batons, and a brief but severe combat ensued . . . Many of the men, seeing the doors closed and the police guarding them, made an attempt to force their way out, and were struck down by the police. A number of visitors to the gallery who had been on the ground floor rooms before the appearance of the crowd found themselves trapped by the closing of the doors, and among them were several women, who were greatly terrified.

These people were let out through a back entrance by a member of the art gallery staff. Some of the unemployed probably escaped subsequently by back entrances, for those taken into custody or to hospital later on were fewer in numbers than had originally entered the building.

(quoted in Braddock and Braddock 1963: 35)

George Garrett, an active member of many leftwing movements (Pridmore 2002), who had spoken at the rally, and was then involved in what he described as the 'storming' of the Walker, later wrote:

Inside the Art Gallery, more police caused pandemonium, men yelped aloud as they were batoned down. Others dashed around panic-stricken. A few desperate ones dropped from an open window into a side street and got away. Those attempting to follow were struck down from behind. The police closed all windows and doors. There were no further escapes. Batons split skull after skull. Men fell where they were hit. The floor streamed with blood. Those lying on it were trampled on by others who were soon flattened out alongside them. Gallery workers were battered, too. The police had gone wild.

(Braddock and Braddock 1963: 36–37)

A trial followed with 161 defendants charged with a series of offences, an event that was later immortalised at Liverpool Unity Theatre (1948), where Bessie Braddock played her mother (Dawson 1985: 74).

The 'storming' of the gallery is significant here because it marks a key period of social change in Britain which dramatically altered the organisation of society and the demand for cultural provision. It was during this period of social upheaval that the Walker Art Gallery dropped out of favour in Liverpool. Indeed, as the NUWCM briefly occupied the public spaces of the gallery to make their political point, so another battle was beginning to rage behind the scenes. This was a battle for professionalisation, played out in the local press, which sought to determine who should occupy and shape the space of the gallery.

This particular attempt to reshape the space of the gallery needs to be understood against wider change then taking place in the town. Most significant here is the dramatic shift, in both size and composition, of the lower middle class. What had been a small class of shop-keepers and small businessmen increased in size during the first decades of the twentieth century as a result of the growth in white-collar occupations (LeMahieu 1988: 8). As the more prosperous classes moved into new private housing, so Liverpool Council began to provide corporation housing. Between 1925 and 1938 the council built over 22,000 new homes, which housed one eighth of Liverpool's population by 1931 (Marriner 1982: 147). The majority of this housing was built in the suburbs, which, aided by the motor car, effectively decanted much of the inner city population from close to the gallery.

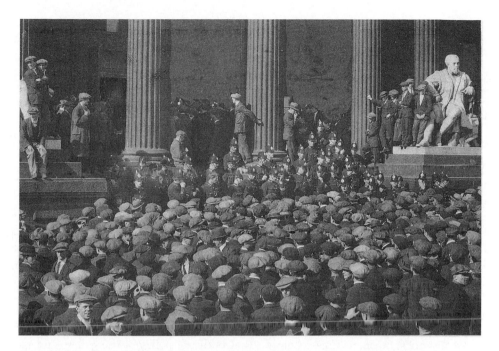

*Figure 6.3* 'Unemployed disturbance in Liverpool. The scene at the Walker Art Gallery just after it was rushed'.

*Liverpool Daily Post and Mercury*, September 13 1921.

The increase in the numbers of salaried workers with disposable incomes and the short-ening of the working week resulted in a shift in the make-up of the audience for cultural provision. As LeMahieu (1988: 9) has argued, it was these circumstances that led to the transformation of the structure of cultural demand and the emergence of a popular culture. In Liverpool, new spaces for leisure opened, including ballrooms and purpose-built cinemas, such as the opulent Forum on Lime Street which opened in 1931, although these were by no means accessible to all. Liverpool's genteel social elite diminished in power, a trend marked by the reinvention in 1922 of the Wellington Rooms, previously a focal point for the Liverpool social season, as a venue for more popular entertainments (Waller 1981: 277). Alongside the picture palaces and other leisure pursuits the gallery stood out as a relic of the past, and it was around this time that the gallery was faced with the most bizarre suggestion for its remodelling. T. W. McLean, a solicitor, acting on behalf of 'a client who is a Liverpool Gentleman of Standing in the Entertainment Business World', desired to rent the basement space of the gallery for the running of a roller-skating rink. The proposal was sent to the architects of the 1930s extension who responded on 11 June 1930 declining on the basis of the additional costs that the plan would necessitate.[2]

By the 1930s, important new attitudes had begun to emerge, evident in government rhetoric, which argued for the arts to be introduced more widely into society. The focus shifted from offering alternate recreations to a mass working class, to a vision of public provision for, as Markham phrased it, 'the average wage earner and his family' (Markham 1938: 173). It was in response to and as part of these shifts, and as increasing amounts of public money went into their running, that museums and galleries across the country began to take on a more publicly oriented role (Minihan 1977: 178). (Liverpool council's allocation of an annual grant for the purchase of pictures in 1929, in response to falling revenues from the annual exhibition, is perhaps indicative of this.)

Central to the success of this shift was the increasing organisation of the museums profession. Museum staff, now with some decades of practical museum experience behind them, began to share information, establish standards and meet regularly. As Kate Hill (2005: 62) has noted, by the early decades of the twentieth century some museum workers could be understood to be professionals with authority, qualifications, staff to manage, a career structure and a peer group. This group, through events such as the annual meetings of the Museums Association, and in line with government policy, began to develop an increasingly sophisticated body of professional knowledge concerning the educational role of the museum.

New expectations were placed on the Walker in April 1931 when a series of letters were exchanged in the *Daily Post* which accused the gallery of failing to fulfil its true function and called for it to take a more active part in the life of the city. The exchange was sparked by a letter from Vere E. Cotton, who wrote in the *Liverpool Post and Mercury* on the 2 April 1931:

> Sir, – The announcement of the retirement of Mr. Quigley from the curatorship of the Walker Art Gallery, coupled with the impending extension of the building, seems an appropriate time to suggest that both the policy of the gallery and its administration require drastic overhaul. While it will generally be agreed that the retiring curator has, within the limits of his office, deserved well of his city, it is useless to expect that, given a continuance of the present regime, the Walker Art Gallery can ever occupy that position in the cultural life of the community which its founders hoped and intended.
>
> (Cotton 1931)

Cotton's main criticisms related to what he regarded as a permanent collection 'unworthy of the second city of the Empire', shaped as it was by local interests and politics (Cotton 1931). He repeated a call that had been made once before in the 1890s for the appointment of a professional Director but which had at that time been overruled by a powerful committee, resulting in the promotion of Quigley. Cotton claimed that the Director should be given powers to do his job; 'he should be trusted and given reasonable freedom of action not only to adopt a definite policy, but to carry it through'. Because, Cotton claimed:

> A sub-committee consisting in the main of city councillors who are elected by the ratepayers for every other reason than their artistic knowledge is no more capable of running the Walker Art Gallery than a committee of the House of Commons would be of running the National or the Tate . . . .
>
> (Cotton 1931)

The letter sparked a long run of responses in the *Post* on almost a daily basis over the following months. In an editorial on 4 April, a number of officials were quoted offering a range of views on the letter. For Alderman Cole, then Chair of the Libraries, Museums and Arts Committee, Cotton's suggestions were impracticable. Professor Budden, chair of art history at Liverpool University, mused rather idealistically, 'It would be a good thing to lift the whole business out of the arena of local politics and local interests' (Anon. 1931). In the letters that followed, some directly criticised specific committee members suggesting that they placed self-glorification, vanity and privilege before a love of art. Others stepped back from this direct assault on the committee members recognising their service to the city and their generosity, instead blaming the committee system for the gallery's decline. In the *Museums Journal*, ex-Walker curator E. R. Dibdin later published what seems to have been a reasonable summary of the official line, which suggested that it was viewed as something of an absurdity to think that the Director should have free reign like the Chief Medical Officer. 'The absurdity of this is evident', he wrote, 'The medical man, like the lawyer, by taking the necessary degrees, gives proof of a knowledge superior to the layman's; there is as yet no institution whose certificate would be a sufficient voucher for the infallibility of an art director' (Dibdin 1931: 87–89). The exchange ended with a petition to the City Council, signed by eighty or ninety prominent citizens of Liverpool.

In actual fact, although Cotton and his supporters clearly perceived Cole and the Arts Sub-Committee as blindly making decisions, there was some evidence of a move to professional values and agendas, and particularly so when it came to reshaping the gallery in this period. Once again, precedents for the alterations were sought in the nationals and other prestigious galleries. This time, however, the latest museum techniques were of consequence and importance. In 1929 a deputation from the Walker visited the new Duveen Galleries at the National Gallery and the Tate Gallery in order to inspect the latest in lighting techniques.[3] Additional visits were made in 1931 to the National Gallery, Tate, the National Portrait Gallery and the Fitzwilliam Museum, Cambridge, again to explore roof lighting techniques.[4] Much time was devoted to discussion of the latest techniques and, as a result of these visits, alterations were made to two of the six galleries planned. These would now be designed as embayments, along the lines of the Duveen Galleries and some of the galleries at the Fitzwilliam. Linked to this, the new technique of bringing light in from the sides of the roof, rather than from a central skylight, was selected.

If the remodelled entrance hall brought a sense of grandeur to the Walker, echoing, if not embracing, the modern architectures of the new pleasure palaces and cinemas in the city, the general design and decoration of the gallery followed professional guidelines of the day, documented in the *Museums Journal* and promoted by such figures as E. E. Lowe, then Director of Leicester Museum and a leading authority on museum practice. The interior decoration was pared back and light colours were utilised throughout so as not to interfere with the objects on display. In the event, perhaps influenced by the row in the *Post*, but perhaps also an inevitable development, Frank Lambert, MA, FSA, previously Director at Leeds City Art Gallery, was appointed, following which it became policy to appeal to areas of broad public interest and offer a wide range of temporary exhibitions, such as *Unit 1*, *Walt Disney Cartoons*, *Everyday Things* and *Industrial Art* (Anon. 1934: 27). Loan cases of exhibits from the Victoria and Albert Museum were introduced in 1934, and in that same year musical concerts were offered in the gallery. Once again, however, a range of interests were shaping the gallery and, as had always been the case at the Walker, the space was conceived and utilised in a variety of ways.

If the programming reveals an attempt to appeal to a broad public, a more inward focus can be detected in the gallery's acquisitions policy. One of the key criticisms levelled at the gallery in 1931 focused on the quality of the permanent collection and the over-reliance of the Arts Sub-Committee on the academic and conventional art of the Royal Academy. As Lambert later wrote:

When the jubilee of the opening of the Gallery came in 1927, it was a disparate and incoherent assemblage of pictures which covered its walls. At one end of the scale stood the Roscoe Collection, at the other the academic 'pictures of the year.' To quote again from the guide of 1895, 'Royal Academicians past and present constitute a liberal percentage of the list of artists whose works are comprised in the collection.' Nothing linked the Italians of the fifteenth century with the Academicians of the nineteenth save perhaps the Pre-Raphaelites, who were inspired by the example of the former and abhorred the productions of the latter. Most deplorable of all in a gallery so widely known (because of the Autumn Exhibition) and in a collection of this size (the catalogue published in 1927 listed more than 2,000 items), great gaps yawned at the beginning and end of the British series, which included no representation either of the glories of English painting in the eighteenth and early nineteenth centuries or of progressive contemporary work. Gainsborough, Reynolds, Turner and their fellows were missing at one end, Steer, Sickert and John, already famous, at the other.

(Lambert 1951: 40)

To truly meet the requirements of an educational institution, a representative collection would be necessary. Under Lambert's directorship, focus shifted from the annual exhibition of contemporary art, to assessment of the permanent collection and an established policy of gap filling in order to develop a representative collection of British painting. The contradiction evident in this shift is that it involved a concurrent shift away from populist works towards an increasingly academic view of art and, in effect, a reassertion of high cultural values. The increasingly professionalised space of the museum would necessitate a sharp distinction between high and low culture, between an academic pursuit and the popular entertainments of the city.

By 1939, the Walker Art Gallery had closed once again as it was taken over for the duration of the war and beyond by the Ministry of Food. The gallery would not reopen until 1951, and when it did it was once again significantly refurbished.

## Conclusion

The literal occupation of the Walker Art Gallery by the National Unemployed Workers' Committee Movement in 1921 took place at a significant moment in the gallery's history. A gallery shaped in response to a very specific set of social conditions, and to enable a specific range of social activities, responses and relations, had, by the 1920s, lost touch with its communities as a result of large-scale social change. The primary inhabitants of the gallery, Liverpool's economic elite, no longer occupied an absolutely central place in society and the larger working population had long ceased to frequent the gallery in any great numbers. If the Walker was to regain its position in the city as a key public site for cultural participation and social cohesion, a significant architectural reshaping would be required.

Where the Walker became a very visible battle ground for a few brief moments in 1921, another battle was raging, albeit in a more subtle and less violent way, to reshape the gallery. During this period the social relations of the gallery space were rewritten and a gallery space which had started life with a broad social remit and audience – but had deteriorated into an institution out of touch with the city and its inhabitants – was ostensibly reinvented as a modern space of formal education and entertainment. The changes were subtle and complex and maintained the difficult mix of public and private, of inclusion and exclusion, that shaped these institutions from the first. Nevertheless, a distinct power shift and change in focus had taken place from the mores and wants of a local art world to the agendas and interests of a national profession.

## Notes

1 What reads now as a shockingly racist comment reveals so much about the dominant systems of value at that time.
2 Walker Gallery Archives, Liverpool (WAG): Old Records – Gallery Extension 1930. Letters and Folders A-F.
3 WAG: Minutes 1929. Minutes of the Libraries, Museums and Arts Committee (Extension of the Walker Art Gallery) Sub-Committee, 29th November 1929, in WAG 1, Box 10.
4 WAG: Minutes 1931. Minutes of the Libraries, Museums and Arts Committee (Extension of the Walker Art Gallery) Sub-Committee, 2nd November 1931, in WAG 1, Box 10.

## Bibliography

Anon. (1877) 'A Great Day for Art', *The Argus*, 15 September, 726.
—— (1931) 'Future of Art Gallery, New Administration Proposals, Local Opinion Divided', *Liverpool Post and Mercury*, 4 April.
—— (1934) 'The Director of the Walker Art Gallery', *Liverpolitan*, 3(7): 27.
Borden, I. and Rendell, J. (eds) (2000) *InterSections, Architectural Histories and Critical Theories*, London: Routledge.
Braddock, J. and Braddock, B. (1963) *The Braddocks*, London: Macdonald and Company.
Cotton, V. E. (1931) 'Letters to the Editor, The Future of the Walker Art Gallery', *Liverpool Post and Mercury*, 2 April.
Dawson, J. (1985) *Left Theatre*, Liverpool: Merseyside Writers.
Dibdin, E. R. (1931) 'The Walker Art Gallery, Liverpool', *Museums Journal*, 31(3): 87–9.
Fraser, D. (1979) *Power and Authority in the Victorian City*, Oxford: Basil Blackwell.
Hill, J. (ed.) (1998) *Occupying Architecture: Between the Architect and the User*, London: Routledge.
—— (2003) *Actions of Architecture, Architects and Creative Users*, London: Routledge.
Hill, K. (2005) *Culture and Class in English Public Museums, 1850–1914*, Aldershot: Ashgate.
King, A. D. (ed.) (1980) *Buildings and Society, Essays on the Social Development of the Built Environment*, London: Routledge and Kegan Paul.
Lambert, F. (1951) 'The Walker Art Gallery, Growth of a Policy (1)', *Liverpool Bulletin, Library, Museum and Arts Committee*, 1(2): 33–40.
Lampugnani, V. M. (1999) 'The architecture of art: the museums of the 1990s', in V. M. Lampugnani and A. Sachs (eds) *Museums for a New Millennium, Concepts, Projects, Buildings*, Munich: Prestel, 11–14.
LeMahieu, D. L. (1988) *A Culture for Democracy, Mass Communication and the Cultivated Mind in Britain Between the Wars*, Oxford: Clarendon Press.
Markham, S. F. (1938) *A Report on the Museums and Art Galleries of the British Isles (other than the National Museums)*, Edinburgh: T. and A. Constable Ltd.
Marriner, S. (1982) *The Economic and Social Development of Merseyside*, London: Croom Helm.
Minihan, J. (1977) *The Nationalisation of Culture, The Development of State Subsidies to the Arts in Great Britain*, London: Hamish Hamilton.
Morris, E. (ed.) (1994) *The Walker Art Gallery*, London: Scala Books/NMGM.
—— (1996) *Victorian and Edwardian Paintings in the Walker Art Gallery and at Sudley House*, London: HMSO.

Newhouse, V. (1998) *Towards a New Museum*, New York: The Monacelli Press.

Pridmore, J. (2002) 'George Garrett and the USA', Glasgow: Centre for Political Song. Online. Available at: www.gcal.ac.uk/politicalsong/research/pridmore.html.

Rathbone, P. H. (1895) *The Political Value of Art to the Municipal Life of a Nation. A Lecture delivered at the Free Library, Liverpool, 1875*, Liverpool: Lee and Nightingale.

Searing, H. (1986) 'The development of a museum typology', in S. Stephens (ed.) *Building the New Museum*, New York: Princeton Architectural Press, 14–23.

Stevenson, M. (2005) 'From cultural institution to cultural consumer experience: Manchester Art Gallery Expansion Project', in S. MacLeod (ed.) *Reshaping Museum Space, Architecture, Design, Exhibitions*, London: Routledge, 65–77.

Till, J. (1998) 'Architecture of the impure community', in Hill, J. (ed.) *Occupying Architecture: Between The Architect and the User*, London: Routledge, 62–75.

Waller, P. J. (1981) *Democracy and Sectarianism, a Political and Social History of Liverpool 1868–1939*, Liverpool: Liverpool University Press.

Wolff, J. and Seed, J. (eds) (1988) *The Culture of Capital: Art, Power and the Nineteenth Century Middle Class*, Manchester: Manchester University Press.

# 7

# MODERNITY AND IDENTITY

## The National Museum of Iran

### Ali Mozaffari

It would seem appropriate for a national museum to embody a narrative of nationalism within its displays. It would also seem appropriate enough that such a public monument embodies sanctioned nationalistic references of its own time in its outward architectural expression. Unlike museum displays, however, which can be adapted to changes of sanctioned ideologies and perceptions of identity by alterations to the curatorial narrative, the aging exterior – the architecture – will gradually transform into a relic, a monument to past times. Abrupt socio-political transformations, particularly revolutions as their ultimate violent form, can almost instantly transform the museum into an anachronistic oddity. Revolution disrupts the assumption of historical continuity upon which museums operate. It redefines the past to which the museum owes its existence, thus challenging and perhaps undermining the relevance of the museum to the present. This problem is compounded when the museum, as a public institution, disseminates an ideology that is largely, if not fully, extraneous to the culture of the public it was meant to address. The National Museum of Iran (NMI) (established in 1937–44) is a case in point. After the Islamic Revolution in 1979, the museum, a showpiece of the sanctioned nationalistic ideology of the outgoing monarchy, the Pahlavis (1925–79), had to embody a new narrative of identity or be committed to oblivion. Furthermore, it had to attract and indoctrinate the public with its post-revolutionary ideologies in order to counter the effects of the previous establishment. This chapter will discuss the evolution of the NMI, from its inception until the present, in order to examine the relationship between state ideology and the museum. It will reveal the effect of the westernising and modernising state agenda during the pre-Revolution period and the Islamicising and assertion of religious identity in the post-Revolution period, both of which have failed to fully capture the public's imagination.

The NMI began as an archaeological museum that was, until 1986, known as the Ancient Iran Museum. It was part of the repertoire of buildings and institutions that marked the intertwined project of nationalism and modernisation that was promoted by the Pahlavi Dynasty and whose built expression in the 1930–40s formed the administrative centre of Tehran. The administrative centre and the National Museum within it comprise a distinctive representation of Iranian national identity. This representation is characterised by a conspicuous blend of Iranian nationalism, western modernity and assertion of material progress (see, for example, Cottam 1964; Katouzian 2003). As will be discussed in the following, the National Museum is itself the outcome of the often hostile encounter between Iran and the West, at least from the early decades of the nineteenth century, in which Iran was usually placed at the humiliating and receiving end of the encounter. By the end of the nineteenth century those encounters had prompted the progressive adoption of essentially western notions of nationalism and progress by the educated elite of Iran. The state and the elite, or the intelligentsia as they will be described here, identified with an earlier period in Iranian history that would, on the one hand, capture and instil their idea of national identity and, on the other hand, serve as a reference for their modernising and progressing aspirations. Tangible heritage as material evidence corroborating that origin was central to the construction of that ideological project. This seems to resonate with the triangular relationship between nationalism, heritage and progress, as previously established by the European ideology of National Romanticism. The focus of the museum on archaeology, its naming as the Ancient Iran Museum and its style of architecture exemplified the official Iranian stance on nationalism and progress.

The Ancient Iran Museum has now evolved into the NMI, which encompasses the pre- and post-Islamic periods in two separate buildings on the same site. Nevertheless, as an institution firmly embedded within the ideology of the time of its inception, the NMI neither forms the unambiguous embodiment of state-sanctioned ideology, nor has it managed to attract and address the public, the ordinary Iranian visitor. It seems the post-Revolutionary transformations have impressed upon the museum an identity crisis that has transformed it into a relic and alienated it from its public. To further examine this possibility, it is useful to explore the historic conditions surrounding the museum's inception.

## Historical background

There were many reasons behind the Iranian aspirations to reform and progress in the twentieth century, which are thoroughly discussed and examined by historians of the Qajar Dynasty (1781–1925) and contemporary Iran. Here, it will suffice to note that during the first decades of the twentieth century those aspirations resulted in a push for progress from the intelligentsia, in alliance with the political establishment of Iran. As Keddie (1999: 89) notes: 'Strong westernization was a reaction against the decentralized or Islamic traditions which . . . [many] saw as stultifying Iran'. This was a comprehensive, top-down effort, largely influenced by European Nationalist Romantic ideologies of the time (Katouzian 2003). Its objective was to break with the immediate traditional past and reconnect with the 'glorious' ancient history of the country (Marefat 1988: 71–2, 97; Grigor 2005: 126). It was exemplified by changes to the administrative institutions of the country, which brought with them massive new infrastructure and building projects reflected in the fabric of the cities and their new architecture. The capital, Tehran, was the site for literal and symbolic erasures of the structures of the immediate past. These structures were perceived as symbols of the previous Qajar Dynasty, who were blamed by their successors, the Pahlavis and the intelligentsia alike, for the country's decadence and backwardness. A new administrative district was constructed in place of the old centre of political power in the city, and within it were planted modern institutions imported from Europe (Marefat 1988: 39).

The NMI (then the Ancient Iran Museum) was conceived in this new, and symbolic, administrative district as part of the repertoire used by the establishment to construct the image of a 'modern' identity linked to ancient origins. The Ancient Iran Museum was located adjacent to the National Library and what would become the site of the Ethnography Museum. Together, these three institutions would provide a tangible representational site within the rapidly modernising capital. This modern identity was fabricated in support of policies of progress, understood as authoritarian modernisation and westernisation. It was intended to disrupt traditional socio-economic and political relations dominated by the ethos of religious Shiism and replace those relations with a modern system (Marefat 1988: 64–5). The post-1979 Islamic Republic would prefer to distance itself from that blend of nationalism and westernisation, as articulated by Ruoh-Allah Khomeini, the late leader of the Islamic Revolution, who stated: 'This nationalism is the source of the miseries of Muslims' (Islamic Republic News Agency).

The notion of establishing a museum in Iran dates back to the late nineteenth century (Samadi 2003: 81–2). However, the Ancient Iran Museum, as the 'mother museum', was established following a Franco-Iranian agreement in 1927, which ended the French monopoly on historical excavations in Iran in return for, among other things, the establishment of a museum and the appointment of a French citizen as its director for three consecutive terms (Hodjat 1995: xi, 148–9; Grigor 2005: 59–62; Marefat 1988: 102–3). The French already had the experience of narrating the Louvre in accordance with their nationalist agenda and of the design and curatorship of the Cairo Museum in 1900, a new institution and direct descendant of the Napoleonic archaeological surveys in Egypt. Both the Louvre and the Cairo Museum would offer precedents for the building of a museum in Iran (Menasseh 2006). The director of the museum in Iran would be André Godard, a Beaux Arts-trained architect with a background in archaeology and experience in the Louvre as well as the archaeological sites of Egypt, Afghanistan and the ancient Sassanid Iranian site of Ctesiphon, then located in the newly created country of Iraq.

The Ancient Iran Museum was built in 1937 and inaugurated in 1944 (Figure 7.1). Godard is credited with the design of the museum, which had exhibition spaces arranged over two levels around a ceremonial axis. Exhibitions were divided into two sections; Ancient Iran on the lower level, with the Islamic period above it (Pope 1946: 78–100). The building is red brick, and the main entry space is a magnificent portal (or *Iwan* in Persian), an entrance that resembles the pre-Islamic Sassanian (241–651 AD) style of architecture. This is flanked by additional rooms, including a lecture hall and library (Figure 7.5). Above the entrance was an inscribed poem, which credited the Pahlavi Dynasty and Reza Shah with the country's progress (including the construction of the museum) and recorded the date of construction (Masoomi 1977: 165). Behind the museum was the National Library, designed by Godard and Maxim Siroux (another French architect and Godard's assistant on the museum). The Ethnography Museum, which could be seen as resembling a Sassanian typology in its plan (Riazi n.d.: 13) was constructed to its east (Figure 7.2). The appearance of this building, however, is very different to the Ancient Iran Museum and resembles the European monumental architecture of the first half of the twentieth century. It was constructed between 1941 and 1953, and it operated as the Ethnographic Museum until 1974. However, in 1975, due to a shortage of space in the Ancient Iran Museum, a decision was taken to annex the building intended for the Ethnography Museum to the Islamic Period section of the Ancient Iran Museum and suitably refurbish its interior to display artefacts of the Islamic Period. This transformation was finally realised in 1996. Meanwhile, in 1986, following the Islamic Revolution of 1979, the Ancient Iran Museum and the annex were renamed the National Museum of Iran (Riazi n.d.: 11).

According to the guide published by the NMI, the interior refurbishment of the Ethnography Museum was conceived with a regard for Islamic art and philosophy. Since 1997 the NMI has existed in its contemporary form, with separate buildings dedicated to Ancient Iran and the Islamic period. The sheer scale of the Islamic period section and the

*Figure 7.1* National Museum of Iran: view of the main façade of the Ancient Iran Museum showing the entry portal.

Photo: the author.

*Figure 7.2* National Museum of Iran: general view of the Islamic Period Section of the museum. Entrance is marked in black stone.

Photo: the author.

wealth of collections on display easily overpowers the Ancient Iran section, potentially turning its display into a mute and neglected relic of olden times.

The NMI is a tangible product of the encounter between traditional Iran and the West, a process that visibly reshaped Iran in the twentieth century. It has been suggested that the effect of the Iran–West encounter was as profound in its depth, breadth and all-encompassing nature, as that of the encounter of Zoroastrian Iran and Arab-Islamic conquerors centuries before it (Behnam 2005: 14). This seems to be a justifiable observation since, as previously mentioned, with the exception of sporadic efforts of the late nineteenth century, it was only in the 1920s and with the subsequent establishment of the Pahlavi Dynasty around 1925, that tangible modernisation of Iranian cities and their institutions was comprehensively enforced as the common goal of both the political establishment and the intelligentsia (Foran 1998: 235–382). The ramifications of the Iran–West encounter and the subsequent modernisation/westernisation efforts have been so profound that some have characterised the Islamic Revolution of 1979 as an 'overtly anti-western' reaction to the modernising agenda of the previous establishment, expressed in the desire for a return to traditionalism (Katouzian 2003: 10, 16, 23, 28). The goal of the Islamic Republic has been to subvert the westernising efforts made in the previous period by reviving an officially sanctioned interpretation of Shiite-Islamic traditions of Iran. As Ruoh-Allah Khomeini, the late leader of the Islamic Revolution, remarked, 'It is regrettable that our country has abandoned Islamic laws, justice and culture and become a follower of the West' (Islamic Republic News Agency).

From the above, it seems that a useful way to characterise the Iran–West encounter is through the dialectic of tradition, couched in the terms and rituals of a theocratic Shiite hegemony and progress, interpreted by the intelligentsia as a 'revival' of the pre-Islamic origins with modernising overtones. From this dialectic emanated different, and even conflicting, attitudes, interpretations and reactions to modernity and progress, and its repercussions have since engulfed all aspects of Iranian socio-political and cultural life. Modern institutions of contemporary Iran have therefore to be examined against this background.

The efforts of both establishments in legitimating their narratives of identity and nationalism, and ultimately their own position in power, have resulted in the manipulation of heritage, with the aim of creating a distinctive cultural expression. Arguably then, in both periods officially sanctioned manifestations of public culture in general and museums in particular were, and still are, ideologically charged, both in their curatorial narrative and in their architecture. The NMI is a case in point, where the representation of sanctioned ideology leads to the unfolding of the drama of nationalism, heritage and progress.

## The international context of Iranian nationalism

Given the profound impact of the Iran–West encounters in shaping the Iranian discourses of nationalism and identity, it is appropriate to position them in relation to the emerging nationalisms in Europe during the late nineteenth and early twentieth centuries. During this period the inter-relationship of heritage–progress–nationalism was tangibly established by Romantic Nationalist movements in Europe, which in turn became sources of inspiration for those in the East (Hobsbawm 1990: 105). Hobsbawm has argued that 'Nation' is in fact a relatively novel concept originating in the late nineteenth century. The main criterion for a 'viable' nation at that time was the existence of a discernible national history – one that substantiated historical evolution of the nation from a discernible origin as informed by

Darwinian concepts (Hobsbawm 1990: 37–8). National history located the authentic origins of the people, as well as the evidence of progress. National origins were located by National Romantic ideologists in the distant past, at a point in which they could locate their national particularity – invariably the time of their peoples' unrivalled glory. At that time in Europe, it was felt necessary to reinvent peoples' national identities, that is, the expression of specificity of their culture, to address the evolving modern conditions. Intellectuals in Europe were confronted with deep socio-political changes largely as a result of the new industrial economy, and aspired to progress while attempting to maintain or construct their national, cultural identity. In these modern conditions, progress was identified with the break with the immediate past – perceived to be decadent – on the one hand, and redefinition of humanity and society in response to socio-political changes on the other hand (Miller Lane 2000: 4, 6–7, 13, 72; Moravanszky 1997: 264). Thus, national identities were redefined to address the evolving modern conditions of humanity, social relations and progress. While the narration of the nation's history relied upon an historical perspective, which historicised traditions as heritage and objects as relics, the evidence of progress linked people with their origin. The National Romantic ideologies of this period were, in effect, intellectual attempts to historicise the status quo of politics and culture; that is, the political and cultural structures characteristic of the hegemonic social groups at that time (Miller Lane 2000: 20). Thus there was a fundamental interconnection, and in fact equation, between nation, progress, history (as heritage) and state (Hobsbawm 1990: 18–19, 38–9).

In redefining humanity consistent with the dominant rhetoric of the time, National Romantics referred to the distant past. History, mythology, literature, folk culture and, above all, archaeological discoveries of material culture became sources for constructing the 'forgotten' origins of modern national groups (Miller Lane 2000: 10, 20–2). There have been a number of classifications of nationalism in the late nineteenth and early twentieth century period. Broadly, they seem to share the following characteristics: a search for a national and cultural origin, the quest for authenticity, the attempt to differentiate 'peoples' as identifiable 'nations' by emphasising their particularities, the goal of reconciling local traditions with world progress, and, finally, self-legitimisation of the state (Schwarzer 1995: 159).

As a cultural product of this ideology, architecture reflected the nationalists' concerns, and architects aspired 'to create a modern, metropolitan architecture capable of expressing a national identity' (Moravanszky 1997: 225). This desire for identity gave rise to the National Romantic tendency in the arts and architecture. This tendency, despite the diversity of representational styles, responded to four tasks: glorification of the State via new governmental buildings in capitals; compilation of repositories such as museums; commemoration of national and mythic heroes; and the creation of new national monuments, one of which was the national museum (Miller Lane 2000: 175). The new museums, in their manifestation as intentional forms within the city, were the architectural expressions of regeneration and progress; in other words, they constituted cultural monuments. Internally, however, they were repositories for material culture, tangible evidence of origins and a visible confirmation of the National Romantic rhetoric (Miller Lane 2000: 20, 207, 223).

The formation of national identity in twentieth-century Iran may be seen in this context. Since the last decades of the nineteenth century, the Iranian intelligentsia saw themselves as agents for 'progress' (Mozaffari 2003: 210–14). They were influenced by European industrialisation and Imperialism, and aspired to western social values. They adopted a mixture of nineteenth-century Romanticism and eighteenth-century classical liberalism, which at times contained the rhetoric of nationalism and racism (Katouzian 2003: 66, 89–90; Hobsbawm 1990: 2). Those ideals, which included a modern, powerful and secular state under the rule of law, were exemplified in efforts that led to the Constitutional Revolution of 1905–11. Later, after the turmoil of the Constitutional Revolution and the First World War was over, with the establishment of a new dynasty, the intelligentsia's aspirations converged with state policies. In Iran, as in Europe, national history had to be narrated or reinvented in relation to progress:

> [t]he government's adoption of earlier Iranian nationalists' glorification of pre-Islamic Iran helped hide the European origin of many of the [modernising and westernising] measures undertaken. There were frequent appeals to the imperial grandeur and achievements of ancient Iran.
>
> (Keddie 1999: 87)

Cultural heritage as an imported construct became the arena in which different theories and concepts such as race theory and progress were played out. It symbolised civilisation and was indexical of national status, ideas that were equally sought in architecture (Grigor 2005: 9). Historical objects were vehicles for that narration, and architecture was its built expression.

As the first National Museum, the Ancient Iran Museum symbolised, in its architecture and its curatorial narrative, the attempt to redefine Iranians by bringing their pre-Islamic past into the present. It was an institution based on a model imported to Iran, and as has been shown elsewhere, its fundamentally French architecture was firmly embedded in the Enlightenment tradition of museum design, perhaps inaugurated by Durand's hypothetical museum design of 1802–5. Nevertheless, it was seen by Iranian nationalists as a modern hybrid aimed at symbolising their ideology of progress in line with the political and cultural agendas of Pahlavi establishment (Mozaffari 2006). This museum, through 'the most comprehensive and systematic collection of material available anywhere', was meant to represent the nation to itself and to the world (Grigor 2005: 137). Here, an officially sanctioned identity was to be constructed by a selection of objects which served as vehicles for the projection and representation of a narrative, be it past glory and rank in the world's founding civilisations, or contemporary spiritual prominence in the eyes of Islamic nations, or even both (Figure 7.3). Thus, as Arthur U. Pope, the American orientalist, described the Ancient Iran Museum in 1946:

> the National Museum is strong in them [specialised classes of artefacts on display in museums of the Hermitage, the Louvre, Vienna, London, New York, the Victoria and Albert, etc.] all, and in every other it is contestably superior. All the museums in the world together could not equal its collection of Persian prehistoric pottery, or its series of Achaemenid stone reliefs. It is unrivalled in architectural ornament – one can follow here in the finest examples the architectural decoration of every period . . . .
>
> (Pope 1946: 78)

The Museum assumed the task of instructing a 'public', a task that has persisted in the museum despite the change in the focus of instruction. Nevertheless, in its first period, the museum fabricated and inculcated identification with the ancient cultural heritage by implying a rupture with the traditional status quo – the immediate Islamic past. Like the

*Figure 7.3* Linear narration of exhibits at the Ancient Iran Museum.
Photo: the author.

European architecture of National Romanticism, the NMI was 'a modern creation that had to use a historically developed language in order to communicate' (Moravanszky 1997: 70). It was meant to fulfil the dual role of commemoration and education in the one building by leaving a 'marked effect on current Persian culture [and making the citizen proud of] the great tradition to which he is heir [as well as presenting today's artisans] with models of the finest quality' (Pope 1946: 100). This role may be deciphered from the planning of the museum and its curatorial narrative.

## The inception and evolution of the National Museum of Iran

The layout of the Ancient Iran Museum was organised around a ceremonial axis. In the manner of French Baroque architecture, the axis marked a hierarchy of spaces. It tied the museum to its urban setting by organising the landscape and a public garden in front of the building (Figure 7.4). It also set the position of the magnificent entry to the museum, and two internal courtyards provided for lighting in relation to the public garden and thus to the urban context. The typology of the plan of the Ancient Iran Museum may be interpreted as an amalgam of pre-Islamic Sassanian palaces, Beaux-Arts architecture and urban planning of the late nineteenth century. The NMI publications claim more than one Sassanian precedent has informed the architectural style of the building. For example, the organisation of spaces in the plan seems to follow a classical Persian palace layout of internal courtyards with surrounding major halls organised along a central axis, as exemplified by the palace of

*Figure 7.4* Model of the Ancient Iran Museum showing the initial axial design with the Beaux-
Arts style front garden forming an enfilade.

Photo: the author.

*Firouzabad* (early third century AD) in the south of Iran (Pope 1965: 50). The main façade
and the entrance, however, have as their origin another Sassanian monument: the *Tagh-e
Kasra*, perhaps the most famous ruin of the Sassanian period (226–650 AD) of Iran in
Ctesiphon, located in present day Iraq (Pope 1965: 54–7). The main entry portal of the
palace, by which it is identified, is significant in classical Persian literature. It allegorises the
fate of the Persian Sassanian Empire at the hands of Arab Muslims. This archaeological site
is woven with the allegory of ultimate human destiny, death, and therefore becomes an
object of reflection, something to take heed from. It therefore made sense for the proponents
of the resurrection of Iranian glory to find a visible and tangible statement of their ideas in
the symbolic resurrection of that palace in the form of the Ancient Iran Museum.

In any event, whether the choice of a Sassanian reference was made by Godard or in
deliberation with, or in fact as an instruction by, the establishment requires further archival
research (Masoomi 1977: 157). There is, however, documented evidence that in the rising
fever of nationalistic sentiments, the palace of Ctesiphon was one of the allegorical topics of
discussion and the subject of some nationalist writings. Furthermore, prompted by such
sentiments, Reza Khan adopted the Sassanian title of Pahlavi when he established the new
dynasty. A booklet published by the NMI after the Islamic Revolution presents a vague
justification of its architectural style. It reads:

In the plans outlined, it was proposed that the architectural style of the museum building should correspond to themes of the items . . . to be displayed and also be in harmony with Persian history, therefore the façade and the entrance doorway of the museum were constructed in the style of *Tagh-e Kasra* . . . the famous [Sassanian] palace in Tisfun [Ctesiphon].

(Riazi n.d.: 1)

The architecture of the Ancient Iran Museum suggests that there would have been a conception of historicity among those who instigated the museum, since it was an eclectic style predicated upon the appropriation of historical motifs. As mentioned, the museum's architectural style lent itself to interpretations that were congruent with the then dominant political and ideological narratives of nationalism. In a similar fashion to the Louvre after the French revolution, the museum was meant to perform an educational role; it symbolised a point of departure from tradition as opposed to a site of its continuation.

The largely unaltered curatorial narrative of the Ancient Iran Museum also reflects the ethos of the establishment of its time. The chronological curation of displays, in what is almost a loop form from the period of prehistory to the end of the Sassanian period, narrated history in accordance with Darwinian conceptions of evolution and progress. The lower level, which was readily accessible from the street, was dedicated to the objects from the time of Iranian antiquities, while the upper level was given over to the objects of the Islamic Period (Figure 7.5). Contemporary descriptions suggest that the museum, in its displays, reflected a balanced presentation of pre- and post-Islamic periods (Pope 1946). However, after the advent of the Islamic Republic, the dominant, ideologically driven view was that the museum was biased in that it favoured the pre-Islamic period over the Islamic period (Hodjat 1995: 111). Although this was pursued as a state policy, and perhaps interpreted from the museum's architecture as an eclectic, historicist style, there seems to be no evidence to suggest that this was an active curatorial policy. However, by virtue of their location at the lower level, the ancient objects on display were given primary exposure to the visitors and thus could be perceived as of greater significance. They were also representative of the specificity of Persian art in contradistinction to the category of Islamic art, which could be perceived as a label that dissolved specificities of culture and race. One could argue that the combination of the nationalist overtones in the style of architecture and the prominence of pre-Islamic objects on display, possibly created the effect of rendering the Islamic display as secondary. Nevertheless, the objects were understood as historical exhibits, and although perhaps revered they did not participate in the practice of the everyday lives of people, thus implying historical distanciation. This effect was consistent with the rhetoric of the establishment, nuanced by the influence of secularisation and westernisation. However, this perceived prominence of the pre-Islamic was, as is shown below, to be reversed after the Islamic Revolution and the Ethnographic Museum dedicated to the Islamic Period exhibits.

## The Islamic Republic

The advent of the Islamic Republic marked the reconsideration, and in many cases reversal, of the past regime's policies in all areas, including culture and heritage. To the Islamic establishment, the ideological and propaganda intent of cultural heritage for the previous regime was evident. The notion of cultural and historical progress was rejected as a secularist

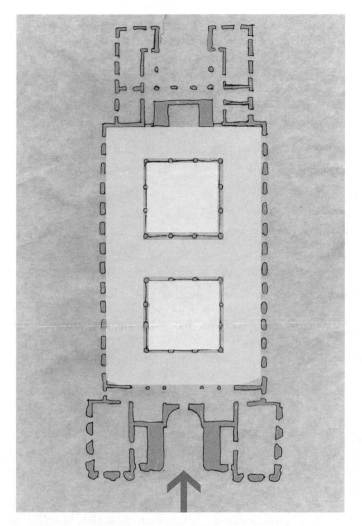

*Figure 7.5* National Museum of Iran: plan of the Ancient Iran Museum. Entrance is indicated by the arrow.

Redrawn by the author.

rupture in the continuity of tradition. An influential line of thought from within the Islamic establishment argued that the West conspired with the Pahlavi establishment to undermine the Islamic part of Iranian identity and heritage under the guise of modernity and progress. In the twentieth century, this 'subversive' movement had three characteristics, which are at the heart of the question of heritage in Iran: 'nationalism, de-Islamization [meaning secularisation], and Westernization' (Hodjat 1996: 162; Kiani 2004). Thus, the ultimate goal of cultural policies would be to reinstate people's Islamic identity through the countering of those three characteristics. The prescribed reaction, then, would be to de-emphasise nationalistic rhetoric of the past, de-secularisation, and the rejection of westernisation, accompanied by an anti-West rhetoric. Opposition to the Pahlavi regime's nationalism (one that was based on identification with Ancient Persia) is apparent in the transformation of the

Ancient Iran Museum to the NMI after the Revolution and in the prominence given to the Islamic Period section of the museum. After all, the belief was that 'Nationalism is planned by plotters to create discord among Muslims and it is being propagandized by agents of colonialization' (Khomeini quoted in Islamic Republic News Agency).

The annexation of the Ethnography Museum in 1996/7 dramatically altered the spatial organisation of the site, previously dominated by the Ancient Iran Museum. The presence of two buildings on the same site, each dedicated to a period of Iranian history, perhaps inadvertently accentuated the rift between the two periods. Indeed, as the visitors' comments book of the Islamic Period section of the NMI suggests, this rift is perceived to be ideologically driven by some of the visiting public:

> Please pay attention to this problem[:] why is the Islamic Period Museum cleaner, nicer, better organized, and larger than the Ancient Iran Museum whilst in terms of civilization, beauty, and spiritual and material supremacy, the Islamic Period is no match for the Ancient times and we have to value [the latter period] above [the former].

The entrance to the site, which was formerly aligned with the ceremonial axis of the Ancient Iran Museum, was now moved to the rather ambiguous position of the void between the two buildings. At present, the exhibition space of the Islamic Period section is arranged in both chronological and thematic fashion over two very large levels. It displays exquisite artefacts, which belong to different origins within Iran and outside of Iran as far as China. Although, from Pope's description of 1946, it appears that the highlights of exhibition have remained the same, the stated intention of the Islamic Period section has been to re-narrate the objects 'in accordance with Islamic art and philosophy' (National Museum of Iran 2002: 1). The wealth of material exhibited in the museum is contextualised in the geographical breadth of Islamic territory after the advent of Islam as a world religion, a territory that rivals that of ancient Persia. The Islamic Period section is also peculiar in that some of the objects on display appear to be part of a living tradition, rather than constituting museological relics characterised by historical distanciation. This peculiarity is pronounced at the heart of the museum; a double-height, domed space at the centre of the cruciform plan of the building. 'Since Islamic civilization and culture stems from the Koran', a square at the centre of the cruciform (Figure 7.6) was purpose designed for the exhibition of Korans (National Museum of Iran 2002: 119). This area is reminiscent of a mosque, symbolised by an altar (mihrab), which, similar to all prayer halls in mosques, points in the direction of Mecca. Facing the altar is the centrepiece of the exhibit, a large manuscript of the Koran. The domed ceiling of the space causes sounds and conversation to reverberate.

There is a well-known precedent for this in the Shah Mosque in Esfahan, which dates back to the Safavid period (1502–1732 AD), the time of the advent of Shiism as the official state religion. The space seems to provide cues for reconnecting with the origins of state Shiism as well as to the quotidian practice of Islam in mosques. Here, the line between the sacred object and the secular, historical relic is rather fuzzy. In the Islamic Period section it seems that for most exhibited objects their 'sacred' aura is intended to be preserved. However, and perhaps because of this, historical distanciation seems to be the key missing element. Thus, the wealth and diversity of objects on display in the Islamic Period section impresses upon the visitor the centrality of Islam in Iranian identity, and supports the cultural policies of the Islamic Republic in two respects. First, it counters the modernising

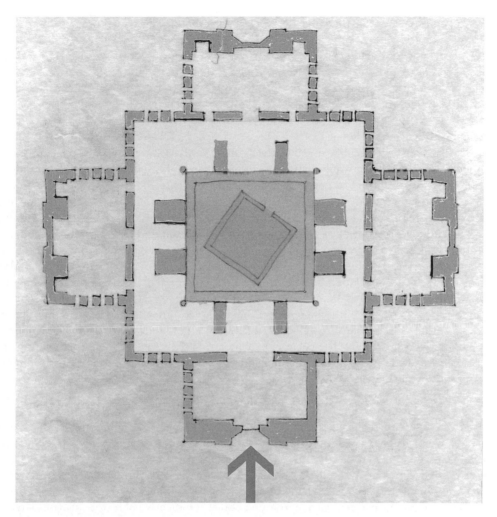

*Figure 7.6* National Museum of Iran: plan of the Islamic Period Section. Entrance is indicated by the arrow and the shaded area in the centre demarcates the exhibition of Korans.

Redrawn by the author.

and historicising rhetoric of the Pahlavi Establishment by reinstating the centrality of religion in daily affairs, including state politics. Second, in so doing it is an attempt to transpose the previously constructed narrative of ancient origins back to one of Islamic, and specifically Shiite, tradition.

In contrast to the previous regime's openness to Western discourses of heritage, now seen to undermine the Islamic traditions of the people, the heritage policies enforced sought to embed Iranian heritage within the normative and immutable body of Islamic laws and Shiite tradition. The immediate impact of embedding heritage into living tradition is the convolution of heritage, marked by historical distanciation, with religious tradition, which is relived through rituals and in 'real time'. This convolution leads to the transposition of formerly secular historic relics back into the realm of the sacred. Thus was the aim of the post-revolutionary narration of relics in the new Islamic Period section. It seems therefore that the result has to be the banishment of objects that do not constitute parts of a living Islamic tradition, especially since the proponents of Islamic revival of heritage in Iran consider genealogy and reverence of past glories to be contrary to Islam (Hodjat 1995: 9). However, in reality, the pre-Islamic objects are still on display. One is led to conclude that such objects are only understood to operate negatively; that is, they provide examples by which the righteousness of religious tradition is confirmed. The rationale for their exhibition has to be for viewers 'to behold ancient works of art, which is to reap admonition and guidance from them' (Hodjat 1995: 110).

In this light, the peculiar mood of the Islamic Period section could be explained. It is argued here that the ambiguous atmosphere of this section stems from the convolution of heritage based on historical perspective and living religious tradition. The participation of objects similar to those on display in the quotidian traditional practices renders them contemporaneous to the viewer. According to the above traditionalist-religious interpretation of heritage, artefacts, by virtue of being part of a sacred tradition, contain a message of truth, which has to be grasped emotionally and intuitively through performing the rituals of the religion. The detached, analytical appreciation of objects and heritage is only secondary (Hodjat 1995: 58–9). One could conclude that the curatorial objective of the museum is for viewers – the majority of whom supposedly come from among the Muslim populace – to 'get admonished, to bear in mind the resurrection, and to acquire knowledge of and faith in the sonnat-ol-lah [God's tradition]' (Hodjat 1995: 111). This is emphasised by the inscription of a Koranic verse, replacing the poem commemorating the deeds of Reza Shah, within the entry portal of the Ancient Iran Museum and in a band above the entrance, which communicates the same message of admonition.

The Islamic Period section is meant to facilitate the construction of truth as a totality. This time, however, unlike the nationalist narrative, which was constructed through the interweaving of mythology, ethnicity, territoriality and material culture, the Islamic narrative is meant to be grasped intuitively. As such, it is predicated upon a notion of a subjectively grasped, transcendental truth that is absolute and is thus ahistorical (Nasr 1989). This section of the museum has to be concerned primarily with enabling the viewer to decipher the immutable truth that is hidden within the object. However, with the exception of the Hall of Korans, the chronological narration of objects indicative of historical evolution and material progress at the lower level and a thematic display of objects at the upper level do little to corroborate the intended spiritual endeavour. One is led to conclude that there is a discrepancy between, on the one hand, the empirical narrative of exhibits and, on the other hand, the metaphysical narrative projected onto them that is coloured by theocratic ideology. This discrepancy seems to suspend the exhibits of the Islamic Period between the realms of the profane and the sacred. The Islamic Period section exemplifies the partial efforts by the Islamic Republic to bring traditional religious practices from the peripheries to the centre, and to reverse the half-complete process of secularisation that began in the twentieth century. It is also an indication that the Islamic establishment's stance on heritage is, paradoxically, static – objectifying the heritage it professes to revive and transforming it into a medium for preaching.

## Conclusion

Thus far, this chapter has shown that the NMI has constituted a register for the battle of ideologies in twentieth-century Iran. Looking back at its evolution, one realises that in each phase of its existence the NMI has symbolised a break with the immediate past while facilitating a form of 'public' education and instruction through its reflection of the dominant ideology of the times. It was initially meant to symbolise a point of departure from tradition, as opposed to being a site of its continuation. However, the efforts of the early twentieth-century intelligentsia backfired in 1979, when an anti-West and traditionally oriented ideology of certain conservative sections of Iranian society took over the apparatus of power. Ironically, the NMI in general, and the Islamic Period section in particular, once again symbolise a rupture that is the result of the new regime's countering of the previous establishment.

Throughout its life, the NMI has symbolised aspects of Iranian identity that have roots in the popular imagination, but their objectification through political ideology has rendered them extraneous to that imagination. Thus, the ambiguities of the NMI in relation to its public become clear. One could argue that had either the nationalist or Islamist ideologies taken root in the popular imagination, the results would have been all encompassing and visible. That is to say, the museum would have been embraced by the populace, attracting devout nationalists prior to the Revolution or devout Shiites taking heed of artefacts after the Revolution. However, this does not seem to be the case.

It is hard to find official documentation of the numbers and attributes of Iranian visitors to the museum in the years prior to the Islamic Revolution. Documented evidence proves that the Ancient Iran Museum was an important site for visiting foreign dignitaries and heads of state (Masoomi 1977: 167–70). This confirms that for the upper echelons of the society, the royalty and the intelligentsia, this museum operated as a representational site for themselves and for foreign visitors. However, one can only make an informed speculation about the relationship between the museum and a broader public. Such an informed speculation suggests that the notion of top-down, or authoritarian, modernisation relied upon enforced public submission to reform, as opposed to democratic participation based on free will. On the other hand, the attitude of the intelligentsia, who, in alignment with the top-down modernisation policies, believed in the rebirth of the Iranian nation out of the corrupt status quo, left little room for voluntary 'public' participation. Some among the intelligentsia even considered that the people (masses) were inferior and undeserving of freedom because 'five million of its seven million populations, in terms of [capacity of] thought are equal to the baboons that Darwin has identified as their ancestors'(quoted in Moazampoor 2004: 118). Naturally, the intelligentsia set the social and cultural norms, and the 'unknowing' populace, presumably, emulated those norms and gradually became cultivated. Thus, the institution of the museum was primarily an instrument for the propagation of the ideology of modernisation, as opposed to a democratic site for public participation.

After the Islamic Revolution, and the change of political rhetoric, the museum has not been flooded with Shiites taking heed of artefacts. The majority of the NMI's visitors seem to be either foreign tourists or to belong to the growing number of organised groups of students on school excursions. It is unclear whether this suggests a belated valuing of the educational and instructive role of the museum or a resurrected nationalism of sorts. This paucity of participation from among the Iranian masses suggests that the museum is disconnected from the populace it is meant to address. Aside from the difficulties associated with ideological projection of the state and the dated narrative of the museum; it may simply be that the link between visiting a museum as a modern cultural practice and other traditional cultural practices in Iran is yet to be established.

It is revealing to contrast the alienated site of the NMI to that of Persepolis (518–330

BC), the ceremonial capital of the Achaemenid Empire and a World Heritage site in Iran (Figure 7.7). Historical evidence suggests that this ancient capital was dedicated to, among other things, the New Year ceremony known as *Nourooz*. The link between Persepolis and the living *Nourooz* tradition was reconstructed in large part by ideological projections of the former Pahlavi monarchy, which designated the Achaemenid Empire as the origin of all Iranians, and furthermore identified Persepolis as their ceremonial capital. Today, however, despite more than twenty-five years of propaganda by the Islamic Republic, the public pilgrimage to this site seems to be stronger than ever. *Nourooz* is a vibrant, non-ideological and non-Islamic traditional practice more than twenty-five centuries old, with a strong basis in popular culture, literature, mores and mythology, and is therefore, unlike the NMI, deeply embedded within traditional Iranian identity. The museum is still waiting for its public.

*Figure 7.7* Persepolis, in the south of Iran.
Photo: the author.

## Acknowledgements

I wish to thank Nigel Westbrook for his helpful comments on this chapter, Mr Mohammed-Reza Karegar, the Director of the National Museum and the Museum's Library, and especially the librarian, Ms. Farideh Shirkhodiee, for facilitating my access to the NMI and its library's resources.

## Bibliography

Adle, C. and Hourcade, B. (eds) (1992) *Teheran Capitale Bicentenaire*, Paris-Teheran: Institut Francais de Recherche en Iran.

Behnam, J. (2005) *Iranian va Andisheye Tajaddod (Farsi)(Iranians and the Idea of Modernity)*, Tehran: Farzan Rouz Publishers, second edition.

Cottam, R. W. (1964) *Nationalism in Iran*, Pittsburgh, PA: University of Pittsburgh Press.

Foran, J. (1998) *Fragile Resistance Social Transformation in Iran from 1500 to the Revolution-Farsi Translation*, trans. A. Tadayyon, Tehran: Rasa Cultural Institute.

Grigor, T. (2005) 'Cultivat(Ing) Modernities: The Society for National Heritage, Political Propaganda, and Public Architecture in Twentieth-Century Iran', unpublished PhD thesis, Massachusetts Institute of Technology.

Hobsbawm, E. J. (1990) *Nations and Nationalism since 1780: Programme, Myth, Reality*, Cambridge: Cambridge University Press.

Hodjat, M. (1995) 'Cultural Heritage in Iran: Policies for an Islamic State', unpublished PhD thesis, The King's Manor University of York.

Islamic Republic News Agency, International Affairs Division Imam Khomeini Cultural Institute. Online. Available at: www.irna.com/occasion/ertehal/english/saying (accessed 17 October 2006).

Katouzian, H. (2003) *Iranian History and Politics: The Dialectic of State and Society*, London: Routledge.

Keddie, N. R. (1999) *Qajar Iran and the Rise of Reza Khan 1796–1925*, Costa Mesa, CA: Mazda Publishers.

Kiani, M. (2004) *Iranian Architecture in the First Pahlavi Era: transformation of Ideas, inception and Formation of the 20-Year period of Contemporary Iran: 1299–1310* (Farsi), Tehran: The Institute for Contemporary Historical Studies.

Manasseh, C. (2006) 'The Cairo Museum, the National Museum of Athens, the Ancient Iran Museum and the Louvre: curatorial practices from East to West and back', in J. Stephens, T. McMinn and S. Basson (eds) *Contested Terrains: Proceedings of the 23rd Annual Conference of the Society of Architectural Historians of Australia and New Zealand (SAHANZ)*, Perth: SAHANZ, 331–8.

Marefat, M. (1988) 'Building to Power: Architecture of Tehran 1921–41', unpublished PhD thesis, Massachusetts Institute of Technology.

Masoomi, G. (1977) *Iranian Archaeology from 2407–2535*, Tehran: The Library of Iranian Centre for Archaeology (*Markaz-e Bastanshenasi ye Iran*).

Miller Lane, B. (2000) *National Romanticism and Modern Architecture in Germany and the Scandinavian Countries*, Cambridge: Cambridge University Press.

Moazampoor, I. (2004) *Study and Critique of Modernist Nationalism in Reza Shah Era (in Farsi: Naghd Va Barrasi-Ye Nationalism-E Tajaddodkhah Dar Asr-E Reza Shah)*, Tehran: The Centre for Islamic Revolution Documents (Markaz-e Asnad-e Enghelab-e Eslami).

Moravanszky, A. (1997) *Competing Visions: Aesthetic Invention and Social Imagination in Central European Architecture, 1867–1918*, Cambridge, MA: MIT Press.

Mozaffari, A. (2003) 'Architecture as a fragment of progress: the case of the Glassware and Ceramic Museum', in G. Hartoonian (ed.) *Progress: Proceedings of the 20th Annual Conference of The Society of Architectural Historians of Australia and New Zealand*, Sydney: SAHANZ, 210–14.

—— (2006) 'The origins of the Ancient Iran Museum (AIM)', in J. Stephens, T. McMinn and S. Basson (eds) *Contested Terrains: Proceedings of the 23rd Annual Conference of the Society of Architectural Historians of Australia and New Zealand (SAHANZ)*, Perth: SAHANZ, 393–400.

Nasr, S. H. (1989) *Knowledge and the Sacred*, New York: State University of New York Press.

National Museum of Iran (2002) *Ancient Iran: A Summary of the Treasures of the National Museum of Iran*, Tehran: Iranian Cultural Heritage Organization.

Pope, A. U. (1946) 'The National Museum in Tehran', *Bulletin of the Iranian Institute* VI, VII, nos 1–4, 1: 78–100.

—— (1965) *Persian Architecture*, London: Thames & Hudson.

Riazi, M. R. (n.d.) *The Iranian National Museum*, trans. S. Bahar, Tehran: Cultural Heritage Foundation and Elam Publication.

Samadi, Y. (2003) *Cultural Heritage in Domestic and International Law Vols. 1–2*, Published in Farsi, 2 volumes, Tehran: Iranian Cultural Heritage Organization, volume 1, 81–2.

Schwarzer, M. (1995) *German Architectural Theory and the Search for Modern Identity*, Cambridge: Cambridge University Press.

# 8

# SCIENCE CENTRES

A museums studies approach to their
development and possible future direction

*Richard Toon*

## The birth of a notion

The notion is the science centre and it was born in North America in the 1960s. Since then, and particularly during the 1980s and 1990s, science centres have spread worldwide. Today there are several national and international professional organizations that together form a global network. The first and largest, with almost 550 members in 41 countries, is the Association of Science-Technology Centers (ASTC) in Washington, D.C. Other groups include the European Network of Science Centers and Museums (ECSITE), which has over 325 members in 45 countries; the Network for the Popularization of Science and Technology in Latin America and the Caribbean (known as Red-Pop), with over 80 members in 15 countries; and the Asia Pacific Network of Science and Technology Centres (ASPAC), with 35 members in 17 countries.

It is virtually impossible to estimate the worldwide audience for science centres as many of the largest belong to more than one network, but ASTC alone estimates 96.5 million visits to its member institutions in 2005; 74.9 million in the United States (Association of Science-Technology Centers 2005). It should also be noted that membership is not confined to museums normally thought of as science centres; indeed, membership is increasingly comprised of natural history museums, nature centres, aquariums, planetariums, zoos, botanical gardens, space museums and children's museums.

However, as one views and counts the results it is clear that in a period of almost forty years a promising new development in museums grew into a worldwide movement. Sheila Grinell provides an often-quoted account of the movement's genesis:

> In the late 1960s, after the decade of reform in science education that followed Sputnik's launch in 1957, several institutions opened that elaborated on the concept of interactivity. The Exploratorium in San Francisco, and the Ontario Science Centre near Toronto eschewed historical and industrial collections in favor of apparatus and programs designed to communicate basic science in terms readily accessible to visitors. These institutions postulated that displays and programs carefully designed to provide first-hand experience with phenomena could captivate ordinary people and, in the best of circumstances, stimulate original thinking about science.
>
> (Grinell 1992: 6–7)

Grinell specifically mentions the Exploratorium and the Ontario Science Centre, both of which opened in 1969, and they have often been recognised as the major pioneers of what has become the science centre movement. It should be acknowledged, however, that other institutions opened earlier that also used the term 'science centre' or were early adopters of the new hands-on or interactive approach to scientific display and interpretation: The Science Center of Pinellas County (1960), The Pacific Science Center (1962), The Center for Science and Industry (1964), The New York Hall of Science (1966), The Fernback Center (1967) and The Lawrence Hall of Science (1968) (Yahya 1996: 124).

Regardless of claims to origins, science centres are undisputedly a product of the 1960s, and Grinell's account describes many of their key elements. Whether they were new institutions or existing museums adopting a new approach, they virtually all embraced a philosophy of learning through interaction or hands-on engagement, which John Durant characterised as involving 'clear, elementary principles [of science] waiting to be discovered by anyone with sufficient child-like curiosity and adult patience' (Durant 1992: 8). The curious and patient proved to be readily available and science centres quickly became popular, not only with the visiting public, but also with researchers exploring museum learning. Indeed a recent review of museum learning literature noted, 'most of what we know about visitors comes from research in this type of museum' (Hooper-Greenhill and Moussouri 2002: 11). The result is that science centres are much studied, but more often than not as sites for the examination of learning rather than as cultural institutions per se. An attempt is made here to redress this balance and to see them more broadly as historically and culturally formed.

## The Cold War context

Our current perspective allows us to see that the founding and growth of the science centre movement took place entirely within the Cold War era – that protracted struggle between the global superpowers of the United States and the Soviet Union and their allies that lasted from about 1947 until the break-up of the Soviet Union in 1991. The era provided inspiration for its content and public support for its potential educational role and pro-science stance. It also had a direct effect on Frank Oppenheimer, the founder of the Exploratorium, often revered as the founder and inspiration of the science centre movement. He was the brother of Robert Oppenheimer and also worked on the Manhattan Project during the Second World War. Like his brother, he became a target of McCarthyism, the anti-communist panic sweeping the United States in the 1950s. He lost his teaching position at the University of Colorado, moving for a time out of professional science altogether. It is perhaps no surprise, therefore, that in the 1960s, when developing ideas for a new museum in San Francisco, he eschewed the political, historical and social dimensions of science and concentrated instead on an abstract mixture of science, aesthetics and experimentation (see Macdonald 1998: 16–17). In the place of the social and historical dimensions of science and technology development, Oppenheimer stressed the individual and creative elements of scientific discovery.

While Oppenheimer's personal biography is relevant to the experience of science the science centre movement promoted, of even greater significance were issues affecting the whole of society at the time, notably the Cold War view that there was a crisis in science and technological education, which was part of an even wider panic about Western society falling behind Eastern bloc achievement. The creation of the Ontario Science Centre, for example, was in part a manifestation of these Cold War fears.

The government of Ontario originally commissioned a new centre as part of Canada's official centennial celebrations (although it did not open in time). Thinking for the project began many years earlier, at the height of the Cold War, with the intention of highlighting and inspiring children and their families to connect to a science and technology that was useful for society. Where the Exploratorium emphasised principles and aesthetic abstractions, the Ontario Science Centre featured applications of science in everyday life. Its designers included historical and contemporary real-life artefacts, but they too believed in the importance of direct experience of science and technology. William O'Dea, the first director general of the Ontario Science Centre, was previously the senior keeper of aeronautics at the Science Museum, London, and as Stella Butler put it, 'His guidance provided a link between the traditional museum approach of artefact-based displays with the new idea of hands-on exhibits' (Butler 1992: 85).

The new science centre approach was meant to intrigue the public and interest them in science activities. The government was also interested because it provided a new means to inform the public about science and technology and perhaps encourage children to develop scientific careers. By the time these new institutions came along the early panic of falling behind the Soviets had somewhat subsided, but the concern in North America to keep up in science and technology was widespread, long lasting, and affected both informal and formal science education for years. As Holdzkom and Lutz described the situation for formal education in the United States:

> The launching of Sputnik aroused public interest, awakened a 'sleeping giant,' and ignited a crash program for curriculum reform in science education. This burst of activity resulted in some of the most current, innovative, and spectacular changes in the history of American public school education. The period that followed has come to be known as the Golden Age of Science Education (1955–74).
>
> (Holdzkom and Lutz 1984: 16)

Many new science curricula were introduced during this period, including a number that Frank Oppenheimer helped develop before he opened the Exploratorium: the Physical Science Study Committee (PSSC) curriculum and the Elementary Science Study (ESS) curriculum (Hein 1990: 13). The affinity between the science curricula reform movement and what was happening in the new museums is clear:

> These new science programs emphasized learning by doing while focusing on current concepts in science. Laboratory activities were an integral part of the class routine. Thus, higher cognitive skills and an appreciation of science were emphasized ... The emphasis was on pure science, doing what scientists do – not on applications of such knowledge.
>
> (Holdzkom and Lutz 1984: 5)

But, by the late 1960s, social values were changing. The rhetoric of science education as laboratory activity was still around, but in San Francisco in particular 'alternative' values were also having an effect on all aspects of cultural life. John Beetlestone *et al.* remarked that, 'Late 1960s San Francisco was not a normal environment, but one where a new, open, evangelical movement could take root' (1998: 17). The need to show national scientific progress diminished and a new ethos, exemplified by the Exploratorium, developed in which the exploration of basic science could be an avenue for personal self-discovery.

Heilde Hein's account of Oppenheimer's new institution reports that the very first exhibits were not, in fact, the type we would now associate with the Exploratorium. Surprisingly perhaps, given the approach the institution is credited with creating, they included a part of the Stamford linear accelerator and 'a collection of materials assembled and contributed by NASA, commemorating the August 1969 lunar landing of the Apollo 11 mission, which coincided with the museum's opening' (Hein 1990: 32). These first exhibits looked back to an earlier era of science display and it was only when the Cybernetic Serendipity exhibition became available a few months later that Oppenheimer felt there was content 'which seemed to embody and harmonize everything the Exploratorium was trying to express' (Hein 1990: 33). The exhibition was first developed by the ICA (Institute of Contemporary Arts) in London and was considered noteworthy enough for the Exploratorium to use it for its official opening in October 1969, keep it running for several years, and to incorporate many of its exhibits into its permanent collection.

The new art and science of cybernetics formed a basic model and inspiration for interactive exhibits, employing feedback mechanisms that changed with human interaction. These exhibits meant cybernetics was not simply an arcane interdisciplinary subject for engineers, mathematicians and early computer scientists, but also, in keeping with the values of the time, a 'technologically utopian structure of feeling, positivistic, and "scientistic"' (quoted in Shanken 2000), an ethos that had a lasting influence on the world of science exhibit design, and certainly longer than in the art world from which it originally sprang.

## Taking the long view

While the Cold War context explains much of the impetus for the development of the first science centres, a longer and broader historical perspective is required to appreciate fully the influences that converged in this distinctive museum form. Indeed, a number of the experiences found in contemporary science centres have significant historical antecedents. It is the packaging of these experiences in a particular institutional form that has proved to be so successful and exportable.

First and foremost is the already mentioned reliance for content on basic scientific principles, using exhibitions illustrating their timeless truths. Indeed, Sharon Macdonald has used this notion to distinguish the science centre from the science museum. As she put it:

> The former [science museums] seek to present science entirely contextualized in a 'slice of history' in a particular community, whereas science centres are more concerned with universal laws and principles which transcend particular times and places.
>
> (Macdonald 1998: 15)

The label texts of interactive science centres – the characteristic 'what to do and what to notice' approach – rarely mentions scientists by name or the historical periods from which so much of their content is drawn. The ahistorical and asocial interpretation of science they present goes virtually unnoticed by visitors and, it must be admitted, by most of those that study them. But the practical advantage of this for a growing movement is clear: if truths of science are universal, then so too are the exhibits that illustrate them. This makes for easy duplication and thematic variation of the basic model in any place, at any time.

The fact that science centre content is characteristically presented ahistorically, however, should not blind us to the fact that this mode of presentation has a history, and one longer than just the past forty years. Indeed, it covers several centuries.

The use of science devices for public teaching purposes goes back at least as far as the mid-seventeenth century, when the subject of experimental philosophy was first taught at Oxford University in England and the University of Leiden in Holland (Turner 1998: 103). The pedagogical science device, therefore, has some roots in *formal* science education, but according to Barbara Stafford there was also an important *informal* educational corollary (Stafford 1994; Stafford and Terpak 2001).

Stafford argues that an important historical change took place as the 'witty and hermetic conceits' of the Jesuits of the high baroque period were transformed in the eighteenth century from devices that 'decorated the surface of privileged leisure' into machines for 'rational recreation' (Stafford 1994: 47–58). Using language that could equally apply to contemporary educational theory in science centres, she describes the intent of those who promoted the study of emerging disciplines of optics, mechanics, astronomy, geometry and physics through 'mechanical amusements': 'Participatory enactment, I suggest, was central to the aim of rational recreation. It made abstraction concrete by picturing the practices of science. Material was internalized interactively' (Stafford 1994: 47). She further comments:

> rational recreations were a sort of joyful diligence. Instructive scientific games were existential rehearsals. They incarnated the unselfconscious art of experimentation fundamental to the laboratory and in ordinary life. Both as instrumentalized performance and as illustrated guide to serious amusements, the genre phenomenologized instruction.
>
> ( Stafford 1994: 51)

Another strand of this history includes the role of public scientific demonstration. Steven Shapin comments, '[Robert] Boyle and his associates developed a variety of relatively novel techniques to assist the transition of experimental and observational experience from the individual to the public domain' (Shapin 1996: 107; see also Shapin and Schaffer 1985). This began with relatively small and closed groups for 'witnessing' scientific experiments in seventeenth-century England and developed into the audiences for the highly popular public science lectures associated with Sir Humphrey Davy and continued by Michael Faraday in the nineteenth century.

By the end of the nineteenth century there had developed in Europe and the United States communities of increasingly professional scientists (who through scientific publications performed 'remote witnessing' for each other) and an interested lay public for them to inform. There were several means by which science went public, including demonstrations and lectures in museums – both 'respectable' museums and the P. T. Barnum-style exhibition (Harris 1973; Alexander 1998) – learned societies, mechanics institutes, as well as popular books and magazines (for a summary, see Gregory and Miller 1998: 19–51).

During this period, new strands of public education and private amusement were added: scientific devices employed in school science experimental demonstrations, the manufacture of scientific toys, particularly those that illustrated the new science of human visual perception (Crary 1990; Turner 1998), and the popularity of World Expositions and World's Fairs (Rydell 1984; The Queens Museum 1989).

Another element from nineteenth-century scientific practice, which is now characteristic of modern science centres, is the way the supposed *objective* truths of science, as they are discovered in interactive exhibits, are experienced *subjectively*. Objectivity and subjectivity merge, or rather the latter guarantees the veracity of the former. This is particularly the case for exhibits of visual perception (although not exclusively so), many of which were first developed in the first half of the nineteenth century as scientific apparatus and soon became domestic amusements. Jonathan Crary in his examination of thaumatropes, phenakistiscopes, zoetropes, kaleidoscopes and stereoscopes (all of which can be found in modern science centres) points to the way they 'collapse' objectivity and subjectivity (Crary 1990: 112). It should also be noted that these devices were developed during a period in which the scientific experimentation was very often performed on the experimenter's own body. Andrew Barry makes the important link between this fact and interactive exhibits:

> Since the late nineteenth century, the significance of a scientist's body to experiment has changed. The body of the practising scientist has become disciplined, capable of performing meticulous practical tasks and making exact observations, but no longer serving as an experimental instrument in itself . . . Experimental events are no longer *experienced* by the scientist; they are *recorded* by the scientists' instruments. By contrast the relatively undisciplined body of the visitor has an increasingly important part to play in the contemporary science museum and what is often called 'the science centre.' . . . In a manner foreign to the practice of contemporary experimental science, the body is itself a source of knowledge.
>
> (Barry 1998: 99–100)

Many contemporary science centre exhibits mediate knowledge through the body, letting the user feel, touch, hear and smell physical forces and explore their own perceptual apparatus. They are, thereby, mimetic, not so much of twentieth- or twenty-first-century scientific practice, but of nineteenth-century practice.

Finally, the major science museums of the twentieth century included elements that are now associated with science centres. For example, the Deutsches Museum demonstrated the actual working of industrial engines from 1925 (Mayr 1990); the Science Museum in London opened the Children's Gallery, which included hands-on exhibits, in 1931 (Science Museum London 1957); and the Chicago Museum of Science and Industry featured push-button devices and live demonstrations in the 1940s (Butler 1992; Caulton 1998). But their approach was directed at the appreciation of scientific and industrial progress, rather than providing an arena for self-discovery through hands-on exploration or demonstration, even in cases where elements of direct involvement were introduced.

What this brief excursion into the history of the formation and content of science centres shows is that even if the historical is eschewed in the interpretations of science by science centres, the influence of the wider historical context has an inevitable influence on purpose and content. As Eilean Hooper-Greenhill suggests, this influence is varied and ever changing:

> There is no essential museum. The museum is not a pre-constituted entity that is produced in the same way at all times. No 'direct-ancestors' can be identified.

Identities, targets, functions, and subject positions are variable and discontinuous. Not only is there no essential identity for museums . . . but such identities as are constituted are subject to constant change as the play of dominations shifts and new relations of advantage and disadvantage emerge.

(Hooper-Greenhill 1992: 191)

## The motley characteristics of the contemporary science centre

The typical contemporary science centre that is heir to this largely unacknowledged past has motley characteristics. The term is not meant pejoratively, but rather an acknowledgement of the variegated form and function that now enables science centres to thrive in so many environments. It is an institution within the museum community, but has considered itself and has been considered by others as a new type of museum with a novel and influential approach to visitor engagement. It is an institution within the education community, but sees itself promoting a new pedagogy in a freer atmosphere than the traditional approach to teaching science. It is an institution in the leisure industry, one among many forms of public entertainment in an entertainment saturated world, but considers itself able to combine fun and learning in a distinctive, compelling and popular way. It is an institution with significant local economic, social and cultural impact, yet is dedicated to promulgating the universal principles of science. In a single institution it claims to combine the four elements that Pine and Gilmore discern in compelling experiences: education, entertainment, aesthetics and escapism (Pine and Gilmore 1999). It even attempts to represent at least two formulations of science: what might be called the 'everyone a scientist' model and the notion that science is the product of specialist knowledge and skills (Rowe 2001). It is, indeed, an institution with diverse goals and aspirations and can be viewed from multiple perspectives.

Inevitably the tensions that develop with such a motley organisation affects both the message (the interpretation of science) and the messenger (the institution proffering the interpretation). These tensions can be treated as a series of dichotomies, each pole of which pulls the centre in a particular direction:

Underlying principle ... Surface phenomena
Learning/education ... Fun/entertainment
Reality ... Appearance
Universal principle ... Particular instance
Certainty of science ... Doubt of experience
Inside/depth ... Outside/surface
Rationality ... Empiricism
Universal truth ... Constructed meaning
Knowledge ... Appreciation
Thinking ... Embodying
Aha! ... Wow!

These form a set of binary opposites. Those on the left-hand side generally belong together, as do those on the right.

The deconstructionist's critique of binary opposites should alert us to the likelihood that one member of each pair is invariably privileged (here the left) and the other marginalised

or denigrated (here the right). Something similar can be found in the literature that criti-
cises science centres for offering their public the triviality of elements of the right-hand side
when their authors consider they ought to be offering them the significance of the left
(Kavanagh 1989; Bradburne 1998; Hughes 2001; Karpf 2002). Two examples illustrate the
tension. First, the virtues of the left-hand side are given in John Durant's description of the
typical science centre:

> Generally speaking, a science centre comprises one or more relatively open spaces
> in which are located a large number of free-standing interactive exhibits. . . .
> Typically, a science centre interactive is a device that embodies an elementary
> scientific or technological principle, and visitors are encouraged to 'play' with this
> device, usually with a minimum of textual or other guidance, in order to 'discover'
> the principle for themselves.
>
> (Durant 1992: 8)

Yet the vices of the right-hand side form James Bradburn's view of science centres:

> The dominant model in which science centres 'vulgarize' knowledge to make it
> palatable to the masses, or sugar-coat science with gratuitous hands-on interaction
> to arouse visitor curiosity, is rarely if ever questioned.
>
> (Bradburne 1998: 120)

A deeper analysis comes from Eilean Hooper-Greenhill, who takes issue with many modern
museum experiences, including those featuring interactive exhibits, because they 'can have
the function, in the apparently democratized environment of the museum marketplace, of
soothing, of silencing, of quieting questions, of closing minds' (Hooper-Greenhill 1992:
214). So, while fun and pleasure are central to the science centre experience, they are also
central to their criticism. Patrick Hughes goes so far as to suggest that science centre entertainment prevents science learning:

> Science centres have proved very popular with visitors, not least because many
> represent science within discourse of fun and spectacle and promote themselves as
> sites where science equals entertainment. Indeed, at many science centres, science
> is totemic – emblematic of the good fortune of contemporary societies – and crit-
> ical appraisal is effectively taboo. The effect is that visitors are prevented from
> acquiring science literacy – the critical resources required to evaluate discourse of
> science representations of science and scientific reports, in order to hold scientists
> to account.
>
> (Hughes 2001: 1)

While some of this is true – science centres do deal in fun and spectacle and critical appraisal
is rare – it is not clear that it is the fun and/or spectacle alone that stops visitors learning or
appraising science. In and of itself, fun does not preclude critical appraisal; indeed, it is the
stock-in-trade of satire, parody and debunking. The taboo against critical appraisal is found
as much in science centres' relationship with other institutions and interests, including
formal educational institutions, government, business interests and their sponsors, who
rarely desire to criticise science and technology. More significantly, the pro and con argu-

ments here all assume the ultimate goal is science learning and that the debate is only over whether the pleasure elements promote or preclude it. But an alternative interpretation of science centres suggests that their goal may not be to provide quasi-classrooms that simply employ entertainment and spectacle to educate. Instead, they can be viewed through the lens of the history outlined above, as theatres or carnivals for science; spaces in which visitors play the role of ritualised scientists for the brief periods they are there.

For ritualised play, science centres do not need to model too closely the actual world of science, which might be thought vital if the goal were 'science literacy' as Hughes suggests. Instead, as argued above, science centres involve their visitors in a symbolic enactment of science activity, drawing on many themes from the history of public science over the past three hundred years. It all takes place, in a special zone, a place set aside, where neither ordinary life nor the world where the work of normal science takes place (Toon 2005). As a form of street theatre it is carnival-like, involving participants in performance, observation, reflection and celebration simultaneously. In this ritualised and liminal safe-space, normal social roles are reversed or combined. Those normally excluded from science become scientists, and visitors' subjectivity and objectivity merge in the cybernetic feedback loop of experience. All of this is temporary, lasting only as long as the visit. Like much else in popular culture, it can be taken as a way of temporarily letting off steam, returning everything back to where it began when the visitor leaves.

The science centre can do all of this and simultaneously reinforce rather conventional views of science. One of its most significant contributions is that in the face of a world dominated by science and technology, the direction and control over which the public has little say, the science centre temporarily transfers control to its visitors as witnesses and enactors of general principles that are not caught up in issues of epistemology, ethics or politics, no matter how much their critics would wish them to be so.

## Future challenge: modernism and postmodernism

Science centres will inevitably change as the movement continues its worldwide expansion and as the relationship of science and technology to society alters. But currently, most science centres exemplify and celebrate the abstract principles of scientific rationalism discovered over many hundreds of years, and they remain wedded to the interactive and hands-on experience that was developed during the Cold War era. In an important sense, they are based on what we might call a modernist view of science, but a postmodernist notion of learning.

The modernist view of science is shown by the fact that despite changes in notions of epistemology in all branches of knowledge (Foucault 1972; McCarthy 1996; Lyotard 1997; Hacking 1999), and in scientific knowledge in particular, science centres largely eschew these concerns, reflecting views of scientific knowledge closer to Thomas Merton's in the 1940s than those of the sociology of scientific knowledge (SSK) movement in the early 1970s. Collectively, SSK critiques and moves away from the philosophical idealism associated with earlier sociologists of science such as Merton, who emphasised the normative structure of science, focusing on its supposed formal characteristics: ethical (scientists use morally and technically efficient methods), universal (science is impersonal and objective), communal (scientific knowledge is public, available to everyone), disinterested (scientific work has no special motives), and possesses organised scepticism (scientific work takes nothing for granted) (Merton 1942 [1973]). While Merton's model still has its supporters –

John Ziman is perhaps an example (Ziman 2000) – those engaged in more relativist and constructivist explorations of scientific knowledge argue that scientific truth it is not independent of the social context of its production in the ways suggested by the Mertonian model.

There is no single reason why science centres' notion of science remains largely Mertonian, but its sense of certainty and objectivity is perhaps more palatable to the public than the unnerving relativism of the constructivist alternative. It must be also be remembered that the science centre model of science closely resembles the model found in contemporary Western schools, which is consequentially one shared by the majority of the 'non-scientific' public. In addition, such an understanding is safe, for its established and universal scientific 'facts' are unlikely to cause offence to visitors or sponsors, compared to those rare exhibits that take on contested social and moral issues. Finally, it is a view of science that many science centre professionals believe in personally.

The science centre movement, however, does not fit perfectly into this characterisation, for while it tends to adopt a realist epistemology when it treats scientific knowledge, it adopts a constructivist view of visitor learning (Association of Science-Technology Centers 1990, 1993). That is, it strongly believes that active participation of the visitor is required for learning through personal meaning making, yet it also believes in an external, objective state of affairs (the truth of those universal scientific principles) that has an existence separate from the learner. One might best characterise it as half-constructivist (the visitor's half): learners construct understandings through interaction and experience with exhibits, or they may come with their own understandings, but these understandings may and often do contain misconceptions, even errors that the science centre experience is specifically designed to address and redress.

So despite the recent crisis of epistemology, which students of museums expect to see manifest in the postmodern museum (Hooper-Greenhill 2000), the scientific modernism of science centres is still extremely popular. Indeed, its popularity may be related to the crisis. Roger Silverstone noted a parallel between the academic deconstruction of certainty and what he considered the public's 'retreat into fantasy' (Silverstone 1989: 187).[1] In the face of this, the science centre may offer a comforting level of certainty. The world is understood in terms of basic principles that can be experienced and even played with. In an age of uncertainty, science centres neither doubt the truths they display nor embrace irrationality. Their optimistic faith in an understandable and controllable nature continues to have broad appeal and gives a sense of security, which, in a reflexive way, makes science attractive.

In North America, where they began, and in Europe, to which they soon spread, science centres developed during a period of unprecedented material domestic progress, progress largely due to scientific and technological innovation. The science centre movement grew rapidly and adapted successfully along the way, contributing to the public's widespread faith in and support for scientific and technological advancement. Perhaps Roger Silverstone's suggestion will come to pass and people in a time of increasing vulnerability and uncertainty will turn to the fantasy end of experience; conversely, they may seek out a deeper understanding of the troubled world around them and be drawn to a deeper exploration, including that provided by science and mediated by science centres. They may even do both. Whatever the outcome, the science centre movement will try to respond. So far, the movement has steadfastly maintained its allegiance to a universal and abstract notion of science mediated to a public through enjoyable interactive encounters. It is not clear, however, if over the longer term such optimism can be sustained and seen as appropriate by its various publics. Thus, changes will continue to be made by science centres as science and the social world alter, and it is to be hoped that future studies will track and interpret these changes.

## Note

1 Silverstone attributes this thought to Christine Brooke-Rose (1981).

## Bibliography

Alexander, E. P. (1998) 'The American museum chooses education', Curator 31(1): 61–80.

Association of Science-Technology Centers (1990) What Research Says About Learning in Science Museums, Washington, DC: Association of Science-Technology Centers.

—— (1993) What Research Says About Learning in Science Museums. Volume 2, Washington, DC: Association of Science-Technology Centers.

—— (2005) ASTC Sourcebook of Science Center Statistics and Analysis, Washington, DC: Association of Science-Technology Centers.

Barry, A. (1998) 'On interactivity: consumers, citizens, and culture', in S. Macdonald (ed.) The Politics of Display: Museums, Science, Culture. London: Routledge, 98–117.

Beetlestone, J. G., Johnson C. H., Quin, M. and White, H. (1998) 'The Science Centre Movement: contexts, practice, next challenges', Public Understanding of Science 7: 5–26.

Bradburne, J. M. (1998) 'Dinosaurs and white elephants: the Science Center in the twenty-first century', Museum Management and Curatorship 7(2): 119–37.

Brooke-Rose, C. (1981) A Rhetoric of the Unreal, Cambridge: Cambridge University Press.

Butler, S. (1992) Science and Technology Museums, Leicester: Leicester University Press.

Caulton, T. (1998) Hands-On Exhibitions: Managing Interactive Museums and Science Centres, London: Routledge.

Crary, J. (1990) Techniques of the Observer: On Vision and Modernity in the Nineteenth Century, Cambridge, MA: MIT Press.

Durant, J. (ed.) (1992) Museums and the Public Understanding of Science, London: London Science Museum in Association with the Committee on the Public Understanding of Science.

Foucault, M. (1972) The Archaeology of Knowledge and the Discourse on Language, New York: Pantheon Books.

Gregory, J. and Miller, S. (1998) Science in Public: Communication, Culture, and Credibility, Cambridge, MA: Perseus Publishing.

Grinell, S. (1992) A New Place for Learning Science: Starting and Running a Science Center, Washington, DC: Association of Science-Technology Centers.

Hacking, I. (1999) The Social Construction of What? Cambridge, MA: Harvard University Press.

Harris, N. (1973) Humbug, the Art of P. T. Barnum, Boston, MA: Little Brown & Company.

Hein, H. (1990) The Exploratorium: The Museum as Laboratory, Washington, DC: Smithsonian Institute.

Holdzkom, D. and P. B Lutz, (eds) (1984) Research Within Reach: A Research-Guided Response to the Concerns of Educators, Charleston, WV: Research and Development Interpretation Service, Appalachia Educational Laboratory.

Hooper-Greenhill, E. (1992) Museums and the Shaping of Knowledge, London: Routledge.

—— (2000) Museums and the Interpretation of Visual Culture, London: Routledge.

—— and Moussouri, T. (2002) Researching Learning in Museums and Galleries 1990–1999: A Bibliographic Review, Leicester: Research Centre for Museums and Galleries, Department of Museum Studies, University of Leicester.

Hughes, P. (2001) 'When 'risk' is taboo: fun, spectacle, and citizenship in science centres', *Open Museum Journal* 4: 1–8. Online. Available at: http://pandora.nla.gov.au/pan/10293/20020120/amol.org.au/craft/omjournal/volume4/hughes_ab.html (accessed 16 November 2006).

Karpf, A. (2002) 'Hands-on museums: just the place to switch minds off'. *The Guardian*, Tuesday 12 March.

Kavanagh, G. (1989) 'Dreams and nightmares: Science museum provision in Britain', in J. Durant (ed.) *Museums and The Public Understanding of Science*. London: Science Museum, 11–14.

Lyotard, J.-F. (1997) *The Postmodern Condition: A Report on Knowledge*, Minneapolis, MN: University of Minnesota Press.

Macdonald, S. (ed.) (1998) *The Politics of Display: Museums, Science, Culture*, London: Routledge.

Mayr, O. (1990) *Deutsches Museum: German Museum of Masterworks of Science and Technology*, Munich: Scala Books.

McCarthy, E. D. (1996) *Knowledge as Culture: The New Sociology of Knowledge*, London: Routledge.

Merton, R. K. (1942 [1973]) *The Sociology of Science: Theoretical and Empirical Investigations*, Chicago, IL: University Of Chicago Press.

Pine B. J. and Gilmore J. H. (1999) *The Experience Economy: Work is Theatre and Every Business a Stage*, Boston, MA: Harvard Business School Press.

Rowe, S. (2001) 'What is "science" anyway? Differing perceptions among science center staff', *ASTC Dimensions*, September/October 2001: 5–6.

Rydell, R. W. (1984) *All the World's a Fair: Visions of Empire at American International Expositions 1876–1916*, Chicago, IL: Chicago University Press.

Science Museum London (1957) *The Science Museum: The First Hundred Years*. London: HMSO.

Shanken, D. A. (2002) 'Cybernetics and art: cultural convergence in the 1960s'. Online. Available at: www.Duke.Edu/~Giftwrap/Ciberartexc.Html (accessed October 2004).

Shapin, S. (1996) *The Scientific Revolution*. Chicago, IL: The University Of Chicago Press.

—— and Schaffer, S. (1985) *Leviathan and the Air-Pump: Hobbes, Boyle, and the Experimental Life*, Princeton, NJ: Princeton University Press.

Silverstone, R. (1989). 'Science and the media: the case of television', in S. J. Doorman (ed.) *Images of Science: Scientific Practice and the Public*, Aldershott: Gower Publishing Company, 187–211.

Stafford, B. M. (1994) *Artful Science: Enlightenment Entertainment and the Eclipse of Visual Education*, Cambridge, MA: MIT Press.

Stafford, B. and Terpak, F. (2001) *Devices of Wonder: From the World in a Box to Images on a Screen*, Los Angeles, CA: Getty Research Institute.

The Queens Museum (1989) *Remembering the Future: The New York World's Fair from 1939 to 1964*, New York: Rizzoli International Publications.

Toon, R. (2005) 'Black box science in black box science centres', in S. MacLeod (ed.) *Reshaping Museum Space: Architecture, Design, Exhibitions*, London: Routledge, 26–38.

Turner, G. L'E (1998) *Scientific Instruments 1500–1900: An Introduction*. Berkeley CA: University Of California Press.

Yahya, I. (1996) 'Mindful play! Or mindless learning!: Modes of exploring science in museums', in S. Pearce (ed.) *Exploring Science in Museums*, London: Athlone, 123–47.

Ziman, J. (2000) *Real Science: What it is, and What it Means*, Cambridge: Cambridge University Press.

# 9

# BEFORE 'TE MAORI'

## A revolution deconstructed

*Conal McCarthy*

Early one morning in September 1984, one hundred Māori elders gathered in the pre-dawn darkness on Fifth Avenue in New York City, outside the Metropolitan Museum of Art. As a *karanga* (call) rang out, they moved up the steps and into the museum, led by warriors in traditional costume. When they arrived at the Rockefeller wing, *tohunga* (priests) wearing feather cloaks proceeded to bless the *taonga* (treasures) in the exhibition. According to *Time* magazine, the opening of 'Te Maori' was the 'most unusual opening' in the 114-year history of the Met (Blake 1984: 40). Hirini Moko Mead, an academic closely involved with the exhibition, described the solemn ceremonies as the 'breakthrough', the moment when their artefacts became art:

> By the time . . . we had finished our *karakia* [prayers], the frenzied clicking of the cameras of the international press present at the ceremony assured us all that this was a historical moment, a breakthrough of some significance, a grand entrance into the world of art. We had suddenly become visible.
>
> (Mead 1984a: 24)

With this dramatic event, the famous 'Te Maori' exhibition entered the international literature, and it has cast a long shadow over museum studies in New Zealand (Clifford 1988: 209–11) (Figure 9.1). This chapter examines the way that objects and their meanings are 'made visible' in museums through contested understandings of cultural heritage. Much research in museum studies investigates changing relationships between museums and native communities, assuming this was a recent development (Shelton in Macdonald 2006; Simpson 1996; Karp and Lavine 1991). Despite twenty years of scholarship in museum history and theory, we still have only a crude and passing acquaintance with the histories of our museums, which are often fashioned to present our recent deeds in a positive light. In the South Pacific, studies from a postcolonial perspective, highly theorised and lacking a detailed historical analysis, tend to present the past as a 'foreign country' (Healy and Witcomb 2006). This chapter argues that museum and heritage studies needs to refine the tools of their analyses in order to deal adequately with the complex realities of post-settler sites. In New Zealand it is important that facile views of the 'dark ages' of New Zealand museology, the period before 'Te Maori', do not distort the particular and localised history of museums and heritage or overemphasise the events of the 1980s. Analysing historical examples of Māori involvement with museums and heritage from the 1930s and the 1900s,

*Figure 9.1* A scene during the welcome ceremony in the Māori Hall after the opening of the 'Te Maori' exhibition, National Museum Wellington 1986.

Reproduced with kind permission of the author.

this chapter attempts to recover Māori responses through an integrated historical analysis that expands museum history and theory beyond presentist readings of colonialism and the Other.

## 'Te Maori' in the longer view

The 'Te Maori' exhibition, which went on a successful tour of US museums in 1984–5, had a profound impact on museums back in New Zealand. The shift from artefact to art and *taonga*, and the move toward 'biculturalism' – the acknowledgement of Māori cultural values alongside those of Pakeha (European) practices, which had been gradually building up since the late 1970s – now suddenly gained momentum with this international exposure. 'The *Te Maori* Exhibition has changed forever the perceived reason for New Zealand museums to hold, study, and display Maori objects', declared the director of the National Museum in 1985. 'No longer can the uninformed public hold the stereotypic idea that Maori culture is "collected" by natural history museums', the director continued, 'as part of an academic and majority culture fascination with things primitive, quaint, tribal, exotic' (National Museum 1985).

When 'Te Maori: Te hokinga mai' returned to tour New Zealand in 1986–7, almost a third of the population saw the exhibition in the four main centres. In particular, the extraordinary response of Māori people to 'Te Maori' revealed an indigenous perspective on cultural heritage. The exhibition established the status of '*taonga*', a Māori culture of display that was closer to the style of presentation of high art rather than the anthropological approach that had dominated in local museums. As Mead explained, the concept of *taonga* was a 'tool of explanation' which allowed Māori to repossess their alienated culture (Mead 1990: 168). But the exhibition was the scene not just for a renaissance of Māori identity but also for Pakeha New Zealanders reforging an independent national identity. Historian Tom Brooking observed that 'Te Maori' marked a turning point in New Zealand history (Brooking 1999: 196–7) and for James Belich (2001: 540–1) the exhibition was a central event in a process of decolonisation.

'Te Maori' certainly had far-reaching consequences for the relationship of Māori to cultural institutions, but there has been a tendency to assume that before 1984 Māori did not attend museums (Mead 1986b). Contemporary commentators thought that when Māori exhibitions were shifted from ethnographic museums to art galleries, or Māori things were displayed in museums in an art gallery style, that this change revealed their artistic and spiritual qualities, which had been neglected by anthropologists for decades (Wilson 1984: 18–19). These carvings, cloaks and other items had always been *taonga* – only Pakeha had just now realised it (Tapsell 2000: 117–18). The awareness that objects, display and audience have a history makes us suspicious of claims for the inherent nature of things, and the discovery of 'new' classes of objects (Kirshenblatt-Gimblett 1995: 148). 'The fact that rather abruptly . . . a large class of non-Western artefacts came to be redefined as art', wrote James Clifford, 'is a taxonomic shift that requires critical historical investigation, not celebration' (1985: 169). It is only by connecting 'Te Maori' to the genealogy of display that the 1980s can be clearly understood in its historical and social context.

It is not the purpose of this chapter to deny the undoubted significance of this exhibition in New Zealand's cultural history. However, twenty years on it is important to assess the frequent claims that 'Te Maori' revolutionised museums, leading to the enlightened 'new museology' of Te Papa, the new national museum, which is often seen as its ultimate expression. It has been regarded as a kind of genesis within a canon of New Zealand museology that was preceded by darkness and ignorance (Te Awekotuku 1985: 54; see also various contributions in *Art Gallery and Museums Association of New Zealand Journal* 16(4) and 17(3), 1986). There have been claims that 'Te Maori' was the first to display Māori carving as *taonga*, and as art, and that before then Māori people had little to do with museums, which effectively ignored Māori people while appropriating their culture (Jahnke 1991: 20; Tapsell 2000: 117). Museum professionals divide museum history into a crude chronology of before and after 'Te Maori', suggesting that everything has now changed (Hakiwai 1990; Tamarapa 1996). The problem is that the period before 'Te Maori' has been constructed as a foil in order to emphasise recent innovations. These views take little account of the complexity of the situation, either now or in the past. This chapter challenges the orthodoxy of the 1980s museology, and in doing so debates issues to do with the study of museums and heritage.

## Museum studies and postcoloniality

At the same time as 'Te Maori' was on display at the Metropolitan Museum, it was business as usual on the other side of Central Park in the American Museum of Natural History, where Māori carvings were presented as artefacts in the Margaret Mead Hall of Pacific Peoples. Meanwhile, downtown at the Museum of Modern Art, the infamous Primitivism show revealed 'affinities' between 'primitive' art and modernism. The 'Te Maori' exhibition attracted a great deal of interest at a time when critics and scholars were debating the politics of representing other cultures. Thomas McEvilley criticised museums for, in effect, colonising non-Western peoples by treating their objects as 'art' (McEvilley 1992: 47). In a series of experimental exhibitions at the Center for African Art in New York, curator Susan Vogel responded to the Primitivism controversy by reviewing a century of different approaches to the display of African objects in American galleries and museums, showing how the presentation became simpler and more aestheticised as African objects became accepted as 'art' (Vogel 1994: 81–95).

Whether they displayed things as beautiful art or as interesting artefacts, anthropologist James Clifford accused both art museums and anthropology museums of ignoring the contemporary lives of tribal cultures 'in the name either of constituting authentic, "traditional" worlds or of appreciating their products in the timeless category of "art"' (Clifford 1985: 171–2). Opinion was divided too about the way carving was enshrined as art in the 'Te Maori' exhibition. While many Māori praised the uncluttered art-style presentation because it approximated Māori responses to object-beings as *taonga*, others were critical and thought the display was cold and lacked a Māori presence (Neich in McCarthy 2004: 232–4). Canadian museum anthropologist Michael Ames described it as 'romantic primitivism' because the 'continuing existence of Māori people' was ignored (Ames 1990: 34). What was absent from this highly theorised debate was a sound historical understanding of how indigenous peoples mediated museum representations of themselves. There was some awareness of Māori agency, but only in the contemporary context. Clifford thought Māori allowed their *taonga* to be appropriated as art in order to enhance their national claims: 'Everybody [was] using everybody', said Clifford, 'and the objects move into new places and old contexts' (Clifford 1987: 150).

Postcolonial studies has followed the lead of the late Edward Said, who urged people to look at culture as a product of colonisation – namely Eastern culture as a product of Western colonisation (Said 1995). However, it seems that much postcolonial writing displays a certain theoretical crudity, which paints a simplistic picture of the process of colonisation and underestimates the complexity of the responses to it. There has been a shift in the literature away from representing the colonised as powerless victims of western hegemony to an exploration of the interactive and cross-cultural nature of orientalism (Hendry 2000; Beaulieu and Roberts 2002). Said himself argued that the best postcolonial writing kept in view both the 'fact of the imperial divide' and the notion of 'shared experiences' (Said 2003: 5). Said has also been influential in the South Pacific, where a small group of scholars have analysed local art and culture in terms of colonisation (Griffiths 1996; Thomas 1994). These writers have tended to concur with Australian cultural historian Greg Dening (1996: 46), who commented that the Pacific, like Said's Orient, was invented by Europe.

Yet analyses of New Zealand museums, in thrall to the theories of cultural studies, have not been attuned to the subtle relations between nation and native in their own distinctive historical context. When it comes to museums, postcolonial literature in and about New Zealand exhibits the failings discussed above (Harple 1996; Corbey 1995; Barrie 1986). Much of this academic research, though useful, lacks a Māori perspective on collection and display, sometimes simply because Māori language material was not used, and it does not consider the possibility of indigenous agency. The application of selected aspects of postmodern or postcolonial theory in relation to contemporary Māori aspirations for self-determination operate in the same colonising mode as the openly orientalist scholarship of fifty years ago (During 1992: 94; Henare 2005: 205–7).

A number of Māori critics have made unreflexive applications of postcolonial language to Pakeha cultural appropriation, portraying colonial history as one-way and one-sided

(Allen 1998; Graham 1995). Linda Tuhiwai Smith sees museums as the result of a Western discourse presenting the indigenous as Other, allowing Pakeha to rule over Māori by studying, describing and authorising their culture (Smith 1999). Others treat colonisation and indigeneity as a more ambivalent and two-sided phenomenon (O'Regan 1999). There is little sense in this work of the historical formation of objects, culture and identity, as if the solution lay in merely 'correcting' the historical record or replacing false representations with 'true' ones. There is an assumption that the essential nature of Māori objects in museum collections remained unchanged through all their 'misrepresentations' until they resumed their 'true' status as *taonga* (Mead 1985; Tapsell 2000, 2006). Simon During (1992: 88) contends that it is the silence of the archive which leads to the production of 'homogenous, a-historical' notions of indigenous tradition. But if the archive is *not* silent, as is shown in this chapter, then traces of indigenous responses to colonisation recovered through a genealogy of display leave open the possibility for future partnerships between museums and their audiences.

International scholarship has begun to move beyond one-dimensional condemnations of colonialism (Loomba *et al.* 2005). New studies focus on the ambiguous nature of relations in settler colonies (Coombes 2006; Henare 2005; Thomas 1999). Exhibitions are now seen as spaces 'where the meanings of objects change', Anita Herle warns, 'spaces for transitive, entangled and contested realities' (Herle *et al.* 1997: 65). Timothy Mitchell (1991), for example, analyses the 'exhibitionary order' through a reflexive approach which incorporates the perspective of the colonial people who are the object of the European gaze, thereby allowing them to become active participants. Christina Kreps (2003) steps outside the western tradition and explores indigenous models for museums and the ways that these have augmented and absorbed western practices.

Within New Zealand, scholars have begun to characterise Māori responses to colonisation in terms of cultural invention, interaction and adaptation (Sissons 1998). James Belich (1996: 271; 2001) has written a new history of New Zealand which foregrounds the 'eager, adaptive and innovative engagement with the things and thoughts of Europe'. His work, part of a worldwide re-evaluation of imperial history (Burdon 2003), provides the historical background against which this chapter views the evidence of Māori agency. Scholars are now critically examining New Zealand's museum history and are situating 'Te Maori' within a 'longer view' (Gathercole 2002; Butts 2003; Henare 2005). A recent study, by the author of this chapter, of Māori exhibitions (McCarthy 2007) examines 'Te Maori' by way of an archaeology of its particular historical moment, suggesting that it was a product of indigenous cultural politics that started in the 1970s. This work all points to 'Te Maori' as the culmination of earlier trends not a 'glorious revolution'. A brief survey of two episodes in this long genealogy of Māori exhibitions demonstrates the richness of the archive and the value of an integrated approach that moves beyond tired reiterations of postcolonial theory.

## 'Symbols of their social life': museums and Māori agency

It was often heard in the 1980s that the new museum displays then coming into fashion were replacing out-of-date representations of 'the Māori as he was'. This section looks closely at how the museum shaped, and was shaped by, its historical setting, prising open the fissures which reveal glimpses of the ways in which Māori became actively involved in museums. When the new Dominion Museum opened in Wellington in 1936, reviews were full of praise for the imposing dimensions of the Māori Hall and its 'priceless treasures', suggesting a celebratory atmosphere in this large open space lacking in the ordered regime of the adjoining ethnographic halls (*Evening Post* 31 July 1936). The centrally positioned meeting house *Te Hau ki Tūranga* symbolised the ambiguous status of Māori culture and its place within the nation. 'The white man, in designing his national treasure house', declared a journalist, 'has certainly given pride of place to the storied history of a proud race' (*Dominion* 1 August 1936).

The way a 'marae' was built into the museum, a house within a house, certainly expressed the assimilationist discourse of the time, the idea that Māori would become brown-skinned Pakeha. Though this may suggest these hallowed halls were an exclusively Pakeha temple of culture, how do we know that there were no Māori visitors, or indeed Māori staff? For these Māori people, did the museum celebrate the glories of their past, or did it signal their absorption into modernity and the nation state? Consider the contemporary photograph of a well groomed young man, a 'modern Maori', visiting the Māori Hall to look 'back into the past' at 'the Masterpieces of his Ancestors' (Anon. 1937: 15). Kingi Tahiwi was a state welfare officer, broadcaster and member of the Ngāti Pōneke Young Māori Club, a man who was at the forefront of the urban migration when many Māori people left their rural homelands for a new life in the cities. As with Pakeha, did Māori like Tahiwi also regard their old carvings as 'masterpieces'? Is it possible that Māori responses to museums did not indicate a preoccupation with the past, but expressed a desire to engage with the present? Despite the rhetoric of assimilation, it is argued here that this space was the site of a Māori attempt to use the treasures of the past to carve out a place for themselves in modern New Zealand society.

The man responsible for articulating a Māori voice was Āpirana Ngata, a lawyer, scholar and MP, who worked to bring about a 'rapprochement' between his people and the state in a number of fields, including anthropology and museums. In 1926 Ngata was instrumental in setting up a School of Māori Arts and Crafts in Rotorua, a state-sanctioned programme to preserve customary practices such as *whakairo* (carving) and *tukutuku* (woven lattice panels) (Walker 2001: 213–14). Through Ngata's involvement in the restoration of *Te Hau ki Tūranga* at the Dominion Museum, the communal revival of Māori arts and crafts and the anthropological category of artefact briefly came together. Apart from the involvement of Māori carver Thomas Heberly (who had been working at the museum for some years), the institution left the project to Ngata and his team of carvers from the School of Arts and Crafts. Despite the fact that it was not completed on schedule, this was the first Māori attempt to conceive, design and install an exhibit in a New Zealand museum (Brown 1995). The old meeting house became a model for the school's plans to reinvigorate the carved meeting house in tribal communities around the country in the form of new houses with carving in a newly traditional style (Ngata 1940).

Rather than endorsing museum anthropology and its display of Māori objects as artefacts, museums were seen as a springboard for cultural maintenance, and display as a means of uplifting Māori pride and unity. Ngata envisaged 'students of Māori art attached to museums', who would eventually take over from the School of Arts and Crafts (Ngata in Sorrenson 1987, vol. 2: 137–8). For example, the school's carvers spent some time at the Auckland Museum with ethnologist Gilbert Archey, studying northern carving styles to use on the new house at Waitangi in the Bay of Islands. This house, *Te Tiriti o Waitangi*, named after the treaty that had been signed nearby in 1840, was the Māori equivalent to the nearby 'Treaty House', which was restored to mark the nation's birthplace. With its spacious interior and pan-tribal iconography, the whare was designed as a monument or museum (Ngata in Skinner 2005: 65).

Ngata's intervention into the culture of display culminated in the 1939–40 Centennial Exhibition in Wellington (Figure 9.2). To an extent, this event shared the ideology of national progress seen at earlier world's fairs, celebrating 100 years since the signing of the Treaty of Waitangi in 1840. Yet Māori were able to present a counter view to assimilation, one which resisted their being consigned to the past or barred from the present. Ngata set up an innovative *whare rūnanga* in the centre of the Māori Court, a 'blend of a beautiful ancient form with modern adaptations' which was said to reflect the 'Māori renaissance' (Anon. 1940: 4). Houses like this, it was claimed, were regarded by Māori themselves not as 'curiosities' or 'relics' but as 'symbols of their social life' (Anon. 1940: 5). According to MP Eruera Tirakātene of Kai Tahu, the exhibition proved that Māori were not dying out, but were 'adapting' to modern life (cited in Palethorpe 1940: 123). Exhibitions of Māori around 1940 were not just European representations of the Other frozen in the ethnographic past, but an indigenous critique of western ideas of heritage and social change. If museums create modern culture by constructing a space where the present is marked off from the past (Prior 2002), then Māori tried to use the past in order to claim the present.

## 'To care for ancient treasures': Pakeha salvage and Māori heritage

Despite its foundational claims, the prehistory of 'Te Maori' stretches back long before the spirited engagement with Western museology that took place in the 1930s. The next case study takes place in the early years of the twentieth century. During the tour of the Duke and Duchess of Cornwall and York to New Zealand in 1901, a large public display of Māori loyalty was staged at Rotorua for the distinguished visitors. During the performances, Māori tribes presented the royal couple with lavish gifts, including rare *kahuwai* (cloaks), old carvings and *mere* (greenstone clubs). Observers were astonished that these objects were given away. A public debate arose about how to prevent the export of such objects, which were coming increasingly to be seen in terms of their value as 'relics'. James Carroll, the Native Minister in Premier Richard Seddon's Liberal government, announced the following year that legislation would be drafted with the aim of 'preserving all Maori works of art' (*New Zealand Parliamentary Debates (NZPD)* 9 July 1901). With a Pakeha father and Māori mother, Carroll was bilingual and had a foot in both worlds. He was a pragmatic politician who worked tirelessly within the government to advance Māori causes, becoming infamous for his '*taihoa*' (wait) policy, which slowed the sale of Māori land. Resistance to Pakeha attempts at assimilation took many forms, but for those Māori who worked within the system, such as the group of parliamentarians known as the Young Māori Party, they were not averse to collaborating with the colonial state (Belich 2001: 210–15). On this issue, however, Carroll received widespread support from Pakeha, and when he presented the Māori Antiquities Act to Parliament in October 1902, it was quickly passed into law (*Herald* 5 October 1901). These parliamentary debates suggest that Pakeha attitudes to Māori material culture were shifting at this time. The elevated status of Māori carving was reflected in the changes to the wording of the bill in committee, where 'antiquity' was substituted for 'relic', and 'curiosities' was replaced by the phrase 'articles manufactured with ancient Maori tools' (*NZPD* 9 October 1901).

But Māori attitudes were also changing. By the late nineteenth century Māori artists had absorbed western ideas about art, which influenced their carving and house design (Neich 2001), and there was ample evidence of a growing sense of cultural heritage which extended and augmented customary practices (McCarthy 2007). In seeking to protect what the Māori

*Figure 9.2* Āpirana Ngata behind the scenes at the Māori court, New Zealand Centennial Exhibition, Wellington 1939.

Reproduced with kind permission of the Alexander Turnbull Library, Wellington, New Zealand (Eileen Deste collection F-18750-1/2).

language version of the bill called 'nga taonga o namata' (treasures of ancient times),[1] the Antiquities Act was not motivated only by Pakeha salvage, but also overlapped with a deep-seated Māori desire to preserve their ancestral heirlooms; what they were increasingly coming to call 'taonga tuku iho' (treasures handed down) (Curnow et al., 2006: 112–17, 174–5). This is demonstrated by the positive reception of the bill in the Māori press, which was not always so approving of government policy. Te Puke ki Hikurangi, for example, welcomed a bill intended to 'care for ancient treasures' (15 November 1901). Others joined in the criticism of gifts lavished on royalty, noting the irony that Pakeha now had more taonga than Māori themselves (Te Pipiwharauroa 1 September 1901). When the Te Arawa whare Rauru was reported to have been sold to a German museum, the editor of Te Pipiwharauroa, Pārākau Maika, called for Māori to hang on to the 'keepsakes' of the ancestors because they were 'chiefly symbols' of the Māori. Rather than selling them off to just any Pakeha and ending up 'hidden in their houses', he urged taonga be given or sold to the government alone so that they can be 'preserved as taonga for the whole tribe' (1 June 1900).

After the legislation was passed, Carroll formed an alliance with a group of sympathetic Pakeha on another scheme of mutual interest: a National Maori Museum. The two leading exponents of this idea were Stephenson Percy Smith and Augustus Hamilton, members of an enthusiastic group of Pakeha who were fascinated by Māori traditions. Hamilton was an English settler who had become famous for his magisterial book on Māori art (1896–1901). When not busy with his day job as Surveyor General, Smith was an indefatigable writer, editor and translator of Māori mythology. Like the Celtic twilight of Irish poet WB Yeats, 'Maoriland' was a romanticised image of an indigenised settler colony constructed through writing, visual culture, music, ethnography and museums. Belich has described how in the late nineteenth century elements of Māori culture were 'collected, laundered and embalmed by Pakeha savants' in order 'posthumously' to provide New Zealand with 'a rich past, runes and ruins.' But the only problem for Pakeha, as Belich pointed out, was that in the midst of this process 'the mummy woke up' (Belich 2001: 124). Māori themselves came to revalue and authorise their 'traditions', participating with the Pakeha salvage project in order to maintain their culture for the future. One chief from Whanganui argued that it was better to 'care for and respect the keepsakes of the ancestors' so that they will 'live long', rather than being 'gnawed by the sun, wind and rain'.[2]

Carroll enthusiastically embraced the proposals for a Māori museum, writing that it had 'long been a desire of mine to see established' (Carroll cited in Pishief 1998: 28). He explained in a letter to Hamilton that he hoped Māori would deposit family heirlooms and tribal history in this museum as a 'constant reminder to the coming generations of the capabilities and taste of the Māori race'.[3] The proposed Māori Museum was meant to be a 'Valhalla for the Maori, a place in which the memories of their great ones can be enshrined and perpetuated' (Hamilton 1902). The plans for the new institution were remarkable for the singular focus on 'the antiquities of the Maori race', as well as the representation on the board: at Carroll's suggestion, three of the seven positions were to be reserved for 'members of the Native race' (Appendices to the Journals of the House of Representatives (AJHR) 1902 G8: 1–3). Sketch plans show a building with a gallery for portraits, statues and pictures of notable events and people in Māori history. The display halls with specimens in cases were a conventional feature of ethnographic museums in the late Victorian period, although the 'application of Maori ornament to modern architecture' was novel. Fully half the space was given over to a large 'winter garden', visible through floor-to-ceiling plate glass windows, showing a village scene with whare (house), pātaka (storehouse) and waka (canoe) animated by papier mâché figures showing activities such as carving and flax weaving (Anon. c.1902).[4] Though these ambitious plans were never realised, Hamilton was ultimately successful in raising the profile and status of Māori collections in museums and of reinforcing the idea of Māori carving as an art form in its own right along the lines of Western arts and crafts. Carroll's support for this campaign was crucial. He was instrumental in having Hamilton appointed as director of the Colonial Museum in Wellington from 1903, found government funding for his numerous additions to the national collection and lobbied for a new building (McCarthy 2004).

A major demonstration of Māori support for Carroll's campaigns for cultural preservation came with the presentation to the government of the meeting house *Tākitimu* by his kinsman the Ngāti Kahungunu chief Tamahau Mahupuku in 1901 (Neich 1994: 303–4). Mahupuku was a wealthy landowner in the Wairarapa region near Wellington (Figure 9.3). He supported the Seddon government, while at the same time hosting major *hui* (meetings) for the *Kotahitanga* (unity) movement which set up an independent Māori parliament (Figure 9.4). His home at Pāpāwai near Greytown was a 'rendezvous for two governments' (Ballara 1993). Mahupuku had his own rifle company, a brass band and a newspaper and was well known for hosting huge picnics and meetings where his friend 'King' Dick Seddon was often present. Regarded by Pakeha as a progressive leader who was trying to modernise his people, 'Sammy' Mahupuku was memorialised in a marble monument designed by the sculptor Nelson Illingworth. A political moderate, he did not support Māori self-determination like

*Figure 9.3* The Pāpāwai marae near Greytown, Wairarapa, showing the meeting house, gateway, palisade fence and monument, 1920s.

Reproduced with kind permission of the Alexander Turnbull Library, Wellington, New Zealand (S.C. Smith collection G-48471-1/2).

*Figure 9.4* This photograph of a *hui* (meeting) with government officials at Pāpāwai marae in the 1890s shows Tamahau Mahupuku (seated on the ground on the left of the table), James Carroll (seated at the table on the left) and probably Tūnuiārangi (standing in front of the house on the right wearing a cap).

Reproduced with kind permission of the Alexander Turnbull Library, Wellington, New Zealand (PAColl-7489-75 F-7886-1/2).

other radical leaders, but favoured a middle path represented by Carroll's Māori Councils Act, which in its early years met some Māori aspirations to local self-government (Hill 2004).

Mahupuku's letter to Carroll is an important statement of Māori heritage values, which not only supports the Pakeha call to 'preserve' history but also expresses a similar agenda from a Māori perspective. While sharing the desire to maintain these cultural objects, he saw them as being alive rather than dead because the past was vitally linked to the present. Evidently, heritage was not something concerned just with the past, but was a marker of modernity because it recycled the past as a regenerative resource (Kirshenblatt-Gimblett 1998: 149–50). The metaphor of *Hine-ahu-one* (the first human or 'earth formed maiden' created by Tāne, the forest god) evokes images of renewal and rebirth. The people will be *physically* reinvigorated, they will literally gain the power of sight through a renewed sense of connection to their ancestral heritage, which will fortify them as they struggle to adapt to modern society. Mahupuku's comments suggest that many Māori at this time had not only come to value and cherish their customary culture and traditions, but had also come to sanction museums as worthwhile places where their material culture might be collected in a way that provided a resource for future generations:

Our hearts were filled with genuine joy . . . when we heard that you had introduced a Bill to Parliament . . . to provide for the collecting, preserving, gathering together the art treasures and insuring the safety of specimens of the handiwork of our ancestors who have passed away from this world – to be kept together in one place and a barrier placed against their removal over-sea . . . That is a step that will cause the minds of the people to reflect on the past, and to cherish, preserve, and venerate the science of their ancestors who are now sleeping in the bosom of their mother Papa-tu-a-Nuku (Mother Earth, wife of Rangi the sky). Such a sentiment stirs the soul, and causes even the eyes that are blind to see, strengthens the muscles that have become benumbed, gives strength to arms and fingers; and the dormant mind is awakened so that it may act with determination, caution, and discrimination, bringing back old time recollections to the heart that had almost forgotten the history of the voyaging hither of the floating vessels of our ancestors . . . Therefore proceed with your work, preserve it in your preserving-chamber, fashion it with the earth of Kurawaka, so that another Hineahuone . . . may arise . . . in the new building-up and collecting-together of our ancient lore, our history, our treasures, our laws, our customs, our sacred rites, and everything that can be preserved of us as a people.

(AJHR 1902 G8: 3–4)

Mahupuku's obituary states that *Tākitimu* was intended to be set up next to parliament 'as a taonga for the whole colony' (*Te Pipiwharauroa* No. 71, January 1904). Another proposal from the Tourist Department was to move it next to the Colonial Museum behind the parliament buildings, in order to 'be used as a museum for Māori implements, ornaments and clothing'.[5] Like a Trojan horse, these plans for the *whare* suggest that Māori saw it as a way of gaining influence in the capital, a statement of bicultural nationhood that reflected their accommodation of Māori self-determination and Pakeha power.

Mahupuku and his people evidently had their own plans for cultural heritage as well. The large *pā* at Pāpāwai was being developed by tribal leaders as a centre for cultural revival. There in 1897, Premier Seddon, the Governor General Lord Ranfurly, and other dignitaries attended the grand opening of the *Aotea-Te Waipounamu* complex, built for meetings of the *Kotahitanga* parliament (Ballara 1993). This modern building was a T-shaped, two-storied, meeting hall with raised dais for speakers. It was a visibly European alternative to the more traditional *whare rūnanga*, the carved and painted meeting houses which were popular among many tribes at this time. Another innovation was the surrounding palisade of the *pā*, which featured carved figures facing inwards to symbolise peace rather than outwards to challenge enemies.

This modern cultural centre was the venue for a number of tribal development projects operating through a Trust, including a *whare wānanga* (tribal university) and 'museum'. Although it is not clear to what extent these plans were implemented, this is a tantalising glimpse of a concrete sense of Māori heritage many years before 'Te Maori'. According to the deed, the Trust was set up with the purpose of:

preserving the specimens of Maori workmanship and carvings and arts and sciences in the said buildings . . . to provide a storehouse or museum for any other such specimens, drawings, sculptures or literature relating to the Maori race.[6]

As well as collecting, it also had a wider social function as a venue for 'religious and tribal observances/meetings affecting the welfare of the Maori race', not just for the *hapu* (sub-tribe) but also for the general public ('Papawai Pa Declaration of Trust' c1907). These initiatives were the work of the *Tāne-nui-ā-Rangi* committee, who worked to collect and record Māori history and *whakapapa* (genealogies) and 'preserve and approve books of Māori tradition' (Ballara 1996). The chairman of the committee was Hoani Paraone Tūnuiārangi, or Major Brown, an educated Anglican of Ngāti Kahungunu descent. Tūnuiārangi led a Māori guard of honour to the Diamond Jubilee celebrations in London in 1897, where he was presented to the Queen (Ballara 1996). He was a member of the Scenery Preservation Society, which set out to preserve native forests and establish national parks (Park 2006: 225–6), and had several articles translated and published in the prestigious *Journal of the Polynesian Society* (Tunuiarangi and Smith 1907). Tūnuiārangi took a leading role in organising large gatherings of *kaumātua* (elders) on *marae* in order to discuss and record traditions. At one *hui* (meeting) in the Dannevirke area, over 200 pages of handwritten *whakapapa* (genealogy) were written down and subsequently stored in the strong room at the local courthouse.[7] After several years, a great deal of material had been gathered, some of which eventually appeared in the *Journal of the Polynesian Society*.

Europeans involved in colonial ethnography understandably have a bad press. But if we are to really understand colonial encounters it is necessary to go beyond simply castigating the coloniser. It has been observed that Pakeha like Augustus Hamilton used Māori culture for their own ends (Mead 1986a). However, it seems just as likely that these Pakeha were used by Māori. Despite Hamilton's at times ethnocentric attitude, his work indisputably earned him the respect of Māori. He acted as trustee for the tribal museum, supported the publication of traditional Māori history, and facilitated research into tribal lore through Māori-speaking ethnologist Elsdon Best (1929). Although the displays at the Colonial and later Dominion Museum looked little different to other ethnographic collections in settler colonies, there is evidence of Māori visitors and considerable interaction with Māori supporters, donors and informants, who were keen to see their knowledge preserved for future generations (McCarthy 2004). That Hamilton's letters and diaries at times reveal the same attitudes as his contemporaries is not surprising, but these should not overshadow his genuine efforts to deal with Māori aspirations, particularly in regard to the efforts of the *Tāne-nui-ā-Rangi* committee to establish a museum and *wananga* (school of learning). Hamilton was given the name '*Tupai-whakarongo-wānanga*' [a counsellor of the tribal wānanga]. Tūnuiārangi (Major Brown) bestowed this honour on Hamilton after he attended a large *hui*, where he told the assembled leaders 'let not the knowledge of your ancestors die away' (*The Advocate* 19 July 1907). It is fitting that on his gravestone the Māori inscription described him as 'someone who cared for the treasures of the past' (Te Papa image library B.10555).

We do not know for sure whether the museum at Pāpāwai was operational, but what is important to note here are the attitudes that lay behind projects even though they may not have come to fruition. It is clear that the intention was to record and disseminate traditional information through the modern media of museums and books, resulting in a 'textual museum' of tribal tradition (Hilliard 2000). Whether in meeting houses, museums or other forms of visual and material culture, Māori always 'found themselves in history' (Johansen in Sahlins 1995: 250). Marshall Sahlins has called this the 'indigenization of modernity' (1993: 21). The remarkable activities of the Ngāti Kahungunu people of the Wairarapa around 1900 represent what we might call the 'indigenization of the museum'.

## Conclusion

Because of the 'Te Maori' effect, studies of museums and heritage in New Zealand have presented an oversimplified view of the formation of the museum, and the audience response to its exhibitions. Postcolonial writing about museums often reproduces North Atlantic ideas in Aotearoa without modification and overlooks submerged histories of indigenous resistance which stretch back long before the 1980s. Even Māori accounts of museums tend to downplay indigenous participation, a surprising history of adaptation that deserves to be recovered as an instructive model for our own times. If indigenous people have *always* challenged Western practices of collection and exhibition, then what does this mean for the museums of the future?

This chapter has demonstrated the usefulness of an integrated model of museum studies which fuses together different approaches – social theory, detailed historical research and a grasp of *te reo Māori me ōna tikanga* (Māori language). Ranging across a broad range of material, and analysing both Māori and Pakeha sources, this research has uncovered a little-known history of active Māori engagement with colonial cultures of display. This history calls into question current orthodoxies about the relationship of museums, indigenous peoples and colonialism. The archive is not silent, and its rich sources may yet lay the foundation for a museum studies which can better serve museums today by more critically reflecting on their past.

## Notes

1 Alexander Turnbull Library, Wellington: 'Ture taonga Maori o namata', [Māori version of the Antiquities Act] 1901, Williams P box q 499M.
2 Te Papa Archives (TPA): Hipango (Ema per Waata Hipango) to Hamilton, October 25 1905. Hamilton correspondence, MU 152, 1/2.
3 Auckland Museum Archives: Carroll to Hamilton, Jun. 8, 1901. Hamilton papers, Ms 131, vol. 11 folder 1 item 5.
4 Archives New Zealand: Anon. (c.1902) 'A rough plan for a suggested scheme of buildings', sketch attached to unpublished manuscript 'Maori antiquities', MA 1, 1906/1413.
5 TPA: Donne to Ward, May 11, 1903. Hamilton Dominion Museum correspondence, MU 152, 9/3.
6 TPA: 'Papawai Pa Declaration of Trust' c.1907, 'Reserve Papawai', MU 152, 4/3.
7 TPA: Hamilton to Carroll, Jul. 20, 1907, 'Dominion Museum correspondence', MU 152, 4.

## Bibliography

Anon. (1937) 'An art inherited', *New Zealand Radio Record*, 10 September 1937.
—— (1940) *New Zealand Centennial Exhibition: The Maori Court. Souvenir*, Wellington: Native Department.
Allen, N. (1998) 'Maori vision and the imperialist gaze', in T. Barringer and T. Flynn (eds) *Colonialism and the Object: Empire, Material Culture and the Museum*, London: Routledge: 144–52.
Ames, M. (1990) 'Biculturalism in exhibits', *Taonga Maori Conference*, Wellington: Department of Internal Affairs, 27–39.
Ballara, A. (1993) 'Mahupuku, Hamuera Tamahau', *Dictionary of New Zealand Biography*, volume 2. Available online at: www.dnzb.govt.nz
—— (1996), 'Tunuirarangi, Hoani Paraone', *Dictionary of New Zealand Biography*, volume 3. Available online at: www.dnzb.govt.nz
Barrie, L. (1986) 'Eurocentrism in a glass box', *Art Gallery and Museums Association of New Zealand Journal* 17(1): 20–2.

Beaulieu, J. and Roberts, M. (2002) *Orientalism's Interlocutors: Painting, Architecture, Photography*, Durham, NC: Duke University Press.

Belich, J. (1996) *Making Peoples: A History of the New Zealanders from Polynesian Settlement to the End of the Nineteenth Century*, Auckland: Allen Lane, Penguin.

—— (2001) *Paradise Reforged: A History of the New Zealanders From the 1880s to the Year 2000*, Auckland: Allen Lane, Penguin.

Best, E. (1929) *The Whare Kohanga and its Lore*, Wellington: Government Printer.

Blake, P. (1984) 'Sacred treasures of the Maoris', *Time*, 24 September.

Brooking, T. (1999) *Milestones: Turning Points in New Zealand History*, Palmerston North: Dunmore.

Brown, D. (1995) 'Te Hau ki Turanga', *Journal of the Polynesian Society*, 105(1): 7–26.

Burdon, A. (ed.) (2003) *After the Imperial Turn: Thinking With and Through the Nation*, Durham, NC: Duke University Press.

Butts, D. (2003) 'Maori and museums: The politics of indigenous recognition', unpublished PhD thesis, Museum Studies, Massey University Palmerston North.

Clifford, J. (1985) 'Histories of the tribal and modern', *Art in America*, Apr: 164–77.

—— (1987) 'Of other peoples: beyond the salvage paradigm', in H. Foster (ed.) *DIA Art Foundation: Discussions in Contemporary Culture, No. 1*, Seattle, WA: Bay Press, 121–9, 142–50.

—— (1988) *The Predicament of Culture: Twentieth-Century Ethnography, Literature, and Art*, Cambridge, MA: Harvard University Press.

Coombes, A. (ed.) (2006) *Rethinking Settler Colonialism: History and Memory in Australia, Canada, Aotearoa New Zealand and South Africa*, Manchester: Manchester University Press.

Corbey, R. (1995) 'Ethnic showcases, 1870–1930', in J. Nederveen Pieterse and B. Parekh (eds) *The Decolonization of Imagination: Culture, Knowledge and Power*, London: Zed Books, 57–80.

Curnow, J., Hopa, N. and McRae, J. (eds) (2006) *He pitopito korero no te perehi Maori: Readings from the Maori-language press*, Auckland: Auckland University Press.

Dening, G. (1996), *Performances*, Melbourne: Melbourne University Press.

Dibley, B. (2005) 'The museum's redemption: contact zones, government and the limits of reform', *International Journal of Cultural Studies*, 8(1): 5–27.

During, S. (1992) 'Post-colonialism: Occasional paper, No. 13', in K. K. Ruthven (ed.) *Beyond the Disciplines: The New Humanities*, University of Melbourne: Australian Academy of Humanities Symposium, 88–100.

Gathercole, P. (2002) 'Te Maori in the longer view', in A. Herle, N. Stanley, K. Stevenson and R. L. Welsch (eds) *Pacific Art: Persistence, Change and Meaning*, Honolulu: University Press of Hawai'i, 271–9.

Graham, B. (1995) 'Trafficking authenticity: aspects of non-Maori use of Maori cultural and intellectual property', *New Zealand Museums Journal*, 25(1): 31–4.

Griffiths, T. (1996) *Hunters and Collectors: The Antiquarian Imagination in Australia*, Melbourne: Cambridge University Press.

Hakiwai, A. (1990) 'Once again the light of day: museums and Maori culture in New Zealand', *Museum*, 42(1): 42–4.

Hamilton, A. (1902) *Notes for the information of Members of both Houses of Parliament, in the matter of the National Maori Museum proposed to be erected in Wellington to carry out the provisions of the Maori Antiquities Act of 1901, and to be a permanent memorial to the past history of the Maori people*, Dunedin: Fergusson and Mitchell.

Harple, T. S. (1996) 'Considering the Maori in the nineteenth and twentieth centuries: the negotiation of social identity in exhibitory cultures', *The Journal of Arts, Management, Law and Society*, 25(4): 292–305.

Healy, C. and Witcomb A. (eds) (2006) *South Pacific Museums: Experiments in Culture*, Melbourne: Monash University Press.

Henare, A. (2005) *Museums, Anthropology and Imperial Exchange*, Cambridge: Cambridge University Press.

Hendry, J. (2000) *The Orient Strikes Back: A Global View of Cultural Display*, Oxford: Berg.

Herle, A., Stanley, N., Stevenson, K. and Welsch R. L. (eds) (2002) *Pacific Art: Persistence, Change, and Meaning*, Honolulu: University Press of Hawai'i.

Hill, R. S. (2004) *State Authority, Indigenous Autonomy: Crown–Maori Relations in New Zealand/Aotearoa 1900–1950*, Wellington: Victoria University Press.

Hilliard, C. (2000) 'Textual museums: Collection and writing in history and ethnology, 1900–1950', in B. Dalley and B. Labrum (eds) *Fragments: New Zealand Social and Cultural History*, Auckland: Auckland University Press, 118–39.

Jahnke, R. (1991) 'Exhibition review: Nga Tupuna at Auckland Museum', *New Zealand Museums Journal* 21(1): 20.

Karp, I. and Lavine, S. D. (eds) (1991) *Exhibiting Cultures: The Poetics and Politics of Museum Display*, Washington, DC: Smithsonian Institution Press.

Kirshenblatt-Gimblett, B. (1995) 'American Jewish life: ethnographic approaches to collection, presentation and interpretation in museums', in P. Hall and C. Seeman (eds) *Folklife and Museums: Selected Readings*, New York: Altamira Press: 143–62.

—— (1998) *Destination Culture: Tourism, Museums, and Heritage*, Berkeley, CA: University of California Press.

Kreps, C. F. (2003) *Liberating Culture: Cross-Cultural Perspectives on Museums, Curation, and Heritage Preservation*, London: Routledge.

Loomba, A., Kaul, S., Bunzl, M., Burton, A. and Esty, J., (eds) (2005) *Postcolonial Studies and Beyond*, Durham, NC: Duke University Press.

Macdonald, S. (ed.) (2006) *A Companion to Museum Studies*, Oxford: Blackwell.

McCarthy, C. (2004) 'From curio to taonga: A genealogy of display at New Zealand's national museum, 1865–2001', unpublished PhD thesis, Museum and Heritage Studies, Victoria University of Wellington.

—— (2007) *Exhibiting Maori: A History of Colonial Cultures of Display*, Oxford: Berg.

McEvilley, T. (1992) *Art & Otherness: Crisis in Cultural Identity*, Kingston, NY: Documentext/McPherson.

Mitchell, T. (1991) *Colonising Egypt*, Berkeley, CA: University of California Press.

Mead, S. M. (1984a) 'Te Maori in New York', *Art New Zealand*, (33): 24–7.

—— (ed.) (1984b) *Te Maori: Maori art from New Zealand collections*, New York: Abrams, American Federation of Arts.

—— (1985) 'Celebrating New Zealand's cultural diversity: A Maori point of view', *Interpreting Cultural Diversity*, Museum Education Association of New Zealand annual conference, Wellington.

—— (1986a) *Te Toi Whakairo: The Art of Maori Carving*, Wellington: Reed Methuen.

—— (1986b) *Magnificent Te Maori: Te Maori whakahirahira*, Auckland: Heinemann.

—— (1990) 'The nature of taonga', *Taonga Maori Conference*, Wellington: Department of Internal Affairs, 164–9.

National Museum (1985) *National Museum Annual Report 1985*, Wellington.

Neich, R. (1994) *Painted Histories: Early Maori Figurative Painting*, Auckland: Auckland University Press.

—— (2001) *Carved Histories: Rotorua Ngati Tarawhai Woodcarving*, Auckland: Auckland University Press.

Ngata, A. (1940) 'Maori arts and crafts', in I. Sutherland (ed.) *The Maori People Today: A General Survey*, Wellington: New Zealand Institute of International Affairs, New Zealand Council for Educational Research: 307–35.

O'Regan, H. (1999) 'If its good enough for you its good enough for me: The hypocrisy of assimilation and cultural colonisation', in J. Brown and P. Sant (eds) *Indigeneity: Construction and Representation*, New York: Nova Science, 193–207.

Palethorpe, N. (1940) *Official History of the New Zealand Centennial Exhibition, Wellington, 1939–40*, Wellington: New Zealand Centennial Exhibition Company.

Park, G. (2006) *Theatre Country: Essays on Landscape and Whenua*, Wellington: Victoria University Press.

Pishief, E. (1998) 'Augustus Hamilton: Appropriation, ownership, authority', Unpublished masters thesis, Museum Studies, Massey University, Palmeston North.

Prior, N. (2002) *Museums and Modernity: Art Galleries and the Making of Modern Culture*, Oxford: Berg.

Sahlins, M. (1993) 'Goodbye to *Triste Trope*: ethnography in the context of modern world history', *The Journal of Modern History*, 65(1): 1–25.

—— (1995) *How 'Natives' Think: About Captain Cook, For Example*, Chicago, IL: The University of Chicago Press.

Said, E. (1995) *Orientalism*, New York: Penguin.

—— (2003) 'Always on top: review of *Civilising Subjects: Metropole and colony in the English imagination, 1830–67*', *London Review of Books*, 20 March, 25(6): 3–6.

Simpson, M. G. (1996) *Making Representations: Museums in the Post-Colonial Era*, London: Routledge.

Skinner, D. (2005) 'Another modernism: Maoritanga and Maori modernism in the twentieth century', unpublished PhD thesis, Art History, Victoria University of Wellington.

Smith, L. T. (1999) *Decolonizing Methodologies: Research and Indigenous Peoples*, Dunedin: Otago University Press.

Sorrenson, M. (ed.) (1987) *Na to hoa aroha: From your dear friend. The correspondence between Sir Apirana Ngata and Sir Peter Buck 1925–1950*, Auckland: Auckland University Press, Maori Purposes Fund Board.

Sissons, J. (1998) 'Introduction: anthropology, Maori tradition and colonial process', *Oceania: Special Issue*, 69(1): 1–3.

Tapsell, P. (2000) *Pukaki: A Comet Returns*, Auckland: Reed.

—— (ed.) (2006) *Ko Tawa: Maori Treasures of New Zealand*, Auckland: David Bateman & Auckland Museum.

Tamarapa, A. (1996) 'Museum kaitiaki: Maori perspectives on the presentation and management of Maori treasures and relationships with museums', *Curatorship: Indigenous Perspectives in Postcolonial Societies: Proceedings of Conference, May 1994*, Canadian Museum of Civilisation, Ottawa: Canadian Museum of Civilisation, 160–9.

Te Awekotuku, N. (1985) 'He tuhituhi noa', *Art Gallery Museums Association of New Zealand Journal*, December 16(4): 54.

Thomas, N. (1994) *Colonialism's Culture: Anthropology, Travel, and Government*, Carlton: Melbourne University Press.

—— (1999) *Possessions: Indigenous Art/Colonial Culture*, London: Thames & Hudson.

Tunuiarangi, H. P. and Smith, S. P. (1907) 'An explanation of certain Maori customs', *Journal of the Polynesian Society*, 15: 129–46.

Vogel, S. (1994) 'History of a museum with theory', in M. N. Roberts and S. Vogel (eds) *Exhibitionism: Museums and African Art*, New York: Center for African Art, 81–95.

Walker, R. (2001) *He Tipua: The Life and Times of Sir Apirana Ngata*, Auckland: Viking.

Wilson, R. (1984) 'A case for the re-evaluation of Maori art', *Art Gallery and Museums Association of New Zealand Journal*, 15(4): 18–19.

# 10

# MUSEUMS, SOCIAL RESPONSIBILITY AND THE FUTURE WE DESIRE

*Robert R. Janes*

This chapter is about the search for meaning among various museums at a time when many of these institutions worldwide are struggling to maintain their stability in the face of the complex challenges of the non-profit world. These challenges range from declining attendance to finding the appropriate balance between earned revenues and public funding, and none of them are easily overcome. At the same time, a growing number of museums are moving beyond the imperatives of the marketplace, with its preoccupation with money and efficiency, to embrace activities that are remote from the bottom line (Janes and Conaty 2005). These museums are not only building new relationships with their communities, but they are also rethinking the meaning of accountability as social institutions. The purpose of this chapter is to explore the meaning of socially responsible museum work, beginning with an overview of several societal issues whose relevance to museum work may not be immediately obvious. This overview is followed by a consideration of why socially responsible museum work is important to the future of museums, including a discussion of several defining characteristics. This chapter concludes with some thoughts on how to embrace the challenges of this kind of work.

## Assumptions

To begin with, the use of the word museum is meant to be inclusive, and includes all types of museums, art galleries and science centres. There are also several assumptions underlying the purpose and intent of this article, the first assumption being that we are the co-creators of our lives and organisations, if we accept this responsibility. By extension, outside experts and advisors do not necessarily know the answers that an organisation needs to solve its problems or improve it (Keating *et al.* 1996: 34). A museum's board, staff and supporters are usually the real experts on the organisation and what is needed, and the challenge is to stimulate further thought through study, dialogue and paying concerted attention to the world outside of the museum. The second assumption is that museums are potentially the most free and creative work environments on the planet. In contrast to the private sector, they do not have production or sales quotas. In contrast to the public sector, they are not forced to administer unpopular government policies. Museums are privileged work environments, because they are organisations whose purpose is their meaning (Handy 1994: 183). Third, it is assumed that the future is not knowable, mainly because the links between cause and effect in organisations are complex, and mostly lost in the detail of what actually happens in between (Stacey 1992: 11). Nonetheless, it is possible to make educated guesses and to influence the evolution of events through the rational application of sound knowledge. Because the future is unknowable, boards, staff and volunteers should not all believe in the same things. They should question every assumption and generate new perspectives through critical analysis, discussion, debate and the testing of alternatives. The fourth assumption is that the purpose of all competent museums and archives is to provide answers to a fundamental question, 'what does it mean to be a human being?' (Postman 1990: 55–8). In short, museums must present the richness and diversity of life, and keep choice and meaningful dialogue alive for all their visitors. As such, museums are valuable social institutions and have no suitable replacement. Finally, it is assumed that learning is essential to intelligent and caring change, and that learning requires that one asks difficult, and often rude, questions in order to challenge conventional thinking. Self-critical thought is now an essential survival skill (Nelson 1989: 45), however reluctant the museum establishment may be to concede this necessity.

## The assault on meaning

It is commonly understood that museums are key agents in the creation of meaning. That is, they create and transfer information and knowledge in an effort to engage visitors in issues that are relevant and significant to them personally and to their communities. In the process, museums assemble and share multiple interpretations, or meanings (Museums Alberta 2003: 44–5). The value of this task has never been more important, especially considering the daily assault on meaning in our lives – a story that began long ago. One observer (McKibben 2003: 15) notes that meaning in human life has been in decline for a very long time, almost since the beginning of Western civilisation. This is in contrast to our hunting and gathering, and agricultural ancestors, whose world and its inhabitants, be they plant, animal or mineral, were saturated with meaning. Nowadays, the widespread belief that nature exists to serve the interests of people has eroded much of what our species once found meaningful. This erosion of meaning is a result of various scientific, technological and societal developments, and it is useful to consider some examples

### *The most ridiculous vehicles ever*

North Americans are obsessed with sport utility vehicles (SUVs), and the production of SUVs and light trucks reached a new record of 18 million in 2005, up some 6 per cent over 2003 (Worldwatch Institute 2005). These vehicles are major consumers of fossil fuel and help to explain why world oil consumption surged by 3.4 per cent in 2004, the fastest rate of increase in 16 years. By forcing a mere 15 per cent improvement in SUV and light truck fuel consumption, Canada and the United States could save more oil each year than the projected annual production of the Arctic National Wildlife Refuge (Roberts 2001: 75). This Refuge is the calving ground for Canada's Porcupine caribou herd, and the Gwich'in First Nation of northern Canada has relied on these animals for 5,000 years. This Refuge is now a target for oil production. Which has the most meaning: fueling SUVs or 5,000 years of cultural diversity?

## Disappearing languages

Moving from vehicles to people, it has been estimated that between 10,000 and 15,000 languages once existed simultaneously in the world (Kane 1997: 130–1). Today, only about 6,000 survive, and only about half of these are being learned by children. As a result, about half of these languages are likely to become extinct within the next century. Every two weeks the world loses another indigenous language (Dalby 2003). In North America, children are learning only 38 of the surviving 187 aboriginal languages. English is now the world's dominant language, with more non-native speakers than native ones. In addition, some 80 per cent of the world's electronically stored information is also in English. Because languages embody the diversity of human experience, and the manner in which we perceive, classify and map the world, we have now constrained the range of our thinking through the loss of these languages. Doesn't this ever-increasing trend towards linguistic homogenisation erode meaning, not to mention our ability to sustain and enhance our understanding of the world?

## Killing our relatives

The last example of the contemporary assault on meaning in our lives has to do with how we treat our closest living relatives – the primates. This is the order of mammals that includes humans, apes and monkeys, and nearly half of the 233 known species of nonhuman primates are now threatened with extinction (Tuxill 1997: 100–1). Our greatest impact on these animals is our practice of taking over their habitat for our own use, in addition to the fact that we are the only primates (with the exception of chimpanzees) who deliberately hunt other primates. In addition, one in four mammal species is in serious decline, mainly due to human activities. In terms of the assault on our own species, every hour the world spends more than 100 million dollars on soldiers, weapons and ammunition (Worldwatch Institute 2005).

Fortunately, there is no international conspiracy on which to blame these senseless developments, although there is good reason to believe that various corporations and governments sometimes work in concert to put profit over people. Nonetheless, one cannot assume that the engineers at Ford, for example, set about to threaten the Arctic National Wildlife Refuge. The problem is much deeper and more insidious, because the problem is all of us (Handy 1997: 28). Many individuals have now entered that deeply perplexing realm of being in conflict with their own sense of values and principles, coupled with a waning sense of meaning.

## The tyranny of economists

All of the previous examples are grounded in a world view based on the belief that continuous economic growth is essential to our well-being, and that the consumption of everything is an appropriate means to achieve unlimited growth. Indeed, capitalism has become inescapable. As philosopher Mark Kingwell (2000: 184) notes 'every moment of waking and sleeping life is shot through with commitment to the goods and services of the global economy'. There is every reason to believe, however, that limitless economic growth is creating genuine and profound dilemmas, and that we are not necessarily happier with buying more material goods (Kingwell 2000: 218).

At the same time, we are faced with a poverty of thought and action, and our reliance on professional economists may be one of the greatest obstacles to achieving some degree of understanding and realism (Wilson 1998: 290). For whatever reasons, traditional economists largely ignore human behaviour and the environment in their analyses and pronouncements. Most importantly, they do not use full-cost accounting, which means that they fail, for example, to recognise the depletion of natural resources as a cost. The general failure of this discipline to acknowledge the real world has not gone unnoticed, however, and economics has been called 'a pseudoscience and a form of brain damage' (Henderson 1980: 22). There is a new sub-discipline called ecological economics, but it is still only marginally influential (Wilson 1998: 292).

It comes as no surprise that museums are not immune to the imperatives of the economists and the marketplace, and there is a growing preoccupation with money as the measure of worth (Perl 2006). This sentiment is now fully installed in the boardrooms of many cultural institutions, with *The Toronto Star* newspaper (Hume 2000) reporting that 'the gap between the haves and the have-nots of the museum world will be greater than ever'. The director of a prominent American art museum is quoted as saying, 'If you want to stay competitive in the cultural arena, you can only do it by investing large sums. That means you have to spend 200 to 300 million just to keep up with the next guy' (Hume 2000: 1–5). Many museums now see no other way but to consume their way to survival or prosperity, failing to recognise that this is an outdated economic perspective.

In pursuit of prosperity, many museums have made the choice to increase their popularity and revenues through high-profile exhibitions and architectural sensationalism, or architectural conceit, depending upon one's perspective. This strategy is so consumptive of staff and money that there is often little left of either to pursue other activities. Yet, various museums are succeeding at this, especially the larger ones, although the long-term sustainability of this approach to business planning is not yet known. A recent research paper prepared for the Getty Leadership Institute (Ellis 2002) concludes that this approach is not sustainable. The problem with the expansion plan, or the galvanising building initiative, as the context to raise funds, refinance and move forward, is cogently summarised as follows:

> this strategy . . . is a form of pyramid selling or Ponzi scheme. Eventually, after the noise has died down and the new building is completed, the logic of the weakening balance sheet kicks in again. Unless the scheme was so successful that it has generated a whole new set of contributed funding opportunities, then the systemic underfinancing reappears, and in a heightened form, given the larger facility and the more ambitious programming on which the facility is premised. The museum stands faced, again, with the three options of crisis appeal, more populist programming, or obfuscatory expansion.
>
> (Ellis 2002: 21)

Some of these museums have also come to resemble corporate entities, with revenues and attendance being the predominant measures of worth. Many of their boards are increasingly indistinguishable from their corporate counterparts, with too many directors being chosen for their business experience, corporate loyalty or ostensible influence in fundraising. Although such qualifications are obviously important, the danger lies in the growing tendency for these boards to self-select on the basis of these criteria, to the exclusion of other attributes such as cultural diversity and community connectedness.

The challenge for museum management is to help governing authorities, staff and society to better understand these complexities and their implications, not the least of which is that the reigning economic growth model is an ideology that has profound implications for museums. This ideology is an integrated set of assertions, theories and aims that constitute a socio-political program. The application of strict economic criteria to museum management is misleading when, for instance, one considers that sound collection management is based on a long-term business plan, not the quarterly results common to business. In contrast, the average lifespan of a multinational corporation (Fortune 500 or its equivalent) is between 40 and 50 years (de Geus 1997: vii).

All of this is puzzling, considering the critical thinking that should accompany the self-proclaimed role of museums as knowledge-based institutions. The belief in limitless growth should be a cause for serious concern among those many museums that have staked their future on attendance figures, architectural vanity and culture as entertainment. Ironically, and despite all of these initiatives, research indicates that the museum sector is struggling to maintain its audiences, and that the visitor base is stagnant or declining (Burton and Scott 2003: 56–7; Cheney 2002; Hill Strategies Research Inc. 2003; Martin 2002), with the exception of public art galleries. Despite the significant progress that individual museums have made in broadening their audiences, there has been little or no diversification in the traditional visitor profile, which is still marked by high income and a high level of education. In addition, there is much anecdotal information that suggests that earned revenues are not infinitely expandable, which is further complicated by the failure of the museum community, at least in Canada, to ponder what constitutes an appropriate balance between public funding, private funding and earned revenues for public museums.

## The marketplace versus social capital

Much of this looming crisis, along with the attendant pressures on museum boards and staff, is a result of a widespread misconception in Western society that markets create communities. The opposite is true, as the marketplace and its activities actually deplete trust (Rifkin 1997). It is the organisations of the non-profit sector, not government or business, which build and enrich the trust, caring and genuine relationships – namely the social capital – upon which the marketplace is based. These organisations range from political parties, to museums, to Girl Guides, and there would be no marketplace without this web of human relationships. Social capital is born of long-term associations that are not explicitly self-interested or coerced, and it typically diminishes if it is not regularly renewed or replaced (Bullock and Trombley 1999: 798).

## Why is social responsibility important?

With this overview of various factors shaping contemporary museums and society, it is appropriate to ask why socially responsible museum work is important. Its importance increases daily, for reasons that are emerging from both the museum community and the larger society. For example, the late Michael Ames, a pre-eminent Canadian museum director, noted:

> My jaded view of museums is a personal view of what we have accomplished here
> and in museums elsewhere. I've always felt that museums should be more interven-

tionist than they manage to be . . . They were designed and constituted to be stabilizing forces, comfortable to work within and pleasant to visit. They don't seem to do much harm, if any.

(Ames 2004)

Ames clearly states that his is a personal view, but there are also societal forces at work which have consequences for museums. In a report (Scott 2003) on the impact of Canada's new funding regime, the Canadian Council on Social Development notes that non-profit and voluntary organisations are constantly juggling their missions to suit the funding agenda in response to a demand for greater accountability. This demand for greater accountability is coming from governments, foundations and private funders, and many of them want museums and galleries to demonstrate their value to their communities, to be more inclusive and to help build stronger communities. In addition, the results of a 2003 survey of 2,400 Canadians indicate that more than half of the respondents believe that 'museums can play a more significant role in Canadian society', although this role was not defined (Canadian Museums Association 2003).

Above and beyond these immediate reasons for paying attention to social responsibility lies another consideration with broader and deeper implications, wherein museums of all kinds could perform an essential service. This consideration is concerned with the management of knowledge, which is done in part by labelling it information, knowledge or wisdom (Hammer in Davis 2005: 2–3). Of particular importance in this hierarchy is wisdom, 'which goes beyond knowledge to incorporate the moral, social, and practical dimensions of solving life-problems in expert fashion'. It can be argued that wisdom is embedded, but too often concealed, in all museums, and that museums are uniquely placed, among contemporary social institutions, in their potential to make the moral, social and practical legacies of human society both visible and accessible – in a way that is free of any particular agenda. Contrary to governments, with their policy agendas, and business, with its profit agenda, museums are empowered to transmit the world's wisdom in a manner similar to a First Nations elder telling meaning-laden stories to her grandchild. This is not a matter of asserting that one cultural tradition possesses the 'right answers', but of making explicit the successes and failures of our species in a manner that could inform and guide contemporary behaviour, whatever the particular society happens to be.

There is a very real and pressing reason for museums to seriously consider their role as brokers of collective wisdom. In a recent book, *The Ingenuity Gap* (Homer-Dixon 2001), the author asks a simple question, 'Can we create and implement useful ideas fast enough to solve the very problems – environmental, social, and technological – we've created?' He looks beyond the conventional panaceas of technological and economic growth, and identifies the lack of ingenuity as our most critical problem. Ingenuity includes new ideas, or innovation, as well as ideas that are not novel, but are nonetheless useful. In short, our world is rapidly exceeding our intellectual grasp.

If human societies are 'knowledge factories', as Homer-Dixon (2001: 36) calls them, then how can the role of museums, as knowledge-based institutions, be ignored in addressing the grim examples of the social and environmental challenges mentioned earlier? It should be noted, however, that the word 'museum' does not appear once in Homer-Dixon's 490-page book. Nonetheless, the role of museums is even more important considering his sombre views on society's inability to solve the problems that are being created (Homer-Dixon 2001: 79–80). He notes that 'an increasingly homogenized, transnational super elite is at work, earning an ever-larger slice of the economic product'. These elite must obviously play a key role in supplying the ingenuity required, but according to Homer-Dixon, 'they are separated from reality, isolated in a land of human construction and human ideas, where reality and illusion are intermingled'.

What social institutions, other than museums, are positioned to demonstrate a sense of place in the scheme of things, a sense of how strange the world is, and of the limits of human knowledge and control? These are critically important as 'we are losing the awe, the respect, and the recognition of mystery that remind us to be prudent' (Homer-Dixon 2001: 95). It is impossible to predict if museums will ever become a source of ingenuity, but there is no doubt that museums are instrumental in generating the social capital mentioned earlier – those dense and meaningful social connections based on trust and reciprocity. It is these social connections and norms that greatly enhance the ability to supply the social ingenuity needed to confront the challenges than humankind faces.

## Two examples of social responsibility

Some museums are fully aware of their role and responsibility in the creation of social capital (Janes and Conaty 2005) and are skilled at creating the trust, empathy and meaning that constitute social capital. The following examples illustrate both substantive and creative commitments to socially responsible museum work.

The first example comes from New Jersey (Koster and Baumann 2005), where the Liberty Science Center took on the role of social activist when they learned that the use of tobacco continues to be the number one adolescent health problem in the United States (Substance Abuse and Mental Health Services Administration 2001). The Liberty Science Center is now actively engaged in telling youth about the realities of smoking, and a key part of their hard-hitting, anti-tobacco program is called 'Live From . . . The Cardiac Classroom'. It uses two-way videoconferencing technology to connect students to a cardiac surgical suite at a major hospital. For two hours, students are immersed in open-heart surgery, which typically begins with a message from the chief surgeon, such as this one:

> Good morning, Liberty Science Center. Today we have a 47-year-old female, over-weight, a lifetime smoker, with no history of heart disease in her family. We antici-pate doing four grafts . . . I can see we have a full room today, tell me a little about your class and your school.

The second example of social responsibility is the McMullen Art Gallery at the University of Alberta Hospital in Edmonton, Canada, a small gallery whose irrelevance had it destined for closure. This purpose-built gallery is located within the hospital, and was founded with the belief that 'art should be where there is hurt and healing' (Pointe 2005: 114). Yet, by 1999, only 4 per cent of the 10,000 annual visitors were hospital patients, and only 15 per cent were hospital staff. All that has changed now, as a result of self-critical analysis and a new sense of purpose. The Gallery now employs visual artists, poets, writers, musicians and a dancer, who work directly with patients and their families in the creative process. Patients paint the windows of their rooms, make murals on hospital walls and create the 'The Poets' Walk', an installation of patients' writing.

After his wife's death in the hospital, a man wrote a note to one of the Gallery's poets. It read:

I want to thank you for your great kindness to my Sofia during her long and horrible ordeal . . . Your visits meant much to her. The words you have written give me solace, and were enormously appreciated by both Sofia and me. Thank-you, they are now treasured mementoes of a difficult end.

These are only two brief examples, and defining what socially responsible museum work means is neither simple nor formulaic, as there are a multitude of possibilities and approaches. It is also important to realise that there are no fixed procedures or rules for engaging in this kind of work, and all museums have the opportunity to explore and discover what is appropriate and useful for them. The underlying premise, however, is the time-honoured assumption that museums exist for the public good. Put another way, social responsibility could be considered the 'will and capacity to solve public problems' (Pew Partnership for Civic Change 2006). Broadly speaking, being socially responsible can also mean facilitating civic engagement, acting as an agent of social change or moderating sensitive social issues (Smithsonian Institution 2002: 9).

## Some characteristics of socially responsible museums

Socially responsible museums have apparently come to a fork in the road, and have chosen a different path for themselves, grounded in a new sense of accountability. In so doing, they have begun to depart from the prevailing preoccupation with money as the measure of worth. A review of several case studies of socially responsible museums (Janes and Conaty 2005) reveals that they all have certain things in common, particularly four values which are apparent in their work (Block 2002: 47–65). These values are idealism, intimacy, depth and interconnectedness, but what do these actually mean with respect to museum work?

Idealism means thinking about the way things could be, and then taking action, rather than simply accepting the way things are. It is this idealism, this striving for constant improvement in the human condition, which lies at the heart of social responsibility. The second value is intimacy, which is about communication, and the quality of the contact that is made. Quality communication lies in direct experience, so it makes sense that electronic and virtual communication are only part of the solution. Although electronic communication lacks quality and intimacy, it does provide broad exposure for museums, which is valuable in its own right. In the end, there is no substitute for human relationships, and all the time, energy and attention these relationships require. Depth is about being thorough and complete, even when this requires a tremendous investment of time and resources. Socially responsible museums have invested enormous amounts of staff time in building relationships with particular groups of people, all in an effort to try to understand what is important. Depth is about thinking, questioning and reflecting, and taking the time to do this. Last, there is interconnectedness, reflected in the growing societal awareness of the deep connections between well-being and families, organisations, the environment and the whole of humanity. It is increasingly difficult, if not impossible, to deny that well-being is fundamentally linked to the health of society and the natural environment (Leonard and Murphy 1995: xi). Even mainstream science is searching for more comprehensive models that are truer to the understanding of the interconnectedness of space and time, and the body and the mind (Kabat-Zinn 1990: 151).

## Some requirements for socially responsible work

In addition to these values of idealism, intimacy, depth and interconnectedness are three other, equally important, considerations that are key organisational ingredients in embarking upon a socially responsible mission. The first of these is the need for shared purpose. Boards of directors, staff, supporters and the community must have an understanding of the museum's purpose, and the commitment to social responsibility must be clearly stated as part of the museum's purpose. The second is the need for active experimentation and the taking of risks. Most innovation occurs from hundreds of small changes and ideas, which add up to enormous differences, and this kind of thinking must be encouraged, recognising that there are never too many ideas. Museums must also confront their traditional belief that they are the authority. Relinquishing some or all of this assumed authority, and becoming more vulnerable, are essential, as socially responsible work is a shared responsibility. Museums must be prepared to reach out to their communities to acquire the expertise and experience they themselves lack. The third consideration is the vital importance of openness. There will always be tension between the individual and the organisation – this is unavoidable. It is important to deal with this tension openly and creatively, so that boards, staff and volunteers feel free to discuss their values and beliefs. This makes for a more authentic museum, and is the foundation for socially responsible work.

## For the sceptics

There are several considerations to keep in mind when thinking about the possibility of museums embracing a larger purpose. First, being socially responsible is not about lowering the intellectual or substantive content of museum work, and latching onto what is the most popular and trendy. The choice of what, and how, to add value to a community is up to the museum, and this inquiry can begin by simply asking if there are any deficiencies in the community that the museum could help to address. Second, being socially responsible is not about abandoning the collections. Collections remain the defining feature of museums, and enhancing their value to the community is only limited by imagination and energy. For example, the Glenbow Museum (Calgary, Canada), in partnership with healthcare professionals, used everyday objects from its collections to help Alzheimer and stroke patients regain their language skills, as objects are powerful memory triggers. Third, being socially responsible is not an either/or proposition. It does not mean putting traditional museum work on hold while doing something new. Regular museum work can continue while also searching for and experimenting with new ways of adding value to one's community.

## Concluding thoughts

There are several suggestions that museum practitioners might consider to enhance their readiness to embrace the possibilities of socially responsible work. The first of these is to 'restore the guardian' (Hawken 1993: 59). As mentioned earlier, governments (or guardian systems) seem to be breaking down, in part because of the money, power and influence exercised by business. There must be a clear demarcation between business and government to ensure that government is accountable for the collective benefits which belong to all of society, such things as justice, peace, clean air and drinkable water. It is common knowledge that various multinational corporations consider the common good to be an arena for private gain.

The so-called experts must also be continually questioned. With science having become the model of explaining reality, along with all of its experts, there is a marked decrease in the reliance of people on their own experience and senses (Franklin 1999: 31). There is inherent and enduring value in local, traditional and experiential knowledge, and it is increasingly important that these resources be respected and used.

A third and final suggestion in contemplating a socially responsible mission is to be aware of postmodernism. This is the school of thought based on the assumption that an 'objective evaluation of competing points of view is impossible, since all points of view are to some extent biased by race, gender and culture' (Woodhouse 1996: 22). The postmodern result can be a mishmash of pluralistic relativism and fragmented pluralism, where everything is of equal weight and value, and everyone does their own thing. Postmodernism has also been called the culture of no resistance, having abandoned the so-called 'arrogance' of trying to figure out the origins, logic, causality and structure of the world we live in (Zernan 2001: 88). Forsaking the effort to understand our shared experience is perilous, especially in light of the consequences of relentless materialism.

It is helpful to consider socially responsible museum work as a purpose-filled experiment, whose intention is just as much about learning as it is about achieving (Block 2002: 3). In doing so, the choice of a worthy destination is more important than simply settling for what will work. This, in turn, requires a willingness to address questions that have no easy answers. This is not as daunting or unrealistic as it may sound, recognising 'that new knowledge comes when you simply bear in mind what you need to know' (Brown in Wilber 2001: 39). Put another way, keep holding the problem in mind and it will yield; it is the will and the passion to do this that are most important. In the words of one of the founders of the voluntary simplicity movement:

> There is nothing lacking. Nothing more is needed than what we already have. We require no remarkable, undiscovered technologies. We do not need heroic, larger-than-life leadership. The only requirement is that we, as individuals, choose a revitalizing future and then work in community with others to bring it to fruition.
>
> (Elgin 1993: 193)

Cultural critic Neil Postman (1985) writes that, as a society, 'we continue to amuse ourselves to death', and museums appear to be increasingly compelled to do the same. Whether it is plastic replicas of Egyptian funerary objects, or the mummified remains of our Neolithic ancestors, many museums have joined the perpetual round of entertainments. The short-term economic necessity of seeing people only as audiences needs no further explanation, but it is also hoped that the search for meaning will survive to inspire the next generation of museum workers, perhaps less beholden to the pressures of the marketplace.

Museums have a role to play in helping to create a continuous sense of a full life, as they are uniquely placed to foster a sense of interrelatedness, along with the deep respect and caring required for intercultural understanding, easing the plight of the disadvantaged and stewarding the environment. Museums, as social institutions, have the potential of one day becoming integral to one's perception of life, a life that is both complete and fully at home in the human community and in the natural world. More practically, socially responsible work is an unprecedented opportunity for museums to renew themselves, and define a more sustainable role in their communities – a role that goes far beyond education and entertainment. This is a choice that any museum can make, and many are already doing so.

In conclusion, what is so often identified as a lack of political will or leadership is, in reality, more often a lack of social or collective will (Homer-Dixon 2001: 331). Museums, art galleries and science centres of all sizes and shapes have a role to play in assuming societal leadership, and together must become more effective in providing insights and answers to the challenges confronting humankind. Understanding does not necessarily mean resolution, as it is 'those problems that we will never resolve that rightly claim the lion's share of our energies' (Conroy 1988: 70). What is essential is the need to keep reflection and dialogue alive, and to avoid stagnation, complacency and the tyranny of economic utility, and thereby address the endless stream of uncertainties, paradoxes and questions that beset any thoughtful museum. The essential task of all sound museum leadership and management is to ensure both individual and organisational mindfulness. It is only through heightened self-awareness, both organisationally and individually, that museums will be able to fulfil the lofty triad of preservation, truth and access (Weil 2004: 75).

## Acknowledgements

This article is based on two public presentations – the first being the '1st Annual Stephen E. Weil Memorial Lecture' at the 2005 Annual Meeting of the Mid-Atlantic Association of Museums (MAAM) in Baltimore, Maryland in October 2005. I wish to thank the Board of Directors and the Executive Director of MAAM for their kind invitation, and for the honour of presenting the first lecture in honour of the late Stephen Weil. The second presentation was a keynote address at 'The Museum: A World Forum' in April 2006, and I thank Simon Knell, Richard Sandell and Barbara Lloyd for both the invitation to speak and their generous hospitality.

I would also like to thank the late Michael Ames, Gerry Conaty, Joy Davis, Joanne DiCosimo, Robert Ferguson, Erica Janes, Joan Kanigen-Fairen, Michael Lundholm, Alan Parry, Kitty Raymond, Michael Robinson, Richard Sandell and Douglas Worts for their insightful comments on earlier drafts of these keynote addresses and the subsequent article. I am indebted to Priscilla Janes for her editorial assistance in reviewing and finalising this text. All of the errors, oversights and fuzzy thinking are mine alone.

## Bibliography

Ames, M. M. (2004) 'Museums – correspondence'. E-mail (23 November 2004).

Block, P. (2002) *The Answer to How is Yes*, San Francisco, CA: Bennett-Koehler.

Bullock, A. and Trombley, S. (eds) (1999) *The New Fontana Dictionary of Modern Thought*, London: Harper Collins.

Burton, C. and Scott, C. (2003) 'Museums: challenges for the 21st century', *International Journal of Arts Management*, 5: 56–68.

Canadian Museums Association (2003) 'Canadians and their museums – a survey of Canadians and their views about the country's museums'. Online. Available at: www.museums.ca/Cma1/Reports Downloads/surveyanalysis2003.pdf (accessed 19 September 2005).

Cheney, T. (2002) 'The presence of museums in the lives of Canadians, 1971–98: what might have been and what has been', *Cultural Trends*, 48: 39–72.

Conroy, F. (1988) *Harper's*, 277: 70.

Dalby, A. (2003) *Language in Danger: The Loss of Linguistic Diversity and the Threat to Our Future*, New York: Columbia University Press.

Davis, J. (2005) 'Mentoring from a social cognitive learning perspective: reflections for the museum sector', unpublished paper prepared for ED-D500 Learning Principles Course. Available from the author.

de Geus, A. (1997) *The Living Company*, Boston. MA: Harvard Business School Press.

Elgin, D. (1993) *Voluntary Simplicity* (revised edition), New York: Quill, William Morrow.

Ellis, A. (2002) 'Planning in a cold climate', unpublished research paper prepared for the Directors' seminar: Leading retrenchment, Los Angeles, CA: The Getty Leadership Institute.

Franklin, U. M. (1999) *The Real World of Technology* (revised edition), Toronto: House of Anansi Press Limited.

Handy, C. (1994) *The Age of Paradox*, Boston, MA: Harvard Business School Press.

—— (1997) 'Finding sense in uncertainty', in R. Gibson (ed.) *Rethinking the Future*, London: Nicholas Brealey Publishing Ltd, 16–33.

Hawken, P. (1993) 'A declaration of sustainability', *Utne Reader*, 59: 54–61.

Henderson, H. (1980) 'Making a living without making money', *East West Journal*, March: 22–7.

Hill Strategies Research Inc. (2003) 'Museums and art gallery attendance in Canada and the provinces'. Online. Available at: www.hillstrategies.com/docs/Museums_report.pdf (accessed 19 May 2006).

Homer-Dixon, T. (2001) *The Ingenuity Gap*, Toronto: Vintage Canada.

Hume, C. (2000) 'Arts story: cultural vacuum' *The Toronto Star* (26 August) 1–5.

Janes, R. R. and Conaty, G. T. (eds) (2005) *Looking Reality in the Eye: Museums and Social Responsibility*, Calgary: University of Calgary Press and Museums Association of Saskatchewan.

Kabat-Zinn, J. (1990) *Full Catastrophe Living*, New York: Bantam, Doubleday, Dell Publishing Group, Inc.

Kane, H. (1997) 'Half of languages becoming extinct', in L. Starke, (ed.) *Vital Signs 1997*, New York: W.W. Norton and Company, Inc. and Worldwatch Institute, 130–1.

Keating, C., Robinson, T. and Clemson, B. (1996) 'Reflective inquiry: a method for organizational learning', *The Learning Organization*, 3: 35–43.

Kingwell, M. (2000) *The World We Want*, Toronto: Penguin Books Canada Ltd.

Koster, E. and Baumann, S. (2005) 'Liberty Science Center in the United States: A mission on external relevance', in R. R. Janes and G. T. Conaty (eds) *Looking Reality in the Eye: Museums and Social Responsibility*, Calgary: University of Calgary Press and the Museums Association of Saskatchewan, 85–111.

Leonard, G. and Murphy, M. (1995) *The Life We are Given*, New York: G.P. Putnam's Sons.

Martin, A. (2002) 'The impact of free entry to museums', *Cultural Trends*, 47: 3–12.

McKibben, B. (2003) 'The posthuman condition', *Harper's* 396: 15–19.

Museums Alberta (1990; 2nd edn 2003) *Standard Practices Handbook for Museums – Book 1*, Edmonton: Museums Alberta.

Nelson, R. F. W. (1989) 'How then shall we live?', *The Post-Industrial Future Project Working Paper No. 2*, Canmore: Square One Management, Ltd.

Perl, J. (2006) 'Arrivederci MOMA', *The New Republic*. Online. Available at: www.tnr.com/index.mhtml (accessed 1 February 2006).

Pew Partnership for Civic Change (2006). Online. Available at: www.pew-partnership.org (accessed 10 October 2006).

Pointe, S. (2005) 'Is art good for you', in R. R. Janes and G. T. Conaty (eds) *Looking Reality in the Eye: Museums and Social Responsibility*, Calgary: University of Calgary Press and the Museums Association of Saskatchewan, 113–27.

Postman, N. (1985) *Amusing Ourselves to Death*, New York: Penguin.

—— (1990) 'Museum as dialogue', *Museum News*, 69: 55–8.

Rifkin, J. (1997) 'The end of work', address on behalf of the Volunteer Centre of Calgary (13 November), Palliser Hotel, Calgary, Alberta, Canada.

Roberts, P. (2001) 'Bad sports', *Harper's*, 302: 69–75.

Scott, K. (2003) *Funding Matters: The Impact of Canada's New Funding Regime on Nonprofit and Voluntary Organizations*, Ottawa: The Canadian Council on Social Development.

Smithsonian Institution (2002) *21st Century Roles of National Museums: A Conversation in Progress*, Washington, DC: Office of Policy and Analysis, 2056000–0039.

Stacey, R.D. (1992) *Managing the Unknowable*, San Francisco, CA: Jossey-Bass Publishers.

Substance Abuse and Mental Health Services Administration (2001) *Summary Findings from the 2000 National Household Survey on Drug Abuse*, US Department of Health and Human Services.

Tuxill, J. (1997) 'Primate diversity dwindling worldwide', in L. Starke (ed.) *Vital Signs 1997*, New York: W.W. Norton and Company, Inc. and Worldwatch Institute, 100–1.

Weil, S. E. (2004) 'Rethinking the museum: an emerging new paradigm', in G. Anderson (ed.) *Reinventing the Museum*, Walnut Creek, CA: AltaMira Press, 74–9.

Wilber, K. (2001) A *Theory of Everything: An Integral Vision for Business, Politics, Science, and Spirituality*, Boston, MA: Shambhala Publications, Inc.

Wilson, E. O. (1998) *Consilience – The Unity of Knowledge*, New York: Alfred A. Knopf Inc.

Woodhouse, M. B. (1996) *Paradigm Wars*, Berkeley, CA: Frog, Ltd.

Worldwatch Institute (2005) 'Vital facts – selected facts and story ideas' from *Vital Signs 2005*. Online. Available at: www.worldwatch.org/press/news/2005/05/12 (accessed 3 April 2006).

Zernan, J. (2001) 'Greasing the rails to a Cyborg future', *Adbusters*, 35: 88.

Part 2

# CHANGING PLACES, CHANGING PEOPLE

# 11

# MAKING PAKEHA HISTORIES
# IN NEW ZEALAND MUSEUMS

## Community and identity in the
## post-war period

*Bronwyn Labrum*

It is a truism that museums have been drawn into debates about the past, its representation and ownership in unprecedented ways (Turner 2001, 2002; Britain 2001, Davidson 2000; Macdonald and Fyfe 1996; Linenthal and Engelhardt 1996, Kavanagh 1996). This recognition has reached beyond the field of museum studies. As other scholars note, 'in our new century there is . . . a growing awareness of the use of museums as powerful institutions for shaping our sense of historical memory' (Adams and Frances 2003: 62). Nevertheless, research in New Zealand and internationally has focused on some topics concerned with representation, ownership of the past and historical memory, to the exclusion of others. Much of the literature in museum studies analyses either indigenous concerns and anthropological collections, particularly in terms of colonialism and post-colonialism (Barringer and Flynn 1998; Simpson 1996; Dorward 1996; Coombes 1994), or the official histories of national institutions in the wake of late-twentieth century debates about the 'nation', national anniversaries and the importance of official collective memory (Neill 2004; McIntyre and Wehner 2001; Boswell and Evans 1999; Dubin 1999; Macdonald 1999; Handler and Gable 1997; Phillips 1996; Kaplan 1994).

Yet, as well as telling important stories about the past, museum collections and exhibitions provide intriguing evidence of the ways that history-making takes place, particularly at the regional or local level. This chapter is concerned with the way that understandings of the 'past' are both made and circulated through such museums, the types of historical narratives that are constructed in this process, and how these might change over time. The chapter focuses on social history collections and displays rather than ethnographic collections and the many different displays and meanings of Maori culture and history within New Zealand museums. This does not mean discussing Pakeha (European New Zealander) history only, but rather the historical stories and events, and the experiences of people that are represented and interpreted in the museum localities. History, in this more specific sense, is most often considered in terms of history curatorship and in examinations of discrete objects and material culture, but is not always linked to historical narratives and people's sense of the past. This is especially so for the period after 1900 in general, and the postwar decades in particular. Most studies of history within museums are conflated with the historical shaping of the modern museum. This means that metropolitan centres and their experiences of the development of the related disciplines of ethnology, anthropology, archaeology and art history in the late eighteenth and early nineteenth centuries are privileged. They take precedence over the formative period of the shaping of history as a discipline in museums in the twentieth century in a wider variety of sites and geographical locations. Studies appear to leap from the imperial/colonial period straight to the postmodern era, as the two key periods of change, with little sense of historical development in between. In other words, history as history easily disappears from consideration.

In a wide-ranging survey of Americans focusing on their myriad connections to the past, historians Roy Rosenzweig and David Thelen concluded that museums and historic sites are 'trusted' by members of the public to convey stories about the past (Rosenzweig and Thelen 2000: 105). Similarly, Chris Healy's examination of history, social memory and colonialism in Australia argued that the way in which the past is constructed in the public imagination produces something called 'Australian history'. His study raises key questions about what history can mean in a postcolonial society (Healy 1997). Writing about the way objects came to be held in contemporary collections in Scotland and New Zealand and the related development of anthropological thought, Amiria Henare refers to the fact that regional history museums and historical/heritage sites are part of 'cultural landscapes', and how they provide evidence of history-making in many different settings (Henare 2005).

This chapter develops these ideas further to include historical developments within and around such collections and their representations. Praising or castigating museums for what they collect or show at one point in time cannot explain how those particular understandings and narratives were arrived at. There is a tendency to analyse contemporary museums, particularly in the field of cultural studies, from a theoretical standpoint which contributes much to the critical literature, but pays less attention to the actual practices in museums and fails to acknowledges their contradictory and complex nature. The tendentious, static and gloom-laden 'readings' of exhibitions that result downplay the multiple ways in which exhibitions may be 'read' and also experienced (Witcomb 2003; Starn 2005). It is as if they were the product of one seamless overarching process or view. As Gaynor Kavanagh has so eloquently put it,

> in many ways, museums are a meeting ground for official and formal versions of the past called *histories*, offered through exhibitions, and the individual or collective accounts of reflective personal experience called *memories*, encountered during the visit or prompted because of it.
>
> (Kavanagh 1996: 1)

For example, sociologist Claudia Bell visited many New Zealand museums in the first half of the 1990s. She saw a Pakeha 'folk-history' in displays that 'appear determined to bowdlerise political issues, offering "untainted" myths of colonial life'. Furthermore, she contended, 'the material in museums tell only one fragment of a single story. Museums lack, at present, ways of telling very many other stories, as preference stays with a decorative version of the past.' She concluded that the 'experience at museums offers a conservative history for undemanding consumers' (Bell 1996: 68, 69, 73, 81). More reflectively, Barbara Kirchenblatt-Gimblett has observed that

> New Zealand tourism projects an imagined landscape that segments the history of the country into three hermetic compartments. The nature story stops with the

coming of people. The indigenous story stops with the coming of Europeans. And the Europeans (and later immigrants) have until recently not been convinced that their story is very interesting.

(1998: 141)

The unanswered questions are why and how have Europeans begun to consider their New Zealand story interesting? For a post-settler nation, part of the explanation lies in more general historical developments and the very recent emergence of a sense of national history. The postwar period, which contrary to many stereotypes was not only a time of conformity, drabness and turning inwards, but also a time of variety, change and experimentation, demands a more critical and close investigation in terms of its relationship to museums, as it has had in relation to other developments (Labrum 2000). Very interesting and important patterns and changes are apparent, decades before the larger shifts in museology and institutions of the late twentieth century which have received so much publicity and analysis.

## The project of finding a country

Until quite recently New Zealand museums, along with those in other former British settler colonies, were devoted to natural history, ethnography or art rather than 'history' per se. They largely ignored the human histories of their own country – still seeing themselves as British and White. These institutions began as museums of natural history then developed collections and displays in industrial, technological and ethnographic knowledge; there were very few non-indigenous historical collections until the 1970s. As Amiria Henare shows, historical collections and displays functioned as memory places for Pakeha, and formed a whiggish, largely triumphalist and laudatory account of settler pioneers, who broke in the land and built up the country into what it had become today (2005). This reflected a 'general absence, or at least a narrow sense, of national and historical consciousness', which only began to change after the Second World War (Gore 2002: 19–20; Labrum 2004). Pakeha New Zealanders were content to see themselves as 'better Britons of the South Pacific' and were late in discovering that they had a history at all (Belich 2001). Historian W H Oliver, author of *The Story of New Zealand* (1960), one of the first general academic histories to be published, said his generation of New Zealanders was involved in 'the project of finding a country by thinking about it' (Oliver 2002). 'New Zealand' was being socially constructed through a discourse of cultural languages – literature, painting, architecture, decorative arts, music and popular culture (McCarthy 2004: 189). The teaching of New Zealand history at universities, the establishment of The Historic Places Trust (the government-supported national heritage organisation), and the growth and reinvigoration of local historical societies all occurred in the late 1950s and 1960s. There were earlier precedents, such as the politician William Pember Reeves' history of labour and social reforms in the late nineteenth century published in 1902; accounts from interwar journalist–historians of the wars between British soldiers and settlers and Maori in the nineteenth century; and the government-sponsored historical commemorations, celebrations and publications of 1940 (the centenary of the signing the Treaty of Waitangi) (Trapeznik 2000; Renwick 2004). But it was the developments of the postwar period that were crucial. James Belich has called the 1960s and 1970s a time of 'decolonisation', both externally, through disconnection from Britain and changing relationships with the rest of the world, and domestically through Maori resurgence and 'the rise of Pakeha groups, notably women, graduates and youths, to a new political and social significance' (Belich 2001: 425).

At the same time as a sense of New Zealand history was quickening, a remarkable number of museums were founded or revived. From just 38 art galleries and museums listed in an official guide in 1958, over the next decade the number of institutions mushroomed: 'especially in collections made on the occasion of the celebration of a local centenary or on the preservation of a house or cottage of some historical merit' (Gamble and Cooper 1969: 5). Of the 112 institutions listed a decade later there were just over 60 'museums', as opposed to art galleries, historical houses or archival collections. Then followed a 'boom period' (McCredie 1999: 14). According to Keith Thomson, however, the:

> apparent rapid increase in the number of museums in the 1970s when more and more communities, celebrating their first century of European settlement, announced their intention of marking the event by providing a material archive of their local history [was] more apparent than real [. . .] as intentions have not always been realised . . . The rosy rhetoric of proud celebrants is more likely to be commemorated in newspaper files than in a rainproof roof sheltering instructive and intriguing exhibits.
>
> (Thomson 1981: 1)

Yet attendance at museums reached more than five million nationwide by 1978, in a total population of just over three million (Thomson 1981: 6).

Developments at the National Museum reflect this overall pattern. The first temporary exhibition of early colonial history was mounted there in 1954 and an honorary curator of cultural history appointed in 1958. The first curator of colonial history began work in 1968 and the Colonial History Gallery was opened in 1969. It remained largely unchanged until the 1990s, however, and was memorably described as

> a mess. The best exhibits are some rooms of English furniture, from the colonial period, and some Victorian dresses. But if you feel a national museum should also try to portray the struggles and achievements of pioneers and settlers . . . the Colonial Gallery doesn't begin to do a good job.
>
> (cited in Gore 2002: 226)

The sense of having an interesting, localised past that is worth representing and preserving in a museum had clearly come into being. Yet why and how that manifested itself at a regional or local level is less clear. A more detailed and critical accounting of the development of 'history' within New Zealand postwar museums is necessary to add depth and clarity to existing generalisations. The rest of this chapter analyses two museums in the Waikato region of the North Island, which are located in areas that witnessed key episodes of Pakeha–Maori interactions in the nineteenth century, through war, religion and trade (Belich 1996). The first one, Te Awamutu Museum, remains a small, localised institution, and in many respects it follows the trajectory outlined above. The Waikato Museum, in contrast, is a larger regional institution located in Hamilton, which is now the fourth largest city in New Zealand. Both these case studies complicate and enrich our understanding of the shaping of history in museums over the twentieth century, and provide important examples of the way that happens in a post-settler society far removed from the metropolitan centres.

## 'Demonstrating the history and culture growth of the area'

The Te Awamutu Museum grew from the formation of the Te Awamutu Historical Society in 1935. With the eminent journalist and historian James Cowan as its patron, the society aimed to 'collect specimens of ancient Maori weapons, implements, carvings, etc. with the idea of later forming a museum' (Evans 1974: 29). Members assiduously recorded local Maori and Pakeha history and historical sites. They also supported and appeared in Rudall Hayward's remake of his silent movie, *Rewi's Last Stand*, a romantic epic set in the Waikato region about the battle of Orakau in 1864, and derived from James Cowan's book *The New Zealand Wars*. The Society suspended its activities during the Second World War although the collection kept growing. Local service club members, the Jaycees, embarked on a building project for the collection and the new premises, known as the Gavin Gifford Memorial Museum, opened on a part-time basis in 1954. As a member recalled,

> In no time at all the building became a depository for items of any description that could be found, scrounged or borrowed. And with them came the cases! . . . A stage was reached where the number and variety of cases and screens were so great that six people could stand in the one display hall and yet remain hidden from each other among the maze of passageways between the ranks of cases.
>
> (J.G.G. 1967. 77)

In the 1960s an archaeological group was formed, the Society began to publish a journal, and members took part in community activities for the centenary of the Battle of Orakau in 1964.

In 1967, the interior of the museum was completely reorganised and painted, with the assistance of a grant from the Queen Elizabeth II Arts Council, because of the 'need to up-date displays and bring them into line with modern trends' (Evans 1974: 31). Several principles guided the Society's planning:

> . . . the Museum, being on a relatively small scale, should confine itself to being a very good folk-museum, telling only the history of its own district, with the provision, however, for displaying any special exhibition which may become available on a short-term basis.
>
> (J.G.G. 1967: 78)

Interestingly, English museum consultant K.A. Webster advocated a national early settlers' park on a visit to New Zealand in the late 1950s, drawing on the contemporary North American and European movement for folk and outdoor museums. The park should be an area 'not just a building housing bygones in glass cases. It is not enough to show series of objects in static display. They must be given life . . . be in the same surroundings as when they were used' (Webster 1959: 14). While the 'collections illustrate the history of the district, Maori, Missionary, Waikato War and pioneering periods' (Gamble and Cooper 1969: 24), over half the entire display space was devoted to 'Maori culture', and there were four cases devoted to the 'Colonial Exhibit'. Many displays had been cut drastically or removed completely, including 'large Boer War and World War' displays, 'which attract very little local interest'. The museum expressed a 'new attitude' on the part of the Historical Society, 'which is aimed at interesting the disinterested visitor by capturing his imagination with vivid display, bringing home to him at least a little of the story of times gone by' (J.G.G. 1967: 79).

Eight years later, supported by Borough Council funding, the Te Awamutu and District Museum was opened in a new building. Staff anticipated longer opening hours and greater accessibility to the public. The museum was still described as a local 'folk' museum, dedicated to 'preserving and demonstrating the history and cultural growth of the area' (Anon 1995: 21). Its 'collections mainly related to Maori culture, Missions, Land Wars and the pioneer period of the district' (Evans 1976: 64). On entering the gallery the visitor encountered the museum's 'fine collection of Maori artefacts', proceeding then to either the Mission section, which emphasised the Otawhao Mission, or the Military section, which concentrated on the district's involvement in the nineteenth-century Land Wars (later called The New Zealand Wars), and included weaponry and medals. (From the 1840s to the 1870s British and colonial forces fought to open up the North Island for settlement. Many Maori died defending their land; others allied themselves with the colonists to settle old scores.) The rest of the museum contained 'small pioneer and natural history displays' (Evans 1976: 65). The upper gallery was used for craft demonstrations, recitals and temporary exhibitions of photography, painting and carving. Pending more funding, it was intended that the pioneer section would be extended to 'village type displays (rooms of a cottage, blacksmith, saddler, shops, chemist, etc.)' (Evans 1976: 65). Because the museum had accumulated a sizable amount of documentary material, including historical documents and records of the early colonial period from official, civic and private organisations and individuals, the institution established a formally-constituted archive, which became a nationally significant registered repository.

Careful consideration of collection and display at the Te Awamutu Museum reveals a rather more complex situation than is often recognised in the literature. Conventional understandings of history and historical importance, with a strong emphasis on pioneering, war and politics, are abundantly represented. Yet we see here, in this post-settler context, a strong interest in Maori culture and artefacts. This is in marked contrast to other colonial contexts where the indigenous are absent from collections, except as literally dead objects of ethnology and anthropology (Healy 1997). Chris Hilliard has written about this systematic and dedicated collecting and recording in New Zealand in terms of an ideology of rescue and salvage of both Maori and Pakeha ways of life (Hilliard 2000). In this respect, the importance of the museum's physical location in terms of its proximity to past mission stations and wars is crucial. This history and heritage was literally all around the museum's staff and supporters. By contrast, other military topics related to empire and the world, more removed from local experiences, were less appealing. The conventions around history and heritage only went so far. Perhaps more unexpectedly, given the small size and meagre resources of the institution, broader trends in museology were self-consciously at work in the positioning of the institution as a folk museum, as well as the awareness of the needs of visitors, a concern with professionalism and standards, and anxiety about being up to date. In the formative period of Te Awamutu Museum's development, it was supported by AGMANZ, the National Art Gallery and Museums Association, which was extremely active. Finally, the constitution and importance of the museum's archive, while itself an act of salvage and rescue, also suggests a different conception of history from that articulated by Bell and Kirschenblatt-Gimblett.

## Experimenting with 'culture history'

The Waikato Museum, situated on the top floor of the Hamilton Public Library, and administered by the Waikato Museum Society, opened to the public in 1965. It was derived from the Waikato Historical Society, founded in 1954, which worked closely with the Waikato Museum Society to establish a stand-alone institution. As well as the Historical Society's collection, it contained 'Maori artefacts, Kauri gum, mineral specimens, shells, coins and artefacts' and 'hunting trophy heads' (Gamble and Cooper 1969: 24). In 1970 Hamilton City Council took over the management and employed professional staff. From 1972 it amalgamated with the art gallery to form one professional and administrative unit and the following year shifted to the top floor of another building. The Waikato Art Museum, as it was named, was really a misnomer in New Zealand terms, because 'it is really a museum of art and history and as such its activities are wide ranging'; they 'cross or at least blur, recognized academic boundaries' (Thomson 1981: 90). There was a strong Waikato regional representation, especially in history:

> the history section is basically devoted to research into and presentation of Waikato history. The collection is still a most diverse one, for history covers all facets of human life. An historical photograph or an old shop sign is as important an item as some piece that has an association with the most important individual the town has produced.
>
> (Thomson, 1981: 92)

In 1973 the museum displayed Te Winika, the century-old newly restored waka taua (war canoe) of the Waikato peoples, just as Uenuku, an ancient carving claimed by the Tainui tribes as a god, was given pride of place at the Te Awamutu Museum. There were also three art exhibitions and a historical exhibition on the development of the Waikato region since the wars of 1863. 'Very few objects are used in this [historical] section with the "storyline" being maintained by the use of maps, photographs and script. The objects in the main are used for visual relief' (Gorbey 1973: 73). The museum was described as combining 'the arts and culture history' and the staff members were listed under the rubric of 'Culture History' (Gorbey 1976: 73). The staff planned to have a full series of displays on the history of the Waikato Region and Hamilton mounted in time for the centennial of local body government in 1978, which was also the centennial of the city of Hamilton. This local orientation was reflected in the development of the collection policy, which focused on 'works and items illustrative of the development of a New Zealand consciousness, whether this be in the fields of history or art' (Gorbey 1978: 17–18).

In 1975, the director reviewed the way that in the past four years, 'four seriously researched and comprehensive displayed exhibitions on subjects that would normally be categorized as falling into the domain of the museum of human history' were mounted. The first exhibition looked at the life of Te Kooti Arikirangi Te Turuki, prophet, religious founder and military leader of the Rongowhakaata tribe in the Gisborne area, who led guerrilla campaigns against the colonial army from 1868–72. It contained an introductory area on the 'culture contact situation' (interactions between Maori and Pakeha) in New Zealand throughout the nineteenth century. The main body of the display dealt with the man, his campaign against the government and his religious ideas. The exhibition concluded with a series of paintings and prints about Te Kooti made by the curator, Hamilton Teachers College lecturer, Frank Davis. The exhibition contained carving, historical artefacts, photographs, contemporary paintings and poetry and it challenged current Pakeha views of the man and the times. The director believed 'It was as successful a fine art exhibition as it was culture history' (Gorbey 1975: 72).

The following year an exhibition about Erueti Te Whiti O Rongomai, the pacifist Taranaki leader and prophet, occupied the same space. After the New Zealand Wars ended in 1872, the King Country, home to the King movement which united Maori tribes against selling land to Pakeha settlers, and a major theatre of war, stayed closed to Pakeha for another decade. South Taranaki too resisted settler incursions until 1881, when the assertive Parihaka community was dispersed by the colonial army. The exhibition contained two key loan items: an Armstrong gun and an old Maori plough, signifying contrasting settler and Maori aims. These were augmented by photographs and maps and 'four hours of total reading material' about the history of Maori–Pakeha interactions in Taranaki, Te Whiti's passive resistance campaign and beyond. The museum displayed a series of related paintings by renowned artists Colin McCahon and Ralph Hotere at the same time. Many visitors criticised the exhibition and felt that it should have been produced as a book; however, television and film companies used a significant amount of the visual material in programmes on Te Whiti and Maori history which were being produced at the time (Gorbey 1975: 72). The reception of this exhibition was an indication that interest in a different kind of New Zealand history was awakening in the 1970s, compared with the earlier focus on pioneering and salvaging remnants of Maori and Pakeha material culture.

The third exhibition focused on the local Waikato campaigns of the New Zealand Wars in 1863–4. In 1861 the new Governor, George Grey, had promised Maori local autonomy, but he also built a military road from Auckland to the Waikato River, the main artery of the Kingite heartland. Grey invaded Waikato in July 1863. Lieutenant-General Duncan Cameron's 12,000 imperial troops faced fewer than 5,000 part-time warriors. The new display began as research for permanent displays then staff decided to mount a whole temporary exhibition. This was later condensed into a permanent display. 'A great deal of emphasis was placed on visual material, maps, paintings, photographs etc., presented in booklet form scattered throughout the gallery' (Gorbey 1975: 75), along with contemporary watercolours on one side and a display of militaria from the period.

An exhibition about the campaign for and eventual granting of women's suffrage in New Zealand in 1893 was the museum's contribution to the United Nations sponsored International Year of Women in 1975. In the view of the director, it was the 'most successful culture history of the four' (Gorbey 1975: 75). It combined photographs, cartoons, labels, notices and other ephemera with the two major petitions signed by 20,000 women in 1892 and 30,000 women in 1893. The displays were set out as a series of panels with the aim of taking the exhibition on tour later and it was accompanied by a booklet written by academic historian Dr Patricia Grimshaw, who had published the first full history in 1972. It was opened by renowned international anthropologist Dr Margaret Mead, which created a great deal of interest in the exhibition.

The Waikato Museum's collections and exhibitions demonstrate Belich's notion of the decolonisation of history. As well as the burgeoning interest in New Zealand history and the rise of museums, from the 1970s many Maori people asserted their identity as Maori and they put renewed value on speaking Maori and on campaigns to settle land grievances, to take just two examples. Pakeha who developed exhibitions about Maori history were aware of these demands. Along with politically aware youth, women and other sectors newly conscious of their place in society, there was a sense that the time was ripe for political and collective change. The Waikato Museum's endeavours show clear links to this overt social change: the displays reflect an increasing interest in New Zealand, a changing notion of what its history was, and recognition of its distinctive place in a rapidly shifting world. 'The pioneer laundress' exhibition at the Manawatu Museum, in 1976–7, reflected both the newly visible groups in society who wanted to know their history and also a more conventional understanding of what that history was, signalled in the use of the term 'pioneer'. Although the Te Awamutu Museum mounted temporary shows, the Waikato Art Museum went further in introducing thematic exhibitions, which combined different kinds of objects, as opposed to displays of single collections. Yet, in common with Te Awamutu, it shared a commitment to the region and locality. Both were firmly aware of the need to appeal to different kinds of audiences and different understandings of the past.

We can see in these and other similar museums a more reflective history developing in the postwar period, which was premised on the interest in and excitement generated by local stories, which grappled with cross-cultural encounter, conflict, settler dominance and disturbance, but also more recent histories and accomplishments. Both institutions experimented with form and content, within their available resources. The collecting and display in these museums is complex, and open to a number of readings. The importance of the local as opposed to the national is clear, as regional museums in this period foreshadowed some of the changes to come in collecting and displaying 'history' that we are more familiar with in the twenty-first century. By attending to local rather than national stories, the distinctive inflection of Pakeha New Zealand cultural history has been traced. A more nuanced reading of these institutions and their histories provides fresh perspectives on questions of identity, history (and heritage), as well as settler–indigenous relations. This detailed case study is important not just for museum history and theory in New Zealand; it is also instructive for those working on similar questions internationally.

## Bibliography

Adams, S. and Frances, R. (2003) 'Lifting the veil: the sex industry, museums and galleries', *Labour History* (Special issue on 'Interpreting Working Life and Culture in Australian Museums and Galleries'), 85: 47–64.

Anon. (1995) 'Historical Society looks back on over 60 years of achievement', *Footprints of History*, 15: 17–21.

Barringer, T. and Flynn, T. (eds) (1998) *Colonialism and the Object: Empire, Material Culture and the Museum*, London, New York: Routledge.

Belich, J. (1996) *Making Peoples: A History of the New Zealanders from Polynesian Settlement to the End of the Nineteenth Century*, Auckland: Allen Lane, Penguin.

Belich, J. (2001) *Paradise Reforged: A History of the New Zealanders from the 1880s to the Year 2000*, Auckland: Allen Lane, Penguin.

Bell, C. (1996) *Inventing New Zealand: Everyday Myths of Pakeha Identity*, Auckland: Penguin.

Boswell, D. and Evans, J. (eds) (1999) *Representing the Nation: Histories, Heritages and Museums*, London and New York: Routledge.

Britain, I. (ed.) (2001) *Meanjin on Museums: Art or Mart*, 60: 4.

Coombes, A. (1994) *Reinventing Africa: Museums, Material Culture and Popular Imagination in late Victorian and Edwardian England*, New Haven, CT: Yale University Press.

Davidson, G. (2000) *The Use and Abuse of Australian History*, Sydney: Allen & Unwin

Dorward, D. (1996) 'Material culture and the construction of "The Other": museums in late nine-teenth-century Australia and New Zealand', *Australasian Victorian Studies Journal*, 2.

Dubin, S. (1999) *Displays of Power: Memory and Amnesia in the American Museum*, New York: New York University Press.

Evans, A. J. (1974) 'New museum at Te Awamutu', *Journal of the New Zealand Federation of Historical Societies*, 1: 4.

Evans, A. (1976) 'Te Awamutu and District Museum', *Agmanz News*, 7: 4: 29–32.

Gamble, B. and Cooper, R. (1969) *Art Galleries and Museums of New Zealand*, Auckland: Art Galleries and Museums Association of New Zealand.

Gorbey, K. (1973) 'New home for Waikato Art Museum', *Agmanz News*, 4: 4: 73.

—— (1975) 'Four historical exhibitions', *Agmanz News*, 6: 4: 70–7.

—— (1976) 'Waikato Art Museum', *Agmanz News*, 7: 4: 67–74.

—— (1978) 'A New Zealand consciousness: a new collection policy for Waikato Art Museum', *Agmanz News*, 9: 2: 17–18.

Gore, J. M. (2002) 'Representations of history and nation in museums in Aotearoa and New Zealand – The National Museums of Australia and The Museum of New Zealand Te Papa Tongarewa', unpublished PhD thesis, History, University of Melbourne.

J. G. G. (1967), '"New Look" at the museum. Extensive alterations and improvements', *The Journal of the Te Awamutu Historical Society*, 2: 3: 77–9.

Handler, R. and Gable, E. (1997) *The New History in an Old Museum: Creating the Past at Colonial Williamsburg*, Durham, NC: Duke University Press.

Healy, C. (1997) *From the Ruins of Colonialism: History as Social Memory*, Melbourne: Cambridge University Press.

Henare, A. (2005) *Museums, Anthropology and Imperial Exchange*, New York: Cambridge University Press.

Hilliard, C. (2000) 'Textual museums: collection and writing in history and ethnology, 1900–1950', in B. Labrum and B. Dalley (eds) *Fragments: New Zealand Social and Cultural History*, Auckland: Auckland University Press: 118–39.

Kaplan, F. (ed.) (1994) *Museums and the Making of 'Ourselves': The Role of Objects in National Identity*, London: Leicester University Press.

Karp, I., Mullen Kreamer, C. and Lavine, S. D. (eds) (1992) *Museums and Communities: The Politics of Public Culture*, Washington, DC: Smithsonian Press.

Kavanagh, G. (ed.) (1996) *Making Histories in Museums*, London: Leicester University Press.

Kirschenblatt-Gimblett, B. (1998) *Destination Culture: Tourism, Museums and Heritage*, Berkeley, CA: University of California Press.

Labrum, B. (2000) 'Persistent needs and expanding desires: Pakeha families and state welfare in the years of prosperity', in B. Labrum and B. Dalley (eds) *Fragments: New Zealand Social and Cultural History*, Auckland: Auckland University Press: 188–210.

—— (2004) 'The "decolonisation" of history or "a demand for the quiet and manageable"? Museums and history in the 1970s', paper presented at *The Seventies: A Decade of Social Change Conference*, Te Papa, November 2004.

Linenthal, E. and Engelhardt, T. (eds) (1996) *History Wars: The Enola Gay and Other Battles for the American Past*, New York: Owl Books.

McCarthy, C. (2004) 'From curio to *taonga*: A genealogy of display at New Zealand's national museum, 1865–2001', unpublished PhD thesis, Museum and Heritage Studies, Victoria University of Wellington.

McCredie, A. (1999) 'Going public: New Zealand art museums in the 1970s', unpublished MA thesis, Museum Studies, Massey University.

Macdonald, C. (1999) 'Race and empire at "Our Place": New Zealand's new national museum', *Radical History Review*, 75: 80–91.

Macdonald, S. and Fyfe, G. (eds) (1996) *Theorizing Museums: Representing Identity and Diversity in a Changing World*, Oxford: Blackwell.

McIntyre, D. and Wehner, K. (eds) (2001) *National Museums: Negotiating Histories*, Canberra: National Museum of Australia.

Neill, A. (2004) 'National culture and the new museology', in A. Smith and L. Weavers (eds) *On Display: New Essays in Cultural Studies*, Wellington: Victoria University Press: 180–96.

Oliver, W. H. (2002) *Looking for the Phoenix: A Memoir*, Wellington: Bridget Williams Books.

Phillips, J. (1996) 'Our history, ourselves: the historian and national identity', *The New Zealand Journal of History*, 30: 2: 107–23.

Renwick, B. (ed.) (2004) *Creating a National Spirit: Celebrating New Zealand's Centennial*, Wellington: Victoria University Press.

Rosenzweig, R. and Thelen, D. (eds) (2000) *The Presence of the Past: Popular Uses of the Past in American Life*, New York: Columbia University Press.

Simpson, M. (1996) *Making Representations: Museums in the Post-Colonial Era*, New York: Routledge.

Starn, R. (2005) 'A historian's brief guide to new museum studies', *American Historical Review*, 110: 68–98.

Thomson, K. W. (1981) *Art Galleries and Museums of New Zealand*, Wellington: Reed.

Trapeznik, A. (2000) *Common Ground? Heritage and Public Places in New Zealand*, Dunedin: University of Otago Press.

Turner, C. (ed.) (2001) 'The future of museums – Part 1', *Humanities Research*, 8: 1.

—— (2002) 'The future of museums – Part 2', *Humanities Research*, 9: 1.

Webster, K. A. (ca. 1959) 'Suggestions by Mr K A Webster as a result of his visit to New Zealand', MS-Papers-3522, Alexander Turnbull Library, Wellington, New Zealand.

Witcomb, A. (2003) *Re-Imagining the Museum: Beyond the Mausoleum*, London: Routledge.

# 12

# HISTORY MUSEUMS, COMMUNITY IDENTITIES AND A SENSE OF PLACE

## Rewriting histories

*Sheila Watson*

Recent research into the production and consumption of meanings in museums (Newman and McLean 2006; O'Neill 2006) suggests that these institutions contribute significantly to the construction of personal and shared identities. In parallel with these sociological studies, historians have taken an increasing interest in the way individuals and communities remember the past, how certain memories are used by groups to articulate a collective identity (Brown 2005: 127), and how such identities are embedded in a sense of place (Schama 1996). While many museums work collaboratively with community groups (Wallace 1986: 155; Crooke 2005), some local histories in professionally run museums are authored by curators, or an exhibition team, who draw on academic histories to construct their narratives but who pay little regard to the way such histories are used by local audiences. This chapter suggests that, by giving more attention to the historiographic needs and historical perceptions of these audiences, museums might more effectively articulate community identities and a sense of place.

In 2004, a new local history museum, *Time and Tide*, opened in the English coastal town of Great Yarmouth in Norfolk. The ground floor of this museum was devoted to two themes chosen by local people, through a series of focus groups, to represent their history and sense of place. The themes selected were the fishing industry and the 'Rows', distinctive and once bustling narrow alleyways which run east to west through the town. Using the records from these focus group meetings, this chapter investigates why the residents of Great Yarmouth have used museums to privilege certain kinds of heritage, and thus certain kinds of identity, in this way. Why, for example, has the fishing industry taken on an iconic status for the town, becoming 'its soul' as one person remarked (Watson 2000a: 3)? Why have certain historical narratives, images, objects, places and working practices become so integral to the ways in which people see themselves and wish to be seen? This study reveals that while these identities appear to be located in an essentialist past, they are, in fact, fluid, complex and emotional, related to perceptions of others and to contemporary contexts, and are dependent as much on material culture as on experience and memory. These are multi-layered identities, richly embedded in a past now managed as heritage, a notion understood here as being 'concerned with the ways in which very selective material artefacts, mythologies, memories and traditions become resources for the present' (Ashworth and Graham

2005: 4). This definition, and the findings of this research, raise questions about the role of local history museums and the nature of the histories they tell.

## Consulting Yarmouth

Ashworth and Graham (2005: 3) have pointed out that 'senses of places are . . . the products of the creative imagination of the individual and of society, while identities are not passively received but are ascribed to places by people'. They are thus 'user determined, polysemic and unstable through time'. Tilley (2006: 8) suggests that landscapes are 'actively re-worked, interpreted and understood in relation to differing social and political agendas, [and] forms of social memory'. While the concept of 'place identity' is complex and depends on a range of factors such as specialist foods, products, landscapes and the built environment, Huigen and Meijering (2005: 20) suggest that heritage may be the outstanding place characteristic.

Great Yarmouth is a seaside holiday town classified as suffering from severe economic and social deprivation (GYBC 2004). After the Second World War, nearly all the surviving Rows were demolished in slum clearance. In the 1960s the fishing industry collapsed and, although the oil and gas industry briefly provided work for some ex-fishermen, these employment opportunities were not enough to prevent the town's economic decline. The holiday industry went down-market. Seasonal holiday work left many unemployed for more than half the year. Like similar towns, Yarmouth became a 'ghetto(s) for the dispossessed' (Girling 2006: 23). In 2000, the Department of the Environment, Transport and the Regions published a review of the Indices of Deprivation and Great Yarmouth ranked fifth worst in ward level intensity out of 354 local authority districts in England (GYBC 2004).

Between 1996 and 2002, the Great Yarmouth Heritage Partnership (consisting of national, county and borough heritage organisations) conducted in-depth consultations with local people and visitors to the town, to establish display themes and an understanding of the role museums and the historic built environment could play in supporting economic and social regeneration. The consultation took the form of focus groups, originally in 1996 facilitated by consultant Susie Fisher, and from 1997 managed and facilitated by Norfolk Museums and Archaeology Service on behalf of the partners. Excepting 1999, focus groups were held annually between 1996 and 2002, at key dates in the development of the borough's museums and the conservation and heritage strategy. They were held with local people within the borough, seaside holiday visitors and, initially, with visitors from Norwich (who proved to have little interest in the project). Stakeholders such as local government officers, elected members and museum staff were also consulted. The focus group work required participants to work collectively on the memories, narratives, episodes and symbols they wished to represent in a museum. In this respect the work was very unlike the production of oral histories where individual accounts are uncontested and located in a personal story.

Consultation involved those living within walking distance of the museums and historic town centre, an area of high economic deprivation, who were mainly social groups C2 and D, and others from the wider borough, predominantly from social groups C1 and B, using the demographic classification system set out in Table 12.1.

Research into the socio-economic profile of visitors to museums has long shown that museums appeal more to the educated and affluent (for a recent example, see Davies 2003). Merriman (2000: 129) has suggested that these visitors privilege a sense of 'impersonal heritage' whereas those of 'lower status' prefer a '"personal past" . . . a sense of the past which is experienced in personal terms, of which the best examples are personal memories and family

*Table 12.1* Demographic classification system

| Social grade | Social status | Occupation |
|---|---|---|
| A | Upper middle class | Higher managerial, administrative or professional |
| B | Middle class | Intermediate managerial, administrative or professional |
| C1 | Lower middle class | Supervisory or clerical, junior managerial, administrative or professional |
| C2 | Skilled working class | Skilled manual workers |
| D | Working class | Semi and unskilled manual workers |
| E | Those at lowest level of subsistence | State pensioners or widows (no other earner), casual or lowest grade workers |

*Source:* Anon. 2006.

histories'. Bourdieu (1984), whose work Merriman acknowledges, suggests that learning, linked to economic status, leads to an aesthetic distancing, a disposition that rejects personal involvement, and conversely a working class popular aesthetic that encourages participation and excitement. Others have suggested that some communities do not necessarily value the historic environment (DCMS 2001: 25, cited Turnpenny 2004: 295). Research here, however, revealed a more complex picture than theory would suggest. Those people at first presumed to be little interested in history or built heritage (i.e. C2s and Ds) displayed a stronger emotional reaction, and a greater sense of loss and neglect than some from more affluent backgrounds who spoke of the need for change. All groups wanted a personal rather than impersonal past, but they did so not out of a sense of nostalgia for an imagined golden era in the town's fortunes. Rather, there was a consensus that the museum displays needed to portray what they saw as the gritty realism of poverty, suffering and endurance (Fisher 1996; Watson 1997, 1999, 2000b, 2004).

## Rediscovering a place

Local people's perceptions of the town were shocking: Yarmouth was a 'superficial place, no decent shops, no identity, on the route to nowhere' (Fisher 1996: 8). C1, C2 and D groups worried about unemployment. Some felt the situation hopeless: 'fractured families, child responsibilities, how can I get out? I'm trapped here'. Summer visitors who 'don't care for the town' were resented. They were believed to bring trouble: 'a danger to my children, drugs, drinks, transients' to a town in rapid decline: 'Broken down buildings, pride slipping away'. The middle classes (predominantly B social group) who lived outside the two most deprived wards damned the town comprehensively. Norwich day-visitors to Great Yarmouth were also contemptuous of it. For them Norwich was 'their spiritual home; old established, cultured, [a] sure touch in Arts and Museums' while Yarmouth was for when they were 'slumming it' (Fisher 1996: 9). Seaside holidaymakers had a kinder view of Yarmouth but they were also 'rueful and resigned' that the town was so 'shabby'.

All groups were asked about the role history and heritage, in particular improved museums, could play in supporting the regeneration of the town by fostering a sense of self-esteem and pride. Local people from all socio-economic groups were enthusiastic about this as were the seaside holidaymakers and heritage-minded visitors. However, participants from the C1 C2 group in Norwich were disapproving of the idea. One remarked: 'Great Yarmouth is trying to make itself better that what it is' (Fisher 1996: 9).

One of the surprises of the study was that heritage professionals and the local public had a fundamentally different sense of heritage focus. The partners had focused on the Quayside museums, ignoring the Maritime Museum on the seafront, which they planned to redisplay at a later date. In contrast, locals were anxious to discuss this museum, which they disliked. In their view, it did not do justice to the importance of the herring fishing industry in particular to the story of the town. A thousand years of fishing was represented by objects in two cases, some ship models, a few Pierhead paintings and some photographs. A fish-curing factory, the Tower Curing Works, shut in 1989 and derelict, was seen as a much better site for the interpretation of the fishing industry. 'For them "Herring, that IS Yarmouth history"' (Fisher 1996: 23).

The Tower Curing Works was bought by the Great Yarmouth Preservation Trust and later leased to the Museums Service. Over the next few years focus groups developed the key themes of the proposed new museum further, which was to be about the history of the town from its origins to the present day. The groups advocated topics such as the 1953 flood, the rise of Yarmouth from a sandbank, the story of the port, the impact of the two wars on the town and the seaside holiday industry in its heyday. However, above all there was one topic which universally engaged local people of whatever social background: the herring fishing industry. Only the Rows aroused similar emotions. Fishing, however, surpassed all else, including the town's association with celebrities and heroes such as Charles Dickens and Admiral Lord Nelson. Given that the participants felt one of the key purposes of the museums was to raise the standing of the town in the eyes of its current inhabitants and visitors, this rejection of the famous is, perhaps, surprising. What the focus groups suggested was that a sense of place was not located in the town's overt links to national events and people, nor with its civic past, but in its longer history, its physical appearance over time, its historic built environment, and particularly with the iconic: the Tower Curing Works, the Rows and, above all else, the fishing industry (Fisher 1996; Watson 1997, 1998, 1999, 2000a, 2000b, 2001, 2004).

## Seeing, remembering, experiencing

While local people thought it was important to have other topics besides fishing, there was consensus that fishing and industrial fish processing should form the core of the new displays. The 2000 focus group report summarised the vision, revealing a complex aspiration for the museum that involved the visual, the act of remembering and the experiential:

> Recreate the Quayside, recreate the atmosphere, noise, bustle, smell, etc. People more important than the process. Tell their stories, living conditions, housing; make it realistic – dangers and discomforts and hardships. Show the scale – the whole of Yarmouth transformed by immigrants and the whole Quayside bustling and exciting. Show what it was like in a boat – people want to go inside a recreated vessel or half vessel.
>
> (Watson 2000a: 3)

Regardless of socio-economic background, everyone had equal regard for the fishing industry. Those who were too young to remember it, or had nothing to do with it, still talked about it as enthusiastically as those who had participated in it, earned income from it or witnessed the great fishing fleets. A historical narrative had emerged from a consensual view of past. This history articulated a sense of community in otherwise socio-economically compartmentalised sections in society. The museum held the potential to make such an identity explicit to members of that community and to outsiders.

However, the more we examine the fishing industry the more puzzling appears the affection in which it is held. Herring fishing was a seasonal activity. It only extended from October to early December and during this period Yarmouth became home to large numbers of, originally Dutch and then Scottish, migrant labourers, as well as gutting girls. The industry peaked in 1913 when 1,163 boats landed some 2,488,140 cwt of fish on the Quay. Herring fishing ceased altogether during the two world wars of the twentieth century, only to be revived in between. After 1945 it was a shadow of its former self, and by 1957 there were only 111 boats fishing for herring. The last landing of the herring was in 1968 from just five boats (Tooke 2006: 11).

From the importance attached to the fishing industry one might assume that it employed more local people than manufacturing and was a great source of wealth to the town. That is certainly the impression given by people talking about the bygone fishing industry. However, the records tell a different story. It is estimated that in 1912 there were only 2,710 regular fishermen and 440 casual workers (Lummis 1985) out of a Yarmouth population of approximately 56,000 (1911 census). Thus, fishing directly employed approximately only 5.6 per cent of the population. Of course, many of the fishermen had dependants and thus the numbers relying on the industry were higher than the statistics suggest. There were also many other trades dependent on fishing, including fish curing and packing, coopering and net mending, but these were mainly seasonal and male. Local women were, according to Lummis, rarely employed in the ancillary trades. Most female workers in the industry were itinerant Scots who arrived in October and left in December, and did not form part of the permanent population of the town. They provided some incomes to those who gave them lodgings but they mainly saved their money for their families back in Scotland. In comparison, nearby Lowestoft that had a population of 38,000 in 1911 with 5,400 regular fishermen in 1912 and 950 occasional fishermen; the ratio of native fishermen to the population as a whole was 16.7 per cent, much higher than in Great Yarmouth. Yet, unlike Great Yarmouth, Lowestoft has not laid claim to fishing as its most important historical industry.

Moreover, evidence suggests that when the fishing ended, its demise was not publicly lamented. One local historian wrote in 1971 'the herring has gone . . . but there has been no decline in the town's prosperity. New industries have grown up to take its place. Yarmouth is still a great seaside resort' (Nobbs 1971: 5). The Maritime Museum on the seafront opened in 1967 to document and display the maritime trades and industries along the East Coast, and there is no record of anyone criticising the museum for having few displays on the fishing industry at this time.

There were, moreover, many other industries that had, during their heyday, been more important economically to the town than fishing. Yarmouth was never dependent on a single line of work. Over the past two hundred years, for example, the seaside holiday trade employed more people in the town than fishing and continues to be a key source of employment.

In the 1960s and 1970s the town remained proud of its beach and its holiday reputation (Nobbs 1971). However, focus groups in the late 1990s did not wish to see the holiday industry given prominence in the new museum. They recognised that it was and is a key to

Yarmouth's economic survival, yet they regarded it with ambivalence. Many of them disliked the influx of visitors, particularly the less affluent. Norwich focus groups made it clear that Yarmouth was 'tacky' and 'tatty' (Fisher 1996: 9). Among holiday destinations, local people understood their town to be regarded as having a low status: 'Yarmouth has been neglected, ignored and despised by the rest of Norfolk, particularly Norwich, so this project will show the rest of Norfolk that Yarmouth has a proud and special place in the world. (P.S. Better than Norwich.)' (Watson 2000a: 4). The focus groups wanted the museum to restrict itself to safe pre- and immediately postwar stories of boarding houses, families with buckets and spades and the occasional scooter boys who flocked to English coastal resorts on bank holidays. In more modern times, the beach has taken on another persona and an identity with which local people are distinctly uncomfortable. Shields (1991: 3) has postulated that there are some marginal places, sites of 'illicit or distained social activities', that carry with them 'the image, and stigma, of their marginality which becomes indistinguishable from any basic empirical identity they might once have had'. In this sense, the seafront, with its beach and amusements, has now become a marginal place: a liability, symbolic of an industry for which the town is despised.

If the modern seaside holiday industry was generally unpopular, there were still many other important local industries which could form the focus for the new museum. Take, for example, the silk industry and Grout's factory (Figure 12.1).[1] Between 1805 and 1815 Joseph Grout and partners built a great mill in centre of the town, powered by steam and, by 1825, they appear to have almost monopolised the market in mourning crêpe. Although the numbers employed fluctuated, at its peak in 1825 they had 3,908 workers, mainly women and girls on shift work (Berry 1971). The factory's massive chimneys and five-storey buildings dominated the appearance of the town. When mourning crêpe went out of fashion, the factory produced quality silk and wool textiles, and manufactured crêpe bandages for the National Health Service and parachutes. In 1972, the company relocated to the outskirts of town and most of the original site was redeveloped. It finally ceased trading in 1996. Grout's was just one of several factories, albeit the largest, that flourished during the past two hundred years and provided local people with employment and a living.

Why, therefore – given the importance of this factory, the number of people it employed, the size of its buildings and their dominant location within the centre of the town, its success (particularly in rivalling the Norwich silk industries), and its survival until after the fishing industry ceased – did local people show so little interest in telling its story? Why, when they mourned the loss of the Rows and the closure of the Fish Wharf, did not one person ever say it was a pity Grout's factory had been demolished? Why did this part of Yarmouth's history vanish virtually without trace from the collective memories of the local population while the fishing continued to exercise such fascination?

There are many possible answers: factories do not have the fishing industry's antiquity; factory work lacks the romance of battling the elements; it was mainly women's work and thus was perceived to lack status; and, above all, factories were perceived to belong to a northern identity, not something one normally associates with East Anglia.

In contrast, the herring fishing industry, gone in 1968 and in decline from the 1930s, nevertheless had a long history dating back in the popular imagination to the establishment of a fishing colony on a sandbank before the Norman Conquest (Lewis 1980: 13). This idea has been repeated as if fact: 'one can never forget that this place owes its origin and prosperity to the herring' (*The Fishing News*, 23 October 1943); ' if the herring had not chosen to visit the Smith's knoll area annually, Great Yarmouth might still have been an uninhabited

*Figure 12.1* Grout's factory occupied a large site in the centre of Great Yarmouth as can be seen from this 1922 photograph.

Reproduced with kind permission of Great Yarmouth Museums.

sand bank' (Butcher 1957: 674). As recently as 2006, *The Eastern Daily Press* published an article entitled, 'The port built on herring', which, quoting a local historian, claimed: 'the town would not have been there if it hadn't been for the herring' (Kennedy 2006: 10). The longevity of fishing clearly forms part of a foundation myth, although this alone is unlikely to explain the importance of fishing in the public's imagination today.

## Re-imagining the past

We have seen how the focus groups, in articulating the importance of the fishing industry, were concerned with the visual, the act of remembering and the experiential. Let us consider these three elements in turn.

The visibility of the fishing industry takes two key forms – in memory and in reproduction through art and photography. In the public memory, during the brief herring fishing season, the River Yare was filled with drifters. The industry was visible and accessible. Local people and visitors from all over Norfolk came to walk among the baskets of fish, to talk to the Scots girls and watch them work and to gaze at the busy river. During the consultation process it was the sight of the fishing industry that appeared important. People described what they saw far more often than what they heard or smelled. The herring fishing industry only lasted for three months each year, but those three months made an indelible impression on all those who saw the Quayside.

This visual aspect of the fishing industry is, perhaps, a key to understanding its importance in the popular imagination and its contribution to identity rooted in a sense of place.

Hall (1995: 181) contends that we see cultural identity in a place, as part of an imaginary landscape or 'scene'. He argues that we give it a background; we put it in a frame in order to make sense of it. National identities are often linked to landscapes and these landscapes are then used to construct a sense of a people.

The other visual aspect alluded to above, is in the reproduction of images of the fishing. All local focus groups of whatever socio-economic background, when shown images of paintings of the fishing by that distinguished group of nineteenth-century landscape painters known as the Norwich school, reacted very enthusiastically to them and wanted them incorporated into displays about the fishing industry rather than hung in an art gallery. Only a group of local artists dissented from this view. The wider public considered these images particularly important, even though they depicted a period beyond memory when fishing boats landed catches of all types on the beach (Watson 1997). The Norwich Castle Museum had, at the end of the nineteenth century, been instrumental in developing the concept of the Norwich School – perhaps to satisfy a middle class desire for a regional identity (Hemingway 2000: 12). However, despite its name, many of its greatest practitioners – men such as John Sell Cotman and John Crome – are closely linked to Great Yarmouth. Their images of the town's beach, the sea, fishermen and women workers formed an enduring image of the past which is central to local identity.

What is interesting about these pictures is the way in which Yarmouth itself is merely a backdrop, the beach, the sea, the sky, the occupations dominate. Such images formed part of a 'picturesque' tradition (Jäger 2003): concealing the hard work, poverty and high risks of the industry, and replacing them with a romantic and artistic conception (Figure 12.2). Here, the identity of Yarmouth lies within the frame of beach and sea, ennobled by work and exposure to the elements. Here, too, the fishermen and women live in harmony with the sea and coastal landscape 'shaping as well as expressing, the specific landscape of the community' (Smith 2003: 36). Together, they and their occupations begin to essentialise the community's identity.

Over time, most of the fishing moved from the beach to the Quayside on the River Yare as new types of fishing vessel were introduced. With the opening of the Fishwarf in 1867 and large-scale commercial processing initiatives, the beach was left to the holidaymakers. Perhaps surprisingly, the romantic view of the fishing moved with the industry to the Quay and, as we have seen, provided the visitors of all social groups with a public spectacle which for them came to identify 'Yarmouth'. But the move to the Quay also marked a move to a more intimate and harsher working life. The Fishwarf during the herring season was filthy, smelly, generally cold and damp, and full of men and women in labourers' clothes swearing, singing and shouting. Very few artists painted the scene but photographers immortalised it with thousands of images (Figure 12.3).

In Smith's (1999: 150) view, people create a collective 'historic and poetic landscape, one imbued with the culture and history of a group, and vice versa', and they and outsiders ascribe part of the group's character to 'the particular landscape they inhabit'. The beach and the Quayside, when devoted to the fishing industry, became part of this poetic landscape whose loss Yarmouth people so lamented, but yet whose image remained publicly displayed.

Memories of the fishing were as important as the visual imagery. Such memories were often contradictory. Thus, the fishing and its associated industries were simultaneously remembered both with affection, with stories of the happy workers and a bustling, wealthy town, and as hard times, when a few made money and most got by as best they could.

*Figure 12.2* Alfred Stannard. Yarmouth Beach 1847. A romantic view of the fishing industry.
Reproduced with kind permission of Great Yarmouth Museums.

However, this dual attitude to the fishing industry did not in any way compromise the firm belief that the museum had to be about the fishing. Yarmouth, everyone agreed, had been a better place, more itself, when the fishing industry existed.

Historians, in other contexts, have recognised that communities define themselves through the adoption of a myth which they know to be only a part reflection of the truth. Individuals in society have a propensity to 'mask elements of reality and to spread myths which belong to . . . [a] social group, and also quite paradoxically to put into operation quite effective powers of observation' (Peneff 1990: 43). Calder's (2004) *The Myth of the Blitz* similarly demonstrates how the nation can remember and celebrate communally through stories, films and anecdotes a triumphant time while contemporary evidence reveals a rather more unsettling aspect. Such myths are developed for a purpose: they serve the community of origin. They are reworked for each generation and are key elements in identity formation (Connelly 2004). In Great Yarmouth, the story of the herring fishing has been reworked over the past 40 years as communities within Great Yarmouth have lost confidence in its future. While individuals remember its harsher aspects, collectively it is celebrated as the 'soul' of town. It has become symbolic.

The third element is the public's appreciation of the fishing industry concerns the experiential. Cultural heritage, it has been suggested, may be experienced not only through material culture but also through its social practices, such as community celebrations that provide 'a focus for the community and an opportunity for interaction, expression and involvement' (Turnpenny 2004: 300). Focus group work indicated that the community participation in fishing embraced not only the active workers, many of whom were, in any

*Figure 12.3* The Fishwarf in 1928. Visitors of all ages enjoyed the spectacle of large quantities of fish on the Quayside.

Reproduced with kind permission of Great Yarmouth Museums.

case, temporary immigrants to the town, but the collective experience of the Quayside spectacle. The desire to recreate the Quayside within the museum, suggests a desire to perpetuate the cultural heritage practices that have been rendered impossible by the cessation of the fishing cycle. Similarly, people wanted not just to look but to 'walk down a Row', enter an original curing house and smell the fish. Bagnall (1996; 2003: 88) has shown how visitors make sense of the past by mapping their consumption of it physically, emotionally and imaginatively. Tilley (2006: 14) also relates identity to how we feel and experience things with our bodies. Evaluation, following the opening of the museum, called *Time and Tide*, in 2004, in the old Tower Curing Works, suggested that while all areas of the museum were popular and successful with visitors, the sensory experiences of the recreated Row, Quayside and smoking houses were particularly well liked and commented upon (Watson 2005).

## Conclusion

Although a sense of place as a significant concept of identity can often be seen as homogenous and static (Hall 1995), in Great Yarmouth it became attached to a changing fishing industry which also moved its geographical centre. Change is also seen in the way the industry has been elevated in importance over the past 40 years. This elevation has taken place partly to counter external perceptions of a town perceived to be in decline. Thus, the identity of Yarmouth has become rooted in an essentialist myth centred on the importance of a fishing industry, which only some within living memory had witnessed. The creation of a new museum within a space that had formerly been dedicated to fish processing, and emphasising the importance of the fishing industry to the history of the town, was a way for local people to express an identity of which they could be proud. Evaluation undertaken since the museum opened suggests that the museum has achieved this goal (Watson 2005).

Great Yarmouth illustrates how communities use such symbols from a selective past to affirm their identities in the present, and by this means achieve community regeneration. But what does this mean for history in museums? There is nothing new in local consultation but historians have seen themselves as guardians of the dispassionate fact rather than exhibitors of golden ages and myths. For many historians, there is much truth in Elton's (1967) perception that history is concerned with 'exact knowledge' (Samuel and Thompson 1990: 1). The empirical traditions of museum curators implicitly endorse such a view; many local history museums still purport to be neutral and impartial. But Turnpenny (2004: 301) has called for heritage managers to acknowledge intangible concepts such as myth, faith and legends. 'These can be understood as having historical, social and spiritual value and are often incorporated into group perceptions of cultural heritage in an attempt to create a position for the community within time and space' (Turnpenny 2004: 301). There are, however, difficulties with such propositions. As Samuel and Thompson (1990: 5) warn, if we do begin to take account of myths, 'we open up a history which . . . pivots on the *active* relationship between past and present, subjective and objective, poetic . . .'. Moreover, if we accept within museums the importance of such myths, how do we identify them and whose myths do we offer up for public consumption? Academic historians understand that the history they write is often constructed for a purpose, that it is affected by the contexts in which they consciously and unconsciously operate (Cannadine 2002; Black 2005). Landscapes and the ideas of place are political, often controlled and manipulated by those with power (Bender 2002). If we accept that all history incorporates much subjectivity, that it is used, as demonstrated here, by communities to locate themselves in place and time as part of community identity formation, and that museums are powerful theatres of public history (Jordanova 2000: 142–6), then the Great Yarmouth model of focus group work suggests a way of democratising that theatre. This is not to suggest that history museums are engaged in the writing of fiction but rather that, like historians more generally, they give emphasis or focus to that aspect which is most important to the narrative.

## Acknowledgements

I am grateful for the help of former colleagues in the Norfolk Museums and Archaeology Service who led focus groups and assisted in the compilation of the final focus group reports. I am also grateful for the assistance provided by my former colleagues in Great Yarmouth museums (part of Norfolk Museums and Archaeology Service) during the writing of this chapter, in particular James Steward. The views expressed in this chapter and any errors are my own.

## Note

1 Most of this information about Grout's factory is taken from research undertaken by an exemployee of Grout's Factory, Gordon Berry, whose papers in the Great Yarmouth Museums Archives proved invaluable in the writing of this chapter.

## Bibliography

Anon (2006) 'Demographics classification' Online. Available at www.businessballs.com/demograph icsclassifications.htm (accessed 25 October 2006).

Ashworth, G. J. and Graham, B. (2005) 'Senses of place, senses of time and heritage', in G. J. Ashworth and B. Graham (eds) *Senses of Place: Senses of Time*, Aldershot: Ashgate, 3–12.

Bagnall, G. (1996) 'Consuming the Past' in S. Edgell, K. Hetherington and A. Warde (eds) *Consumption Matters: The Production and Experience of Consumption*, Oxford: Blackwell, 227–47.

—— (2003) 'Performance and performativity at heritage sites', *Museum and Society*, 1(2): 87–103.

Bender, B. (2002) 'Contested landscapes: Medieval to present day', in V. Buchli (ed.) *The Material Cultural Reader*, Oxford: Berg, 141–74.

Berry, R. G. (1971) 'Great Yarmouth textiles', unpublished manuscript, Great Yarmouth Museum Archives.

Black, J. (2005) *Using History*, London: Hodder Education.

Bourdieu, P. (1984) *Distinction: A Social Critique of the Judgement of Taste*, London: Routledge and Kegan Paul.

Brown, C. G. (2005) *Postmodernism for Historians*, Harlow: Pearson/Longman.

Butcher, L. G. (1957) 'Herring Fair', *East Anglian Magazine*, 16(12) October 1957: 672–79.

Calder, A. (2004) *The Myth of the Blitz*, London: Pimlico.

Cannadine, D. (ed.) (2002) *What is History Now?* Basingstoke: Palgrave Macmillan.

Connelly, M. (2004) *We Can Take It! Britain and the Memory of the Second World War*, Harlow: Pearson Education Limited.

Crooke, E. (2005) 'Museums, communities and the politics of heritage in Northern Ireland', in J. Littler and R. Naidoo (eds) *The Politics of Heritage: The Legacies of 'Race'*, London: Routledge, 69–81.

Davies, S. (2003) *Renaissance in the Regions: A Further Analysis of the Baseline Exit Interviews 2003*, Museums, Libraries and Archives Council. Online. Available at www.mla.gov.uk/resources/assets// R/ren_baseline_exit_rep_doc_4389.doc (accessed 17 May 2007).

DCMS (2001) *The Historic Environment: A Force for Our Future*, London: Department of Culture, Media and Sport.

Elton, G. (1967, 1976 edition) *The Practice of History*, London: Methuen.

Fisher, S. (1996) *A Heritage Trail for Great Yarmouth*, October 1996, job no. 687, Great Yarmouth Museums.

Girling, R. (2006) 'No, we don't like to be beside the seaside', *The Sunday Times Magazine*, 23 April 2006: 14–27.

GYBC (2004) Great Yarmouth Borough Council, 'Indices of Deprivation', internal memo in the Department of Regeneration.

Hall, S. (1995) 'New cultures for old' in D. Massey and P. Jess (eds) *A Place in the World? Places, Cultures and Globalization*, Oxford: Oxford University Press, 175–211.

Hemingway, A. (2000) '"Norwich School": Myth and reality', in D. Brown, A. Hemingway and A. Lyles (eds) *Romantic Landscape: The Norwich School of Painters*, London: Tate Gallery Publishing Ltd, 9–23.

Huigen, P. and Meijering, L. (2005) 'Making places: a story of De Venen', in G. J. Ashworth and B. Graham (eds) *Senses of Place: Senses of Time*, Aldershot: Ashgate, 19–30.

Jäger, J. (2003) 'Picturing nations: landscape photography and national identity in Britain and Germany in the mid-nineteenth century' in J. M. Schwartz and J. R. Ryan (eds) *Picturing Place: Photography and the Geographical Imagination*, London: I.B. Tauris & Co Ltd, 117–40.

Jordanova, L. (2000) *History in Practice*, London: Arnold.

Kennedy, A. (2006) 'The port built on herring,' *Eastern Daily Press*, 8 April 2006, 10–11.

Lewis, C. (1980) *Great Yarmouth, History, Herrings and Holidays*, Cromer: Poppyland Publishers.

Lummis, T. (1985) *Occupation and Society: The East Anglian Fishermen 1880–1914*, Cambridge: Cambridge University Press.

Merriman, N. (2000) *Beyond the Glass Case: The Past, the Heritage and the Public*, London: UCL, Institute of Archaeology.

Newman, A. and McLean, F. (2006) 'The impact of museums upon identity', *International Journal of Heritage Studies*, 12(1): 49–68.

Nobbs, G. (1971) *Bygone Yarmouth, An Illustrated History of a Seaside Resort*, Norwich: Macklow Publications.

O'Neill, M. (2006) 'Museums and identity in Glasgow', *International Journal of Heritage Studies*, 12(1): 29–48.

Peneff, J. (1990) 'Myths in life stories', in R. Samuel and P. Thompson (eds) *The Myths We Live By*, London: Routledge, 36–48.

Samuel, R. and Thompson, P. (1990) 'Introduction' in R. Samuel and P. Thompson (eds) *The Myths We Live By*, London: Routledge, 1–22.

Schama, S. (1996) *Landscape and Memory*, London, Fontana Press.

Shields, R. (1991) *Places on the Margin: Alternative Geographies of Modernity*, London: Routledge.

Smith, A. D. (1999) *Myths and Memories of the Nation*, Oxford: Oxford University Press.

—— (2003) *Chosen Peoples: Sacred Sources of National Identity*, Oxford: Oxford University Press.

Tilley, C. (2006) 'Introduction. Identity, place, landscape and heritage', *Journal of Material Culture*, 11(1/2): 7–32.

Tooke, C. (2006) *The Great Yarmouth Herring Industry*, Stroud: Tempus Publishing Ltd.

Turnpenny, M. (2004) 'Cultural Heritage, an ill-defined concept? A call for joined-up policy', *International Journal of Heritage Studies*, 10(3): 295–307.

Wallace, M. (1986) 'Visiting the past: History museums in the United States', in S. P. Benson, S. Brier and R. Rosenzweig (eds) *Presenting the Past: Essays on History and the Public*, Philadelphia, PA: Temple University Press, 137–61.

Watson, S. (1997) *Follow up Focus Group Work Report*, Great Yarmouth Museums Archives.

—— (1998) *Focus Group Report*, Great Yarmouth Museums Archives.

—— (1999) 'Using focus groups: the Great Yarmouth experience', *Social History Curators' Group News*, 44: 6–9.

—— (2000a) *Tower Curing Works Display Themes Report*, Great Yarmouth Museums Archives.

—— (2000b) 'The Great Yarmouth Experience', *Significant Others: Society of Museum Archaeologists*, special issue of *The Museum Archaeologist*, 25: 35–8.

—— (2001) *Tower Curing Works Display Themes Report*, Great Yarmouth Museums Archives.

—— (2004) 'Museums and social inclusion: managing consultation with specific target groups: A British case study', in M. Dreyer and R. Wiese (eds), *Zielgruppen von Museen: Mit Erfolg erkennen, ansprechen und binden*, Freilichtmuseums am Kiekeberg, Rosengarten-Ehestorf, 85–98.

—— (2005) 'Museums and communities: Time and Tide, a case history', unpublished paper.

# 13

# MUSEUMS AND THE SHAPING OF CULTURAL IDENTITIES

## Visitors' recollections in local museums in Taiwan

*Chia-Li Chen*

Museums play an important role in shaping and defining a person's cultural identity and this chapter investigates ways in which such identities are made. If we accept that visitors are not passive but active participants in the museum experience and engage with the museum through memory and reminiscence then, by examining this process, we can begin to understand how such changes in identity are produced.

This research explores the memories of local residents in their museum visits in Taiwan. Regular local museum visitors, through the deployment of reminiscence and memory, form personal links to the past, thus developing their cultural identities. They use historical houses and local history exhibitions as aides-mémoire. For them the museum visit is an emotionally laden, memory-rich experience. This chapter, therefore, investigates how regular museum visitors remember and how material culture in the museum helps to trigger their memories. After a brief discussion of the development of museums in Taiwan and the nature of memories in the museum, this chapter considers ten categories of museum memories found in interview data. In the first part of the chapter, memory in relation to museum architecture will be discussed. Overall this research aims to provide an insight into the way that visitors deploy memory and reminiscence within a museum setting.

## A brief history of museum development in Taiwan

The development of museums in relation to cultural identity in Taiwan is inextricably linked to their histories. Museum development in Taiwan can be divided into three phases. From 1895 Taiwan was a colony of Japan for 50 years until the end of Second World War in 1945. In this first period from 1895–1945 the museum concept was brought into Taiwan by Japan during Japanese colonial rule and, during this time, the Taiwan Museum was established. Its main purpose was to collect the artefacts of aboriginal peoples and species of plants and animals on the island of Taiwan, to provide useful information for the colonial rulers.

The second phase occurred during the rule of Chiang Kai-shek and his son Chiang Ching-kuo, 1949–1987. At the 1943 Cairo Conference, it was decided that Taiwan should return to mainland China once the Allied Forces won the war. The reunion with mainland China however only lasted for four years. In 1949 China's ruler, Chiang Kai-shek and his political party, the KMT (Kuomingtang), were driven out of China by the Communists and took refuge in Taiwan.

To legitimate and consolidate his regime in Taiwan, Chiang Kai-shek declared martial law, restricting political rights and freedom of speech, and extending the powers of the presidency to an extreme degree. During this period, people were taught that Taiwan was only their temporary objective and the ultimate goal was to employ Taiwan as a bastion from which to re-conquer mainland China. The National Palace Museum and National Museum of History were founded to collect artefacts and works of fine art brought back from mainland China. Their main purpose was to display Chinese culture and enhance political hegemony by promoting Chinese cultural identity in Taiwan.

The third phase is from the 1987 to the present. The lifting of martial law in 1987, which re-established freedom of speech, led to changes in the cultural and political environment. During the process of democratisation, formerly proscribed political ideas surfaced and people in Taiwan experienced a period of identity confusion. Formerly held beliefs were now questioned. No longer was unification with China perceived by all to be the ultimate aim. The independence of Taiwan from China became publicly acceptable. As Mercer observes: 'identity only becomes an issue when it is in crisis, when something assumed to be fixed, coherent and stable is displaced by the experience of doubt and uncertainty' (Mercer 1990: 43). This uncertainty is what most Taiwanese people have been experiencing in the decades following political liberation and social transformation.

During this period, Taiwan experienced rapid social and political transformation along with a rapid growth of local museums, many located in renovated historical houses which were built during the Japanese colonial period. While the decision to re-use colonial buildings on the one hand indicates an intention to shape local identity based on the preservation of historical buildings, it also emphasises colonial history, which elicits very complex responses from people towards the colonial past. This chapter therefore aims to reflect on this issue by investigating local residents' museum experiences in relation to the shaping of cultural identities.

## Memories in the museum

Memories are embodied in various artefacts and cultural forms (Radley 1990; Urry 1996; Zelizer 1995). Museum memories are thus expressed through tangible material culture. In other words, objects and the physical context of the museum prompt visitors' memories. They provide opportunities for recollection and stimulate remembering. Therefore, memory in the museum is very often triggered and mediated through images or objects. At the same time, objects in the museum constitute a part of the story that the museum presents and this narrative affects the act of remembering within an exhibition space.

Second, memory in the museum is selective and institutionalised. By collecting and exhibiting, the museum has had to subject itself to the cultural politics of memories. That is to say, the museum is an institution which officially decides what is worthy of preservation and what is not. On the one hand, it constructs what is to be remembered, but on the other hand, it also chooses what is to be forgotten (Hallam and Hockey 2001; Urry 1996). As Urry (1996: 50) explains: 'forgetting is as socially structured as is the process of remembering'. Therefore, the museum solidifies memories' meanings and transforms private memories into the material of public memories (Sherman 1995: 52–3). Research suggests that once living memories enter into the museum, they become mummified, lose their relationship with the original group of people for whom they had complex, confused, individual and collective meanings, and provide instead official, coherent meanings for visitors (Assman 1995; Brower 1999; Sherman 1995). Herrmann and Plude (1995: 55), however, think that memories prompted by a museum visit do allow for some individual responses and that they 'include some sense of rarity or uniqueness with associated feelings of reverence and a philosophical content regarding the relationship between the visitor and the museum exhibits'.

However, despite these theories that see visitors passively accepting the formal museum memory, visitors themselves make sense of, interpret and construct meanings in the museum. Museum professionals have become aware that visitors, though limited to the objects selected and presented by the museum, are able to associate an exhibition with their own memories and create individual meanings and memories during their visits (Hooper-Greenhill and Moussouri 2002; Silverman 1995). The museum is not only a place for learning but also a site for memory and reminiscence, which provides infinite opportunities for individual meaning-making. This process of memory creation by local visitors to museums will be explored further in this chapter.

## Methodology

Five museums in Taiwan were chosen to illustrate how visitors interact with exhibits in different types of museums in various areas of Taiwan. The five museums were all small to medium-sized. Two, the Bai-mi Clog Museum (Figure 13.1) and the Peitou Hot Springs Museum, are community-engaged museums. The former provides a case study of how the Bai-mi community tackled local issues by building a museum, while the latter shows how the Peitou community rediscovered past prosperity in part through the establishment of the museum. In contrast, the I-Lan Museum of Local Political History and the Hsinchu Municipal Glass Museum (Figure 13.2) were both established and managed by local government authorities to implement local political and cultural agendas. The former demonstrates how the I-Lan county government endeavours to promote pride in being an I-Lan resident through the presentation of I-Lan's history, while the latter is designed to regenerate the traditional glass-making craft of Hsinchu.

In contrast to all of these, the first holocaust museum of Taiwan, the Taipei 228 Memorial Museum (Figure 13.3) presents the most traumatic event in twentieth-century Taiwanese history, and illustrates the cause, and ongoing process, of the emergence and formation of Taiwanese identity through the understanding of the 288 Incident. The worst massacre in modern Taiwanese history occurred on 28 February 1947 and is known as the 288 Incident. It occurred two years after the Japanese colonial period came to an end when Taiwan was reunited with China after 50 years of separation. However, tension between the Taiwanese people and new immigrants from China led to a series of disputes. The 288 Incident began when monopoly officials attempted to arrest a woman who sold untaxed cigarettes and beat the woman unconscious. Their brutal behaviour angered people, and fury at the new immigrants exploded among the Taiwanese. After a short period of unrest, the Chinese government and representatives of the Taiwanese people started negotiations for political reform. While promising to bring about a peaceful solution, General Chen asked Chiang Kai-shek to send back-up troops from China. As soon as the troops arrived in Taiwan they massacred large numbers of Taiwanese people and arrested the people's

*Figure 13.1* The Bai-mi Clog Museum with colourful wall decorated and installed by local residents.

Photo: the author.

*Figure 13.2* The Hsinchu Municipal Glass Museum.

Photo: the author.

*Figure 13.3* The Taipei 228 Memorial Museum, a former broadcasting station.
Photo: the author.

representatives. About 20,000 innocent people died and most Taiwanese intellectuals and members of the elite were killed or disappeared forever.

To explore local residents' museum experiences in all the case study museums, qualitative in-depth interviews were held with visitors chosen on the basis of residence, age and frequency of visits. First, they had to be local residents who had lived in the community or the county for more than five years. Second, they had to be over 20 years old, to ensure they had some community memories and were able to compare the past and present. They had to be motivated individuals who visited independently and regularly and who had been to the museum at least twice in the year before this research was carried out (March and April 2001). Based on these criteria, five visitors were interviewed in each museum so 25 people were interviewed altogether. Interviewees are anonymous and are identified by an English letter followed by an Arabic number to indicate the museum where they were interviewed. The background information of interviewees is listed as in Table 13.1.

*Table 13.1* Background information of the interviewees

| Museum | Visitor | Gender | Education |
|---|---|---|---|
| The Bai-Mi Clog Museum | B-1 | M | Junior High School |
| | B-2 | F | Junior High School |
| | B-3 | M | Senior High School |
| | B-4 | M | Senior High School |
| | B-5 | F | College |
| The I-Lan Museum of Local Political Theory | L-1 | M | College |
| | L-2 | F | College |
| | L-3 | M | College |
| | L-4 | M | College |
| | L-5 | M | Senior High School |
| The Taipei 228 Memorial Museum | T-1 | F | Senior High School |
| | T-2 | M | Post Graduate |
| | T-3 | F | Senior High School |
| | T-4 | F | College |
| | T-5 | M | College |
| The Peitou Hot Springs Museum | P-1 | M | College |
| | P-2 | F | Senior High School |
| | P-3 | F | Senior High School |
| | P-4 | M | Post Graduate |
| | P-5 | F | Senior High School |
| The Hsinchu Municipal Glass Museum | G-1 | M | College |
| | G-2 | F | Junior High School |
| | G-3 | M | College |
| | G-4 | M | College |
| | G-5 | M | Senior High School |

For example, B-1 refers to the participant who was interviewed in the Bai-mi Clog Museum. All interview data was transcribed and analysed by Nudist computer software, and the memories were put into two categories: those stimulated by historical buildings and those stimulated by exhibits.

## Memories stimulated by historical buildings

Research has indicated that most visitors have memories prompted by the museum's environment and buildings (Falk 1988). Lowenthal (1985: 16) has suggested that the surrounding milieu very often works as the repository of memories. Similarly, Halbwachs (1980: 140) claims that collective memories are always associated with a place and location. He argues that: 'every collective memory unfolds within a spatial framework . . . we can understand how we recapture the past only by understanding how it is, in effect, preserved by our physical surrounding'. Notably, revisiting a place very often brings back those memories of the past. Summarising Lowenthal's concepts of heritage, Urry (1999: 224) identifies four characteristics of old houses: solidity, continuity, authority and craft. For him the concept of solidity is not only determined by the fact that they have survived over time but also by their continuity between the past and present. All five case study museums were housed in historic buildings. All of them had been used for official purposes and had not been open to the general public. However, they had all, nevertheless, played a part in local residents' lives. When asked if they had been to the historical buildings before their conversion into museums, 13 respondents said that they had some impression of the buildings and 5 of them had been into the historical buildings on special occasions. Comparing their impressions of the past with the present, they recalled various feelings and thoughts during their visits. Five different types of memories in the historical buildings have emerged and each type will be discussed separately below.

### Remembering life episodes

Respondents recalled memories in and about historical houses in terms of an event or life episode. Some of them could remember details of the event including the people they were with, the location and its surroundings in the historical buildings, but they were not sure about the exact time. The memory unfolded like a scene in a film which flashed back to an uncertain time in the past. G-5 remembered how he once visited the historical house:

> Before . . . I went here once. In the air force . . . I used to work at the railway station, because there was a driver who worked at the American Military Consultancy. He went to the railway station to take films for them to watch. I was poor then and I did not have a car. I had to walk. He drove me home and we went by the building.
>
> (Interviewee G-5)

Since the building was occupied by the American Military Consultancy during those years after the Second World War and very few people were allowed into the building, a visit to it was an unusual event for G-5.

### Memories of domestic life in the past

Since these museums are open to the public, people are able to walk around, chat with friends in the garden or reminisce in the museum. They become places of contemplation. Older people, who had lived in Japanese houses or stone-built houses, respond very personally to the building because visiting the museum reminds them of their domestic life in the past. Many traditional houses have been demolished, victims of international style and the linear progressive concept of modernism, and only a few traditional or stone houses have been left for domestic use. The museum building thus provides material evidence of the lifestyle of earlier days. One interviewee, who had lived in a stone house, expressed his fondness for it and made a very precise comparison between the stone house and the modern building. He said:

> The stone house is warm in the winter but cool in the summer. In winter, it is hard for the wind to break in and in the summer, the heat penetrates slowly. For example, if there is sunshine from nine o'clock in the morning, you won't feel the heat until four in the afternoon. Unlike a concrete house where you have to turn on the air-conditioner around eleven in the morning, otherwise it will get too hot.
>
> (Interviewee B-3)

Since Taiwan was a colony of Japan from 1895 to 1945, many people acquired a Japanese lifestyle and have experience of living in traditional Japanese houses. One respondent remembered how he liked to live in a Japanese house:

> I lived in Japanese accommodation when I was little because my father was a civil servant. I grew up in Japanese accommodation . . . The old house was warm in winter and cool in summer. It was not afraid of typhoons because its structure was not tall, but was wide and strong. The beams were very strong. I liked the environment.
>
> (Interviewee L-5)

Whether talking about a traditional stone house or a Japanese building, both respondents expressed the view that the traditional buildings had more comfortable temperatures. Of course, it is generally accepted that global warming has resulted in higher temperatures so there may be an element of nostalgia in these memories. However, the visit provides an opportunity to compare lifestyles in the past with those of the present, and creates the possibility of questioning how we have lived and the paths we have taken.

### Childhood memories

For those who never went into these historical houses when young, visiting the museum did not evoke a memory of a particular event, but some general childhood memories of being in the vicinity of the house. For example, the I-Lan Museum of Local Political History was first built as the residence of the Japanese governor of I-Lan County and was in continuous use as the residence of the mayor of I-Lan County for nearly a century. To most people in I-Lan, it was an inaccessible place and this made it a place of mystery. As L-4 remembered:

> As a child, I felt this Japanese house was very serious, and mysterious. Beside it, there was a river with bending willows and clear transparent water flowing by. It was also the place that I first learned how to swim in childhood.
>
> (Interviewee L-4)

Likewise, local residents also found the stone house of the Bai-mi Clog Museum full of mystery for different reasons. Unlike the other examples, the house was not built for the privileged but for the employees of the Taiwan Compost Company. Made of stone, it was a popular style of residence for people in the Bai-mi community in the 1960s and 1970s. As it had been deserted before its renovation, it acquired a reputation for being haunted. One young woman remembered:

> As deserted accommodation, there were weeds everywhere and the whole building was very old and crumbling. Little children used to call it a haunted house because it was always closed and the doors and windows were creaking making sound of y-y-wi-wi . . . The weeds were as tall as a man. Children used to peep in from outside and called it a haunted house.
>
> (Interviewee B-5)

In general, these old houses appeared particularly grand and mysterious to children. Difficult of access, they emanated an enigmatic aura – a world of closure and mystery, which continues to inspire local residents' imagination linked to their childhood memories.

### Reconstruction of a historical event

For those who do not have memories of the historical house, a visit to the museum is an invitation to reconstruct historical events in their minds. Taking the 228 Memorial Museum as an example, some respondents do not have particular memories of the building itself. However, when visiting the museum and walking around the historic house, one visitor imagined the historical event happening there. Looking at the exhibition, she learned that it was from this place, the former broadcasting station, that people received news and information about the incident. T-4 liked the idea of using this building as a museum and said:

> I think it is great because this is the historical site. It wouldn't mean so much if you chose other places. Because this was the centre of Taiwan – the headquarters of the 288 Incident, resolution and messages were sent from here . . . in Taipei. Because there were 17 committees in Taiwan, they all sent their messages to Taipei. Mr Wang went here to read the news every day. This was the place that stirred up the movement. There is no better place than this place as the museum
>
> (Interviewee T-4)

Although she did not witness the actual event, through the information provided by the museum and visiting the historical site, she was able to experience the historical event in her imagination.

### Reflection, association and creation of memories

For the younger generation, who did not have any experience of colonialism nor of the 288 Incident, visiting the museum was more about gathering information and learning history. However, one young respondent did not think the lack of previous personal memory would prevent him from generating new memories. He emphasised that visiting the museum in the historic building inspired him to recreate the past and make it part of his memories. Historic houses, he pointed out, link experiences and understanding across generations. He said:

> So if one looks at things of ten years ago, they will bring back many memories. Um, of course there is happiness or pain – all kinds of memories. But I feel we should make people think about our history . . . In other words, if you encounter an old building in Taipei, it reminds you that it was this school that you went to or it was where you worked. Or maybe a grandmother or a grandfather talks to their children, tells their grandchildren that this was the place that I went to work or went shopping.
>
> (Interviewee P-1)

The historic house museum thus serves as a theatre in which people learn of memories which they themselves did not experience firsthand, and where their imagination allows them to create their own memory of these things.

## Memories prompted by exhibits

Research has shown that objects play an important part in our lives, in constructing our self and symbolising our identities. Csikszentmihalyi and Rochberg-Halton (1981) studied 82 American families to investigate how people attributed meanings to objects in their daily lives. In this research, they found that 'the potential significance of things is realized in a process of actively cultivating a world of meanings, which both reflect and help create the ultimate goals of one's existence' (Csikszentmihalyi and Rochberg-Halton 1981: xi). From the data, they discovered that gender, rather than social class, plays an important role in the process of generating meanings of objects. They found that men emphasised the usage value of objects more and regarded objects as the extension of self. In contrast, women tend to cherish objects because of their quality of contemplation and their association with relationships with others. Likewise, Pearce (1998) conducted a survey investigating the relationship between objects and personal culture. She also found that women tend to value the intrinsic and emotional meanings of objects and make a connection between the past and present, while men tend to value objects for their practical purpose in the present and future. Research conducted at Wakefield Museum with different age groups found that younger people would prefer to see things in relation to their present experience while older people are more interested in objects which remind them of their earlier lives (Johnstone 1998).

These research projects have provided significant insights into the relationship between people and objects, although most of the studies are limited to everyday objects owned by the respondents. Once objects are selected and exhibited in museums, their status and meanings are transformed significantly. They are no longer mundane and disposable; they are preserved carefully to represent customs, values or lifestyles of certain periods in time. In these circumstances, objects in the museum were not owned or used by visitors individually, their relationship with visitors is impersonal. However, such objects can function as a link between private and public memories. How do they trigger visitors' memories? This research supports what Silverman (1990) found previously: that visitors in different types of museums have different responses to exhibits. For example, many objects in local history museums resemble something that visitors have been familiar with or used before, and through free association or recollection, the artefacts very often invite and stimulate visitors' memories of things in the past. The objects in the 228 Memorial Museum, a holocaust museum, on the other hand, are more about the ritual of commemoration than materials for personal recollection. They are a series of icons and images as well as a means of healing collective grief. In another example, objects in an art museum provide aesthetic pleasure and a novel experience for visitors. Bearing in the mind that people's reactions depend on the type of museum they are in, the five case studies will be examined further to analyse how people remember in response to museum exhibits. By so doing, it is hoped to provide some insights into how visitors understand, make meanings and construct their personal memories and identities through museum objects.

### The experience of using objects

The interview data indicated that visitors are most interested in objects that they have used before. Of course, the museum exhibits are not items that they have owned and used, but they very often remind them of the experience of using similar ones at home. This experience was most common in local community museums or history museums where exhibits have been collected locally. In the case of the I-Lan Museum of Local Political History, the exhibit that attracts most people's interest is the old bathtub, which has been gradually replaced by the modern bathtub and is rare in households now (Figure 13.4). One interviewee told me that he felt it was particularly dear to him because he had used a similar one in his childhood:

> Such as the bathtub, the pulo for bath (pulo is bathtub in Japanese), we used it when we were little. Such as the toilet, the veng kan (toilet in Taiwanese dialect), the one with a top, I used them all in Japanese accommodation when I was little . . . Because in the old days, there were no modern facilities, it was stuck there and stank, so we used the top . . . We used them all, so I feel it is very dear to me.
>
> (Interviewee I-5)

Familiar exhibits tend to invoke memories of past usage and comparisons of the past with the present. Visitors to the Bai-mi Clog Museum like to compare the products made by traditional craft with modern ones made by machines. B-2 pointed out:

> It is good to let younger generations see – they are solid. If you compare . . . well, they were better. Even though we produce shoes quickly by machine now, the hand-made products before were really nice. They were really smart. I feel people before were more practical and produced solid objects.
>
> (Interviewee B-2)

*Figure 13.4* The old bathtub exhibited in the I-Lan Museum of Local Political History.
Photo: the author.

Others talked about the strengths of traditional crafts. B-3 compared the clogs with modern shoes and thought:

> Wearing clogs is good for your health. Our feet don't stink. Good circulation and sometimes it can give you a foot massage. It helps your blood circulation. If you wear modern shoes, your feet smell.
>
> (Interviewee B-3)

Visiting the local history museum not only brings back memories of using those objects but also encourages visitors to compare the handmade objects of the past with their modern equivalents, revealing a tendency to think that things were better in the past. Lowenthal (1985: 4) called this modern-day 'nostalgia' and criticised it for the underlying assumption that something very old was 'necessarily good'.

### Economic conditions in the past

Visitors' memories are complex and they can often hold apparently contradictory views of the past. For example, memories of hardship in the old days are sometimes mixed with remembrances of happy family times. In the case of the Bai-mi Clog Museum many older visitors had memories of wearing clogs which not only reminded them of family life but also of the economic conditions in their childhood.

> The way we wore the clogs was not like now . . . In the past, we could only wear clogs in the evening, only in the evening after taking a bath, cleaning our feet and hands. In the daytime, we had to walk on bare feet.
>
> (Interviewee B-1)

Such memories can be seen within the context of the changing use of clogs. Plastic shoes have made clogs virtually redundant as everyday footwear. Clogs are now mainly made and worn for aesthetic pleasure and entertainment. Through the regeneration of the traditional craft by the Bai-mi Clog Museum, they have become both artworks and means of experiencing an older lifestyle.

### Family relationships

Recollection is seldom independent from its context (Halbwachs 1980). Falk and Dierking (2000) also emphasise that memories and learning in the museum are situated within personal, physical and sociocultural contexts. Many memories in the museum are therefore linked to friends or family members and the time spent with them. At the Peitou Hot Springs Museum, P-3 found that the tatami, a Japanese mattress which is commonly found in household furniture in Japan, interested her most (Figure 13.5). Since she had had some tatami in her house, it stimulated memories of using them and the relationship between her and her children. She said:

> Because I had had tatami in my house, I had six at my home because they were very useful, particularly good for . . . the touch and contact between parents and children. Though they were little then, my children still remember the tatami very

*Figure 13.5* The Hall of Tatami of the Peitou Hot Springs Museum.
Photo: the author.

much because we used to sleep, play games and tell stories on it. It was a very good way to contact and touch.

(Interviewee P-3)

Visiting the museum and seeing objects they had used before, therefore, not only enabled interviewees to recall the experience of using objects but also brought to mind their past relationships and time spent with family members.

### The collective trauma of historical tragedy

The previous three patterns of remembering were found in the local history museums or the community museum. However, when it comes to the holocaust museum, the communication between visitors and museum exhibits became more painful and intense. In the case of the Taipei 228 Memorial Museum, because of the nature of the museum, many visitors appeared very solemn when looking at exhibits. Apart from photography and newspaper cuttings, many objects exhibited had belonged to victims of the 288 Incident. During the process of collecting and exhibiting, ordinary objects had been re-contextualised and acquired a symbolic association with the dead. Here, the objects represent the absent victims of the incident (Hallam and Hockey 2001). It is this symbolic power that touches, even overwhelms, visitors. One respondent revealed that he even felt like crying when he saw the photographs of an execution:

When they executed those people, their hands and feet were pierced by shackles. I think it hurts a lot . . . I have read about it in documentary. Today, when I see the photography, maybe because I am a little bit older now, I can feel others' pain . . . I feel great pain.

(Interviewee T-2)

In this case, for those who experienced the tragedy or lost relatives in the incident, objects or photographs on display have a direct emotional, distressing effect on them; for others who did not have this firsthand experience, the exhibits still provide powerful material evidence of a link with historical tragedy. Exhibits are charged with mixed emotions and they sometimes even evoke direct sensations in visitors such as the feeling of being hurt. Seeing, in this case, strangely involves and activates other senses. Barthes (1981: 26) explains this effect and describes it as 'punctum' in his discussion of photography. He writes: 'It is this element which rises from the scene, shoots out of it like an arrow, and pierces me. A Latin word exists to designate this wound, this prick, this mark made by a pointed instrument'. This 'punctum' effect, indeed, occurred to visitors in the Taipei 228 Memorial Museum. It was the 'punctum' effect that struck T-2 when he looked at the scene in which people's hands were chained.

In this particular case, visitors not only looked at exhibits but also felt pain when they did so. Objects owned and used by the victims here have the power to transmit grief and pain to visitors. When these particular objects, which are related to and symbolise death, are exhibited in the museum, their 'punctum' effect is further carried to wider society, thus embodying a collective national trauma.

### The loss of youth

When the visitor is a family member of the victim, looking at objects or photographs used by his or her own dead relative arouses complex memories. The exhibits provide a direct link to his or her personal life. During my fieldwork, I saw a lady who stood in front of Tei-Dong Wang's photographs and stared at the books and wristwatch used by Mr Wang for a long period of time. After chatting with her, I realised that she was a relative of Mr Wang, the representative of the people's committee who was executed during the 288 Incident. Without telling anybody, she came to the museum alone. Visiting the museum took her back to painful memories throughout her childhood and adulthood. She not only lost her uncle, Mr Wang, but also her brother in the early 1960s. Following the 288 Incident, there was a long period of White Terror. Anyone who said anything against the government or talked about the 288 Incident might be questioned, sent to prison or, worst of all, executed secretly. Her own brother was executed during that White Terror period because he joined a study society. This incident changed her whole life and left her with unforgettable trauma. She recalled:

At that time, our family was wealthy. My second brother was very able at school and worked in the post office. And because of that, my Dad felt very sad . . . After that, my Dad stopped sending us to school . . . For me, I just got to the primary school. Not until recent years did I continue my junior high school education in the evening when it became compulsory. My father used to say: 'No need to study, especially girls! Why study? Those who don't study are safe. And him, study and lose his life.'

(Interviewee T-1)

She sometimes could not help weeping when we walked around the museum as she recalled these memories during my interview with her. Kavanagh (2002) has highlighted the risks of dealing with traumatic experience in the museum suggesting that, although there is an increasing emphasis on the therapeutic role of museums, this role is not suitable for those visitors who have just recently experienced trauma. In this case, the Incident happened when the respondent was little. However, having lacked professional support and having suppressed her feelings for decades, she was not able to talk about her traumatic experience in public. Visiting the 228 Memorial Museum gave her comfort to see how justice had been done and, chatting and sharing her experience with the researcher to a certain extent, also helped her express the anxiety and disquiet which had been deeply repressed for a long time.

The museum exhibits, owned by her dead uncle, not only triggered her childhood memories but also made her think of the passage of time and loss of her youth. She said:

> it happened during our youth, which should be our golden age. It stopped my brothers and sisters doing many things. I felt . . . very frightened and dared not to talk to others, many things . . . Now we are too old to do many things.
>
> (Interviewee T-1)

Exhibits in museums thus elicit visitors' childhood memories, inviting them to review the past, and cause them to reflect on the passage of time.

## Conclusion

This exploration of the role of local museums in the shaping of visitors' museum experiences and cultural identities in Taiwan has resulted in a range of findings that suggest the local museum is a significant site through which local residents construct a sense of locality and knowledge of themselves through their memories. During fieldwork participants were very eager to talk to the researcher about their memories and childhood experiences, and both the historical buildings and their local exhibits played particularly important roles in facilitating these discussions. This research also demonstrates that memories of local residents have varied layers of meaning. They provide a vivid portrait of personal experiences. As a form of important intangible history revealing sentiments and feelings they also offer new insights into the past of a local area.

The research also illustrates the complex relationship between past and present in museum visitors' minds. Visitors actively compare past and present and, in most cases, they adopted a positive attitude to the past-exhibiting 'nostalgia' (Lowenthal 1985). However, it is worth noting that visitors do not naively accept everything in the past as good; they are able to give reasons for their point of view. Although modern society is usually considered to be more advanced in material achievement, respondents constantly reflect and question the modern way of life through comparison with architecture and artefacts of the past.

Moreover, memories are not passively received in the museum; they are actively recalled and constructed. For example, in the case of the 228 Memorial Museum, visitors are able to reconstruct historical events. Finally, memories in the museum on the one hand have the therapeutic power to make people feel and express suppressed feelings. On the other hand they sometimes, especially in the case of the holocaust museum, elicit feelings of suffering and evoke sympathy towards those who experienced a particular historical event. Therefore, visits to the museum can be very emotionally-laden experiences since they trigger visitors' memories of earlier days, open the dialogue between the past and the present and invite visitors to articulate their memories and identities.

# Bibliography

Assman, J. (1995) 'Collective memory and cultural identity', *New German Critique*, 65: 125–33.

Barthes, R. (1981) *Camera Lucida: Reflections on Photography*, trans. Richard Howard, London: Vintage.

Brower, B. C. (1999) 'The preserving machine: the "new" museum and working through trauma – the Musee Memorial pour la Paix of Caen', *History and Memory*, 11(1): 77–103.

Csikszentmihalyi, M. and Rochberg-Halton, E. (1981) *The Meaning of Things*, Cambridge: Cambridge University Press.

Falk, J. H. (1988) 'Museum recollections', in S. Bitgood Jr., J. Roper and A. Benefield (eds) *Visitor Studies 1988: Theory, Research and Practice: Proceedings of The First Annual Visitor Studies Conference*, Alabama: Pyschology Institute of Jacksonville University, 60–5.

Falk, J. H. and Dierking, L. D. (2000) *Learning from Museums*, Oxford: Altamira Press.

Halbwachs, M. (1980) *The Collective Memory*, trans. F. J. Ditter, Jr. and V. Yazdi Ditter, New York: Harper Colophon Books.

Hallam, E. and Hockey, J. (2001) *Death, Memory and Material Culture*, Oxford: Berg.

Herrmann, D. and Plude, D. (1995) 'Museum Memory', in J. H. Falk and L. D. Dierking (eds) *Public Institutions for Personal Learning: Establishing a Research Agenda*, Washington, DC: American Association of Museums.

Hooper-Greenhill, E. and Moussouri, T. (2002) *Researching Learning in Museums and Galleries 1990–1999: A Bibliographic Review*, Leicester: Research Centre for Museums and Galleries.

Johnstone, C. (1998) 'Your granny had one of those!', in J. Arnold, K. Davies and S. Ditchfield (eds) *History and Heritage: Consuming the Past in Contemporary Culture*, Dorset: Donhead Publishing Ltd, 67–77.

Kavanagh, G. (2002) 'Remembering ourselves in the work of museums: trauma and the place of the personal in the public', in R. Sandell (ed.) *Museums, Society, Inequality*, London: Routledge, 110–22.

Lowenthal, D. (1985) *The Past is a Foreign Country*, Cambridge: Cambridge University Press.

Mercer, K. (1990) 'Welcome to the jungle: identity and diversity in postmodern politics', in J. Rutherford (ed.) *Identity, Community, Culture, Difference*, London: Lawrence & Wishart, 43–71.

Pearce, S. M. (1998) 'Objects in the contemporary construction of personal culture: perspectives relating to gender and socio-economic class', *Museum Management and Curatorship*, 17(3): 223–41.

Radley, A. (1990) 'Artefacts, memory and a sense of the past', in D. Middleton and D. Edwards (eds) *Collective Remembering*, London: Sage Publications, 46–59.

Sherman, D. J. (1995) 'Objects of memory: history and narrative in French war museums', *French Historical Studies*, 19(1): 49–74.

Silverman, L. (1990) 'Of us and other "things": the content and function of talk by adult visitor pairs in an art and a history museum', unpublished thesis, University of Pennsylvania.

—— (1995) 'Visitor meaning-making in museums for a new Age', *Curator*, 38(3): 161–70.

Urry, J. (1996) 'How societies remember the past', in S. Macdonald and G. Fyfe (eds) *Theorizing Museums*, Oxford: Blackwell Publishers, 45–65.

—— (1999) 'Gazing on history', in D. Boswell and J. Evans (eds) *Representing The Nation: A Reader*, London: Routledge, 208–32.

Zelizer, B. (1995) 'Reading the past against the grain: the shape of memory studies', *Critical Studies in Mass Communication*, 12(2): 214–39.

# 14

# POLITICAL AND SOCIAL INFLUENCES AFFECTING THE SENSE OF PLACE IN MUNICIPAL MUSEUMS IN PORTUGAL

*Marta Anico and Elsa Peralta*

Heritage is increasingly being used as a means of identifying and articulating a sense of 'place' in the context of the globalisation and postmodernisation of culture. One of the ways in which this focus on 'place' manifests itself is by investment in local museums that allow the production, representation and regulation of a discourse of both the loss and preservation of heritage in public. In Portugal, as in many other European countries, we have witnessed several examples of this trend, reflecting recent radical transformations in Portuguese society.

This chapter analyses the different types of this investment in local museums, focusing on identifying those involved in the construction of a discourse about the past in the local public sphere, such as the politicians and those that originally participated in the activities represented, as well as their motivation. It argues that symbolic investment in the past and in local heritage is designed to create an impression of cultural vitality in localities (Zukin 1995) which encourages the political and social advancement of those who participate in these activities. In addition, this chapter emphasises the point that this impression of vitality not only embodies local factors but that it also incorporates and reflects diversity and global patterns, creating a syncretism that influences various dimensions of peoples' lives, such as their relationships to work, leisure and cultural practices.

Thus, these local museums do not exist only in, and for, the 'place'. They are part of broader cultural landscapes, translating and materialising the global–local nexus (Robins 1999), as well as the polymorphism and plurality of Portuguese society. Two case studies in two different regions of Portugal will illustrate this point.

## Recent changes in Portuguese society

To understand the present state of local municipal museums in Portugal, it is important first to look at some of the main changes that have occurred in Portuguese society which have resulted in what has been described as a state of unfinished modernity (Silva 1994). This state has been influenced by two decisive events. First, the Revolution of April 1974, that brought democracy to the country after 40 years of dictatorship and, second, the entry of Portugal into the European Economic Community in 1986. These two events, which had profound historic, political and social consequences related to the loss of the former overseas colonies and the development of closer ties with Europe, produced deep changes in Portuguese society.

After years of backwardness in relation to other European countries, Portugal opened up to the principles and values of modernity (Viegas and Costa 2000) and a set of interrelated changes began to take place, including the democratisation of education and culture, the emergence and growth of middle classes, social mobility and the expansion of consumption (Machado and Costa 2000). This growth of the middle classes, along with improvements in educational standards and the development of the service sector, are also related to two other phenomena that are equally important for this chapter's analysis: the concentration of population in coastal areas and urbanisation (Conde 2000). The growth of the main cities (Lisbon and Oporto) and the development pattern experienced by smaller towns (Gama 1993) has resulted in the movement of people from the interior regions of the country to the coast and helped to establish the framework for an intermediate stage of development (Santos 1994), placing Portugal in an state of multi-directional and unfinished modernity.

Consumption is another well-known feature of modernity (Lash and Urry 1994), a condition where knowledge, culture and information are regarded as instruments of empowerment for both individuals and populations, increasingly appealing to a wider public. This explosion of consumption has been realised in, among other things, the increase in leisure and cultural pursuits. In recent years an escalation in the number of exhibitions, concerts, music festivals, dance and theatre performances has been evident. These forms of expression, which would have been regarded as part of a 'cultivated culture' restricted to the aristocratic and bourgeois elite just a few decades ago, are now part of a qualitative change in Portuguese lifestyles illustrating how different sectors of Portuguese society are increasingly interested in a wide range of cultural products.

As a consequence, both supply and demand in the cultural sector has expanded, and cultural practices have become increasingly economically and socially important to the general population. However, this is most evident in the urban areas along the coast, where the above changes are more far-reaching. The depopulated interior regions of the country lag behind in economic and cultural development.

Nevertheless, in both rural and urban areas, there has been a considerable investment in the cultural sector, which has been sponsored by local agencies, especially by local authorities. The sector has also benefited from European Union funding programmes that have been available since 1986. Local authorities have become important agents of change, especially since the promulgation of the Local Government Act in 1979. Since then, municipal councils have assumed the task of promoting 'culture' as a fundamental political responsibility, and this helps to explain the creation and development of many municipal museums, such as the Maritime Museum of Ílhavo and the Ceramics Museum of Sacavém. Furthermore, membership of the European Union brought new possibilities for local authorities and local museums, in terms of European and other international contacts, the establishment of networks, the development of projects and funding opportunities.

The modernisation of Portugal and the recent transformation of Portuguese society can be placed in the context of globalisation. The dissemination of local and global cultures throughout the world has contributed to changing concepts of place and identity. Places are described and promoted as part of broader cultural landscapes, and previous territorial and spatial concepts are now giving way to new configurations based on local, regional or national characteristics that more often than not reveal the mingling of different layers of social and cultural identity. In this context local authorities and local populations see municipal and other local museums as strategic resources for cultural representation.

## The Ceramics Museum of Sacavém and the Maritime Museum of Ílhavo

The Ceramics Museum of Sacavém is located in the metropolitan borough of Loures, the fifth largest in the country in terms of population (approximately 200,000 inhabitants). Situated on the outskirts of Lisbon, its socio-demographic profile changed radically in the second half of the twentieth century with the return, in the 1970s, of thousands of people from Portugal's former, and recently independent, colonies. In parallel with these migration flows, which brought diversity and change to the area, economic changes also considerably affected society.

Loures contains both rural and urban landscapes. In the past, it not only supplied agricultural products to Lisbon, but districts such as Sacavém were also heavily industrialised in the mid-nineteenth century. It is close to the country's capital, has good transport systems and a regular supply of labour. The ceramics factory of Sacavém is typical of this industrial development, which continued to flourish in the first decades of the twentieth century.

However, in recent decades Loures and Sacavém underwent several changes. There was an abrupt economic decline. Agricultural production dwindled and many industries, including the ceramics factory of Sacavém, closed down. Despite this, the local population continued to increase dramatically as a result of both internal migration to the suburbs of the main cities such as Lisbon, and immigration from the former Portuguese overseas territories, Eastern Europe and, more recently, from Brazil.

The Maritime Museum of Ílhavo is located in the centre-north region of Portugal, in the town of Ílhavo, not far from the city of Oporto. In the past, Ílhavo's industries were of national importance. Near to a vast lagoon, its population made use of a considerable coastline and, traditionally, relied on agriculture and fishing, particularly cod fishing. But employment patterns changed dramatically when fishing and agriculture declined as industrial employment grew, as well as the employment in the service and administrative sectors of the local economy. Given its proximity to the sea, the tourist sector is also important in Ílhavo, due to the seasonal flow of tourists (mainly Portuguese) who arrive in the town each summer.

Ílhavo lies within a wider conurbation and exhibits growth intensity that is found in much larger towns, benefiting as it does from its location and good road and rail links. With approximately 37,000 inhabitants, Ílhavo attracts people from neighbouring localities. In addition, migrants tend to settle in this coastal zone, as do foreign immigrants. This rapid demographic growth has led to considerable pressures on the area, and house-building has proceeded at a rate that far outstrips the infrastructure and basic services (access routes and public health), which are, on the whole, inadequate.

This is, then, a diverse area, in a process of transition, with development taking place at different rates. This is apparent in the co-existence of modern social practices alongside other, more traditional ones. Such disjunction is seen in the changes that have been wrought on the physical landscape and on the social and economic structure of the area. It can also be observed in blurred distinction between the rural and urban environments, the fluidity of the community's cultural and physical boundaries, the interaction of industry with the growth of the service and administrative sectors in the local economy, and with complementary forms of subsistence farming and fishing.

In both Loures and Ílhavo, change and diversity help to explain the context in which the museums have developed. Our argument is that the disjunctions and differences (Appadurai 1990) caused by these changes promoted new forms of (re)imagining 'culture' and 'place' (Macdonald 1997). One way of doing so is through the (re)assessment of the past and the construction of a heritage discourse, in particular through the creation of and investment in local museums.

The Ceramics Museum of Sacavém, created with the aim of preserving the cultural memory and legacy of the ceramics factory, opened in the year 2000. The factory was founded in 1856 by the Portuguese entrepreneur Manuel Joaquim Afonso and specialised in the production of glazed tiles, ceramic mosaic, sanitary ware, tableware and hospital and pharmacy ware. Owned and managed by English proprietors since 1861, it operated for more than a century and achieved considerable international recognition for its products. But the factory also had important national and local significance. It became a significant part of Portugal's industrial and artistic history and influenced not only the lives of its workers but also the lives of other sectors of the local population because of its presence in the daily routines and activities of this community. However, from the 1960s onwards the ceramics factory of Sacavém began to experience economic difficulties, aggravated by the oil crisis in the 1970s, and it never recovered its previous prominent position. After controversial bankruptcy proceedings (officially declared in 1995) the factory was closed down and completely demolished and all of its remaining equipment and grounds were sold.

The municipal council of Loures decided to intervene and create a museum dedicated to the factory's artistic production and social history. This was not without its problems, due to the fact that private developers had bought the site and intended to construct a luxury residential unit on it. Nevertheless, after intense negotiations between the municipal council and private contractors, consensus was finally achieved in 1997 with the donation of part of the land and the museum's collection to the municipality. Under this agreement, the new urban development plan included a residential scheme and the Ceramics Museum, which both parties saw as contributing to urban regeneration.

The museum was then built on the site where the factory had previously stood. Its displays focus on two main themes: the social history of the industry in Sacavém and the artistic production of the factory. The Ceramics Museum of Sacavém was opened in July 2000 by the President of the Portuguese Republic, Jorge Sampaio, whose presence was regarded by its promoters as proof of this local municipal museum's national relevance.

Two years after its opening ceremony the museum was given a new reason to celebrate. Despite the fact that it had been so recently opened, the Ceramics Museum of Sacavém was awarded the Micheletti Prize in 2002, an award given by the European Museum Forum and the Luigi Micheletti Foundation to the most promising technical or industrial museum of the year. The jury considered the Ceramics Museum of Sacavém, housed in a modern building, with attractive surroundings and good amenities, to have presented the history of the ceramics industry in an engaging and sympathetic manner. The assessment also pinpointed two other important factors: the involvement of local people in some of the museum's educational programmes, such as ceramics workshops and storytelling, and the offer of inclusive exhibitions and other museum activities that take into consideration the specific needs of disabled visitors.

This award raised the profile of the museum which now no longer possessed just local and national significance but also international status. Therefore, while asserting the locality's particular characteristics, the Ceramics Museum of Sacavém has also assimilated good international practices.

Let us now consider the Maritime Museum of Ílhavo. At the current time it is mainly devoted to the commemoration of the cod fishing industry. However, this was not always the case. Founded in 1937, the museum has undergone many transformations since then. Its collections, its themes, its displays and even the building that houses the museum have all been overhauled at one time or another.

Originally it was a regional museum, with a historic and ethnographic orientation, with various local cultural displays. Today, the Museum of Ílhavo occupies a new building, with a very bold design, which opened in 2001. That was when the museum chose to specialise and focus on maritime activities and, in particular, on the representation of cod fisheries which at one time employed many local families. In fact, local people mostly define themselves by their special relationship with the sea, in particular the cod fishing. The harsh conditions endured by the fishermen had an epic quality: in a fleet of single manned white-sailed boats (dories) they plied the icy waters of Newfoundland and Greenland. This type of fishing was called *faina maior* (literally, 'harder work'), and it gained a place in the local collective imagination, providing the foundation for a discourse of differentiation.

However, from 1970 on, the unsustainable exploitation of cod and the crisis of stocks led to the reduction of the catch, resulting in an abrupt decline in fishing. This accelerated when Portugal entered the European Union, with the subsequent introduction of a quota policy. Cod fishing then underwent a definitive slump. Following this, a group of people linked to cod fishing, in particular masters and ship-owners, became actively involved in the representation of a memory of an industry in which they had once participated. Their activity was expressed largely in increasing involvement in the local ethnographic museum, which up to that point had not had any significant displays related to cod fishing.

After 1997, the recently-elected mayor of Ílhavo set about establishing a new direction for the museum focusing on this theme. The mayor noted the degree of consensus generated in this community (where legends associated with the sea and fishing still persist), by seafaring in general and cod fishing in particular. He therefore associated himself with the views of the masters and ship-owners. However, this led to a certain amount of conflict between them as the latter lost their exclusive control over the representation of the fishing past. Both aimed to be identified as the main proprietors of this memory while the common fisherman was almost absent from the process as he did not participate in it and was not represented.

Within the new council, the historical and symbolic importance of the sea, and cod fishing in particular, became a key element in the development of the town's identity. In order to raise the profile of this symbol, thereby gaining political dividends, and to capitalise on the image, the new mayor decided to establish monuments to evoke this memory. At the same time, a marketing slogan *Ílhavo: The Sea by Tradition*, promoted the new image of the town.

The most important element of this scheme involved remodelling the museum of Ílhavo. What used to be an ethnographic, regional museum now became, exclusively, a maritime museum, after it had been subjected to a bold, revolutionary design process, which received various awards in Portugal and abroad. At the same time, it was essential that the museum should be managed by someone whose 'image' was compatible with the new needs of this completely reconstructed museum, freeing it from local constraints and placing it within the cosmopolitan circles of global demand. The man invited to be the Museum's director was Álvaro Garrido, a lecturer in the University of Coimbra. He was, on the one hand, able to use the museum to give publicity to his own research and, on the other hand, to use his contacts in the academic and 'high culture' worlds to raise the museum's profile. Under this leadership, the museum's displays have started to match the standards of cosmopolitan cultural facilities: its exhibitions are being referred to more and more frequently in the media – both local and national.

In these two cases, whether built from scratch or totally refurbished, both museums incorporate a cosmopolitan aesthetic and design and, at the same time, they focus on a specific cultural symbol which is considered to be 'the most expressive' or 'the most differentiated' in terms of representing the locality's distinctiveness and therefore promoting its public profile.

## Champions of municipal museums

Municipal councils are the main promoters of local heritage and local municipal museums in Portugal. There are many reasons for this. Public demand has led to local authorities' assumption of responsibilities in the cultural sector. It has become a given that 'culture is good and necessary', which predisposes a warm and positive reaction by the public to initiatives in this sector. Thus, local populations interpret the lack of a cultural programme, a cultural centre or even a museum, as an unacceptable void that local authorities should fill. However, we should not forget that the politicians themselves have promoted this way of thinking since they were the ones responsible for the construction of a discourse on the importance and relevance of the cultural sector, which led to the investment in local cultural production, enabling them to enhance their role as patrons, offering culture to the local communities.

In this sense, municipalities' investment in heritage is a particularly effective strategy, since it is based on identity references previously agreed to by local populations (Prats 2005). This has resulted in the construction of a heritage discourse based on local figures and heroes, historical events or other symbols of local identity. This means that heritage discourses, in particular those in local museums, are frequently based on pre-existing cultural elements accorded high value by communities and are regarded as symbols of their unique lives.

In Ílhavo, the heritage discourse is mainly based on the fishing activity, an activity that impacted considerably on the job market in the municipal area. This explains why the local population are so enthusiastic about the representation of the fishing activity in the Maritime Museum. In Sacavém (Loures), this discourse is related to an industrial and artistic activity: the production of faience. As in Ílhavo's case, the factory of Sacavém employed large numbers of the local population until very recently, which explains the local community's enthusiasm for the Ceramics Museum.

Therefore, the abandonment of certain types of occupations has important social and cultural implications, generating a sense of loss of cultural references. This is especially significant when such dislocation is accompanied by major socio-demographic changes. This is precisely the case with Ílhavo and Loures, which have experienced considerable demographic growth associated with migration flows. The co-existence of different cultures and populations in these municipalities has resulted in the fragmentation of local cultural references, which also leads to a sense of loss regarding objects, places and expressions that refer to a locality's collective memory.

In these contexts of change and decline (Hewison 1987), municipal councils also turn to heritage as an instrument of local development, based on turning former industrial sites into cultural tourist attractions. These new attractions are related to a new kind of value, which links heritage and development. Under the slogan 'local', 'endogenous' or 'sustainable development', politicians promote benefits brought about through tourism generated by local cultural heritage. They argue that these support a differentiated tourist industry, following international trends. However, whether we see these as the preservation of local identity references or the transformation of old productive facilities and traditional cultures into tourist attractions, the authors would argue that we are witnessing a generalised phenomenon that could be called the 'musealization of frustration' (Prats 2006).

On the other hand tradition, heritage and museums represent the 'quality of life' of local areas, helping to attract outside resources. In Portugal, as in many other countries, local areas wish to be recognised as centres of major importance, the focus of administrative, commercial, cultural or political activities of their region. In this sense, the accumulation of 'cultural capital', expressed through the strategic positioning and differentiation of local areas at a national level, offers the necessary theoretical arguments for negotiating financial support with the government and the European Union. Such strategies stress the translocal and relational condition of these localities and their cultures.

Therefore, in the context of increasing competition between cities and localities, local museums are instruments used to promote the distinctive characteristics of a place (Augé 1998). In this sense, the municipal councils' political investment in local municipal museums enables them to position themselves not only on the national stage but, increasingly, to attract international prestige, acquiring visibility in a new global context (Dicks 2003).

By investing in heritage and local museums, municipal councils aim to achieve political legitimacy. This legitimacy translates at a local level into electoral benefits, since people see this kind of cultural project as an indicator of the efficiency of their political promoters. Furthermore, on a broader level, it translates into the reputation and visibility of local politicians in their parties' hierarchies, since a good performance in the local government is often seen as a doorway to higher political achievements.

Besides the municipal councils, there is another group of active promoters, which could be called the 'preservationist lobby', who intervene in the establishment and management of local museums in Portugal. These include heritage movements and other local groups which mobilise support and resources to use heritage as a way to affirm and protect their particular interests (Colardelle 1998).

These groups have different motives. Some wish to preserve those cultural elements that supposedly define the distinctiveness of the locality and which, at the same time, operate as indicators of prestige and distinctiveness for those that hold or preserve them. Others were strongly implicated in the activities represented in these local museums, and therefore wish to be associated with this representation in order to maintain a symbolic status within the local community. Finally, we have one other group that participates in these processes with the aim of obtaining social prestige.

The Sacavém faience collectors are fairly typical of this trend. Although they do not fit into the category of local groups, some of them have been actively engaged in the Ceramics Museum. These collectors collaborate with the museum in all sorts of ways, including taking part in artistic and market assessments. But they also loan items for temporary exhibitions or even donate items to the museum's collections. In all of these cases the outcome is purely symbolic, a benefit that confers cultural and social prestige upon these patrons.

The same can be said about the Friends of the Maritime Museum of Ílhavo. This group was set up in the early stages of the museum's creation, instigating it, in fact. It is currently composed of people who, in one way or another, have been linked to cod fishing, especially people who were prominent in that activity. When the industry declined, these people sought other ways to preserve it, trying simultaneously to perpetuate its symbolic status nationally and also locally in the heart of the community to which it belongs.

A third group of active promoters of the museum is linked to economic interests. Financial supporters are increasingly important in many Portuguese museums, sponsoring special temporary exhibitions, the publication of catalogues, the conservation of items and collections, and even the building and refurbishment of museums. However, unlike the United Kingdom, the Portuguese private sector does not play a major role in heritage and museum management.

Finally, we have a group that could be called 'cultural intermediaries' (Bovone 2001). This group conceives and delivers projects (museums, exhibitions, publications), in a professional manner. Working side by side with local authorities, these cultural intermediaries have several roles. First, they create a set of heritage narratives with academic and technical credibility. They also communicate and promote them in the public domain. Academics and heritage/museum professionals are the two most relevant categories of cultural intermediaries. While the former play an important role in providing local museums with academic credibility, the museum professionals are responsible for the formal languages of the heritage narratives. By providing local museums with academic and technical expertise, they are actively involved in a group survival strategy that aims to justify their own existence and that of their work.

All these groups are simultaneously involved in the construction of the heritage narratives found in municipal museums. Sometimes their interests are at cross purposes, leading to conflict and tension between the groups; this is not so much because they have different versions of the same past, but because each can claim the right to represent the same memory. However, because in Portugal these museums depend on municipal councils for their funding and administration, it means that such tensions are neutralised by central management control arising out of public guardianship.

This chapter set out to analyse the background to investment in local museums in Portugal, focusing on those involved in their development and what inspired them and, in doing so, to show that the processes involved are complex and characterised by the presence of different participants motivated by particular interests and aims.

Despite the fact that each group seeks to achieve specific benefits for itself, benefits that are related to reputation, political legitimacy, social distinction and professional prestige, municipal and other local museums are important for the cultural regeneration of localities. Regarded as public assets of matchless value, these museums contribute to the creation of an image of vitality and modernisation which, while being rooted in the past, nonetheless allows the negotiation of change and positioning the local in the global context.

Strong attachment to the place, quite often supported by local authorities, thus complements and helps to develop each area's relationship with the wider world. This research finds, therefore, an opening up to the global space alongside the appearance of new spaces taking root, generally via investment in territorially-based historical facts. This is a way of affirming difference and negotiating a favourable position in the new, global, cultural and economic space.

So it is the disjunctions occurring in the context of a changing, heterogeneous society that promote the development of new ways of imagining difference. They explain the present reassessment of the past, and the intensifying of cultural awareness, along with the expansion of the national network of museums and the use of the significance of the past.

All of this also enables the construction of an ideal image for each locality that can serve as a reference point for identity when previously existing references begin to disappear. In this context, 'time', rather than 'space', which is all too often fragmented, emerges as a fundamental category in a discourse on belonging. This time is the 'time of tradition', perceived as a time identified by the present that idealises it. It is afterwards structured in the social space through the agency of 'places', as local museums, which are agents and repositories of local memory.

## Bibliography

Appadurai, A. (1990) 'Disjuncture and difference in the global cultural economy', in M. Featherstone (ed.) *Global Culture: Nationalism, Globalization and Modernity*, London: Sage, 295–310.

Augé, M. (1998) *Não Lugares: Introdução a uma Antropologia da Sobremodernidade*, Lisboa: Bertrand.

Bovone, L. (2001) 'Os novos intermediários culturais: considerações sobre a cultura pós-moderna', in C. Fortuna (ed.) *Cidade, Cultura e Globalização*, Oeiras: Celta, 105–20.

Colardelle, M. (1998) 'Les acteurs de la constitution du patrimoine: travailleurs, amateurs, professionnels', in J. Le Goff (ed.) *Actes des Entretiens du Patrimoine. Patrimoine et Passions Identitaires*, Paris: Fayard, 123–35.

Conde, I. (2000) 'Context, culture, and identity', in J. Viegas and A. Costa (eds) *Crossroads to Modernity. Contemporary Portuguese Society*, Oeiras: Celta, 71–100.

Dicks, B. (2003) *Culture on Display: The Production of Contemporary Visibility*, London: Open University Press.

Gama, A. (1993) 'Espaço e sociedade: uma situação de crescimento urbano-difuso', in B. S. Santos (ed.) *Portugal. Um Retrato Singular*, Porto: Afrontamento, 441–73.

Hewison, R. (1987) *The Heritage Industry: Britain in a Climate of Decline*, London: Methuen.

Lash, S. and Urry, J. (1994) *Economies of Sign and Space*, London: Sage.

Macdonald, S. (1997) *Re-imagining Culture. Histories, Identities and the Gaelic Renaissance*, Oxford: Berg.

Machado, F. and Costa, A. (2000) 'An incomplete modernity. Structural change and social mobility', in J. Viegas and A. Costa (eds) *Crossroads to Modernity. Contemporary Portuguese Society*, Oeiras: Celta, 15–40.

Prats, L. (2005) 'Concepto y gestión del patrimonio local', *Cuadernos de Antropología Social*, 21: 17–35.

—— (2006) 'Activações turístico-patrimoniais de carácter local', in E. Peralta and M. Anico (eds) *Patrimónios e Identidades. Ficções Contemporâneas*, Oeiras: Celta, 191–200.

Robins, K. (1999) 'Tradition and translation: national culture in its global context', in D. Boswell and J. Evans (eds) *Representing the Nation: A Reader. Histories, Heritage and Museums*, London: Routledge, 15–32.

Santana, A. (1998) 'Patrimonio cultural y turismo: reflexiones y dudas de un anfitrión', *Revista Ciencia y Mar*, 6: 37–41.

Santos, B.S. (1994) *Pela Mão de Alice. O Social e o Político na Pós-Modernidade*, Porto: Afrontamento.

Silva, A. S. (1994) *Tempos Cruzados. Um Estudo Interpretativo da Cultura Popular*, Porto: Afrontamento.

Viegas, J. and Costa, A. (2000) 'Introduction: overlapping processes of social change', in J. Viegas and A. Costa (eds) *Crossroads to Modernity. Contemporary Portuguese Society*, Oeiras: Celta, 1–12.

Zukin, S. (1995) *The Cultures of Cities*, Cambridge and Oxford: Blackwell.

# 15

# ECOMUSEUMS AND SUSTAINABILITY IN ITALY, JAPAN AND CHINA

## Concept adaptation through implementation

*Peter Davis*

In previous studies, I have described in detail the origin and development of ecomuseums (Davis 1999), explored the ways in which they have provided a more democratic museum model (Davis 2004) and their relationship to small-scale cultural tourism (Davis 2005). The concept has now been practised for some 35 years and, despite being regarded with some scepticism (see, for example, Howard 2002; Sauty 2001), the movement is still very strong. The principal web-based database on ecomuseums[1] suggests there are currently some 400 worldwide, with major growth in recent years in Scandinavia, Italy and Asia. Ecomuseums are dedicated to conserving the special nature of individual places, an idea that has resonance with those promoted by the organisation Common Ground. Clifford and King (1993), when promoting the aims of that body, noted that 'every place is its own living museum, dynamic and filled with sensibilities to its own small richnesses . . . symbolism and significance cling to seemingly ordinary buildings, trees and artefacts . . . places are different from each other'. Ecomuseums have provided a platform for such 'living museums' by promoting the distinctiveness of individual places, sustaining heritage resources and aiding community development. Their basic tenets are (Corsane *et al.*, 2007a; 2007b):

- The adoption of a territory that may be defined, for example, by landscape, dialect, a specific industry, or musical tradition.
- The identification of specific heritage resources within that territory, and the celebration of these 'cultural touchstones' using in-situ conservation and interpretation.
- The conservation and interpretation of individual sites within the territory is carried out via liaison and co-operation with other organisations.
- The empowerment of local communities – the ecomuseum is established and managed by local people. Local people decide what aspects of their 'place' are important to them.
- The local community benefits from the establishment of the ecomuseum. Benefits may be intangible, such as greater self-awareness or pride in place, tangible (the rescue of a fragment of local heritage, for example) or economic. There are often significant benefits for those individuals in the local community most closely associated with ecomuseum development.

These criteria were debated extensively during the first major growth phase in the establishment of ecomuseums (Varine 1988; Rivard 1988) in order to reach a workable definition of the ecomuseum. While Rivard's comparison of the traditional museum (= building + collections + experts + public) to the ecomuseum (= territory + heritage + memory + population) is useful, it fails to capture the diversity of ecomuseum activities. In my opinion, after several years of exploring ecomuseums in different parts of the world, the most practical definition is 'a community-driven museum or heritage project that aids sustainable development'.

## Sustainability

There has been a major shift from the notion of sustainability as a biological phenomenon (O'Riordan 1990) to having a much more inclusive meaning. It is regarded now as the maintenance of our total environment, the social, economic and cultural environments, as well as safeguarding natural resources. In Sweden, for example, the Ministry of the Environment (now the Ministry for Sustainable Development) developed an Environmental Code for sustainable development that highlights the relationship between nature and culture, and states the need for action at national, regional and local level (Regeringskansliet 1999). This document also recognises that sustainability and democracy go hand-in-hand, with community decision-making seen as essential to achieving viable outcomes. These ideas of locally-based democratic approaches to maintaining the environment have obvious connections to ecomuseum philosophy and the concept of sustainable tourism.

Ideas of sustainability are being promoted through new approaches to tourism, including ecotourism and cultural tourism. It is here, in the development of low-level, sustainable tourism, that the idea of conserving elements of the heritage of places and providing economic and community benefits collide. Place marketing, with an emphasis on material culture, local traditions, landscapes and wildlife, is regarded as an increasingly important aspect of sustainable tourism (Walsh et al. 2001). It is perhaps not surprising therefore that the principles promoted by the *Charter for Sustainable Tourism* (Martin 1995) share similarities with those of the ecomuseum. The *Charter* notes the significance of natural and cultural destinations, and the need to promote only low impact activities at a local level. The *Charter* suggests that sustainable tourism should raise environmental awareness and provide empowerment and other tangible benefits for local communities.

The concept of sustainability prompts the following three questions about ecomuseum projects. Are ecomuseums a model of process and practice that will sustain local tangible and intangible heritage? Can ecomuseums aid the sustainability of local communities by providing tangible, intangible or economic benefits? Are ecomuseum projects sustainable entities? These three key issues are discussed below in relation to a sample of ecomuseums that have been established in Italy, Japan and China.

## Ecomuseums in Italy

The Piemonte (Piedmont) region in northern Italy has seen the decline of traditional industries, migration to urban areas and consequent changes to the rural landscape. It is a region of particular museological interest because of the energy and enthusiasm with which ecomuseum approaches to heritage conservation and interpretation have been adopted. The growth in the number of ecomuseums has been remarkable. In 1998 there were 15 ecomuseums in the whole of Italy (Davis 1999); in 2006, in Piemonte alone there were 50 officially recognised by provincial and regional governmental agencies (Maggi, *pers. comm.*, 2006).

One of the many recently-established ecomuseums in Piemonte is the Ecomuseo della Canapa (The Cannabis (Hemp) Ecomuseum), in the town of Carmagnola, which lies south of Turin. The descriptions and comments given below are based on an interview conducted by the author at the ecomuseum with Catterina Longo Vaschetti, leader of Il Gruppo Storico di S. Bernardino, and Loredana Bove, a representative of the Municipality with responsibility for museums.

At the height of the industry in the late nineteenth century there were 87 rope factories in St. Bernardo, a 'borgata' (Parish) of Carmagnola. These were usually family-run businesses, with the hemp (*Cannabis sativa L.*) being supplied by local farms. The factories were covered sheds (rope-walks) where the hemp was processed and spun into rope. The rope-making industry went into decline in the 1930s and the last ropeworks in St. Bernardo closed in 1955, and by 1975 only one had escaped demolition.

The St. Bernardo Historical Association initiated the project to save this last remaining ropeworks. A public fête, exhibition and demonstration of rope-making by the Association was held in 1991, an event that was well received by local people, many of whom had some association with the former industry. Several local people had collections of related material culture, photographs or memorabilia that were donated to the project. Demonstrations of rope-making were given in other places to raise the project's profile and Municipal support was ensured when national television showed an interest and produced a documentary profiling the Association's work. This enabled the purchase of the ropeworks site and its subsequent restoration in 1997. Since then a strong volunteer force has been established that manages the site and gives demonstrations (Figure 15.1). The volunteers have forged links with local artists and work in association with the other museums in Carmagnola, being considered one element in a suite of local attractions marketed to the public.

The Historical Association was surprised by the enthusiasm and support of local people, but there have been other unexpected outcomes, including invitations to give rope-making demonstrations in other countries, and a demand for hemp rope from visitors and specialist design companies. The Association, encouraged by the response from schools, is extending its educational remit and building a small classroom on site. The Municipality has also begun to recognise the importance of the ecomuseum, and what it represents in terms of capturing local identity, and has harnessed its potential to aid cultural tourism in Carmagnola, the local museums being part of a strategy that promotes distinctiveness, local products, agricultural tourism and 'slow food'.

However, audience figures are still low, with some 800 visitors from April to August, consisting mainly of schoolchildren, middle-aged people and cultural associations. Because the ecomuseum is part of the Carmagnola museums network, the Municipality sets the entrance fee and provides some financial and promotional support. The low attendances are not considered to be problematical, and the overall impression is of a very professional operation; there is good interpretation on site, the informative demonstrations being supported by high-quality graphics.

The site was designated as an ecomuseum from the start of the project at the suggestion of the Provincial government, and was never seen as a 'traditional' museum in any sense. The site is historically important, but undoubtedly the process of working together to conserve and interpret it was more significant, the local people involved having the

*Figure 15.1* Rope making demonstration, Ecomuseo della Canapa.
Photo: the author.

common purpose of conserving an important fragment of their heritage. The volunteers – all of whom are local people – share a sense of place through the common bond of the rope-making industry and take an active role at the site. When working on-site the volunteers use local dialect, keeping an important intangible heritage alive. The site itself has become a meeting place (for mass, for example) and a focus for collective community pride in place, a means of celebrating the past and demonstrating pride in the history of the industry. The original aim of the project – to sustain memories of the industry and value them – seems therefore to have been achieved.

The interview suggested that the volunteers had independence within the broad supportive framework provided by the local authority and that the major benefit from this cooperative approach was that the sustainability of the project was ensured. With some additional capital funding the ecomuseum was extending its range of activities, even though the restricted size of the site prevents any major development. The interviewees gave a clear impression that the processes of developing and maintaining the site, celebrating manufacturing skills and maintaining local dialects were extremely important, but it seems that one of the most significant outcomes was that the volunteers had profited personally by accruing social and cultural capital (Corsane *et al.* 2007b). The only significant sustainability issue is the age profile of the volunteers themselves, and they were only too aware of the need to recruit younger people to help manage the site and learn traditional skills.

## Ecomuseums in Japan

Ohara (2006) notes that Soichiro Tsuruta formally introduced the concept of the ecomuseum to Japan in the 1970s, referring to it as an 'environmental museum' in a talk introducing contemporary museological practices that were being discussed by the International Council of Museums (ICOM) at that time. Although initially failing to attract any interest, it was reintroduced into Japan in the 1980s, a period when there was increased spending by the government on projects in rural areas. Ecomuseums gained increasing favour in the 1990s, when many municipalities became interested in the phenomenon. Ohara suggests this might have been because the ecomuseum was seen as an alternative vision for a museum, a less expensive option that did not require the building of permanent and expensive buildings with their associated revenue costs. The 1992 UN Conference on Environment and Development in Rio de Janeiro also had an impact, and steered Japanese ecomuseums towards conservation of the natural environment and the development of sustainable communities. As a result, in the early 1990s the creation of on-site interpretive facilities in conservation areas were often (erroneously) labelled as ecomuseums.

Ohara notes that there is no official system that promotes ecomuseums in Japan, but that the Ministry of Agriculture, Forestry and Fisheries' 'rural environmental museum' programme, adopted in 1998, encourages the formation of museums that conserve natural environments, cultural landscapes and traditional cultures. This programme seeks to prepare the ground for such conservation projects, and some 50 areas in Japan have already been selected and developed. Ohara lists the key features of such developmental projects, which include encouraging developers to be faithful to local histories and traditional cultures, and to take a holistic approach by developing footpath links between core facilities (such as a reception centre) and other key sites in the area. Emphasis is placed on appreciation of traditional agriculture and encouraging local people to recognise the importance of the landscape. The scheme promotes public participation. Interestingly, the programme recognises that in order for such areas to be sustainable, local governments or semi-public enterprises should be entrusted to run them – in other words they are 'top-down' initiatives. However, in all other respects there are recognisable links – territory, holism, public participation, a respect for traditions – between this programme and ecomuseum approaches and practices.

However, even before this programme came into being several local community activities in Japan demonstrated ecomuseum qualities. Ohara (1998) suggested that Japan had 'spawned one ecomuseum plan after another in a very short time, with each now groping for clues as to . . . [the] direction [in which] it should proceed'. The interest in ecomuseums has been promoted by the Japanese Ecomuseological Society (JECOMS), founded in March 1995. Its international symposia have involved some of the key proponents of ecomuseum philosophy, and the *Journal of the Japanese Ecomuseological Society* provides a vehicle for debate and comment. The Japanese Ecomuseological Society's literature identifies several ecomuseums scattered throughout the Japanese archipelago, in both urban and rural locations, and fulfilling a variety of roles. The 'Ecomuseum Map of Japan' published in 2002 showed nine diverse sites, including Tamagawa, a site with a complex of religious buildings and industrial heritage along the banks of the Tama river, the Kounotori Ecomuseum, devoted to the conservation of the endangered Japanese Stork (*Ciconia boyciana*) and the Asian Live Museum, which encompasses three small towns in Tokushima Prefecture with an emphasis on conserving and interpreting traditional industries. Two further examples provide a contrasting picture of how the ecomuseum philosophy has been adopted in Japan. These are Hirano-cho and Asahi-machi.

In the fourteenth century, Hirano-cho in Osaka Prefecture in Japan was an autonomous town, and as a result of its past status has numerous historical sites, including temples, shrines, secluded gardens and traditional wooden houses which form a network of protected sites. The ecomuseum, founded in 1993 by a group of local residents and coordinated by Ryonin Kawaguchi, the priest of the Senkouji Buddhist Temple, included some of these historic areas among its seven original sites. By 2003 the ecomuseum included 15 sites and involved some 40 people; there is no coordinating body, simply a loose confederation of local people who share the vision of preserving local heritage and encouraging dialogue between local people, young and old. A sweet shop museum, a bicycle museum, Hirano no Oto 'the smallest museum in the world' (a CD playing everyday sounds of bygone Hirano), vernacular local houses with shady courtyards (Figure 15.2), the old headquarters of the local newspaper and a film museum (video and audio recordings of more than 40 years of Hirano's festivals and events) attract significant numbers of visitors when the ecomuseum opens its doors every fourth Sunday.

Although there is a map depicting the scattered ecomuseum sites, the exact locations have been made difficult to find, which Kawaguchi (*pers. comm.*, May 2003) suggests 'makes visitors ask for directions and encourages interaction with local people'. It was the view of the priest that 'most Japanese museums are very boring and don't touch normal people', that 'people should be the focus', 'people make the town' and that the ecomuseum would help

*Figure 15.2* A traditional Japanese house and garden, a feature of the Hirano-cho ecomuseum.
Photo: the author.

local people develop and begin to understand the intangible nature of their heritage. He also suggested that

> The ecomuseum is part of our efforts to recognise the cultural and historical assets we have and to get residents involved in such activities. In a way all local residents are curators. A town is revitalised when the people there are revitalised.
>
> (Kawaguchi, *pers. comm.*, May 2003)

He was also anxious not only to preserve tangible landmarks and objects, but also the craft skills and other intangible heritages, including traditional forms of play and 'local wisdom' saying 'we are trying to pass such knowledge and skills on to future generations'.

Hirano is an unusual ecomuseum in many respects, but especially because it is very intro-spective. Kawaguchi was convinced of the value of the ecomuseum for local people, but had little interest in the greater impact that it could have by attracting tourists and their spending power. No effort has been made to actively promote the ecomuseum beyond the town itself, simply because attracting additional visitors was not a primary objective. What was important was giving local residents pride in their own place, an ability to reflect on their history and recognise its significance. In terms of sustainability, and of ecomuseum theory and practice, Hirano appears – on the surface at least – as an excellent example. The ecomu-seum embraces past and present, the tangible and the intangible, and succeeds by being inti-mate and low key, encouraging the visitor to discover its secrets. By doing so it is, of course, creating its own cultural identity and mythology; whether this is a positive or negative result only time will tell. What is clear is that the loose structure being implemented here provides a mechanism for the preservation of fragments of the town's heritage that would not neces-sarily be conserved by conventional means. Unfortunately, it is a mechanism that is sustained by a number of key individuals, and if they lose enthusiasm, or their collections are not passed on, aspects of heritage now deemed important might still be lost.

A second example is Asahi Town in the prefecture of Yamagata. It is the site of Japan's first ecomuseum, the local authority exploring the ecomuseum concept as early as 1989, and formally adopting an ecomuseum plan in 1991 as part of the town's development strategy. Although it is in a mountainous and scenic area that attracts winter-sports enthusiasts, there has been a gradual population decline and the ecomuseum philosophy has been used as a tool to foster local pride in the region, to re-establish a spirit of place, and as a means of attracting summer visitors. An ecomuseum headquarters was opened in the town's council offices in 2000, acting as a base where the professional staff work alongside the not-for-profit Asahi-machi Ecomuseum Association to act as a catalyst within the area, promoting its attractions and encouraging local residents to participate in ecomuseum activities.

The designated sites in Asahi are a unique blend of natural, cultural and spiritual sites that make full use of the distinctive features of the area. The apple orchards support the main industry of the town and a significant collection of rare apple varieties from all over the world has been made, located on a hillside site that incorporates a charcoal kiln, an apple museum and an apple spa. Asahi is also famous as a wine-producing area and a local vineyard and winery is also incorporated into the ecomuseum. Smaller cottage industries also feature in the Asahi Ecomuseum, including a beeswax candle workshop.

One of the most remarkable attractions in Asahi is the lake known as Onuma Ukishima. Set in among cedar and beech forest, the lake is remarkable for its 'moving islands' – mats of floating vegetation that are said to move of their own accord, without the assistance of wind or water currents. Because of this curious phenomenon the lake is thought to have magical and religious properties, and has its own shrines; guides lead visitors to viewpoints to witness the movement of the islands. Equally fascinating is the 'Air-Shrine' (Figure 15.3), a contemporary sculpture in stainless steel, erected on a mountaintop which rises from the beech forest, that reflects the sky and surrounding vegetation; the footpath to the shrine incorporates prayer wheels that encourage contemplation. The numerous mountain roads provide scenic views of terraced rice paddies (Figure 15.4) which are an important part of the cultural landscape of Asahi-machi.

In contrast to Hirano, the Asahi-machi ecomuseum has been developed by the local authority, and the ecomuseum sites are an essential feature in the town's promotional literature. Most of the key sites are owned and managed by the local authority, or receive their financial support. Major businesses such as the vineyard and the apple orchard see the ecomuseum as a means of promoting their products and sustaining their businesses, as do the smaller cottage industries. However, despite the seeming lack of direct community involvement, Ohara (*pers. comm.*, May 2003) suggests the view of the Ecomuseum Association is that local people feel much more positive about their town because of its ecomuseum activities. In a remote rural area with limited employment prospects it is perhaps not surprising to see the local authorities taking a lead role in sustaining it. What is more interesting is the way that local people have embraced the ideas and activities promoted by the Association, becoming actively involved in the conservation of traditional landscapes and ways of life, and in so doing becoming ambassadors for their locality and actors for sustaining it.

*Figure 15.3* Festivities at the Air Shrine, Asahi-machi ecomuseum.
Photo: Kazuoki Ohara.

*Figure 15.4* Traditional rice fields, Asahi-machi ecomuseum.

Photo: the author.

## Ecomuseums in China

China has some 56 ethnic minority groups, which together account for a mere 8.41 per cent of the population, the remainder being the dominant Han Chinese (Chinese Government 2006a). The cultural heritage of these minority groups, and the remote areas within which they live, are the focus for ecomuseum development in China, making them distinctive. Probably the only other countries to adopt ecomuseological practices to sustain and represent indigenous minorities are Mexico (Camarena and Morales 1997, 2004; Peña Tenorio 2000) and Sweden (Davis 1999: 120–1).

An and Gjestrum (1999) suggest that the attempt to establish ecomuseums in China was influenced by the Chinese government's recognition that previous attempts to open up rural areas and minority cultures for tourism and economic benefit had resulted in failure. As a consequence, a new approach was required 'in order to provide local minority communities with the tools needed to handle the balance between the protection of their cultural identity and rational social and economic development'. They have described in detail the procedure that was followed to establish the first ecomuseum in China at Soga in Guizhou Province, which was carried out with specialist and financial aid from the Norwegian government, and the dedicated involvement of museum specialists from the Chinese Society of Museums.

Myklebust (2006) reflects on this process, and on the ways in which the Chinese museologists benefited from a seminar and field visits in Norway, but also how the young participants from the Chinese villages 'made a deep impression on us Norwegians by their critical reflections on what they had seen and what could and could not be used in their local setting'. The outcome of the preparatory work was a set of guidelines named *The Liuzhi Principles* after the town where discussions took place. These principles are:

- The people of the villages are the true owners of their culture. They have the right to interpret and validate it themselves.
- The meaning of culture and its values can be defined only by human perception and interpretation based on knowledge. Cultural competence must be enhanced.
- Public participation is essential to ecomuseums. Culture is a common and democratic asset, and must be democratically managed.
- When there is a conflict between tourism and preservation of culture the latter must be given priority. The genuine heritage should not be sold out, but production of quality souvenirs based on traditional crafts should be encouraged.
- Long term and holistic planning is of utmost importance. Short time economic profits that destroy culture in the long term must be avoided.
- Cultural heritage protection must be integrated in the total environmental approach. Traditional techniques and materials are essential in this respect.
- Visitors have a moral obligation to behave respectfully. They must be given a code of conduct.
- There is no bible for ecomuseums. They will all be different according to the specific culture and situation of the society they present.
- Social development is a prerequisite for establishing ecomuseums in living societies. The well-being of the inhabitants must be enhanced in ways that do not compromise traditional values.

These principles were agreed by all the participants and set out a firm basis to develop the ecomuseum projects in Guizhou. Myklebust (2006) suggests that the principles are applicable to most ecomuseum projects, but especially so if they are focused on sustaining minority cultures.

The 'fragmented' model for the ecomuseum is one that identifies scattered heritage sites over a large geographical area, and is one that has been implemented widely in Scandinavia to aid tourism and local economies. Hamrin (1996) has suggested that this emphasis on turning the cultural landscape into a museum is so different from French approaches that is should be called the 'Scandinavian ecomuseum model'. A further feature of this model is that a reception centre is provided that provides orientation, and frequently houses a documentation centre where oral testimonies, photographs and objects are held. Not surprisingly, with the influence of Norwegian museologists, all seven Chinese ecomuseums that have so far been created utilise this model. However, unlike anything in Scandinavia (with the exception of the Sami Museum, Ajtte), all the Chinese ecomuseums are dedicated to sustaining ethnic minority groups. The apparent exception is Longli, populated by Han, China's dominant ethnic group. Longli Ecomuseum is dedicated to what is regarded as 'traditional' Han culture, based in a beautifully preserved Ming Dynasty city, with a castle and defensive walls. However, in this area of China the Han are identified as a minority.

Detailed descriptions and illustrations of the ecomuseums that have been created so far can be found in Su (2005a). Reflections on ecomuseum development in China resulting from a major conference (*Communication and Exploration*) on ecomuseums held in Guiyang, (the principal city of Guizhou) in 2005 have been briefly described by Su (2005b). More detailed descriptions have been published in Chinese (Su *et al.* 2006) and in English (Davis *et al.* 2006). What is evident is that the Chinese have identified ecomuseums as a major means of promoting sustainable development in poor rural areas, and that further initiatives in other provinces will be considered. In Guangxi, for example, which has established its first ecomuseums at Lihu and Sanjiang, a strategic plan already exists to create several more ecomuseums, aided by the governmental support for cultural heritage development expressed in China's '11th Five Year Plan of Development 2006–2010' (Rong 2006). Two Chinese ecomuseums will be discussed in more detail, here: the Soga Ecomuseum of the Qing Miao and the Nandan Lihu Ecomuseum of the White-trousered Yao.

## The Soga Ecomuseum

An and Gjestrum (1999) note that the Miao are the fourth largest ethnic minority in China, and that half the population live in Guizhou. The smallest branch of the Miao – the Qing Miao – is found in Liuzhi District, a mere 4,000 people scattered in twelve remote mountain villages. The unique nature of this group of people is symbolised by head ornaments of long ox horns worn by the women, which are enhanced at festivals, weddings and other special occasions by elaborate hair-pieces made of wool (Figure 15.5). The Qing Miao also have a rich intangible heritage including unique music and dance traditions. The local economy is based on mixed agriculture, weaving and embroidery, and the religion is polytheistic with a shaman (Guishi) acting as religious and spiritual leader of the village.

*Figure 15.5* A young Miao woman in ceremonial dress.

Photo: the author.

Soga Ecomuseum, based in the small Qing Miao village of Longga, became the first ecomuseum in China on 31 October 1998, with a key feature being its Information Centre that houses the local 'Memory project'. The design of the Centre was decided by an architect in consultation with village people to ensure a sympathetic approach to the local landscape and respect for local building materials and techniques. Local people also carried out much of the construction work for the Centre, again promoting ownership. The memory project initially sought to document collective memories of the village inhabitants through oral recording in their own language; the Miao have no written language of their own. The project has since grown to include the collection of photographs and material culture, and the documentation of village practices and rituals.

The ecomuseum project was closely tied to raising the standards of living for the villagers. Significant improvements include the renovation of houses in the old village and the provision of new housing, piped water, an electricity supply, a new school and medical facilities. These changes are the first to be seen by an ecomuseum visitor, travelling along a newly-constructed road into the 'new' village where the school and clinic are located. A short walk brings the visitor to the square where festivals are celebrated, and where local people give demonstrations of dancing and music; the Information Centre is close by, and houses a very professional exhibition about aspects of the Qing Miao and their culture. From here the visitor is free to roam through the old village (Figure 15.6), meet local people and purchase craft souvenirs.

*Figure 15.6* In the old village, Soga Ecomuseum.

Photo: the author.

## The Lihu Ecomuseum

The Lihu Ecomuseum of the Yao, based in Huaili Village in a remote mountainous area of Nandan County was opened in November 2004, the first to be created in Guangxi Province. It was developed with the professional assistance of museologists from the Guangxi Ethnography Museum, and all participants received training from the Chinese Society of Museums. Ecomuseum experience was also provided by specialists from neighbouring Guizhou; this assistance has meant that the Yao ecomuseum resembles closely those established in that province. Financial support was provided by business sponsors from regional electronics, engineering and telecommunications companies, with some international aid being made available to support the provision of water and sanitation in the village. Local government funding was dedicated to developing the tourist infrastructure, in particular the construction of a road into the mountains (Rong 2006).

The White-trousered Yao are so called because the village men always wear white trousers. However, the women's ceremonial clothing is much more colourful, and is a feature of the exhibition in the museum's Information Centre (Figure 15.7), representing the weaving, printing and embroidery skills of the village women. Intangible heritage in the community is again very strong, notable features being the large bronze drums that provide a rhythmical and hypnotic accompaniment to ritual dances (Figure 15.8) and antiphonal songs. The village features specially-constructed elevated barns that store the subsistence crops grown there, and visitors can explore ancient tombs, old roadways and wells that are scattered through the surrounding forest. Su (2005a) suggests that 'The village has almost escaped from the impacts of mainstream modern civilisation as its natural environment and social structure remain intact and its people adhere to their ancestors' lifestyle and religion'. Ritual

*Figure 15.7* Costume display, White-trousered Yao Ecomuseum.
Photo: the author.

*Figure 15.8* Traditional dancing and drumming, Huaili village.

Photo: the author.

ceremonies, especially those associated with funerals, or the naming of a new bronze drum are a feature of Yao culture. As with Soga, the ecomuseum is seen as a means of capturing these rich community memories, the Information Centre being a base for this documentation; specialist ethnologists from the Ethnography Museum in Nanning have used the ecomuseum as a base to carry out their research.

Rong (2006) suggests that developing ecomuseums in Guangxi Province has had significant benefits, noting in particular the increased pride expressed by local ethnic minority groups in their culture, and increased interest in those cultures from researchers and academics. He also points to the educational benefits for local schools, the promotion of cultural exchanges to and from the Province, and the gradual rise in interest in tourist visits to the ecomuseums, which is beginning to have some economic benefit for local people.

The development of ecomuseums in these remote rural areas of China has clearly had major tangible benefits for local indigenous cultural minorities. They have achieved better living conditions as a result of the restoration of local houses, the provision of essential utilities such as water and electricity, the building of new facilities including schools and hospitals, with a resulting improvement in educational standards and medical care. Every effort has been made to make interventions – guided by the Liuzhi Principles – in a sympathetic manner with respect for local people, their customs and beliefs. The conservation of the distinctiveness of local cultures is central to these projects, with resources being devoted to the documentation of local memories, customs and material culture. To date there has been a sensitive approach to cultural tourism, with a careful development of the sites in consultation with local people. New infrastructure, in particular extensive road-building programmes, has enabled low-level cultural tourism that has started to bring small economic improvements to the lives of local people. Central to the success of the projects has been the development of a national network of ecomuseums that has enabled information exchange between sites.

An and Gjestrum (1999), referring to their Chinese experiences, state that 'people should not be separated from their cultural heritage but that they should have the opportunity to create their future based on it'. The implication here is that ethnic minority peoples can use their cultural assets to aid sustainable development via cultural tourism. This process is not without risk. The focus on ethnic minorities in China's ecomuseums is fraught with potential problems, in particular the danger of transforming living cultures into mere exhibitions. There is a real threat of the loss of authenticity and the change to the social fabric and values of these isolated communities as the 'outside world' impinges on their lives.

Ecomuseum theory demands that these organisations originate within and are led by local communities. However, there is little evidence to demonstrate that this has been the case in China. They appear to be very 'top-down' organisations, and indeed would never have been possible without outside financial and expert help. During my own visit to the sites it was impossible to discover if there was real autonomy for local village leaders, or how much influence local people had in the operational and strategic management of the ecomuseums. It was unclear how the financial benefits from cultural tourism were distributed within the communities, or even, as Maggi (2006) notes, to know what priority tourism has for these new institutions. While increasing numbers of tourists will bring in additional revenue, this too poses dangers to the community, as change will be inevitable. The key question – what is the driving force behind the development of ecomuseums in China? – remains unanswered. While the sincerity of local actors is unquestionable, to what extent are major political strategies relating to tourism and rural development shaping ecomuseum development?

Tourism is a major growth area in China. The Chinese National Tourism Authority (CNTA) is responsible for strategic planning, and its Chairman, Shao Qi Wei, makes reference to tourism being 'one of the fastest developing industries in China . . . in 2000 China hosted 83.44 million inbound tourists'. He also indicates that according to the forecasts of the World Tourist Organisation China will become the world's largest tourism destination by 2020 (Shao 2006) having progressed from being ranked 18th in the world in terms of tourism in 1980 to 5th in 2000 (CNTA 2006a).

The stated principles being followed by the CNTA include two contrasting and arguably incompatible strategies, namely the road to mass tourism ('Principle 6 – it is imperative to persist in the direction of development featuring (sic) by large production, large market and large tourism') and sustainability ('Principle 7 – it is imperative to stick to the principles of sustainable development') (CNTA 2006b). Despite this paradox, in 2000 CNTA stated that during the 10th five-year plan period China's tourism would 'find an effective way to develop tourism and protect the environment, and build the tourism industry into an environmentally-friendly sector' (CNTA 2006c). Tourism (other than a reference to Hunan) is not explicitly mentioned in China's 11th Five-Year Guidelines (Chinese Government, 2006b). However, there can be little doubt that tourism will be part of a wider strategy to build 'a new socialist countryside', one of the major policies for the next five years in China. Rural development is a key strategy for the Chinese government, and will include a wide range of agricultural reforms and subsidies. It is against this complex political backdrop that Chinese ecomuseums will evolve and further develop. It is difficult to forecast the impact of increased tourism or the opening up of the countryside to development on isolated rural communities, and whether ecomuseums will provide a sustainable solution to conserve the extraordinary cultural distinctiveness of China's minority cultures.

## Conclusions

This chapter set out to ask three basic questions, one being whether ecomuseums are sustainable entities. This is especially relevant if we consider that ecomuseums are diverse organisations, each with its own specific objectives related to its 'place' and its local cultural and natural resources. It would appear that to be sustainable most ecomuseums require outside financial and expert assistance. The ecomuseums featured here demonstrate a reliance on external help: Hirano-cho appears entirely self-sufficient, but even small voluntary museums such as in Carmagnola benefit from being part of a larger network. Perhaps the greatest threat to sustainability in these voluntary organisations is the age and skill profile of the individuals involved, with an urgent need to pass on knowledge to a younger generation. A second question was whether ecomuseums can help to sustain local heritage resources, and all the ecomuseums described above can demonstrate characteristics and achievements which indicate that they actively sustain local cultural and natural assets; however, once again specialist curatorial and financial expertise is necessary. The third question asked if ecomuseums can sustain local communities, and indications are that they can have a positive impact. It is evident that some ecomuseums are introspective, with benefits limited to maintaining local pride within the community. However, others are specifically geared to cultural tourism with a view to sustaining communities by providing real tangible and economic benefits for local people. Ecomuseum development in China has taken the concept into new territory, with a focus on sustainable development in areas populated by ethnic minorities.

## Note

1 www.ecomuseums.eu

## Bibliography

An, L. and Gjestrum, J. A. (1999) 'The ecomuseum in theory and practice: the first Chinese ecomuseum established', *Nordisk Museologi*, 2: 65–86.

Camarena, H. and Morales, T. (1997) 'Los Museos Comunitarios y la Organización Indigena en Oaxaca', *Gaceta de Museos*, Coordinación Nacional de Museos y Exposiciones, INAH, No. 6, June, 11 18.

—— (2004) 'La Unión de Museos Comunitarios de Oaxaca A.C.'. Online. Available at: www.inter-actions-online.com/page_news.php?id_news = 120 (accessed June 2006).

Chinese Government (2006a) 'Ethnicity in China'. Online. Available at: www.china.org.cn (accessed 27 September 2006).

—— (2006b) '11th Five Year Guidelines'. Online. Available at: www.china.org.cn/english/2006/Mar/160397.htm (accessed 27 September 2006).

Clifford, S. and King, A. (eds) (1993) *Local Distinctiveness: Place, Particularity and Identity*, London: Common Ground.

CNTA (2006a) 'Tourism rankings'. Online. Available at: www.cnta.com/lyen/2fact (accessed 27 September 2006).

—— (2006b) 'Tourism principles'. Online. Available at: www.cnta.com/lyen/2policy/principles.htm (accessed 27 September 2006).

—— (2006c) 'Tourism policies and the environment'. Online. Available at: www.cnta.com/lyen/2policy/environmental.htm (accessed 27 September 2006).

Corsane, G., Davis, P., Elliott, S., Maggi, M., Murtas, D. and Rogers, S. (2007a) 'Ecomuseum evaluation in Piemonte and Liguria, Italy', *International Journal of Heritage Studies*, 13(2): 101–16.

—— (2007b) 'Ecomuseum performance in Piemonte and Liguria, Italy: the significance of capital', *International Journal of Heritage Studies*, 13(3): 224–39.

Davis, P. (1999) *Ecomuseums: A Sense of Place*, London: Leicester University Press/Continuum.

—— (2004) 'Ecomuseums and the democratisation of Japanese museology', *International Journal of Heritage Studies*, 10(1): 87–104.

—— (2005) 'Ecomuseums and the democratisation of cultural tourism', *Tourism, Culture and Communication*, 4: 45–58.

Davis, P., Maggi, M., Su, D., Varine, H. de, and Zhang, J. (eds) (2006) *Communication and Exploration, Guiyang, China – 2005*, Trento, Italy: Provincia Autonoma di Trento.

Hamrin, O. (1996) 'Ekomuseum Bergslagen – från idé till verklighet', *Nordisk Museologi*, 2: 27–43.

Howard, P. (2002) 'The eco-museum: innovation that risks the future', *International Journal of Heritage Studies*, 8: 63–72.

Maggi, M. (2006) 'Report on my visit to some Chinese ecomuseums in Guizhou and Inner Mongolia Provinces', in P. Davis, M. Maggi, D. Su, H. de Varine and J. Zhang (eds) *Communication and Exploration, Guiyang, China – 2005*, Trento, Italy: Provincia Autonoma di Trento, 217–23.

Martin, C. (1995) 'Charter for sustainable tourism', unpublished document, presented at the World Conference on Sustainable Tourism, 27–28 April 1995, Lanzarote, Canary Islands.

Myklebust, D. (2006) 'The ecomuseum project in Guizhou from a Norwegian point of view', in P. Davis, M. Maggi, D. Su, H. de Varine and J. Zhang (eds) *Communication and Exploration, Guiyang, China – 2005*, Trento, Italy: Provincia Autonoma di Trento, 7–14.

Ohara, K. (1998) 'The image of "Ecomuseum" in Japan', *Pacific Friend*, 25(12): 26–27.

—— (2006) 'The current status and situation of ecomuseums in Japan', in P. Davis, M. Maggi, D. Su, H. de Varine and J. Zhang (eds) *Communication and Exploration, Guiyang, China – 2005*, Trento, Italy: Provincia Autonoma di Trento, 131–39.

O'Riordan, T. (1990) 'The Politics of Sustainability', in R. K. Turner (ed.) *Sustainable Environmental Management: Principles and Practice*, London: Belhaven Press, 29–50.

Peña Tenorio, B. (2000) 'Los Museos Comunitarios en México', in *Dimensión Antropológica-INAH*. Online. Available at: http://paginah.inah.gob.mx:8080/dAntropologica/dAntropologica_Texto.jsp?sldArt = 172&sVol = null&sTipo = 1&sFlag = 1 (accessed June 2006).

Regeringskansliet (Swedish Ministry of the Environment) (1999) *The Swedish Environmental Code*. Online. Available at: www.sweden.gov.se/sb/d/574/22847 (accessed June 2006).

Rivard, R. (1988) 'Museums and ecomuseums – questions and answers', in J. A. Gjestrum and M. Maure (eds) *Okomuseumsboka – identitet, okologi, deltakelse*, Tromso: ICOM Norway, 123–8.

Rong, X. (2006) 'Ecomuseums in Guangxi: establishment, exploration and expectations', in P. Davis, M. Maggi, D. Su, H. de Varine and J. Zhang (eds) *Communication and Exploration, Guiyang, China – 2005*, Trento, Italy: Provincia Autonoma di Trento, 19–21.

Sauty, F. (2001) *Écomusées et musées de société au service du développement local, utopie ou réalité?*, Clermont Ferrand: Collection 'Jeunes auteurs', Centre national de resources du tourism en espace rural.

Shao, Q. W. (2006) 'Chairman's remarks'. Online. Available at: www.cnta.com/lyen/2cnta/chairman.htm (accessed 27 September 2006).

Su, D. (ed.) (2005a) *China Ecomuseums*; Beijing: Forbidden City Publishing House.

—— (2005b) 'Ecomuseums in China', *ICOM News*, 58(3): 7.

Su, D., Davis, P., Maggi, M. and Zhang, J. (eds) (2006) *Communication and Exploration: Papers of the International Ecomuseum Forum, Guizhou, China*, Beijing: Chinese Society of Museums.

Varine, H. de (1988) 'Re-thinking the museum concept', in J. A. Gjestrum and M. Maure (eds) *Okomuseumsboka – Identitet, Okologi, Deltakelse*, Tromso: ICOM Norway, 33–40.

Walsh, J. A., Jamrozy, U. and Burr, S. W. (2001) 'Sense of Place as a component of sustainable tourism marketing', in S. F. McCool and R. M. Moisey (eds) *Tourism, Recreation and Sustainability: Linking Culture and Environment*, Wallingford, Oxford: CABI Publishing, 195–216.

# 16

# MĀORI, MUSEUMS
# AND THE
# TREATY OF WAITANGI

The changing politics of
representation and control

*David Butts*

Indigenous peoples are increasingly seeking meaningful governance relationships with museums that hold elements of their tangible and intangible cultural heritage. With the revision of New Zealand's national and metropolitan museum legislation in the 1990s, moderate advances have been made in Māori participation in the governance of these institutions based on the recognition of the principles of the Treaty of Waitangi. During the same period more radical governance changes based on Treaty principles were made in a number of regional museums as they made the transition from incorporated societies to charitable trust museums. It is argued in this chapter that to understand the nature of these changes in Māori participation in museum governance, and of the ongoing relationships between Māori and museums, and their significance in new Zealand society, it is necessary to acknowledge the tensions within New Zealand politics surrounding the recognition of Māori indigenous and Treaty rights, particularly within the context of public institutions.

## Strategies for indigenous recognition

Museums in North America, Australia and New Zealand, countries with similar colonial histories, have begun to make the transition from operating within the discourse of colonialism to engaging in the politics of indigenous recognition. In large part this has been in response to and in partnership with indigenous communities and collectives that have been proactive in engaging with heritage institutions that currently hold elements of their cultural heritage.

There has been a continuous tradition of resistance to colonisation by indigenous peoples. This resistance has taken many forms, from passive resistance to armed conflict, and in current times indigenous peoples' resistance to the appropriation of their cultural property and interpretation of their cultures by public institutions, including museums, continues to find many forms of expression. Indigenous agency in the assertion of cultural property rights is evident at international, national and local levels: in international initiatives such as the Draft Declaration of the Rights of Indigenous Peoples and the Mataatua

Declaration; in domestic legislation, such as the Native American Graves Protection and Repatriation Act 1990, and treaty settlements, for example, the Nisga'a treaty settlement with the Canadian Federal Government and the Provincial Government of British Columbia 1998; and in the establishment of local indigenous cultural centres (Watt 2005). Māori have been actively engaged at all three levels. They participated in the drafting and negotiation of the Draft Declaration of the Rights of Indigenous Peoples and initiated the conference that drafted the Mataatua Declaration. They have concluded Treaty settlements with the New Zealand government which resulted in the return of cultural property (Mead 1995) and domestic heritage protection and maintenance legislation in New Zealand (e.g. Historic Places Act, Resource Management Act, Protected Objects Act) increasingly takes account of Māori cultural property rights guaranteed by the Treaty of Waitangi. This chapter, however, will focus on another area of engagement: that at a local level.

## Recognising the Treaty of Waitangi

While this chapter focuses on the relationships between Māori and museums in the late twentieth and early twenty-first centuries, it is important to acknowledge the long history of Māori activism in seeking redress from the British Crown and the government of New Zealand (Walker 2004). The Treaty of Waitangi, signed in 1840, provides the foundation of Māori–Crown relationships (Orange 1992). Broadly speaking, and taking account both of the English and the Māori language versions of the Treaty, the Treaty ceded to the Crown the right to govern the colony of New Zealand, protected Māori rangatiratanga, that is, Māori rights in relation to their lands and taonga (their precious possessions), and granted Māori the same individual rights as British citizens (Kawharu 1989). Unfortunately, as has occurred for many indigenous peoples, these Treaty rights, negotiated at the onset of colonial occupation, were not honoured by successive colonial governments. New Zealand courts considered the Treaty a 'simple nullity' in the nineteenth century and those Māori seeking redress for Treaty grievances struggled to gain recognition of their Treaty rights in the courts. Treaty grievances include: the loss of whānau (family), hapū (sub tribe or collective of families) and iwi (tribal) lands as a result of the individualisation of land titles, legislative and raupatu land alienations (the confiscation of land from tribes that resisted government purchase of their lands for European settlement); loss of fishing rights; and decline of Te Reo Māori (Māori language) through the enforced use of English in the compulsory state education system.

However, Mason Durie (2000) has argued that the existence of the Treaty of Waitangi between Māori and the Crown of New Zealand has led to a level of engagement that might not otherwise have occurred. The Treaty of Waitangi has always been central to Māori understanding of their destiny as indigenous peoples within the nation-state of New Zealand and since 1975 successive governments have increasingly recognised the significance of the Treaty in this regard. In 1975, the Waitangi Tribunal was created to make recommendations to government on the settlement of Treaty grievances (including, from 1985, historical grievances dating back to 1840) and the Treaty provisions have been recognised in a number of important Acts of Parliament. Much attention has been given to defining the principles of the Treaty and these are now generally agreed to include the notions of tribal self-regulation, partnership, participation, active protection and redress. Some legislation gives more force to the recognition of these principles than others; none more forcefully than in section 9 of the State-Owned Enterprises Act 1986 which states: 'Nothing in this

Act shall permit the Crown to act in a manner that is inconsistent with the principles of the Treaty of Waitangi' (Durie 1998: 28).

However, this recognition of the Treaty in legislation in the 1980s and the optimism that broadly characterised the 1990 sesquicentennial celebrations of the signing of the Treaty can now be seen as the high watermark of official biculturalism. There has always been an undercurrent of resistance to the recognition of indigenous collective rights within wider New Zealand society. In recent years, under the banner of 'one law for all', the centre-right political parties have begun to call for an end to Treaty settlements, the removal of Māori representation in Parliament and the deletion of Treaty clauses in legislation. These tensions in the recognition of individual and collective rights have had the effect of drawing the centre-left coalition government of the past eight years progressively to the centre-right in order to retain its popular majority. This has, however, been made more difficult under the country's proportional electoral system (MMP) adopted in 1996. In the early 1990s, the government became much more cautious about making reference to the principles of the Treaty in legislation. This has reduced Māori opportunity for legal redress for Treaty breaches by government or government agents, including museums established by Act of Parliament. However, the Waitangi Tribunal continues to deal with claims where legislation offers no protection.

In 2004, in his annual speech to the Orewa Rotary Club in Auckland, Dr Don Brash, Leader of the Parliamentary Opposition and the National Party, stated that he was concerned about:

> the dangerous drift towards racial separatism in New Zealand, and the develop-ment of the now entrenched Treaty grievance industry. We are one country with many peoples, not simply a society of Pākehā and Māori where the minority has a birthright to the upper hand, as the Labour Government seems to believe.
>
> In parallel with the Treaty process and the associated grievance industry, there has been a divisive trend to embody racial distinctions into large parts of our legis-lation, extending recently to local body politics. In both education and healthcare, government funding is now influenced not just by need – as it should be – but also by the ethnicity of the recipient.

Public support for the sentiments expressed in this speech was apparently so widespread that the Labour government responded by attempting to replace 'race-based' government funding in areas such as education and health with 'needs-based' funding.

In 2003, the New Zealand Court of Appeal ruled that the Māori Land Court had the jurisdiction to investigate customary title to the seabed and foreshore.[1] The government responded by enacting The Foreshore and Seabed Act 2004 and the Resource Management (Foreshore and Seabed) Amendment Act 2004, making the foreshore and seabed Crown property. Provision was, however, made for the recognition of customary rights in the Customary Rights Orders and Territorial Customary Rights. Prior to the 2005 national elec-tions, the Māori Party was formed largely in response to the government's seabed and fore-shore legislation and party candidates were successful in four of the seven Māori seats in the New Zealand Parliament. In June 2006, Māori Party MP for Waiariki, Te Ururoa Flavell, in a speech addressing the Historic Places Amendment Act, connected Dr Brash's Orewa speech and the government's reluctance to make specific provision for Māori trustees on the Board of the Historic Places Trust in new legislation:

217

Our particular concern was the removal of ethnicity, the deletion of Māori as one of the key factors in board membership. The Bill serves to reduce and dilute the strength of Māori representation to having knowledge about Māori – rather than being Māori.

The Historic Places Trust, the Māori Heritage Council, and other submitters opposed this, but the Select Committee chose to ignore their submissions and instead continue the practice of targeting Māori. Post Orewa, Post Budget – the word we are getting very clearly is don't mention the word Māori, don't ask for any budget money for Māori, don't be Māori.

While many commentators focus on the increasing resistance to the recognition of Treaty rights by 'mainstream' politicians, there are still those who point to 'a small but increasing number of Treaty settlements, the incorporation of Māori interests and values in a wide range of legislation, and the growing capacity of Māori to participate in the state' as reasons for optimism about the future place of the Treaty in New Zealand society and constructive relationships between the Treaty partners (Belgrave *et al.* 2005: xx).

## Māori and museums

Within this evolving political environment, museums in New Zealand have maintained their relationships with Māori at the local, regional and national levels. Recent research has demonstrated that relationships between Māori and museums prior to the 1990s were largely based on sustained individual and family relationships, although the depositing of major cultural treasures such as wharenui (meeting houses), pataka (storehouses) and waka (canoes) was sometimes the result of decisions made by iwi or hapū (Butts 2003; McCarthy 2004). Many Māori cultural treasures were collected through processes which most museum practitioners today would consider inappropriate, even though these were quite normal practice within colonial societies.

The international exhibition 'Te Maori', in the 1980s, and subsequent Māori advocacy for changes in museum practice, combined with increasing recognition of the need for change by many museum practitioners, resulted in a number of fundamental attitudinal shifts in relationships between New Zealand museums and Māori. Māori collections were reconceptualised and revalued, not as ethnological curiosities, but as cultural treasures handed down through the generations (referred to in Māori as taonga tuku iho) and the link between these collections and the people for whom they have particular significance was increasingly acknowledged. The manner in which Māori collections were exhibited began to shift from an emphasis on long-term typological displays towards recognition that the collections are part of a living heritage. There was a shift from Māori inclusion in museums, primarily as the subject of collecting and representation, to Māori participation in all aspects of museum activity, from employment as museum managers and practitioners to engagement in the governance of institutions.

The composition of the museum sector in New Zealand is varied and complex. Of the more than 400 museums, only about 120 have one or more full-time salaried employees. There is also a clear hierarchy of institutions holding significant collections of taonga Māori (Māori cultural property). The four major metropolitan collections, in Auckland and Wellington in the North Island and Christchurch and Dunedin in the South Island, were founded in the nineteenth century as part of the colonial scientific establishment. In contrast to regional institutions, these museums have larger organisational structures and have larger collections drawn from iwi throughout New Zealand. The regional museums are located in regional cities throughout New Zealand. They are smaller and tend to be regionally focused.

The legislation defining the purpose, governance and funding mechanisms for each of the metropolitan museums has been revised since 1990. In each case modifications have been made to the nature of Māori representation in their governance arrangements. Two issues arise as a result. The first concerns the degree to which the revisions include reference to the Treaty of Waitangi or recognise the role of Māori within the institution. The second concerns the level and nature of Māori representation in the governance of the institution.

In these areas the four museum acts show no consistency. The legislation for the two museums in the South Island, the Canterbury Museum (passed 1992) in Christchurch and the Otago Museum (passed 1996) in Dunedin, made no reference to the Treaty of Waitangi and provided for only one Māori community representative. This was, however, an improvement for the Otago Museum which had not had any legislative provision for Māori representation on its trust board. The museum had, nevertheless, had two Māori advisors attend board meetings since 1986, initially as a result of planning the 'Te Maori' exhibition. Neither of these museums has had Māori directors, senior managers or curators of their Māori collections. These institutions have, however, made significant efforts to engage local iwi in the management and care of their taonga Māori collections.

The Museum of New Zealand Te Papa Tongarewa Act 1992 makes no reference to the Treaty of Waitangi and no provision for Māori representation on the museum trust board. However, the act does require that the museum:

> Endeavour to ensure both that the museum expresses and recognizes the mana and significance of Māori, European, and other major traditions and cultural heritages, and that the museum provides the means for every culture to contribute effectively to the Museum as a statement of New Zealand's identity.

In the First Schedule to the museum's legislation, consistent with the State Services Act, the museum is required to recognise the aims and aspirations of the Māori people, the employment requirements of the Māori people and the need for substantial involvement of Māori people as employees of the board. The museum's trustees are appointed by a government minister and since 1992 there have always been two Māori trustees on the trust board. However, this is not a Māori (i.e. hapū or iwi) controlled mandating process. The museum is actively engaged in becoming a bicultural organisation (Nesus 2004), a process symbolised by the appointment of a Māori co-director known as the Kaihautu. There are a number of Māori on the senior management team and the museum has employed Māori staff throughout the organisation and particularly in the care and interpretation of the taonga Māori collections. Through the activities of Te Papa National Services, the Museum of New Zealand has supported the development of dialogue and projects designed to enhance museum engagement with Māori throughout New Zealand (Hakiwai and Barnicoat 2002). Despite this level of Māori participation within Te Papa, Tapsell argues that the museum will not meet its Treaty obligations until provision is made for the mana whenua (the iwi holding customary authority in the area where the museum is located) on the trust board (Tapsell 2005: 277).

The Auckland War Memorial Museum Act 1996 created the Auckland Museum Trust

Board and the Māori committee known as the Taumata-a-Iwi. The Taumata-a-Iwi consists of five Māori representatives from the mana whenua iwi in the Auckland metropolitan area and has the responsibility of assisting the trust board to ensure that its policies accord with Māori values and the Treaty of Waitangi. This advisory committee has developed a Kaupapa or policy document that articulates five principles which have been adopted by the museum trust board. These five principles, derived from the Treaty principles, are the right to advise, partnership, Māori expectations, active protection and redress for past misunderstandings. The Taumata appoints one representative of the local iwi to the museum's trust board of ten members. The museum has appointed a Director–Māori at senior management level and Māori curatorial staff have been appointed to care for and interpret the Māori collections.

The level of Māori representation on the trust boards of these metropolitan institutions is very similar (one or two representatives), but the mechanisms for appointment and the nature of the mandate is different in each case. The level of Māori representation in all four institutions means that Māori trust board members depend on the goodwill of the non-Māori majority and the museum's senior management to advance Māori initiatives. Thus, while the term 'partnership' is liberally used to describe these governance relationships, the reality is that the partnerships are heavily biased in favour of the majority population. Dr Merata Kawharu (2002: 300) whose father, Professor Sir Hugh Kawharu, was the sole iwi representative on the Auckland Museum Trust Board until 2006, states:

> As primarily an advisory body, the Taumata has minimal decision making powers in comparison with the Board. Despite the act requiring the Board's policies to accord properly with matters provided for in the Treaty, and despite principles two and four in the Kaupapa relating to partnership and active protection of Māori interests, little in the way of equal partnership exists.

Although there may be no real partnership at the governance level, in the case of the two North Island metropolitan museums, the Museum of New Zealand Te Papa Tongarewa and Auckland Museum, the trustees have sought to operationalise the notion of partnership at the management and curatorial levels, and beyond. It would take a more detailed analysis than can be presented here to determine whether this has improved museum services to Māori or interpretation of Māori culture. Much of the goodwill seen here is also evident within the South Island metropolitan institutions, but here less progress has been made in developing meaningful partnerships at the governance and management levels or in operationalising the Treaty principles within the institutions.

## Regional museums, governance and the Treaty of Waitangi

Provincial museums, such as Hawkes Bay Art Gallery and Museum and Nelson Provincial Museum, also hold significant Māori collections. Some of these institutions have their origins in the nineteenth century, while others, although established later, have nevertheless inherited material from that period. Some are combined art galleries and museums. There are also a number of more recently established regional and local museums with much smaller and more localised Māori collections.

Regional museums can be arranged in three governance categories: independent charitable trusts, local authority controlled organisations with charitable trusts (generally referred to as Council Controlled Organizations (CCOs)), and local authority departments or business units. At the present time in New Zealand there is a significant change taking place in the governance and management of a number of these regional institutions.

All regional museums depend on local authority funding for 50 per cent or more of their annual budgets. Many charitable trust museums began as incorporated societies, later pursuing trust status in order to broaden their stakeholder base. In other cases, local authorities pushed for trust status in response to the rapidly increasing costs of museum provision apparent in the 1990s. The transition to charitable trust status meant a reconsideration of governance arrangements and in particular the mechanisms for Māori participation. Of the six well-established museums that made this transition in the 1990s, four provided one or two places for local iwi representatives, making for little change to existing levels of representation, and two went much further in developing radically new models. Of the four that made little change, only one included reference to the Treaty of Waitangi in their trust deed.

The two museums that adopted new models were the Tairawhiti Museum on the east coast of the North Island and Whanganui Regional Museum on the south-west coast of the North Island (Butts 2002). In 1999, the Tairawhiti Museum introduced a trust board of eleven members, five of whom were to be representatives of the major iwi of the Tairawhiti region. The local authority was to appoint two members and the Museum Society four members. Each of these latter organisations included one Māori person in their appointments to the board resulting in a Māori majority. This is the only museum trust board where this has consistently been the case. The relative ease with which this has been accepted in the wider community can be linked to the fact that Māori constitute 45–50 per cent of the population in the Tairawhiti region. The new museum trust constitution was influenced by elements of the Auckland War Memorial Museum Act 1996. Section three of the deed, entitled Treaty of Waitangi, reads as follows:

> The Board and each individual member of the Board shall at all times act in accordance with the principles of the Treaty of Waitangi and will:
>
> (a) observe and encourage the spirit of partnership and goodwill envisaged by the Treaty, the implications of Mana Māori and elements of care of Māori cultural property which only Māori can provide; and
> (b) actively pursue a policy of involvement of Maori in such a way that will retain the trust and confidence in and support of Māori for the objectives of the Trust and that will promote among Māori a sense of ownership, in common with the rest of the community, of the museum and its undertaking.[2]

While the Auckland Museum legislation was influential in this formulation of underlying principles, the Gisborne institution went much further than the legislation, which provided for only one Māori trustee, by providing places on the trust board for all the iwi in the Tairawhiti region. This is the type of governance partnership that Kawharu (2002: 300) suggests has not been achieved at Auckland Museum.

Since these governance changes were made, the name of the museum has been changed from the Gisborne Museum and Arts Centre to the Tairawhiti Museum. This new name shifts the emphasis from the city where the museum is located to the region the museum serves, and connects the museum very directly to the territory of the iwi represented in the museum's governance. While there has been very little negative response to the governance changes there have been comments made about the change of name and a perceived increase in 'Māori exhibitions'. An analysis of the exhibition programme shows that there had in fact only been a slight increase in the number of exhibitions that could be characterised as having a Māori art or history focus.

The constitution of the Tairawhiti Museum is seen by both Māori and Pākehā (here meaning non-Māori New Zealanders, or those people who are in New Zealand by right of the Treaty of Waitangi) trustees to provide the basis for a meaningful partnership between the museum and iwi in the region. In an interview with Dr Apirana Mahuika, Ngāti Porou representative on the trust board, in 2001, he stated:

> My understanding of governance in the Tairawhiti Museum is that there is now a greater involvement of Māori people in looking after the taonga tuku iho [treasures handed down from previous generations]. Gone are the days when another culture determines what should be done to this culture. We are working closely together now. I feel we have a real partnership now.
>
> The key to this governance is the enhancement and retention of mana [authority] of each of the groups and nobody rides slipshod over one another's mana. For us here in Tairawhiti, it is recognition of mana, the understanding of mana and what it means to people who own the mana and what it means for us to share mana with other people and vice versa. And that's real governance. The name also provides a sense of governance . . . If you get the name right, you get the whakapapa [genealogy, connections, history] right. Tairawhiti has been around for a long time. It's an ancient name. Our people say it's the eastern border, but within the eastern seacoast are iwi, hapū and whānau representatives. It's their rohe potae; it's the hat that embraces us as a region, but within this are their individual hairs, there are individual people with individual mana. And this is the significance of the name Tairawhiti.

The relationships between Tairawhiti Museum and some local iwi have strengthened significantly as a result of the new governance arrangements. This is usually the result of the proactive engagement of the iwi representatives on the trust board. Within two years of the new constitution being adopted, the museum had developed innovative policies in the areas of Koiwi Tangata (human remains), Repatriation and Kaitiakitanga (guardianship).

The relationship between the museum and Te Aitanga-a-Hauiti at Tolaga Bay (Uawa) has led to initiatives such as an exhibition of Te Aitanga-a-Hauiti taonga tuku iho in the museum, followed by a cultural festival at Tolaga Bay that included taonga tuku iho loaned from the museum collection. The museum also established an education exhibition and teaching space in a spare classroom at the area school in Tolaga Bay and the museum educators used this facility as a base from which to service schools further north along the coast. Planning is progressing on the development of further cultural heritage initiatives at Tolaga Bay and the museum is taking a constructive part in these discussions (Spedding 2006). These plans may include the establishment of a cultural centre.

In February 2006, Tairawhiti Museum appointed Dr Monty Soutar as director of the museum. Doctor Soutar is a member of Tairawhiti iwi Ngāti Porou and of the Waitangi Tribunal. He is only the second Māori to be appointed as director of a regional museum. In June 2006, Dr Apirana Mahuika, the Chairman of the Ngāti Porou Runanga (Tribal Council), was elected chairperson of the museum trust. These two appointments indicate the increasingly active participation of iwi in this institution. Prior to the changes in the constitution, the museum had recognised the importance of employing Māori staff and this policy has been continued. In 2006, 50 per cent of the museum staff was Māori.

Unfortunately, however, these changes in the relationship between the museum and iwi do not ensure the financial sustainability of the institution.

The Whanganui Regional Museum, first opened to the public in 1895, adopted a radical new bicameral governance structure in 2001 (Butts *et al.* 2002). The structure is based on two houses, the Tikanga Māori House and the Civic House. Each house nominates six members to a Joint Council that governs the museum. The representatives of each house have a right of veto over any matter coming before the Joint Council, or, put in a more positive light, a majority of the representatives from each house must support a motion before it will pass. The reality is that the Joint Council works by consensus and the veto provisions have not been used. The trust deed is based on the principles of partnership and 'two peoples development', and makes reference to the Treaty of Waitangi. In an interview in 2003, Grant Hwyler, former Ngāti Apa representative on the Joint Council, described the principle of two peoples development:

> I think partnership is a straightforward term: it's two distinct groups cooperating, working together. I think the key to it is the next principle which is two peoples development, which says that, right we have partnership, but the expectation is that both groups will move forward; whereas in the past we've had this thing called partnership where, from a Māori perspective, one group still holds all the power and is pushing ahead; the other group has to do as it's told and follow along. So, the two principles can't be separated. It's Māori whānau, hapū and iwi basically forming their own strategies and their own visions for the future, for the non-Māori doing the same, and then somehow they come together, because there's limited resources. We're all living in the same space and negotiating: How are we going to do this? How is each group going to reach a level of development that's acceptable to them?

In an interview in 2003 with Karanga Morgan, Ngā Rauru trustee, she remarked on the principle of two peoples development:

> It is that we would develop in a way that we would enhance one another rather than take away from one another, that I would still be able to retain who I am, without taking away from you who you are, but we would still have the opportunity to grow and develop and work together.

She confirmed that the constitution recognised the principles of the Treaty:

> In terms of the Treaty, it's a true recognition of how partnership can work and that's why this model is a good model. It's a fair model for everyone and I think that the model is wonderful, but the effectiveness is determined by the people inside it. So it can only be as good as the people that sit at the table.

Dr Mahuika's reference to the recognition of iwi mana in his statement above is similar to Hwyler's and Morgan's references to the principle of two peoples development. It is evident from these statements that it is at the governance level that the customary authority of iwi to maintain their kaitiakitanga of taonga, guaranteed in the Treaty, should be recognised. It is increasingly unacceptable to iwi that this authority should be exercised through advisory committees. Morgan's statement reminds us that no matter how good the constitution, it is the quality of the trustees that determines how effectively the principles of the Treaty will be observed. Thus, it is important that the mandating processes for both Māori and Pākehā trustees are robust in ensuring that the people appointed have the time and ability to be effective members of the board.

At Whanganui Museum, the transition from an incorporated society to the new trust was not as smooth as in the case of the Tairawhiti Museum. In 1998–9, three local politicians publicly objected to the proposed governance arrangements in the newly drafted constitution, stating that their community was multicultural, not bicultural, and that the proposed changes were not consistent with the commonly held notion of democracy in their community (Butts 2006). This might be seen as an example of the majority culture seeking to deny indigenous recognition while preserving its power base under the guise of multiculturalism. In other words, if colonialism espoused a blatantly intolerant racism in order to exert control, today a tolerant multiculturalism is increasingly being turned to the same effect in the contemporary politics of New Zealand. These were the very sentiments echoed at the national level in Dr Brash's 'Orewa Speech' in 2004. However, the museum society persisted with its proposed new governance model and, at the time of writing, the new trust had been operating for five years.

In a 2002 interview, Michael Payne, Pākehā trustee on the Joint Council, made the following comment regarding the opposition of the local politicians:

> They fear that their authority might be diminished by sharing it . . . I think the underlying thing may be partly racist, it's a word I don't like and don't use frequently, but I think there's an unwillingness to share, to see that in a circumstance like this that the sharing of power could only enrich the whole rather than diminish it.

Unfortunately, the museum's resourcing has been seriously constrained since the establishment of the new trust, to the extent that public programmes have been reduced and the level of staffing has remained static. The museum has also been constrained in its ability to operationalise the principles of the constitution within the museum. A collection policy framework for taonga Māori (known as Te Pou Arahi) has been partially completed and a new Taonga Māori Repatriation Policy was ratified in 2005. Although the return of koiwi (Māori skeletal remains) to iwi has been identified as a priority, by May 2007 remains had been returned to only one iwi. This reflects both the complexity of such transactions and the limited capacity of the museum to progress this issue at a governance and operations level. The museum has only one part-time Māori employee, funded from an external contract for education services, despite the appointment of Māori being a priority for the trustees. There is a danger that a failure to deliver on the expectations of the new governance arrangements will alienate both the conservative Pākehā and Māori. Having been a trustee at Whanganui Regional Museum from 2001 to 2005, I can attest to the level of frustration these constraints have engendered for both trustees and the museum director. A Constitutional Review Panel is due to report to the Joint Council of Whanganui Regional Museum in October 2006 and the preliminary indications are that this report will find that the bicameral bicultural governance model is working effectively, although there is a need to more actively develop relationships with all the museum's stakeholder communities.

In 2005, the Whanganui District Council decided it wanted more control over the museum and art gallery and moved to amalgamate these institutions with the city library under a newly created management structure inside its own organisation. In order to achieve the expected organisational and professional synergies between the three institutions, and save money, the city disestablished the directors' positions in the three institutions and created two new positions for cultural managers within its own bureaucracy to oversee the three institutions. Although the trustees have taken legal advice, the Joint Council has been constrained in its resistance to this takeover because the Wanganui District Council provides more than 70 per cent of the museum's budget: all museum staff have their employment contracts with the council and the council claims to own the museum building. The only major asset the trust board owns is the collection but it does not have the resources to care for the collection without council support. At the present time it is unclear what part the trust board will have in the long-term planning of the museum. The trustees were given only very limited involvement in planning for the 'Heart of the City' project, which will result in the redevelopment of the museum facilities. This is indicative of their recent marginalisation.

The local authority's desire for control is driven by a combination of factors: minimising increases in ratepayer funding of museums; facilitating organisational synergies; developing museums as key components of regional development strategies, especially regional tourism strategies; demonstrating its commitment to community well-being as required in recent legislation; and remedying perceived ineffective trust board governance.

It is evident that there may be a tension between what is good for museum practitioners and what is best for the community. Moving within the local body structures may bring a greater level of autonomy from trustees for managers, security of tenure for staff, and a close engagement with annual funding cycles. Security of funding and professional independence is highly valued by professional museum practitioners. But in making this move within the local bureaucracy the museum may significantly constrain its potential to act as a common ground where different peoples within the community can meet, establish and maintain connections and relationships on the basis of understandings they negotiate, and then work collaboratively together to govern the institution and determine its strategic direction. There is an argument to be made in support of the structural, if not financial, independence of trust museums from local government to allow them to operate as vital interconnecting nodes in the social, cultural and intellectual networks that sustain our civil society.

## Conclusion

While significant progress has been made in Māori–museum relationships within New Zealand's metropolitan and regional trust museums, there are currently forces at large at the national and regional levels that threaten the continuing evolution of these relationships. The metropolitan museums are working creatively within the constraints of their legislation to engage with the local tangata whenua and the many other iwi whose taonga tuku iho they care for in their collections. As the regional charitable trust museums are drawn ever more closely within the influence and even organisational structures of district councils, the opportunities to continue governance negotiations with iwi may be constrained. And where significant progress has been made in developing new bicultural governance models, these may be challenged within the environment of local body politics that tends to polarise communities around issues such as separate provision for Māori, and Māori treaty rights. The Treaty of Waitangi is increasingly characterised by many mainstream politicians at all levels in New Zealand society as an instrument primarily for the resolution of historic grievances and the inappropriate advancement of a privileged minority. Hence, New Zealanders have been encouraged to think that when the historic grievances are settled the Treaty will no longer be relevant to contemporary New Zealand life and thus consigned to a few paragraphs in the history books. Contesting this view are those members of our society, Māori and Pākehā, who recognise the Treaty as a living treasure, a taonga tuku iho, and one of the founding constitutional documents of our nation state, designed to protect and promote the well-being of Māori, while facilitating the continuing development of the nation. In the process of negotiating Treaty-based constitutional arrangements, museums are providing a forum for the exploration of governance models that may in time have wider application within New Zealand's public institutions. In so doing they will be working in the service of New Zealand society.

## Notes

1 Attorney-General v. Ngāti Apa [2003] 3 NZLR 634(CA).
2 Gisborne Museum and Arts Centre Charitable Trust Deed 1999: 4.

## Bibliography

Belgrave, M., Kawharu, M. and Williams, D. (2005) *Waitangi Revisited: Perspectives on the Treaty of Waitangi*, Melbourne: Oxford University Press.

Butts, D. (2002) 'Māori and museums: the politics of indigenous recognition', in R. Sandell (ed.), *Museums, Society, Inequality*, London: Routledge, 225–43.

—— (2003) 'Māori and museums: the politics of indigenous recognition', unpublished thesis, Massey University, Palmerston North.

—— (2006) 'Museum governance, indigenous recognition and (in)tolerant multiculturalism', *New Zealand Sociology*, 21(1): 89–106.

Butts, D., Dell, S. and Wills R. (2002) 'Recent constitutional changes at Whanganui Regional Museum', *Te Ara: Journal of Museums Aotearoa*, 27(2): 37–40.

Durie, M. (1998) *Te Mana Te Kawanatanga: The Politics of Māori Self-Determination*, Auckland: Oxford University Press.

—— (2000) 'Universal provision, indigeneity and the Treaty of Waitangi', *Victoria University of Wellington Law Review*, 33: 591–601.

Hakiwai, A. and Barnicoat, W. (2002) 'Te Papa national services', *Te Ara: Journal of Museums Aotearoa*, 27(1): 35–36.

Kawharu, I. (1989) *Waitangi: Māori and Pākehā perspectives of the Treaty of Waitangi*, Auckland: Oxford University Press.

Kawharu, M. (2002) 'Indigenous governance in museums: a case study, the Auckland War Memorial Museum', in C. Ffords, J. Hubert and P. Turnbull (eds) *The Dead and their Possessions: Repatriation in Principle, Policy and Practice*, London: Routledge, 293–30.

McCarthy, C. (2004) 'From curio to taonga: a genealogy of display at New Zealand's national museum, 1865–2001', unpublished thesis, Victoria University of Wellington.

Mead, H. (1995) 'The Mataatua Declaration and the case of the carved meeting house Mataatua', in J. Wong *et al.* (eds) *Material Culture in Flux: Law and Policy of Repatriation of Cultural Property*, Vancouver: University of British Columbia, Faculty of Law, 69–75.

Nesus, C. (2004) 'Making the connection: biculturalism at work', *Te Ara: Journal of Museums Aotearoa*, 29(1): 12–15.

Orange, C. (1992) *The Treaty of Waitangi*, Wellington: Bridget Williams Books.

Spedding, M. (2006) 'Te Aitanga-a-Hauiti and the Tairawhiti Museum', *Te Ara: Journal of Museum Aotearoa*, 31(1): 27–31.

Tapsell, P. (2005) 'From the sideline: Tikanga, Treaty values and Te Papa', in M. Belgrave, M. Kawharu and D. Williams (eds) *Waitangi Revisited: Perspectives on the Treaty of Waitangi*, Melbourne: Oxford University Press, 266–80.

Walker, R. (2004) *Ka Whawhai Tonu Matou: Struggle without End*, Auckland: Penguin.

Watt, L. (2005) 'American Indian tribes and their museums', *Te Ara: Journal of Museums Aotearoa*, 30(1): 10–13.

# 17

# CULTURAL ENTREPRENEURS, SACRED OBJECTS AND THE LIVING MUSEUMS OF AFRICA

*Evelyne Tegomoh*

This chapter is about sacredness and how this notion holds within it museological elements which permit us to look beyond traditional conceptions of the museum. In this respect, it contrasts the imposition of non-African models for cultural management and appreciation with long-established and highly successful cultural practices rooted in the African landscape, which often remain invisible or incomprehensible to community outsiders, both African and non-African, but which suggest another museology.

Implicit within the notion of sacredness are concepts of inclusion and exclusion: those who believe and those who do not; those who control and those who cannot. Particular practices are preserved and maintained in each society in order to uphold the sacredness or secrecy of its cultural 'matri-patrimony'. This term has utility here because both genders are often involved in the management of the sacred inheritance to be found in African societies. In contrast, the term 'patrimony' is at very least ambiguous in its inference of gender. Most African societies are hierarchical and the production, distribution and consumption of their cultural matri-patrimonies lies in the possession of sub-units of society, located in particular social fields, where roles, relationships, tensions, fears, beliefs and power distributions are clearly understood. This chapter suggests that if one inserts a 'cultural entrepreneur' or museum-maker into such a society one disrupts these social fields and socio-cultural change – perhaps in the very thing the entrepreneur is attempting to capture, preserve or represent – is an inevitable result. This is true whether the entrepreneur is an outsider or not (Barth 1981; Grønhaug 1978).

Drawing on an example taken from northern Cameroon, this chapter illustrates and analyses the risks and cultural changes that can result from the intrusion of a cultural entrepreneur, with newly acquired museological knowledge, into an African society. The Mbum community of Ngaouha in the Adamawa province of Cameroon is the point of focus. My involvement in the creation of a palace or public museum, which aims to use this community's sacred objects (known as Fembum, meaning the power of the Mbum) as the centrepiece of its exhibition, has permitted a firsthand view of the effects of this museum-making on the different social fields that manage the cultural matri-patrimonies which bind the community together. The cultural entrepreneur in this story is Baba, a well-intentioned individual and member of the Mbum.

## Baba's story

'Mboriangha' is the annual celebration of the Mbum people of Ngaouha, and an important and central festival of the Mbum people of Northern Cameroon as a whole. It is not simply a time for merriment; it is also a moment to take stock of the events of the past year, a time for sacrifices, rite and rituals, a way of calling on the ancestors to bless and guide the people. With its preservation of purpose and revisiting of rites, ceremonies and other cultural signifiers, the festival might well be understood as a kind of public open-air museum. But it also holds within it another kind of museum, for it is during this festival that the Fembum, the Mbum 'sacralia and regalia', is brought out of Rau Fembum (the 'holy mountains') This museum is a 'closed' museum, a space for preserving the Mbum's sacred, revered, and ritualised art objects (Tegomoh, 2001). Only male members of a specific lineage are permitted to handle the Fembum during the rituals and festival. The Fembum consist of regalia, throwing knives, bracelets, gongs, spears, swords, trumpets and so on which, from the Rau Fembum, are taken to Pak Fembum, the house of the revered objects. Here, the regalia – beautifully covered with cowries and beads – are strictly reserved and worn solely during the Mboriangha by the 'Belaka', the divine king of the Mbum of Ngaouha.

Having grown up with stories and myths about Fembum, and challenged and inspired by an Italian friend while in Italy on a course in tannery, in 1993 Baba started work on his developmental project, the creation of a museum. Without knowing exactly where the Fembum were, Baba spent a year travelling between Ngaoundere, where he worked, and Ngaouha, before finally obtaining confirmation that the Fembum actually existed. Armed with this small piece of information, and driven by the vision that through his museum project Ngaouha could achieve development, he started sourcing funds. In time, he found success in a 'self help' programme run through the US embassy, but before the funds could be received, the ambassador had to assure herself of the truth of the revered Fembum. She wished to visit Ngaouha to see it.

Baba returned home to Ngaouha to inform the Belaka and his court of events. Although the Belaka had the gist of the project's potential for the community, the court was doubtful and suspicious and when it finally met to take a decision, for or against this project, its members began with a cross-examination of Baba's personality and identity. On this point the court agreed that being the son of a princess, he was of the house though not of the lineage that handled the Fembum. As a result, opinions varied as to the potential of the project. Lengthy discussions went on into the early hours of the morning but failed to settle the matter. Then the Belaka intervened: the Fembum would be retrieved from Rau Fembum but would not enter the village settlement area.

When informed about this decision, Baba asked the Belaka if he was also going to welcome and receive the ambassador outside of the village. The Belaka asked him to bring the Fembum, which had been found, into the village, believing the notables who were opposed to the idea of having the Fembum brought out of the Rau Fembum would be scared and would not approach them. Baba was obliged to bring a sheep that would be sacrificed on the day the Fembum were to be taken out of the Rau Fembum, believing that this would appease the ancestors who in turn would grant blessings on their transaction. On the agreed day, 3 people, instead of 12 as had previously been arranged, showed up for the trip to the Rau Fembum. When Baba went out to find the missing men, he was told that some were ill and that others had gone away. Then he came across one man, Ibrahim, who was clearly in disagreement with his mother. The mother, with her breast in hand, was requesting from Ibrahim that her breast milk be returned before the son could go to the mountain. There is no more absolute way within Mbum society for a mother to forbid a child from doing something. With the intervention of the Belaka, however, a team of six left the village for the Rau Fembum. Some members, at least, had an idea of where some of the Fembum were located.

From Rau Fembum, they brought what they could find to Nyamounake, a prince who was a supporter of the project. This prince later organised search parties to locate more Fembum since these were kept in a number of different rau or caves. Around the time of the Ambassador's visit an increasing number of individuals became interested in the project, but political change in the US Congress, meant that American interest in the project waned and financial support was suspended. However, Baba was not deterred. A new search for funding brought him into contact with Ngaoundere Anthropos, a joint research programme between the Universities of Tromsø in Norway and Ngaoundere in Cameroon. It was then, in 1995, that I was recruited into the project, as I was then reading creative arts, and specialising in art history and museology at the University of Maiduguri in Nigeria. I have been involved in the project since that time (Tegomoh 2002: 40–8).

## Cultural entrepreneurs and cultural change

The mobility and interaction of people and events, or the introduction of new technologies and ideas, foster change. When a person's newly acquired knowledge and skills are brought into his or her society, they introduce risks and entrepreneurship (Barth 1963). When this entrepreneurship involves the use of cultural symbols such as sacred objects to create something new, such as a museum, the social fields that have traditionally managed the matri-patrimonies are disrupted. Of course, societies are never static; change is constant whether visible or invisible, conscious or unconscious. But cultural entrepreneurship presents rather different challenges for it engages with and challenges those traditional practices which form the essence of one's sense of being: the customs, beliefs, laws and arts that bind people together into a cultural unit (Barth 1963; Beck, 1992). While the target of the entrepreneur is development it will inevitably affect a people's way of being, their essential nature. This essential sense of self is derived from a way of living, which is perceived and re-enforced in living, which embodies processes of production and consumption within the natural environment, and which is socially structured in space and time. Clearly, to view this cultural infrastructure as 'cultural heritage' is to misrepresent it. Matri-patrimony better reflects an active and bi-gendered culture, and a materiality that exists within the political and socio-economical dimension of a living African culture. As Baba's example shows, cultural entrepreneurs can cause anxiety and mistrust, making the elders – the traditional custodians of the cultural matri-patrimony – resistant. This forces cultural entrepreneurs to take their negotiations elsewhere, to members of the community more amenable to the use of cultural symbols as emblems for advertisement, enhancement and the cultural development of their people.

In the example of the Fembum and the Mbum palace museum project, these sacred objects had already existed within a closed museum whose knowledge was carefully managed and handed down through a lineage of initiated members. Inevitably, the entrepreneur, with his foreign backing and his desire to make the private public, met with resistance from this group. The issue centred on control and the fears of those who had traditionally possessed the powers of management in the production, distribution and consumption of these cultural matri-patrimonies, that they would lose them. This sense of loss overrode any support they might have for the project's potential to bring development opportunities to the community. To the court, the Fembum are not mere objects but representations of that which cannot be represented. The Fembum embody the history of the Mbum's origins, and attest to the legitimacy of the cosmic and social order that replaced the primal time and its events. The Fembum are given 'auratic values' by the Mbum people and especially so by the lineage that handles them (Godelier 2002; Röschenthaler 1999).

In the modern state of Cameroon where the politics of identity are important for daily interaction and the running of the state, cultural entrepreneurs have taken the opportunity to launch cultural and development associations. These locate and generate funds for the revitalisation of their cultural matri-patrimonies. Their attentions are geared towards socio-cultural development, especially where the government has failed. Some of these funds, especially those from foreign organisations, come with strings attached, which could result in traditional managers losing control of their society's cultural inheritance. Even the uniforms of these associations, identified as they are by the cultural symbols imprinted on them, have appropriated and made public those matri-patrimonies formerly regarded as sacred and venerated by the people. The purpose of the entrepreneur is not only to generate funds but also to make these matri-patrimonies publicly accessible.

These cultural associations very often engage in the process of reinvention and revitalisa-tion of the dances and languages of their societies. In Cameroon, several local language centres have been established for the promulgation of languages that are fast dying out under pressure from stronger neighbouring languages and the official languages of English and French. And as in other cultures, it has now become very common for cultural and develop-ment associations to be invited to grace and animate official or state occasions with tradi-tional songs and dances. It could be argued, therefore, that cultural entrepreneurs in this way keep alive their matri-patrimonies by giving the people a sense of being.

However, cultural entrepreneurs might also be seen as acting like many non-govern-mental organisations, where founders sell their societies for self-gratification. It is through cultural entrepreneurs, that funding bodies can acquire control and blindly destroy the thing that most interested them by the introduction of alien practices and values rather than acting to simply promote, revitalise, preserve and sustain. What happens to the wealth of seemingly unwritten (in the eyes of other peoples) knowledge that will be lost as a result? Every society has its written language that is not readily understandable to others.

Thanks to Baba, the cultural entrepreneur, we can vividly see how African peoples have maintained and continue to strive to preserve, conserve and sustain open, closed, mobile, private, public, natural and sacred spaces. These natural environments were adopted, adapted, preserved, conserved, maintained and transformed into cultural resources which are then sustained through their various social formations and, most importantly, through their role as symbolic spaces of performance. To suggest this, is to visualise an African land-scape of museums, to which outsiders remain blind (Figure 17.1).

These cultural resources may be material or immaterial, tangible or intangible, objects or actors, but all are imbued with meanings and values within the space of performance. Differences of access to these spaces has prompted the classification of the 'museums' as open, closed, private, public and mobile. The natural resources – turned cultural resources – automatically become actors in these spaces with the roles attributed to them by the soci-eties and communities which draw on these 'objects' to perform rituals and engage in other

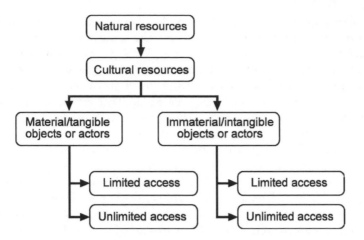

*Figure 17.1* A museological interpretation of the African environment.

socio-cognitive behaviours. The communities in their turn become co-actors in these same spaces and hold a symbiotic relationship to these natural resources. Table 17.1 reflects the multiple identities and functions attributed to these resources and indicates how each is regarded and in what type of museum they might be found. The suggestion that the material culture of these peoples already exists in other and different conceptualisations of the museum should raise doubts about the validity of attempts at traditional museum engagement.

The Barombi, the Sanaga, just like the birds (owl), animals (elephant), forests (Kovi-Fem) and mountains (Gbea (Buea)), are 'sacralised' and socialised; they are acculturated by the perceptions, interpretations and cultural needs and uses of the communities. For example, on its sacred day of recollection and celebration, Barombi lake is out of bounds to every member of the community. The same is true for the elephant or the owl which cannot be hunted casually and without prescription. Hunting the elephant becomes special theatre with both hunters and animal involved in performance. Here, the elephant is given a specific role: honoured by the hunters, it is anthropomorphised; it becomes human. The theatrical drama continues to the final act, where the elephant is seen as accepting death in order to give life to the community. Similarly, on Ngaouha mountain, the Mbum perform special sacrifices before any transaction takes place there – the space is sacred and venerated by the people. Forests, like Kovi-Fem of the Nso, is revered as the sacred dwelling of their founding ancestress and ancestors. Kovi-Fem becomes an anthropomorphic forest as well as a deified-ancestralised museum space for the performances of the living and the ancestors. In the same way, the Bukwe-forest (tropical forest with all its resources) of the Kwa (Pygmy) embodies the ancestral spirit of that people. Birds like the owl and eagle are regarded as sacred or totems and are not eaten. If they are eaten then it is only as part of a sacrifice which, like the consumption of the sacred Lamb of Christ of the Christians, seeks salvation.

Africans have always had sustainable and balanced notions of the complementary relationship between human and natural worlds. These complementarities are maintained through the stories African parents tell their children where animals, trees, birds, rocks, waters (rivers, lakes, seas) play real, humanly-defined roles in the society.

*Table 17.1* The multiple identities and functions attributed to cultural resources

| Natural resources | Cultural resources | Types of museum |
|---|---|---|
| Birds and animals | Eagles, owls and elephants, pigs – for food, sacrifice and totem | Open, closed, private, public and mobile |
| Forest | Kovi-Fem (sacred forest) – for food/ fuel/medicinal plants, burial place for royals and sacrificial grounds | Open, closed, public. |
| Mountains | Ngaouha, Buea – for food/fuel/ medicinal plants, burial place for royals and sacrificial grounds | Open, closed, public |
| Lakes/rivers | Sanaga/Barombi – for food/ medicinal plants, burial place and sacrificial grounds | Mobile, public, private, open, closed |

The various forms of 'museum' created through this process might be understood as follows:

- *Open museums*: these are actually those 'open' natural spaces that have been adopted and adapted, and organised by human communities for special cultural, ritual and heritage celebrations and observations. They include the sacred mountains of Rau Fembum in Ngaouha, Buea Mountain for the Bakweri, the lakes Oku (for the Oku people) and Awing (for the Awing people), the river Wouri (for the Ngondo of the Douala) and the Sacred Forests and market spaces. In some places shrines restrict access.
- *Public museums*: are museums that are created by communities, nations and public organisations. These are museums where access is accorded to the public without any restrictions, like markets, palaces (places where people seek asylum), the sea spaces, the mountains, some of the lakes, etc.
- *Private museums*: these are museums created by private individuals, families or solidarities of confraternities and sororities, like the AFHEMI Museum (African Art, Handicraft and Environmental Management Institute) in Yaounde or the Musa Art Gallery in Kumbo. Where it is a secret society, as with the Mfuh or Kwifor House, access is restricted only to members. Management and use here is determined by an individual or 'chosen few' and access can be open or closed.
- *Closed museums*: these are the opposite of open museums. They are accommodated in buildings and other closed spaces like the Rau Fembum and royal graveyards which give limited accessibility to the public.
- *Mobile museums*: these are usually the performing art museums which can move and make their performance wherever they wish. They include dance groups, theatre groups, masquerade groups, demonstration groups and so on. They can be public or private, open or closed.

These natural museums perform functions we understand as museological but yet they do not conform to traditional Western conceptions of what the museum can be. These are living spaces without any contaminating notion of heritage or preservation. Acts of keeping and preserving are replaced by socially embedded beliefs and values which are woven into the act of living. These are not ecomuseums. Do we actively promote the creation of more traditional museums or maintain Africa's natural museums by preventing the de-contextualisation of her cultural matri-patrimonies? If we aspire to the latter goal, then how can access be managed? How can societies aspire to Baba's dream of inward investment and development, without sacrificing the very thing that makes them distinctive? And finally, in an increasingly pervasive technological age, how can such museums be accessed and understood by a global community? Clearly these kinds of museum do need to be understood but that understanding also risks their destruction.

## Acknowledgement

I wish to acknowledge my mentor and colleague Dr Fongot Kinni, for his insightful discussions on my thoughts around African's cultural matri-patrimonies. He is currently working on a book entitled *Redefining African Heritage and Museology*.

## Bibliography

Barth, F. (1963) *The Role of the Entrepreneur in Social Change in Northern Norway*, Bergen: Arbok for Universitetet.

—— (1981) 'On the Study of Social Change', in *Process and Form in Social Life. Selected Essays of Fedrik Bart*, London: Routledge and Kegan Paul.

Beck, U. (1992) *Risk Society: Towards a New Modernity*, London: Sage.

Godelier, M. (2002) 'Some things you give, some things you sell but some things you must keep for yourselves: what Mauss did not say about sacred objects', in E. Wyschogrod, J.-J. Goux and E. Boynton (eds) *The Enigma of Gift and Sacrifice*, New York: Fordham University Press

Grønhaug, R. (1978) 'Scale as a Variable in Analysis', in F. Barth (ed.) *Scale and Social Organisation*, Oslo: Universitetsforlatget.

Röschenthaler, U. (1999) 'Of objects and contexts: Biographies of ethnographica' in *Journal des Africanistes*, 69(1): 81–103.

Tegomoh, N. E. (2001) *The Destiny of Belaka Saliou Saoumboum*. Tromsø, University of Tromsø.

—— (2002) *The Task of Becoming Visible: Mbum Sacralia and Regalia*. Mphil Visual Anthropology, Tromsø, University of Tromsø.

# 18

# CHARTING
# THE BOUNDARIES

Indigenous models and parallel practices
in the development of the post-museum

*Moira G. Simpson*

The globalisation of the museum concept has seen the idea of a public institution for collecting and displaying culture spread throughout the world as part of local strategies for nation-building, reinforcing or asserting cultural identity, preserving material culture and cultural expressions, and communicating knowledge, ideas and histories. Although often considered to be conservative and immutable, the museum actually possesses a changing and contested history of development and purpose, evolving in response to the cultural, political and epistemological frameworks in which it operates both within the Euro-American or Western context (Bazin 1967; Bennett 1995; Hooper-Greenhill 1992, 2000) and, increasingly, in numerous other global cultural arenas (Ardouin and Arinze 1995, 2000; Bedekar 1995; Bolton 1994; Eoe and Swadling 1991; Geismar and Tilley 2003; Healy and Witcomb 2006; Kreps 2003; Simpson 1996, 2006 a and b).

There are, nevertheless, some activities which are generally regarded as underlying principles central to the idea of the museum; in particular, the emphases on the preservation of collections of objects and on the utilisation of exhibitionary techniques to display and interpret objects in conjunction with textual and visual interpretive materials. Yet the emphasis on materiality does not reflect the full diversity of ways in which heritage and preservation are conceived among different peoples of the world. The Western museum's emphasis on objects does not readily accommodate the need for preserving 'living' culture, an important limitation for those in societies in which less emphasis is placed on preserving the materiality and more on maintaining the intangible aspects of heritage, including the relationships, knowledge and activities that give objects meaning. This is of particular concern in societies where languages, ceremonies, traditional knowledge and other cultural practices are under threat of continued loss or extinction.

Discussing the potential for the idea of the museum to be transferred successfully into diverse cultural contexts, the Indian academic Vasant Bedekar noted in 1988 the existence of a wide variety of situations in which museums in India operated (Bedekar 1988). While claiming that non-Western countries had already contributed to the character of contemporary museology, he maintained that the post-museum stage of the institution's development would need to be marked by substantial change to satisfy the need for a variety of forms of museology to suit differing cultural circumstances. His words echoed those of Zbynek Stransky who, in 1981, stated that 'the institutionalized form [of the museum] is not the final end; it fulfils a certain socially conditioned mission' and predicted that the museum would, as it had before, continue to change 'and in the future it will have eventually completely new forms' (Stransky 1981: 21).

The focus of this chapter is on observing and analysing new forms of the museum that can be perceived in disparate manifestations emerging out of the utilisation of parallel practices of traditional cultural preservation and contemporary museology by local communities in different parts of the world. In particular, this chapter considers what influence traditional concepts of heritage preservation and protection have on the development of community museums in indigenous societies and how communities are using museums as sites of intercultural engagement and resistance. These, in turn, impact on our understanding of museums more broadly and contribute to the reshaping of museums and museological praxis in the twenty-first century. In an earlier text, *Making Representations: Museums in the Post-colonial Era* (Simpson 1996), I examined some of the early developments in this process. The second part of that book, 'The "new" museum paradigm', outlined some historical and cultural precedents of collection and display practices that can be observed in a number of diverse societies. I then discussed examples of contemporary museums established in Maori, Native American and Australian Aboriginal communities, as well other culturally-specific, community museums established by immigrant minority groups in North America and the UK.

In recent research, I have been continuing to explore the influence of indigenous knowledge and cultural practices on potential forms of the future museum, which Bedekar (1988) referred to as the 'post-museum'. This notion of the post-museum as the future, but as yet ill-defined, shape of the museum-to-come, has gained further ground in a number of recent writings which examine the development of the museum as an institution that has both shaped, and been shaped by, Western knowledge and continues to change under the influences of post-modernist perspectives and new technologies (Duclos 1994; Hooper-Greenhill 2000; Russo and Watkins 2005; Thornton, 2005). Hooper-Greenhill notes that the post-museum 'is a new idea that is not yet born, but whose shape is beginning to be seen' (2000: 8). However, its shape will be as difficult to define in the future as it has been in the past for, as Hooper-Greenhill has shown in her study of *Museums and the Shaping of Knowledge*, 'There is no essential museum . . . cabinets, *studioli Theatrum sapientiae*, repositories, and "museums" have been constituted according to the prevailing epistemological context' (1992: 191). Changes that she identifies in the post-museum are an increased focus on the use of existing collections of objects rather than further accumulation, an equal concern for the intangible aspects of heritage, and 'a feminisation of the museum . . . the post-museum will negotiate responsiveness, encourage mutually nurturing partnerships, and celebrate diversity'. She also predicts that 'much of the intellectual development of the post-museum will take place outside the major European centres which witnessed the birth of the modernist museum' (Hooper-Greenhill 2000: 153).

Such changes in museological philosophy arise in large part from the interactions between museums and the communities of traditional owners of museum collections, a process of intercultural dialogue and contestation that, over the past few decades, has illuminated the diversity of concepts associated with the term 'heritage' and broadened the way in which heritage is defined in international discourse, and practised in the globalised museum.

UNESCO is particularly active in encouraging heritage in all its forms, tangible and intangible. It is these changes that are the subject of my current research interests, which have focused on traditional practices and new museum models in North America and the Pacific, in particular in indigenous communities in Canada and Australia. A number of changes can be seen in examples of museums in different cultural contexts including: the shaping of local models formed by museum–community interaction; the incorporation of parallel practices of contemporary ethnomuseology and indigenous curation; influences derived from religious and spiritual beliefs; an overlap of museum–community–ceremonial social worlds; and the deconstruction of the idea of the museum as a physical entity contained within the boundaries of a building (and especially one whose classical architecture speaks so loudly of its European philosophical and architectural origins) with a complementary idea of the landscape as museum. In a global context, the post-museum takes many forms.

For many, the process of globalisation has negative connotations associated with homogenisation, universalisation and 'compression of the world' (Robertson 1992). For some, it raises fears of the merging of the universal with the particular, and the loss of identity and diversity. However, others recognise that globalisation can also be a stimulus for heterogenisation, as communities respond by asserting local differences more forcefully (Albrow 1990; Appadurai 1990; Robertson 1994 and 1995). This process of global localisation, which Roland Robertson called 'glocalisation', is related to indigenisation, and is evident when intersections occur between the global and the local: local responses display local characteristics demonstrating differences marked by culture, ethnicity and religion. Within this context, many communities are embracing the museum concept but adapting it to suit their own cultural and social needs, often in parallel with local methods of managing knowledge and caring for culture. If a museum is to be effective in preserving cultural material and knowledge, it must operate within the cultural and epistemological framework of those whom it is intended to benefit. As the notion of the museum spreads, the concept is changing and adopting new roles and forms that reflect alternative approaches to heritage, preservation and interpretation, and these developments can be seen worldwide as the idea of the museum continues to spread and evolve in local contexts (Ardouin and Arinze 1995, 2000; Bolton 1994; Geismar and Tilley 2003; Kassarherou 1998; Kreps 2003; Simpson 1996, 2006 a and b).

The examples of indigenous museum models discussed here illustrate the impacts that cultural specificities can have on the conceptualisation and adaptation of the museum concept when it is adopted by communities in different cultural contexts and used to serve the cultural and political agendas of the local community. This is part of a larger study examining the influences that indigenous spirituality and world views are having on the development of contemporary museums, as the concept of the museum is subjected to forces of change imposed by the processes of globalisation and indigenisation. As noted by Appadurai (1990: 295): 'at least as rapidly as forces from various metropolises are brought into new societies they tend to become indigenized in one or other way'. In theory at least, the Museum, like other forces from the metropolis, can be 'indigenised', its functions and methods adapted to suit the needs of the local context. This is resulting in great diversity in the forms of cultural preservation facilities being developed or established in indigenous community contexts and extends the parameters of the museum beyond those conceptualised within a Western frame of knowledge.

The modern museum developed as a cultural construct reflecting Western epistemologies and socio-political agendas and there are a number of aspects of museum practice which reflect the inequities of the power–knowledge relationship between museums and the communities represented in their collections. In the early modern museum, the collecting and telling of history reflected the perspectives of the dominant, and were based on gender, class and race so that the voices and the material culture of women and children, the working classes, and ethnic minorities were less in evidence (Porter 1990, 1996; Kavanagh 1990). In European countries and in the settler societies of former European colonies, such as the USA, Canada and Australia, museums were associated with empire or nation-building, a role that the globalised museum maintains. Colonial collecting activities and the interpretation of ethnographic collections supported the political, social and religious ideologies of the colonisers and the activities of the colonial project in bringing 'civilisation' and Christian values to peoples considered to be racially and culturally inferior. Thus, museums contributed to and reflected the creation of a cultural hegemony which gave primacy to Western knowledge, scientific rationality and educational methodologies. Through collecting and research activities, indigenous peoples were disassociated from their material heritage and, although they were used as subjects, resources and informants in the professional activities of anthropologists and museum curators, they were largely excluded from the processes of representation, the management of heritage and the construction of professional and institutional policies regarding display and interpretation.

Postmodernism and the concerns for social relevance and inclusivity expressed in museological discourse over the past 40 or so years have resulted in critiquing and re-evaluation of the modern museum. Indigenous peoples, whose communities had suffered dispossession of lands, heritage and rights under colonialism, have been vocal critics of Western museums, challenging their authority and their possession of indigenous heritage materials and human remains. These efforts to erode the hegemony of Western historicity and increase social agency have opened the museum to alternative interpretations and viewpoints. At the same time, many indigenous peoples have been adopting the idea of the museum as a community cultural facility for protecting and preserving cultural materials as well as enabling them to communicate their own histories and interpret their cultures.

The globalisation of the museum has seen the transposition of the museum idea into many different cultural contexts where it has been adopted first as a European cultural and discursive system and then adapted to local needs to become part of the indigenous field of discourse. Variously referred to as museums, interpretative centres, cultural centres, art centres, keeping places, treasure houses and other indigenous names, these localised models grow out of, and are perceived within, a social world where situated knowledges form the frameworks within which they operate. Situated knowledges, according to Haraway,

> require that the object of knowledge be pictured as an actor and agent, not a screen or a ground or a resource, never finally as slave to the master that closes off the dialectic in his unique agency and authorship of 'objective' knowledge.
>
> (Haraway 1991: 188)

This chapter argues that knowledge and collection management are situated processes that are used to regulate access and knowledge transmission in museums and related cultural facilities and which create diverse models of museums and museum-related cultural facilities that are appropriate to the needs of those who operate them. Based on these considerations, a variety of different models of museums can be identified operating within the epistemologies that prevail in different cultural contexts, some of which challenge accepted principles of the idea of the museum, particularly with regard to public access and open dissemination of knowledge. Particularly relevant here are the ways in which public and private aspects of culture and knowledge and the implementation of cultural protocols or customary laws impose restrictions on access to objects and knowledge and so shape local museums and related cultural facilities.

In examination of a number of museums and cultural facilities operating within indigenous communities in Australia and North America, it became clear that traditional mechanisms for preserving cultural practices and their material manifestations, and social frameworks for controlling and transmitting knowledge, are important factors in determining the acceptability of conventional museological methods and models in indigenous communities. Analysis of specific indigenous museums and related cultural facilities provides evidence of the central role of non-Western epistemologies in reshaping the Western museum concept to create culturally-appropriate facilities, for there is no one universal model of the Museum that will suit all cultural contexts. Community museums allow indigenous values to be given prominence, which may be reflected in many aspects of indigenous community museums including architecture, display techniques, collection management and interpretation. Differing approaches to cultural preservation and the control of knowledge are key factors in determining access to indigenous museums and the knowledge that they contain. Indigenous epistemologies and protocols concerning knowledge management in public/private domains are therefore primary determinants in the formation of protocols of access to these facilities.

It is beyond the scope of this chapter to discuss the full range of indigenous museum models that have been examined in this project; this will be dealt with more fully in a forthcoming book. Rather, the focus is on the particularities of localised models of museums that can be observed within the context of indigenous communities in Australia where museum methods and related cultural practices operate in parallel, enabling Indigenous Australians to preserve and protect culture and control knowledge and access in the context of both intra- and intercultural exchanges. Focusing on the tensions between the public/private aspects of cultural knowledge, this chapter will concentrate on two apparently dialectical models that have quite differing agendas in terms of knowledge management and audiences and yet are both concerned with the preservation of material culture and associated knowledge. It should be emphasised here that secrecy and gender divisions in the ritual domain in Aboriginal communities are not simple binaries of sacred or secular, secret or public, male or female; rather ritual life is a complex of activities in which there are gradations of secrecy. Some rituals are performed in secret by men, some by women; some are shared, others are public and unrestricted. Secrecy itself may be merely a mask that creates or enhances power only when the secrecy itself is public knowledge (Keen 1994: 251–4; Morphy 1991: 98–106).

These examples demonstrate that Aboriginal political agendas and protocols concerning ritual knowledge affect the forms of cultural facilities that are established by communities to preserve, protect and transmit cultural knowledge and the degree to which that knowledge is made publicly available. The interpretative centre model has primary functions of research, archiving, display and communication of publicly accessible knowledge, while the Keeping Place model establishes boundaries that limit access in order to protect objects considered to be both secret and sacred, and restrict knowledge dissemination to a narrow group of community members. These examples of the post-museum illustrate the diverse nature of museum-related facilities in differing cultural contexts when the cultural and religious protocols of indigenous knowledge management are applied to collection management. They raise interesting issues about indigenous uses of the museum concept and the tensions that occur between public and private dimensions of culture in some indigenous communities.

## The interpretative model

The interpretative model is the type of community museum that conforms most closely to the Western modernist museum. Indigenous communities utilise the idea of the museum as a facility for storing and preserving material culture, collecting and storing documents and photographs and other archival records and displaying and interpreting cultural materials in order to communicate to visitors, both insiders and outsiders, aspects of their own histories and cultures. The interpretive model may be a standalone facility or part of a larger network of cultural facilities that contribute to the community's cultural and heritage preservation strategies, designed to protect, conserve and interpret the cultural and historical record of an area or people for the benefit of community members and/or visitors from outside the community.

Indigenous museums often present a rival discourse to the dominant historical narrative – a re-reading of history from an indigenous perspective. As noted by Clifford (1997: 213–14), these local models of museums and cultural centres 'respond to histories of exclusion and silencing . . . and can provide sites for . . . "minority" and "tribal articulations" of a discrete culture and history'.

For indigenous visitors the exhibitions can provide cultural reaffirmation and an opportunity to balance the historical record, by conveying indigenous accounts of history during the relatively brief but turbulent period of post-European settlement. Like the movement among some historians towards the reinterpretation of Australia's frontier history and the relationships between coloniser and colonised, these insiders' emic perspectives (Pike 1967) presented in indigenous museums and interpretive centres, provide historical perspectives that are meaningful to Aboriginal people and which act as interjections to the more familiar dominant historical narratives and museological discourses about indigenous peoples presented in mainstream museums (Russell 2001). So, in Brambuk Living Cultural Centre in Victoria, Australia, visitors can read diary entries giving accounts of frontier violence which refer to individual settlers poisoning or shooting Aboriginal people to acquire land. In Bunjilaka, the Aboriginal Centre in Melbourne Museum, an audio-visual display presents images, excerpts and quotations from official records, personal diaries, memoirs and other contemporary accounts that give insights into the views and actions of government agents and settlers in south-east Victoria in the post-settlement years. Again, these include firsthand accounts of atrocities perpetrated against Aboriginal peoples.

Indigenous museums also provide a means of reaffirming cultural identity. In the post-European settlement period, many Indigenous Australians suffered post-contact trauma or experienced the dislocation from lands and communities that resulted from re-settlement on mission stations or from the forced removal of the 'stolen generations'. For others, mixed heritages and imbalances in the dominant historical record and in the teaching of history in schools, may leave individuals feeling uncertain about their identity and history. Genealogical records can be an important resource for reconnecting people with their indigenous ancestry and asserting identity to others. A travelling exhibition developed by Yugambeh Museum, Language and Heritage Centre in Queensland, comprises pictorial displays that provide genealogical links between contemporary community members and various indigenous historical figures, filling a gap in the dominant historical record presented in the school curricula and most history texts. The interpretative model enables indigenous people to control the interpretation process and address such historical inequities. It also provides a mechanism for intercultural communication through which indigenous staff can seek to establish a dialogue and present an insider or emic view to an audience of outsiders or non-indigenous visitors.

Using forms of communication with which outsiders will be familiar, the interpretive strategies generally include the use of objects, photographs, written labels and texts, although in some cultures, the communication methods may emphasise oral and visual methods of communication reflecting traditional, historical record-keeping and teaching methods. For example, the Navajo Community College in Arizona, USA, has visual displays with no labels. These are used by elders as the focus for storytelling, which is the traditional method of teaching in Navajo culture (Simpson 1996: 161–3). Exhibitions in Djomi Museum in Maningrida and Buku-Larrnggay Mulka Museum in Yirrkala, two indigenous museums in Arnhem Land in Northern Australia, present items of material culture, photographs, historical artefacts and contemporary art works, with limited textual information. The displays are primarily intended for visitors to Maningrida and Yirrkala who are drawn to the museums mainly by the presence of the very successful art centres with which they are associated.

Interpretive museum models can provide visitors with insights into indigenous world views and those aspects of culture considered to be open and public. However, other aspects of Aboriginal culture may be considered private and are not open to outsiders. In many Indigenous Australian communities, knowledge management processes involve the observation of cultural protocols and customary laws that restrict access in order to preserve the integrity of sacred knowledge, objects and sites. Various facilities and strategies may be used to protect and preserve the private or sacred aspects of culture in combination with economic development initiatives designed to attract visitors to the area and create employment opportunities within the community.

In Indigenous Australian settlements and community museums, spaces in which restricted aspects of culture are located are protected by the establishment of boundaries which confine visitors to public spaces and protect the community from unwanted intrusions (Simpson 2006b: 152–77). These boundaries and the regions that they create may be physical, symbolic or imaginary. The construction of boundaries is both a strategy to protect cultural and intellectual property rights but also a means of protecting the immanent aspects of culture from inappropriate access, and such boundaries have varying degrees of permeability depending on the nature of the material, knowledge, places or events that they are designed to protect and the degree to which they are restricted. They include regulations administered by Aboriginal community and land councils in central and northern Australia that require visitors to obtain permits before travelling to communities, and impose imaginary and symbolic boundaries that limit their access to public areas such as the art centre and village store. Additional boundaries, both physical and symbolic, delineate areas around or within an indigenous museum, publicly presenting some aspects of culture while protecting and concealing aspects considered to be sacred and secret. In this way an interpretive museum model in an Indigenous Australian community may have areas that are open and accessible, presenting exhibitions of cultural material for public consumption, while an area may be set aside for the storage and concealment of that which is sacred and secret.

## The restricted Keeping Place model

In communities in which knowledge management involves the privileging of certain aspects of knowledge to specific sub-groups based on gender, age or status, preservation may be achieved through concealment in order to maintain the integrity of the objects and the knowledge associated with them. In a number of Indigenous Australian communities, restricted storage facilities called Keeping Places, are used to house sacred and ceremonial objects, especially items considered to be secret and sacred, and other items of a culturally sensitive nature.

In parts of Australia, especially New South Wales and Victoria, some indigenous community museums are referred to as Keeping Places even though their primary role is as an interpretive centre. They may also contain a restricted storage space. In Central Australian communities the term Keeping Place more commonly refers to a building constructed primarily as a secure storage facility for sacred and restricted objects, referred to in many anthropological texts by the Arrernte word *tjurunga*. The Keeping Place is a modern version of the traditional sacred storehouses where custodians hid tjurunga and other important ritual objects (Berndt 1974: 1–25; Gillen 1896: 179–80; Spencer and Gillen 1904/1969; Stirling 1896, 76–82; Strehlow 1947). These were often caves, piles of rocks or simple structures built from tree branches and brush. Items considered to be particularly sacred were subject to restrictions on who could handle or even see them and infringement could lead to severe punishment or even death (Gillen 1896: 179). Access to the traditional storehouses was, therefore, strictly limited to custodians and to initiates when they were under instruction.

Due to their potential value on the art market, sacred and ceremonial objects are no longer safe from misappropriation or theft and require more secure storage facilities than was previously the case, so while traditional bush storehouses are still used, some Indigenous Australian communities have constructed buildings to provide a more secure storage facility. This has often been facilitated by the assistance of staff of the National and State museums, who have been involved in repatriating sacred objects from museum collections back to traditional owners. Depending on the availability of funding, the Keeping Places vary greatly in the quality of construction and consequent levels of security that they would afford if subjected to an attempt at forced entry. Likewise, climatic controls may include dehumidifiers and air-conditioners or simply provide physical barriers, such as glass panes rather than louvres, to provide protection against the elements and the penetration of dust and insects.

Many anthropological studies of Indigenous Australian religious life detail rituals, such as initiation ceremonies, in which various sacred items were displayed and used. Rituals took many forms and often comprised several parts taking place over a number of days or weeks, with some parts being public and others restricted to varying degrees. During and after the ceremony, initiates would learn the meanings of patterns on sacred objects, and the myths, songs and rituals associated with the objects, a process that might continue for many years (Berndt 1974: 17–18; Strehlow 1947). When required for a ceremony, the objects were removed from their storehouses and taken to the ritual site. Sacred sites and locations of ceremonies are demarcated by time–space boundaries, usually imaginary rather than physical, although visual makers might be used to warn anyone approaching of the restricted nature of the site (Wallace and Wallace 1977: 12–15, 70). Depending on their nature, both ceremonial sites and objects might have varying levels of restriction associated with them at different times, the boundaries therefore displaying temporal–spatial fluidity according to the occasion and the status of the objects.

Although many anthropological accounts of Aboriginal ceremonial life have suggested that ritual secrecy and care of secret/sacred objects was the domain of the men, most of these studies were carried out by male anthropologists; complementary work by female anthropologists such as Phyllis Kaberry (1939), Catherine Berndt (1965) and Diane Bell (1983; 1987) have revealed a parallel domain within the ritual lives of Aboriginal women, in which some aspects are also gender-restricted, while others are shared (see also essays in Brock 1989). When members of the Warlpiri community in Yuendumu in Central Australia sought more secure storage for sacred objects in the 1970s, they established two Keeping Places, which they called museums, one for men and one for women.

Restricted Keeping Places have no public or interpretive dimension for those outside the groups holding access rights. Access is limited to individuals who hold the custodial rights to the secret/sacred objects through status on the basis of gender and others factors such as clan membership, age and initiation. However, certain privileges may be extended to visitors such as anthropologists who are conducting research in the community, or have been involved in establishing and maintaining the Keeping Places and facilitating the repatriation of sacred objects from State and National museums.

## The boundaries of the post-museum in Indigenous Australia

How precisely are these divergent models to be perceived and understood in the context of museology? Museums are both repositories of objects of knowledge and also objects of knowledge in themselves. Each museum or cultural centre is a construct of the social world and the epistemological framework in which it operates. Consequently, the form, activities and functions of glocalised museums vary according to the ways in which cultural heritage is conceived and preserved in the community, such as what forms of cultural heritage are valued, how preservation is enacted, how knowledge is managed and transmitted, and who are the intended audiences. Reflecting alternative concepts of knowledge management, indigenous museums may emphasise other forms of heritage than collecting objects, such as cultural landscapes and intangible heritage (performative, intellectual and relational aspects of culture). In applying local frames of knowledge and fulfilling indigenous cultural and political agendas, indigenous community museums apply protocols concerning public/private aspects of culture and restrictions on accessibility. The implementation of cultural protocols concerning ritual secrecy and restrictions on access to places, objects and knowledge creates boundaries which protect aspects of culture considered to be private or secret, and demarcate regions within the particular locale of the museum, thereby defining and controlling the public/private aspects of culture.

The term 'locale' is a useful descriptor for the social worlds in which specific museums operate, as its meaning, as defined by Giddens, refers to a space that is 'used as a *setting* for interaction' (Giddens 1979: 206–7). As a place where temporal and spatial attributes can be combined and in which there is no division between the cultural and the natural landscapes, the idea of locale reflects the multidimensional nature of tangible, intangible, cultural and natural heritages. It thus accommodates the interactions and integrated nature of the cultural and natural worlds of many indigenous peoples which encompass cosmology, cultural history and ceremonial life, including concepts of traditional ownership rights and inherited custodianship responsibilities for objects and knowledge, and for land and sea.

The creation of boundaries within a locale in turn creates regions which Goffman refers to as spaces demarcated in terms of time–space relations and variable in the degree of 'boundedness' imposed or permeability that they allow. According to Goffman, 'a region may be defined as any place that is bounded to some degree by barriers to perception' (1959: 107).

The indigenous museums and their activities are enmeshed within a locale that comprises a network of relationships between people, objects, places and events. Central to this are rights and responsibilities of people to objects, places, knowledge and performative aspects of culture which are managed and transmitted according to local cultural conventions. The creation of boundaries in the context of the sacred in Indigenous Australian cultures and museums, creates regions in which intra- and intercultural activity can be managed and controlled. This practice has been extended from the traditional locale of ceremonial life and custodianship of country, to the locale of the museum or Keeping Place and the custodianship of the objects and knowledge that they protect.

It may appear that there is a conflict between the conventional philosophy of the museum, in which public access, display and dissemination are central aspects, and the role of the restricted Keeping Places, where boundaries are imposed, limiting the 'audience' and level of access on the grounds of cultural values such as religion or gender. However, museums, like most other public institutions and organisations, comprise both public and private regions demarcated within physical and imaginary boundaries to which access is controlled as a result of the institution's function and as a reflection of its power and control over the knowledge it holds within. Knowledge is both a resource that can be collected, organised, stored and accessed in the context of institutions such as museums, libraries, archives and other collecting institutions, but it is also the subject of a situational process of management which determines who can and cannot access or acquire cultural knowledge.

As objects change location culturally, physically and temporally, they pass through different hands and are attributed with multiple uses and meanings. In the process, they develop complex 'social lives' (Appadurai 1986) which can be recounted in the writing of 'cultural biographies of objects' (Kopytoff 1986; Hooper-Greenhill 2000). The act of removal of an object from its original cultural context and its relocation to a museum or art gallery abruptly and profoundly changes its meaning – it alienates it from everyday life and subjects it to reinterpretation by curators and visitors. Within their original social context or locale, objects are linked to peoples, places and cultural practices and their meaning or significance is understood within that epistemological framework; in other words, they take their meaning from the knowledge, skills, beliefs and values of the participants in the social worlds in which they are used. In their original context, they were familiar cultural tools with functions which might be part of everyday and/or ceremonial life. Relocated to a new locale – the museum – they take their place in a new social world, a world of public display and interpretation that adds further layers and new relationships to their biographies.

This transformative process applies to any object removed from its original context and placed within a museum collection where new relationships are built, intercultural as well as intracultural, and new meanings are assigned by curator, designer, conservator and visitor. The object becomes a specimen, one example within a particular typology, a piece of historical evidence; 'meaning and understanding become a conglomeration of assorted biographies, of the collector, of the curator and of the object specimen itself' (Pearce 1999: 29). In the locale of an ethnographic museum exhibition, objects are redefined within a Western epistemological framework and meaning is constructed by the values and beliefs of the curator and the visitor. In the politically-charged environment of the ethnographic museum, whose history is embedded in colonial activities, objects and their owners became exotic Other; the process of recontextualisation is simultaneously a process of subjectification and objectification and of (de)mystification.

In the modernist museum, curatorial staff and museum designers controlled the selection of objects, the contexts in which they were presented, and the narratives in which they were placed. While it is now well-recognised within the museum profession that museum visitors make their own meanings based on previously-held knowledge, values, opinions, conceptions (and misconceptions), meaning can be influenced as much by what is not presented as by what is, by what remains unspoken as much as by what is stated. Within the narratives presented in exhibitions of the histories and cultures of the Other, have been 'painful silences; powerful absences . . . in the collection of another culture, the museum constructs a history which situates that Other in the theoretical and institutional framework of the collector's world' (McLoughlin 1993).

Modernist museums have boundaries that control and limit what visitors see and where they move within an institutional framework based on security concerns and museological functions that are performed by staff in different fields of work: research, collections management, display, conservation. Objects may be located within one of a number of regions of the museum – the galleries, stores, conservation laboratories – each region having differing levels of public accessibility. The objects move from one region to another at different times, their status and their accessibility changing according to the type of the boundary that defines each region. Objects may, for example, play a central role in display and interpretation and be located in a gallery, a region of the museum that is accessible to the general public with few restrictions. Many other objects remain in the stores where they are arranged, classified, documented, conserved, studied and preserved. In this semi-restricted region, they are less accessible but still available to members of the public who receive permission to access them, such as bona fide researchers, students or others who are considered appropriate on cultural or academic grounds. In the laboratories of the conservators, objects are restricted even more as their fragility or value require that they are afforded greater protection and care while their material needs are tended. Essentially, in the modernist museum:

> a division was drawn between the private space where the curator, as expert, produced knowledge (exhibitions, catalogues, lectures) and the public space where the visitor consumed those appropriately presented products. By introducing strategies to make museums more inclusive and relevant 'the closed and private space of the early public museums has begun to open, and the division between the private and the public has begun to close.
>
> (Hooper-Greenhill 1992: 200)

In Australia's state and national museums, however, such strategies have also had to accommodate the cultural values and protocols of indigenous heritage management which are now observed when developing policies for collection management. Most of these museums now involve indigenous peoples in collection management and exhibition development as advisors, community consultants or as curatorial staff. This has brought indigenous perspectives into exhibitions and led to the development of culturally appropriate collections management praxis. Any objects classified as secret/sacred, or otherwise considered to be culturally sensitive, are stored separately in clearly marked areas or designated Keeping Places. The only staff who can access them are individuals approved by the traditional custodians, and any researchers wishing to view them must first seek and receive the permission of the traditional custodians as well as the museum curators. In these institutions, the opening of the museum has been paralleled by even stricter limitations surrounding Indigenous Australian materials that are classified as secret/sacred, and their relocation in closed and private areas of the museum stores.

The restricted nature of the Keeping Place may seem to undermine the philosophy of the museum, yet it can also be perceived as the development of culturally-appropriate ethno-museology, in which indigenous values and Western museology operate in parallel. In establishing the Keeping Place, the community has adopted the idea of a secure facility for collections of important cultural material utilising those museum technologies, such as environmental controls, material conservation and security, that are considered useful, culturally appropriate and affordable. Simultaneously, the community has rejected the Western museum philosophy of open public display and interpretation, instead restricting display and access only to those with appropriate status or to occasions when the objects are used in ritual. The application of indigenous knowledge management practices in parallel with selected aspects of Western museology enables communities to create cultural facilities in which curation, conservation and interpretation conform to the cultural and religious values and customary laws of the community, and so maintain the integrity of the objects in relation to the social world in which they operate. Consequently, the Keeping Place as an indigenous museum fulfils museological functions appropriate to its operation within an indigenous knowledge system, while reflecting the indigenous community's cultural imperatives and knowledge-management processes.

In this way, the Keeping Place contributes to the preservation of cultural materials, and the transmission and maintenance of traditional knowledge and ceremonial practices associated with the objects. It provides a facility for the secure storage of the collection of sacred and ceremonial objects so that they can be cared for by traditional custodians, accessed for display and other ceremonial purposes and used by elders to teach young initiates about their meanings and related ceremonies as they prepare them to take on custodial responsibilities. Within the context of the specific Aboriginal communities, the Keeping Place therefore plays a parallel role to a museum: maintaining collections, preserving them for future use, interpreting the objects and displaying them at appropriate times through their use in ceremonies. These tasks are carried out within the epistemological framework of indigenous cultural law, according to the protocols of knowledge management associated with sacred and ceremonial aspects of culture, which determine that secret/sacred material is accessible only to those with the appropriate status. Indeed, it could be argued that unrestricted exposure in public displays is so alien to their function that it would render the objects devoid of meaning. Cultural preservation is therefore achieved not just through preservation of the objects themselves, but also through their continued use, and through the protection and concealment of restricted aspects of culture. As opposed to the historicity of the modernist museum which preserved the past for the future by separating objects from their original context and discouraging or forbidding handling and use, the Keeping Place maintains the links between the objects and their function so that they remain active within the present, part of contemporary life.

## Conclusion

As a result of the glocalisation process, epistemological variations and differing conceptualisations and approaches to the management of heritage impact on the ways in which a museum is conceived within a specific locale and the ways in which objects will be curated, displayed and interpreted. The boundaries that are imposed by indigenous knowledge management systems therefore create a variety of forms of museums designed to fulfil the specificities of cultural/political concerns in particular locales.

The restricted Keeping Place and the interpretative model are two examples of many types of indigenous community museums that are being established within different Indigenous Australian cultural contexts. These, and related cultural facilities, operate along a private/public continuum of indigenous knowledge management from highly restricted to open and accessible determined by the status of the materials that they contain. The 'audiences' range from small and narrowly defined groups of community members, who hold the appropriate authority to view secret/sacred materials, to large and diverse audiences who can view unrestricted materials. Museums in indigenous communities in Australia, and elsewhere, may therefore be different from the Western museum model and some may challenge basic ideas of the museum that are grounded within Western epistemology. They operate within the framework of indigenous knowledge systems and socio-political agendas and are diverse in form and purpose. While these facilities share similar goals with the Western modernist museum, such as collection management, cultural preservation and knowledge dissemination about the objects or sites that they preserve and present, they achieve this through mechanisms applicable within specific local socio-cultural and epistemological frameworks, and within boundaries determined by the community to manage cultural knowledge. Boundaries and regions are established as part of culturally-determined approaches to the management of knowledge, designed to create demarcations between public and private and control the movement of knowledge among and between community members and visitors. The public/private dimension of indigenous museums is therefore determined by the nature of the materials stored and the agenda of the community in terms of protecting, communicating and preserving aspects of their culture.

The tensions that exist between the public and private aspects of culture provide one example of the cultural specificities that indigenous world views may impose on community-based, culturally-appropriate museum models. Such differences illustrate the need to accept alternative values and divergent viewpoints as part of the heterogeneity of contemporary museology and ensure that the twenty-first century museum will reflect and preserve the diversity of human cultures.

## Bibliography

Albrow, M. (1990) 'Introduction', in M. Albrow and E. King (eds) *Globalization, Knowledge and Society*, London: Sage Publications, 3–13.

Appadurai, A. (1986) 'Introduction: commodities and the politics of value', in A. Appadurai (ed.) *The Social Life of Things*, Cambridge: Cambridge University Press, 3–63.

—— (1990) 'Disjuncture and difference in the global economy', in M. Featherstone (ed.) *Global Culture: Nationalism, Globalisation and Modernity*, London: Sage, 295–310.

Ardouin, C. D. and Arinze, E. (1995) (eds) *Museums and the Community in West Africa*, Washington, DC: Smithsonian Institution Press.

—— (2000) *Museums and History in West Africa*, Washington, DC: Smithsonian Institution Press.

Bakhtin, M.M. (1981) *The Dialogic Imagination. Four Essays by M. Bakhtin*, edited by Michael Holquist, translated by Caryl Emerson and Michael Holquist, Austin, TX: University of Texas Press.

Bazin, G. (1967) *The Museum Age*, Brussels: Desoer.

Bedekar, V. H. (1988) 'Third World opportunities for expanding museology discipline', in *Museology and Developing Countries – Helper or Manipulation?* Papers of a symposium of the ICOM Committee for Museology held in Hyderabad, New Delhi, November, ICOFOM Study Series No. 14, 81–7.

—— (1995) *New Museology for India*, New Delhi: National Museum.

Bell, D. (1983) *Daughters of the Dreaming*, North Melbourne: Spinifex.

—— (1987) 'Aboriginal women and the religious experience', in W. H. Edwards (ed.) *Traditional Aboriginal Society: A Reader*, South Melbourne: Macmillan.

Bennett, T. (1995) *The Birth of the Museum: History, Theory, Politics*, London: Routledge.

Berndt, C. H. (1965) 'Women and the "secret life"', in R. M. Berndt and C. H. Berndt (eds) *Aboriginal Man in Australia: Essays in Honour of Emeritus Professor A.P. Elkin*, Sydney: Angus and Robertson, 238–82.

Berndt, R. M. (1974) 'Australian Aboriginal religion, chapter 5: Central Australia', Published in the series *The Iconography of Religions*, volume 5, Leiden: E.J. Brill, 1–21.

Bolton, L. (1994) 'The Vanuatu Cultural Centre and its own community', *Journal of Museum Ethnography*, 6: 67–78.

Brock P. (1989) (ed.) *Women, Rites and Sites: Aboriginal Women's Cultural Knowledge*, Melbourne: Allen and Unwin.

Clifford, J. (1997) *Routes: Travel and Translation in the Twentieth Century*, Cambridge, MA: Harvard University Press.

Duclos, R. (1994) 'Postmodern/postmuseum: new directions in contemporary museological critique', *Museological Review*, 1(1): 1–13.

Eoe S. M. and Swadling, P. (1991) (eds) *Museums and Cultural Centres in the Pacific*, Port Moresby: Papua New Guinea National Museum.

Geismar, H. and Tilley, C. (2003) 'Negotiating materiality: international and local museum practices at the Vanuatu Cultural Centre and National Museum', *Oceania*, 73(3): 170–88.

Giddens, A. (1979) *Central Problems in Social Theory: Action Structure and Contradiction in Social Analysis*, London: Macmillan.

Gillen, F.J. (1896) 'Notes on some manners and customs of the Aborigines of the McDonnell Ranges belonging to the Arunta Tribe', in B. Spencer (ed.) *Report of the Work of the Horn Scientific Expedition to Central Australia. Part IV. Anthropology*, London: Dulau and Co, 161–96.

Goffman, E. (1959) *The Presentation of Self in Every Day Life*, New York: Doubleday.

Haraway, D. J. (1991) *Simians, Cyborgs, and Women: The Reinvention of Nature*, New York: Routledge.

Healy, C. and Witcomb, A. (2006) (eds) *South Pacific Museums: Experiments in Culture*. Melbourne: Monash University Press.

Hooper-Greenhill, E. (1992) *Museums and the Shaping of Knowledge*, London: Routledge.

—— (2000) *Museums and the Interpretation of Visual Culture*, London: Routledge.

Kaberry, P. (1939) *Aboriginal Women, Sacred and Profane*, London: George Routledge and Sons, Ltd.

Kassarherou, E. (1998). 'Museums and cultural diversity. Ancient cultures, new worlds in the Pacific region: The Tjibaou Cultural Centre, Noumea'. Paper presented at ICOM Conference, Melbourne, Australia, 11 October 1998. Online. Available at: www.mov.vic.gov.au/icom/spkr3.html (accessed 31 March 2001).

Kavanagh, G. (1990) *History Curatorship*, Leicester: Leicester University Press.

Keen, I. (1994) *Knowledge and Secrecy in Aboriginal Religion*, Oxford: Oxford University Press.

Kopytoff, I. (1986) 'The cultural biographies of things: commoditization as process', in A. Appadurai (ed.) *The Social Life of Things*, Cambridge: Cambridge University Press, 64–91.

Kreps, C. K. (2003) *Liberating Culture: Cross-cultural Perspectives on Museums, Curation, and Heritage Preservation*, London: Routledge.

McLoughlin, M. (1993) 'Of boundaries and borders: First Nations' history in museums' *Canadian Journal of Communication* (18), 3. Online. Available at: www.cjc-online.ca/viewarticle.php?id = 184&layout = html (accessed 22 November 2006).

Morphy, H. (1991) *Ancestral Connections: Art and an Aboriginal System of Knowledge*, Chicago, IL: University of Chicago Press.

Pearce, S. (1999) *On Collecting: An Investigation into Collecting in the European Tradition*, London: Routledge.

Pike, K. L. (1967). *Language in Relation to a Unified Theory of Structure of Human Behaviour*, 2nd edition, The Hague: Mouton.

Porter, G. (1990) 'Gender bias: representations of work in history museums', *Continuum: Australian Journal of Media & Culture*, 3(1). Online. Available at: wwwmcc.murdoch.edu.au/Reading-Room/3.1/Porter.html (accessed 22 November 2006).

—— (1996) 'Seeing through solidity: a feminist perspective on museums', in S. Macdonald and G. Fyfe (eds) *Theorizing Museums: Representing Identity and Diversity in a Changing World*, Cambridge, MA: Blackwell, 105–26.

Robertson, R. (1992) *Globalization: Social Theory and Global Culture*, London: Sage.

—— (1994) 'Globalization or Glocalization?', *Journal of International Communication*, 1(1): 33–52.

—— (1995) 'Glocalization: time–space and homogeneity–heterogeneity', in M. Featherstone, S. Lash and R. Robertson (eds) *Global Modernities*, London: Sage Publications, 25–44.

Russell, L. (2001) *Savage Imaginings: Historical and Contemporary Constructions of Australian Aboriginalitie*, Kew: Australian Scholarly Publishing.

Russo, A. and Watkins, J. (2005) 'Post-museum experiences: structured methods for audience engagement', in H. Thwaites (ed.) *Proceedings of the Eleventh International Conference on Virtual Systems and Multimedia*, Brussels, 173–82. Online. Available at: http://eprints.qut.edu.au/archive/00003985/01/3985.pdf (accessed 14 May 2006).

Simpson, M. G. (1996) *Making Representations: Museums in the Post-colonial Era*, London: Routledge. Revised 2001.

—— (2006a) 'A world of museums: new concepts, new models', in A. Pinto and A. P. Ribeiro (eds) *The State of the World*, Lisbon: Fundação Calouste Gulbenkian, 90–121.

—— (2006b) 'Revealing and concealing: museums, objects and the transmission of knowledge in Aboriginal Australia', in J. Marstine (ed.) *New Museum Theory and Practice: An Introduction*, Oxford: Blackwell Publishing, 152–77.

Spencer, B. and Gillen, J. G. (1969) *The Northern Tribes of Central Australia*, The Netherlands: Oosterhout N.B. (reprint of the 1904 Macmillan edition).

Stirling, E. C. (1896) 'Anthropology', in B. Spencer (ed.) *Report of the Work of the Horn Scientific Expedition to Central Australia. Part IV. Anthropology*, London: Dulau and Co. and Melbourne: Melville, Mullen and Slade, 1–160.

Stransky, Z. Z. (1981) Untitled essay in *Interdisciplinarity in Museums*, Museological Working Papers (MuWoP), (2), 19–21.

Strehlow, T. G. H. (1947) *Aranda Traditions*, Carlton, Vic.: Melbourne University Press.

Thornton, M. (2005) 'The Museum as an intercultural site' presented at *Politics and Positioning*, Museums Australia National Conference 2005. Online. Available at: www.mia.id.au/ma.htm (accessed 14 March 2006).

Wallace, P. and Wallace, N. (1977) *Killing Me Softly: The Destruction of a Heritage*, West Melbourne, Vic.: Thomas Nelson.

# 19

# WHERE TO FROM HERE?

## Repatriation of indigenous human remains and 'The Museum'

*Michael Pickering*

Over the past several years there have been major developments in international repatriation debates and activities regarding indigenous human remains. As a result, many museums, Australian and British in particular, but also mainland European and American, large and small, now find themselves either implicitly or explicitly, voluntarily or compulsorily, involved in complex domestic and international repatriation exercises. However, because of the delicate professional, cultural, national and international 'politics' of the repatriation debate, and a prevailing popular belief that repatriation is being forced on institutions, there is still a tendency for many institutions, their departments, and the staff not directly involved in the activity, to disassociate themselves from the issues, and from those active in the area. As a result, repatriation activity is often treated as an isolated event to be contained and marginalised – even spoken about in hushed voices. It is deemed to occupy isolated individuals who are left to get on with their work of collection destruction in private. Other professionals, both those within, and those outside, the institution, criticise participants or, at best, turn a blind eye to the activity thanking the heavens that their collections are safe. Indeed, Rudyard Kipling's (n.d.) 'Smuggler's Song' comes to mind:

> If You wake at midnight, and hear a horse's feet,
> Don't go drawing back the blind, or looking in the street,
> Them that asks no questions isn't told a lie.
> Watch the wall, my darling, while the Gentlemen go by!

Only, the boxes in transit do not contain 'brandy for the parson', nor 'laces for a lady'.

As a result, repatriation runs the risk of being reduced to an applied exercise in logistics and process. Its capacity to deliver real contributions to multidisciplinary and museological theory, policy, practice and knowledge as a whole is neglected and thus compromised.

Changes in legislation, changes in industry and institutional policy and changes in the philosophies of individuals are making it difficult for museums to resist engagement at some level. Involvement may be active, based on negotiating the management of remains in the institution's care, or passive, where an institution without collections of remains is nonetheless affected by the repatriation debates within the museums industry. Some see repatriation as something they want to do; others see it as something they are forced to do. Whatever the motivator, museums are increasingly obligated to return remains and, whether we acknowledge it or not, all industry practice is being affected by the issue.

The contribution of the British and Australian museum industries deserves special acknowledgement. Australian Museums have been engaged in proactive repatriation for a number of years (Museums Australia 1993, 2005). While, following the agreement between the British and Australian Prime Ministers in 2000 (Prime Minister 2000), the British museum industry has engaged with the issue, and has admirably and comprehensively participated in an important consideration of repatriation of the remains of indigenous people (Department of Culture, Media and Sport 2003).

It is typical of most repatriation papers that they are delivered to confined audiences – usually practitioners of repatriation, curators of ethnographic collections or disciplinary conferences such as archaeology or anthropology. These professions are not the target audience for this chapter. Rather, this chapter is intentionally pragmatic. It is hoped that its message will reach and inform a wider museum community, not just those directly involved in repatriation. Nor does the chapter explicitly try to convert people to supporting repatriation of remains through moral, philosophical, historical or legal argument. This aspect of the debate is adequately covered by other sources (for example, Department of Culture, Media and Sport 2003; Fforde et al. 2002; Fforde 2004; Museums Australia 2005; Pickering 2002; United Nations 1994). Instead, it is intended to encourage recognition of the opportunities and benefits, tangible and intangible, that the simple act of engagement with the issue of repatriation brings to the institution – regardless of whether engagement has led to a repatriation exercise or not. This is illustrated through the experiences of the National Museum of Australia in repatriating Aboriginal and Torres Strait Islander human remains.

## Repatriation at the National Museum of Australia

Australian State and Territory museums have been returning ancestral remains to Aboriginal and Torres Strait Islander people for more than 25 years, although with varying levels of enthusiasm in the early years. Since the late 1990s, along with growing appreciation of the various merits of repatriation, all state and territory museums have had the opportunity to be proactive in repatriation of indigenous remains. This is primarily due, first, to an Australian museums industry-wide commitment to the ethics of repatriation (Museums Australia 1993, 2005) complemented more recently by the provision of special funding through the 'Return of Indigenous Cultural Property Program' (Australian Government 2006a), as well as support funding for special collections, such as those returned from overseas (Australian Government 2006b).

This commitment to unconditional return of Aboriginal and Torres Strait Islander remains by the Australian museums industry is reflected in, and articulated by, Museums Australia (2005), the peak industry professional body, in its document 'Continuous Cultures, Ongoing Responsibilities. Principles and Guidelines for Australian Museums working with Aboriginal and Torres Strait Islander Cultural Heritage'. While not binding on museums, the document enshrines the philosophies and principles expected from practitioners in the Australian museums industry.

The National Museum, like most Australian museums, had been returning remains to Aboriginal and Torres Strait Islander people on request since its inception in 1980. The returns were slow but consistent over 20 years. In 2001, the National Museum of Australia established a Repatriation Program Unit to manage the return of indigenous remains both in its own collections and those returned from overseas. The National Museum's own holdings of human remains derive from many sources. It is important to acknowledge, however, that the National Museum is 'new' enough not to have deliberately collected human remains as a strategy. This is in contrast to much older Australian state museums dating back to the mid-nineteenth century. These museums had, at some time in their past, actively pursued indigenous remains. The National Museum has benefited from not having the burden of this legacy in being considered more impartial than some other institutions. Most of the remains in the National Museum's past and current holdings derive from the now defunct 'Australian Institute of Anatomy' collections, transferred to the National Museum in 1985. The Institute was established in the 1930s and made large collections of human and animal biological specimens, as well as an enviable collection of other cultural objects. The National Museum has also contracted to the Australian Government's 'Office of Indigenous Policy Coordination'. In this capacity it acts as the temporary repository and repatriation point for collections returned to Australia from Edinburgh University, the Royal College of Surgeons in London, Manchester Museum, Horniman Museum and Exeter Museums in the UK, the Bishop Museum and Michigan University in the USA and from the Museum of Ethnography in Sweden.

The National Museum's repatriation activities are guided by the *Policy on Aboriginal and Torres Strait Islander Human Remains* (National Museum of Australia 2005). Over the five years of the Museum Repatriation Unit's operations, and at time of writing, the remains of 700 individuals have been returned to Aboriginal communities across Australia and consultations are ongoing over another 64. Fifty-four have had title returned but are held at the Museum by the request of communities until resources become available for final treatment.

The National Museum's experiences in repatriation are not unique, although they have probably been a little more intensive and diverse than the experiences of the other seven major Australian State museums. Despite its 'National' prefix, the National Museum has no more legislative authority, and in some cases less, than the state museums. Its 'Federal' status has certainly meant that it attracts the attention of other federal and international agencies. Nonetheless, at the end of the day, it is an Australian museum doing what Australian museums do. All in all, however, the National Museum has been quite successful. It has certainly satisfied its obligations to the Australian Museum industry's commitment to repatriation, it has satisfied contractual obligations to external government funding agencies, and has returned enough remains to satisfy most indigenous advocates. Most importantly, however, it has been privileged to witness the impact on the grass-roots Aboriginal communities who have received remains. It is at this level of engagement that the most significant contributions of repatriation are to be seen and appreciated.

Nonetheless, setting sentiment aside, through its industry-endorsed, applied exercises in repatriation, the National Museum has also reaped a number of unexpected benefits. These include outcomes in research, community alliances, public programmes, policy development, reputation, management processes, museum practice and media profile, among others. Specific examples follow.

## Research

Research is close to the heart of any curator. With regard to indigenous human remains it can include research *on* remains, research *about* human remains, and research *about the issues of repatriation* of human remains. In Australia, at least, research *on* indigenous human remains held in museum collections is minimal. This is primarily because such research requires indigenous community approval – something few prospective researchers into biological anthropology are prepared to accept as a condition of access (Pickering in press). The partial exception is to in-house research done for the purpose of establishing provenance and drafting community reports. This research is usually restricted.

More significantly, research *about* human remains is increasingly common. The research by National Museum repatriation staff contributes to what is known about the history of the collections. These histories not only provide interesting reading in themselves, but also inform the ethics and practice of repatriation. Authors such as Turnbull (1991a, 1991b, 1994, 1997, 1998, 1999, 2001, 2002) and Fforde (2002, 2004), in particular, have written extensively on the history of the collecting of indigenous human remains, providing revealing insights into the profiles of collectors, infringements of the law, contemporary museological theories and practices and the biases within collections, among other interesting historical issues. This research has typically focused on issues in social history and relationships between the colonial institutions, individuals and indigenous peoples, not specifically on advocating repatriation. However, such research has both informed and been informed by the repatriation process. Robertson's (2004) research, for example, has recently shown that the National Museum's domestic collections of remains, long used as the basis for many statements about Australian indigenous populations and health in prehistory, are in fact highly biased and unrepresentative as a population sample. This simple finding has a major impact on debates in Australian archaeology.

Of course, the greatest contribution of the National Museum has been with regard to research *about* repatriation. This is encouraged by the increasing profile of the repatriation debate. The National Museum has contributed to a number of discussions on the repatriation process and associated ethics, method and theory and has hosted several successful repatriation workshops and conferences. Staff are regular lecturers at academic and public forums. This engagement is, of course, not unique to the National Museum and reflects international museum trends towards a growing interest in repatriation. Nonetheless, the National Museum, through its engagement and experiences, does have a higher than average profile in Australia.

The Museum has also been instrumental in encouraging research about human remains and repatriation beyond the conventional disciplinary boundaries of anthropology and archaeology. Once dominated by archaeologists, the debate is now attracting input from philosophers, historians, journalists and art historians, among others, who bring new, and very important, perspectives to the debates. In a 2005 conference hosted by the National Museum, the Australian National University, Griffith University and the World Archaeological Congress, a number of speakers from across the world presented papers on a diverse range of repatriation themes, providing a welcome shift away from the familiar critical 'rhetoric of allegation' and simple case studies in favour of wider philosophical, historical and cultural considerations (Centre for Cross-Cultural Research 2005). Indeed, we should look forward to the day when a repatriation session includes a paper by a museum's Chief Finance Officer reflecting full institutional involvement. Such research has been stimulated by the questions surrounding repatriation, by the prospect of repatriation and by the outcomes of repatriation.

## Community alliances

The National Museum has, in the processes of both consultation and/or physical return of remains, developed closer relationships with the communities involved. This has informed not only the activities of the repatriation programme but also wider museum knowledge about contemporary Aboriginal and Torres Strait Islander cultures. Through such engagement we learn much about the cultures, lives and histories of contemporary indigenous Australians. The repatriation process occurs within cultural and political scenarios structured by modern circumstances, often far different to the so-called 'traditional' cultures so beloved of conservative museums. The 'new ethnographies' – stories of modern lives, experiences, cultural beliefs and social change – inform new research, exhibitions, content development and delivery as well as the philosophical and theoretical basis of modern museology. It should be remembered that among the agendas of the museums of 100 years ago was often the desire to showcase and communicate prevailing knowledge, beliefs and social theories not only through reference to the objects of the past, but also through consideration of the objects and cultural attributes of other then-contemporary cultures. For example, the spears collected by Baldwin Spencer in Central Australia in 1899 were not collected as ancient relics but as contemporary tools of a foreign culture. To satisfy the more conservative among us it may be argued that, in today's museums, through attempting to communicate contemporary indigenous lives and cultures, museums may be returning to, rather than departing from, traditional agendas (although, it must be hoped, with more realistic sets of cultural theories).

Repatriation staff have also become another informal point of contact when queries arise about museums in general. Staff assist communities with advice regarding the development of local community museums or 'keeping places', in particular ways of caring for and displaying materials. Some communities, convinced of the commitment of the Museum, are starting to ask for assistance in obtaining further research on repatriated remains.

However, it must be acknowledged that the National Museum of Australia does have the advantage of being effectively 'on the doorstep'. Communication between Aboriginal and Torres Strait Islander communities and the Museum is easy and straightforward. Some of the Museum's staff are indigenous or have spent their professional careers working with Australian indigenous communities, which facilitates the communication process. The situation is different for overseas museums, separated in space, experience and money.

Engagement is, however, still possible and beneficial. An excellent example of a repatriation exercise resulting in an international alliance developing between an institution and indigenous communities is the return of remains from Sweden to groups in North Western Australia in 2004. In this case the Swedish Government and the Swedish Museum of Ethnography wished to return remains collected in 1909. The National Museum of Australia provided advice to the Swedish Embassy in Australia and to the Australian Government on appropriate communities, organisations and professional expertise that could assist in facilitating the return. An embassy representative visited the community. Later, a contingent of indigenous representatives travelled to Sweden to receive the remains and to escort them home. The National Museum provided a reception venue on their return and assisted with final return of remains. Following on from this event, however, several researchers have continued to investigate the original collecting expedition. Published and unpublished documents in the Swedish language are being located and translated into English for the first time in 100 years, providing a valuable resource to both non-Swedish speaking scholars and the indigenous community. The biographies of the expedition's members are being investigated, often with surprising outcomes. The descendants of the original expedition also participated willingly in the repatriation. In 2005 the King and Queen of Sweden visited Australia, a visit in part influenced by the success of this return. When they visited Western Australia they were presented with artworks by representatives of the Aboriginal groups involved in the repatriation (Western Australian Government 2005). The overall outcome is that everyone involved, the Swedish and Australian Governments, museums, researchers, individuals and the indigenous communities entered into, and are maintaining, a cooperative relationship with benefits and contributions that continue long after the physical return of the remains. In short, over nearly 100 years, more goodwill, more information and more knowledge has been generated through the repatriation of the remains than was ever achieved through the life of the museum collection (Hallgren 2005; Australian Government 2004).

### Internal development

The National Museum's experiences are also having an internal expression, influencing generic in-house, opinion, process and policy. Repatriation within the National Museum is guided by institutional policies and protocols specific to Aboriginal and Torres Strait Islander human remains (National Museum of Australia 2005). These policies reflect wider Australian museum industry philosophy and practices (Museums Australia 2005). While relatively minor in the grand scheme of the National Museum's activities, these policies, informed by experience, have also influenced the characteristics of other Museum policies related to the management of non-indigenous materials, including the 'Deaccessioning Policy' (National Museum of Australia 2006a) and the 'Return of Cultural Objects Policy' (National Museum of Australia 2006b). The principle and practice of consultation with indigenous interests has also influenced protocols for consultation with non-indigenous interests in other exhibition and content areas. The National Museum thus engages closely with *all* community groups and interests, not just indigenous, represented through its exhibition and content delivery agendas.

Other Museum staff have embraced repatriation activities with a commitment beyond that required of their normal duties. For example, the hand-over of remains often involves a small ceremony that can include smoking the remains and the storage site in a traditional ritual cleansing. This requires special security arrangements, in particular the temporary isolation of smoke detectors. The process for this is well established with security and facilities staff providing much appreciated assistance. Similarly, where indigenous custodians authorise a more public event, the Museum's visitor services staff provide valuable assistance to both indigenous community members and invited guests.

Repatriation activities also require development of financial management processes that reconcile the often highly informal administrative structures and processes of many indigenous communities with the rigorous demands of Government institutional accountability. The Museum's processes have become tolerant of the concept of 'sole-supplier', where the suitable service provider for the receipt of remains is clearly the community from where the remains derived – this can be at odds with conventional government procurement protocols process. It also allows for the often-slow progress of any repatriation project – something at odds with the concept of 'financial year'. The members of the National Museum's repatriation unit and finance sections have, through appreciating the formal demands of each other's duties, learned how to cooperate to streamline and facilitate the repatriation process.

In summary, repatriation exercises at the National Museum have regularly involved staff from all areas of the institution. Their engagement not only informs them about repatriation but also reminds them that they are an integral part of the activity. Repatriation has thus become an institutional activity, not just the preserve of a small team.

## Media

Now, to turn to that objective and impartial arbiter of success, the media. Due to the domestic cultural and political sensitivities of repatriation, the National Museum has not *actively* sought to promote its activities in this area through the media. The offer is routinely made to communities that if they desire some media exposure the museum is happy to assist with contacts or arranging a media reception, but it is only with the approval of the community that the media are invited into the process. The Museum also responds to media enquiries where a request is received in relation to generic repatriation issues or museum process and does not compromise a community's privacy or rights. Often, media engagement is instigated by the community itself, or by the facilitating organisation, and the National Museum is invited to comment on specific events.

So, despite this relatively passive approach to media engagement where repatriation is concerned, the National Museum of Australia has had a considerable media profile. By way of experiment, the Museum has, at times, engaged an independent media-monitoring agency to assess the commercial value of the Museum's media exposure across all museum activities (the process assesses column space and what the Museum would have paid for that space if advertising). In 2002–3 repatriation was valued at $270,000 (of $6,700,000), in 2003–4 at $617,819 (of $10,376,000) and in 2004–5 at $86,708 (of $6,700,000), a total of nearly $980,000 dollars (AUD) in what has been consistently favourable coverage. These figures compare well with the annual budget allocation to repatriation. Indeed, in total, the figure exceeds the actual budget allocation over the same period. In short, repatriation paid for itself in positive media coverage. In addition, through this coverage it is reaching audiences not usually exposed to the concept and issues of repatriation. Not bad, when it is remembered that repatriation is a relatively minor function of the National Museum.

## Museums have rights too

Advocates of repatriation often argue that museums have a responsibility to return human remains, particularly where those remains have been acquired inappropriately, such as without free and informed consent, in violation of tradition or in breach of the law, among other reasons. I personally support all of these reasons.

However, it must be recognised that museums also have responsibilities to other charters, protocols and groups – not least to their present and future audiences. Indeed, an institution would be failing in its duty if it neglected to consider the impact of its repatriation actions in the context of how the activity might serve the best interests of its wider client base. It is all too easy for advocates – of any issue – to see the immediate exercise, their discrete passion, as the 'centre of the universe' and to read institutional caution or delays to respond to requests as deliberate conspiracy. Advocates must recognise, however, the obligation on the museum to behave ethically in all of its activities. Indeed, the responsibility of an institution to considerations of long-term, institutional and audience impacts, among other issues, makes any museum's decision to engage in a discussion about repatriation, let alone proceed to the return of remains, all the more significant. A museum has a responsibility to its clients. Its audience is the primary client and includes the public, other institutions, amateur and professional scholars, future users of the facilities and knowledge, sponsors, funding agencies, governments and interest groups (communities). Applicants for repatriation are also clients, whether local or international, when they seek the advice and assistance of an institution. Because of these responsibilities, the museum has a right to a degree of 'self-interest' to ensure that its capacity for delivery of all things to all clients is facilitated and continued. Museums therefore have a right to expect some return through their financial, moral, logistic, intellectual and philosophical investments in the repatriation process. An institution has a responsibility to make wise investments on behalf of its clients. The generic return on this investment is knowledge.

A museum is therefore justified in considering its repatriation activities in the light of what tangible and intangible benefits the activity brings; not only to the group receiving the remains but also to other groups affected by the return. It is not selfish, it is not unethical, for a museum to ask 'What's in it for us?', when the 'us' embraces not only the museum, but its local, national and international audiences, its clients, its contributors, the ethics of the industry and associated professions, the obligation to contribute to knowledge and to the advancement of society. I restate my belief that museums should return remains, and that returns should be timely and unconditional. However, it is in everyone's interests that the museums, and their clients, should be allowed to benefit from the activity.

## Conclusion

The National Museum experience suggests that museums have not only much to contribute, but also much to learn and much to gain through active engagement with the repatriation debate and process. Experience has also shown that, no matter what part of a museum a person works in, be it curatorial, conservation, finance, visitor services, security, marketing, administration, and so on, it is important that staff be aware of and informed by the debates, the issues and considerations that they address, and how they might implicitly or explicitly affect their work and their professional development.

It is to be hoped that institutions will eventually recognise that repatriation of indigenous remains is appropriate. At the same time it will not be unreasonable for museums to ask that there be some return, either implicit or explicit, that helps the museum fulfil its philosophical and intellectual obligations to its audiences. This return will ideally be realised through new knowledge and new relationships. To engage openly and willingly in the repatriation debates and process is not to surrender; rather it should be recognised as an opportunity. It is, however, correspondingly important for advocates of repatriation to recognise that museums have rights too.

## Acknowledgements

The contents of this chapter have been tested on, and benefited from comments by, staff of the National Museum of Australia including, Freda Hanley, David Kaus, Leanda Kitchen, Lynne McCarthy, Craddock Morton, Kipley Nink, Sarah Robertson, George Taylor and Peter Thorley.

# Bibliography

Australian Government (2004) *Closing the Circle: The Return of Indigenous Australian Ancestral Remains from Sweden*, DVD, Canberra: Department of Immigration and Multicultural and Indigenous Affairs, Office of Indigenous Policy Coordination.

—— (2006a) *Return of Indigenous Cultural Property Program*, Department of Communication Information Technology and the Arts. Online. Available at: www.dcita.gov.au/arts/councils/return_of_indigenous_cultural_property_(ricp)_program (accessed 9 June 2006).

—— (2006b) *Repatriation Program*, Office of Indigenous Policy Coordination. Online. Available at: www.oipc.gov.au/programs/Repatriation.asp (accessed 9 June 2006).

Centre for Cross-Cultural Research, Australian National University (2005) *The Meaning and Values of Repatriation*. Online. Available at: www.anu.edu.au/culture/repatriation/index.php (accessed 13 June 2006).

Department of Culture, Media and Sport (2003) *Report of the Working Group on Human Remains*. Online. Available at: www.culture.gov.uk/NR/rdonlyres/D3CBB6E0–255D-42F8-A728–067CE53062EA/0/Humanremainsreportsmall.pdf (accessed 9 June 2006).

Fforde, C. (2002) 'Collection, repatriation and identity', in C. Fforde, J. Hubert and P. Turnbull (eds) *The Dead and Their Possessions: Repatriation in Principle, Policy and Practice*, London: Routledge, 25–46.

—— (2004) *Collecting the Dead: Archaeology and the Reburial Issue*, London: Gerald Duckworth & Co.

Fforde, C., Hubert, J. and Turnbull, P. (eds) (2002) *The Dead and Their Possessions: Repatriation in Principle, Policy and Practice*, London: Routledge.

Hallgren, C. (2005) 'Eric Mjoberg and the Rhetorics of Human Remains'. Online. Available at: www.anu.edu.au/culture/repatriation/index.php (accessed 13 June 2006).

Kipling, R. (n.d.) *A Smuggler's Song*. University of Newcastle. Online. Available at: http://whitewolf.newcastle.edu.au/words/authors/K/KiplingRudyard/verse/p3/smuggler.html (accessed 9 June 2006).

Museums Australia (1993) *Previous Possessions, New Obligations: A Plain English Summary of Policies for Museums in Australia and Aboriginal and Torres Strait Islander People*, Canberra: Museums Australia Inc.

—— (2005) *Continuous Cultures, Ongoing Responsibilities. Principles and Guidelines for Australian Museums working with Aboriginal and Torres Strait Islander Cultural Heritage*, Canberra: Museums Australia Inc. Online. Available at: www.museumsaustralia.org.au/dbdoc/ccor_final_feb_05.pdf (accessed 9 June 2006).

National Museum of Australia (2005) *Policy on Aboriginal and Torres Strait Islander Human Remains*. Online. Available at: www.nma.gov.au/shared/libraries/attachments/corporate_documents/policies/atsi_human_remains_policy/files/9463/POL-C-011%20Aboriginal%20&%20Torres%20Strait%20Islander%20human%20remains-2.0%20(public).pdf (accessed 13 June 2006).

—— (2006a) *Collections – Deaccessioning and Disposal Policy*. Online. Available at: www.nma.gov.au/shared/libraries/attachments/corporate_documents/policies/collections_deaccessioning_and_disposal_policy/files/14195/POL-C-035%20Collections%20-%20Deaccessioning%20and%20disposal-4.0%20(public).pdf (accessed 14 June 2006).

—— (2006b) *Return of Cultural Objects Policy*. Online. Available at: www.nma.gov.au/shared/libraries/attachments/corporate_documents/policies/return_of_cultural_objects_policy/files/14172/POL-C-037Returnofculturalobjects-2.0(public).pdf (accessed 14 June 2006).

Pickering, M. (2002) 'Repatriation, rhetoric, and reality: The repatriation of Australian Indigenous Human remains and sacred objects', *Journal of the Australian Registrars Committee*, June: 15–19, 40–1. Online. Available at: http://amol.org.au/arc/papers/S&LMichael_Pickering.pdf (accessed 9 June 2006).

—— (in press) 'Policy and research issues affecting human remains in Australian Museum collections', in Museum of London, *The Politics of Human Remains and Museum Practice: Ethics, Research, Policy and Display*, London: Museum of London.

Prime Minister of Australia, John Howard (2000) *Press release Joint Statement with Tony Blair on Aboriginal remains*. Online. Available at: www.pm.gov.au/news/media_releases/2000/Aboriginal_4–7.htm (accessed 9 June 2006).

Robertson, S. (2004) *A Critical Evaluation of the Application of Cribra Orbitalia in Australian Archaeology as a Correlate of Sedentism*, unpublished BA Hons. thesis, Australian National University.

Turnbull, P. (1991a) 'Science, national identity and Aboriginal body snatching in nineteenth century Australia', *Working Papers in Australian Studies*, Working Paper no. 65, Sir Robert Menzies Centre for Australian Studies, Institute of Commonwealth Studies, University of London.

—— (1991b) 'Ramsay's regime: The Australian Museum and the procurement of Aboriginal bodies, c.1874–1900', *Aboriginal History*, 15(2): 108–21.

—— (1994) '"To What Strange Uses" The procurement and use of Aboriginal Peoples bodies in early Colonial Australia', *VOICES*, 4(3): 5–20.

—— (1997) 'Ancestors, not specimens: reflections on the controversy over the remains of Aboriginal people in European scientific collections', *Electronic Journal of Australian and New Zealand History*. Online. Available at: www.jcu.edu.au/aff/history/articles/turnbull.htm (accessed 9 June 2006).

—— (1998) '"Outlawed subjects": The procurement and scientific uses of Australian Aboriginal heads, ca.1803–35', *Studies in the Eighteenth Century*, 22(1): 156–71.

—— (1999) 'Enlightenment, anthropology and the ancestral remains of Australian Aboriginal people', in A. Calder, J. Lamb and B. Orr (eds) *Voyages and Beaches: Pacific Encounters 1769–1840*, Honolulu, HI: University of Hawaii Press, 202–25.

—— (2001) '"Rare Work for the Professors": The entanglement of Aboriginal remains in phrenological knowledge in early colonial Australia', in J. Hoorn and B. Creed (eds) *Captivity*, Melbourne: Pluto Press, 3–23.

—— (2002) 'Indigenous Australian people, their defence of the dead and native title', in C. Fforde, J. Hubert and P. Turnbull (eds) *The Dead and Their Possessions: Repatriation in Principle, Policy and Practice*, London: Routledge, 63–86.

United Nations (1994) *Draft declaration on the Rights of Indigenous peoples*. Online. Available at: www.unhchr.ch/huridocda/huridoca.nsf/(Symbol)/E.CN.4.SUB.2.RES.1994.45.En?OpenDocument (accessed 9 June 2006).

Western Australian Government (2005) *Speech by Hon. Dr Geoff Gallop MLA. Premier of Western Australia. State visit by the King and Queen of Sweden*. Function Centre, WA Maritime Museum. Saturday 12 November 2005, 1.10 p.m. Online. Available at: www.premier.wa.gov.au/docs/speeches/121105_Swedish%20King%20and%20Queen_WEB.pdf (accessed 14 June 2006).

# Part 3

# ARTICULATING CHANGE
## Media, message, philosophy

# 20

# BEYOND NOSTALGIA

## The role of affect in generating
## historical understanding at heritage sites

*Kate Gregory and Andrea Witcomb*

Affect is increasingly recognised as an important means to achieve audience participation in the process of making meaning. As Dipesh Chakrabarty (2002) argues, in a world which is increasingly defined by experiential and immersive technologies, traditional ways of producing and disseminating knowledge are no longer sufficient to equip contemporary citizens. Rather than analytical didactic approaches to representation, Chakrabarty argues that it is embodied forms of knowledge apprehended by the senses rather than through analytical processes that we need to understand. This shift in knowledge production privileges performative models of democratic engagement rather than pedagogical ones. In his schema it is the body rather than the mind which is the privileged site of knowledge production. For Chakrabarty, it is the subjective, felt response that is the most relevant for contemporary forms of political engagement.

This chapter aims to understand how embodied forms of knowledge production, such as affect, can be mobilised to produce new forms of historical understanding in contemporary audiences. It explores how emotional responses open up possibilities for interpretation that engage with the politics of representation and identity formation. In doing so, this chapter engages with recent work on affect which attempts to connect it to the cultural and political sphere. Chakrabarty's own work is part of this attempt. While at first glance Chakrabarty's arguments would appear to reinforce a Cartesian split between the mind and the body, he does suggest that embodied forms of knowledge, while working through the senses, also draw upon memory. He thus opens the door to developing an understanding of how affective forms of knowledge might connect with social and individual identity and therefore with the political. This approach relates to a number of writers who are exploring the importance of affect for the maintenance and production of memory as well as social and cultural understanding.

In the context of museological forms of display, for example, Marius Kwint (1999) has explored the importance of objects for their capacity to invoke memory and sensory engagement. In his analysis, objects are productive forces. They both trigger memory and carry meaning. They therefore open a space of evocation which, as he argues, implies an open dialogue between the object, the maker and the consumer in constructing meaning.

Likewise, Susan Stewart (1999) has long argued that objects have the power to touch, to move and summon something else. Brian Massumi (2002) similarly understands affect as being about potentialities and a productive force. Concerned to understand how and why we are being shaped by media and architectural environments in contemporary society, he posits 'a physiology of perception' in which he analyses sensory forms of knowledge as being driven by affect. Massumi understands affect as a moment of confrontation in which there are many possibilities, a moment embedded with potential responses, reactions and directions which is characterised by a sense of openness.

Massumi's understanding of affect might be seen to be similar to Walter Benjamin's notion of the dialectical image. For Benjamin (1999: ref. N10a, 3 475; 1970), the dialectical image was the product of a confrontation between the past, present and future, in which linear understandings of time, such as chronology, disappeared and were replaced with insights produced out of a sense of historical difference. A sense of shock or surprise was essential to the production of such insights. Benjamin was thus highlighting the affective and experiential aspect of historical understanding, an insight which is useful for exploring the use of affective modes of interpretation in both museums and heritage sites.

## What is an affective experience?

There have been various attempts to describe affect in operation, usually by art historians in their analysis of art, but also by architectural writers and cognitive theorists. An early attempt to theorise affect was that of Silvan S. Tomkins and Carroll E. Izard (1964). Psychologists, Tomkins and Izard argued that there were nine innate affective states, most of which operate along a continuum: interest-excitement; enjoyment-joy; surprise-startle; distress-anguish; shame-humiliation; disgust (dis-taste); dissmell (dis-smell, or bad smell); anger-rage; fear-anxiety. What is clear from this classification is that affective states document emotional responses to experiences, which can range from the pleasurable to the abject.

Art and architectural critics have provided another perspective on affect, by showing how affective experience registers on the body. They have done this by addressing the affective dimensions of spatial interaction between art object, installation or space and the viewer. Such critics have recognised how viewers' bodies register this interaction through their sensory and physical responses – such as crouching, touching, listening, recoiling or the feeling of being enveloped by a space (Best 2001–2). They have pointed to the affective power of the art object by exploring how art induces interest and sensory engagement leading to a range of affective responses (Bennett 2001; Ednie-Brown 1999; Prown 1980).

Cognitive theorists working on fiction have theorised affect in relation to narrative. Some types of fiction, they argue, work through simulation which enables the reader to respond empathetically with characters and their situations. Other cognitive theorists have argued for a wider understanding of our affective engagement with fiction by suggesting that fiction works through the creation of possible worlds rather than exclusively through character-based simulations (Meskin and Weinberg 2003). This understanding prioritises the notion of space as a productive entity full of new possibilities for affect which are not simply narrative driven.

The emphasis on the productive possibilities of space in the creation of meaning is relevant to exhibition contexts. As Suzanne MacLeod (2005) argues in the introduction to her edited collection *Reshaping Museum Space*, exhibition narratives are the product of both spatial and content-driven considerations. Museum spaces are 'active in the making of meaning' offering transformative possibilities (MacLeod 2005: 1). Importantly, she argues that there is a history to the spatial characteristics of museums and therefore that these characteristics are open to change. Her recognition of the role of space in creating meaning is one that we wish to explore by linking it to the notion that narratives both create and are the result of 'possible worlds'. It may be possible to take this further by arguing that exhibitions are potential gateways to other possible worlds, that is, they offer moments of dialectical possibility in the way that Benjamin argued the photographic image did. This is because the narratives produced through affect are the result of the tensions and interplays between form and content or space and objects and the viewer.

Heritage sites also offer this potential because of the way they mediate between past and present, space and objects, absence and presence. The idea of the past as another world is evident in historical re-enactments and reconstructions, and in the ubiquitous idea of time-travel. This chapter explores how heritage sites might be thought of as possible worlds which work through affective corporeal and imaginative engagement to develop historical understanding. It does this by analysing the production of affect in two different types of heritage sites in Western Australia belonging to the National Trust of Australia (W.A.). The first are the historic house museums interpreted during the 1970s. The second are early twenty-first century interpretations of a remote historical settlement. The chapter traces how differences in these exhibition sites produce different modes of historical understanding. The Trust's interpretation of historic house museums during the 1970s facilitated the affective responses of pleasure and empathy producing nostalgia that was not based on historical veracity. In one of the twenty-first century interpretations, pleasure and nostalgia have been replaced by an altogether different manifestation of affect which is based in corporeal sensation, intellectual shock and disorientation which ultimately opens up a critical awareness of the past. In another recent interpretation which uses pleasure and nostalgia, these are supplemented with archival evidence generating a more balanced celebration of past community life. In the 1970s nostalgia worked through simulation or reconstruction; in the later interpretation, nostalgia works through evocation or suggestion. All these interpretations use different forms of affect to produce historical understanding that speaks to different audiences.

## Nostalgia one: the still life

Historic house museums potentially enable an affective engagement with the past. The perception of intangible traces of past life incites a range of emotional and cognitive experiences from interest or curiosity to pleasure, delight and wonder. When we perceive the imprints of past lives that are somehow embodied within the house, despite their actual presence being long gone, we experience a collapse of the present with the past, and momentarily enter another world. Such an affected response is heightened by the silence of the house, the absence of real life living within it. For in silence, in gaps, there is presence. Just as a sculpture gives shape to emptiness, to space, as much as to material form, the historic house plays with a delicate balance between presence and absence. As Monica Risnicoff de Gorgas (2001: 10) has observed, historic houses invoke 'a particular type of mental and emotional reaction' which is 'produced by the presence and absence of the people who once lived in the house'. Absence is in fact integral to its ability to invoke the presence of the past. Potentially, historic houses open up a space in which the intangible past can be *sensed*. This might commonly be described as a house having 'atmosphere'. However, this delicate balance can frequently collapse into mute, static pictures of the past, which do not affectively speak in the present.

In the 1970s, the Trust aimed to use its historic house museums to represent 'living homes', wanting to avoid 'museum-like' display methodologies. They were furnished to denote the lives of past inhabitants. Because the original furnishings were rarely intact in the Trust's historic houses, furnishings were used which were not provenanced to the house but lent an authentic air and gave the impression of the house being lived-in. The houses illustrate what Barbara Kirshenblatt-Gimblett (1998) has termed 'in-situ' displays that recreate settings and present them as a pre-existing and authentic 'slice of life'. The Trust ideally wanted visitors to feel as though they were stepping into the past, or as if the owners 'had just stepped out for a moment'. As Mrs Viva Johnstone commented in a letter to Mr Dunnett, 'In furnishing the cottage we aim to avoid a museum look, but to make it as true to history as possible but also as though the occupants had just stepped out into the garden for a moment'.[1] This was important if the Trust was to 'touch' the public, engage visitors emotionally and mnemonically, and enable an affective experience of the past which would in turn both educate and inspire the public to participate in heritage preservation. The Trust's policy of representing 'living' history thus aimed to facilitate an 'embodied knowledge' of the past. It had an implicitly pedagogical objective.

A visitor to the house museum Woodbridge was so affected by the site that she was inspired to put pen to paper (Figure 20.1). She submitted her poem for publication in the Trust's newsletter.

*Woodbridge* by Betty Lloyd-Mostyn (1978)

The house is full of ghosts today!
Do you see, on the lacy verandahs,
Puff-sleeved ladies taking the air
Flower-scented, whisping from the garden?

There is a child – one in the nursery
Rocking a surprise-eyed doll
In a miniature chair.
And look there, the parasol waits
To shade her walk across
The lush green curving to dim
Water's rim.

Downstairs the table gleams,
Immaculate with linen, starch-stiff,
Appliqued intricately;
Polished crystal rainbow-shafted,
Silver, sheened, unmarked by finger-prints –
'They' leave none, you see.

A posy and a fan lay here,
A fur wrap casually draped around a chair
By one lately returned
From some elegant festivity.

The geranium hedges hide the lives
Of flesh and blood inhabitants
While we, intruders too,

Walk whispering through the corridors
Of this still world.

Time
Holds its breath.

For audiences of the 1970s, the Trust's historic houses operated as a type of theatre set filled with furnishings which acted as props designed to trigger individual and cultural memory. Objects, as Marius Kwint, has observed, 'stimulate remembering' and arouse dormant memories. Furthermore, Kwint argues, objects are record-like in their capacity to hold cultural memory that speaks beyond individual experience. This collective memory is transmitted to us through the senses (Kwint 1999). Thus, filling the houses with historical objects was vital for the audience's mnemonic engagement. Ironically, however, as the Trust's collection grew through the 1970s and 1980s, many houses were filled with far too many objects, which actually prevented an affective response because there was no room for the important ingredient of absence. Unlike Sir John Soane's Museum in London where the density of objects operates to reveal the interior space and its meanings, the density of objects in the reconstructed historic houses owned by the Trust in Western Australia resulted in closed meaning and flatness – in a picture rather than a space unfolded and expanded into carefully contrived possibilities for viewing.

The objects furnishing Trust houses, and their arrangement, denoted nineteenth-century middle-class gentility. The house interiors were largely created by troops of volunteer

*Figure 20.1* Woodbridge dining room, property of the National Trust of Australia (W.A.), 2005.
Photo: Kate Gregory.

women in the Furniture and Furnishings Committee and in Property Management Committees and there is evidence to suggest that many of these women were 'playing house'; enacting their own style and taste, as informed by their own memories and experiences of middle-class gentility, through the furnishing. As Linda Young (2003) has found, middle-class gentility was an extremely broad category of experience, one which would have resonated with the vast majority of historic house visitors. Many visitors immediately empathised with the houses because they recognised objects and arrangements which were akin to their own middle-class family histories or, if not, the picture of gentility was one that they aspired to. Visitors' books of the 1970s provide evidence for this. Visitors were charmed by what they saw; noting that they'd 'like a house like it' and that they'd had a 'very pleasant experience' or a 'good excursion to nostalgia' which prompted their remembrance of 'the golden days'. Other visitors were flooded with specific memories of their own 'mothers and grandmothers'. Many visitors commented on the 'lovely old furnishings' which reminded them of 'days gone by'. The houses therefore 'spoke' to an audience who shared a cultural memory and recognised a rosy version of their own heritage. A consequence of this is that historic houses today have much less relevance because younger audiences do not share the same cultural memories nor the value of gentility. The houses therefore do not speak affectively to today's audience who are not subject to the same sense of pleasure or nostalgia and do not have memories of the objects held within the house.

Although each house was a picture of middle-upper class gentility, the lives of some of the original pioneering inhabitants were far from genteel. Hardship was glossed over, evidence of the role of servants or Aboriginal labour was wiped away, even bathrooms as sites of bodily ablution and therefore distasteful, were largely absent from the Trust historic houses. Indeed, in one house, a bathroom dating from the 1940s was transformed into a sewing room because this was thought to be more palatable and pleasure-inducing.[2] Affect therefore worked to erase history but promoted social cohesion among a particular audience which saw its own values and aspirations reflected in the house.

The houses enabled pleasure and nostalgia because they represented the past in romantic terms. The knowledge which each house reinforced and created was mythical, generalised and essentialist. It was story-like rather than being based in historical accuracy. The aim was to enter the house and step into another realm which unfolded like a story book beginning with 'Once upon a time'. The visitor moves past the entrance hall and proceeds to marvel at the lovingly kept objects, the strange contraption in the kitchen, the gleaming silver, the perfect arrangements and the permanently set dining table. But frustratingly, we are kept at bay; prevented from fully inhabiting the rooms, running our fingers over the velvet-covered chairs, holding that delicate teacup or admiring the view from the window. Red rope barricades at the entrance of each room keep us in a state of longing and curiosity. Our imagination is pricked, but not fully permitted to wander. Corporeal engagement is kept to a minimum. Instead of being inhabited, each room is viewed from a designated vantage point and becomes a 'picture' (*Trust News* 1978: 8). The red rope barricade transforms the fiction of a living house into a static picture. The house becomes a still-life and its capacity for affect is reduced.

## Disrupting the past

If the limitations of the historic house trope are the inability to actually inhabit the space, touch the objects and the simplicity of the historical information being conveyed, these limitations are explicitly addressed in more recent interpretations of historic sites. This is because, rather than inviting the visitor to inhabit a ready-made narrative and to make it their own through the trope of nostalgia, these sites are invitations to inhabit a space, not a picture. And one of the markers of this difference is the emptiness of the sites. While the initial affective responses are a sense of alienation and disorientation, the result is to demand a more inquisitive approach from the visitor, requiring them to produce their own interpretative narratives as a means to breach the gaps left open. In contrast to the 1970s historic house, which achieves affective responses through its saturation of the site with objects in the effort to reconstruct the past, more recent interpretations of a different kind of historical site are marked by their emptiness. The consequences of this emptiness are an initial sense of alienation and disorientation which is then transformed in the act of interpretation by the visitor into an active critical reading of the past. The particular range of affective responses produced by this style of interpretation is also different, working particularly through the production of shock and surprise, enabling what Walter Benjamin called the production of a dialectical image in which a new awareness of the past is produced in the clash between received ideas about the past and the sense of radical difference from the present moment. For Benjamin this moment of recognition of difference was the moment in which critique was enabled. This chapter suggests that new forms of site interpretation also work in much the same way.

By way of example, we want to discuss the interpretation of Greenough by the National Trust of Australia (W.A.) which was done by Mulloway studio architects in consultation with Paul Kloeden from Exhibition Services, both of which are based in Adelaide, South Australia. Central Greenough is a historical site, abandoned after a flood in the 1950s. It lies just outside Geraldton, a regional centre and major port 420 kilometres north of Perth, capital of Western Australia (Figure 20.2).

The site's emptiness and relative isolation are part of its emotional attraction. It speaks of the past, it appears to be redolent with meaning, and yet that meaning is not nostalgic – if anything there is a sense of desolation and foreboding in walking and exploring what is left – an experience which is physically, visually and emotionally heightened by the effect of the wind – seen not only in the bent trees but viscerally felt on your face as you walk around. That sense of emptiness is reflected in the style of interpretation chosen for the entry to the site itself via the original settlement store. There is no attempt to recreate the store. Nor is there any attempt to flood you with contextual information through a more traditional social history type of display. Rather, there is a sense of emptiness with a few clues here and there. To get anything out of it you have to take your time and explore the space. In the process you begin to immerse yourself in the space itself as part of the effort to generate a narrative about this particular building and more generally about the site as a whole.

Entering the settlement through the shop door is most definitely not an invitation to enter a recreation of the past – unlike the remaining gate to the main street of the settlement, a leftover from a 1970s interpretation scheme. To begin with the door is made of heavy glass, is hard to push open and very clearly announces itself as a new element in the fabric of the building. On entering, you are faced not only with a sense of emptiness but also of whiteness (Figure 20.3). The building clearly announces that it has been cleaned up, renovated. The act of reconstruction can only be done by the visitor using the bare clues provided by the interpretation on offer – a kind of minimalist 'graffiti' on the walls with dates of major events in the life of the building, a few paint scrapes left bare to expose traces of the building's previous lives. The dominant aesthetic is clearly a modernist one – clean

*Figure 20.2* Greenough settlement, property of the National Trust of Australia (W.A.), 2005.
Photo: Kate Gregory.

*Figure 20.3* Greenough general store, property of the National Trust of Australia (W.A.), 2005.
Photo: Kate Gregory.

lines, no fussiness. The emptiness produced by this aesthetic treatment leaves open the necessary space to then react to the small amounts of introduced interpretative material which are provided. All of it clearly announces itself as introduced fabric – the map on the wall, the text on the wall, reproductions of historical photographs in light boxes and a few replica objects displayed as if they were art objects. The interesting thing is that almost all of these introduced fragments deal with a dark past – the moment of colonisation and what it meant. The imaginary landscape that is produced through these fragments of interpretation could not be a stronger contrast to the whiteness of the building the visitors are in.

The first clue that we are being asked to use our imaginations, comes with the large map that connects the store to the landscape it sits in, and beyond that to the history of settlement/invasion (Figure 20.4). For the map is an orientation both to geography and to the

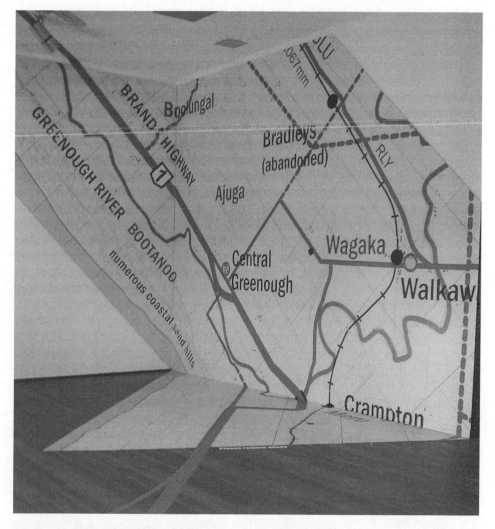

*Figure 20.4* View of map in Greenough general store, property of the National Trust of Australia (W.A.), 2005.

Photo: Kate Gregory.

presence of two cultures – coloniser and colonised. As the label for the map printed directly onto the wall proclaims:

> A map is nothing more than a series of clues, clues as to where we are, where we have come from, and where we are going. Contour lines provide clues as to the natural landscape. Yamagi words provide clues as to the natural landscape. Yamagi words provide clues to the indigenous occupation of the land, their meeting places and yam grounds. Survey lines, roads, fences and building markings provide clues as to how it was settled by Europeans. But these are only clues. The reality lies beyond the map, all around us.

In approaching the map to read it more carefully, the viewer inevitably stands on it, replicating the position of the mapper/explorer. Unlike the earlier explorers, however, we cannot hide under the pretext of Terra Nullius for the map signals the presence of the indigenous people loud and clear. The viewer is thus implicated within this history.

The theme is continued in a simple but disturbing display consisting of four plinths supporting four props which are treated as if they were art objects and lit individually from above. The first one of these appears to be a dress pattern for an old-style dress but on closer inspection the pattern turns out to be by 'Buckaroo Bobbins' © 2003 with a 'Bonus Pattern for making your own sandbags ideal for protecting your home against rising floodwaters' with a little diagram of water lapping against sandbags. A sense of humour is clearly at play with a reference to the flood that led to the settlement's abandonment. The second prop offers a joke at the expense of the Trust itself and its past approaches to the interpretation of heritage. The prop consists of two bars of soap (Figure 20.5). Their labels, which form their wrapping, read: 'This soap is Sarah's Conservation Soap' with the words 'Sanitises before public display', 'Try it on your site', 'Extraordinary Cleansing Powers', 'Removes All Unsightly Buildings and Stories', 'Produces Absolute Cleanliness on Heritage Sites'. Two Union Jack flags make up the brand emblem. This clearly alerts the visitor to the constructed nature of all heritage sites. It warns the visitor not to take everything at face value, to read beyond the immediately obvious.

Almost as if by way of example, we are immediately presented with the value of reading beyond the obvious. For the next prop is some coiled barbed wire fencing, appearing to all intents as if still wrapped up in its original wrapper. Closer inspection, however, reveals its dark side for the wrapper reads: 'Settler's Own ideal for disrupting nomadic lifestyles and keeping people out'. In a Benjaminian moment, we recoil, almost in horror at the matter-of-fact way in which this simple object is made to stand for the process of colonisation. The shock is really to realise how simple it was to prevent people from entering their traditional lands. Given that many of the pioneering families still live in the district and indeed facilitated the Trust's acquisition of this landscape, the comment could be considered brave or, alternatively, as alienating to the local community. The last prop, a tin with a wrapper around it reads: 'Extract of Rust – For debility and impoverishment. Free for all wheat farmers after 1865'. Despite being 'the granary of the colony' for a time, rust was a disease that affected the Greenough crops of wheat and sent many farmers into ruin.

Confronted by the messages contained in such innocuous looking objects we are now in a heightened state of shock. We are ready, however, to undertake a reading of the site which is open to its hidden messages and which refuses to understand the site through the rubric of a romanticised nostalgia for a bygone past. For the past is now full of ghosts and traces of

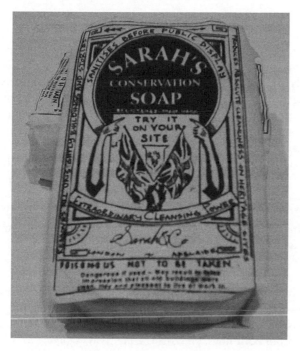

*Figure 20.5* Greenough general store prop, property of the National Trust of Australia (W.A.), 2005.

Photo: Kate Gregory.

traumatic experiences. Almost as if recognising our need to take a break and to verbalise this new information, we walk out past an inviting seat in front of an extract from a diary printed onto the wall. The extract, taken from explorer George Grey's 1839 diary, represents perhaps one of the earliest Aboriginal accounts of European exploration in Western Australia. Grey recorded Noongar man Warrup's description of the journey he took looking for the men that Grey had left behind, only to find them dead.

The words in front of our eyes crystallise our thoughts and confirm, through their documentary status that which we have always found difficult to face – that pioneering was in fact the process of invasion. Nostalgia is turned on its head. And all of this takes place before we even buy our ticket and enter the settlement itself!

## Nostalgia two: layering the past

This does not mean, however, that nostalgia is not used as a productive force in contemporary practices of interpretation. In St Catherine's Hall, which was the local church and community hall, nostalgia is used to evoke a lost community. This is done through a combination of video footage, sound installation, photographs and archival documents set up in the darkened hall as if a performance is about to begin. In contrast to the whiteness of the settlement store which engages with dark and unsettling stories of colonisation, the darkened hall gives form to the lighter side of community life. A video of interviews with former local residents who lived in Greenough up until the 1950s is projected onto a large screen positioned in the centre of the stage at the front of the hall. Empty deck chairs nearly fill the hall, invoking the absent community members and past performances while also inviting the visitor to sit and take a walk down memory lane with key protagonists. What they encounter is a layered historical account of Greenough told through a number of perspectives. A local historian provides the wider historical context of the Greenough settlement, while former residents recall family and community life. Their stories are highly subjective, enlivened by laughter, tears, song and family photographs. A complex picture is created which illustrates the hall's significance in the building and reinforcement of community identity. Its loss of function as a community hall is poignantly drawn through these layered stories, resulting in an emotional landscape tinged with nostalgia.

Another major interpretative tool in the hall – a sound installation built into an old hall piano – further mobilises the sense of nostalgia. The visitor is prompted to sit down and play the piano by two red keys standing out amongst the ivory thereby triggering the sound installation. The space echoes with the sound of old dance-hall music and the visitor is filled with a desire to dance, at once inhabiting the emotional state of community dance-goers as they laugh and dance their way around the hall with family and friends. Former community celebrations at the hall are not just invoked but for a moment felt corporeally, viscerally and emotionally. As the music plays on, however, it dawns on the visitor that this is a lost activity; the site is imbued with the loss of its former life and role as a hub of community activity. Nostalgia is used to generate historical understanding and appreciation for the social dimensions of community history. A more traditional exhibition form, a free-standing interpretative panel which is read from both sides, presents the archival evidence for what we have already felt about the history of the hall – notices for dances, performances, reports about community hall activities and photographs. The imaginary and historical are brought together, each indispensable to the other in generating historical understanding. In St Catherine's Hall nostalgia is balanced with archival evidence. The result is to layer the past with different meanings. This gives the interpretation greater potency and impact than the use of nostalgia in the 1970s interpretations of historic houses which were limited in their rosy, idealised vision of the past.

## Conclusions

While these interpretative styles produce affective forms of embodied knowledge they do so for different generations and thus have different outcomes. In the 1970s historic house, the ambition was to recreate the past so that temporal distance was minimised. However, the living windows they created, although enabling audiences to glimpse aspects of the past, did not permit the visitor to fully enter this other world. The resulting distance produced a romantic vision of the past, creating nostalgia. Nevertheless, the picture presented created recognition, working to build consensus and a sense of a shared past. In contrast, more recent forms of interpretation have sought to create a disjuncture between past and present in order to open up a space of understanding or empathy. While the former is comforting, the latter is troubling and complex, revealing traces of the past in the present. That it does this through an intervention that critiques former attempts to recreate the past by using design tools that disrupt a closed text and allow for the creation of intentional gaps, should not come as a surprise. The visual elements of this form of interpretation are familiar to younger audiences who inhabit a consumerist space in which contemporary style is both message and medium. It is the contemporary equivalent of 'living history' as the 1970s attempt to engage with popular culture. At the same time, it reflects our contemporary understanding of history as fragmentary, partial and impossible to recover. What we now need to understand is how such interpretations of historical sites are received by the audiences who visit them.

## Acknowledgements

This chapter forms part of a research project on the history of ideas about heritage in Western Australia which was funded by the Australian Research Council and the National Trust of Australia (W.A.) under the Linkage scheme.

## Notes

1   Letter from Mrs Viva Johnstone to Mr Dunnett, 25 January 1966, in Mrs Johnstone's file, Furnishing and Historic Objects Committee, Box 69, National Trust of Australia (W.A.) Archive, Woodbridge.
2   Minutes of the Furniture and Furnishing Committee, 6 February 1980 and 3 December 1980, File 1 June 1965 – October 1982, Box 67, National Trust of Australia (W.A.) Archive, Woodbridge.

## Bibliography

Benjamin, W. (1970) 'Theses on the Philosophy of History' in H. Arendt (ed.) Illuminations, trans. Harry Zohn, London: Jonathan Cape, 255–66.
—— (1999) The Arcades Project, trans. H. Eiland and K. McLaughlin, Cambridge, MA: The Belknap Press of Harvard University Press.
Bennett, J. (2001) 'Stigmata and sense memory: St Francis and the affective image', Art History, 24(1): 1–16.
Best, S. (2001–2) 'What is affect? Considering the affective dimension of contemporary installation Art', Australian and New Zealand Journal of Art, 2–3(2–1): 207–25.
Chakrabarty, D. (2002) 'Museums in late democracies', Humanities Research, IX(1): 5–12.
Ednie-Brown, P. (1999) 'Falling into the surface: Towards a materiality of affect', Architectural Design, 69(9/10): 8–11.
Kirshenblatt-Gimblett, B. (1998) Destination Culture: Tourism, Museums and Heritage, Berkeley, CA: University of California Press.
Kwint, M. (1999) 'Introduction: The physical past' in M. Kwint, C. Breward and J. Aynsley (eds) Material Memories, Oxford: Berg, 1–16.
Lloyd-Mostyn, B. (1978) 'Woodbridge: a poem', Trust News, December, 8.
MacLeod, S. (2005) 'Introduction', in S. MacLeod (ed.) Reshaping Museum Space: Architecture, Design, Exhibitions, London: Routledge, 1–5.
Massumi, B. (2002) Parables for the Virtual: Movement, Affect, Sensation, London: Duke University Press.
Meskin, A. and Weinberg, J. M. (2003) 'Emotions, fiction and cognitive architecture', British Journal of Aesthetics, 43(1): 18–34.
Prown, J. (1980) 'Style as evidence', Winterthur Portfolio, 15(3): 197–210.
Risnicoff de Gorgas, M. (2001) 'Reality as illusion, the historic houses that become museums', Museum International, no. 210, 53(2): 10–15.
Stewart, S. (1999) 'Prologue: From the museum of touch', in M. Kwint, C. Breward and J. Aynsley (eds) Material Memories, Oxford: Berg, 17–36.
Tomkins, S. S. and Izard, C. E. (1964) Affect, Cognition and Personality: Empirical Studies, New York: Springer Publishing Co.
Trust News (1978) no. 93, 19 April: 8.
Young, L. (2003) Middle Class Culture in the Nineteenth Century: America, Australia and Britain, New York: Palgrave Macmillan.

# 21

# VISITORS AND LEARNING

Adult museum visitors'
learning identities

*Lynda Kelly*

Current theories of learning focus on the meanings an individual makes based on their experience – alone, within a social context and as part of a community (Matusov and Rogoff 1995; Hein 1998; Woolfolk 1998; Malone 1990; Falk and Dierking 2000; Falk and Dierking 1992). One way to better understand the process of learning for an individual is to find out how people view themselves as learners across the rich array of both formal and informal learning experiences available to them. As informal learning environments, museums are increasingly positioning themselves in the market as places for rich learning experiences. Research has shown that when asked why they visit museums people often say to learn (Falk 1998; Falk *et al.*; 1998 Prentice 1998; Jansen-Verbeke and van Rekom 1996; Combs 1999; Kelly 2001) but there has been little exploration into what learning means for visitors. What do museum visitors think learning is, what is their *learning image*? Recent museum literature has focused on identity and the role it plays in the visitor experience (Rounds 2006; Falk 2006; Spock 2006; Leinhardt *et al.* 2002a; Leinhardt and Knutson 2004). However, little evidence has been gathered to date about the influence of museums on a person's identity and how visitors view themselves as learners within the context of a museum visit – their *learning identity*.

This chapter reports on recent research that explored the interrelationships between visitors' views of learning and their learning experiences at a museum, within the context of debates surrounding education and the visitor experience. Other issues examined include the relationship between learning, education and entertainment, as well as how exhibitions can influence adult museum visitors' learning identities. Implications of these findings for museological practice are outlined at the end of this chapter.

Museums have always seen themselves as having an educational role. Yet, more recently there has been a conceptual change from thinking about museums as places of education to places for learning, responding to the needs and interests of visitors (Bradburne 1998; Carr 2003; Falk and Dierking 2000; Falk and Dierking 1995; Hooper-Greenhill 2003; Falk 2004; Rennie and Johnston 2004; Weil 2002). Weil (1999) stated that museums need to transform themselves from 'being *about* something to being *for* somebody' (Weil: 229, emphasis in original). Hooper-Greenhill (2003) noted that the conceptual change from education to learning was an important development in the ways museums think about their visitors and provide services for them. She also argued that this shift required museums to concentrate on the visitor rather than on their internal systems of delivering programmes.

An emphasis on learning requires that museums focus on an individual's learning processes. It has been proposed that, if learners thought about their learning rather than merely learning how to learn, their learning outcomes would be better (Saljo 1979; Marton and Svensson 1979; Taylor 1996; Clarke 1998; Pramling 1996). Saljo (1979) concluded that the focus of research should be on how learners conceptualised their ways of thinking about learning, rather than how they thought they learned.

When visitors are asked why they visit museums the overwhelming reason they give is for some type of learning experience, usually described as education, getting information, expanding knowledge or doing something worthwhile in leisure. Often the word 'learning' was used, which was linked to higher-order fulfilment of personal needs and enhancing self-esteem (Hood 1995; Jansen-Verbeke and van Rekom 1996; Combs 1999; Falk *et al.* 1998). There is a large body of literature about how people learn, where they learn and what they learn. However, less work has been published on what the word learning actually means as defined by the learner, especially in a museum context (Environmetrics 1998; Rowe 1998; Combs 1999; Kelly 2006).

A learning focus may also prove problematic due to the potential confusion between the words 'learning' and 'education'. Falk, Dierking and Holland observed that 'if researchers use the term "learning" to talk with visitors it might affect the outcome of the study, since many of them might [associate] "learning" with formal education and [therefore] have difficulty with the question' (Falk *et al.* 1995: 27). A review of the literature showed that education was perceived to be passive, formal, being told to do something, imposed, not chosen, associated negatively with school and teachers, hard work, structured and systematic (Hooper-Greenhill 2003; Taylor and Spencer 1994). Roberts stated that 'The term "education" has long been associated with the kind of information-based instruction that occurs in classroom settings' (Roberts 1991: 163). Taylor and Spencer reported that, when comparing education to learning, one respondent in their study commented that 'Learning is *you* doing it and education is somebody doing it *to* you.' (Taylor and Spencer 1994: 5, emphasis added).

Prince (1990) investigated a range of attitudes and perceptions that were key to museum visiting. He suggested that if museums were perceived as educational this could be a deterrent, due to peoples' past negative experiences with formal education. Prince proposed that people made positive choices to do things in their leisure time because they valued and enjoyed them. He then concluded that, if people valued the concept of learning more highly than education, museums may be doing themselves a disservice if they portrayed themselves as being educational. To illustrate this problem, a study of school-museum learning uncovered an unintended outcome (Griffin 1998). When students were asked about learning generally, or what they had specifically learned during their visit to a museum, they expressed the view that they didn't consider they were learning when looking, playing, using interactives, watching videos and participating in other hands-on experiences. Griffin concluded that students thought they weren't learning unless they were undertaking a formal task, as they 'identified learning almost exclusively with the type of activities that go on at school, especially pen and paper activities' (1998: 91).

A related issue is that entertainment as a concept has become problematic, with the belief that if museums were entertaining they were somehow 'dumbing down' to the audience and not being as educational as they are expected to be (Kilian 2001; Kimmelman

2001; Kelly 2003). However, can learning experiences in museums be both educational and entertaining? Do visitors think there are real or perceived differences between the concepts of learning, education and entertainment? Do they think that if museums offer entertaining experiences they are failing in their learning goals or 'dumbing down'?

## Investigating adult museum visitors' learning identities

Identity is a concept that has received increased attention across a range of research disciplines (Sfard and Prusak 2005; du Guy et al. 2000; Kidd 2002; Maslow 1999) and most recently in a museum context (Leinhardt et al. 2002a; Leinhardt and Knutson 2004; Falk 2006; Rounds 2006; Spock 2006). Rounds (2006) recognised that identity was crucial in what visitors learn, how they learn and whether they are changed by their museum experiences. A visit to a museum influences both a person's identity (Leinhardt and Gregg 2002; Hooper-Greenhill 2003; Falk 2006) and their sense of self (Leinhardt et al. 2002b; Hooper-Greenhill 2000). The interplay between the backgrounds that visitors bring with them and their reactions to objects and experiences can lead to subtle changes in views of themselves, their identity and meaning-making, both individually and collectively (Hein 1998; Silverman 1995; Stainton 2002). Ivanova (2003) recognised that a two-way process of exchange occurred between the visitor's identity and the sense of identity that was present within the content of the museum. She noted that museums preserved history and memory as well as constructing them. She felt that it was important that 'museums in general need to understand how they influence the development of identity, explicitly or implicitly' (2003: 22).

Museums also have objects which can strongly resonate with a person's experiences, both forming and affirming a visitor's identity (Leinhardt et al. 2002a; Paris 2002; Hooper-Greenhill 2000; Ivanova 2003; Gurian 1999). Identity can be shaped by visitors' interactions with museum objects: 'visitors recall meaningful objects during museum visits that elicit feelings relevant to their own personal identities' (Paris and Mercer 2002: 418). In researching visitors' responses to objects, other manifestations of identity examined by Paris and Mercer were 'gender, ethnicity, historical generation, self and family' (2002: 418). Hooper-Greenhill recognised that museums played a key role, not only in maintaining and transforming culture on a broad scale, but also through 'the recognition of the significance of objects in relation [to] the construction of the self' (2000: 150).

Rounds suggested that visitors used museums for 'identity work', which he defined as 'the processes through which we construct, maintain, and adapt our sense of personal identity, and persuade other people to believe in that identity' (Rounds 2006: 133). Sfard and Prusak (2005) argued that learning played a key role in shaping identities. A learner-centred approach to museum visiting means that it is vital to further understandings about how visitors describe learning and how they see themselves as learners within a museum context. Research undertaken at the Australian Museum, Sydney, examined the interrelationships between visitors' views of learning and their learning experiences at a museum (Kelly 2006). The first part of the study investigated an individual's personal philosophy and views about learning – their learning image (van Rossum et al. 1985), and how this related to the concepts of education and entertainment. Eight in-depth interviews, 100 questionnaires with adult museum visitors and a telephone survey of 300 Sydney adults were conducted. The second stage explored how engagement with a museum exhibition impacted on visitors' learning identities, defined as an individual's learning image within a socio-cultural context, including future views of learning and the roles learning plays across a person's life. Ten groups of visitors were interviewed before and after a visit to the *Uncovered: Treasures of the Australian Museum* exhibition, with conversations being audio-taped and detailed behavioural observations undertaken.

Analysing findings across all data sets suggested that a person's learning image was fluid and strongly influenced both by the context of a visit and the roles played during the visit. Participants strongly supported the ideas of meaning-making, social learning, physical learning, and learning based on a person's interests, choices and motivations. Also, they recognised the key roles that prior knowledge and experience played in learning. Looking at these findings in conjunction with the museum learning literature suggested that museum learning could be framed under five interrelated categories – person, people, place, purpose and process – the 5P model of museum learning (Figure 21.1), explained further below.

### *Person*

The category of person relates to the individual learner, their prior knowledge, experience and lived histories, their cultural backgrounds and gender, as well as the roles played at different times in their everyday lives. It also covers individual changes that result from learning through meaning-making and seeing things in different ways. The framework of constructivism, with its emphasis on the learner (Fosnot 2005; Hein 1998; Woolfolk 1998) is the theoretical construct that underlies the person category. The aspects of constructivism with strong support were learning that builds on what people already know, personal interest, personal change and seeing something in a different way. When describing learning, the role that prior knowledge played was also mentioned, for example 'expanding your knowledge, a new aspect on life' (Interview #11); 'an expansion of what you already know' (Interview #47), and 'new things that add to your body of knowledge' (Interview #78).

Museums have been described as socially-mediated meaning-making environments (Falk

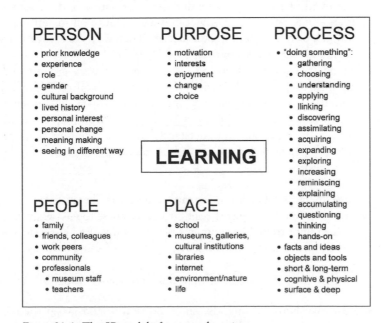

*Figure 21.1* The 5P model of museum learning.

and Dierking 2000). People make meaning from their museum experiences in many different ways based on a conjunction between what the museum provides and the social norms of the group they visit with (Fienberg and Leinhardt 2002). In the study strong support was found for learning as meaning-making. For example, 82 per cent of museum visitors rated the statement 'Constructing meaning based on my own experiences' as important/very important in learning something new. In the open-ended responses people talked about learning as a process of gaining some knowledge, thinking about it and then making new meanings. Learning was described as making sense of something in order to draw conclusions and reach new understandings: 'Finding your place in the world. Engaging with the world in a way to discover more about it and make sense of things. That's the big picture.' (Interview #40).

### People

People is the social dimension of learning. A range of people involved in learning were identified by participants in the study, including family, friends, colleagues, work peers and professionals such as museum staff, teachers and university lecturers. Learning that is community-based within a 'community of practice' is also covered by this dimension. The role of people in learning has been well-recognised in the learning literature (Kelly 2006). In-depth interviewees in the study felt that the social dimension of a visit was an important way in which learning happened through people's interactions with others in the group and the roles they played in a museum visit. The recognition that family and the general community were valuable learning units was a particularly strong result. When discussing their museum experiences participants recognised that they learned with and through others, thus learning about themselves and others as well as the subject matter. Study participants talked about interacting with both the content of the exhibition and the other people in the group they had visited with. For example, one discussed the nature of the learning between himself and his friends as a social event: 'sometimes we'd bounce off something of interest to ourselves, then we'd look at it a bit more, wander off. Then we'd come together a few times to have a look at things.' (Interview Transcript 3.4 24/02/01).

Morrissey reported that adults exhibited learning behaviours that were group-based, resulting in people learning '*about* each other while they learn *through* each other' (Morrissey 2002: 285, emphasis in original). This was illustrated by one of the study participants when describing his visit to the Australian Museum's *Body Art* exhibition with a group of friends who shared the same interest in the topic and an understanding of it as a cultural practice. The learning discussed was both personal and social, with a resulting change in attitudes and seeing things in a different way:

> You have this stereotype about people who've got tattoos and it really gives you a different perspective on it . . . I probably just thought it was an abuse to your body, sort of, beforehand . . . And since then, like, when people have piercings I just look at it, not stare at it, and think about where they got it, what sort of thing they had done.
>
> (Interview Transcript 3.4 24/02/01)

Through social engagement, both as an individual and within the group, he reported learning more about himself and others: 'I also learned a bit more about my friends. I didn't know they had an interest in [tattoos] either, and you sort of learn more of what they're about as well'.

(Interview Transcript 3.4 24/02/01)

Parents can also gain new insights into what interests their children, for example in this taped conversation between a mother (K) and daughter (m) about the coral display they were looking at:

m. Oh mum, I know what that is.
K. What?
m. Coral.
K. Good girl.
m. That's coral, that's coral.
K. It's all different types of coral.
m. Mum, which is the prettiest coral?
K. I don't know, which one do you like?
m. Probably that one.
K. I knew you'd say the pink one.
m. No, purple!

(Conversation Transcript F3 29/09/2004)

### Process

Process includes the myriad ways that learning actually happens. The words listed in the 5P model under process were used by participants in the study, demonstrating the enormous diversity in the ways people described the learning process. Across all samples learning was seen as a way of acquiring and gathering something, for example, information, skills or knowledge, and doing something with it, such as understanding, applying, expanding, discovering, assimilating, experiencing and exploring. Learning was associated with change, both profound and surface, as well as engaging with facts and ideas. Learning was also mentioned as a cognitive process (inside a person's head) and a physical process (such as a hands-on, manipulative experience). Some examples of responses that illustrated process were: 'Opening the mind to new experience' (Interview #4); 'Acquiring new knowledge and applying that' (Interview #5); and 'Expanding your knowledge about an area by a variety of means' (Interview #11).

In the second stage of the study there were many instances that demonstrated how process was closely linked with people, person and place. For example, the mother in one family (K) called her son (z) to her and, through processes of questioning, exploring, thinking and linking, while drawing on prior knowledge and experience she encouraged him to identify an object for himself in the context of a shared place. Also, z used the tools provided in the exhibition (object and accompanying text) to reach an understanding of what he was looking at:

K. Come and look at this. What is that? Where's that from z?
z. Bali.
K. Yes, good boy.
z. I knew that.

281

K.  How did you know that?

z.  Because it has all these on it 'Javanese and Balinese' [reading from text] in the second line. I'll tell you why I knew it was Balinese, because I saw those little gold things in Bali.

(Conversation Transcript F3 29/09/2004)

## Purpose

Purpose includes the motivations behind learning that include a person's general interests, enjoyment and fun, choosing learning and learning for change. Purpose is closely related to the person and process aspects of learning. The issue of choice, especially when comparing learning with education, was one area people in the study felt particularly strongly about. The differences seemed to lie in the word 'teach' which was associated with being 'talked to' or 'told to do something' in an educational sense, and the word 'learn' that was connected with personal choice. Choice was seen as an important way of facilitating learning, for example: 'learning never, never ends . . . it's a choice . . . a very natural process . . . [whereas] education is more given to you' (Interview Transcript 3.5 5/03/01). Another participant mentioned that 'Obviously [learning is] something that's not boring, something that's not passive, so it's more of an active thing . . . Something where you choose to be involved, that you're interested in doing' (Interview Transcript 3.1 22/11/00).

## Place

Place encompasses where learning happens. While learning was viewed as contextual, taking place across all aspects of a person's life, there were specific places nominated by individuals when thinking about where they learned. These included the formal education environments of school, university and libraries, as well as informal contexts such as cultural institutions and the environment/nature (specifically holiday and travel destinations). The internet also emerged as important in learning and is included in this category as people spoke about it as a 'virtual place'. Although it was recognised that the internet was a convenient and easy place to retrieve information, there were strong opinions about the range, depth, reliability and credibility of information available, especially when compared with books/libraries and cultural institutions.

## Learning compared with education and entertainment

As discussed earlier, it had been suggested that the word 'learning' may be confused with 'education' and therefore be negatively perceived; however, these assertions have not been researched from the visitors' perspective. In the study, visitors were asked to describe their views of learning, education and entertainment, in order to explore the differences and potential relationship between them. What emerged was that, although the concepts of learning, education and entertainment shared some similar characteristics, there were five major differences in how they were perceived.

The first was that responses to the word 'learning' were more varied than for 'education' and 'entertainment'. Second, the general language used to explain each concept differed. More active words were used to talk about learning, such as discovering, exploring, applying and experiencing. Museum visitors described education in more concrete ways, including words and phrases such as 'structured/formal' and 'something you are told to do/tell others to do'. Third, although previous research established that people had generally negative views of education as a passive process over which they had no control, the study demonstrated that negative views of education emanated from the perceived lack of choice it offered. Fourth, although there were differences in the language used to describe these concepts, there was still an appreciation of the role that education played in both acquiring facts and information and in delivering learning. Education and learning were closely linked in people's minds, with education leading to learning and learning being a part of education. Education was not seen as necessarily negative, just different – something everyone experiences at some stage of their learning lives.

The fifth difference emerged when comparing entertainment with learning. Entertainment was described as fleeting, short term, a good time, with the recognition that the medium or delivery mechanism (such as film, videos and multimedia programs) formed an important part of the entertainment experience. In contrast, people felt that learning used your brain, built on previous knowledge, was long term and could be entertaining as well. A strong finding was that descriptions of entertainment included words and phrases that were based on feelings and emotions in contrast to learning and education.

Compared with other literature that has discussed entertainment in museums (Roberts 2001; Moore 1997; Witcomb 2003; Roberts 1997; Combs 1999), the study found that learning, education and entertainment were related in positive ways (Figure 21.2).

From the descriptions provided it is proposed that the *museum experience* links the three concepts. Museums have a strong learning focus, with the educational role being one way to deliver museum learning, and entertainment representing the enjoyment, leisure, emotional and sensory aspects of a museum visit. In relation to the 5P model of museum learning described earlier, education is a *process* that occurs within a defined *place*. It is a formal way of delivering learning, grounded in sites such as schools, adult education courses and universities. Entertainment also happens within a defined *place*, either real or imaginary, yet is *person*-centred – being sensory, escapist and relaxing, undertaken both individually and

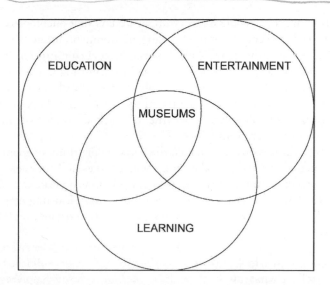

*Figure 21.2* Learning, education and entertainment.

with others. Learning, while it involves other *people*, is essentially an individual *process* that happens inside a person's head and at their own instigation. It is also *place*-centred, occurring across a broad range of contexts, both formal and informal.

## Implications

The study found that an individual's learning image was *fluid*, responding to the situation and social circumstances at a particular point in time. In addition, individuals didn't have a single learning image, rather, they had a series of learning images or personal frameworks for themselves as a learner which changed according to the context, including their identity, roles, the social group and the experiences offered. Adult museum visitors in the study tailored their learning style to suit their particular situation, rather than seeking learning experiences that matched how they stated that they liked to learn. In this sense learning was an adaptive process, both a structured and unstructured experience, where learners used a set of tools in accordance with both the learning image they were functioning in at the time as well as the socio-cultural context. For example, in a museum visit how an individual saw themselves and the role they played within the social and physical environment influenced both how they experienced the museum as a learner, as well as what they were learning. This is an interesting and potentially controversial finding and poses the question: do museums facilitate visitor learning despite themselves?

Second, it also emerged that a person's learning image was an integral part of their *identity*. For example, one participant described learning as a complex multi-layering of material/artefacts, stories, spirituality and identity:

> [Learning is] not only just about the physical form, it's about the environment, it's about spirituality, it's about, at the end of the day, identity. That's what it's all linked back to and, again, learning is very much a part of that.
>
> (Interview Transcript 3.7 13/03/01)

It was concluded from these findings that people have a *learning identity* that encompasses not only a person's learning image, but accounts for the learning environment, future views of learning and the self, and the role learning plays across a person's life. Learning identity covers a broad range of socio-cultural factors that impact on a person visiting a museum, including the context of the visit, the roles played and the tools interacted with, as well as their prior knowledge and life experiences. These come together in ways that shape, not only what is learned, but how people see themselves as a learner during and after a visit and how that influences their future learning activities.

Third, the study suggested that exhibitions can change the ways people think of themselves as learners. During a museum visit people take on a range of roles and they learn together about the content or subject of an exhibition as well as each other's interests and points of view. Parents, in particular, direct both the visit and their child's learning more than they perceive they do, as illustrated in this conversation segment between a mother (J) and her two children (n and a):

n, a. [both shouting out] Look at this, look at this!
J. Okay . . . you want to tell me what it is?
n. What do you think it is?

J.   I don't know, but what do you think all those are?
a.   Sticks.
J.   Sticks?
a.   Yeah, sticks.
J.   Do you think they are sticks? Well, I'll read it to you and it says [reading from text] 'it's feathers and fibre'. So they're actually feathers.
n.   Feathers?
J.   C'mon, let's get moving!

(Conversation Transcript F2 28/09/2004)

There were also many examples of visitors using the objects in the exhibition as triggers for family memories:

m.   Mummy, come here.
K.   I'm here.
m.   Look at all those butterflies.
K.   Where did we see butterflies like that?
m.   Camp.
K.   Where was that again? We saw big butterflies in, it starts with 'B'.
m.   Bali.
K.   Mm.
m.   They were big black ones.
K.   Some of them were coloured.
m.   I love them.
K.   Tell me which one you like the best.
m.   I like them all. Maybe that one the best [points]. Which one do you like the best?

(Conversation Transcript F3 29/09/2004)

Finally, it was found that interacting with an exhibition reinforced in visitors' minds how they did *not* want to learn. For example, when asked how the exhibition fitted with the ways they liked to learn, one couple reported that although the exhibition was full of interesting trivia, they didn't develop any new knowledge or insights into the content. They stated that although there were interesting 'snapshots' there were no 'deep learning opportunities'. They felt overall that the exhibition didn't engage them on an emotional level when compared with their recent experiences of visiting museums in other countries.

## Implications for museums using the 5P model of museum learning

Museum learning is a dynamic process dependent on the individual and their environment within a social context and a community of practice. It is focused on some change in a person through inspiring individuals to find out more and changing how they see themselves and their world. Learning is a positive process, well-regarded and appreciated by individuals. The study suggested that museum learning experiences are enhanced through giving attention to the learner and the multiple roles they play in a visit, the social context in which they operate, the objects and tools the museum provides, and the interpretive

285

approaches employed within the 5P framework of person, people, place, purpose and process (Figure 21.3), discussed further below.

Under the *person* dimension museums need to encourage visitors to think of themselves as learners and open them to new ways of seeing themselves as learners, while recognising that a person's learning image is fluid and changes during their visit. The multiple roles a person plays at various times during the one visit need to be appreciated, along with an understanding of the general nature of learners' prior knowledge, experiences and interests, which can be done through a rigorous programme of front-end evaluation. The capacity for visitors to apply information to a variety of other contexts and life experiences should be a facilitation role that museums play. The recognition that visitors' construct their own narratives and make their own meanings, which may be different from those intended by the exhibition developers, needs to be accounted for when researching the experiences visitors have.

Regarding *people*, it needs to be recognised that museum visits are mediated experiences with knowledgeable others who facilitate discussion and sharing of opinions and understandings. Exhibitions need to be designed to encourage conversation and promote group interaction and group activities, yet also allow for private reflection. Different people in a group play different roles, and some individuals play more than one role at any one time, therefore, museums need to keep in mind that everyone learns a wide variety of things in an exhibition in a diverse number of ways, ranging from 'simple' facts, to aesthetic appreciation, to deep changes in attitudes, behaviours or self-perceptions.

Adults accompanying children have different requirements. Comfortable spaces throughout exhibitions where 'visitor management' can take place (such as plenty of chairs, resting and eating spaces, as well as activities to distract cranky, bored children) are needed. Guides and texts with conversation starters and information detailing key messages of an exhibition could be provided to enhance the visitor experience and the learning that takes place.

The *process* of learning also requires the attention of exhibition developers. Exhibitions that are heavily focused on objects need to provide access to collections and other real material for visitors to use actively and manipulate. Objects that make an impact because they

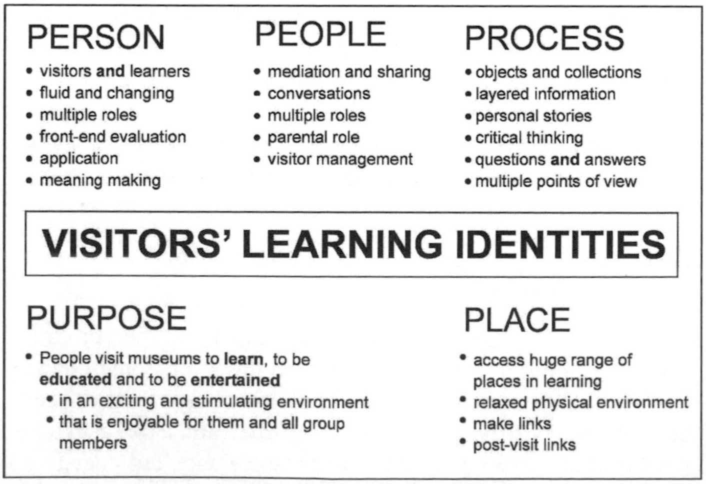

| PERSON | PEOPLE | PROCESS |
|---|---|---|
| • visitors **and** learners | • mediation and sharing | • objects and collections |
| • fluid and changing | • conversations | • layered information |
| • multiple roles | • multiple roles | • personal stories |
| • front-end evaluation | • parental role | • critical thinking |
| • application | • visitor management | • questions **and** answers |
| • meaning making | | • multiple points of view |

## VISITORS' LEARNING IDENTITIES

| PURPOSE | PLACE |
|---|---|
| • People visit museums to **learn**, to be **educated** and to be **entertained** | • access huge range of places in learning |
|   • in an exciting and stimulating environment | • relaxed physical environment |
|   • that is enjoyable for them and all group members | • make links |
| | • post-visit links |

*Figure 21.3* Implications for museum practice: the 5P model of museum learning.

are big or tiny, unusual or familiar, bizarre or mundane are enjoyed and appreciated by visitors. Layered information and personal stories behind objects, as well as access to curators who work on the collections, are regarded as important by visitors. Planning for diverse modes of presentation for self-direction and choice in interpretive styles and levels of information needs to be considered. Both social and learning experiences will be enhanced by opportunities for visitors to engage in critical thinking and questioning, with exhibitions that raise questions, yet also point to answers. Presenting multiple points of view to enable visitors to reach their own conclusions and make their own meanings is a must.

The *purpose* of a museum visit constantly cited by people is to learn, to be educated and to be entertained in an exciting and stimulating environment that is enjoyable for them and all members of their group. Giving learners choice and control over their museum experience and their learning through providing multiple pathways through an exhibition is required. Making exhibitions relevant by making explicit why it is important to know something will have better learning outcomes for visitors.

Visitors make links from unfamiliar to familiar *places* that they have been and shared as a group. A relaxed physical environment that is welcoming and enjoyable, as well as sensual and stimulating needs to be accounted for in planning exhibitions. Activities and material that can be accessed after a visit for further discovery and exploration at the learner's own pace and discretion should be included. Using the internet as an information resource to provide deeper layers of content accessible either on-site or off-site would be appreciated by visitors.

## Conclusion

The findings of the study suggest that, as people access a large and varied range of places when learning takes place, museums need to position themselves as unique and accessible learning settings where visitors can experience the real and be together in an enjoyable, safe environment. The study found that museums can shape adult visitors' learning identities. Through access to objects and information visitors see reflections of themselves and their culture in ways that encourage new connections, meaning-making and changes to their learning identity. Given the opportunity to articulate their personal views about learning, adult museum visitors revealed wide-ranging and deep understandings of themselves as learners (their *learning image*). These learning images are fluid, shaped by the socio-cultural context of the museum in conjunction with the multiple roles people play during a visit (their *learning identity*). The literature review revealed that visitors learn a great deal from museums across a diverse range of content areas and at many different levels. However, the study revealed that visitors could also learn more about the concept of learning as well as their own learning processes and learning identity if they were encouraged to think about their learning image before they engaged with an exhibition.

## Bibliography

Bradburne, J. (1998) 'Dinosaurs and white elephants: the science centre in the 21st Century', *Museum Management and Curatorship* 17: 119–37.

Carr, D. (2003) *The Promise of Cultural Institutions*, Walnut Creek, CA: AltaMira Press.

Clarke, J. (1998) 'Student's perceptions of different tertiary learning environments', *Higher Education Research & Development*, 17: 107–17.

Combs, A. (1999) 'Why do they come? Listening to visitors at a decorative arts museum', *Curator*, 43: 186–97.

Conversation Transcript F2 (28 September 2004) *Family #2*, unpublished manuscript.

Conversation Transcript F3 (29 September 2004) *Family #3*, unpublished manuscript.

du Guy, P., Evans, J. and Redman, P. (2000) (eds) *Identity: A Reader*, London: Sage.

Environmetrics (1998) *Staff Perceptions of Learning*, Sydney: Australian Museum.

Falk, J. (1998) 'Visitors: who does, who doesn't and why', *Museum News*, 77: 38–43.

—— (2004) 'The director's cut: toward an improved understanding of learning from museums', *Science Education*, 88: S82–S96.

—— (2006) 'An identity-centred approach to understanding museum learning', *Curator*, 49: 151–66.

—— and Dierking, L. (1992) *The Museum Experience*, Washington, DC: Whalesback Books.

—— (eds) (1995) *Public Institutions for Personal Learning: Establishing a Research Agenda*, Washington, DC: American Association of Museums.

—— (2000) *Learning from Museums: Visitor Experiences and the Making of Meaning*, Walnut Creek, CA: AltaMira Press.

—— and Holland, D. (1995) 'How should we investigate learning in museums? Research questions and project designs', in J. Falk and L. Dierking (eds) *Public Institutions for Personal Learning*, Washington, DC: American Association of Museums, 23–30.

—— and Coulson, D. (1998) 'The effect of visitors' agendas on museum learning', *Curator*, 41: 107–20.

Fienberg, J. and Leinhardt, G. (2002) 'Looking through the glass: reflections of identity in conversations at a history museum', in G. Leinhardt, K. Crowley and K. Knutson (eds) *Learning Conversations in Museums*, Mahwah, NJ: Lawrence Erlbaum Associates, 167–211.

Fosnot, C. (2005) *Constructivism: Theory, Perspectives, and Practice*, New York: Teachers College Press.

Griffin, J. (1998) *School–Museum Integrated Learning Experiences in Science: A Learning Journey*, unpublished PhD Thesis, University of Technology, Sydney.

Gurian, E. (1999) 'What is the object of this exercise? A meandering exploration of the many meanings of objects in museums', *Daedalus*, 128: 163–83.

Hein, G. (1998) *Learning in the Museum*, London: Routledge.

Hood, M. (1995) 'Audience research tell us why visitors come to museums – and why they don't', in C. Scot (ed.) *Evaluation and Visitor Research in Museums: Towards 2000*, Sydney: Powerhouse Publishing, 3–10.

Hooper-Greenhill, E. (2000) *Museums and the Interpretation of Visual Culture*, London: Routledge.

—— (2003) *Museums and Social Value: Measuring the Impact of Learning in Museums*, Paper presented at Annual Conference of the Committee for Education and Cultural Action (ICOM-CECA), Oaxaca.

Interview Transcript 3.1 (22 November 2000) *Brenda*, unpublished manuscript.

Interview Transcript 3.4 (24 February 2001) *Scott*, unpublished manuscript.

Interview Transcript 3.5 (5 March 2001) *Stephen*, unpublished manuscript.

Interview Transcript 3.7 (13 March 2001) *Louise*, unpublished manuscript.

Ivanova, E. (2003) 'Changes in collective memory: the schematic narrative template of victimhood in Kharkiv museums', *Journal of Museum Education*, 28: 17–22.

Jansen-Verbeke, M. and van Rekom, J. (1996) 'Scanning museum visitors', *Annals of Tourism Research*, 23: 364–75.

Kelly, L. (2001) *'Developing a Model of Museum Visiting'*, Paper presented at National Cultures, National Identity, Museums Australia Annual Conference, Canberra.

—— (2003) *'Museums, "Dumbing Down" and Entertainment: A Visitor Perspective'*, Paper presented at UNCOVER – graduate research in the museum sector Conference, Sydney.

—— (2006) *Visitors and Learners: Adult Museum Visitors' Learning Identities*, Sydney: University of Technology.

Kidd, W. (2002) *Culture and Identity*, Hampshire: Palgrave Macmillan.

Kilian, M. (2001) *The Culture of Popular Science or 'Star Wars'? Museums Struggle to Align Education and Entertainment*, Chicago, IL: Chicago Tribune.

Kimmelman, M. (2001) *Museums in a Quandary: Where Are the Ideals?*, New York: New York Times.

Leinhardt, G. and Gregg, M. (2002) 'Burning buses, burning crosses: student teachers see civil rights', in G. Leinhardt, K. Crowley and K. Knutson (eds) *Learning Conversations in Museums*, Mahwah, NJ: Lawrence Erlbaum Associates, 139 66.

—— and Knutson, K. (2004) *Listening in on Museum Conversations*, Walnut Creek, CA: AltaMira Press.

——, Crowley, K. and Knutson, K. (eds) (2002a) *Learning Conversations in Museums*, Mahwah, NJ: Lawrence Erlbaum Associates.

——, Tittle, C. and Knutson, K. (2002b) 'Talking to oneself: diaries of museum visits', in G. Leinhardt, K. Crowley and K. Knutson (eds) *Learning Conversations in Museums*, Mahwah, NJ: Lawrence Erlbaum Associates, 103–33.

Malone, J. (1990) *Theories of Learning: A Historical Approach*, Belmont, CA: Wadsworth Publishing Company.

Marton, F. and Svensson, L. (1979) 'Conceptions of research in student learning', *Higher Education*, 8: 471–86.

Maslow, A. (1999) *Toward a Psychology of Being*, New York: John Wiley & Sons, Inc.

Matusov, E. and Rogoff, B. (1995) 'Evidence of development from people's participation in communities of learners', in J. Falk and L. Dierking (eds) *Public Institutions for Personal Learning*, Washington, DC: American Association of Museums, 97–104.

Moore, K. (1997) *Museums and Popular Culture*, London: Cassell.

Morrissey, K. (2002) 'Pathways among objects and museum visitors', in S. Paris (ed.) *Perspectives on Object-Centered Learning in Museums*, Mahwah, NJ: Lawrence Erlbaum Associates, 285–99.

Paris, S. (ed.) (2002) *Perspectives on Object-Centered Learning in Museums*, Mahwah, NJ: Lawrence Erlbaum Associates.

Paris, S. and Mercer, M. (2002) 'Finding self in objects: identity exploration in museums', in G. Leinhardt, K. Crowley and K. Knutson (eds) *Learning Conversations in Museums*, Mahwah, NJ: Lawrence Erlbaum Associates, 401–23.

Pramling, I. (1996) 'Understanding and empowering the child as a learner', in D. Olsen and N. Torrance (eds) *The Handbook of Education and Human Development: New Models of Learning, Teaching and Schooling*, Cambridge: Blackwell Publishers Ltd, 534–63.

Prentice, R. (1998) 'Recollections of museum visits: a case study of remembered cultural attraction visiting on the Isle of Man', *Museum Management and Curatorship*, 17: 41–64.

Prince, D. (1990) 'Factors influencing museum visits: an empirical evaluation of audience selection', *Museum Management and Curatorship*, 9: 149–68.

Rennie, L. and Johnston, D. (2004) 'The nature of learning and its implications for research on learning from museums', *Science Education*, 88: S4–S16.

Roberts, L. (1991) 'Affective learning, affective experience: what does it have to do with museum education?' *Visitor Studies: Theory, Research and Practice*, 4: 162–8.

—— (1997) *From Knowledge to Narrative: Educators and the Changing Museum*, Washington, DC: Smithsonian Institution Press.

Roberts, L. B. (2001) 'Outcomes and experience: new priorities for museums', *Curator*, 44: 21–6.

Rounds, J. (2006) 'Doing identity work in museums', *Curator*, 49: 133–50.

Rowe, S. (1998) *Learning Talk: Understanding How People Talk and Think About Learning in the St. Louis Science Center*, St. Louis, MO: St. Louis Science Center.

Saljo, R. (1979) 'Learning about learning', *Higher Education*, 8: 443–51.

Sfard, A. and Prusak, A. (2005) 'Telling identities: in search of an analytic tool for investigating learning as a culturally shaped activity', *Educational Researcher*, 34: 14–22.

Silverman, L. (1995) 'Visitor meaning making in museums for a new age', *Curator*, 38: 161–69.

Spock, D. (2006) 'The puzzle of museum educational practice: a comment on Rounds and Falk', *Curator*, 49: 167–80.

Stainton, C. (2002) 'Voices and images: making connections between identity and art', in G. Leinhardt, G. Crowley and K. Knutson (eds) *Learning Conversations in Museums*, Mahwah, NJ: Lawrence Erlbaum Associates, 213–57.

Taylor, P. (1996) 'Reflections on students' conceptions of learning and perceptions of learning environments', *Higher Education Research & Development*, 15: 223–37.

Taylor, S. and Spencer, E. (1994) *Individual Commitment to Lifelong Learning: Individuals' Attitudes: Report on the Qualitative Phase. Research series No. 31*, Sheffield: Employment Department.

van Rossum, E., Diejkers, R. and Hamer, R. (1985) 'Students' learning conceptions and their interpretation of significant educational concepts', *Higher Education*, 14: 617–41.

Weil, S. (1999) 'From being *about* something to being *for* somebody: the ongoing transformation of the American museum', *Daedalus*, 128: 229–58.

—— (2002) *Making Museums Matter*, Washington, DC: Smithsonian Institution Press.

Witcomb, A. (2003) *Re-Imagining the Museum: Beyond the Mausoleum*, London: Routledge.

Woolfolk, A. (1998) *Educational Psychology*, Boston, MA: Allyn and Bacon.

# 22

# MUSEUMS – DRAMA, RITUAL AND POWER

*Jem Fraser*

This chapter explores the implications of a general model for the development of a new critical pedagogy of museums. Unlike most existing models its starting point is an acknowledgement of the role of museums within the existing power structure in society, and the assumptions museums make about the appropriate power relations between the curator and the visitor. It provides an understanding of the impact of the museum visit and lays the foundation for improved displays.

The model focuses on the museum visit as a drama with visitors in role, sometimes as audience and sometimes as performers, making meaning, rather than simply acquiring information or, in some abstract way, appreciating beauty. Visitors are active in their choices throughout their visit and their meaning-making is influenced, but not wholly determined, by how well the museum drama works for them. The museum experience is one of transaction between the visitor and the displays constructed by the museum, not one of one-way communication – no matter how effective this is. Within this model the museum's displays and curatorial authority can be rejected by visitors on the basis of their prior knowledge and life experience, the two can be aligned and the visitor's sense of identity reinforced, or there can be a negotiation, in which visitors change their sense of themselves in response to the encounter with the museum.

At its best, the museum drama can engage visitors' emotions and imagination and enable them to experience intellectual, psychological, emotional and perhaps spiritual growth. At its worst, visitors' negative experiences alienate them not just from the museum but from trying such experiences again in the future

In this model, authority, power and the task of creating knowledge are shared between visitors and curators and the model presents four key factors which affect how people make meaning of displays – transaction, ritual, identity and power. It proposes that if museums recognise and embrace the complex transactions of ritual, identity and power, they would enable visitors to experience not just learning but growth, and greatly revive and enhance the educational and cultural value of museums, leading to a new pedagogy for museums.

## Museums – drama, ritual and power

In the past 15 years many larger museums have considered it a priority to undertake visitor surveys which provide information on who their visitors are, their ages, where they come from, whether or not they have a job, their education, etc. (Lampost Index 2006, ALVA 2005, MORI 2001).

Alongside this mainly quantitative activity there has been an increase in more qualitative research to investigate the effect of the museum experience on people, the sense that visitors make of their visit, and the meaning they take away with them when they leave (Durbin 1996; Borun *et al.* 1998; Serrell 1999; Falk and Dierking 2000; Hooper-Greenhill 2001). Many of these studies have focused on research into learning in museums by schoolchildren, although there are examples of the experience of adult and family group visiting and meanings made by visitors.

This word 'meaning' embraces more than learning in its narrow sense – meaning is about the impact the visit has on people's lives – their memories, feelings, values, sense of wonder – and the overall impact on them of the experience of the particular place, object or set of objects. It is useful at this point briefly to review some current models of the meaning that visitors make in museums based on the visitor experience, and then propose a model which helps us gain an insight into the sometimes profound and long-lasting effect that museum experiences have on people. Through an understanding of their visitors and the process through which they make meaning, museums will be helped to create displays which enhance that process.

One very influential model of the visitor experience is that of Falk and Dierking (2000). This recognises the relationship between visitors and their background, both personal and social, their interpretive community, their motivation for visiting and the museum environment. It proposes that individual learning in museums takes place as a result of the interaction at a moment in time of three contexts – the personal, the socio-cultural and the environmental. It recognises that learning is an active process involving the connection of past experiences to more recent ones and that memory is an important constituent of that process.

This model has been useful in contributing to a better understanding of the visitors' experience. However, it does not acknowledge the museum as an instrument of power within society, nor the implications for the authority of museums of visitors being conceived of as active rather than passive.

This could be due to the notion that there is an understanding in the museum world that museums have an inbuilt authority and power. For example, Hooper-Greenhill writes:

> Museums are deeply involved in all these areas, and especially in their interrelationships with power; the power to name, to represent common sense, to create official versions, to represent the social world, and the represent the past.
>
> (Hooper-Greenhill 2000: 19)

Carol Duncan explores these ideas in her theory of museum visiting which focuses almost entirely on the power of the museum in society (Duncan 1995). She argues that, while museums and exhibitions might appear to be morally and politically neutral, their purpose is to uphold the current power structure of society. According to Duncan this is a primary not a secondary purpose: it is what museums are for.

> To control a museum means precisely to control the representation of a community and its highest values and truths. It is also the power to define the relative

standing of individuals within that community. Those who are best prepared to perform its ritual . . . are also those whose identities (social, sexual, racial, etc.) the museum most fully confirms.

(Duncan 1995: 8)

Museums carry out this function by providing a ritual of belonging for the dominant groups in society. Museum visiting, she argues, shares many of the characteristics of ritual, in particular a strong separation of the museum from everyday life in preparation for the reflections and symbolic meaning to be made within.

Duncan explicitly acknowledges that her model is theoretical and political and is not based on an analysis of the experiences of real visitors. All such theories relating to the power of the museum tend to assume that visitors passively accept the message of the museum, and only have the power to make meaning depending on whether or not they have the appropriate cultural background.

A third major contribution to understanding museum experiences is that of Lois Silverman, whose description of visitors' engagement as meaning-making is a significant improvement on the traditional interpretation or communication model (Silverman 1995). The latter emphasises the museum's message and the processes by which it can be transferred as nearly intact as possible into the visitors' heads. Silverman recognises that visitors have and value a far wider range of experiences than the acquisition of cognitive knowledge or even the aesthetic satisfaction of viewing art and artefacts. These experiences may involve reminiscences, social interaction with their companions on the visit, and a whole range of idiosyncratic links made between their life experiences and the objects on display (Silverman 1990). Despite the unpredictability of individual meanings implicit in this, an effective model of museum visiting would need to take into account this range of experiences and enable staff to build on visitors' meaning-making capacity in a positive way.

Finally, mention should be made of the model presented in Canada by Douglas Worts, who analysed visitor responses to different interpretive methods in the Art Gallery of Ontario (Worts 1994). As a result of his investigations into visitor comments and drawings Worts offered a *Conceptual Model of Museum Experience* which emphasises individual identity and the many processes and products of the experience that happen during interactions with people, objects and places. He writes, 'People want to see themselves reflected either literally or symbolically in their imagery and in their writing' (Worts 1994: 182). Visitor responses gave a range of personal insights that the gallery itself could not articulate and illustrated the emotional power of the objects in the displays. 'While it is true that we as an institution have something unique to offer the public in the collections and our intellectual insights, the visitor centred half of the creative process is based on personalising the symbolic objects' (Worts 1994: 190).

The model itself is very complex and, while it brings together many of the issues highlighted above, in its present form it is rather unwieldy and I have failed to find any evidence of it being applied, modified or developed.

Against the background of these four perspectives, an alternative model will now be presented based on the museum visit as a drama comprising four elements, the first of which is identity.

# Identity

Worts, among other researchers, demonstrates that a study of visitor comments data can be a rich resource for the study of meaning-making. This was the chosen methodology for studying visitor experiences in analysing 3,000 visitor comments in St Mungo's Museum of Religious Life in Glasgow (Fraser 2005). The first notable thing in the comments was that the encounter between the visitor and the museum is a very personal one, with the visitors addressing not so much staff, as a museum persona. Visitors write of personal connections which they make to their own life experience, to that of their family, to their own knowledge. They reminisce about objects they are familiar with; they try to make sense of the new objects or new information about the objects in the light of their own worldview. These findings verify Silverman's and Wort's premise that self-identity is a key influence on visitors' meaning-making and that individual visitors may make different meanings depending on their background and life experience.

When visitors' individual identity is affirmed, they had a good and positive experience, when it is not their experience was less positive and could, depending on the circumstances, lead to their rejection of not just one particular museum, but all museums – the 'museums are not for me' response. This rejection could be experienced as a result of what they saw in the displays or through their encounters with other people in the museum, through not being able to find their way about or through not feeling comfortable within the museum environment. Identity and the opportunity to make connections through that identity with the objects on display, to increase knowledge (cognitive, aesthetic or experiential) and to enhance one's self-esteem and confidence is the first of four components in a new model of visitor meaning-making.

# Transaction

The second element in this model is Transaction, which is the mechanism of *how* visitors relate to the displays and to the museum environment. The term 'transaction' is preferable to terms like 'communication' and 'interpretation', because these do not adequately capture the interchange between visitors and the museum and, in particular, between visitors and objects in displays.

Objects, including buildings, are capable of containing very significant meanings, through the power of association and the semiotic power of the visual languages which shape them. Even the most basic apparently functional objects and specimens collected from nature are also vehicles for communication, and many objects have an element of intentional expression of meaning, most clearly acknowledged in museums in the Western concept of art. These communicative intentions are overlaid with associations which may be with people or communities we know or have knowledge of from history, with a place, an incident, a smell, a touch or texture, an emotion. The fundamental premise of museums – that people are interested in looking at objects – implies that those objects which are associated with emotions are those which are the most memorable and in which we invest a great deal of our identity.

Falk and Dierking's model proposes that when people relate to objects in displays they evaluate and make meaning of the object, taking into account many factors – the display itself, whether or not they are interested in it, how it looks, what the museum says about it, the museum itself and how they perceive the museum on that day, which might depend on the purpose of their visit, who is with them, the time they have to spend and their own experience of the object, what they have read or seen or been told about the object or the displays. Viewing this as transaction gives a sense of how visitors experience these factors, taking most of them into account almost instantaneously. They assess the level of interest for them and decide to either engage with the object or not according to their own life experience. They may accept the museum meaning or negotiate a meaning which is satisfactory for them – one they can live with. These transactions with the objects and can be powerful intellectual, emotional and psychological experiences which, at their most intense, may be akin to a transformative religious or aesthetic experience in a church, a musical concert, a play in a theatre or a natural landscape.

At the other extreme the transaction can be such that the individuals finds the evaluation socially, psychologically, intellectually or emotionally at odds with his or her experience and that they reject it outright – perhaps most frequently by not visiting that museum again.

Transaction between objects and visitor identity is integral to the whole meaning-making process within the museum environment.

## Ritual

But what of this museum environment itself? This leads into the third element of the new model – Ritual. Ritual is a concept with which we are familiar in many aspects of our lives, whether these are sacred or secular, such as weddings, funerals, first communions, birthdays, bar mitzvahs and other ceremonies associated with the life cycle. Both secular and sacred rituals acknowledge a wider authority which validates the ritual, which in turn provides for continuity of the way of life and traditions of the community or individual. The ritual also provides the potential for change of status or identity within the group or individual change as with rites of passage. In our media-focused culture, people create new rituals to meet new needs and respond to new communicative opportunities. These confer roles on individuals by enabling them to choose to take part – for example, by placing flowers by the roadside to show sympathy with and sorrow for a death, or by wearing a coloured ribbon or wristband to associate oneself with a cause. In the performance of the action, the individual is both actor and audience – he or she wears the ribbon to be associated with the cause and to be seen by others in that light too. The action is performative in that it both acts out and confers an identity and role on the individual.

Rituals contain elements of two kinds of drama – the aesthetic and the social (Chaney 1993). For example, during a wedding ceremony the aesthetic drama takes place when the couple make individual commitments one to the other in an exchange of vows, the ritual focusing on the couple and their change of status. The guests are the audience for this part of the ceremony which is akin to those attending a theatrical or musical performance where, seemingly passive, they listen to the words of the play or music and have an expectation that they may be uplifted spiritually and emotionally. At other times in the wedding the guests themselves perform, moving around, meeting each other, talking, laughing, dancing, eating in a variety of social situations: this is a social drama in which the guests have roles to play. The role people play in a drama, whether social or aesthetic is important to the meaning people make. Museum visiting has elements of both social and aesthetic drama, and visitors play different roles depending on their particular motivation and background. A grandmother visiting with her grandchildren plays a different role from when she visits on her own or with her peer group and the meanings she makes may also differ.

Visitors are not passive. They play many different, active roles in the museum ritual – that of the scholar, the tourist, the expert, the cultured person, the romantic, the leader of a group and so on. Visitors are active in their meaning-making as they engage with the museum ritual.

In the aesthetic drama visitors act as audience for the displays which represent the performance of the curatorial script. While engaged with the aesthetic drama, visitors both serve as fellow members of the audience for other visitors and at the same time perform roles in the social drama with their companions and possibly with museum staff with whom they interact. Many visitors engage with the ritual, respond to the script and perform both for themselves and for other people in the museum, as they make meaning. This performance is overt when they write in the comments book, when they chat to their companions, when they point objects out to others or when they participate in a guided tour.

## Power

Duncan identifies the social purpose of ritual as a key to understanding museum visiting, which brings us to the fourth dimension of the new model, that of power. The success of any ritual depends on the recognition of its covert authority and legitimacy. As Duncan puts it, museums 'are one of those places in which politically organized and socially institutionalized power most avidly seeks to realize its desire to appear as beautiful, natural and legitimate' (Duncan 1995: 6). The aura of objective knowledge, or of a universal aesthetic, of historic treasures and artistic masterpieces, of scientific specimens and academic rigour are all deployed to secure the authority of the museum. In the nineteenth century it was assumed that people would be educated by simple exposure to objects laid out according to typologies. We now know that this idea of learning is too simplistic and that learning is an active process. Many museums, however, simply copy the Victorian intention to transmit information from the museum to visitors. In the best museums the acknowledgement of the active mind of the visitor is accompanied by a full acknowledgment of his or her meaning-making capacity, with a transformative effect on the displays. This is particularly evident in places like Te Papa in Wellington, New Zealand or the Museum of World Cultures in Gothenberg, Sweden.

## A new model of the visitor experience

The following section will sum up the new model of the visitor experience with its four components – identity, transaction, ritual and power (Figure 22.1).

This model acknowledges both the position and the authority of the museum's role in society and the power of visitors to draw upon the knowledge, values and ideals of their own life experience and to use the specially prepared displays as a resource to make and take ownership of their meaning.

This model recognises the validity and integrity of many of the meanings made by all visitors who engage with the museum, not just those intended meanings of the display team. The meaning-making process is an individual and social process that is influenced, but not wholly determined by the museum ritual.

Visitors' responses to the objects will be affected by their perceptions and expectations of

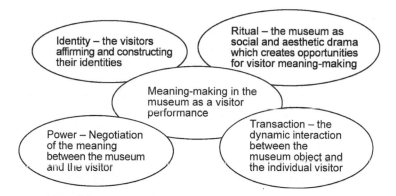

*Figure 22.1* A model of the visitor experience.

the museum and the museum visit. Visitors' reaction or performance may be conscious or unconscious and can have positive or negative effects on how they subsequently view the museum and similar objects. At best the museum drama, a product of the whole staged performance scripted by curators, educators, designers and architects, may enable visitors to experience powerful meanings if their emotions, intellect and imagination are engaged, leading them to construct new knowledge, new identities and new experiences. At worst, visitors may have negative experiences which alienate them from the museum and lead them to construct knowledge and experiences which adversely affect not only whether or not they visit museums in the future, but which also limit their opportunities for personal growth.

No matter how sophisticated the design or how psychologically informed the communication methods, issues of identity, transaction, ritual and power will predominate. A new model will enable museums to develop further in a direction which the best are already taking. Museums will become more alert to their role in validating and, where appropriate, challenging attitudes and values which are embedded in their identities; that they will become more aware of the need to support visitors in their transactions with objects, but in an open-ended way that enables their meaning-making; that they will become more conscious of the need to create spaces and displays that support ritual, both social and aesthetic; and that they will bring to awareness their own power to influence and the visitor's power to accept or reject that influence. By engaging consciously with identity, transaction, ritual and power museums will increasingly become places which enable individuals to grow in understanding of each other, of their similarities and their differences, and to examine and reflect on themselves and their values within the changing society in which they live.

## Using the new model to explain experiences in museums

At the American Association of Museums (AAM) conference in 2001, a senior museum professional, Kathy McLean, described her reaction to two recent exhibits which she had visited. The first was the *Armani* show at the Museum of Modern Art in New York, which she visited when it was very crowded. She described gorgeous floor-to-ceiling apparel, mood lighting, amazing fabrics but no information other than small labels which, as there was no chronology in the layout, was confusing and difficult to contextualise. She described the meaning of the museum as a celebration of Western culture values and the cult of the celebrity which presented her with a dilemma. Although she hated the idea of the exhibition, in particular the 15 million dollar sponsorship by Armani, as it went counter to her own identity and values, she had a great time and came out of the museum with a feeling of well-being and belonging.

The other exhibition, *Without Sanctuary – Lynching Photography in America*, she found in a 40-year-old style of history exhibition – small photographs on walls, labels text in small type beside each photograph, a few dark brown objects in cases – in the New York Historical Society. As she went round she became distressed by the images and looking up caught the glance of another visitor – an African American woman – whose eyes she described as seeming 'to sear right through her'. Feeling uncomfortable she made her way to the comments book to which Afro-America high school students had spent some time contributing. One comment caught her eye. 'Having people look at these photos is like doing the lynching all over again'. She finished her narrative – 'No longer a museum visitor but instead a voyeur I had to leave'.[1]

No explanation was offered for the different responses. However, the new model offers an insight and explanation for these experiences. In the first Armani exhibition, even with her intellectual reservations about the huge commercial funding, the narrator felt comfortable, knew she belonged and she had a positive and identity-affirming experience. The situation within the exhibition was not threatening to her either as an individual or as a member of the museum profession. She had the power to counteract the commercial aspects of exhibition-making in her own museum and in her own network. She could appreciate the aesthetic ritual of the exhibition and enjoy the company of peers, other visitors and the occasion. The exhibition reinforced her identity as a white professional American female with the power of choice. In the model of meaning-making in this event the ritual component is dominant along with that of identity.

In the second exhibition, her role in the museum drama changed from museum visitor and even museum professional to one where she felt excluded. The meaning she made was that she no longer belonged. She had become alienated in a performative process – not solely by the objects and the actions of other people in the museum but by the meaning she made of them, the transaction she had made with the photos and other people in the museum, the drama she had enacted.

The transaction component of the meaning-making model dominated in this case along with the power of the museum as an institution. She felt identified by the museum and by other people in the museum with the racial hatred which had perpetrated the lynching and other atrocities in the photographs. Her alienation was produced performatively within the engagement, she felt powerless and she excluded herself from the museum.

This new meaning-making model based on a performative society can offer insight into the meanings made by this same person in the two exhibitions in the USA as well as the many comments to visitors in research for this chapter and other qualitative studies by Hooper-Greenhill (2001) and by Falk and Dierking (2000). Many visitors are unable to challenge the boundaries that are set for them by their life experience. Their own frame restricts the discourse available to them to make meaning.

If museums wish to take the opportunity to continue to open up the range of discourses and give visitors an opportunity to explore new understanding, then the application of the model will complement and accelerate the re-examination, already begun, of the educational role of museums in today's society.

## A new pedagogy for museums – the museum visit as a drama

This chapter has constructed a theory of the museum visit, which examines the museum visitor experience and uses the metaphor of performance to describe the components which constitute that experience – transaction, ritual, identity and power ('TRIP'). The outcome of the museum meaning-making process is performative, not just for the curator and the museum team but for visitor and curator alike. Each contributes to the process. The meaning made by both at a conscious or unconscious level becomes part of her or his future meaning-making repertoire, part of her or his self.

This understanding of the reciprocal nature of meaning-making as well as the identification of the factors which contribute to the process presented in the 'TRIP' model, encourage a fundamental shift in the way people see the educational function of museums. Only by adopting a museum pedagogy which recognises the way that the practice of drama, ritual and power construct and offer human beings particular views of themselves and the world can museums truly fulfil their potential. These views are always implicated in the discourse and the relations of ethics and power. To invoke the importance of pedagogy is to raise questions not just about how visitors make meaning but also about how curators construct the ideological and political positions from which they speak. Giroux, an American educator, defines pedagogy as 'a configuration of textual, verbal and visual practices that seek to engage the processes through which people understand themselves and the ways in which they engage with others and their environment' (Giroux 1992: 3). If museums can understand the pedagogical practice, which can be used to bring this about, then they may better fulfil their educational purpose.

Such definitions move away from an older pedagogy, which used the information transmission model for mass education and was rooted in the UK in the needs of an industrial age and colonial empire, embedded in a single dominant white British culture. As educators recognised and took on board changes in thinking in a variety of disciplines, pedagogy in formal institutions slowly changed from subject-centred to child-centred throughout the twentieth century. The holistic development of each individual and their involvement in their own learning, championed by Dewey (1938), has become the goal of education.

Globalisation and the movement of people across geographical and cultural boundaries has accelerated this process and made it more urgent (Stiglitz 2002: 9). People of different cultures with different interpretative communities live alongside each other. They have to learn new practices and new ways of being, in order to recreate their identities. The transactions between peoples are active and performative – they affect and are affected by the process.

Jerome Bruner, the American psychologist, writes that the critical enabling factor, the one that brings the mind into focus, is culture (Bruner 1996: 87). He argues:

> What now comes to the centre of attention is the individual's engagement with established systems of shared meaning, with the beliefs, values and the understandings of those already in place in society as he or she is thrown in among them. The critical 'test frame' from this point of view is education – the field of practices within which such engagement is, in the first instance, effected. Education is not simply a technical business of well managed information processing, nor even a matter of simply applying learning theories to the classroom or using the results of subject-centred achievement testing. It is a complex pursuit of fitting a culture to the needs of its members and their ways of knowing to the needs of the culture.
>
> (Bruner 1996: 43)

This new model of the visitor meaning-making process has been developed within a drama metaphor – the exhibition as the staging of a production: a production which recognises the ideological and social basis on which meaning is constructed and creates an environment in which new meaning is formed and new identities are transacted. By focusing on the visitor in performance the museum team can create environments where the boundaries of different cultural frames are made explicit and the opportunities to investigate those boundaries are presented. Through the medium of the museum drama visitors can explore their feelings, values, identities and knowledge just like the audience for a dramatic play. In the exhibition visitors can confront, contest or collaborate their own values, attitudes and experiences within the museum, thus making their boundaries explicit. Bhabha writes that it is by:

> focusing on those moments or processes that are produced in the articulation of cultural differences [that] provide the terrain for elaborating strategies of self-hood that initiate new signs of identity and innovative sites of collaboration, and contestation, in the act of defining the idea of society itself.
>
> (Bhabha 1994: 10)

The museum exhibition as a dramatic production can provide such moments.

The role of museum staff is central to the visitor meaning-making process. Those who work on exhibitions should acknowledge and celebrate the differences presented by visitors rather than retreat from them. A curator does not have to 'be one to know one' (Fay 1996: 9). All museum staff, from whatever background, can still speak about, and to, the experiences of racism, sexism and class discrimination in a way that mobilises rather than destroys mutual hopes for the future. The curator can distinguish knowing from being. Knowing an experience means being able to say what it is. Those who work in a museum can interpret the experience through a process of understanding, rather than necessarily having the experience themselves.

This new pedagogy shifts the knowledge/power relationship away from the limited emphasis on transfer of knowledge towards the strategic issue of engaging with the ways in which knowledge can be reconfigured in the minds of the visitors. Ideally, visitors should be offered scripts that both affirm and interrogate the complexity of their identities, and enable them to use, refine and enhance their interpretive strategies.

Giroux writes that:

> A new pedagogy is more than simply opening up diverse cultural narratives and spaces to visitors, it means understanding how the multi-layered and often contradictory voices and experiences intermingle with the weight of particular histories that will not fit easily into the master narrative of a single culture. The value of the museum is its fragmented character, which can enable the reading of many stories and narratives, even previously unknown ones. Museums and those who work in them should be seen as sites for both critical analysis and as a potential source of experimentation, creativity and possibility.
>
> (Giroux 1992: 80)

If museum staff recognise and use the relationship between knowledge and power they will create an environment that will allow the voices of visitors to be heard. Visitors will thus create new meanings within a framework of explicit values. It is in the creation of a meaningful ritual that visitors make connections with their own experience and are willing to make an investment in the display – that is taking time to make meaning and to create knowledge. This is akin to the flow experience, which has been described by Csikszentmihalyi, where the challenge of the task is appropriate to the knowledge and skills of the visitor, neither too difficult (which leads to anxiety) nor too easy (which leads to boredom) and a high degree of unselfconsciously concentrated engagement becomes possible (Csikszentmihalyi and Kermanson 1995). Emotional investment in the display is essential for the creation of meaning. The museum task is to create displays which enable the visitor to engage critically with the meanings on display, examine their context and create new meaning.

A new museum pedagogy based on the perspective of human beings making meaning as a process of enacting their identity will open up the possibility for incorporating into the museum cultural and social practices that no longer need to be mapped or referenced solely on the basis of the dominant models of Western culture. Visitors will be encouraged to cross ideological and political boundaries as a way of furthering the limits of their own understanding in a setting that is pedagogically safe and socially nurturing rather than being authoritarian or infused with an over-literal political correctness.

Giroux also argues that:

> Pedagogy is about the intellectual and emotional and ethical investments we make as part of our attempt to negotiate, accommodate and transform the world in which we find ourselves. The purpose and vision that drives such a pedagogy must be based on a politics and view of authority that links teaching and learning to forms of self and social empowerment that argue for forms of community life that extend the principles of liberty, equality, justice and freedom to the widest possible set of institutional and lived relations.
>
> (Giroux 1992: 81)

Raising awareness among museum staff of the potential and the nature of the meaning-making process that they share with each other and with visitors is key to the successful application of this model. This will require the museum team to articulate their own meaning(s), acknowledging and exploiting the ritual they are constructing by using the objects in space with the technologies of text, lighting, audio and visual elements. If they imagine, study and empathise with all their audiences, including those unfamiliar with the museum persona, and focus on enabling the visitor experience – cognitive, physical, psychological, emotional and spiritual – they will design exhibitions which encourage visitors to grow and become enriched through their encounters with the objects. Thus they will enable responses and meaning-making from a wide range of visitors.

This new model, providing as it does a theoretical understanding of the museum experience, has the potential to support the development of a new museum pedagogy which could, in turn, make a real difference in people's lives.

## Note

1  AAM 2001.

# Bibliography

ALVA (2005) 'Visits made in 2005 to visitor attractions in membership of the Association of Leading Visitor Attractions (ALVA)'. Online. Available at: www.alva.org.uk/visitor_statistics (accessed 19 November 2006).

Bhabha, H. K. (1994) *The Location of Culture*, London: Routledge.

Borun, M., Dritsas, J., Johnson, J., Peter, N., Wagner, K., Jangaard, A., Stroup, E. and Wenger, A. (1998) *Family Learning in Museums: The PISEC Perspective*, Washington, DC: Association of Science-Technology Centers.

Bruner, J. (1996) *The Culture of Education*, Cambridge: Cambridge University Press.

Chaney, D. (1993) *Fictions of Collective Life: Public Drama in Late Modern Culture*, London: Routledge.

Csikszentmihalyi, M. and Kermanson, K. (1995) 'Intrinsic motivation in museums. What makes visitors want to learn?' *Museum News*, 74(3): 34–7.

Dewey, J. (1938) *Experience and Education*, New York: Kappa, Delta, Pi.

Duncan, C. (1995) *Civilising Rituals*, London: Routledge.

Durbin, G. (ed.) (1996) *Developing Museum Exhibitions for Lifelong Learning*, London: The Stationery Office.

Falk, J. H. and Dierking, L. D. (2000) *Learning from Museums*, Walnut Creek, CA: AltaMira Press.

Fay, B. (1996) *Contemporary Philosophy of Social Science*, Oxford: Blackwell.

Fraser, J. W. (2005) *Museums – Drama, Ritual and Power*, unpublished dissertation, University of Leicester.

Giroux, H. A. (1992) *Border Crossings*, New York: Routledge.

Hooper-Greenhill, E. (2000) *Museums and the Interpretation of Visual Culture*, London: Routledge.

—— (ed.) (2001) *Visitors Interpretive Strategies at Wolverhampton Art Galley*, Leicester: Leicester Research Centre for Museums and Galleries.

Lampost index (2006) Library, Archives, Museums and Publishing, Statistical Tables, Loughborough University:

    'Breakdown of museum visitors by social grade 2004'

    'Museum visits 2003–4'

    'Museum visitors 2004/2005'

    'Museum visitors age profile 2003–4'

    'Museums reasons for visiting 2004'

Online. Available at: www.lboro.ac.uk/departments/dils/lisu/lampost.html (accessed 19 November 2006).

MORI (2001) *Renaissance in the Regions – A New Vision for England's Museums*, London: Resource, The Council for Museums, Archives and Libraries (now MLA).

Serrell, B. (1999) *Paying Attention: Visitors and Museum Exhibits*, Washington, DC: American Association of Museums.

Silverman, L. (1990) *Of Us and Other Things: The Content and Functions of Talk by Adult Visitor Pairs in an Art and History Museum*, unpublished dissertation, University of Pennsylvania.

—— (1995) 'Visitor meaning making for a new age', *Curator*, 38(3): 161–70.

Stiglitz, J. (2002) *Globalization and its Discontents*, New York: Penguin.

Worts, D. (1994) 'Extending the frame: forging a new partnership with the public', in Pearce, S. (ed.) *New Research in Museum Studies 5*, London: Athlone Press: 168–81.

# 23

# CRITICAL MUSEUM PEDAGOGY AND EXHIBITION DEVELOPMENT

## A conceptual first step

*Margaret A. Lindauer*

In *The Educational Role of the Museum* Eileen Hooper-Greenhill states, 'The development of a critical museum pedagogy that uses existing good practice for democratic purposes is a major task for museums and galleries in the twenty-first century' (Hooper-Greenhill 1999: 4). I take her remark to be a reference to critical pedagogy – an educational philosophy initiated in the 1960s by Paulo Freire, which enacts particular teaching techniques for socially activist purposes (Freire 1995). Among the educational practices in which museums engage, the task of applying critical museum pedagogy to the development of educational exhibitions is particularly challenging insofar as critical pedagogy has been conceptualised historically as classroom practice that relies on the presence of a dynamic teacher acting as a democratic facilitator working towards social justice. Unlike classrooms, museum exhibitions typically teach without the benefit of full-time instructors responding to visitors' ideas. Thus, the objectives of critical pedagogy applied to exhibit development may diverge somewhat from the objectives of enacting critical pedagogy in a classroom context.

In this chapter I recount the origin of critical pedagogy and describes its compatibility with some aspects of new museum theory. Critical pedagogy is here distinguished from other educational philosophies represented in museum studies literature and professional museum practice. It then describes three central features of critical pedagogy, and acknowledges ways in which critical pedagogy has been critiqued among teachers who subscribe to its tenets but question some of its assumptions. The chapter concludes by offering a conceptual first step towards applying critical pedagogy to the development of an exhibition about the history of the tourist industry in the south western United States.

## The origins of critical pedagogy

The overarching social purpose of critical pedagogy is to engage in teaching and learning that redresses social inequities. Its deepest roots sprouted from the practices and politics of Paulo Freire, who, as a young boy in Brazil during the early twentieth-century economic depression, was jolted from a precarious middle-class lifestyle into poverty and felt the effects of acute hunger on his physiological ability to engage in the intellectual demands of learning (Shaull 1995). From that experience, he vowed to fight against endemic hunger. As a young adult, he came to recognise that endemic hunger is associated with entrenched poverty, which is sustained systemically – through a confluence of economic, social and political mechanisms of which many people are unaware, or uninformed or (in essence) unschooled. He therefore turned his attention to the field of education as an arena in which to combat entrenched poverty, teaching illiterate peasants not only how to 'read the word' but also to 'read the world' in which they had been subjugated, exploited and oppressed. Freire invoked the term '*conscienticizao*' (usually translated as 'conscientisation' or 'critical consciousness') to characterise the political objective of his teaching practice as one in which oppressed people come to understand the social mechanisms through which poverty is sustained and also become engaged in transforming those mechanisms (Freire 1995). As education theorist Henry Giroux explains, 'students can be educated to take their places in society from a position of empowerment rather than from a position of ideological and economic subordination' by analysing and resisting ways in which they have been exploited consumers of socially constructed representations (Giroux 1986: 49). In other words, freedom from subjugation begins with the recognition that one's place in a social structure is constructed. From that recognition, a flame of resistance might be ignited, potentially fuelling the strategic desire to change that structure, even if in small or incremental ways.

Freire's teaching method, which had been widely adopted in literacy campaigns throughout north eastern Brazil, was perceived as enough of a threat to social order that he was jailed shortly after the military coup in 1964 and then essentially exiled from his country. He continued working on literacy programmes in other countries and began publishing articles and books about his philosophy and methods. While he did not use the term 'critical pedagogy', he explained the relationship of critical theory to his pedagogical principles. Critical theory recognises schooling to be a mechanism that maintains inequities, as students of different socio-economic classes have been 'tracked' differently from one another, not in overtly socio-economic terms but rather in terms of skills and achievement. This tracking, generally speaking, has resulted in students of lower socio-economic status becoming 'schooled' to fill low-skilled, low-paying jobs while students of middle and upper socio-economic status are 'schooled' to embark on professional, managerial, entrepreneurial and executive careers (Willis 1981). Readers of Freire's articles and books recognised that his teaching principles and methods were applicable to a wide range of educational contexts beyond rural peasant communities of Brazil. Insofar as formal schooling is but one social institution that historically has sustained social inequities, it is also but one arena in which people may engage in critical pedagogy.

## Connecting critical pedagogy to new museum theory

During the late twentieth century – at the same time that teachers and education theorists were contributing to professional literature about critical pedagogy – museum professionals and scholars contributed to the development of new museum theory, which posed questions regarding what, how and in whose interests knowledge is produced and disseminated in museums. (Following Janet Marstine (2006), I use the term 'new museum theory' as a synonym for 'new museology' and 'critical museum theory'.) A number of exhibition critiques, historical analyses and sociological studies cast modernist museums in disparaging light, characterising them as authoritative, elitist, exclusionary and conservative (Marstine

2006). Each of these qualities is intimately entwined with the others. A museum's authoritative quality, generally speaking, could be manifested in either a positive or negative sense. In a positive sense, the museum is a respected institution that can be trusted to present factual information that has been well-documented and is widely shared among experts in a given field. In a negative sense, its authority can be patronising and/or paternalistic if an authoritarian curatorial voice presumes to deliver a singularly correct interpretation of artworks or artefacts on behalf of a so-called general public assumed to be in need of proper edification. Looking back to the late nineteenth-century proliferation of museum development, Tony Bennett has argued that museums historically provided a means through which immigrants and members of the working-class 'might learn, by imitation, the appropriate forms of dress and comportment exhibited by their social superiors' and thereby might 'progressively modify their thoughts, feelings and behavior' (Bennett 1995: 24–8). In this sense, museums have been accused of being exclusionary; while people from all walks of life have been invited (indeed encouraged) to attend, only some people's histories and cultures have been celebrated. For example, natural history museums historically cast Anglo-Saxon cultures as teleologically more advanced than other cultures, while history museums typically commemorated the achievements of government and business leaders, usually upper-class white men. At the same time, art museums have celebrated the artistic genius of men, while allowing token representation of work by women artists. Thus, while everyone is welcome to walk through the museums' doors, the kinds of histories, truths and values celebrated and enacted in museum exhibitions have surreptitiously enforced exclusionary distinctions. Insofar as these histories, truths and values instil and are instilled by tradition, museums are conservative. And because museums are trusted authoritative institutions, the programmes they produce may be perceived to provide factual information rather than a vehicle for sustaining socially constructed cultural myths and values.

Exhibition critiques and historical analyses published during the late twentieth century instilled a heightened sensitivity towards the complexities of representation, especially in terms of how exhibitions are inscribed with implicit (often unintended) messages about race, gender, class and other aspects of identity. The development of new museum theory inspired visions for postmodern and postcolonial practice, as well as an institutional model for which Hooper-Greenhill has coined the term 'post-museum' (Hooper-Greenhill 2000). Exhibitions in the post-museum would be discursive, in the sense of fostering debate or generating conversation. Furthermore, a post-museum would be more democratic than the modernist museum, inviting community members to contribute to decisions about what histories will be told and the polysemic ways in which artworks and artefacts can be interpreted. Museums would thereby become inclusive, as people contribute opinions shaped by diverse life experiences associated with (though not determined by) being a person of a certain race, class, ethnicity, gender, physical ability, sexual identity and/or religion. Understanding ways in which people experience the world differently from one another ideally improves social relations; the museum thus becomes a progressive institution, in the sense of becoming a site for combating prejudice and nurturing appreciation of cultural diversity.

This distinction between what the modernist museum *has* been and what the post-museum *could* be (or *should* be) paints a useful, albeit oversimplified, picture of divergent models. It is oversimplified in the sense that museums are not monolithic institutions that stay locked in step with one another. A combination of modernist qualities (authoritative, elitist, exclusive and conservative) and post-museum qualities (discursive, democratic, inclusive and progressive) can probably be found in many museums at the turn of the twenty-first century. Nonetheless, the binary construct of modernist/post-museum is useful insofar as it compels museum professionals to examine the political implications of their practices. No exhibition, indeed no institution, can present everything there is to know. Choices are always made, even if tacitly, regarding what, how and in whose interests knowledge will be produced and disseminated. In this sense, all exhibitions enact social relations of power; they are inherently political even if exhibition developers claim to engage in apolitical practice.

Of course, not all museum professionals share the same political agenda. Debates over the social purpose of museums permeate the history of the profession. For example, the dispute over the extent to which museums could or should explicitly engage in contemporary social issues was fuelled by a group of protestors who disrupted the opening session of the 1970 American Association of Museums annual conference. Carrying picket signs that read 'Strike Against Racism, Sexism, War and Repression', they demanded that the conference focus on increasing direct action with which museums would fight for civil rights and USA military withdrawal from the Vietnam War. Reflecting on the event over 25 years later, Stephen Weil, former scholar at the Center for Museum Studies, Smithsonian Institution, recounted, 'Most of us then and still today would [agree] . . . Museums cannot . . . be the agents of such sweeping dramatic change, that they could single-handedly stop a war, end injustice, or cure inequality' (Weil 1996: 65). Weil certainly was correct in stating that museums could not *single-handedly* redress social issues, though a number of museums and museum professionals remain committed to doing what they can, thereby tacitly endorsing the overarching objective of critical pedagogy (Sandell 2002; Janes and Conaty 2005).

## Distinguishing critical pedagogy from other pedagogical models

At the same time that museum professionals subscribe to different overarching political agendas for their practice, they enact various educational models for exhibition development (Lindauer 2005). Among those models, one based on critical pedagogy has not yet been articulated in the museum studies literature. For example, in his book entitled *Learning in the Museum*, George Hein characterises learning theories in terms of a continuum with one end marked by a transmission-absorption model of learning and the other end marked by a constructivist model (Hein 1998). He places various pedagogies along that spectrum, characterising constructivism as both a learning theory and a teaching method/philosophy. His spectrum is not wide enough to include critical pedagogy, which overlaps with and resides to the political left of what he characterises as constructivist pedagogy.

Constructivist and critical pedagogies share an opposition to the transmission-absorption model and a commitment to problem-posing teaching methods, but they differ from one another in terms of the overarching social purpose of education. The transmission-absorption model, which Freire characterised as a 'banking' approach to teaching, casts learners as empty vessels that become filled with prescribed knowledge didactically delivered by teachers. A transmission-absorption teaching model corresponds to a behaviorist learning theory for how the human brain acquires new knowledge through a process of trial and error. If the learner does not successfully absorb knowledge on its initial transmission, the teacher delivers a subsequent transmission. Through trial and error, knowledge is eventually achieved.

Constructivist pedagogy enacts generative teaching methods, casting learners as active participants in problem-solving activities. Generative teaching methods correspond to constructivist learning theory, which asserts that learning occurs as people actively participate in new experiences and build on previous experiences to construct new knowledge, or 'make meaning'. The teacher's role is to provide an engaging environment and pose provocative questions with which to explore ideas, study objects and draw interpretations, explanations or conclusions. The overarching social purpose of constructivist pedagogy is to help learners develop useful and/or valued skills, e.g. reading, building a robot, writing software, appreciating artworks, speaking a second language, designing a bridge, etc. The list is infinite, though a twofold rationale is constant: insofar as generative teaching methods are most educationally effective (given the ways in which the human brain builds knowledge), they also are more humane than transmission-absorption methods.

Critical pedagogy enacts transformative teaching methods. Like generative teaching methods, it casts learners as active participants and is structured around posing questions. It is distinct from generative teaching methods in terms of *what* knowledge is taught and *for what purpose* knowledge is constructed. Whereas generative teaching methods are designed to help learners construct knowledge that enables them to participate variously in different professional and cultural contexts, transformative teaching methods are designed to help learners understand knowledge as 'cultural capital', identify the uneven distribution of cultural capital and redress the social consequences of uneven distribution. For example, as the critical pedagogy dictum 'read the word and read the world' implies, transformative teaching methods pose questions that might focus on identifying ways in which a modernist museum celebration of a town's history inadvertently inscribes a hidden curriculum of prejudice: a story about men who cleared the land, built new buildings and established a sustained system of governance also 'celebrates' the displacement of native people and sustains a portrait of 'ideal' leader as a strong, able-bodied, heterosexual white man whose wife tends to home, family and charity. Critical pedagogy focuses on identifying cultural myths and reflecting critically on ways in which they pervade the histories we celebrate, the stories we tell, the policies we enact, the laws we pass and the punishments we deliver. The purpose of identifying the dissemination of prejudicial 'ideals' is to become equipped to conscientiously transform exploitative social relations, as well as to guard against unknowingly perpetuating prejudicial cultural myths. The *particular* ways in which this might be accomplished will vary among educational settings; however, three *general* features of critical pedagogy collectively provide an armature that conceivably is transportable from one context to another.

## Three central features of critical pedagogy

Inspired by Freire, a generation of classroom teachers dedicated to the tenets of critical pedagogy addressed the very questions posed by new museum theory: what, how and in whose interests will knowledge be produced and disseminated? In response to the question of *what* knowledge will be disseminated, critical pedagogy prescribes 'critical content'. In response to questions of *how* knowledge will be produced, it endorses 'progressive pedagogical principles' and 'emancipatory authority'. These three general features, as explained below, are interrelated; critical content becomes transformative when it is experienced according to progressive pedagogical principles and within the context of emancipatory authority. When the three features are enacted simultaneously, critical pedagogy theoretically educates learners to actualise social justice, thereby addressing the question of whose interests will be served (Gore 1993). As Gore (1993) notes, not all proponents of critical pedagogy share the same vocabulary to name the central features of critical pedagogy. They do, however, agree on the gist and interrelationship of the terms as Gore describes them.

In advance of describing each of these features and their interrelationships, it is important to add a word of caution: what appears to be a formulaic approach [*critical content + progressive pedagogical principles + emancipatory authority = educating for social justice*] risks misrepresentation of the complex means through which historically entrenched social inequities persist. In fact, some of the critical pedagogy literature refers explicitly to Marxist philosopher Antonio Gramsci's theory of hegemony, which describes how dominant groups govern without imposing overt force but rather by securing consent from subordinate groups to abide by social-cultural practices that implicitly sustain the authority of a dominant group (Gramsci 1971). In other words, discrimination and exploitation are not always recognised as such, and they may in fact be most powerful when perceived as educational programmes designed to empower victims of subjugation.

Education theorists Stanley Aronowitz and Henry Giroux characterise curricula in terms of different kinds of intellectual discourse: hegemonic, accommodating, critical and transformative (Aronowitz and Giroux 1993). Hegemonic intellectual discourse, which is paradigmatic of the modernist museum, unabashedly recounts histories and celebrates values that preserve the dominance of a particular culture or group, whereas accommodating intellectual discourse appears to diverge from, though surreptitiously sustains, those values. For example, a museum exhibition that features multi-vocality (presenting perspectives of people who have historically been marginalised in museum representation) may appear to redress historical inequity in museum representations. However, if that exhibition invokes multiple perspectives while recounting the histories and values paradigmatic of a modernist exhibition, it upholds myths of a dominant culture. Such was the case in a 1997 exhibition at the Heard Museum, in Phoenix, Arizona, entitled *Inventing the Southwest: The Fred Harvey Company and Native American Art*.

The exhibition title, *Inventing the Southwest*, alluded to post-structural analyses of how knowledge is constructed (analyses that are central to new museum theory), but the exhibition text celebrated a quintessentially Anglo-American rags-to-riches narrative about an immigrant-turned-entrepreneur. Fred Harvey established a foodservice company on the Santa Fe Railway in the late-nineteenth century. By the early-twentieth century, his company had expanded into a multifaceted corporation that managed distinctive hotels, opened souvenir shops and choreographed tourist experiences at the Grand Canyon and throughout Arizona and New Mexico. The company played a pivotal role in the cross-cultural representation of Native Americans to Euro-Americans and western Europeans, and it fuelled production of Native American art, as it became the major supplier of American Indian baskets, pottery, jewellery and textiles to individual collectors, tourists and museums across North America and Western Europe.

Many of the written text panels in the exhibition recounted the circumstances and historical context of Harvey's successes. For example, one text panel stated, 'As the Harvey Company prospered, it bought and sold vast quantities of art prized by travelers, not only as mementos of their trip, but also as home décor popularized during the Arts and Crafts movement'. The active subject here is the white male protagonist with entrepreneurial savvy, and the text is an example of hegemonic discourse insofar as it alludes to a potent cultural myth about America as the land of opportunity where individuals who work hard can climb the socio-economic ladder of success. A subsequent text panel quoted the words of Anita Abieta, a community member of Isleta Pueblo, who said,

> There was a depot here, and the train used to stop. We would sell fruit, potteries and whatever souvenirs we had. Sometimes people would get out of the train and sometimes they wouldn't, and so we would go from one box to another. It helped the people of the Pueblo.

Here the text enacts the post-museum quality of inclusivity, but it invokes the voice of the other to cast the white male protagonist in complimentary light. This particular instance of inclusivity does not challenge, or even relativise, the dominance of Western cultural values, which is what makes it an example of accommodating intellectual discourse.

Among the four kinds of intellectual discourse that Aronowitz and Giroux describe, neither hegemonic nor accommodating intellectual discourses are compatible with critical pedagogy. Critical intellectual discourse, in their words, is 'ideologically alternative to existing modes of thought but not actively engaged in redressing social inequality and injustice' (Aronowitz and Giroux 1993: 47). It is more closely aligned with critical pedagogy than accommodating intellectual discourse, but it does not exemplify the content that critical pedagogy prescribes. For example, critical intellectual discourse might accompany a photograph of Fred Harvey and his business partner in the manner set out in Figure 23.1.

This hypothetical photo-caption offers factual information that disrupts uncritical celebration of Anglo-American myth by alluding to historic victimisation of Native Americans. However, it also casts American Indians as *merely* victims rather than as people who have resisted domination, continue to enact their own cultural values and, at the turn of the

While native people were pushed to ever more remote and inhospitable regions, Euro-Americans amassed hundreds, then thousands, then millions of Indian artifacts.

*Figure 23.1* Critical intellectual discourse might accompany a photograph of Fred Harvey and his business partner.

Photo: Special collections, University of Arizona Library, AZ 326, Box 11, Folder 3, N-12062.

twenty-first century, are gaining strategic power in cross-cultural political negotiations over natural resources, sovereignty and appropriation of sacred material culture. Thus, critical intellectual discourse does not directly challenge historically entrenched social hierarchies; it just makes us feel badly about them. In that sense, it does not adequately redress social injustice. According to Aronowitz and Giroux, only transformative intellectual discourse offers such potential. In their words, it 'connects a struggle for meaning' with a struggle over power relations, explicitly making 'the pedagogical more political and the political more pedagogical' (Aronowitz and Giroux 1993: 46). Distinguishing it from critical intellectual discourse relies on other central features of critical pedagogy – progressive pedagogical principles and emancipatory authority.

Progressive pedagogical principles, the foundation on which problem-posing teaching methods developed, become transformative when they enact what Ira Shor and Paulo Freire call 'liberatory praxis' – the word 'praxis' referring to practice that is deliberately, conscientiously informed by theory, and 'liberatory praxis' being the antithesis of authoritarian practice (Shor and Freire 1987). In addition to providing a catalyst for dialogue, conversation or debate, liberatory praxis reflects a conviction that, when the educational objective is to 'read the world', learners potentially contribute just as much to the production of knowledge as teachers do. The point is not merely to pose questions and/or generate multiple interpretations but rather to exchange stories, ideas, questions and information, through which teachers and learners alike gain new understanding of the different ways in which people variously experience a socially and culturally diverse world.

Critical pedagogy does not, however, call for teachers to relinquish their expertise. Indeed, it respects authoritative knowledge as long as that authority is delivered in a way that fosters emancipation from domination and subjugation. As education theorist Peter McLaren explains, emancipatory authority invokes both a language of critique and a language of hope (McLaren 1998). A language of critique involves identifying, analysing and deconstructing hierarchical social relations while also recognising (although not resigning oneself to) one's place in historically entrenched hierarchical structures of power. A language of hope involves fuelling a strategic desire to change those structures, and it involves understanding how people actively construct their identities and social relations through signs, signifiers, images and discourses.

The significance of emancipatory authority is perhaps best illustrated in a counter-example. The 1991 exhibition at the Smithsonian's National Museum of American Art (now called the Smithsonian American Art Museum) entitled *The West As America: Reinterpreting Images of the American Frontier, 1820–1920* was notoriously controversial as it presented revisionist art historical interpretations of iconic paintings. For example, Frederick Remington's 1903 painting *Fight for the Waterhole* was described as an image of cowboys in the west defending their claim on natural resources. The accompanying object label explained that the image resonated with white viewers in the industrialised cities of the eastern United States who were unsettled by immigrant labourers on strike for better working conditions and higher pay. The critical content was accompanied by a quote from the artist, who said, 'Jews, injuns, chinamen, Italians, Huns, the rubbish of the earth I hate' (Wood 2004). The interpretative label, intended to represent new critical scholarship, ultimately denigrated a previously celebrated national artist and tainted the cultural myths of the nation's history with which the artist had been associated. Some text panels posed questions, but they were largely rhetorical and supported the curatorial thesis that 'artworks were carefully staged fictions, constructed from both supposition and fact in order to justify the hardship and conflict of westward expansion' (Dubin 1999: 172). The debate fuelled by the exhibition compelled politicians and newspaper columnists to harden their staunchly held belief that the national museum ought to celebrate nationhood. However, even visitors who appreciated the curators' methodological approach commented that the exhibit text had a patronising tone, asserting hierarchical expert authority over visitors' presumed lack of knowledge (Wallach 1994). After members of Congress threatened to eliminate federal funding for the Smithsonian and plans for the exhibition to travel to other museums were cancelled, art historian Alan Trachtenburg noted, 'what was missing from the exhibit was the effort to construct a different way of thinking about the nation' (Trachtenburg 1991: 121). In other words, *The West As America* offered critical content but did not inscribe transformative intellectual discourse because it lacked a language of hope.

## Critical pedagogy and exhibition development

With my admittedly brief description of critical pedagogy I return to the question: what would critical pedagogy applied to exhibit development look like? However, before attempting an answer, it is essential to acknowledge critiques of critical pedagogy by classroom teachers who subscribe to its philosophy but have found that enacting its features does not necessarily generate the intended results. These teachers discovered that it is not possible to control what, how and in whose interests knowledge is produced, in part because the prescribed progressive pedagogical principles require the not-yet-achieved outcomes that critical pedagogy portends. Teachers and learners cannot engage in a non-hierarchical debate because an already existing social order cannot be left willy-nilly outside the classroom (Ellsworth 1989). Such observations did not cause teachers to abandon critical pedagogy but rather to proceed with cautious humility and to articulate a 'post-structural critical pedagogy', which resists the tendency to rely on 'expert' knowledge, does not claim to know what social justice looks like and recognises that we always operate in a field of power/ knowledge even as we attempt to disrupt it (Biesta 1998).

Each of these points should be borne in mind as we turn back to the history of the Fred Harvey Company to make a conceptual first step toward applying critical pedagogy to exhibition development. In response to Biesta's advice to resist the tendency to rely on expert knowledge, it is wisest not to set out to answer the 'who, what, why, where, when and how' questions that, according to visitor studies, people like an exhibit to answer. I would consider photo captions that throw the reader slightly off balance, perpetually displacing the locus of authority and gently suggesting that knowledge of the past is always incomplete (Figure 23.2).

A complete absence of explanatory text cannot really be sanctioned, but when captions are didactic, they should disrupt Anglo-American myths that sustain cultural domination. For example, some histories of the early twentieth-century renaissance of Native American art inscribe what cultural theorist Ann McClintock calls 'male birthing stories' (McClintock 1995). In these stories a beneficent Euro-American entrepreneur (usually a man) is heralded for 'teaching' Native American artisans about their cultural histories (which ironically were presumed to have been forgotten as a result of Euro-American expansionism), 'instructing' them to re-establish lost material culture traditions while also 'helping' them to tailor their production for a tourist market. Entrepreneurs, including Fred Harvey, have been accorded active agency while makers are presumed to have passively followed instructions from a market expert regarding specific sizes, selected colours or particular design motifs. McClintock's

You may not remember something that is remembering you.

*Figure 23.2* Photo captions can be used to throw the reader slightly off balance, perpetually displacing the locus of authority and gently suggesting that knowledge of the past is always incomplete.

Photo: Courtesy of the Heard Museum, Phoenix, AZ.

aptly paradoxical term 'male birthing' expresses scepticism toward the particular nature of these relationships while also acknowledging that paternalistic social relations did indeed develop between merchant and producer. In the same way that it is difficult to fathom the biological possibility of male birthing, it is hard to believe that native peoples played a thoroughly passive role in the hand production of their goods. In fact, anthropologist Kathleen M'Closkey has demonstrated that one such trader could not possibly have exerted the degree of design direction that he claimed to have wielded (M'Closkey 1994). Thus, the male birthing tale can be told differently to accord the producers some agency (Figure 23.3).

As Biesta cautioned against claiming to know what social justice looks like, she coined the term 'emancipatory ignorance' to refer to teaching that 'does not show the way . . . [or] say what to think' but implicitly inquires, 'What do you think?' (Biesta 1998: 505). It seems to me that, in an exhibition about the Fred Harvey Company, ignorance cannot be emancipatory unless it is recognised to be equally shared. Thus, photo captions would address an ambiguous 'you', as both viewer and depicted subject(s) (Figure 23.4).

Finally, as it must be acknowledged that an author cannot work outside a field of power/knowledge (e.g. I bring a certain 'expert' knowledge, acquired through relative privilege, to this endeavour), it would be disingenuous to demonise power or to deny asymmetrical cross-cultural relations. However, readers' attention should be drawn to various ways in which people participate in fields of power/knowledge. The phrase 'power/knowledge', as Gayatri

Native arts and crafts people produce tourist art that reflects careful anthropological study of Euro-American tastes and shopping habits.

*Figure 23.3* The male birthing tale can be told differently to accord the producers some agency.
Photo: National Anthropological Archives, Smithsonian Institution (02331803).

Your way of doing things is not neutral.

*Figure 23.4* Photo captions would address an ambiguous 'you', as both viewer and depicted subject(s).

Photo: Courtesy of the Heard Museum, Phoenix, AZ.

Spivak explains, is better characterised in the French *pouvoir/savoir*, translated as something like 'to be able to know' and referring to ways in which ways of knowing constitute 'ways of doing and not doing' (Spivak 1993: 37). My initial conceptual step toward applying critical pedagogy to exhibition development feels like it falls short of being transformative intellectual discourse. At this point, I do not claim to know that an exhibition can disrupt prejudicial cultural ideals, exploitative stereotypes or oppressive histories. However, I do know that exploring the history, features and critiques of critical pedagogy can unsettle and invigorate one's sense of doing (and/or not doing) theoretically informed museum practice.

## Bibliography

Aronowitz S. and Giroux, H. (1993) *Education Still Under Siege*, Westport, CT: Bergin and Garvey.

Bennett, T. (1995) *The Birth of the Museum: History, Theory, Politics*, London: Routledge.

Biesta, G. (1998) 'Say you want a revolution . . . : suggestions for the impossible future of critical pedagogy', *Educational Theory*, 48(4): 499–510.

Dubin, S. C. (1999) *Displays of Power: Controversy in the American Museum from the 'Enola Gay' to 'Sensation'*, New York: New York University Press.

Ellsworth, E. (1989) 'Why doesn't this feel empowering? Working through the repressive myths of critical pedagogy', *Harvard Educational Review*, 59(3): 297–324.

Freire, P. (1995 [1970]) *Pedagogy of the Oppressed*, New York: The Continuum Company.

Giroux, H. (1986) 'Radical pedagogy and the politics of student voice', *Interchange*, 17(1): 48–69.

Gore, J. (1993) *The Struggle for Pedagogies: Critical and Feminist Discourses as Regimes of Truth*, New York: Routledge.

Gramsci, A. (1971) *Selections from the Prison Notebooks*, New York: International Publishers.

Hein, G. (1998) *Learning in the Museum*, London: Routledge.

Hooper-Greenhill, E. (1999) *The Educational Role of the Museum*, London: Routledge.

—— (2000) *Museums and the Interpretation of Visual Culture*, London: Routledge.

Janes, R. J. and Conaty, G. T. (eds) (2005) *Looking Reality in the Eye: Museums and Social Responsibility*, Calgary: University of Calgary Press.

Lindauer, M. (2005) 'From salad bars to vivid stories: four models for developing "educationally successful" exhibitions', *Museum Management and Curatorship*, 20: 41–55.

McClintock, A. (1995) *Imperial Leather: Race, Gender and Sexuality in the Colonial Conquest*, New York: Routledge.

McLaren, P. (1998) 'Revolutionary pedagogy in post-revolutionary times: rethinking the political economy of critical education', *Educational Theory*, 48(4): 431–62.

Marstine, J. (2006) *New Museum Theory and Practice: An Introduction*, Malden, MA: Blackwell Publishing.

M'Closkey, K. (1994) 'Marketing multiple myths: the hidden history of Navajo weaving', *Journal of the Southwest*, 36(3): 185–220.

Sandell, R. (ed.) (2002) *Museums, Society, Inequality*, New York: Routledge.

Shaull, R. (1995) 'Foreword' to P. Freire, *Pedagogy of the Oppressed*, New York: The Continuum Company: 11–16.

Shor, I. and Freire, P. (1987) 'What is the "dialogical method" of teaching?' *Journal of Education*, 169(3): 11–31.

Spivak, G. C. (1993) *Outside in the Teaching Machine*, New York: Routledge.

Trachtenburg, A. (1991) 'Contesting the West', *Art in America*, 79(9): 118–23, 152.

Wallach, A. (1994) 'The battle over "The West as America" 1991', in M. Pointon (ed.) *Art Apart: Art Institutions and Ideology Across England and North America*, Manchester: Manchester University Press: 89–101.

Weil, S. E. (1996) 'The distinctive numerator', *Museum News*, 75(2): 64–65.

Willis, P. E. (1981) *Learning to Labour: How Working Class Kids Get Working Class Jobs*, New York: Columbia University Press.

Wood, M. (2004) 'The West as America: reinterpreting images of the frontier, 1820–1920'. Online. Available at: www.people.virginia.edu/~mmw3v.html (accessed 20 June 2006).

# 24

# LEARNING AT THE
# MUSEUM FRONTIERS

## Democracy, identity and difference

### Viv Golding

This chapter contends that the museum frontiers – museums acting in partnership – are ideally placed to promote learning that involves recognition of complex layering of ideas: difference *and* similarity, between *and* within communities, at a local *and* a global level. To explore this concept the chapter draws on Black[1] theoretical perspectives and applies them to case studies in the Horniman Museum, London. The case study examples[2] focus on collection-based themed projects with school groups including underachieving pupils in danger of disaffection. Overall it is argued that negative media portrayals of 'Other' cultures and peoples as starving and 'primitive' have a detrimental effect on the self-esteem, motivation and academic attainment of all pupils (both Black and white), which frontier project-work can counter by providing a vital reflexive space; where dialogical exchange can replace stereotypical and prejudiced views with greater intercultural understanding. In this way museums benefit all members of Britain's plural, multicultural society by developing a new collaborative praxis.

Audre Lorde, speaking of difference as a creative interconnection between the individual and her community identities, states:

> *Difference* must not be merely tolerated, but seen as *a fund of necessary polarities between which our creativity can spark* like a dialectic. . . . Within the interdependence of mutual (non-dominant) differences lies that security which enables us to descend into the chaos of knowledge and return with *truer visions of our future*, along with the concomitant power to *effect those changes* which can bring that future into being. *Difference is that raw and powerful connection from which our personal power is forged.* . . . Without *community* there is no *liberation*, only the most vulnerable and temporary armistice between an *individual* and her oppression. But community must not be a shedding of our differences, not the pathetic pretense that these differences do not exist.
>
> (Audre Lorde 1996: 159, emphasis added)

What is vital to the definition of difference and identity here is Lorde's emphasis on the power of creativity to promote non-dominant *connection* within and through difference, which permits learning and understanding of similarity. In short, Lorde takes a *both and*

315

profoundly anti-essentialist stance to the concepts of difference and identity. The notion of 'pure' origins with impermeable boundaries hinders human connection and it is, Lorde contends, only through forging new alliances: between Black and white, man and woman, lesbian and straight that an effective challenge to discrimination, prejudice and stereotype can be mounted (Audre Lorde 1996).

Audre Lorde's writing, which is poetic, theoretical and, crucially, political, has been important for developing feminist-hermeneutic dialogue and progressing 'thick democracy' at the museum frontiers (Golding 2004a, 2004b, 2006a, 2006b, 2008; Apple 2003: 12).[3] This notion is distinct from the association of democracy with the Western system of power, whose ultimate aim often appears to be to extend the market-place of consumers within twenty-first-century capitalism, rather than raise new voices. The Western notion of democracy arose from a brief period of history – fifth century Athens – importantly characterised by freedom of expression, communal decision-making, sovereignty of the law and equality before it. Yet democracy was narrowly defined for 'citizens' of the nation state – including only those born of Athenian parents – excluding women and slaves. In the context of the museum frontiers the concept of 'thick democracy' is more concerned with the raising of new voices in a critical dialogue to promote the rule or power and 'strength of the people' (COED 1976: 272). Precisely defined: 'government by all the people, direct or representative; form of society ignoring hereditary class distinctions and tolerating minority views . . . demos = the people + –cracy = "rule of, ruling body of, class influential by" . . . Greek Kratia = power (Kratos = strength)'(COED 1976: 237, 272). Briefly, thick democracy highlights a need to reconfigure notions of the rights and responsibilities of citizenship in a new context, one of a global political economy that transcends the nation state, yet is disassociated from military intervention in non-Western politics.

In this chapter a strong argument is made that language proficiency is crucial not only to all learning but to participation in democracy. An expanded view of language is presented vitally to include art as a powerful sign system for human communication with those who have learnt the necessary decoding/encoding tools. Overall, the need for museums and their educational partners to engage in dialogue with sensitivity and creativity is highlighted, for language and communication to progress community cohesion through 'shared values and common citizenship' in a plural, multicultural society (The Home Office 2001: 3).

Gloria Azuldua casts light on the way in which language can impact on identity in a negative sense, for people who speak English in addition to their mother tongue. Azuldua contends:

> So, if you want to really *hurt me, talk badly about my language. Ethnic identity is twin skin to linguistic identity* – I am my language. Until I can accept as legitimate Chicano Texas Spanish, Tex-Mex and all the other languages I speak, I cannot accept the legitimacy of myself . . . and as long as I have to accommodate . . . English speakers rather than having them accommodate me, my tongue will be illegitimate. I will no longer be made to feel ashamed of existing. I will have my voice: Indian, Spanish, White. I will have my serpent's tongue . . . *I will overcome the tradition of silence.*
>
> (Anzaldua 1987: 59, emphasis added)

Opening this chapter with the creative voices of two Black women marks a personal attempt to break the 'silence' or erasure of Black voices in the traditional museum discourse, imbued with eighteenth century, 'either-or', Enlightenment thought. It highlights a democratic faith in the powerful contribution twenty-first century museums might make in maintaining a democratic way of life, in establishing a new 'culture, which has a voice' and presents an optimistic view of learning 'in-*between*' locations, at the 'frontiers' of traditional disciplinary boundaries, and beyond the confines of institutional spaces (Freire 1972: 58; Philip 1992).

The frontier or borderland location outlined below has long been peopled by many 'community of communities', with ties both real and imaginary, to the UK *and* to other areas of the globe (Parekh 2002: preface; Anderson 1998). Specifically, this chapter considers a spatio-temporal site of collaborative effort between institutions – the museum, university and school – all geographically located in 'culturally rich' areas of south London that nevertheless, 25 years after the Brixton uprisings, still suffer from 'severe' levels of 'social deprivation' (Scarman 1981; Anon. 2004a; Anon. 2004b).

## Issue-based learning at the museum frontiers to develop critical thought

It is 'issue-based' active learning, to develop 'critical' thought in participants at these museum frontiers, which this chapter will outline (Freire 1996: 78). The author initiated the development of issue-based project work at the Horniman Museum Education Department, in collaboration with a self-selecting multi ethnic research team, of 25 local schoolteachers and their pupils, and the Postgraduate Certificate of Education (PGCE) Art Department of Goldsmiths College University of London in 1995 (Golding 2000). This issue-based project work was distinctive in addressing the broader historical and current socio-political issues affecting the pupils' lives outside the museum/school, within the context of the National Curriculum, especially Art, English, Information and Computer Technology (ICT) and Citizenship (QCA 2006a).

All collaboration centred on museum objects and focused on the creative arts to equip pupils with subject specific 'knowledge, understanding and skills' across the curriculum from Foundation level through to Key Stage 4 (QCA 2006b). A major pedagogical concern was to empower pupils and nurture 'informed and critical citizens . . . socially and morally responsible' to participate more fully in the democratic life of the school and beyond (QCA 2006b). To this end pupils were engaged in 'dialogical' exchange as active 'subjects', to construct new, unbiased interpretations, not only to empathise with and to celebrate a common humanity underpinning the diversity of world culture housed in the Horniman, but also to recognise the continuing importance of taking action to protect universal human rights and responsibilities and drawing attention to the tension between individual freedoms and the necessary constraints of the social group (Freire 1996: 64–7). This is a perspective, with its attention to globally shared values, which is rooted in the 'grand narratives' of modernism, for example, the discourses of Marx and Freud, with their huge universalising claims *and* the more 'postmodernist' aim of raising new voices or 'mini-narratives' at the local level.

In working to achieve this end the creative research partnerships placed world arts and culture at the *centre* of a multicultural-antiracist curriculum, drawing attention to the socio-political basis of what counts as knowledge and culture to de-center and subvert the assumption of cultural authority of 'one true' civilization, that of the Western world, by forming a series of mini-centres over an intensive six-year collaboration. The partnerships were not engaged in a series of tokenistic 'add-on' one-day events, 'saris, samosas and steel band' sessions during Black History Month, nor were they idealistic long-term schemes that simply set out to replace Black pupils' low levels of achievement in potentially high-earning skills such as literacy and numeracy with high achievement in less work-related skills such as Ghanaian drumming and dance, but rather ventures that might increase levels of motivation, enhance feelings of self-worth and ultimately achievement, through the sparking of imaginative effort (Klein 1997: 52–61).

While recognising their inevitable entanglement in webs of power, the team leaders made an effort to work non-hierarchically alongside other visiting artists, creative writers, storytellers, musicians and ICT specialists. Engaging in dialogue together, key objects from Horniman's exhibitions and an accompanying key theme or word was selected for the focus of project work, which would resonate with the lived experiences of pupils in each school group by connecting the personal, social and physical context of active and embodied learning – a holistic mind *and* body – in an essentially relational experience (Falk and Dierking 2000). Dialogue around the key object and key word also benefited from intensive work utilising original objects from around the world in the special Horniman handling collection (numbering more than 3,000 historical and contemporary items), which furthered learning connections by applying familiar concepts and usage to new objects of knowledge, in a movement from the 'known' to the 'unknown' (Falk and Dierking 2000). Handling such a variety of objects can uniquely promote a wide range of multi-sensory learning, appeal to diverse learning styles and develop the full range of students' multiple intelligences, which is necessary for pupil learning in general and specially important for pupils in danger of disaffection, as is demonstrated below with reference to a selection of object-based case studies (Cassells 2000; Gardner 2000, 2005).

## Nkisi: power and Kemnell Technical College

Minkisi (plural of nkisi) or power figures, traditionally made by unknown carvers and 'nganga' or ritual experts, from the Kongo people of central Africa are displayed in the Horniman Museum's *African Worlds* exhibition. The kingdom of Kongo, which was flourishing during the fifteenth century when diplomatic links were established with Europe, Portugal and Brazil, was undermined by the seventeenth century and the nation remains fragile today. One nkisi provided the key object that inspired a wealth of creative activity around the key theme of *power* from Year 9 pupils at Kemnell Technical College, a boy's school in Bromley, South London.

Tony Minnion and Jaqui Callis (Directors of the Cloth of Gold Arts Company), the Writer/Director Sola Oyelele and the author decided to use the concept of power, or more precisely transgressing established power structures, in an effort to work non-hierarchically as multiracial team-leaders at Kemnell. The power project was one of 16 collaborative museum/school projects, in which the team leaders were forcefully dedicated to challenging discrimination in general and racial prejudice in particular, but without lecturing in the traditional teaching manner. This was an especially important aim throughout the Kemnell work, with a majority white school group, academically 'underachieving', who had little personal contact with the wider multicultural society of inner London (Anon. 2006a).

Kemnell boys began their eight-week project with an introduction day at school that featured three distinct sessions. First, in the morning until break, Horniman handling objects from historical and contemporary Africa were utilised to develop the boys' multiple intelligences as part of discussion, reflection, music, dance and drama, and creative writing activities led by the writer/director Sola Oyelele. Specifically, the following intelligences were encouraged: naturalistic (recognising features of the natural world); musical (making and listening to music); spatial (using mental models of the spatial world); bodily kinesthetic (using the body to express ideas and emotions); linguistic (manipulating words and meanings); interpersonal (understanding other people's motivations and aspirations) and intrapersonal (using self-understanding to navigate the world) intelligence (Gardner 2000: 36). Next a period of computer research developed the boys' skills in ICT as well as their logical-mathematical (using logic, abstract models and theories) intelligence (ibid.). Then, after lunch, the boys spent the whole afternoon working on art activities led by the artist Tony Minnion, learning the skills of screen-printing and further developing the full range of their multiple intelligences in the construction of their first banner on the theme of power.

The introductory day prepared the boys for a visit to Horniman on the following day, where the current author's talk engaged the whole pupil group in a critical exploration of power with reference to the minkisi collection – museum fragments in the wider socio-political context of power structures. The boys' previous computer research revealed that minkisi were often referred to by the vague but always derogatory term 'nail fetish', even in otherwise scholarly circles, until the late twentieth century. In deconstructing the term 'fetish' at school the underlying discourse of historical prejudices, defining a white European 'self' against the 'savage', the absolute 'other', were uncovered and, at the museum, the roots of this inappropriate European term, with racial and political implications for the Kongo objects and practices, were further interrogated. This critical work of interpretation was progressed by the museum interpretation panels, constructed by a five-person African–British Anthropology Advisory Panel (AAP), which emphasised indigenous interpretations that could be traced to hybridity – images of the passion of Christ on the cross *and* an African judicial system. The AAP text highlighted the previous imposition of Western notions of evil witchcraft onto the minkisi use – a blinkered Western perspective, associated with racial discrimination and fear of organised resistance to colonial rule – when actually minkisi were used as witnesses to personal vows or public oaths in judicial disputes. In this respect the original use of minkisi bears certain similarities to swearing on a bible, since hammering a nail or blade, together with a personal item such as a piece of cloth, hair or saliva into the figure would seal the pledge.

Following the museum introduction the pupils were set to work first in pairs and then in teams of four boys in an attempt to raise further ideas from the quieter boys and more personal interpretations. The team leaders stressed that creativity was of the utmost importance and, to this end, the boys were asked to resist censorship of ideas and concerns for correct spelling or grammar, but to relax and use their imaginations. They were also provided with linguistic tools such as the acrostic technique to structure their creative effort. An acrostic poem is a poem or rhyming puzzle, in which the first, or first and last, letters of lines, spell a word or words. One nkisi example written at this time is:

Never looks away
Kindling the fire in his eyes
I try to stare him out
Staring, starin
I loose

At the museum the boys were most fascinated to see demonstrated by X-ray analysis, that their key object nkisi's power was derived from 'magical' substances: earth, beads, animal teeth and a cartridge case, which were stored inside a small carved section of the body and covered with a mirror. These magical power substances were thought to persuade the spirit of a hunter, returned from the land of the dead, to reside in the nkisi and this notion led to a discussion of myth-making around the world as a way of making sense or attempting to understand the existential questions of human life – why are we alive and how should we act? Then Sola told a Nigerian story of how music came to the world through the drumming of Ayan (a traditional name for boys of drumming families), which involved all the group in more musical drama work around the gallery space before boarding the bus back to school.

Dialogical engagement was successfully used, with reference to objects at the museum, to raise issues and binary notions inherited from media images of starving powerless Africans needing powerful Western aid and to open the pupils to newer, more critical and complex thought. The team leaders facilitated many pupil discussions around 'power' during the subsequent project work at school to inform their poetry – these included political power, the power of love, patriarchal power and the disadvantages/advantages of being a man or a woman.

While one pupil wrote:

> Womens' Rights.
> Stand up. Shout out.
> Treat as equal.

Another pupil thought that:

> Women get away with things.
> They have more rights and a power in pregnancy,
> that men don't have.

Different forms of poetry were explored and developed – rhythmic, non-rhythmic, haiku, elegy, acrostic and frame. For example, each pupil was also asked to write a line beginning with the frame sentence 'Give me the power to . . . ' At the beginning of the project these were mostly all based around Western notions of power but were rewritten on the last day to include many personal hopes, wishes and desires around:

- finding cures for their particular ailments, those of their family or friends
- stopping animal cruelty
- environmental issues/saving the planet
- ending racism, crime and bullying
- overcoming their fears – of heights, spiders, enclosed spaces
- bringing family members together again
- bringing back lost loved ones.

These poems were all extremely moving. They reflected real wishes that might have been taken to the nkisi power figure as this example shows:

*Grandad*

The grandad that was liked by so many
isn't now remembered
by any
only by me
and this fond memory
prevents me from
wasting a penny.
The grandson of
old honest Ron
still grieves that
he has now gone.
The cap he used to wear
to cover up the grey old hair,
the way he would walk and
the funny way he would talk
still leads me to believe
that it wasn't his turn to leave.

On the last day, the pupils wrote out their personal memory and 'Give me the power to . . .' poems. The personal memories were not read out and shared with the group but placed inside their individual artwork, drawstring bags screen-printed with images symbolising personal power. These bags were pinned to the mono-printed recesses inside the group artwork, an impressive Power Book. The Power Book is approximately 1 metre by 1 metre by 0.25 metre deep when closed; when opened 18 recesses are revealed, which are designed to contain the individual drawstring bags. It has screen-printed representations of two power figures on the front and back covers, and the act of pinning the individual bags with the secret poems inside was intended to activate it in a manner reminiscent of an nkisi ceremony (Anon. 2006a).

Finally the book was closed and groups of pupils made *tableaux vivants* or still picture sculpture for the word 'power' in front of their group artwork. Pupils worked silently with the expressive powers of the body, to further articulate positions of power that connected the museum with the wider world. For example, they practised standing tall with a clenched fist of freedom visible in nkisi and in protest marches. Thus the creative features of this project present an idea that knowledge is not simply something out there in the museum or in the minds and books of scholars but rather something that can be gained by any museum visitor through embodied engagement *with* the museum. In other words, as the next case studies will reinforce, a range of activities including handling objects, ICT research, art, drama and creative language work can combine to provide a unique sensory threshold for promoting knowledge as embodied experience.

## Mende mask: beauty and Sandhurst Primary School

A multicultural group of Key Stage 2 pupils aged 10–11 years old at Sandhurst Primary School, inner London, engaged with a Mende mask as their key museum object. These masks, which were used by the Sande Women's Society of Mende-speaking people, have been subject to diverse interpretations by anthropologists. These different meanings were shared with the pupils as a means of discerning what constitutes 'fact' and 'fiction' for whom and why, before the key word *beauty* was selected as their key theme and they interrogated its meaning.

The wooden Mende mask features thin eyes, pointed chin, elaborate hairstyle and rings around the neck – aspects that represent signs of beauty, aging, wealth and well-being in Sierra Leone, West Africa. The notion of beauty proved a particularly powerful one for this age group, enabling them to address health and aging issues as part of the Personal, Social and Health Education (PSHE) and citizenship curriculum. Engaging pupils in critical dialogue, creative writing and art on the theme of beauty cross-culturally formed a vital part of antiracist-multicultural education to build positive self-image and self-esteem and counteract media messages from the wider world. Images of beautiful people usually present a young, thin and white person, which can lead to feelings of insecurity about other body shapes and colours. In cases of sensitive children who fail to fit the thin, white stereotype, illnesses such as bulimia and anorexia can threaten their welfare.

The central use of the Mende mask in traditional Sande societies is part of an initiation rite. It marks the emergence of girls from the world of childhood to that of young womanhood. Clitoredectomy, or female circumcision, essentially marks the final masquerade, in which the elder women (wearing the masks) lead the younger girls back into the village following the genital mutilation; an actual physical change that has taken place. This aspect of the mask presents problems of power and control to the project team leaders who questioned the possibility of attacking the sexist practice of female circumcision, without endorsing the familiar racist perspective of the 'primitive other'. It was decided that the young age of the pupils made it inappropriate to consider the control of female sexuality in patriarchal societies. Instead, the attention focused on the more positive aspects of maskmaking and the possibilities of making temporary changes to bodies through art was explored.

At the planning stage of this project the class teacher Rachel Emery explained how the students' young bodies were beginning to change in the natural movement from childhood into puberty and they felt anxious about it. Her class work included some discussion on this bodily process of growing up, but it was always 'a bit embarrassing' for the pupils. It was easier to explore these issues and concerns through the intensive project work, because the focus was on ideas and issues as they related to an external object, the Mende mask. Pupils could begin to discuss their personal anxieties in an indirect way through this museum artefact, which presented an alternative perspective on what it means to be beautiful in Sierra Leone, West Africa.

The rituals in which the masks are worn mark an important movement of aging, from girlhood to womanhood in this part of the world, which inspired a wealth of artwork. Using individual mirrors the class began by drawing portraits of themselves as adults, adjusting their features, the shape of their faces and hairstyles. Many of the girls drew sophisticated hairstyles with complex braids and plaits whilst the boys drew beards, moustaches, receding hairlines and bald heads. They adjusted their facial shapes and features to resemble their adult faces and humorously added flashy jewellery, body piercing, scars and tattoos to create the characters they might grow into. Thus change – bodily change and the forthcoming change from primary to secondary school (another anxiety) – began to be seen as something to be welcomed rather than feared.

Mende mask work clearly provides a cross-cultural challenge to Western hegemonic views, which can be reinforced through storytelling and drama activities. For example, when the pupils were asked what words conveyed beauty to them one boy said 'what is on the inside not only on the outside'. He went on to write an acrostic poem – influenced by 'Pia' – a traditional African tale retold by the visiting writer Sola Oyelele and enacted by the pupils.

Mirrors reflect what's on the outside not on the inside
Effect is not always the best
No show off will get attention
Don't think you're the best
Everyone's not perfect, everyone's the same inside.

In the story Pia, although she is one of the plainest girls in the village, is able to win the most handsome and kindest young man for her husband, following acts of kindness to his grand-mother. Sola led activity work to develop 'kinaesthetic intelligences' and facilitate 'embodied knowledge' by using the freeze technique of drama lessons, where the pupils are asked to express an idea with their bodies and then act as if they are frozen into this pose (Golding 2004a). The series of freeze frames in the Pia tale really emphasised the nastiness of excluding someone (in this case the plain Pia from the girl gang), since exclusion was clearly seen and *felt through the body* in pose, raising their hands and then turning their backs to poor plain Pia.

The young pupils produced a quantity of creative work based on the notion of multiple intelligences, the cross-cultural concept of beauty and the effects of the passage of time on the body. Their frame poems on these issues, which portrayed themselves as they imagined they might look and feel in years to come, were printed onto strips of paper 'hair' and attached to the mask head-dresses. The Sandhurst pupils used the frame 'When I am [age]. These [part of the body] will [sense].' For example 'When I am fifteen. These lips of mine will kiss cute boys.' Fifteen seems very old to many ten-year-olds! Another example of frame poetry expresses a positive acceptance of the aging process.

When I am fifteen
These eyes of mine will see the future and what it brings
This nose of mine will smell fresh air and not pollution
This mouth of mine will taste fresh fruit and taste clean water

When I am fifty
This face will turn wrinkled
This hair will turn grey
My body will go crippled and short.

Interestingly, for an *Inspiration Africa!* project, it was the Japanese Haiku form that influenced the crispness and clarity of this frame poem, from a pupil who found the counting of syllables a stimulus to creativity. This pupil perceives differences, similarities and interconnections between languages of the world and uses imagination to explore personal and group identities, local and global responsibilities, which is a theme that will be expanded in the final case study.

## *See Me – Automatic Rap* and Stockwell Park Secondary School

*See Me – Automatic Rap* was an art project developed by Deborah Benjamin while under-going a Post-Graduate Certificate of Education (PGCE) course at the Art Education Department of Goldsmiths College, University of London. There were two elements to this project – *See Me* graphic work and *Automatic Rap* textual work, which a multicultural group of 'underachieving' year 9 pupils 'in danger of disaffection' from Stockwell Park School, inner London, tackled through a term-long project with the Horniman's Mask Collection and dialogical exchange around the key word 'identity' (Golding 2000, 2004a, 2004b).

The Stockwell pupils considered two main aspects of masking – dissimulation and trans-figuration – alongside the transformatory aim of masquerade. This facilitated much playful artwork on image, personal identity and transformation, since the masquerader in perfor-mance challenges established notions of an individual self and agency. Masks are not simply devices to hide behind but involve a concerted attempt to 'make contact' with forces that are beyond the individual experience and affect the well-being of the social group.

Most importantly, this African-centric artwork presented a potent challenge to negative portrayals of Black cultural experiences, both implicit and explicit, that arise from everyday language and are rooted in ubiquitous media representations of Africa as simply a land of war and famine. For the project team leaders the Black psychoanalyst Franz Fanon's work on the notion of masking illuminated our concern to raise new voices in opposition to these disparaging views. Briefly, Fanon argues the totality of colonial imposition lingers today, deep in the individual psyche of the post-colonial world, which forces Black people to wear 'white masks' in order to survive (Fanon 1993). White masks not only transform and contort Black bodies; they suppress the expression of the authentic Black voice and experience (Golding forthcoming). Fanon states:

> I ascribe a basic importance to the phenomenon of language. . . . which should provide us with one of the elements of the coloured man's [sic] comprehension of the other. For it is implicit that to speak is to exist absolutely for the other. . . . To speak means to be in a position to use a certain syntax, to grasp a morphology of this or that language, but it means above all to assume a culture, to support the weight of a civilization.
>
> (Fanon 1993: 17–18)

At a semantic level, Fanon analyses the problematic comprehension of the other for the Black person in a white hegemonic world. The Black consciousness of the Black subject uncritically taking on wholesale negative beliefs about the Black self, through a cultural consumption intended primarily for a white market, leads to a belief in inferiority not just of the Black self but critical aspects of this self such as language. Nourbese Philip, a visiting lecturer to the school during this project, echoes Fanon in her articulation of this view. She notes:

> Language as the house of being (Heidegger) Straight English, Queen's English, received pronunciation – I prefer to call it the King's English – a more honest description of its pedigree. None of these is really the house of my being – I am always a stranger. Dialect or what I prefer to call the demotic English should have been my house, my home.
>
> (Philip 1997a: 50)

Philip highlights the way in which the dominant language, 'standard English', transports the reality and rightness of the Black child to a location that can only be found elsewhere. Philip further speaks of cultural imperialism, the imposition of a power to name things by their English proper names and the acculturisation into the dominant culture through school, which functions as an engine imposing dreams and visions of goodness and beauty equated with whiteness, that leads to 'linguistic schizophrenia, or an alienation' from the first language (Philip 1997b: 129).

These are complex issues that directed the aims of See Me–Automatic Rap, which were made accessible to the underachieving year 9 pupils through both parts of the project work. First, in See Me pupils investigated the concept of personal and group identity, focusing on the human body, their own face as an image and the power to transform this through creative effort. Each pupil was given two photocopied 'portrait' photographs, which they had taken on disposable cameras during their museum visit (Golding 2006a). These self-portraits were then transformed – coloured 'alien green and proud' as well as in naturalistic dark hues, 'red eyed devils', tattooed in a linear manner reminiscent of the Ifa museum heads, or Janus-faced like the museum's skin-covered Cross Rivers masks from Nigeria and the Chinese opera masks in the handling collection.

Next, in the Automatic Rap work, pupils were encouraged to investigate the textual body-language. In lively discussion team leaders and pupils explored the general use of language/s to communicate and express ideas and emotions through different forms – oral, written and, once again, the sign system of art. More specifically, pupils considered the fact that 'collectors' and not 'makers' of the older Horniman masks were 'named', which provoked attention to the importance of grasping language and claiming the power to name and actively take ownership of the individual place in a global world.

Finally, these notions were related to the rights and responsibilities of individuals and the groups that are enshrined in law. For example in The International Convention on the Rights of the Child certain articles highlight the right 'to preserve identity, including nationality, name and family relations' (Article 8), the right to 'freedom of expression . . . either orally, in writing . . . in the form of art or through any other medium of the child's choice' (Article 13), and the right of 'ethnic, religious or linguistic minorities or persons of indigenous origin . . . to enjoy his or her own culture, to profess and practice his or her own religion, or to use his or her own language' (Article 30) (Anon. 2006b).

The dialogue continued while pupils expressed their Automatic Rap ideas in a mixed media piece involving both visual and textual elements on an overhead transparency (OHP) that was eventually overlaid on top of the self-portrait. Each pupil first wrote their name decoratively in their own language (more than sixty different languages were represented in the school) on their OHP and then they worked together, in a respectful sharing of the group's diverse languages, through including one other pupil's name in another language on each other's transparencies.

Issues of power and equality emerged during this linguistic identity work and, as an adjacent activity to naming, year 9 also wrote a statement about 'equal opportunities' (a key theme for the school at the time) on their individual transparency. They made some brave attempts to articulate precisely what this concept meant to them following the classroom discussion. Three examples, from the pupils Lady Di, Hafiq and Hafida, appear on their artwork and are taken as representative of the group.

Equal opportunities for all means equal rights for all

No matter what the colour of your skin is, what race you are, what sex you are (male/female), what age you are, what ever your sexual persuasion, what ever your abilities or disabilities are, and what ever your religion

Help us. Help your children have good health and go to a good school.

The project team leaders argue that the *See Me – Automatic Rap*, Mende masks and Nkisi projects were part of a 'good museum–school' curriculum, promoting 'respect for all' and good mental 'health' in the pupils by ensuring inclusion in creative democratic education, 'valuing diversity' and presenting a strong 'challenge to racism' (Anon. 2006c). This contention will be justified with reference to the voices of Black pupils in the conclusion.

> *Racism is not just about what people say*, it can be about what they don't say. They isolate you, *make you feel different and alone.* . . .
> Some of the racism in schools is about *the assumptions that people have.* . . . They are trying to be supportive but they are also labelling you.
>
> (Anon. 2000: 11)

> We only do black history during Black History Month. The same posters of the same black leaders are put up every year, and then taken down again at the end of the month. *It's tokenism.* . . .
> There's a lot of negativity in schools, there should be *more positivity*.
>
> (Ibid.: 23, emphasis added)

These comments exemplify feelings that were allowed to emerge during collaborative projects, when pupils were given the opportunity to 'question and challenge' what constitutes personal 'identities', as well as explore the way in which identities relate to aspects of our shared humanity, such as language, and overlap with notions of ethnicity, power and equality. Both visual *and* textual vehicles were important in encouraging pupils to experiment and articulate these questions of social justice and in this chapter's concluding remarks the key factors of effective collaboration are outlined.

## Conclusion: promoting intercultural respect and challenging injustice

First, the team leaders were determined to challenge fears of being 'different and alone' by developing a new praxis to raise new voices and visibilities at the museum frontiers through a museum–school multicultural-antiracist curriculum, which put an inclusive ethos into practice. It was vital not to 'add on' insights to an unchanging centre, but to proceed from postcolonial and Black feminist texts, which privileged critical thought, respectful dialogical exchange, self-reflexivity and transformative action. This approach facilitated community sharing and celebration during creative art and language work, so that pupils could perceive their multiple intelligences as a source of difference and pride, *and* view their linguistic skills including bilingualism in a global context of language users. Second, meticulous research and planning of the pupils' work provided them with key museum objects that acted as 'hooks' to engage curiosity, and motivating key theme 'tasks' that not only matched and stretched 'skills' but also attached to 'personal' interest and experiences, which presented a means to engage in long-term or 'flow' learning (Csikszentmihalyi and Hermanson 1995; Golding 2004a).

Most importantly, this permitted pupils to gain high grades in the end of Key Stage Standard Attainment Tests (SATs). For pupils who had previously experienced many negative assumptions about their abilities, academic success provided them with positive experiences, challenging and overturning what appeared to be socio-historically determined conditions. A special learning space is critical to this success. The museum frontier location prevents education from stagnating in isolated pockets where school and museum work separately, to the benefit of all participants. School pupils can adopt new behaviours and make new connections, while educator team-leaders benefit from sharing ideas, enthusiasms and expertise with colleagues in different fields.

Perhaps what needs to be emphasised is a postmodern oppositional strategy, which stresses the potential of employing 'fragmentation' and a series of subversive strategies as techniques of resistance when a grand logic of emancipation may prove impossible (Lyotard 1984). In other words, certain radical and liberating features of the modernist discourse might be incorporated into work at the museum frontiers, which is essentially engaged and not an 'anything goes' abandonment of the socio-political world (Crimp 1985: 44). In contradistinction, as educators we need to recognise our own entanglement in wider webs of power and must take responsibility for constructing projects that open the museum to the 'discourse of others' to 'heterogeneity of texts' and multiple re-writings (Foster 1985: viii–ix).

Re-writing the museum at the frontiers benefits the development of new audiences. For example, the art projects discussed here address some of the attitudinal barriers to museum visiting by ethnic minorities that recent research has highlighted (Desai and Thomas 1998). In Desai and Thomas's research, Black and Bangladeshi respondents spoke of feeling out of place, self-conscious and ill at ease in museums and galleries, because they were underrepresented among the largely white visiting groups. Despite this, the respondents, often the 'better educated', felt that museums had the capacity to broaden people's horizons and offer an enriched view of the world, by introducing aspects of other people's cultural life that 'could result in greater mutual respect and harmony in society' (Desai and Thomas 1998: 25).

The team leaders contend that feelings of 'discomfort' are unlikely to be prevalent in project participants, who were facilitated in a critical thought process of making connections with the world of the museum and their everyday lives, while developing visual and literacy skills. Perhaps most importantly, they saw their culture positively reflected not only in their museum/school creative curriculum, but also in the ethnically mixed museum/school team-leaders who delivered this curriculum and were 'visibly committed to equal opportunities' and to the development of antiracist strategies for the 'field of education' with the aim of 'eliminating racism from our society' (Anon. 2000: 8; Macpherson 1999: 14, 45; Golding 2000, 2008).

In conclusion, the collaborative frontier team of art department, university and museum regarded it as a matter of political urgency to revisit preconceptions and prejudices concerning damaging notions of the failing child, too often the Black child but also white working class children. Most importantly, the impact of the Power project on the Kemnell boys demonstrates the wider value of the new ways of working at the museum frontiers. During collaborative project work notions of failure and inadequacy were interrogated, destabilised and reconstructed in new alliances that redefined the terms 'self' and 'other', and demonstrated that in a twenty-first century world of suspicion and misunderstanding, museums can provide a new space of coherence, relevance and meaning for democratic society.

## Notes

1 The capital 'B' is used throughout as a gesture of feminist politics.
2 One case study discusses 'Inspiration Africa', which is a DfES/DCMS funded project for progressing partnerships between schools, artists and museums. The Horniman museum worked with 12 schools and the Cloth of Gold Arts Company. The second case study was part of Horniman collaboration with Goldsmiths College PGCE (Post Graduate Certificate in Education) Art Department and a teacher member of my PhD research group.
3 Briefly, Feminist-hermeneutics conjoins the politics and creativity of Black feminist thought with the interpretation and understanding that Hans Georg Gadamer contends can be gained in respectful dialogical exchange (Gadamer 1981).

## Bibliography

Anderson, B. (1998) *Imagined Communities*, New York: Verso.

Anon. (2000) *Challenging Racism and Promoting Race Equality: Guidance to Schools*, London: London Borough of Lambeth

—— (2004a) 'Report on the Borough of Lambeth'. Online. Available at: www.lambeth.gov.uk (accessed 27 March 2004).

—— (2004b) 'Report on the Borough of Lewisham'. Online. Available at: www.lewisham.gov.uk (accessed 27 May 2004).

—— (2006a) 'Inspiration Africa!'. Online. Available at: www.clothofgold.org.uk/archive/inafrica (accessed at 17 September 2006).

—— (2006b) *The International Rights of the Child*. Online. Available at: www.unicef.org/crc (accessed 10 November 2006).

—— (2006c) *Respect for All: Valuing Diversity and Challenging Racism Through the Curriculum*. Online. Available at: http://qca.org.uk/8859.html (accessed 20 June 2006).

Anzaldua, G. (1987) *Borderlands/La Frontera, The New Mestiza*, San Francisco, CA: Spinsters/Aunt Lute Press.

Apple, M. (2003) *Official Knowledge*, London: Routledge.

Cassells, R. (2000) 'Learning styles', in G. Durbin (ed.) *Developing Museum Exhibitions for Lifelong Learning*, London: The Stationery Office, 38–45.

COED (Concise Oxford English Dictionary) (1976) London: Oxford University Press.

Crimp, P. (1985) 'On the museum's ruins', in H. Foster (ed.) *Postmodern Culture*, London: Pluto Press, 43–56.

Csikszentmihalyi, M. and Hermanson, K. (1995) 'Intrinsic motivation in museums: why does one want to learn?', in E. Hooper-Greenhill (ed.) (2001) *The Educational Role of the Museum*, 2nd edition, London: Routledge, 146–60.

Desai, P. and Thomas, A. (1998), *Cultural Diversity: Attitudes of Ethnic Minority Populations Towards Museums and Galleries*, London: Museum and Galleries Commission (MGC) Report, BMRB International Ltd.

Falk, J. and Dierking, L. (2000) *Learning in the Museum*, Walnut Creek, CA: AltaMira Press.

Fanon, F. (1989) *Studies in a Dying Colonialism*, London: Earthscan Publications, 59–65.

—— (1993) *Black Skin, White Masks*, London: Pluto Press.

Foster, H. (1985) (ed.) *Postmodern Culture*, London: Pluto Press.

Freire, P. (1972) *Cultural Action for Freedom*, Harmondsworth, Penguin.

—— (1996) *Pedagogy of the Oppressed*, London: Penguin.

Gadamer, H. G. (1981) *Truth and Method*, London: Sheed and Ward.

Gardner, H. (2000) 'Multiple intelligences', in G. Durbin (ed.) *Developing Museum Exhibitions for Life-long Learning*, London: The Stationery Office, 35–7.

—— (2005) 'Multiple Lenses on The Mind'. Online. Available at: www.pz.harvard.edu/PIs/HG.htm (accessed 7 November 2006).

Golding, V. (2000) *New Voices and Visibilities at the Museum Frontiers*, Leicester: unpublished PhD thesis, University of Leicester.

—— (2004a) 'A field-site of creative collaboration: Inspiration Africa!', *Journal of Museum Ethnography*, 16. 19–36

—— (2004b) 'Using tangible and intangible heritage to promote social inclusion amongst young people with disabilities'. Online. Available at: http://museumsnett.no/icme/icme2004/golding.html 1–12 (accessed 5 May 2006).

—— (2006a) 'The Museum clearing: a metaphor for new museum practice', in D. Atkinson, and P. Dash (eds) *Social and Critical Practice in Art Education*, London: Trentham Books, 51–66.

—— (2006b) 'Carnival connections: challenging racism as the unsaid at the museum/school frontiers with feminist-hermeneutics', in J. Anim-Addo (ed.) *Swinging her Breasts at History*, London: Whiting and Birch, 289–309.

—— (forthcoming) *Learning at the Museum Frontiers: Identity Race and Power*, London: Ashgate.

Hooks, B. (1994), *Teaching to Transgress, Education as the Practice of Freedom*, London: Routledge.

Klein, G. (1997) *Education Towards Race Equality*, London: Cassell.

Lorde, A. (1996) 'The master's tools will never dismantle the master's house' in *The Audrey Lorde Compendium. Essays, Speeches and Journals. The Cancer Journals. Sister Outsider. A Burst of Light*. London: Pandora, 158–61.

Lyotard, J. F. (1984), *The Postmodern Condition*, Manchester: Manchester University Press.

Macpherson, W. (1999) *The Stephen Lawrence Inquiry: Report of an Inquiry by Sir William Macpherson of Cluny*, London: The Stationery Office.

Parekh, B. (2002), *The Future of Multi-Ethnic Britain*, London: Profile Books.

Philip M. N. (1992) *Frontiers. Essays and Writings on Racism and Culture*, Ontario: The Mercury Press.

—— (1997a) 'The absence of writing or how I almost became a spy', *A Genealogy of Resistance and other essays*, Ontario: The Mercury Press.

—— (1997b) 'Father tongue', in *A Genealogy of Resistance and Other Essays*, Ontario: The Mercury Press.

QCA (2006a) 'Art and Design Subjects', Qualifications and Curriculum Authority. Online. Available at: www.qca.org.uk/7914 (accessed 13 November 2006).

—— (2006b) 'About Citizenship', Qualifications and Curriculum Authority. Online. Available at: www.qca.org.uk/7907 (accessed 13 November 2006).

Scarman, Lord (1981) *The Brixton Disorders, 10–12 April 1981* (Cmnd 9453), London: HMSO.

The Home Office (2001) *Building Cohesive Communities*. Online. Available at: www.irr.org.uk/reports/index.html (accessed 16 March 2005).

# 25

# MORAL LESSONS AND REFORMING AGENDAS

History museums, science museums,
contentious topics and
contemporary societies

*Fiona Cameron*

Contemporary discourse casts museums as socially responsible (Janes and Conaty 2005), as organisations with the capacity to sustain societal health (Anderson 2005; Sutter and Worts 2005: 132) and improve the human condition. Similarly, the American Association of Museums 2002 study, *Mastering Civic Engagement*, presents museums as sites that can exert greater influence in society, as places where values are generated and as incubators for change (American Association of Museums 2002: 9). Interestingly, the desire to improve the human condition, to act as sites for the formation of values and incubators for change, appears reminiscent of the older and now unacceptable moralising and reforming treatise.

Museums have always acted as sites of social transformation and social responsibility. According to theorist Tony Bennett (1995; 1998), the history of the modern museum is that of instilling dominant moral codes of conduct, values and reforming behaviours. Working alongside other institutions of symbolic, coercive, political and economic power, such as the prison service, the police, church, state, education system and the media, museums were established for the delivery of moralising and reforming discourses. All this raises interesting questions. Are the contemporary discourses of social responsibility simply a revisionist version of the older ideal? What roles do museums perform as moralising and reforming spaces in contemporary society? And how do audiences imagine museum roles and the shifting foundations of museum authority and legitimacy?

The induction of contentious and divisive topics such as 'hot' contemporary issues, political topics and revisionist histories into museum exhibitions offers an ideal starting point to examine the contemporary roles of history and science museums as moral and reforming technologies. Such topics raise moral dilemmas, questions about what is right and wrong and circumscribe acceptable forms of behaviour. They engage the self in ways other topics may not, as they speak to values, beliefs and moral position.

This chapter draws on the findings from the international research project 'Exhibitions as Contested Sites – the roles of museums in contemporary societies' to examine these questions.[1] This project examined the relevance, plausibility and practical operation of history and science museums as civic centres for the engagement of contentious topics. A range of research methods was employed, including literature review, quantitative and qualitative research. Quantitative research involved telephone surveys in Sydney and Canberra drawing on a sample of 500 respondents. Participants were asked to respond to 16 topics that Australians might consider controversial and to a series of role-positioning statements using a five-point Likert scale (strongly agree to strongly disagree). Exit surveys were conducted at the Australian Museum and the Australian War Memorial with 197 and 248 visitors respectively, and at three Canadian Museums with a total of 286 visitors. Here participants were asked to respond to a range of questions comparable to the phone survey. Surveys were then analysed using SPSS (data analysis software) to compare datasets. The qualitative phase of the research involved five visitor focus groups (40 participants) in Sydney and Canberra. The findings of the quantitative research – museum visiting experiences, functions and activities, and notions of authority, expertise, trust and censorship – were discussed.

The perspectives of museum staff, stakeholders and media were also investigated using an online survey, in-depth interviews and focus group discussions with over 100 participants in 26 institutions in Australia, New Zealand, Canada, the USA and the UK. Participants were asked to identify topics that might be considered controversial for their institution and country in order to capture current thinking about museum roles and emerging controversies. Other questions related to museums and social responsibility, authority, expertise and censorship, controversies and their impact on institutional functioning, as well as successful programming and funding arrangements. This comparison of geo-political, social, cultural and institutional contexts was able to illuminate the multifarious challenges, limitations and opportunities that institutions face in presenting contentious subjects. The research revealed a diversity of opinions about museums as sites for cultural politics, characterised broadly by an apolitical/political divide.

## Apoliticality

Opinions about whether museums have a responsibility to represent contentious topics are founded on the belief that museums are apolitical. For those respondents who saw museums as having such a role (60 per cent in phone surveys in Sydney and Canberra), maintaining an apolitical position was imperative to securing institutional legitimacy and trust (Market Attitude Research Services 2002a; Market Attitude Research Services 2002b). Stronger support, around 80 per cent, was given to this apolitical position by visitors sampled through exit surveys at the Australian Museum (AM), the Australian War Memorial (AWM), the Museum of Anthropology (MoA), Vancouver, the Canadian War Museum (CWM), Ottawa, and the Musée d'Art (MA), Montreal. So how is apoliticality perceived as an exhibitory strategy and what are the implications for institutional power, legitimacy and trust?

According to 90 per cent of focus group participants, apoliticality is linked to a museum's information credibility factor. Participants identified museums as places that present trusted and reliable information; 'the museum has always been factual – we can rely on it . . . ' (Sydney Adults 30–49). Knowledge claims are factual because of collections. As one visitor commented, 'If history is facts why cloud it with viewpoints . . . Museums have artefacts why cloud it with opinions' (Exit Survey CWM). Similarly, exhibitions are perceived as based on quality and rigorous scholarship. Typical responses included, 'museums have a reputation like university professors, you expect to show things which have the backing of scientific method. It is not just propaganda, it's a well thought out established viewpoint' (Sydney Adults 18–30).

Apoliticality is predicated on the belief that a museum's voice is impartial and value neutral. As one participant stated, 'In principle, museums should deal with something confrontational in a non-judgmental way . . . it's not there to manipulate, its simply there to say here it is' (Sydney Adults 30–49). Impartiality refers to maintaining a non-judgmental position where the ability for audiences to self-regulate has primacy. For one participant this meant that 'museums give a non-biased view and allow people to form their own opinions' (Exit Survey CWM). And impartiality is about emotional distance, 'Museums need to be distanced from public opinion. To base museum information on public opinion can be a false premise' (Sydney Adults 50–64).

In Bennett's (1998) analysis of nineteenth-century museums as pedagogical civilising institutions, the normative belief was that museums should be accessible to all citizens. This idealised notion of access for all is linked to concepts of the museum as apolitical and as a space where all values are equal, 'Museums should present for the largest number of people and not for certain categories' (Canberra Adults 50–64). In taking a political stance on hot topics, some respondents feared that this right of access might be violated. For example, one visitor commented, 'with an exhibition about asylum seekers . . . people might use it to push their own political angle . . . you've got to be very careful' (Sydney Adults 18–30).

Apoliticality refers to museums as safe, physically protected, calm and civil spaces for people to interact, 'Museums are a protected environment you can't get anywhere else for dealing with contentious topics' (Exit Survey MoA). Safeness also relates to values and beliefs, 'The challenge for museums is to put something forward that holds up to all our values and truths' (Sydney Adults 30–49). Legitimacy is a key factor in this. Legitimacy can be undermined when museums present unsubstantiated opinions and openly engage in a partisan debate, 'As long as you present the facts, both sides, but as soon as anything political comes up, someone's extreme view, it won't be a success' (Canberra Adults 50–64).

Clearly, many audiences have a utopian view of museums as democratic spaces, although this is changing. For some, the apolitical–political divide is becoming less certain. This confusion is sustained by a longing for objectivity on the one hand and the realisation that topics and their interpretation are contingent and subjective on the other. As one participant stated, 'when you talk about these things emotion comes into it and you may not be able to present the facts. Depending on who is presenting the exhibition . . . they put their own point of view so you have to be careful' (Canberra Adults 50–64). Still others, while acknowledging that objectivity no longer exists, fear museums may suffer from government interference. One focus group participant commented, 'The information provided on a topic is going to depend on what government is in and who is funding an exhibit' (Sydney Adults 30–49). The blurring of the boundaries between an apolitical and political stance and the potential for social manipulation for many is summed up by one focus group participant, 'My concern with a lot of topics is that there is tremendous scope for social engineering . . .' (Sydney Adults 30–49).

Apoliticality is about the power museums hold as cultural authorities, and underscores institutional legitimacy. Many staff expressed the need to uphold this belief otherwise institutional power and credibility is relinquished. As one member of staff noted, 'we should be inciting debate not championing single points of view. If we become too politicized we lose our power and perhaps our funding' (Staff Web Survey). The belief in apoliticality and, in particular, aperspectual objectivity is shared widely, 'This museum should be a place of neutrality, the places for contestation in western societies are academia' (Staff, national museum, USA). Apoliticality is synonymous with Elaine Gurian's observation that 'museums are safe places for the exploration of unsafe ideas' (Gurian 1995: 33).

## Politicality

This research suggests that many history and science museums, when engaging contentious subjects, are inextricably political, acting as moralising technologies for stakeholder values. According to Bennett (1995) the work of museums as moral technologies in the nineteenth century operated from within government, culture and an economic rationale to influence and modify thoughts and behaviours. In *Discipline and Punish*, Foucault (1991a: 30, 101, 110) refers to this process of civilising espoused by Colquhoun as a new technology of power over the mind where pedagogy becomes one of the tools of ideology.

> Since recreation is necessary to Civilised Society, all Public Exhibitions should be rendered subservient to improvement of morals, and to the means of infusing into the mind a love of the Constitution, and a reverence and respect for the Laws.
> (Colquhoun 1806: 347–48 quoted in Bennett 1995: 19)

Antonio Gramsci (1971: 261) extends moral hegemony in civil society to the bourgeoisie as they possess the economic power to recruit for moral projects. Moreover, Gramsci (1971) views moral hegemony as descending flows of cultural and ideological power countervailed from below. Foucault (1991a) and Bennett (1995; 1998), on the other hand, direct their attention to institutional properties and mechanisms that frame and facilitate moral projects. This research reveals that the moralising apparatus in contemporary museums is governmental and class related, but also extends beyond to include the moral projects of a range of diverse social groups. It engages ideological struggles from above and below and technologies such as exhibitions for framing public morality.

Robert Janes, in his introduction to *Looking Reality in the Eye: Museums and Social Responsibility* (Janes and Conaty 2005: 12), states that museums are among the most free and creative work environments and, unlike the public sector, are not forced to administer unpopular government policy. This research refutes his claim and suggests that moral projects are still mobilised by government to serve political agendas and secure economic advantage. As one UK director explained, the political and moral values of conservative boards and politicians is one of the major defining acts of moral leadership for extending political power, although this varies. This reflects Bennett's interpretation of 'governmentality' and Gramsci's ruling class recruitment for moral projects:

> museum boards and politicians, often funders, tend to be conservatives . . . active in politics and socially upwardly mobile. They support their own values in their work to get approval. Everything comes down to values, will, determination, money and politics.

The relationship between morality, political agendas, capitalist aspirations and exhibition content is clearly expressed in the case of one state museum in Canada. Here, economic and political drivers were instrumental in recruiting the museum to support neo-liberal government policy on the clear felling of forests.

The current government is very pro-business, right-wing. It is now possible in Ontario to clear thousands of hectares of forests but the museum can't talk about that because we get so much money from the province. In the environmental community this is a very serious issue.

(Staff, state museum, Canada)

Moral projects may also be counter-governmental, at times leading to undesirable consequences. The Aboriginal Gallery at the National Museum of Australia, in presenting revisionist histories of frontier conflict and massacres of Aborigines over neo-liberal discourses of European settlement, was deemed at odds with the conservative right and the Howard government's political position (Edwards 2003; Mcdonald 2003). This controversy sparked a review that re-cast exhibitions on the nation's post-1788 history in a more celebratory tone and resulted in the loss of the Director's job (Attwood 2003; National Museum of Australia 2003a, 2003b; Mcdonald 2003).

The Museum was planning a major Aboriginal Gallery for a nation . . . public figures had been claiming that Aboriginal people had received preferential treatment . . . Massacres had been exaggerated or even invented. There was no stolen generation, and if Aboriginal children had been removed from their families, it was for their own good.

(Management, national museum, Australia)

The induction and support of moral projects by museums beyond government and class into the broader ideological and cultural apparatus of civil society is highlighted by the 2003 *Treasures of Palestine* exhibition at the Powerhouse Museum in Sydney. Under pressure from the Jewish lobby, this travelling exhibition promoted Jewish political aspirations in the Middle East by the removal of controversial photos and documentaries showing Palestinian dispossession and life under Israeli military occupation (ABC Online 2003: 1; Legislative Council General Purpose Standing Committee 2003). The exhibition was transformed into a celebration of Palestinian art and culture (Abdul-Nabi 2003). Similarly, the diversity of moral projects serving social groups can originate from below. This was highlighted by the exhibition *Anita and Beyond* at the Penrith Regional Gallery on the rape and murder of Anita Cobby in 1986 (Loxley 2002). Framed according to the sensibilities of the family, the exhibition of artworks, video and personal memorabilia was used as an introduction to a discussion of the repercussions of the rape and murder for the community rather than the violence itself or the forensics surrounding the murder.

The selection of moral projects for image marketing and to legitimise the aspirations of particular social groups above those of audiences is illustrated with the Australian War Memorial. Here the values of ex-service personnel prevail and are mobilised to legitimise and affirm their service while excluding discussions of the moral and political implications of conflicts even though 80 per cent of audiences surveyed wanted these topics discussed (Exit Survey AWM).

Our mission statement is very loaded and says to commemorate the sacrifice of Australians in war. The word sacrifice . . . can be moulded to exclude controversial views that might upset some stake-holders . . . We are not a war museum so you can't easily look at the political motives why Australians went to war. We are in danger of hiding the truth.

(Staff, AWM)

The promotion of a moral project to serve diverse ideological, political, economic and social ends, from the support of government agendas, to the protection and legitimisation of the values and experiences of stakeholders was evident with the exhibition *September 11: Bearing Witness to History* at the National Museum of American History. Changes were made by the curatorial team to the number of people who died in the aircraft that hit the Pentagon from 64 to 59 innocent people. This reflected the views of victims' families, affirmed the Bush administration's discourses portraying the USA as the innocent victim, while legitimising the War on Terror.

We had a controversial issue about the number of people who died in the airplane that hit the Pentagon, we said 64 and the families said they did not want the terror- ists counted in that number, we changed it to 59 innocent people. They wanted to remember what happened to Americans . . . not to give terrorists credence . . . The American public did not want us to explain to them why Islamic fundamentalists hate Americans – not on September 11th . . . it's not a role that the museum could play at this moment.

(Staff, national museum, USA)

Here, the process of exhibition development acted as a vehicle for mapping out the discur- sive territory, a moral universal wherein moral boundaries and values were drawn that had purchase in the collective consciousness of the time. In this sense the National Museum of American History helped to set the agenda for discussion as part of the wider cultural and moral conversation around terrorism. That is, not as a definable and closed text but as a series of symbolic hooks on which to make anxieties around terrorism and loss represent- able. This included the mapping of discourses around American supremacy and innocence and the construction of a moral angle to stake out the limits of transgression in which to formulate collective solutions, the War on Terror and for the cultural policing of Muslims as potential terrorists.

Many institutions, when exhibiting contentious subjects, act as moral guides as part of a broader process of social moralisation, to valorise, affirm and represent moral values that structure social life in certain ways. Exhibitions act as tools for constructing and justifying a moral system in a tangible form by constructing a field of visibility through the choice of topics, content including material objects, the moral angle and censorship decisions. For example, *Treasures of Palestine* constructed a visible field that omitted reference to the Israeli occupation and the plight of Palestinians.

The confluence of contentious topics and moral projects suggests a broadening of moral authority to a range of social groups beyond government and class, reflecting institutional commitments and pressures to engage diversity and the complex interests that museums mediate. Institutions surveyed, however, still tend to define moral projects around conten- tious topics as lessons according to one dominant moral universal. Moral projects are selected according to the perceived and actual symbolic, social, economic, political and cultural power of specific individuals or groups and the persuasiveness and functionality of a particular moral angle. For example, Anita Cobby, the murdered Blacktown nurse and beauty queen, accrued symbolic power by being posthumously sanctified as a symbol for all victims of sexual violence (Taylor 2004). The exhibition used Anita's story as a symbolic hook to set a moral agenda around sexual violence, to validate and reassert accepted values and act as a reflexive agent for a discussion about its negative impact in the community.

Overwhelmingly, the economic and political power and the interests of the ruling classes as argued by Foucault (1991a) and Bennett (1998) in the nineteenth century still tend to be the defining logic behind the representation of a particular moral universal. These groups have the clout to pursue their own interests and to intervene in exhibition development. The National Museum of Australia example shows how a clash of moralities and the political objectives of government can coalesce to redefine moral projects for exhibitions. Recommendations for the revision of the Horizons gallery sought to redefine its content to project Australian society's 'sense of itself' according to a celebratory vision detailing exemplary individual, group and institutional achievements (National Museum of Australia 2003a: 6).

Therefore, it is useful to conceptualise institutional cultures as moralising, as a hierarchical, complex and dispersed web of values held by heterogeneous actors. These are moralising spaces that are created, opened, closed and reshaped according to the topics and the values that institutions select to achieve particular political, social, economic and cultural ends.

## Audiences and the legitimisation of a moral paradigm

Surprisingly, many audiences sanctioned the strategic deployment of power by museums to define moral projects. Although many focus group participants expressed the importance of museums being non-judgmental, to show both sides, there are some topics like terrorism and drug use that were deemed unworthy of a balanced consideration (Ferguson 2006). In these cases, presenting the 'other side' was seen as legitimising certain 'extremist' values and 'deviant' behaviours; for example, in relation to the 9/11 perpetrators or drug use. One participant stated, 'presenting these topics could give legitimacy to something that has no legitimacy' (Sydney Adults 50–64).

Clearly, topics with a certain moral force, those symptomatic of particular social problems or which threaten a dominant moral universal, are deemed problematic. This suggests that museums have a role as moral protector; that is, in setting moral standards, offering moral certainty, in providing lessons that protect the dominant morality against violation and avoiding moral panic by curating topics according to a certain moral angle. Here, safeness refers to the protection of moral standards against deviation.

## Reforming agendas, a moral and responsible society

Museum reforming agendas are integral to the moral apparatus. In analysing nineteenth-century reformatories Foucault (1991a: 126, 238–9) argues that these institutions acted as mechanisms directed to the future, to prevent crime and transform the criminal in habits, behaviour, morality and conscience. Likewise, in engaging contentious topics in museums, the concept of reform is centred around morality and the deployment of tools such as exhibitions for providing moral direction in reforming future conduct.

Bennett (1998: 67) argues that modern systems of rule are distinguished from their predecessors in terms of the degree and kind of interest they display in the conditions of life of the population. Contemporaneously, this interest according to Bennett (1998) and Witcomb (2003) has shifted from instilling a sense of morality and good behaviour to fostering an acceptance of cultural diversity. This research suggests that the acceptance of cultural diversity is just one reforming agenda, but rather broadly embraces the idea of improving society by producing moral and responsible citizens. And reform, 'the betterment of society', is replaced by the terms 'social change' and 'social responsibility'. According to a UK museum director, in discussing edgy topics, museums have a role in defining, creating and promoting the views, values and activities of an open and tolerant society:

> To institute change on a broad scale we need to work with other organizations, who are working towards a more tolerant, open society that's honest about difficult issues. Museums can provide the backdrop for raising these issues. We have to think about what sort of society a museum aspires to help create.

Reform, like moral direction, often operates from within government – as Bennett argued of the nineteenth century. For example, the social inclusion agenda under New Labour mobilised museums as reformers in response to government discourses of access and equity (Department for Culture, Media and Sport 2000). An older notion of civic reform within government based on a pedagogical format still prevails, especially for national museums. Curators at the Smithsonian are under pressure to produce exhibitions that portray national history in a celebratory tone and produce a shared national identity that excludes controversy and difference, affirms civic pride and forms better citizens.

> There is a notion that we need national civic lessons and that the Smithsonian Institution is one of the few national institutions administering this . . . we are a place where you understand American history in such a way that makes you a better citizen and creates a shared ideal that excludes controversy and difference.
> (Staff, national museum, USA)

Reforming projects, like moral ones, are diverse and can be initiated from below. The Lower East Side Tenement Museum, for example, a museum of urban immigrant history in New York, uses history to help create a more equitable society by challenging prejudices, promoting tolerance and encouraging humanitarian and democratic values (Abram 2005: 19–42).

Defining and promoting what a better, more open, morally responsible society might be depends on the topic, an institution's mission and the values and interests promoted. Reform, the cultural shaping of the population, is generally predicated on a moral universal and can encompass a range of objectives from political affirmation and persuasion, image marketing to civilising rituals and self-improvement projects.

## Audiences, reform and technologies of self

Prevailing discourses on museums as reformers (Bennett 1995; 1998) engage with the concept of institutions as technologies of power where the power of the state submits individuals to strong ideological manipulation. Foucault's (1988) technologies of self are less well known and offer a useful tool for understanding the complex relationships between museums, audiences and reforming agendas. Technologies of self acknowledge an individual's ability to transform themselves, their conduct and way of being, through their own means or with the help of others (Foucault 1988: 18). Overwhelmingly, audiences in focus group discussions share a similar interest in reforming self and society. Here it is useful to embrace Foucault's later definition of 'governmentality' to understand the link between the strategic deployment of museum power and how this works with technologies of self in co-determining reform (Foucault 1991b).

For around 25 per cent of focus group participants, reform equates with historical reflexivity. Here, museums act as sites for information on contentious topics and events in the historical record. Audiences use this symbolic content to look and learn about the past by engaging their capacities for inner reflection to evaluate their own values and beliefs; 'Museums are reflective, there is . . . an opportunity to reflect on the past' (Sydney Adults 30–49). This is similar to Thompson's (1995: 42–3) analysis of media content. He argues that audiences appropriate messages and make them their own in a process of self-formation and self-understanding.

Current hot topics were seen as too political, emotionally charged, value laden and opinion based, having the potential to undermine a museum's reputation as an 'impartial', 'safe', 'apolitical' and 'trustworthy' information source:

> a museum is not there to foster discussion on contemporary issues. Contemporary issues become historical issues with the passage of time, a lot of these are very political, very contemporary and to me they just don't fall into the ambit of a museum.
> (Canberra Adults 50–64)

This reflective reasoning is based on the idea that topics become safer with time, when opinions and views have been carefully considered and a body of scholarly information has time to emerge.

Many staff endorsed historical reflexivity, providing shape and form to what people remember, as a reforming agenda where collections and scholarly information act as impartial tools for reflection, 'We have a role retrospectively . . . by giving a context and shape to what they remember . . . everyone remembers market scenes in Sarajevo but they are not quite sure who was being killed and who was killing and who was fighting' (Sydney Adults 50–64).

Likewise, many staff reiterated the relationship between historical reflexivity and the emergence of scholarly information in constructing reliable information, 'A certain amount of time should pass for reflecting on events so we have time to sift through the scholarship' (Staff, national museum, Australia). Clearly, a tension emerges between audience views of the impartiality of information and the role of staff in shaping reforming projects.

For the majority, 55 per cent, contextualisation acts as a reforming tool. Applied to current as well as historical topics and events, this approach enables audiences to understand their origin, complexities and likely ramifications, 'with September 11 and the Bali bombing for example, a museum's role is to build up a historical picture of where these events originated' (Canberra Adults 50–64).

Symbolic content is deployed for locating, constructing and reforming self, understanding others, in reshaping stocks of knowledge, testing feelings and attitudes, re-evaluating moral positions and expanding horizons of experience, 'It is important to get some reference to where you sit in the scheme of things – where is my place in all this' (Canberra

Adults 50–64). It resonates with diagnostic reporting by deconstructing problems, analysing causes and in portraying the context in which the story is taking place (Tester 2001: 39). Several staff expressed a similar diagnostic treatise of past-present-future options and opinions, 'Historical museums can pick topics that can allow you to understand why you have come to the place that you are now in the dialogue' (Staff, history museum, USA).

For around 20 per cent, reforming agendas also involve the active reshaping of individuals' behaviour to bring about change. That is, by opening people's minds to alternative views on a given topic and offering suggestions on how audiences might become active to bring about change, 'If museums are to continue to exist as people friendly institutions, they have to have programs to educate people about the history of terrorism, why it happens and the role of civil society to combat terrorism' (Canberra Adults 50–64). Here, symbolic content acts with self to interrogate choices, motivations and frame action. As one participant stated, 'I like the idea of an exhibition being empowering – in presenting good ideas and how do you turn that into action' (Sydney Adults 18–30).

For staff, reform also involved inciting audiences to perform a morally right action; 'Its not simply preserving the past or doing the housekeeping well. It's also what we think of the future, what are the options, are there things we should be doing that might be ameliorating damage, and improving the situations' (Director, national museum, UK).

The instrumental nature of curatorial endeavour in influencing thoughts and action around contentious topics is expressed by one participant, 'Museums are sanctuaries from the raging world. We also need to offer the other alternatives, the other perspectives, ideas in order to get them better prepared to go out there with a better perspective' (Staff, state history museum, USA). All this resonates with a public service institutional model. It positions museums as uniquely qualified to judge what matters in society, what audiences need to know in order to act as good citizens and make informed choices, and in defining the morality on which action is based.

## Conclusion

Clearly, reform and the relationships between museums and audiences require a new account of self as a symbolic project that is self-acting, more open-ended and reflexive than Bennett's concept of self as a product of an external system of power. According to 80 per cent of audiences surveyed, institutions are seen as having the power to challenge people's ways of thinking and shift an individual's point of view. The means of constituting and reforming self, however, refers to a greater ability to self-regulate, evaluate and process a range of information on their own terms, 'museums should not express an opinion, they should provide good information and arguments. . . . We have our own opinions' (Sydney Adults 30–49). For 90 per cent, this also refers to offering opportunities to express their opinion, to engage with other visitors, the institution and to leave evidence of debates in exhibitions, 'with more discussion, people would be better informed and therefore form their own opinions' (Market Attitude Services 2002: 20). And for 70 per cent of respondents, strategies involve techniques that facilitate critical thinking and personal resolution. That is, providing carefully selected and authoritative scholarly information, multiple perspectives and opinions on given subjects, source transparency, interpretive guidance and the framing of content to show how judgments are formed and decisions made.

To this end, audiences avail themselves of museums as systems of expertise to construct autobiographical narratives such as self-identity, moral position, attitudes, values and action around certain topics and events. Museum information is utilised along with a stock of resources such as face-to-face dialogue and alternative perspectives to construct these narratives, 'everything that you read is somebody's opinion. The best you can do is try and get as many different opinions as you can and try and formulate your own' (Sydney Adults 18–30). Here museums' symbolic power is mobilised to persuade and confront, to influence actions and beliefs and to cultivate trust and shape the course of actions. Thompson (1995: 215) calls this the paradox of reflexivity/individualism and dependency/institutionalisation. And, as Foucault puts it, the technologies of domination, in this instance museums as spaces for structuring and shaping a field of action, have recourse to the processes in which the individual acts upon him or herself.

This research suggests that museums have a strong moralising and reforming task to perform as a system of social, cultural and self development. On the one hand, audiences want open debate and a range of perspectives, but on the other hand require museums to set moral standards and reforming agendas that can be used to understand and evaluate societal conduct. The belief in many institutions as apolitical or aperspectual is located within institutional practices and civic purposes that are rooted in the pedagogic genre. These practices have served as a useful tool to disguise institutional politicality, frame institutional legitimacy and trust with audiences and to orchestrate consent for moralising and reforming practices. As symbolic forms, museums have been successful in sustaining a belief in legitimacy, although this is changing.

Historian Dipesh Chakrabarty (2002) argues that admitting emotion and embodied experiences into the museum's repertoire offers an antidote to analytic pedagogic knowledge and reasoning, and has the potential to democratise museums. However, this research reveals that the majority do not want a radical democracy. Rather, a pedagogic and authoritative system of relations is still longed for when engaging contentious topics countervailed by new technologies for self-regulation, reflexivity and self-consciousness.

## Note

1 The project was funded by the Australian Research Council and the Canadian Museums Association in partnership with the History Department, University of Sydney, Australian Museum and the Australian War Memorial (2001–04). Contested Sites began as an Australian study and now has an international profile involving 28 museums in Canada, the USA, the UK, New Zealand and Australia.

## Bibliography

ABC Online, The World Today – Tuesday 18 November 2003, *Powerhouse Museum accused of censorship*. Online. Available at: www.abc.net.au/worldtoday/content/2003/s991934.htm (accessed 27 June 2006).

Abdul-Nabi, R. (2003) *The tactics of the Israel lobby in the West*. Online. Available at: http://world.mediamonitors.net/content/view/full/2331 (accessed 27 June 2006).

Abram, R. (2005) 'History is as history does: The evolution of a mission-driven museum', in R. Janes and G. Conaty (eds) *Looking Reality in the Eye: Museums and Social Responsibility*, Calgary: University of Calgary Press, 19–42.

American Association of Museums (2002) *Mastering Civic Engagement: A Challenge for Museums*, Washington, DC: American Association of Museums.

Anderson, D. (2005) 'New lamps for old', keynote paper presented at the Museums Australia 2005 national conference *Politics and Positioning*, 1–4 May 2005.

Anita and Beyond (2003). Online. Available at: www.penrithcity.new.gov.au/penrithgallery/archives/anita.htm (accessed 28 June 2006).

Attwood, B. (2003) 'Whose dreaming? Weekend Review', *Australian Financial Review*, Friday 8 August 2003, 6.

Bennett, T. (1995) *The Birth of the Museum: History, Theory, Politics*, New York: Routledge.

—— (1998) *Culture: A Reformer's Science*, Sydney: Allen and Unwin

Cameron, F. R. (2005) 'Contentiousness and shifting knowledge paradigms: the roles of history and science museums in contemporary societies', *Museum Management and Curatorship*, 20: 213–33.

—— (2006) 'Beyond surface representations: museums, edgy topics, civic responsibilities and modes of engagement', *Open Museum Journal*, 8. Online. Available at: http://amol.org.au/craft/omjournal/journal_index.asp (accessed 7 November 2006).

Chakrabarty, D. (2002) 'Museums in Late Democracies', *Humanities Research*, IX(1): 5–12.

Department for Culture, Media and Sport (2000) *Centres for Social Change: Museums, Galleries and Archives for All: Policy Guidance on Social Inclusion for DCMS Funded and Local Authority Museums, Galleries and Archives in England*, London: Department for Culture, Media and Sport.

Edwards, F. (2003) 'Has politics interfered in the governance of the National Museum?', *The Canberra Times*, 18 December 2003. Online. Available at: http://canberra.yourguide.com.au/detail . . . ory = opinion&story_id = 274770&y = 2003&m = 12 (accessed 29 June 2006).

Ferguson, L. (2006) 'Pushing buttons: controversial topics in museums', *Open Museum Journal*, 8. Online. Available at: http://amol.org.au/craft/omjournal/journal_index.asp (accessed 7 November 2006).

Forgacs, D. (2000) *The Antonio Gramsci Reader: Selected Writings 1916–1935*, New York: New York University Press.

Foucault, M. (1988) 'Technologies of self' in L. H. Martin, H. Gutman and P. H. Hutton (eds) *Technologies of Self: A Seminar with Michel Foucault*, Amherst, MA: University of Massachusetts Press.

—— (1991a) *Discipline and Punish: The Birth of the Prison*, trans. from French by Alan Sheridan, London: Penguin Books.

—— (1991b) 'Governmentality', in G. Burchell, C. Gordon and P. Miller (eds) *The Foucault Effect: Studies in Governmentality*, Hemel Hempstead: Harvester Wheatsheaf, 87–104.

Gramsci, A. (1971) *Selections from the Prison Notebooks*, selected and translated by Q. Hoare and G. Lovell-Smith, London: Lawrence and Wishart.

Gurian, E. (1995) 'A Blurring of the Boundaries', *Curator*, 38(1): 31–37.

Janes, R. and Conaty, G. T. (2005) *Looking Reality in the Eye: Museums and Social Responsibility*, Calgary: University of Calgary Press.

Kelly, L. (2006) 'Museums as Sources of Information and Learning: The Decision Making Process', *Open Museum Journal*, 8. Online. Available at: http://amol.org.au/craft/omjournal/journal_index.asp (accessed 7 November 2006).

Legislative Council Standing Committee, Questions and Answers No. 37, December 2003. Online. Available at: www.parliament.nsw.gov.au/prod/lc/lcpaper.nsf/0/6EB558049C11DA1CCA56DF10043F818/$file/37-QUESTIONSANDANSWWERSWEDNESDAY3DECEMBER2003.PDF (accessed 7 November 2006).

Lemke, T. (2000) 'Foucault, governmentality and critique', paper presented at the *Rethinking Marxism Conference*, University of Amherst (MA), 21–24 September 2000.

Loxley, A. (2002) 'An angel in disguise', *Sydney Morning Herald*, 11 September 2002.

Lull, J. and Linerman, S. (1997) *Media Scandals: Morality and Desire in the Popular Culture Marketplace*, Cambridge: Polity Press.

Mcdonald, J. (2003) 'National lampoon', *Australian Financial Review*, Thursday 24 July 2003.

Market Attitude Research Services, (2002a) Detailed Report on Museum Issues: Sydney Pulse – April/May 2002, unpublished manuscript, University of Sydney.

—— (2002b) Preliminary Report, Canberra Pulse, 14 November 2002, unpublished manuscript, University of Sydney.

National Museum of Australia (2003a) 'Review of the National Museum of Australia', *Terms of Reference*. Online. Available at: www.nma.gov.au/about_us/exhibitions_and_public_programs_review/review_report/terms_of_reference (accessed 28 June 2006).

—— (2003b) *Review of the National Museum of Australia its Exhibitions and Public Programs*. Online. Available at: www.nma.gov.au/aboutus/council_a . . . view/report/the_exhibitions_section_two (accessed 28 June 2006).

Sandell, R. (2003) 'Social inclusion, the museum and the dynamics of sectoral change', *Museum and Society*, 1(1): 45–62.

Simons, J. (1995) *Foucault and the Political*, London: Routledge.

Sutter, G. and Worts, D. (2006) 'Thinking like a system: Are museums up to the challenge?', *Museums and Social Issues* 1(2): 203–18

Taylor, D. (2004) *Anita died in Vain: Anita and Beyond*. Online. Available at: www.onlineopinion.com.au/view.asp?article = 2671 (accessed 7 November 2006).

Tester, K. (2001) *Compassion, Morality and the Media*, Buckingham: Open University Press.

Thompson, J. B. (1995) *The Media and Modernity: A Social Theory of the Media*, Cambridge: Polity Press.

Witcomb, A. (2003) *Re-imagining the Museum*, London: Routledge.

# 26

# 'WHO KNOWS THE FATE
# OF HIS BONES?'

Rethinking the body on display:
object, art or human remains?

*Mary M. Brooks and Claire Rumsey*

Collecting and displaying bodies, a practice giving once living people the anomalous status of 'objects' or 'art', is increasingly contested. The challenge that bodies pose to contempo rary museum and gallery practice through their potent blend of attraction and repulsion is the central issue addressed in this chapter. The ethical and legal issues involved in the recovery and display of bodies have been discussed by many commentators (Kåks 1998; Nail 1994; Parker Pearson 1995; Steel 2004; Vaswani 2001). This important debate has led to changes in practice in repatriating human remains (Department for Culture, Media and Sport 2003). This chapter focuses on the conceptualisation of the body in the museum and how this enables human remains to be collected, displayed and viewed. Emotional reactions – and how these inform the boundaries of the acceptable – will be considered using experimental evidence exploring reactions to human-like animal flesh and human hair and teeth. Issues relating to the use of human remains in art practice are discussed and changing practices in the display of human remains are reviewed.

Three contrasting exhibitions are referenced throughout, selected for their different approaches to presenting and representing human remains. *London Bodies, The Changing Shape of Londoners from Prehistoric Times to the Present Day* at the Museum of London (27 October 1998 to 21 February 1999) used seven skeletons with other body parts, supported by objects and images, to explore how Londoners' bodies have changed from prehistory to the present day. *Spectacular Bodies* at the Hayward Gallery, London (19 October 2000 to 14 January 2001) explored the interaction between anatomical and artistic representations of the body through medical wax models and works by anatomists, painters and sculptors including skeletons, human remains and casts. *Body Worlds: The Anatomical Exhibition of Real Human Bodies* at the Atlantis Gallery, London (23 March 2002 to 9 February 2003) showcased dramatically posed contemporary bodies preserved using Gunther von Hagens' unique plastination process. These three exhibitions are clearly linked by the use of human remains but their context and goals differed. *London Bodies* and *Spectacular Bodies* both operated within the established framework of museum and gallery exhibition conventions. The former positioned itself as archaeological and historical exploration of the body while the latter sought to 'blur boundaries between art and science' (Kemp and Wallace 2000: 8). *Body Worlds*, located outside the traditional museum in both physical context and interpretative techniques, aimed to give visitors an understanding of the human body drawing on the scientific and artistic tradition of anatomical representation explored in *Spectacular Bodies* but as contemporary – and controversial – practice.

## 'But who knows the fate of his bones . . . '

In his 1658 *Urne-Burial: A Brief Discourse of the Sepuchrall Urnes Lately Found in Norfolk*, Thomas Browne asked 'But who knows the fate of his bones, or how often he is to be buried? Who hath the Oracle of his ashes, or whither they are to be scattered' (Keynes 1968: 115). This question had both theological and archaeological significance when most Western Christians believed that preservation of the earthly body was necessary to ensure the resurrection of the body and, hence, eternal life. Contrary to what might be expected, the general secularisation of Western culture has not lessened the significance of appropriate burial. People still care desperately about the whereabouts of loved ones' bodies and wish to ensure that these are 'properly' treated, although there are poignant examples of conflicting views on how this is achieved. A bitter controversy between bereaved families followed the discovery of the sunken British trawler *The Gaul*. Some relatives wished the fishermen's bodies to lie undisturbed while others thought it more respectful to recover and bury the remains (Hometruths 2003). Similar emotions were aroused by the organ retention scandal, centred on Alder Hey Hospital, Merseyside. A major review of the law on the removal, retention and use of human organs and tissues from both the living and the dead followed (Department of Health 2003). These changes are now impacting on museological practice. Curatorial and conservation responsibilities are not dissimilar to those of medical professionals but with the additional challenge of displaying bodies to the public.

Rumsey's research (2001) found that people felt less strongly about bodies from the distant past. Respondents to her survey clearly distinguished between the acceptability of displaying prehistoric human remains versus twentieth century remains, dry bones as opposed to flesh and adults as opposed to babies. Nevertheless, family links can produce emotions and actions across the centuries. In the eighteenth century William Corder was executed for the murder of Maria Marten and his body was eventually displayed at the Royal College of Surgeons. It was recently claimed – and cremated – by a distant descendant, Linda Nessington, who commented that 'to have his body on public display was horrible and very undignified' (Gooderham 2004). Recognising concerns among the modern maritime community, one of the 92 skeletons recovered from Henry VIII's sunk flagship *Mary Rose* was interred with full ceremony at Portsmouth Cathedral including a Requiem for those who lost their lives. Nevertheless, removing the bodies from their marine grave remains a contentious issue locally.

## Attraction and repulsion

A moment in the seventeenth century – the evening of 27 February 1662/3 – serves as a touchstone here. The ever-curious Pepys attended a dissection at the Barber-Surgeons Hall and returned later to the anatomy theatre 'to see the body alone'. His intellectual, rational interest contrasts with his visceral, emotional reaction. Compelled to touch, he nevertheless recoils 'I did touch the dead body with my bare hand: it felt cold, but methought it was a very unpleasant sight' (Wheatley 1938: III, 51). The results of two small experiments conducted to explore just such reactions of fascination and distaste to body-like materials based on Rumsey's initial research (2001), and then revisited in 2005, were very revealing. In the 2005 experiment, a group of students were asked to talk about their immediate reactions to a pig's heart, trotter and skin, a plait of human hair, wisdom teeth in a glass box and false teeth. The glistening, fleshy nature of the animal parts and their smell aroused repulsion although one student, with a medical background, took a more detached view and praised the heart for its beauty. Most found the pig's trotter and skin – the latter seeming particularly like human skin – repugnant. Some were also reluctant to touch the human hair although for others it evoked memories such as brushing a mother's hair or the sight of a grandmother's locks. One student speculated about the feelings of the person whose hair had been cut off. Ironically, as they were the only man-made item, the false teeth were viewed with repulsion by all. One student explicitly made the connection between this intimate, internal – but disquieting – artefact and old age and decay, remembering the sight of a grandparent's teeth in a glass. Calls to close *Death Threads*, Karah Benford's exhibition of puppet figures incorporating used false teeth, were the results of similar emotion, 'These things have been part of someone's body' (Bayman n.d.). In contrast, students perceived the wisdom teeth as sentimental keepsakes, naturally lost and associated with the tooth fairy. Possibly the fact that they were presented in the decorative glass box led the students to perceive the adult teeth as baby teeth, despite their size and shape. One student commented that the box 'protected' her from the teeth and therefore she felt able to handle them. What does this experiment suggest about how visitors view bodies in museums?

Bodies in museums are, obviously, not in their expected final resting place. Their removal may be the result of interventions which may be viewed – depending on one's perspective – as desecration and theft or as scientific, archaeological and medical research. Scheper-Hughes's observation that bodies are both 'objects and semi-magical symbolic representations' is useful here (Scheper-Hughes and Wacquant 2001: 2). In most urban Western cultures, viewing a body is a relatively rare and usually a stressful experience – unless the body in question is in a museum where they draw audiences although also arousing controversy. Even in this culturally defined framework, looking at a dead body may encourage reflections on mortality and be disturbing. Indeed, it might even be considered more disturbing if visitors – and museum professionals – lost the ability to react emotionally to human remains (Downes and Pollard 1999: xi). There remains a curious tension between attraction and repulsion aroused by the display of human bodies and body parts in the museum: they generate crowds, controversy – and income (Brooks and Rumsey 2006: 279–81). Freud's 1919 essay on 'The Uncanny' (*unheimlich*) discusses the complexity of attitudes to the inside of the body: 'something hidden and dangerous' (Strachey and Dickson 1985: 340). Seeing on public display what is normally unseen, potentially shameful – and the same as the inside of our own bodies – is both intriguing and unsettling.

Attitudes to appropriate approaches to displaying human remains are complex and often contradictory. Hill, Curator of Iron Age Collections, Prehistory and Early Europe, British Museum, observed that the preserved bodies are the most popular exhibits in the museum (Brooks and Rumsey 2006: 280). The well-known children's author Edith Nesbitt recorded her vivid memories of her childhood encounter with mummified bodies in a Bordeaux charnel house, contrasting it with her experience of viewing Egyptian mummies in the British Museum:

> My fancy did not paint mummies for me apart from plate-glass cases, boarded galleries, and kindly curators, and I longed to see them . . . My sisters . . . believed

too that the mummies would be chiefly interesting on account of their association with Bloomsbury. The vision of dry boards, and white light and glass cases vanished, and in its stead I saw . . . with a ghastly look of life in death – about two hundred skeletons. Not white clean skeletons, hung on wires . . . but skeletons with the flesh hardened on their bones, with their long dry hair hanging in each side of the brown faces, where the skin in drying had drawn back from their gleaming teeth and empty eye-sockets.

(Nesbitt 1966: 59, 61)

Nesbitt's shocked reaction echoes some of the students' reactions to human-like animal flesh. It highlights the contrast between her expectations of seeing 'clean bones' in cases and behind glass with the reality of preserved flesh on exposed skeletons. The differences between flesh and bones – wet and dry – become critical. A skull with desiccated skin and the skeletons of a child with rickets and a mother with a foetus caused most concern among visitors to *London Bodies* (Ganiaris 2001: 271). This greater emotional response seemed to be due to the presence of flesh as well as links with gestation and perceived deformity. When the body becomes too like us, the viewer, it becomes threatening. The frequent phenomenon of giving friendly names to exhibited human remains humanises the dead body. In the British Museum, a Late Predynastic mummified Egyptian man nicknamed 'Ginger' is displayed not far from the body of 'Pete Marsh', named after the peat bog in which he once lay. In Freud's terms, the nickname makes them *heimlich*, reducing the threat of the alien by drawing their bodies into the living world.

## Conceptualising the body in the museum

How is a body defined in the context of a museum? The very words used – body, corpse, human remains, human preparation, specimen preserved in fluid – are strongly indicative of underlying attitudes and assumptions, sometimes acknowledging the human source, sometimes denying it. The UK Museums Ethnographers Group defines human remains 'as including both prehistoric and historic biological specimens as well as artefacts (i.e. items made from human remains which have been altered by deliberate intent)' (1994: 22). The Department for Culture, Media and Sport (2005) definition excludes hair and nails but includes:

> osteological material (whole or part skeletons, individual bones or fragments of bone and teeth), soft tissues including organs and skin, embryos and slide preparation of human tissue.

The Human Tissue Authority (HTA), charged by the Department of Health to licence the display of certain categories of bodies in museums, uses the phrase 'relevant material' (2006: 7) as a catch-all term but excludes hair, nails and blood.[1] Remains which have been altered in form, such as crematory 'slag' in burial urns and Egyptian mummies ground to a powder for pigment or medicine, are thus given the same status as a complete body. This was implicit in the British Museum's recent return of human ashes, gathered from a cremation fire and preserved as an amulet, to the Tasmanian Aboriginal Centre (Kennedy 2006). The Pitt Rivers Museum (2003), Oxford, has been consulting with the source community about a group of hair samples in their collection, implying that they view this as comparable to other human remains.

Mary Douglas' (1984) anthropological exploration of concepts of order and disorder in social life is useful in understanding how the way in which the dead body is conceptualised acts to enable the display of what would normally be seen, in public contexts in Western society, as an unacceptable practice. Douglas examined the boundaries of the acceptable in terms of purity and impurity. A body on display, potentially 'polluting', is 'purified' by the Western perception of a museum as a sacred space: it is both sanitised and sanctified. Taboos associated with dead bodies are overcome in this conceptual framework which enables objectification so the experience of viewing becomes culturally acceptable. Geary's argument that bodies and body parts are both 'persons and things', serving to connect the past with the present, the dead with the living and offering succour, solace and inspiration, is exemplified by such museological practice (1986: 169). As Nesbitt's experience indicates, cases and barriers have both a physical and symbolic purpose. Part of the violent reaction aroused by the London Body Worlds exhibition may have been due to the fact that the bodies were on open display and not in a traditional museum space and so did not benefit from its culturally 'cleansing' protection. The appearance of the plastinated bodies may also be an issue: their very life-likeness and glistening fleshiness makes them ambiguous – part object, part human remains. However, it is clear that the hegemony of the museum no longer goes without challenge. Some comments on a feedback board placed near the display of mummies in Manchester Museum forcefully reclaimed the individuality of the human beings on exhibition and proposed they should no longer be displayed.[2] In contrast, one visitor to London Bodies thought too few skeletons had been displayed (Swain 1998).

Reliquaries literally incorporate bodies in objects whereas museological conceptualisation of the body as object enables their collection, storage and display. This objectification enables the experience of viewing to become an educational, historical or scientific process rather than an emotional or spiritual experience. Bodies become nonbodies. The ambivalent status of the bodies/objects in Body Worlds has taxed legal minds; the Mannheim court in Germany ruled that the preserved bodies were legally 'things' and not human bodies, which enabled them to be displayed (Linke 2005: 18). The catalogue entries for Spectacular Bodies follow standard gallery practice by including the names of artists in its entries (Kemp and Wallace 2000). This resulted in human remains being listed as made by 'Anon', a literal dehumanisation (Brooks and Rumsey 2006: 268).

What are the implications of such conceptualisation of human remains as 'art'? Spectacular Bodies displayed body parts such as a preserved baby's head from the Anatomisch Museum, Leiden alongside art as if these had the same status. In his Poetics, Aristotle commented on the ability of art to transform the dead body: 'we enjoy looking at the most accurate representations of things which in themselves we find painful to see, such as . . . corpses' (Dorsch 1965: 35). Artists have long depicted the dead body, often in disturbing poses. Rembrandt's The Anatomy Lesson of Dr Nicholaes Tulp (1632) and de Ribera's 1637 painting of Apollo Flaying Marsyas are notable examples. Gunter von Hagens has overtly aligned himself with this tradition. Sawday (1995: 186) has explored the blend of the erotic, the horrifying and the scientific in both visual and textual depictions of the dead body, citing Golding's retelling of the flaying of Marsyas in his 1567 translation of Ovid to support his case. This description might almost be of one of the skinned and exposed bodies in Body Worlds:

For all his crying ore his eares quight pulled was his skin.
Nought else he was than one whole wound. The griesly bloud did spin
From every part, his sinewes lay discovered to the eye,
The quivering veynes without lay beating nakedly.
The panting bowles in his bulke ye might have numbered well
And in his breast the shere small strings a man might tell.

Depictions of Christ's passion, death and resurrection are common in Christian art, allowing artists to represent the dead or dying male body as both symbol and physical reality. One – rather extreme – example will suffice here. In Ruiz's *Christ Consoled by Angels* (1760), Christ's shattered physical body is supported by angels while others collect his blood in communion chalices and place his torn flesh on patens as his 'eucharistic body' (Clifton 2002: 70–1).

Artists have long used body parts for casts in a tradition linking anatomy, art and medicine. Sawday notes that Rembrandt is reported to have owned 'four flayed arms and legs anatomized by Vesalius' (1995: 148). In 1801, with the encouragement of Benjamin West, President of the Royal Academy and the painter Richard Cosway, the artist Thomas Banks and the anatomist Joseph Constantine Carpue used a plaster cast of a murderer's body to make the *Anatomical Crucifixion* (Kemp and Wallace 2000: 85–7). William Hunter, who taught anatomy to artists and doctors, flayed the body of a smuggler hung for his crimes. Hunter cast the body in the pose of the famous third century Roman sculpture *The Dying Gall*, creating the *écorché* figure called *Smugglaris* (1834, original cast 1775). Modern artists are continuing this tradition although this practice may not be perceived as ethically acceptable or, indeed, legal. Anthony-Noel Kelly stole body parts from the Royal College of Surgeons from which he made carefully gilded casts. He was convicted and imprisoned in a case which reversed the established English legal position that a body could neither be owned or stolen as it was not property (Wildgoose 2002). Despite this precedent, Damien Hirst, who has been photographed with a dead head (Molyneux n.d.), is proposing to cast a human skull and stud it with diamonds (Dowell 2006: 49).

Some contemporary artists, however, have moved from making representations of the dead body or using it as the basis for casts to using actual bodies, body parts or bodily fluids. Christine Borland has worked with both actual bones and representations of bones (Brown 2001). *From Life*, short-listed for the 1997 Turner Prize, was a forensic reconstruction of the skeleton of an Asian woman whom Borland had purchased by mail order. A reconstruction of the women's face, modelled first in clay and then as a bronze cast, was the climax of the exhibition, allowing the bones the dignity of a face and giving the commoditised skeleton a recognizable identity (Barrett 1997). The issue here is less the nature of the art itself but how this different conceptualisation and presentation of the human body might impact on museum or gallery practice at a time when approaches to displaying the human body are under review. Moore and Mackenzie Brown (2004) have argued that one of the reasons why von Hagens has attracted such controversy is that he crosses – and confuses – perceived boundaries between scientific and artistic approaches to the presentation of the body. The situation becomes even more complex where blood or less identifiable elements of the human body are involved. Marc Quinn first made *Self*, a sculpture of his own head made from his own blood frozen at −70°C, in 1991; this has been remade every five years using fresh blood. Kieran Crowder's multidisciplinary staged work *Here Lies* includes sound, performance and abstract paintings which incorporate a mélange of cremated human remains that are assembled in layers of paint, bone and other material elements. These layers are then shaped, split or 'cracked' in various ways and may also be built up as geometric figures such as circles and spirals (Quinn 2004). Crowder views these human ashes as 'not . . . just some gimmick or novelty, but [a] . . . rethinking – not just of art, but also of its publics, its orthodoxies, and its promise' (Wiltshire 2004). Crowder first worked in a crematorium at the age of 16 and much later took a philosophy degree to explore and develop his artistic ideas. With the permission of the local authority, he had collected crushed bones, furnace waste, dental and medical items from the cremulator; this 'waste' would otherwise have been placed in the pond in the crematorium gardens. Crowder has reflected carefully on the use of this material, being aware that its use in art could be sensationalised by the media. He only began using the crematorium remains in highly personal paintings after the death of his mother, feeling that his own experience of family bereavement 'qualified' him to create this work.[3] Crowder has not yet offered the paintings integrating crushed human remains for sale and they are rarely displayed.

## Codes of ethics and the storage and display of human remains

Museums are in the challenging position of balancing their duty to the dead with the needs of researchers and visitors in an increasingly sensitised and multicultural context. Codes of ethics, such as those of the International Council of Museums (2002), the UK Museum Association (1999) and the American Association of Museums (1994), acknowledge the importance of respect in caring for human remains. However, these codes tend to provide general principles rather than specific guidelines so many institutions have developed policies which reflect both respect for the bodies in their care and their responsibilities to visitors and researchers. Sometimes this means setting limitations. The Mary Rose Trust (2000) made a conscious decision not to use the human remains from its collection in exhibitions or advertising.[4] Access is restricted and a protocol has been set for appropriate behaviour in the store containing human remains. Similarly, the National Museum of Australia's Human Remains Policy stipulates that 'All persons entering the Human Remains Keeping Place shall conduct themselves in a respectful manner' (Wholley 2001: 278). It is important to remember that 'respect' is necessarily culturally dependent; some cultures might wish to honour their dead with music, flowers or offerings of food. Conservators have long been aware of the issues involved in the preservation of human remains (McGowan and Laroche 1996). Other initiatives are seeking ways to balance the responsibilities and needs of cultural groups, museum professionals and scientists involved in human remains. The National Science Foundation has funded Connective Tissues, based at the Illinois Institute of Technology and the Chicago Historical Society, to develop ethical guidelines for biohistorical research.

## Statutory and non-statuary codes for the display of human remains

New legal requirements and codes in England, Wales and Northern Ireland are more specific about the definition of good practice for the collection, storage, curation, display and deaccessioning of human remains in museums. The non-statutory guidance issued by the Department for Culture, Media and Sport (DCMS) (2005) focuses on human remains more than 100 years old. The Human Tissue Authority (2006) regulates the licensing of the public display of bodies and tissue from persons who have died since 1 September 1906 following on the 2004 Human Tissue Act which made consent a statutory requirement. It is instructive to consider how the art works discussed above might be influenced by these developments.

Crowder's work would seem to fall within the HTA's definition of the human body and hence would require a licence for display. However, does the consent he obtained from the local authority, but not, self-evidently, from the – unidentifiable – humans whose bodies form some of the crematorium 'waste', satisfy the requirement that the views of the deceased person or their relatives and friends be considered? Quinn's head, although presumably satisfying HTA's criterion of consent, would seem to be excluded as blood is not considered as a 'relevant material' in their framework. The problem for Borland's installation might be establishing the date of the skeleton which would influence whether a licence was required or not – although other legislation relating to the sale of human remains needs to be considered.

The DCMS's Guidance (2005) provides procedural and ethical frameworks. Notwithstanding the Statement of Dissent which accompanied the 2003 *Working Group in Human Remains Report*, this document argues that most research into human remains in the UK is 'uncontroversial' while acknowledging the rights of indigenous communities. It makes specific mention of 'artworks composed of human bodily fluids and soft tissue' (DCMS 2005: 9) and describes appropriate good practice for display. This lists possible justifications for exhibiting human remains including medical, scientific, historical and anthropological reasons but also acknowledges, albeit in a rather tentative way, the role of human remains to 'encourage reflection' (DCMS 2005: 20). The recommendation that displays should 'prepare visitors to view them [human remains] respectfully, or to warn those who may not wish to see them at all' (DCMS 2005: 20) might involve a change of practice for art works using human remains. Such art pieces may not be conceptualised as 'human remains' and their viewing may not previously have been specifically restricted or preceded by warnings. Concern over the use and abuse of bodies obtained and sold for medical research was part of the point of Borland's work *From Life*. This piece did, in fact, attract the attention of the police concerned that the purchase of the skeleton was linked to commercial exploitation of human remains. Nevertheless, it would be ironic if the effect of current legislation was to curtail contemporary interpretations of the long-established tradition of the artistic exploration of the dead body. It remains to be seen how this physical and metaphysical framing of human remains in the context of both commercial and public museums and galleries will evolve.

## Changing practices in the display of human remains

One of the most interesting developments in rethinking the body in the museum is the decision to engage the visitor in the viewing decision. One of the goals of the Petrie Museum's touring exhibition *Ancient Egypt: Digging for Dreams* was to 'test new approaches in presenting Egyptian archaeology to a wider audience' (MacDonald 2001). Visitors were given the choice whether or not to lift the shrouds covering the mummies and to contribute to a comment board debate as to whether dead bodies should be displayed. MacDonald notes 'Hundreds of visitors, most of them children, have contributed their thoughts and feelings. So far they are roughly evenly divided in favour and against the display of dead people' (2001). A similar interest in debate and engagement led the American National Museum of Health and Medicine, which holds a permanent collection of human remains drawn mainly from military sources, to establish links with descendant families to the mutual benefit of both (Sledzik and Barbian 2001).

There were more parallels than may initially appear between the display of naturally preserved dry archaeological skeletons in *London Bodies* and plastinated curiously lifelike contemporary bodies in *Body Worlds*. The final part of this chapter explores the fundamental differences in ethical and intellectual frameworks which underpinned these different displays – and hence both created and mediated visitor reactions.

Although the Museum of London was clearly aware of their crowd-pulling potential and its Director was explicitly seeking an attention-grabbing income-generating exhibition (Swain 1998: 14), the special nature of this material was recognised right from the start. The aim was to 'safeguard the interests of the other key part of the team, the human skeletons at the centre of the exhibition' (Swain 1999). Two ethics papers were developed to define practice. Although von Hagens is clearly a master of the media, he also displays sensitivity to ethical and religious issues. Essays in the *Body World* catalogue addressed visitors' reactions to the display of bodies and debated legal, ethical and theological questions (Kunkel 2002). von Hagens places great stress on the fact that the displayed bodies are all the result of donations. A shrine to the donors with a plastinated body holding its own heart is included in the displays. Nevertheless, he has repeatedly been accused of obtaining his bodies from inappropriate, if not illegal, sources; a court case is pending in Siberia (BBC News 2002). Rumsey (2001) reviewed issues relating to consent relating to the display of plastinated babies and foetuses.

Before visitors entered *London Bodies*, large signs made them aware of the nature of the exhibition allowing anyone with religious, ethical or personal objections to choose whether to enter. Visitors were asked to show appropriate respect in the exhibition while unaccompanied children were not allowed and parental permission was required for school visits. Nobody joining the long queues outside *Body Worlds* could have been in doubt about the nature of the display they were waiting to see. Some *Body Worlds* installations included warnings before visitors entered the section devoted to gestation. Such a warning was not included in the first *Body Worlds* London exhibition which also had a rudimentary café overlooking the display hall – a juxtaposition which was hardly conducive to respect. *Body Worlds* positively encouraged children with free entry for those under six and the giving out of free information packs.

The physical nature of the display sends a strong subliminal message about attitudes on the part of the curatorial and design team – and those expected of the visitor. In *London Bodies*, the skeletons were displayed in cases like transparent coffins. All the skeletons were fully enclosed and labelled using established museum conventions. *Body Worlds* combined dramatically posed bodies on easily touchable open display with specimens in (sometimes rather unstable) display cases. Walter notes that the relationship between the visitor and these standing bodies changes the nature of the viewing experience, making them both 'real and unreal' (2004: 605, 619). Ironically, the only theft from a *Body Worlds* exhibition was that of a foetus from an unlocked display case (Jablon 2005). The labelling of the posed bodies tended to focus more on artistic explanations of the pose and why a particular individual had been chosen, such as muscle tone. The cased exhibits were accompanied by text which stressed health issues but varied uncertainly between 'layman's' vocabulary and medical terminology, rather undermining the exhibition's educational claims.

The Museum of London's research showed that visitor response was overwhelmingly positive, a justification of the careful balance achieved by the exhibition (Swain 1999). In

351

contrast, *Body Worlds* attracts – and seems to court – extreme reactions. Displays have been physically attacked (Chrisafis 2002) and criticised by religious and civil authorities but the touring shows continue to attract huge crowds, drawn by the intriguing frisson of seeing bodies defying the normal pattern of life and death.

## Conclusion

The HTA necessarily focuses on the legal requirement of consent in its guidelines and does not venture into the potentially complex territory of context and content of the display. It relies on the DCMS (2005: 16) guidance which stresses the need for 'dignity and respect', both culturally determined concepts, in the preservation, representation and interpretation of human remains. As noted, the display of human remains can evoke attraction and repulsion, both powerful forces which may easily trigger conscious and unconscious reflections which may be disturbing and can evoke – and cross – individual and cultural taboos. Williams (2001) has argued that one of the roles of the postmodern museum is to provide an emotional and philosophical space in which to explore such 'taboo' subjects. Doing this in relation to the display of human remains involves museum professionals in a challenging complex of potentially conflicting priorities and obligations in cultural, scientific and artistic practices within a rapidly altering multicultural social and legal context. Rethinking the fate of human remains in the museum, whether conceptualised as object, art or body, means engaging overtly with these issues in a creative and humane way and, in the most significant shift in practice, engaging visitors constructively in the debate.

## Acknowledgements

Special thanks to Oscar Embola, Konstantinos Hatziantoniou, Florence Maskell and Narell Thomas for their participation, to Dinah Eastop, Senior Lecturer, for constructive feedback and to Nell Hoare MBE, Director, Textile Conservation Centre, University of Southampton for permission to publish.

## Notes

1 The exclusion of blood was stated at a consultation meeting held by the Human Tissue Authority on 22 June 2006 attended by Mary Brooks.
2 Personal observation, Mary Brooks, Manchester Museum 2006.
3 Personal communication, Kieran Crowder in conversation with Claire Rumsey, 29 June 2006.
4 Personal communication, Dr Mark Jones, Head of Collections, The Mary Rose, 19 July 2001.

## Bibliography

American Association of Museums (1994) *Code of Ethics for Museums*, Washington, DC: American Association of Museums.

BBC News (2002) 'Russians charged over body parts', *BBC News World Edition*, 20 July. Online. Available at: http://news.bbc.co.uk/2/hi/europe/2140333.stm (accessed 30 March 2006).

Barrett, D. (1997) 'Christine Borland', *Frieze*, 35. Online. Available at: www.royaljellyfactort.com/davidbarrett/articles/freize/fr-borland.htm (accessed 23 June 2006).

Bayman, H. (n.d.) 'Anger at student's body parts art', BBC News Online, Portsmouth. Online. Available at: http://news.bbc.co.uk/2/hi/uk_news/england/hampshire/dorset/3632333.stm (accessed 23 June 2006).

Brooks, M. M. and Rumsey, C. (2006) 'The body in the museum', in V. Cassmann, N. Odegaard and L. Powell (eds) *Human Remains: A Guide for Conservators, Museums, Universities, and Law Enforcement Agencies*, Berkeley, CA: AltaMira Press, 261–89.

Brown, K. M. (2001) *Christine Borland. Progressive Disorder*, Dundee: Dundee Contemporary Arts Book Works.

Chrisafis, A. (2002) 'Lecturer's body blow costs exhibition £30,000', *The Guardian*, 28 March. Online. Available at: www.guardian.co.uk/uk_news/story/0,675134,00.html (accessed 1 October 2004).

Clifton, J. (2002) 'A fountain filled with blood: representations of Christ's blood from the Middle Ages to the eighteenth century', in J. N. Bradburne (ed.) *Blood Art, Power, Politics and Pathology*, Munich: Prestel, 65–87.

Department for Culture, Media and Sport (2003) *Working Group in Human Remains Report*, London: DCMS.

—— (2005) *Guidance for the Care of Human Remains in Museums*, London: DCMS.

Department of Health (2003) *Human Bodies, Human Choices*. Online. Available at: www.culture.gov.uk/global/publications/archive_2003/wgur_report2003.htm (accessed 3 December 2003).

Dorsch, T. S. (1965) *Aristotle. On the Art of Poetry. Classical Literary Criticism*, Harmondsworth: Penguin.

Douglas, M. (1984) *Purity and Danger. An Analysis of the Concepts of Pollution and Taboo*, 1st edition 1966, London: Ark Paperbacks.

Dowell, B. (2006) 'Arts diary', *New Statesman*, 26 June, 49.

Downes, J. and Pollard, T. (1999) 'Preface', in J. Downes and T. Pollard (eds) *The Loved Body's Corruption. Archaeological Contributions to the Study of Human Mortality*, Glasgow: Cruithne Press, x–xiii.

Ganiaris, H. (2001) 'London Bodies: An exhibition at the Museum of London', in E. Williams (ed.) *Human Remains. Conservation, Retrieval and Analysis*, Oxford: Archaeopress.

Geary, P. (1986) 'Sacred commodities: the circulation of medieval relics', in A. Appadurai (ed.) *The Social Life of Things*, Cambridge: Cambridge University Press, 169–94.

Gooderham, D. (2004) 'Murderer laid to rest after 200 years', *East Anglian Daily Times*, 17 August. Online. Available at: www.eadt.co.uk/content/news/story (accessed 20 August 2004).

Hometruths (2003) 'The Gaul Tragedy', 20 September. Online. Available at: www.bbc.co.uk/radio4/hometruths/0338gaul_tragedy.shtml (accessed 20 September 2003).

Human Tissue Authority (2006) *Guidance – Public Display*. Available at: www.hta.gov.uk/_db/_documents/20060906_Public_display_guidance_final_pdf_200609151404.PDF (accessed 12 July 2006).

International Council of Museums (2002) *Code of Professional Ethics, Section 6.7: Human Remains and Material of Ritual Significance*, Paris: ICOM.

Jablon, R. (2005) '*Body Worlds* fetus stolen from display', *Chicago Sun–Times*, March 31. Online. Available at: www.findarticles.com/p/articles/mi_qn4155/is_20050331/ai_n13506838 (accessed 12 July 2006).

Kåks, P. (1998) 'Human remains and material of ritual significance', *ICOM '98 Special Issue*, 10–11.

Kemp, M. and Wallace, M. (2000) *Spectacular Bodies*, Berkeley, CA: University of California Press and Hayward Gallery.

Kennedy, H. (2006) 'Knowledge or humanity?', *The Guardian*, 28 March. Online. Available at: www.guardian.co.uk/australia/story/01741036,00.html (accessed 29 March 2006).

Keynes, G. (ed.) (1968) *Sir Thomas Browne. Selected Writings*, London: Faber & Faber.

Kunkel, A. (ed.) (2002) *Prof. Gunther von Hagen's Body Worlds: The Anatomical Exhibition of Real Human Bodies*, Heidelberg: Institut für Plastination.

Linke, U. (2005) 'Touching the corpse. The unmaking of memory in the body museum', *Anthropology Today*, 21(5): 13–19.

MacDonald, S. (2001) *An Experiment in Access*, paper presented at ICOM International Conference, Barcelona, July (unpaginated). Online. Available at: http://publicus.culture.hu-berlin.de/umac/2001/macdonald.html (accessed 29 March 2006).

McGowan, G. S. and Laroche. C. J. (1996) 'The ethical dilemma facing conservation: care and treatment of human skeletal remains and mortuary objects', *Journal of American Institute of Conservation*, 35: 109–21.

Mary Rose Trust (2000) 'Code of Practice', unpublished document, The Mary Rose Trust, 8.

Molyneux, J. (n.d.) '*Body Worlds*. A matter of opinion', *The Anatomists*. Online. Available at: www. channel4.com/science/microsites/A/anatomists/opinions4.html (accessed 30 March 2006).

Moore, C. M. and Mackenzie Brown, C. (2004) 'Gunther von Hagens and *Body Worlds* Part 1: The Anatomist as prosektor and proplastiker', *The Anatomical Record Part B: New Anatomy*, 276B: 8–14.

Museum Association (1999) *Codes of Ethics*, 3rd edition, London: Museum Association.

Museum Ethnographers Group (1994) 'Professional guidelines concerning the storage, display, interpretation and return of human remains in ethnographical collections in United Kingdom museums', *Journal of Museum Ethnography*, 6: 22–24.

Nail, N. H. (1994) 'Treasured bones', *Museums Journal*, 94(7): 32–34.

Nesbitt, E. (1966) *Long Ago When I Was Young*, London: Ronald Whiting and Wheaton.

Parker Pearson, M. (1995) 'Ethics and the dead in British archaeology', *The Field Archaeologist*, 23: 2–3.

Pitt Rivers Museum (2003) *Human Remains in the Pitt Rivers Museum*, Press Release. Online. Available at: www.prm.ox.ac.uk/human.html (accessed 7 December 2004).

Quinn, N. (2004) *White Trash*. The Arts Institute at Bournemouth. Online. Available at: www.aib. ac.uk/aj/htmls/gallery-info/crowderandquinn.htm (accessed 30 March 2006).

Rumsey, C. (2001) 'Human remains: are the existing ethical guidelines for excavation, museum storage, research and display adequate?', unpublished MA dissertation, University of Southampton.

Sawday, J. (1995) *The Body Emblazoned*, London: Routledge.

Scheper-Hughes, N. and Wacquant, L. (eds) (2001) *Commodifying Bodies*, London: Sage Publications.

Sledzik, P. and Barbian, L. (2001) 'From privates to presidents: past and present memoirs from the anatomical collection of the National Museum of Health and Medicine', in E. Williams (ed.) *Human Remains. Conservation, Retrieval and Analysis*, Oxford: Archaeopress, 227–35.

Steel, P. (2004) 'Close to the bone', *Museums Journal*, 104(8): 22–5.

Strachey, J and Dickson, A. (eds) (1985) *Sigmund Freud. Art and Literature*, Harmondsworth: Penguin.

Swain, H. (1998) 'Displaying the Ancestors', *The Archaeologist*, 33: 14–15.

—— (1999) *Displaying the Ancestors*, unpublished paper.

Vaswani, R. (2001) 'Remains of the day', *Museums Journal*, 101(2): 34–5.

Walter, T. (2004) 'Plastination for display: a new way to dispose of the dead', *Journal of the Royal Anthropological Institute*, 10: 603–27.

Wheatley, H. B. (1938) *The Diary of Samuel Pepys*, London: Bell & Sons, III, 51.

Wholley, A. L. (2001) 'The attraction of the macabre: issues relating to human soft tissue collections in museums', in E. Williams (ed.) *Human Remains. Conservation, Retrieval and Analysis*, Oxford: Archaeopress, 275–81.

Wildgoose, J. (2002) 'The business of flesh', *The Guardian*, 31 October. Online. Available at: http:// society.guardian.co.uk/news/story/0,7838,821587,00.html (accessed 6 July 2006).

Williams, C. (2001) 'Beyond good and evil? The taboo in the contemporary museum: strategies for negotiation and representation', *Open Museum Journal*, 4. Online. Available at: http://amol.org.au/ omj/abstract.asp?ID = 12 (accessed 9 May 2005).

Wiltshire, S. (2004) *Here Lies. Kieran Crowder. The Artist in Conversation with Stephanie Wiltshire*. Online. Available at: www.kierancrowder.com (accessed 27 June 2006).

# 27

# FROM THE DOCUMENT
# TO THE MONUMENT

## Museums and the philosophy of history

*Beth Lord*

How will museums think about the relations between objects, concepts and history in the twenty-first century? Will the presentation of history in the museum be different from its twentieth-century form? These questions are pertinent in light of the current trend to dehistoricise museum displays in favour of a purely aesthetic approach. Many new museum displays are rich in objects and light on interpretation: this appears to be based on the dual aims of reducing didactic content and returning power to objects. Such displays – often realised as Enlightenment-style rooms or exhibits modelled on visible storage – fit in with the need to soften the overbearing voice of curatorial authority and to make the interpretive process more open to the visitor. The object alone is believed to be sufficiently powerful to engage the visitor and to prompt him or her to make connections with concepts and with the past. On this basis, objects are increasingly being displayed in a way that is aesthetic, decontextualised and ahistorical.

But stripping objects of interpretation and removing their historical context runs up against the problem of communicating history. Communicating history in the museum seems to require more than just an aesthetic arrangement of objects. Some explanatory material, it seems, must be provided to fit the objects to historical events and eras, and to explain the historical circumstances around the production and use of objects. However open-ended and plural the museum's presentation of history may be, it appears it cannot avoid including certain 'closed' and fixed facts of time and place. It seems that history museums, perhaps uniquely, need to tell an objective historical story, and cannot take up the aesthetic approach that minimises authoritative interpretation. This points to a tension between communicating history (risking didacticism), and returning power to objects (risking aestheticism). How can objects be used to communicate history without presenting history didactically? How can museums return power to objects without making the experience merely aesthetic? Does the apparently unique position of history museums mean that they will remain didactic and objective, giving visitors the historical narrative through which to understand the objects, while other types of museums minimise interpretive text and focus on subjective responses?

These stark questions put the issues around object display into a very crude dichotomy between 'objective' and 'subjective' modes of presentation. Of course, matters are not as simple as that. The complexity of the situation is evident when we see that the mode of presentation supposedly open to greater 'subjectivity' in interpretation – the aesthetic approach – is also the most object-centred. Similarly, the mode of presentation that appears to offer an 'objective' interpretation – the didactic approach – is actually built on a particular subject-position with respect to history. Yet despite these complexities, it is often in terms of a simplistic subjective–objective dichotomy that the question of object display is discussed (e.g. Hein 2000). Whether the dichotomy is cast in terms of 'subjective vs. objective', 'visitor-centred vs. collection-centred' or 'experience-driven vs. object-driven', museum thinkers take the view that if museums do not fall in with one side of it, they must fall in with the other (O'Neill 2006). Such dichotomies then become too easily conflated with political alignments, as if liberal or conservative political positions could be directly inferred from epistemological positions on object knowledge. The fact that the debate around object display is trapped in this dichotomy, and the fact that the history museum demands a model that is neither 'objective' didacticism nor 'subjective' aestheticism, suggests that we need a new way to think about the object in the twenty-first century museum. We need a new way to think about how the object is related to concepts, a new way to think about how it is related to history, and a new way to think about the power it has to engage the observer.

## The old model: recognition, recollection, replay

We need a way around the dichotomy, a mode of display that enables museums to communicate history without doing so didactically, and that enables them to promote plural interpretations without falling into mere aestheticism. This requires a shift in the *philosophical* understanding of how the present particular object is to be related to the past. In thinking about this relation, museums in the twentieth century have been dominated by two philosophical models: a Platonic model that characterises the relation of particular to universal in terms of recognition, and a hermeneutic model that characterises the relation of past to present in terms of replay. The Platonic and hermeneutic models are conflated in their reliance on *memory* as the cognitive means by which the visitor moves from encountering the object to recognising a fixed true idea. It is this move that is implicitly at work in both the didactic and aesthetic approaches, and it is this move that will need to be overcome to find a new way of thinking.

The Platonic model offers two powerful figures of thought that have endured over two thousand years: first, that objects are particular instances of universal concepts, and, second, that we recognise the universals through our encounters with the particulars. For Plato, as set out in dialogues such as Meno (Plato 2002), we see a particular object (such as a spear) and we recognise a universal concept (of spears, of tools of war or of warfare generally) that, consciously or not, we already knew. The basis for Plato's assertion that we already know these concepts – the famous Platonic Forms or Ideas – is rooted in his doctrine that the soul gains such universal and eternally true knowledge in its eternal state, before it lodges itself in a particular human being. Whether we accept that doctrine or not, the broadly rationalist notion that universal concepts are already known is an implicit assumption of modern museum practice: the tendency to display selected exemplary objects of a type or era assumes the viewer's ability to connect it to universal concepts. Whether those concepts are the 'right' ones or not is less important than the fact that the universal–particular connection is made.

On the Platonic model, understanding a particular object involves the recognition in it of an already-known universal. In this sense, all understanding is *recollection* of something already known. Understanding involves a silent transition from present particular experience to knowledge of universals acquired in the past; it involves the transition of memory. To understand an object is to have it prompt the 'memory' of the universal that it represents. Recollection is experienced as the recognition of the universal in the particular: we instantly recognise *this* object as a spear, as a weapon, as an implement of ancient warfare, and so on. Understanding and memory are a single movement from the present particular encounter to the fixed universal concept acquired in the past.

Hermeneutics, the second model governing twentieth-century museum display, urges the same transition of memory, not in the sense of recollecting something already known, but in the sense of making something from the past *replay* through the present (Gadamer 2004: 102–29). Hermeneutics – meaning the art of interpretation – has a long heritage concerning our understanding of texts, objects and artworks from the past. The nineteenth- and early twentieth-century hermeneutics of Friedrich Schleiermacher and Wilhelm Dilthey argued that the meaning of historical texts and objects could be accessed only by the historian bracketing off his present circumstances and trying to immerse himself fully and 'scientifically' in the circumstances of the past. Understanding historical objects, on this account, is an imaginative projection into the past that requires the knower to *negate* his present situation to traverse the distance of time separating him from his object. But philosopher Martin Heidegger argued, in 1928, that our situatedness in the present is fundamentally *not* separable from our ability to understand the past. Rather, the knower's present situation is always constitutively involved in *any* process of understanding (Heidegger 1996: 134–43). This shift led the foremost thinker of hermeneutics in the twentieth century, Hans-Georg Gadamer, to claim that our situatedness in the present is the *only* possible starting-point for understanding, and that it is a *productive* starting-point (Gadamer 1976; 2004). Our immersion in the present does not cut us off from the past, as the hermeneuticians of the nineteenth century supposed, but is precisely what allows the past to be opened up to us.

Hermeneutics is recognised as having been influential on thinking about object interpretation in museums in the late twentieth century (Hooper-Greenhill 2000: 116–19). Indeed, the shift from Schleiermacher's 'scientific' hermeneutics to Gadamer's 'philosophical' hermeneutics is mirrored by a shift in museum pedagogy. In the twentieth century, museums ceased to believe that objects had a single fixed meaning that had to be accessed through careful study in a museum environment closed off from the present world, and began to claim that the meaning of objects was constructed from the present circumstances and attitudes of the people viewing them (Hooper-Greenhill 2000: 124–50). This shift towards 'meaning-making' is directly (although not solely) attributable to Gadamer's philosophical hermeneutics.

It may seem that hermeneutics, which promotes multiple subjective interpretations, is at odds with the Platonic model which relies on fixed universals to give meaning to particulars. In fact, hermeneutics and Platonism are closer than first appears. The possibility of plural meanings presented by hermeneutics does not, in fact, mean that there is no fixed truth about the object. On the contrary, it is precisely their 'truth' that prevents objects' multiple interpretations from being arbitrary (Gadamer 2004: 117). The object has a certain fixed identity that is present in each of its interpretations. Although this identity is realised only *through* its multiple interpretations and never appears as itself, it survives and transcends its interpretations as the criterion of their validity. In other words, for hermeneutics there are certain fixed truths that are instantiated only in particular interpretations, just as, for Plato, there are fixed universals that are instantiated only in particular objects. To make a particular interpretation is, in fact, to draw out the truth of the object, to *replay* that fixed truth in a particular way. The 'particular way' will depend on the present circumstances, attitudes and knowledge of the particular visitor, but it will be tied to the fixed truth of the historical object. The present visitor 'remembers' the object by 'replaying' in the present the truth of the object that was fixed in the past. Both Platonism and hermeneutics maintain that there are fixed true ideas, separated from present particulars by a gap that can be bridged only by memory.

The other side of hermeneutic replay (replaying the truth of the past in the present) is hermeneutic projection: projecting the present self, with all its assumptions, into the past in order to *rediscover* the self. In the museum visitors are encouraged to understand the past by relating it to their own present circumstances, possibly to leave with an enriched sense of self. This is most commonly achieved through encouraging *empathy* with the past: drawing attention to the similarities between present and past, telling the stories of individuals with whom the visitors can connect emotionally, and encouraging visitors to put themselves in past circumstances. The most extreme, and perhaps most effective, use of empathy is found in museums that give visitors an identification card connecting them with someone who lived during the events depicted – an approach used in the United States Holocaust Museum, Washington DC, and In Flanders Field Museum, Ypres. If replay brings a past truth into the present, empathy projects the present self into the past. Both these movements between past and present involve memory: replay of the past in the present, and rediscovery of the present self in the past. Platonism and hermeneutics are conflated in a single movement where understanding and memory meet: an arc from the present encounter between self and object to the recognition of universal concept, historical truth and self-identity, all of which are already-known, fixed entities. Museums have implicitly relied on this philosophical conflation of understanding and memory: understanding and interpreting the museum object involves recognising its concept, replaying its truth and rediscovering the self through empathetic connection with the object. Both didactic and aesthetic modes of display rely on the visitor 'remembering' fixed truths in these ways.

The combination of Platonism and hermeneutics has placed limits on the way that objects are used in the museum to present history, on the way the visitor is expected to relate to history, and on our *thinking* about objects' relation to the past. Objects refer to universal concepts and fixed truths; they refer to a past that is already known, already finished. The past is presented as a fixed whole that is no longer open to development and change, but that can only be remembered. It is remembered through its particular remnants, the objects that visitors encounter and which prompt their memory. For the visitor, the museum object is a tool of memory and history is a closed box which the object pries open. The visitor is asked to transport him or herself back through recognition and empathy and to *remember* the past, to replay it as a fixed whole. The Platonic–hermeneutic model rests on the notion of a fixed truth that cannot be changed but can only be repeated.

There are different ways in which we might think about the relations between objects, people and the past; ways that do not close the past down but that open it up; ways that do not cast object-encounters as repetitions of fixed ideas of the past, but as starting points for constructing the past anew; ways that do not use objects as tools of memory, but as tools of productive thinking. Ideas of universal truths or single fixed histories are ideas that that the best museums are trying to challenge. If objects are to be genuinely open, they cannot be anchored in fixed concepts; the concepts themselves have to be broken open. If the past is to be genuinely open, it cannot be presented as a fixed truth that can only be remembered.

Both concepts and the past must be presented as something to be created and developed. We want a model that promotes history instead of memory, and thinking instead of empathy.

But how could history ever be presented without reference to a fixed past or to universal concepts? Can we really do away with the didactic presentation of historical fact, while still communicating history? Can visitors make connections between present and past without reliance on Platonic-hermeneutic memory? The answer to these questions can be found in the post-structuralist philosophy of Michel Foucault and Gilles Deleuze that seeks to 'reverse Platonism' (Deleuze 1994: 59; cf. Foucault 1984: 93). This philosophy gives us a new way of thinking about historical objects and their experiences without relating them to fixed ideas. Although Deleuze's work on memory and the past is highly relevant here, a discussion of it is beyond the scope of this chapter. Here, Foucault's philosophy of history will be examined. The shift that Foucault advocates from 'total history' to 'general history' in *The Archaeology of Knowledge* shows that objects can be used to communicate history without a return either to didacticism or to aestheticism; 'history that severs its connection to memory' (Foucault 1984: 93). This can be presented through the following example.

### Presenting history: an example

The Museo de America (Museum of the Americas) in Madrid is Spain's museum of its colonial past. Its oldest collections, of both natural and cultural objects, were first displayed in the Royal Cabinet of Natural History in the mid-eighteenth century, were transferred to the National Museum of Archaeology in 1868, and were put in the new Museo de America in 1941. The permanent exhibition discussed here opened in 1994. It is a typical story of a European museum with collections from that country's colonised lands.

However, this museum is remarkable for a number of reasons to do with its presentation of history. The museum does not present objects as pieces of evidence for a continuous historical narrative; it does not take 'the story of Spanish colonialism' as its starting point and then punctuate that story with illustrative objects. In fact, one of the striking things about the museum is the absence of any historical story of discovery, colonisation or exploitation. Similarly, the museum does not take 'indigenous American culture' to be its general topic, specified into Inca, Mayan and Aztec cultures represented by their objects. The museum refuses to assume that those cultures – or their history, religion, or ways of life – exist as static *things* or universal concepts which could then be represented by particulars. Instead of starting with one continuous history or one total concept of a culture and using the objects to illustrate it, the Museo de America starts with the *objects* and relates them to develop discontinuous historical series.

This may sound unremarkable given the general belief that starting with objects is what museums are all about. And, as we have seen, withdrawing the historical narrative to focus on particular objects is not unique. With the aesthetic approach discussed earlier, museums are increasingly taking objects out of heavily contextual displays and giving them a 'purer' display, organised non-chronologically in closely-packed glass cases with minimal interpretation. These kinds of displays give people more access to more objects, and allow them to make their own interpretive connections between things, rather than relying on the museum's authority to do so. If there is any rhetoric around these displays, it involves returning power to the objects, and getting rid of the contextual furniture in galleries that distracts from the object experience. For example, the Chinese galleries in the Royal Ontario

Museum in Toronto were last year redeveloped using aesthetic rather than contextual display. The previous displays featured a gallery environment resembling a Chinese court-yard, with display cases housed in Chinese architectural features and organised around different aspects of Chinese cultural life. In the 2005 redesign all atmospheric scene-setting and most interpretive material have been removed. The galleries now have plain white walls and feature objects arranged in no clearly apparent order in rows of tall glass cases. The effect is to decontextualise the objects, stripping them of their material and cultural functions and making them into art objects. As is also the case in most art galleries, the visitor is not offered any suggestion of how, why or even *that* historical development occurred among objects of the same kind: all are treated as being comparable on the same terms, because the only terms the visitor has to compare them are aesthetic.

The Museo de America, however, is not an example of this kind. The new displays at the Royal Ontario Museum are not intended to exhibit history: they are intended to exhibit objects as beautiful and intriguing; they are intended to show the extent and character of the collection or of Chinese bronzes generally; they are intended to show the similarities and differences between objects, to suggest different and multiple classificatory orders, to allow the visitor to explore with the eye before understanding through text. Where the museum's aim is to communicate nothing other than the objects themselves, perhaps aesthetic displays are suitable. (The author remains agnostic on whether that aim is a good one.) The Museo de America, however, like most other history museums, aims to communicate the history of a certain time and place through objects. Its decision to 'start with the objects' is therefore fundamentally different from the current trend for object-centred, decontexualised aesthetic displays. It is also fundamentally different from the standard presentation of history in the museum.

To make this clearer, let's take a contrasting case: the Imperial War Museum (IWM) North in Salford. For all its audiovisual innovation and striking building, this is a very traditional museum of the history of warfare in the twentieth century. The museum is organised around a timeline which runs along its walls, with relevant objects arranged near the key dates. The objects illustrate the points on the timeline and fit neatly into the chronology. The space is punctuated by 'silos' which use objects to illustrate big concepts that don't fit neatly into the chronology: propaganda, women at war, and so on. In traditional style, the visitor moves through time as he or she moves through the museum (Bennett 1995: 181–2), following the trajectory and development of the twentieth century through its wars. Even the audiovisual events that take over the whole space and interrupt the visit at regular intervals seem designed to represent the total and terrifying interruption of normal experience that war brings. In a two-hour visit you experience the progression of the twentieth century.

Now, there is nothing intrinsically wrong with this kind of display; arguably it is a good way of communicating a long and complex history in a short time and small space. According to one of its designers, the original concept was for an experience modelled on the cinematic with a clear three-act narrative structure, offering 'a panoptic view of twentieth-century conflict' (Greenberg 2005: 233). As Greenberg also points out, this approach has potential to be creative, transforming and vitally engaging for audiences. The point here is not to criticise this method of display, but to show that history is understood here as a fixed and continuous line along which events and objects are placed. Similarly, big concepts such as 'propaganda' are presented as stable totalities (physically manifested by silos) illustrated by objects. We can see both the Platonic and hermeneutic models at work here.

Particulars are used to recognise the universal concept that we already know, to replay the truths of the past, and as a means of projecting one's present understanding into the past. A soldier's letter is a tool both for recognising and for connecting with the events on the time-line. These imaginative and empathetic leaps back in time through such objects can, of course, be very powerful. Ultimately, perhaps, the aim is to be able to imaginatively recon-struct, replay or 'remember' the whole of the twentieth century through objects.

The Museo de America does not give the visitor the experience of historical progression, the possibility of replay or the chance for projected empathy. Nor does it aestheticise objects such that the experience is primarily one of beauty and wonder. It treats its artefacts as historical documents, but not as particulars through which the visitor is supposed to connect with a universal concept or fixed continuity of history. Objects are not made to refer to anything, but *taken together* in small groups they are starting points for developing micro-histories. A seventeenth-century Peruvian pot is shown amid Peruvian pots from different centuries, up to the present day. In the next case, Mayan religious objects are shown along-side Catholic religious objects, used around the same time in the same area. Relating the objects within each case yields short historical series of causation and development (e.g. between pot designs in one culture through time, or between multiple cultures influencing one another around the same time). But the museum does not suggest that these series contribute to an overarching story of the development of American culture. These series, built up through the visit, are discontinuous with one another – no single continuous story of development or of destruction emerges. Removing the objects from a single narrative and from well-defined concepts means that the visitor is not encouraged to make the empathetic leap back in time, or to personalise the encounter with the object. Instead, he or she is encouraged to *do a kind of history*: to relate objects to construct cause–effect series and to bring the discontinuous strands together into a complex whole. At the end of the museum visit, the visitor will not be able to remember or reconstruct the history of Spanish colo-nialism; nor will he or she have gained an understanding of 'the Incas' or 'the Aztecs' as stable concepts. That is because there is no such continuous history and there are no such stable concepts. What emerges from the visit as a whole is the experience of history and culture as complex, puzzling and irreducibly multiple – and of history as a practice that *involves* the visitor.

Of course, this museum is not completely without conceptual or curatorial order. The museum's organisation – around ways of knowing, types of societies, religious practices and means of communication – allows it to display material from all cultures together within the same spaces, including those from the Spanish settlers, the Catholic church, the indigenous populations, African and Asian slaves and the *Mestizos*. All these objects are treated as being equally puzzling and as contributing to multiple different micro-histories. Most strik-ingly, the opening gallery of the museum is called 'the Instruments of Knowledge', which examines the different ways the new world was understood, described and mythologised before and during the colonial period. Among the sources of knowledge displayed in the gallery (literature, scientific accounts, maps, drawings, etc.) is the museum itself: an eigh-teenth-century cabinet of curiosities is presented as one way in which Europeans repre-sented and mythologised the Americas. Right from the beginning of the visit, the museum puts itself on display and tells the visitor that objects can and will be used to construct history in multiple different ways. The curatorial voice initiates this historical process but the visitor must carry it out.

## The new model: history, genealogy and thinking

The difference between the IWM North and the Museo de America exemplifies a shift in the philosophy of history identified by Foucault in his 1969 book *The Archaeology of Knowledge* and his 1971 essay 'Nietzsche, Genealogy, History'. Foucault's argument in the book is partly targeted at the mid-twentieth century *Annales* school of history, which aimed to delve 'beneath' the major events of a historical era to reveal the more permanent social relations and structures that determine the events of that era. These historians address long periods

> as if, beneath the shifts and changes of political events, they were trying to reveal the stable, almost indestructible system of checks and balances, the irreversible processes, . . . the great silent, motionless bases that traditional history has covered with a thick layer of events.
>
> (Foucault 2002: 3)

The philosopher Jacques Rancière, who has also written about the *Annales* school, argues that the effect of such an approach is to negate events and subjects, and thus to render both history and politics meaningless (Rancière 1994). Foucault argues for a post-*Annales*, post-*structural* history that returns to events and the documents that are evidence for them, but that refuses to refer those events to total concepts of social relations or historical tendencies thought to underlie them. Foucault's analysis is not only a critique of the *Annales* school: it is a critique of all history that relies on Platonic assumptions of eternal truths (Foucault 1984: 87).

The shift that Foucault identifies in the philosophy of history is described in *The Archaeology of Knowledge* as that from 'total history' to 'general history' (Foucault 2002: 10), and in 'Nietzsche, Genealogy, History' as that from 'traditional history' to 'effective history' (Foucault 1984: 88). This distinction is intricately bound up with how we use documents as evidence for the past. Foucault believes that history practised as 'total history' assumes that the past can be understood in its totality according to a single principle, and that its task is to reconstitute 'the overall form of a civilization' (Foucault 2002: 10–11). Total history assumes single coherent principles under which phenomena and their material traces can be united. It assumes that all such phenomena are continuous with one another, that they can be derived causally from one another, that they all express or relate to a central developmental principle. Total history understands the past primarily in terms of its 'monuments' – historical eras, societal and economic structures, and total concepts. This kind of history uses documents (including artefacts and objects) as evidence for these monuments. It interprets the documents of the past in terms of the assumed continuity of historical eras and the assumed coherence of universal concepts. The IWM North gives us the example here: the monuments of 'the twentieth century' and 'the First World War' have to be assumed to be coherent, stable and fixed *things* before the soldier's letter can be interpreted as evidence for them.

Foucault, of course, is not denying that the First World War happened, nor that the soldier's letter is a valuable document that can be used to understand it. Rather, he is advocating a reversal in the way we approach the document and the monument. He argues for performing history as archaeology, examining particular documents and developing how they fit into multiple, discontinuous historical series. General history does not assume that all such documents will be evidence for a single principle governing the time and place they are from; it takes their differences, specificities and discontinuities as primary. That is, the 'monument' of the First World War must be built up through relating documents into micro-series and constructing series of series. There will be no ultimate unity or continuity to the monument that results, and no single trajectory along which it can be plotted. The unities and continuities that will be found will be *within* and *between* documents that make up series, but the monument will have the character of complexity, discontinuity and difference between series. The task is to determine

> what form of relation may be legitimately described between these different series . . . what interplay of correlation and dominance exists between them; what may be the effect of shifts, different temporalities, and various rehandlings; in what distinct totalities certain elements may figure simultaneously; in short, not only what series, but also what 'series of series' . . . it is possible to draw up. A total description draws all phenomena around a single centre – a principle, a meaning, a spirit, a world-view, an overall shape; a general history, on the contrary, would deploy the space of a dispersion.
>
> (Foucault 2002: 11)

When put into practice in the museum, this means that objects will not be used as evidence for a single historical trajectory, nor as illustrations of universal concepts. Rather, objects will be understood as particulars, as fundamentally puzzling things to be opened, developed and connected with other things into series. They will be interpreted in terms of their changing relations to other particulars, not in terms of how they fit into unchanging total concepts.

It is significant that Foucault uses the term *general* history for his project, for with this term he distances himself philosophically from the Platonic model discussed earlier. Whereas the *universal* is known in advance and recognised in the particular, the *general* is something conceptual that is built up from sets of particulars. Significantly, it is an Aristotelian term rather than a Platonic one. Foucault rejects the Platonic doctrine of understanding as the recognition of eternal forms, and also the hermeneutic model of understanding as self-discovery through the truths of the past. For Foucault, understanding must be divorced from recognition, recollection and memory, and aligned instead with disruption, instability and dissolution of fixed identities. The object must cease to be the tool of memory and become a tool for knowledge that cuts through those assumed identities. Foucault identifies and announces his departure from the old model of recollection:

> Documents have [always] been used, questioned, and have given rise to questions; scholars have asked not only what these documents meant, but also whether they were telling the truth, and by what right they could claim to be doing so. . . . But each of these questions, and all this critical concern, pointed to one and the same end: the reconstitution, on the basis of what the documents say, and sometimes merely hint at, of the past from which they emanate and which has now disappeared far behind them; the document was always treated as the language of a voice reduced to silence.
>
> (Foucault 2002: 7)

The traditional devices for constructing a comprehensive view of history and for retracing the past as a patient and continuous development must be systematically dismantled. Necessarily, we must dismiss those tendencies that encourage the consoling play of recognitions. Knowledge, even under the banner of history, does not depend on 'rediscovery', and it emphatically excludes the 'rediscovery of ourselves'. History becomes 'effective' to the degree that it introduces discontinuity into our very being.

(Foucault 1984: 88)

For 'document' here we can read 'museum object'. In standard history museums, as can be seen with the case of IWM North, the object is treated as the remnant which prompts the recognition of the past, which prompts the empathetic leap backwards, which enables us to reconstitute the 'monument' of a historical era. But in new history museums, such as the Museo de America, the object will be developed into series and relations that build *forward* in unforeseen directions. It is a move away from history as memory and towards history as construction.

> Now . . . history has altered its position in relation to the document: it has taken as its primary task, not the interpretation of the document, nor the attempt to decide whether it is telling the truth or what is its expressive value, but to work on it from within and to develop it: history now organizes the document, divides it up, distributes it, orders it, arranges it in levels, establishes series. . . . The document, then, is no longer for history an inert material through which it tries to reconstitute what men have done or said, the events of which only the trace remains; history is now trying to define within the documentary material itself unities, totalities, series, relations. History must be detached from the image that satisfied it for so long, and through which it found its anthropological justification: that of an age-old collective consciousness that made use of material documents to refresh its memory; history is the work expended on material documentation. . . . The document is not the fortunate tool of a history that is primarily and fundamentally *memory*; history is one way in which a society recognizes and develops a mass of documentation with which it is inextricably linked.

(Foucault 2002: 7)

Just as this model undoes the Platonic doctrine of universal concepts and recollection, it offers us a shift away from didactic displays that present history as a *fait accompli* and that present cultures in terms of stable universal concepts. It is a shift away from the power of the curator to tell the visitor the story, and towards the power of objects to unfold multiple stories. But, unlike the current trend for object-rich displays, Foucault's model of general history does not make the experience of the object primarily aesthetic or evocative. The object is mysterious, but it is not simply to be appreciated for itself or related to the viewer's subjectivity. Foucault refuses the hermeneutic leap of connecting with the past through our present subjectivity, for he denies that there is a stable subject that leaps back or rediscovers itself in the process. 'The purpose of history . . . is not to discover the roots of our identity, but to commit itself to its dissipation' (Foucault 1985: 95).

Foucault's model actually gives more power to the visitor than the aesthetic model, for here the visitor must be the historian: history has become the activity of developing objects into different series, and the object has become a living site of differences. It contains infinite differences and specificities to be opened up, related to other things and arranged in discontinuous series. The museum object is not the inert trace of a fixed past with which we can only connect through memory or empathy. Rather, in working with the object, in developing it into different causal series and multiple micro-histories, we will recognise the object as an integral part of what we are, and understand how these causal series have been the condition of possibility of present circumstances. Thus, there is a link with the self, but not the hermeneutic link that relies on self-identity and the fixed truth of the object. The self is an open question whose determinations change as history is performed. The historical object is no longer a tool of memory, but a way of developing and opening up what makes us what we are.

In this way, history becomes genealogy. We no longer treat the past as a total object that is other than us, but as that which is contained in multiple, changing ways in what we are. We can understand our present in a new way, through opening up new historical series as its conditions of possibility. Genealogy, for Foucault, is a methodology that opposes itself to the search for origins and universal structures of knowledge typical of total history. Genealogy is a localised 'descent' into the contingencies of our past (Foucault 1984: 80–3). Through genealogy we reveal the contingent series and accidental events that are the condition of possibility of our present. Foucault believes genealogy to have a progressive purpose: not teleological progress towards a goal, but rather progress as the development of capacities to get out of fixed ways of thinking, particularly our thinking of certain power structures as necessary and unchangeable. Genealogy aims simultaneously to identify the contingent historical conditions of the self and to liberate the self from those contingencies.

This means that while history museums like the Museo de America refuse the possibility of empathy with the past, the experience they offer is deeply relevant to the self. In performing history in this way, opening up objects and relating them into new and different series, the visitor performs his or her own genealogy, and understands his or her present situation in new ways. The visitor is able to consider the present both as the effect of multiple different relations of the past, and as radically open to different relations of power and causation. This points to a positive programme for the museum to achieve what Foucault hoped genealogy could achieve: liberation from the belief that particular concepts, interpretive frameworks and ways of thinking are metaphysically necessary or essential (Lord 2006).

## Conclusion

The twenty-first century museum can give power to both objects and visitors, avoiding the heavily didactic displays of the past. It can do this in a way that avoids aestheticism by arranging objects in groups that encourage the visitor to practice 'general history': developing them into multiple discontinuous series. Rather than matching objects to assumed historical continuities or universal concepts, the visitor starts with the object and builds up historical discontinuities and dispersed groupings. Rather than the visitor starting with his or her subjectivity to understand the past, the visitor starts with the puzzling object and discovers new ways of thinking about what has made the self and its present relations to society and power possible. Instead of the work of memory, the visitor engages in the work of history. What this means is perhaps that the museum experience is much less personal, but much more productive for thought.

This chapter concludes with a question: in presenting history without narrative, without memory, and without empathy, does the Museo de America sanitise history by refusing to tell of the appropriation, violence and enslavement that colonialism involved? Does the museum evade these issues through presenting history differently? Or is the absence of violence part of the museum's refusal to engage visitors through memory, replay and empathy? I do not have a good answer to these questions. Perhaps for many histories – the First and Second World Wars among them – it is too soon to treat them without reference to memory, for the memories of events are still active. Perhaps it is precisely when memory becomes solidified, when it becomes assumed as a fixed and completed whole and becomes a presupposition at the very foundations of a culture, that it must cease to be the mode of communicating history in the museum and new ways must be found. Perhaps we do not yet know what histories will be suitable for that kind of treatment in the twenty-first century.

## Bibliography

Bennett, T. (1995) *The Birth of the Museum: History, Theory, Politics*, London: Routledge.

Deleuze, G. (1994) *Difference and Repetition*, trans. P. Patton, London: Athlone.

Foucault, M. (1984) 'Nietzsche, Genealogy, History', trans. D. F. Bouchard and S. Simon, in P. Rabinow (ed.), *The Foucault Reader*, New York: Pantheon.

—— (2002) *The Archaeology of Knowledge*, trans. A. M. Sheridan Smith, London: Routledge.

Gadamer, H.-G. (1976) *Philosophical Hermeneutics*, trans. and ed. D.E. Linge, Berkeley, CA: University of California Press.

—— (2004) *Truth and Method*, trans. J. Weinsheimer and D. G. Marshall, London: Continuum.

Greenberg, S. (2005) 'The vital museum', in S. MacLeod (ed.) *Reshaping Museum Space*, London: Routledge, 226–37.

Heidegger, M. (1996) *Being and Time*, trans. J. Stambaugh, Albany, NY: SUNY Press.

Hein, H.S. (2000) *The Museum in Transition: A Philosophical Perspective*, Washington, DC: Smithsonian Books.

Hooper-Greenhill, E. (2000) *Museums and the Interpretation of Visual Culture*, London: Routledge.

Lord, B. (2006) 'Foucault's Museum: Difference, Representation, and Genealogy', *Museum and Society*, 4(1): 1–14.

O'Neill, M. (2006) 'Essentialism, Adaptation and Justice: Towards a New Epistemology of Museums', *Journal of Museum Management and Curatorship*, 21(2): 95–116.

Plato (2002) *Five Dialogues*, trans. G. M. A. Grube, Indianapolis, IN: Hackett.

Rancière, J. (1994) *The Names of History*, trans. H. Melehy, Minneapolis, MN: University of Minnesota Press.

# 28

# EDUCATION, POSTMODERNITY
# AND THE MUSEUM

*Eilean Hooper-Greenhill*

## Museums, education and cultural change

The educational role of museums today is of high priority, and while the emphasis on education and learning varies from country to country (Moffat and Woollard 1999; Stöger and
Stannett 2001), this reprioritisation can be seen as part of an international movement to
renegotiate the purposes of museums as they reshape their nineteenth- and twentieth-
century philosophies to respond to the demands of the twenty-first century. This renegotiation may entail considerable change within museums as institutional goals are reviewed,
different sources of funding are investigated and new posts are created. In England, for
example, education is high on government cultural agendas, outlined through a number of
policy documents and supported by a range of 'capacity-building' strategies. However, the
insistence by government and associated organisations on the growth and development of
the educational capacity of museums, and especially of museum–school services (DCMS
1998, 2000, 2001, 2005), has been controversial, both welcomed and resisted.

It is commonplace today to describe the public museum as one of the outcomes of modernity. Huyssen, for example, calls museums 'a direct effect of modernization' (Huyssen 1995:
15) and it is the modernist museum that frames current views of what museums should or
should not be. Rapid change is sometimes resisted in what Bennett has called institutions of
'slow modernity' (Bennett, 2004: 187), where to a large extent, modernist ideals still shape
the practices of the present. But, equally, many of those most intimately involved want to
democratise museums further through developing appropriate ways of thinking about education and learning in postmodern times.

'Museum education' consists of a range of discourses within what is now a dynamic and
fast-developing discursive field (Belsey 1980; Weedon 2004). Any analysis of museum
education today, therefore, must encompass social and cultural change and it is here that
postmodernism, which opens up key questions about the relationships between the past and
the present, and which offers tools for the analysis of large-scale historical change, may
prove useful (Lyon 1999; Best and Kellner 1997; Jencks 1992). Postmodernism as a set of
ideas is not straightforward; there is no unified postmodern theory (Best and Kellner 1991:
3). Rather, a large group of disparate theorists can be identified working to analyse postmodernity, understood as an emerging form of society. Postmodernity is sometimes understood
as being 'after' and therefore implying the dissolution of modernity, but at other times it is
seen as the latest stage of modernity (which is sometimes referred to as 'late' modernity)

(Ashcroft *et al.* 1998: 147). Theorists disagree about the value and intentions of postmodern theories. Seidman, for example, states:

> Postmodern thinkers are heirs to the Enlightenment, but critical heirs. Their aim is to preserve the core ethical convictions or values of the Enlightenment and its hope for a better world but to offer different understandings of knowledge, social life, politics, the self, and social evolution.
>
> (Seidman 2004: 202)

Delanty, on the other hand, finds postmodernism, and in particular its deconstructionist semiotic methodology, inadequate because in his view it fails to explore the interrelationships of agency, culture and structure, legitimates cultural relativism and endorses nationalism (Delanty 1997: 108). While these are serious charges, postmodern theorists have raised important issues about those ideas and institutions which emerged during the nineteenth and early twentieth centuries and which still structure social life to a large degree. The theorists of postmodern times offer some ways of reflecting on the complex discourses of museum education.

Postmodern writers suggest that any understanding of the here and now cannot be achieved without digging into the past to expose the critical ways in which the past moulds the present through reshaping ideas, renegotiating relationships and repositioning practices. The values and attitudes of the past live on in new guises, and are rarely completely jettisoned (Best and Kellner 1997: 26). Current changes in museums have been described as a paradigm shift (Anderson 2004). But this is a claim too far; while there are substantial ongoing changes within museums, these proceed on the basis of interrogating and renegotiating earlier practices and philosophies, many of which continue in one form or another to underpin the identity of museums today. It might be more accurate to think of the position of museum education today as one of *trying to establish* new paradigms in relation to long-established frameworks. Very few writers on museum education have integrated historical perspectives into their analysis (but see Hein 1998 and Roberts 1997), but the mapping of these modernist frameworks is essential in understanding how they may be rearticulated, set to one side or reinforced in the further building of an appropriate pedagogy for the post-museum (Hooper-Greenhill 2000).

One of the most useful ways of using postmodernism is as an attitude or a critique, a way of thinking (Usher *et al.* 1997: 8). Lyotard proposed postmodernism as an attitude of incredulity (Lyon 1999: 16), scepticism towards modernist ideas which have attained the status of 'common sense' or 'myth'. There are three 'myths' that are of particular relevance to museum education, these are: the project to produce single explanations of the world through knowledge that apparently has universal relevance, the idea that the self is a fixed and stable entity and the concept that learning consists of absorbing and reproducing a fixed body of approved knowledge. Postmodern writers suggest that concepts of knowledge, the self and learning have been substantially reworked in the last half century. Each of the three 'modernist myths' will be examined in turn and some of the implications for present-day practice drawn out through the themes of pathways to knowing, meaning and subjectivity and epistemological ethics.

The public museum emerged in Europe during the modern period, and education seems to have been an important component of its identity. One of the signs of modernity, it is suggested, was the shift in museum purposes and philosophies through the setting out of displays in the public museum for educational rather than celebratory or decorative purposes (McClellan 1994: 2). It is frequently claimed that education was a founding purpose of museums, but the early history of museum education has not yet been fully written. Certainly this claim can be substantiated for some museums, but education was not always seen as a primary purpose in others. Ruskin, for example, distinguished between a national art gallery, whose purpose is 'treasuring', and educational museums (Taylor 1999: 78). It is also hard to fully understand what educational purposes in museums might have been during the nineteenth end early twentieth centuries and to what extent these purposes might resonate with our ideas today. The basic parameters and assumptions of our present-day lives, such as mandatory schooling for everyone up to the age of 16, equality (at least in theory) between the sexes and a dynamic multi-racial social mix, were not in place.

Schooling in England was haphazard and undeveloped until towards the end of the nineteenth century. The Elementary Education Act which would make possible the introduction of free and compulsory education was not introduced until 1870 (Lawson and Silver 1973: 314; Minihan 1977), and the school leaving age not raised to 11 years until 1893 (Williams 1961: 158). Visiting museums could not be counted as part of schooling until 1894 (Lewis 1989: 24). It is partly because of the lack of an integrated school system that museums were seen as useful for adults in search of self-improvement (Stephens and Roderick 1983).

At this time, participation in public life was narrowly proscribed. While museums purportedly addressed their visitors as 'citizens', this was not as inclusive as might be imagined. In England, for example, the Reform Act of 1832 still excluded 80 per cent of men and all women from the franchise (Taylor 1999: 39), and while the Reform Act of 1867 extended the franchise to working men (Taylor 1999: 80), women were not expected to move out of the domestic sphere until much later. The complex ethnic mix produced as a result of colonial diaspora was incomplete; British history has been described by Bhabha as taking place both in the British Isles and overseas and to a large extent these historical processes remained separate (Bhabha 1994: 6). Indigenous peoples from the colonies and empire were rarely seen in Britain. Their artefacts, however, were exhibited within museums and helped to produce specific attitudes and perceptions towards them through processes of 'Othering'. Bennett, for example, describes how, in the second half of the nineteenth century, 'the archaeological conception of the person' proposed that indigenous peoples were on the lowest rungs of the evolutionary ladder and were therefore incapable of becoming fully civilised (Bennett 2004: 63). This view also positioned women as (variously) naturally timid, dependent and a drag on progress and improvement (Bennett 2004: 112).

If museums were proposed as having educational value during the modernist period, and if this purpose was underscored by contemporary ideas about knowledge, the self and learning, what do we know about those ideas and to what extent do those nineteenth-century ideas shape the discourses of museums today? What alternative ways of thinking about knowledge, learning and the self are available to museums and what opportunities do they suggest? It is beyond the scope of this chapter to do more than suggest the outlines of some of the contradictory discourses that cut across the complex discursive field that constructs how 'museum education' is understood today. However, it is hoped that in identifying these diverse discursive strands it will become possible to engage in deeper discussions of 'museum education' such that colleagues from across the museum can explore and share their views, ultimately constructing a collective approach that can open up the potential of museums for what Giddens calls 'life politics' – human self-actualisation on both individual and collective levels (Giddens 1991: 9).

## Knowledge theories: rethinking epistemologies

The modern period oversaw the emergence of a positivist/empiricist epistemology which proceeded on the basis of an abstracted model of scientific logic, viewing science as a linear, cumulative process that produced increasingly more accurate descriptions of an objective world that could be mastered through verifiable knowledge. Superstition and magic were set aside as unreliable and unworthy, as knowledge was developed that could be accepted as objective, rational and unified. Fields of knowledge – disciplines – were constructed that proposed universal truths and it was the task of educational systems as they emerged to transmit this canon of disciplinary knowledge through approved curricula. Educational discourses shaped and maintained the project of modernity through the development of educational systems where subject disciplines were clearly defined, and where space and time was monitored and controlled with the aim of producing a bounded, centred and autonomous self (Usher *et al.* 1997).

Museums were one of the social systems where these values were produced and transmitted in such a way that they could, theoretically, be absorbed by all. During the modernist period, displays acted like textbooks, setting out the structure of individual disciplines such as art or natural history (Hein 1998: 20). Education in museums was expected to be achieved through exhibition and display, where to look was to learn. There were few ancillary aids to learning such as labels or catalogues; through looking at things laid out in the correct order, learning was expected to occur 'naturally'. Looking itself was expected to be dispassionate, rational and objective. As the structures of the subject-matter (art, science, etc.) were absorbed, so the attitudes and values encoded within this disciplinary pedagogy would shape viewers according to their social station (Hooper-Greenhill 2000: 31–2). Education in the modernist museum thus included the laying out of objects in disciplinary taxonomies and also the shaping of disciplined (or civilized) attitudes, values and behaviours. The educational work of museums was conceived in a broad-brush rather than a fine-grained way. Prior to the emergence of society-wide educational systems that could provide anchors to specific curricula and pathways to specific groups of learners, the educational purposes of museums could only be conceived in an abstract way for a general public, which, although differentiated, was understood as massed.

As Henry Forbes, Director of Liverpool's Free Public Museums, put it in 1894:

> A biological Museum should . . . be as it were a Book of animals and plants, explained in words understandable of all persons of ordinary education, commencing with the description of the simpler forms and leading step by step to the higher and more complex.
>
> (Cited in Bennett 2004: 72–3)

At the present time, the idea of universal knowledge that is true, objective and verifiable is no longer tenable (Delanty 1997; Fay 1996). Post-BSE, post-AIDS, post-Chernobyl, belief in scientific ways of knowing is always conditional. The ambition to provide a single unified objective explanation of the world and its people that would be applicable in all circumstances has been exposed as the embodiment of a limited Eurocentric masculinist perspective. With the rise of oppositional voices, such as those of women, and those who were 'Other' but who are now very much within (Bhabha 1994: 6), knowledge is now understood as perspectival rather than universal. Interpretive philosophical frameworks have shown how beliefs are tied in to location in history, culture and geography through family, community, upbringing and personal biography. Forms of knowing have multiplied.

Knowledge as a unified body, an approved canon, is no longer either desirable or possible to sustain. Knowledge is no longer enshrined in books that can be managed and controlled, but is available at the touch of a mouse. Through the internet, anyone can find out about anything whenever they like; bits and pieces can be combined and made meaningful and this can be broadcast worldwide in an instant, in text and/or still or moving images. As Plant points out, when knowledge takes the form of information, it circulates through networks that evade the control of educational institutions (Plant 1995, quoted in Usher *et al.* 1997: 14).

In postmodernity, knowledge is perceived as fluid, changing and unstable. The universal meanings and approved curricula that formed the basis for modernist education have become problematic. Increasingly, nineteenth-century disciplines are breaking down as new disciplines emerge and inter-disciplinarity is found to be productive. The separation between spaces dedicated to education and non-educational spaces is seen to be spurious as it is acknowledged that lifelong learning can take place anywhere.

But how deep is this change? While we see everyday how knowledge embodies different viewpoints, is more fluid and less controllable, older views and desires are still held by many, especially in the museum. In 1984 it was still possible to make the following statement:

> The philosophies which lie behind the great monolithic museums vary, but all work towards a universal view of man's achievement or knowledge.
>
> (Wilson 1984: 54)

## Identity and the self

Educational discourses during modernity were based on apparently coherent and objective structures of knowledge, which, through the search for unity, truth and certainty made the world intelligible and able to be mastered. As knowledge was shaped, so was the self. Disciplinary knowledge was expected to create a centred, stable and sovereign self, governed by reason and free will. This 'Cartesian subject' came to know through rational cognition, which simultaneously confirmed his identity (Woodward 2002: 6). The humanist self assumed a male subject, 'man', which it was posited stood for all humankind (Woodward 2002: 6). However, this gendered subjectivity not only failed to represent women, it rendered those who were 'Othered' as invisible (Bhabha 2000: 96), still in many cases condemned to haunt the present as, in Rutherford's terms, 'ghosts' (Rutherford 2005). During the modern period, education was experienced as preparation for identities which were to a large extent ascribed, pre-given. Education shaped the self through grand narratives that emphasised the value of scientific knowledge in the achievement of human betterment. The aim was a self with specific qualities and attitudes, the liberal citizen with faith in this benevolent progress which would be achieved through science and truth (Usher *et al.* 1997: 11). Through the experience of education, individuals would become self-regulating.

In postmodernity, issues of identity have come to the fore and it is acknowledged that identities are both multiple and open to change. As Giddens pointed out, where large areas of life are no longer set out in advance, individuals are continually required to 'negotiate life-style options', each of which constitutes different aspects of self and identity (Giddens

1992: 75, cited in Woodward 2002: 3) The unified and reductive 'man' of humanism has been challenged and largely dismantled (Weedon 2004: 9). Now it is understood that subjectivity is always gendered, and rooted in class, race, ethnicity and sexual orientation (Hutcheon 1989: 39). Identities are both diverse and hybrid. It is no longer necessary to be white, educated, able-bodied, metropolitan, Western and male in order to be regarded as fully human, although in some contemporary discourses which divide the world into the civilised and the uncivilised it is clear that these earlier ways of thinking and forms of domi-nance are far from eradicated (Weedon 2004: 3).

Identity, meaning and self-determination are key issues in the production of a powerful sense of an active self. Active selves are able to go beyond reactive responses to external forces. It is in the production of active, empowered selves that socio-cultural and construc-tivist ideas about learning are important.

## Learning processes

Learning in the modernist period was expected to be hard intellectual work, a form of disci-pline. Linear and incremental step-by-step models of teaching, like the taxonomies of Bloom and Gagné (Hein 1998: 26), led learners through the exercise of their cognitive faculties towards individual improvement, and towards a pre-allotted social position. With spaces for learning kept rigidly apart from everyday spaces, learning styles were limited to reading and writing. Teachers adopted the position of expert and did not expect to have to consider any special or individual needs of their pupils. Teaching focused on transmitting the bodies of knowledge to be learned, and the proof of learning was the ability to repeat what had been transmitted. The experience of learning could be tough, as measurement in relation to external norms placed pupils in hierarchically graded positions that largely deter-mined self-perceptions (Gallagher 1992: 297). The expert–novice relationship between teacher and learner positioned the learner as insignificant except as a passive receiver. Successful educational processes were expected to produce a world that was mastered through order and liberal citizens who knew their place within this hierarchised world.

This repressive patriarchal dream has still not been eradicated, but lifelong learning and socio-cultural learning theories have opened up new ideas which are having an impact in schooling and for adult learners. Learning has been found to be more effective if it is enjoy-able, thus collapsing the separation between education and play (Usher et al. 1997: 17). The emotions play a strong role in learning, and the separation between cognitive and affective learning, and between mind and body as resources for interpretation, has been shown to be artificial. Experience is seen as raw material for learning, available for transformation (Usher et al. 1997: 101), as the everyday world is repositioned as a classroom for learners. Learning has been found to be more like a process of bricolage, a picking up of bits and pieces to patch over the gaps in knowledge when they are exposed, rather than a steady accumulation of incremental facts in a linear way. Learning today is conceptualised as interpretive, open-ended and identity-focused. There is a far greater attention to learners and awareness of their different intelligences and learning styles.

Teachers pay as much attention to the structure of learning experiences as to the struc-ture of the subject-matter to be learned (Hein 1998), and are no longer seen as guardians and disseminators of canonical knowledge, but as facilitators who enable the sifting and judging of useful material. Learners are no longer conceived as empty vessels, but are understood to always have some level of prior knowledge that needs to be acknowledged and built upon.

Constructivist and socio-cultural learning theory makes it clear that learners do not always learn what teachers teach (Jarvis *et al.* 1998). Lifelong learning theories show how learning is not limited to formal and approved sites, but can happen anywhere, at any time.

What is learned, therefore, cannot always be controlled and what is learned is not always what teachers would define as worthwhile or appropriate (Usher *et al.* 1997: 2.). To a large degree, learning is now closely linked to lifestyle, particularly for adults, who learn what they need for what they want to do.

## Museum education in postmodernity

This chapter has staked out, somewhat schematically, six moments within the discursive field of museum education. What are the implications? The final section of this chapter will draw out some of the issues in relation to three themes: pathways to knowing, meaning and subjectivity, and the ethics of museum epistemologies.

With the advent of constructivist and socio-cultural theories of learning, there has been a shift in the understanding of how people learn and, as a result of this, pathways to knowing have changed. In the modern period, it was thought that learning would occur through rational cognition; in the museum, it was thought that the meanings of objects could be grasped through the power of thought alone, the mind acting independently of the body. George Godwin, the Honorary Secretary to the London Art-Union, described in 1840 how the fine arts could work:

> The influence of the fine arts in humanizing and refining – in purifying the thoughts and raising the sources of gratification in man – is so universally felt and admitted, that it is hardly necessary now to urge it. By abstracting him from the gratification of the senses, teaching him to appreciate physical beauty, and to find delight in the contemplation of the admirable accordances of nature, the mind is carried forward to higher aims, and becomes insensibly opened to a conviction of the force of moral worth and the harmony of virtue.
>
> (Godwin quoted in 'The Art-Union of London', *Art-Union*, 2, [May 1840]: 67; cited in Minihan 1977: 78–9)

This *disembodied* approach to learning, with the mind 'abstracted from the senses' was typical of the period. Trodd describes how, for Hazlitt for example, to understand art involved abstraction from the physical body into the language of the image (Trodd 1994). Carlyle's remarks concerning portraiture also convey this sense:

> in . . . Historical investigations it . . . is one of the most primary wants to procure a bodily likeness of the personage inquired after; a good *Portrait* if such exists; failing that, even an indifferent if sincere one. In short, *any* representation made by a faithful human creature, of that Face and Figure, which *he* saw with his eyes, and which I can never see with mine, is now valuable to me, and much better than none at all.
>
> (Quoted in the National Portrait Gallery catalogue 1949 and discussed in Hooper-Greenhill 2000: 38–9)

In the face-to-face encounter between viewer and sitter, a faithful rendition will enable the viewer to see through the artist's eyes and, communing directly with the sitter, enter both the sitter's mind and the mind of the artist. Learning in the gallery was thought to involve the highest form of thinking, the exercise of the consciousness, cognition, while the body was seen as a source of pollution (Trodd 1994) and the use of the senses as a lower form of knowing. The sublimation of the body to the mind was a constant theme during the modern age, where asceticism and bodily restraint were both religious and social virtues.

Today, one of the strongest claims made by museum educators is that of the value of learning through the senses. The use of the sense of touch, smell, hearing and taste have been added to sight as museum educators have developed powerful ways of teaching based on museum collections. Pathways to learning that include embodied approaches – opportunities to handle artefacts, to act out ideas and to design and produce creative products as a response to museum collections – are effective in engaging learners of all ages and abilities. This is fully acknowledged in most museums, and, indeed, these ideas lie behind recent changes in display technologies. But there are still strong calls for the reinstatement of earlier approaches, which mock attempts to broaden the curriculum and the teaching methods of museums as 'dumbing down' or 'political correctness' (Appleton 2001).

Modernist educational approaches were used to produce a hierarchised and controlled world where personal fulfilment was largely closed to all but a few. Being forced to conform to this view of individual potential is immensely damaging and should be strongly resisted. Multiple pathways to knowing, that accept cultural and social difference as a given, open up more opportunities for learning for a broader range of people.

The second issue to address is that of meaning and subjectivity. The modernist tradition emphasises that there is a correct way of approaching objects and works of art (Tapia and Barrett 2003: 202), and that meaning is stable and can be transmitted. In the case of paintings, for example, the focus is on the artist and the subject-matter of the painting. The modernist tradition suggests that the meaning of a painting can be given to a viewer intact. However, postmodern writers suggest that meanings are never merely passively received, but are appropriated through processes of interpretation where new information or experience finds a place in relation to what is already known and as meaning is evolved through these articulations, views about the self and identity are also developed.

Subjectivity is formed through interpretation (Atkinson 2005: 28). As students, for example, look at paintings and respond to what they see, they may well address the content of the work, but they also produce their own identities. People don't just decode pre-existing meanings, but produce their own meanings that shape both ideas about the paintings and ideas about themselves. There are many examples of this from research carried out by the Research Centre for Museums and Galleries. The examples that follow form part of the evidence collected during research for Museums, Libraries and Archives Council carried out in 2005 (Hooper-Greenhill et al. 2006). Two 'flip-books' were also produced which contained the writing and drawings of school students. The quotes reproduced below are from the flipbooks. For example, Achese aged 9 wrote:

> The artist who painted the picture made it look real. You can imagine the story behind the paintings. The painting inspired me to do fascinating drawings as well.

Vincent aged 18 wrote:

> The most (un) interesting thing about today was . . . not that the gallery was bad because I'm sure boring people love to pore over things like this all day. I have

better things to do than ask questions about a picture. Its [sic] very boring, also I think a lot of the so-called art in this museum is over pretentious and hence depresses me. This art gallery has given me an insight into other peoples' boring and drab lives, and it will make my life feel a lot more fulfilling.

In each of these examples, the student inscribes him/herself into the response to specific works and experiences. Their interpretations include opinions about the art, artist or gallery, and also a view of how this relates to themselves. Learning in museums is never just about learning about the collections, it is also about the shaping of views about the self.

If interpretation of objects and collections always shapes subjectivities, then questions of ethics arise, and this is the third issue that needs to be examined briefly. What cultural narratives can be seen in museums and what are invisible? How do the interpretations produced by museums impact on individual subjectivities and identities? As Macdonald points out, museums are institutions of recognition and identity *par excellence* (Macdonald 2006: 4). Museums are places where the past is incorporated into the present, where heritage and history are made (Rutherford 2005). Here there are opportunities to expose the ghosts, to review the hidden histories and to bring to visibility that which has been hidden.

Stuart Hall has shown how the national heritage as a whole is a powerful source of symbols and meanings about the imagined community which forms the nation, and points out that those who cannot see themselves represented by these symbols cannot properly belong to the nation (Hall 2005). Museums today are able to use their colonial collections to picture more diverse and hybrid nations than were represented during modernity and in so doing both empower learners and exercise their ethical responsibilities by addressing the unspoken pasts that haunt the present (Museums Association 2002; Bhabha 1994: 12).

The value of this for learners is easy to see; Ivie aged 12:

The most interesting thing about today was . . . sketching all the different instruments. Also I think the handling session was interesting and I was very proud because some of the instruments were from my country (Nigeria).

Learning processes in museums engage both minds and bodies in imaginative and highly successful ways; it is well understood that successful learning about and through collections enables the growth of self-esteem and pride in personal achievements; and many museums are working in innovative and creative ways with relevant interpretive communities to produce cultural narratives appropriate to post-colonial times. The power and promise of museum education should not be in doubt.

However, the fear remains that the future may prove more difficult to realise than might be expected, because of our own ghosts, the ghosts of the modernist 'myths' that still threaten this future. After all, up until the early 1990s, students of museum studies could read in the official training manual about how they should think about visitors:

The museums' client is generally intelligent and able to read or use libraries to look up background. He must be led to this process . . . .

(Wilson 1984: 58)

And about how they should think about making displays accessible:

Imagination must be stirred, but tiresome rhetoric, fussy comparisons and gimmicky flourishes are to be avoided at all costs. Good taste and restraint are vital. It is the objects that are important: they must speak for themselves.

(Wilson 1984: 58)

These are the ghosts of modernity, barely exorcised. They must be recognised, faced and challenged.

## Bibliography

Anderson, G. (ed.) (2004) *Reinventing the Museum: Historical and Contemporary Perspectives on the Paradigm Shift*, Walnut Creek, CA: AltaMira Press.

Appleton, J. (2001) 'Museums for "The People"', main essay in *Museums for 'The People'?: Conversations in Print*, London: Academy of Ideas, 14–26.

Ashcroft, B., Griffiths, G. and Tiffin, H. (1998) *Key Concepts in Post-colonial Studies*, London: Routledge.

Atkinson, D. (2005) 'Approaching the future in school art education: learning how to swim', in D. Atkinson and P. Dash, *Social and Critical Practice in Art Education*, Stoke-on-Trent: Trentham Books, 21–30.

Belsey, C. (1980) *Critical Practice*, London: Methuen.

Bennett, T. (2004) *Pasts Beyond Memory: Evolution, Museums, Colonialism*, London: Routledge.

Best, S. and Kellner, D. (1991) *Postmodern Theory: Critical Interrogations*, Basingstoke: Macmillan.

—— (1997) *The Postmodern Turn*, New York: The Guilford Press.

Bhabha, H. (1994) *The Location of Culture*, London: Routledge.

—— (2000) 'Interrogating identity: the post colonial prerogative', in P. Du Gay, J. Evans and P. Redman *Identity: A Reader*, London: Sage Publications, 94–101.

Delanty, G. (1997) *Social Science: Beyond Constructivism and Realism*, Buckingham: Open University Press.

DCMS (Department for Culture, Media and Sport) (1998) *A New Cultural Framework*, London: DCMS.

—— (2000) *Centres for Social Change: Museums, Galleries and Archives for All: Policy Guidance on Social Inclusion for DCMS-funded and Local Authority Museums, Galleries and Archives in England*, London: DCMS.

—— (2001) *Libraries, Museums, Galleries and Archives for All: Co-operating Across the Sectors to Tackle Social Exclusion*, London: DCMS.

—— (2005) *Understanding the Future: Museums and 21st Century Life: the Value of Museums*, London: DCMS.

Fay, B. (1996) *Contemporary Philosophy of Social Science: A Multicultural Approach*, Oxford: Blackwell.

Gallagher, S. (1992) *Hermeneutics and Education*, New York: State University of New York Press.

Giddens, A. (1991) *Modernity and Self-identity: Self and Society in the Late Modern Age*, Cambridge: Polity Press.

Hall, S. (2005) 'Whose heritage? Un-settling "the heritage": re-imagining the post-nation', in J. Littler and R. Naidoo (eds) *The Politics of Heritage: the Legacies of 'Race'*, London: Routledge, 23–35.

Hein, G. (1998) *Learning in the Museum*, London: Routledge.

Hooper-Greenhill, E. (2000) *Museums and the Interpretation of Visual Culture*, London: Routledge.

Hooper-Greenhill, E., Dodd, J., Phillips, M., Gibson, L., Jones, C. and Sullivan, E. (2006) *What Did You Learn at the Museum Today? Second Study. Evaluation of the Outcomes and Impact of Learning Through the Implementation of the Education Programme Delivery Plan Across Nine Regional Hubs (2005). RCMG (Research Centre for Museums and Galleries) Leicester: University of Leicester.* Online. Available at: www.le.ac.uk/museumstudies/rcmg

Hutcheon, L. (1989) *The Politics of Postmodernism*, London: Routledge.

Huyssen, A. (1995) *Twilight Memories: Marking Time in a Culture of Amnesia*, New York: Routledge.

Jarvis, P., Holford, J. and Griffin, C. (1998) *The Theory and Practice of Learning*, London: Kogan Page.

Jencks, C. (1992) *The Postmodern Reader*, London: Academy Editions.

Lawson, J. and Silver, H. (1973) *A Social History of Education in England*, London: Methuen and Co. Ltd.

Lewis, G. (1989) *For Instruction and Recreation: A Centenary History of the Museums Association*, London: Quiller Press.

Lyon, D. (1999) *Postmodernity*, 2nd edition, Buckingham: Open University Press.

McClellan, A. (1994) *Inventing the Louvre: Art, Politics and the Origin of the Modern Museum in Eighteenth Century Paris*, Berkeley, CA: University of California Press.

Macdonald, S. (ed.) (2006) *A Companion to Museum Studies*, Oxford: Blackwell Publishing.

Minihan, J. (1977) *The Nationalisation of Culture: the Development of State Subsidies to the Arts in Great Britain*, London: Hamish Hamilton.

Moffat, H. and Woollard, V. (1999) *Museum and Gallery Education: A Manual of Good Practice*, London: The Stationery Office.

Museums Association (2002) *Code of Ethics for Museums*, 1st edition, London: Museums Association.

Roberts, L. (1997) *From Knowledge to Narrative: Educators and the Changing Museum*, Washington, DC: Smithsonian Institution Press.

Rutherford, J. (2005) 'Ghosts: heritage and the shape of things to come', in J. Littler and R. Naidoo (eds) *The Politics of Heritage: The Legacies of 'Race'*, London: Routledge, 82–93.

Seidman, S. (2004) *Contested Knowledge: Social Theory Today*, 3rd edition, Oxford: Blackwell.

Stephens, M.D. and Roderick, G.W. (eds) (1983) *Samuel Smiles and Nineteenth Century Self-help in Education*, Nottingham: Nottingham Studies in the History of Adult Education, University of Nottingham.

Stöger, G. and Stannett, A. (2001) *Museums, Keyworkers and Lifelong Learning: Shared Practice in Five Countries*, Austria: published with support from the SOCRATES Adult Education Programme of the European Union, the Swedish National Council for Cultural Affairs and the Büro für Europäische Bilungskooperation, SOKRATES-Büro.

Tapia, J. and Barrett, S. (2003) 'Postmodernism and art museum education: the case for a new paradigm', in M. Xanthoudaki, L. Tickle and V. Sekules, *Researching Visual Arts Education in Museums and Galleries: An International Reader*, Dordrecht: Kluwer Academic Publishers, 197–212.

Taylor, B. (1999) *Art for the Nation: Exhibitions and the London Public 1747–2001*, Manchester: Manchester University Press.

Trodd, C. (1994) 'Culture, class and city: the National Gallery, London and the spaces of education, 1822–57', in M. Pointon (ed.) (1994) *Art Apart: Art Institutions and Ideology across England and North America*, Manchester: Manchester University Press, 33–49.

Usher, R., Bryant, I. and Johnston, R. (1997) *Adult Education and the Postmodern Challenge: Learning Beyond the Limits*, London: Routledge.

Weedon, C. (2004) *Identity and Culture: Narratives of Difference and Belonging*, Maidenhead: Open University Press.

Williams, R. (1961) *The Long Revolution*, Middlesex: Penguin Books.

Wilson, D. (1984) 'National museums', in J. M. A. Thompson (ed.) *Manual of Curatorship: A Guide to Museum Practice*, London: Butterworths, 54–8.

Woodward, K. (2002) *Understanding Identity*, London: Arnold.

# INDEX